UNITED NATIONS

ECONOMIC SURVEY OF EUROPE IN 1984-1985

Prepared by the
SECRETARIAT OF THE
ECONOMIC COMMISSION FOR EUROPE
GENEVA

NEW YORK, 1985

NOTE

The designations employed and the presentation of the material in this publication do not imply the expression of any opinion whatsoever on the part of the Secretariat of the United Nations concerning the legal status of any country or territory or of its authorities, or concerning the delimitation of its frontiers.

UNITED NATIONS PUBLICATION
Sales No. E.85.II.E.1
ISBN 92-1-116319-6 ISSN 0070-8712

03500P

PREFACE

The present *Survey* is the thirty-eighth in a series of reports prepared by the secretariat of the Economic Commission for Europe to serve the needs of the Commission and to help in reporting on world economic conditions.

The *Survey* is published on the responsibility of the secretariat, and the views expressed in it should not be attributed to the Commission or to its participating Governments.

The pre-publication text of this *Survey* was completed on 8 March 1985 and made available to the 40th session of the Economic Commission for Europe. The final text, incorporating minor changes, was completed on 26 April 1985.

EXPLANATORY NOTES

The following symbols have been used throughout this *Survey*:

A dash (-) indicates nil or negligible;

Two dots (. .) indicate not available or not pertinent;

An asterisk (*) indicates an estimate by the secretariat of the Economic Commission for Europe;

A slash (/) indicates a crop year or financial year (e.g. 1980/81);

Use of a hyphen (-) between dates representing years, for example, 1981-1983, signifies the full period involved, including the beginning and end years.

Unless the contrary is stated, the standard unit of weight used throughout is the metric ton.

The definition "billion" used throughout is one thousand million.

References to dollars ($) are to United States dollars unless otherwise stated.

Minor discrepancies in totals are due to rounding.

The following abbreviations have been used:

CMEA   Council for Mutual Economic Assistance
ECE   United Nations Economic Commission for Europe
EEC   European Economic Community
FAO   Food and Agriculture Organization
GDP   Gross domestic product
GNP   Gross national product
IMF   International Monetary Fund
NMP   Net material product
OECD   Organisation for Economic Co-operation and Development
OPEC   Organization of the Petroleum Exporting Countries
SDR   Special drawing rights

CONTENTS

CHAPTER FOUR

Eastern Europe and the Soviet Union

CHAPTER FIVE

International trade and payments

Statistical appendices

LIST OF TABLES AND CHARTS

Chapter One

Chapter Two

Appendix A.   Western Europe and North America

Chapter 1

THE ECONOMIC SITUATION IN THE ECE REGION

In 1979 the world economy went into a phase of declining economic growth accompanied by a worsening of inflation and considerable shifts in the current account balances between regions and countries. The slowdown in overall economic activity was to last for a period of more than three years (chart 1.1.1) during which strong and sometimes even drastic economic policy measures were adopted by governments to fight internal and external imbalances.

The influence most immediately shaping the general course of the world economy was the upsurge of oil prices. Oil prices more than doubled from the end of 1978 to the beginning of 1980 and overshadowed the sharp price rise of other commodities. Non-oil commodity prices had already started to increase before the eruption in oil prices, in response to the strengthening of world demand. The underlying rate of inflation in the developed market economies was already considered to be too high in early 1979 before the oil shock gave it further momentum. In these circumstances the immediate priority of economic policy became not only the containment but the reduction of inflationary pressures

which had been increasing since the 1960s. In the centrally planned economies, where a slowing of growth had been evident in the latter part of the 1970s, economic performance in 1979 remained well below the targets set in the annual plans. Unusually bad weather, as well as the disturbances in the world economy, contributed to this outcome. The unexpected increase in world market prices may have caused greater than planned cuts in imports and thus intensified the already tight supply constraints in eastern Europe. Although 1979 was still a year of recovery for the developing countries as a whole, imbalances were appearing which increased their vulnerability to adverse changes in the world economy.

This chapter first gives an overview of the developments and policy issues in the ECE region following the disturbances at the turn of the decade. The discussion then continues with a short analysis of the upturn in economic activity since 1983 and a separate treatment of trade developments, particularly of east-west trade. The chapter ends with an appraisal of the overall situation.

1.1 ECONOMIC DISTURBANCES IN THE EARLY 1980s

(i) Output performance

In the faltering economic climate depressive factors emerged in 1979 and were further strengthened in 1980. The deceleration of growth became a world-wide phenomenon. International trade, which slowed down even more than output, spread the deflationary impulses throughout the world economy.

The *developed market economies* experienced a major recession which hit both North America and western Europe. The timing of the cyclical movements, however, was somewhat different. In the United States industrial output did not grow after the first quarter of 1979 while for western Europe 1979 was still a year of output recovery. The downturn came in the second quarter of 1980. The fall in output was steeper in the United States than in western Europe but it lasted only two quarters. The recovery in the United States was shortlived. It continued only into the first quarter of 1981 and then stagnated before a new downturn started in the last quarter. In western Europe output declined through most of 1980. At the beginning of 1981 there were signs of a hesitant recovery but, in fact, the decline continued until the last quarter when there was a brief respite until the first quarter of 1982. The decline in output resumed in the second quarter. The fall in the United States was again much larger than in Europe.

The greater variability of economic activity in the United States than in Europe is also reflected in the annual changes in total output. In 1980 GDP growth in western Europe was 1.5 per cent whereas there was a small decline in the United States. In 1982 total output fell in the United States by over 2 per cent compared with virtually stagnant GDP in western Europe (table 1.1.1).

TABLE 1.1.1

Output performance in developed market economies
(*Annual percentage change of real GDP*)

	1979	1980	1981	1982
Developed market economies . . .	3.2	0.6	1.3	−1.0
North America	2.9	−0.2	2.6	−2.3
Western Europe	3.5	1.5	−0.1	0.5
Southern Europe	3.1	1.5	2.0	2.6

The recovery from recession, which, on the basis of previous experience, should have followed the downturn in 1980 within a year or two, did in fact appear, but it petered out. A second re-

CHART 1.1.1.

Growth performance

(Average annual growth rates of real gross domestic product, in per cent)

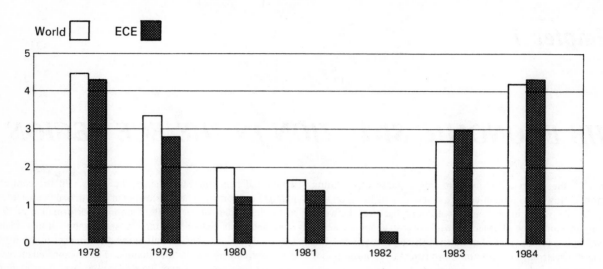

Source: Department of International Economic and Social Affairs of the United Nations Secretariat; ECE secretariat.

cession was then superimposed on the first which resulted on both sides of the Atlantic in a renewed fall in output in 1982. The developed market economies experienced a *double recession* in which both external shocks and economic policies played an important role in shaping the direction and pattern of economic developments.

The origin of the double recession can be located on the supply side although the restraints on the demand side were also a drag on economic activity as, after the onset of the second oil shock, economic policies were in general pro-cyclical, not supporting but restraining economic activity in the downswing. There were mainly two channels through which the price shocks from the supply side influenced developments. The immediate effect was a rise in production costs which resulted in a profit squeeze, which in turn led to an acceleration in the rate of inflation with a subsequent curb on output and an increase in unemployment. The market economies experienced a short period of stagflation during which both inflation and unemployment increased. The second channel was the effect of the profit squeeze on fixed investment and hence on the growth of productive capacity. A change in the relative prices of raw materials of the size that took place in 1979-1980 required considerable adjustment in the structure of prices and production. Thus, as a result of shocks on the supply side, the short-run cyclical problems became interwoven with problems of growth and structural adjustment.

Non-accommodating monetary policies led to very tight monetary conditions in most countries. Short-term nominal interest rates rose by several percentage points in late 1979 and early 1980. Although the inflation rate increased, the real rate of interest tended to grow. By 1981 real long-term interest rates in most countries had risen considerably. In 1982 real rates remained high or, as in the United States and the United Kingdom, increased further.

Fiscal policy also became substantially more restrictive in many countries by active moves to limit the growth of public spending.[1] In many countries large budget deficits were increas-

ingly perceived as reflecting structural problems and this motivated governments to adopt medium-term strategies designed to gradually reduce budget imbalances.

The policy-induced character of the second recession is easily recognized. The tightening of economic policies accompanied by high and rising interest rates weakened investment prospects during 1981-1982. Fixed investment dropped in 1982 both in western Europe and in the United States.

The monetary factors did not only contribute to the second recession within national economies. The international banking system also began to show signs of fragility which led to the emergence of new forces of contraction with a negative impact on developments in the industrialized countries.

The non-oil *developing countries* were faced after 1979 with several external disturbances at the same time: first, higher oil prices raised directly and indirectly the cost of imports; second, the economic policies of the industrialized countries raised interest rates in world financial markets; and the recession led to a reduction in the demand for imports from the developing countries. However, the international markets, by recycling the balance of payments surpluses of the oil exporting countries, provided the necessary financing for the growing deficits of the non-oil developing countries. These countries were thus able to keep up a reasonable rate of output growth and to increase their imports and to support economic activity in the rest of the world. Although the oil exporting countries surpluses fell sharply in 1981, international financing continued to expand at only a slightly lower rate than before. The non-oil developing countries were still able to increase their imports considerably. In 1982, however, the developing countries' capacity to import was drastically affected by falling terms of trade, rising debt service costs, and above all, by the shrinking availability of external credit. Their imports declined, adding further deflationary pressure on economic activity in the rest of the world. Output growth nearly stagnated in the developing countries as a whole in 1982.

The *south European* countries were greatly affected by the two oil shocks due to their high dependence on energy imports. The return of migrant labour, due to labour shedding in the advanced western countries, was also an important factor adding to their

_____
[1] About fiscal policy, see various issues of OECD *Economic Outlook*, Paris (biannual).

economic difficulties. Although the timing of the adjustment to the first oil crisis differed in each of them, the adjustment was generally made later and was sharper than in the more advanced economies of western Europe. This delay stemmed from a variety of factors, but in general there was an inadequate perception among policy makers of the length and depth of the first post-1973 recession. Consequently, policies tended to maintain domestic demand at the cost of increased borrowing abroad. In the early 1980s, the emergence of a serious foreign payments constraint led to the introduction of harsh policies to check domestic demand and, particularly, private consumption.

In the *centrally planned economies* an upturn in economic activity was planned for 1980. It was expected that the adverse conditions which had prevailed in 1979 would not be repeated. In the east European countries, however, the recovery did not materialize. Some countries experienced serious difficulties in adjusting to imbalances and to adverse economic developments. For the trade-intensive economies of eastern Europe the problem was to adjust to a worsening of their terms of trade and to curtail the increase in their external deficits at a time when world trade was slowing down sharply and export prospects were weakening. Supply shortages held down production and thus hampered the achievement of the planned targets. In the Soviet Union economic performance was less vulnerable to unexpected changes in external conditions because of the availability of domestic fuels and of the relatively small share of foreign trade in total output. In fact a favourable terms-of-trade movement permitted a substantial acceleration of imports without a binding external constraint. Consequently, in the Soviet Union there was a marked upturn in output growth in 1980 and the target set in the plan was nearly achieved.

In the domestic productive sectors of the centrally planned economies imbalances rose mainly from the supply side as shortages of raw materials and other inputs increased. The demand side influenced developments for the most part through changes in exports. This effect, however, was indirect: export performance determined the possibilities to import and so provided the necessary foreign inputs for productive activity.

TABLE 1.1.2

Output performance in centrally planned economies
(*Annual percentage change of real NMP*)

	1979	1980	1981	1982
Eastern Europe and the Soviet Union	2.1	2.7	1.7	2.8
Eastern Europe	2.0	0.1	−1.9	0.1
Soviet Union	2.2	3.9	3.3	3.9

For all of the centrally planned economies, 1980 was the closing year of a five-year plan period. A deceleration of output growth had already been foreseen in the plans for this period but actual developments were even below these reduced plans (table 1.1.2). Factors such as the slowdown in the growth of the labour supply and increasing scarcities of energy and raw materials severely restricted the possibilities of further strong expansion. Besides these more fundamental restraints on growth, various unexpected events and developments, such as the oil price increase and, particularly, the deepening recession in the developed market economies during the latter part of the five-year period, contributed to the weaker than planned output growth in the centrally planned economies. The medium-term plans for 1981-1985, reflecting a further accommodation to the less favourable environment for growth, projected a slowdown from the

growth rates of the previous quinquennium. The general strategy emerging from the plans was to make short-run adjustments to the changed external environment while pursuing long-run policies aimed at easing the constraints on stable growth in the future. The strategies involved structural changes in the domestic economies and, particularly, in foreign trade. The necessity of raising economic efficiency as well as improving the management and planning systems was emphasized.

In the context of the restrained policy stance, governments opted in 1981 for a slow rate of growth in the domestic use of output in order to provide room for improvements in foreign trade balances without endangering consumption. The deceleration of production, in this policy framework, had a severe impact on investment, which had been faltering already before 1981. Weak investment inevitably delayed the implementation of the necessary structural adjustments.

The output performance in 1981 of the centrally planned economies lagged behind the plan targets because of unforeseen developments. The events in Poland directly influenced the aggregate result with an unprecedented drop in output of 13 per cent. The spillover effects on other centrally planned economies were considerable as shortfalls in committed deliveries from Poland disrupted production in other countries. The difficulties in meeting the various targets for material input production, exports and import reductions were also an important cause of the failure to achieve planned growth rates. In the Soviet Union output growth was only slightly lower than in 1980, mainly because of a third successive year of poor agricultural performance.

In 1982 there was near stagnation in the world economy and in all the major regional groupings of the world. The centrally planned economies registered one of their weakest performances of the post-war period although their growth was nonetheless positive in contrast to that in other parts of the world economy. The rapid changes in the international financial conditions during 1981 had a profound impact on the east European economies. As financial difficulties became serious, for Poland and Romania in particular, international lending institutions became more cautious in their lending policies and credits to all the centrally planned economies began to dry up. In 1982 certain financial institutions also withdrew their deposits from east European countries and thereby added to the liquidity shortage in these countries. In these external financial conditions some of the most indebted countries had to adopt adjustment measures which involved abrupt and sharp import cuts and strong export promotion, hence aggravating internal imbalances and inhibiting the achievement of the modest growth targets. As a result the east European countries succeeded in turning their current accounts from deficit into surplus in 1982. The counterpart of these strong adjustment measures which led to the improvement in the external balance was, however, a further slowdown in output growth in all the east European countries. However, in Poland the fall in output was less dramatic than in 1981. In the Soviet Union the situation was quite different: an increase in the terms of trade permitted imports to continue to rise substantially and there was little change in the rate of output growth from that in the two previous years.

(ii) **Tight policies**

Since 1979 the world economy passed through a period of faltering economic activity reaching a low point in 1982. It needs emphasizing that the economies of the ECE region contributed in a very important way to this negative overall development: the policies of the ECE countries, aiming at adjustment and stabilization, were highly restrictive and had serious consequences for the growth of output.

After the second oil shock the reduction of inflation became the primary objective in most industrialized countries and the main burden of achieving it was to be borne by monetary policy. This emphasis was based on the view that inflation is basically a monetary phenomenon and, therefore, it was believed that by restraining the rate of increase in money supply the rate of increase of nominal incomes would be reduced relative to output and this would create favourable conditions for curbing inflation. It was also thought that a policy following a monetary rule would have only a minor impact on real output and so the inflation rate would respond quickly to changes in the money supply. This view, however, was refuted by actual events: when monetary policies were set to achieve the announced targets for money supply growth, real output responded quite strongly to monetary restraint. The cost of bringing down the rate of inflation, from a double-digit rate in 1980 to below 9 per cent in western Europe and to less than 5 per cent in the United States at the end of 1982, was very high losses of output and employment. The rate of unemployment increased by 3-4 percentage points on both sides of the Atlantic and the total number of unemployed reached over 22 million in 1982.

In this period another major aim of most governments was the reduction of budget deficits. Only in the United States was there a move towards greater ease. The efforts in many countries to reduce deficits were, however, partly frustrated because the actual deficits were swollen by the "automatic stabilizers", rising interest rates and rising indebtedness. Nevertheless, the fact remains that many countries adopted tighter fiscal policies simultaneously and these had a deflationary impact in addition to that induced by stringent monetary policies. This coincidental tightening meant that the recession was probably more severe than any single government expected. The aim of disinflation was to lay the foundation for a return to non-inflationary economic growth, but although the period 1980-1982 witnessed the most marked break in inflation since the 1960s the process was not considered to be complete. Inflation continued to be an important policy concern.

When, after the oil shock, strong inflationary pressures encountered restrictive money supply targets high interest rates emerged. The uncontrolled upward drift of interest rates in the United States led eventually to interest rate differentials *vis-à-vis* the rest of the world which began to strengthen the US dollar. In other countries relatively high interest rates were generated because their exchange rates were vulnerable to international capital movements. Particularly in Europe the external constraints on monetary policy gradually overshadowed purely domestic considerations as interest rates were raised to levels which were incompatible with domestic objectives for economic activity and employment. Developments in the United States thus reduced to a considerable extent the policy options available elsewhere.

Confronted with large fluctuations in interest rates in the

United States monetary authorities in the other major centres consistently acted to limit the fluctuations in their own interest rates. In doing so they accepted large net declines in their holdings of foreign exchange to moderate falls in their exchange rates. They were, however, prepared to accept increases in interest rates in order to meet exchange market objectives, to control inflation at home and to assist in coping with fundamental imbalances in the external account. A policy of relative stability of interest rates in Europe could only be achieved at the expense of large fluctuations in and a weakening of exchange rates against the dollar. From mid-1980 to the end of 1982 the effective dollar exchange rate appreciated by some 30 per cent. The inflationary consequences of these developments were considerable since world market prices of many important basic commodities are fixed in dollars. The dollar appreciation held down costs and prices in the United States but elsewhere it was an additional source of inflationary pressure. Effectively, some of the inflation in the United States was shifted to Europe and contributed to the differential inflation performance between the United States and Europe.

The restrained policy stance in eastern Europe was evident in the measures adopted for purposes of adjustment. Aggregate domestic demand (as measured by NMP used) had already been increasing in volume terms more slowly than domestic production (NMP produced) in the latter part of the 1970s reflecting *inter alia* the policy goal of cutting trade deficits with the market economies. Once the balance of payments constraint became binding in 1980 there was an immediate need for a large and rapid shift of resources away from domestic use. As a result, the volume growth of aggregate domestic demand declined sharply in 1981 and in some countries there was even an absolute fall. Finally, in 1982, when eastern Europe had attained a surplus in the current account with the market economies, the volume of aggregate domestic demand fell by several percentage points. The shifts of resources into the foreign sector were carried out by import controls rather than through gains in exports. This combination of policies had a direct, restraining effect on domestic production through input shortages but may have also added some further deflationary pressures on the market economies which in 1982 were already in a serious recession. In the Soviet Union, on the other hand, there was no strong need for drastic adjustment measures. Therefore, the development of aggregate domestic demand could roughly follow that of production.

The tight stance of policy in eastern Europe was also necessitated by the changing situation in intra-CMEA trade. The big rise in world commodity prices was absorbed into intra-CMEA trade prices with a time lag, and was eventually reflected in changes in the terms of trade between the Soviet Union and the east European countries. Hence adjustment efforts were also needed in this part of their foreign trade. In 1981-1982 the volume of east European exports to the Soviet Union increased considerably while their imports fell. The counterpart of this development was a corresponding restraint on domestic absorption out of domestic production in the east European countries.

1.2 UPTURN IN 1983-1984

In 1983 the economies of the *ECE region* began to recover from the longest post-war slowdown in real growth. After practically no growth in 1982, output for the region as a whole increased by some 3 per cent in 1983. While there was an upturn throughout the region its strength was uneven: in the centrally planned economies the output growth was somewhat stronger than in the market economies; among the market economies the recovery in the United States gathered considerable momentum whereas output growth in western Europe lagged behind. The recovery in 1983 continued in 1984 with more strength than was generally expected at the beginning of the year. The rapid growth in the United States, which continued to lead the world recovery, took most analysts by surprise. As regards developments in the centrally planned economies the continued revival in most countries was stronger than envisaged in the annual plans for 1984. For the ECE region as a whole real output growth was over 4 per cent, the highest rate of growth since 1978.

The upswing of economic activity in the ECE region has spread its influence to the rest of the world. The dominating sources for this uplift were the United States and, outside the ECE region, and to a lesser extent, Japan. The developing countries' exports increased sharply and as their balance of payments constraints eased somewhat they were able, as a group, to raise their imports. Thus the revival in the industrialized countries provided the impetus to some modest growth in the developing countries in 1984 after a period of stagnation in 1982 and 1983. World output growth picked up in 1983-1984 although with a lag with respect to the recovery in the ECE region (chart 1.1.1).

In the *United States* expansionary fiscal policy accompanied by an easing in monetary policy sparked off a very strong recovery towards the end of 1982. Although the upturn conformed quite closely to a "normal" post-war recovery the pace of growth was still unusually strong in the first half of 1984. The expansion was supported by a very rapid growth of fixed investment—its growth was exceptional not only in relation to the other main components of demand but also to previous post-war recoveries. Fears of overheating led to a tightening of monetary policy which may have contributed to the sharp slowdown in the second half of 1984. Although there was then also a drop in the rate of growth of fixed investment it still provided strong support to the growth of demand. Through 1983 and 1984 domestic demand increased at very high rates in the United States and domestic output responded strongly. Nevertheless, the balance of payments moved into considerable deficit and thus stimulated economic activity in the rest of the world.

The recovery in *western Europe* compares unfavourably with that of the United States. The weaker productive performance of western Europe goes back to the first oil crisis and there has been very little growth since 1980. Supply-side factors may have contributed to this development but it seems that the performance in western Europe has reflected above all the weak growth of demand which has led to the emergence of several growth-impeding factors. In addition economic policy developments have had an important impact on the output performance. The persistent weakness of western Europe during the present upturn is shown in the output figures: real output growth in 1983 was about 1 per cent on average and in 1984 around 2 1/2 per cent.

The weak recovery in western Europe reflects in a considerable

measure the stance of economic policies. In contrast with the United States, European fiscal policies have tended to remain tight although monetary policies have provided some room for recovery in real output. The main stimulus to growth came from private consumption due *inter alia* to falls in the savings ratios. Although exports improved, net exports have not provided an important source of European growth. The better export performance was due more to increasing intra-European trade than to the large deterioration in the United States trade balance: this reflects the limited direct impact of United States' import demand on western Europe's total exports. On average investment did not make a contribution to the upturn in its early stages although in 1984 both fixed investment and stockbuilding played an increasing role.

The recovery had a marked effect on unemployment only in the United States where it fell from 10 per cent in 1982 to around 7 per cent in the fourth quarter of 1984. In western Europe, in contrast, unemployment remained on a rising trend and at the end of 1984 the rate of unemployment was around 10 per cent. Thus the recovery in western Europe had failed to create enough employment to check the upward trend in unemployment.

A notable feature of the present recovery has been the continued fall in *inflation* rates. Contrary to often expressed views, fiscal stimulus such as that experienced in the United States has not led to accelerating inflation. There were, at any rate, several factors at work which tended to reduce inflation during the revival of economic activity: conditions of large excess supply in goods and labour markets continued to dampen inflation; inflationary expectations were on the decline; and inflationary pressures from the international commodity markets did not flare up although there was some upward pressure in the early stage of recovery.

As a reflection of the existing labour market conditions, with high unemployment, increases in money wages moderated or remained stable and labour cost pressures were considerably eased by rises in productivity. Inflationary cost pressures weakened as the US dollar appreciated. The impact, however, was greater for the United States than for western Europe. In the last quarter of 1984 inflation in western Europe was on average still significantly higher than in the United States.

The immediate impact of the downturn following the second oil price shock was a *profit squeeze* with very unfavourable consequences for economic activity and growth. Falling labour cost pressures, including productivity increases due to labour shake-outs, however, provided scope for a recovery of profits. And profit shares, in fact, have been rising strongly during the present recovery and even before in some countries. At the macroeconomic level one of the most important adjustments required after the second oil shock was the restoration of profits. By 1984 the adjustment process had already gone a long way to raise profit shares to their pre-recession levels.

The export-led recovery of output growth in *southern Europe* in 1984 (nearly 3 per cent)—although relatively favourable compared with the more industrialized countries of western Europe—has not prevented a further increase in unemployment or stopped the persistent and dramatic fall in fixed investment. The still high levels of inflation in southern Europe, where external price shocks were superimposed on domestic supply rigidities and where the external constraint remains, have required caution towards any stimulus of domestic demand.

The upturn in the rate of growth of the *centrally planned economies* got under way in 1983. However the pace and timing of development was not uniform. After stagnating in 1982 total output growth in eastern Europe rose sharply in 1983 by over 3 per cent and accelerated further, to about 5 per cent, in 1984. In the Soviet Union, on the other hand, output growth, hovering between 3 and 4 per cent, did not vary much from the rates of the immediately preceding years. Although the east European countries had made substantial adjustments to the changing internal and external economic environment, governments still remained cautious with respect to accelerating the growth of output. The very severe external constraints encountered previously led governments to continue to emphasize the need for improvements in the current account as their central concern. Since significant progress had been achieved in the easing of supply bottlenecks, material inputs were more efficiently used and the balance of payment constraint was loosened: output growth could resume while further improvements in the current account balance could be attained. In the Soviet Union there were also favourable changes in the structure of economic growth in 1983-1984. In particular, the output of a number of sectors which had constituted supply bottlenecks increased at significant rates. Industrial output grew strongly in both years supported by increased labour productivity growth. The overall growth rate in 1984 was marginally lower than that in 1983, mainly because of a fall in the growth of agricultural output.

In the centrally planned economies as a whole total domestic demand (NMP utilized) continued to expand at a slower pace than output (NMP produced) reflecting the overall policy targets with respect to external balance. As regards the structure of domestic demand consumption had remained relatively protected during the austerity period, but in 1983 growth in consumption was less than that of total domestic demand in several countries because of stronger fixed investment. In 1984

consumption again rose considerably thus leaving correspondingly less room for expansion in fixed investment.

The strong *investment* performance during the present recovery in the United States has restored the ratio of gross fixed investment to total output (GNP) to the level attained during the previous peak in 1979. However, this investment boom has been financed to a great extent by foreign savings through a growing current account deficit. In a longer run perspective this may suggest that in spite of the striking investment recovery, the conditions for a sustained improvement in productivity and growth are not as yet securely based. It should also be borne in mind that a considerable part of the strength of the present recovery represents a rebound from the most severe recession in the post-war period. In western Europe the investment ratio has not increased during the present recovery and has remained well below the ratios of the late 1960s and early 1970s. Thus it is not only western Europe's present phase of slow growth which is a matter of concern: weak investment activity compromises the possibility of attaining future rates of output growth that would provide for growing employment and a fall in unemployment.

In the centrally planned economies investment growth has become somewhat more buoyant since the recovery began during 1983. Levels of investment, however, are running well below their long-term trend. The plans for the current quinquennium had already incorporated targets which were well below trend, but with the likely exception of the Soviet Union even these modest targets may not be fulfilled. External constraints and the need to maintain consumption have reduced investment resources. Growth rates, and in some countries the absolute level, of investment have been cut. Given the problems facing those countries, which require far-reaching changes in the structure of output, a resumption of investment growth and greater investment efficiency is essential if the centrally planned economies are to continue to adjust to the unfavourable conditions which have affected them in recent years. Much will depend on whether the underlying strength of the recovery in 1983 and 1984 can be maintained in 1985 and beyond.

1.3 INTERNATIONAL TRADE AND PAYMENTS

(i) World trade

The sharp increase in oil prices caused a significant deterioration in the terms of trade of the oil importing countries while the oil exporting countries experienced a large improvement in their terms of trade. These shifts in relative trade prices were reflected in changes in the pattern of current accounts: the imbalances that emerged in 1979 worsened considerably in the course of 1980. The developed market economies and the oil-importing developing countries saw their balances weaken while the oil-exporting developing countries experienced a very significant strengthening. Among the centrally planned economies, the deficits of the east European countries were slightly enlarged while the Soviet Union—a net exporter of oil—recorded a large surplus. The following discusses changes in trade and payments, first, during the period of world recession (1980-1982) and then during the subsequent recovery (1983-1984).

World trade did not provide much independent impetus to growth in 1980. In parallel with the decline in world output growth, the volume of world imports decelerated sharply from 1979 to 1980 (see table 1.3.1). Imports into the ECE region stagnated because of the developing recession in the region. The fall in oil imports in particular was very sharp. However the imports of the developing countries, OPEC in particular, continued to expand and give some stimulus to world economic activity. OPEC import demand, in fact, boosted the growth of exports from the developed market economies. Thus the volume of exports of the ECE region, in contrast to imports, increased.

TABLE 1.3.1

Trade developments, 1979-1984
(*Annual percentage changes, in volume*)

	1979	1980	1981	1982	1983	1984
World imports	6.9	1.7	−0.5	−0.6	0.9	8.5
ECE imports	7.7	−0.5	−2.6	−0.1	4.8	10.7
ECE exports.	7.2	3.0	0.6	−0.7	2.3	8.4

The dampening effect of the recession in the developed market economies continued to spread in 1981-1982 through the channels of international trade. World trade, as a whole, fell slightly in 1981 and in 1982. Neither the developing countries nor the centrally planned economies were in a position to provide a counter-weight to the impact of the deflationary forces. The recession of the developed market economies radiated outwards through imports: imports into the ECE region declined in real terms in 1981 and stagnated in 1982.

Some regions continued to stimulate world trade until 1981. Thus, the imports of OPEC rose in 1981 by 20 per cent in volume and even the oil-importing developing countries, benefiting from the favourable conditions in the financial markets, were still able to manage some real import growth in spite of their growing balance of payments difficulties. However, in 1982 the trade of the developing countries was very severely affected by the recession in the developed countries. The substantial fall in the world market prices of commodities worsened dramatically their terms of trade, their exports declined or stagnated, and many of

them were facing a very serious debt problem. These developments forced these countries to resort to various measures to restrain imports. Thus, the volume of imports into the non-oil developing countries declined by 8 per cent in 1982. Reflecting the sharp decline in oil consumption in the developed market economies, the exports of the oil-exporting countries fell throughout the whole period of 1980-1982. Notwithstanding the unfavourable tendencies in their export markets the oil exporters still continued to expand their imports in 1982 although at a sharply reduced rate.

The centrally planned economies did not impart any significant stimulus to world trade in 1981-1982. Although the growth of imports into the Soviet Union remained buoyant in this period, east European imports were sharply curtailed.

In 1982 the configuration of balance of payments current accounts was in some respects different from what it had been only two years earlier, after the second oil shock. The biggest change was in the OPEC current account. After declining sharply in 1981 the OPEC surplus disappeared in 1982. The aggregate deficit of the non-oil developing countries fell slightly in 1982. Although their trade deficits contracted, the invisible balances deteriorated because higher interest rates had to be paid on a rapidly expanding stock of foreign debt. As a counterpart to the disappearance of the OPEC surplus, there was some improvement in the aggregate current account of the developed market economies in 1981. There was little change in their aggregate deficit in 1982, but there were a number of shifts in the position of individual countries. The biggest change was in the United States where the current account moved into substantial deficit.

The improvement in the world economy that got under way towards the end of 1982 gave only a weak stimulus to world trade in 1983. The pronounced upturn in the United States (and Canada) gave a major contribution to the growth of trade, but several restraining factors were still at work and the result was a modest growth in the volume of world trade of 1 per cent. The main characteristic of the growth of world trade volume was its geographical unevenness. The substantial rise in imports into the United States was mainly due to a relatively strong recovery in aggregate demand. In addition, the appreciation of the US dollar made imports very competitive with domestic production. In the developed market economies outside of North America sluggish economic growth and depreciating currencies led, in contrast, to little or no expansion in import volumes. Thus, the considerable recovery in the imports of the ECE region mainly reflected developments in North America, although there was some pick-up in imports into the centrally planned economies. Developing countries were under strong pressure to reduce their imports. During 1983 the oil-exporting countries were affected by falling oil prices and a slackening in the demand for oil. Faced with persistently falling export earnings these countries also had to reduce their imports sharply. In many non-oil developing countries, the need to make room for debt servicing payments, which were taking a large percentage of export earnings, also contributed to the reduction of imports into these countries.

The economic recovery strengthened during 1984 and stimulated a marked upswing in world trade after three years of decline and stagnation. The volume growth was some 8-9 per cent with a very strong increase during the first three quarters of the year. As in 1983, import developments differed substantially between regions. The rapid expansion of imports into the United States persisted and rose above their pre-recession peak. Imports into Japan also rose considerably, but in Europe—both in western Europe and in the centrally planned economies—they increased at a somewhat slower pace. Thus, much of the large increase in the volume of ECE imports reflected developments in the United States, although western Europe also made an important contribution.

The countries benefiting most from the boom in the United States in 1983-1984 were Japan, the Asian developing countries, Canada and Latin America. The impact on exports from Europe—both western Europe and the centrally planned economies—was less significant because the trade of the European countries is dominated by intra-European trade. Yet another feature of trade developments was that the significantly diverging dollar prices of major categories of traded goods in 1983-1984 left their mark on the terms of trade. The average price of manufactured goods declined by 7 per cent, that of oil by 16 per cent while primary commodity prices rose by some 7 per cent. A large deterioration in the relative trade prices of the OPEC countries was largely reflected in the terms of trade gains of the developed market economies. The non-oil developing countries also had some improvement in their terms of trade, although primary commodity prices were falling in the latter half of 1984 after a considerable increase in 1983 and early 1984.

The changes in current balances in 1984 reflect the widespread adjustments that had been under way in earlier years. These adjustments were mostly concentrated in the trade account. Large imbalances, with opposite signs, developed in the United States and Japan. The continued widening of the United States deficit stemmed mainly from the upsurge in imports, while for Japan the spectacular growth in the surplus was caused by its strong export performance. In Europe—both western Europe and the centrally planned economies—there were some improvements in current accounts, mainly because of favourable export developments. In the non-oil developing countries the strong growth of exports led to a further large improvement in their trade and current balances. Finally, the current account deficit of the OPEC countries was reduced, mainly because of recovery in the volume of oil exports.

(ii) East-west trade

The economic disturbances which followed the second oil shock had profound effects on east-west trade. After a period of uninterrupted growth in the second half of the 1970s the volume of western imports from eastern Europe fell for three consecutive years from 1980. This trade flow developed even less favourably than the volume of western imports from the world. This weakening export performance of the east European countries reflected above all the general slowdown in the western market economies, but western trade policies may have also contributed to this development. In addition, domestic economic factors and policy measures adopted in eastern Europe also played a role in the weak performance. The volume of western imports from the

Soviet Union had declined quite steeply since 1979, but there was a sharp upturn in 1982. This reversal was mainly due to the growth of energy imports.

The volume of western exports to eastern Europe had stagnated in the latter half of the 1970s and declined after 1980. The balance of payments situation was aggravated by accumulating debt and, for some countries, by increasing difficulties in obtaining access to credits and so strong adjustment measures were directed at imports from the west. Having succeeded in a considerable adjustment of their external balances in 1980 and 1981, the east European countries achieved a convertible currency current account surplus in 1982, at about the same time as the supply of new credits largely dried up.

By contrast, western trade with the Soviet Union was more dynamic than the rest of east-west trade. Although the volume of oil sales from the Soviet Union to the west declined, its export revenues still increased considerably following the rise in oil prices. Higher revenues, in turn, permitted a faster growth of imports. On the other hand, when oil prices weakened in 1981-1982 Soviet export revenues remained largely intact because the volume of oil exports was sharply increased.

Western trade with eastern Europe showed definite signs of recovery after 1982. Following a period of decline in 1980-1982, western imports increased sharply in 1983 and accelerated in 1984. This turnround was caused by the general economic recovery in the west, by strong export efforts and by recovery of supply capacities in eastern Europe. The eastern export growth mainly reflected higher sales of oil and oil products and, in the case of Poland, the regaining of lost coal markets. Western imports of manufactured goods also rose at high rates.

Western exports to eastern Europe, which had also fallen for several years, started to recover in 1983 and continued to grow at a modest rate in 1984.

The pattern of adjustment in eastern external balances was different from that in 1980-1982, when adjustment was achieved through the reduction of imports at a faster rate than the fall in exports. In 1983-1984 east European exports were growing rapidly and imports began to rise again, although slowly. As regards western trade with the Soviet Union, energy was mainly responsible for the continuation of western import growth in 1983-1984. By contrast the formerly dynamic western exports to the Soviet Union stagnated in 1983 and fell in 1984. This probably reflected the winding down of contracts linked to the Yamal pipeline project.

The changes in east-west trade flows were reflected in improvements in eastern convertible currency current accounts. The east European surplus of $3 billion in 1983 increased to $4 billion in 1984, while the $6 billion surplus of the Soviet Union improved considerably, to $8 billion in 1984.

The favourable balance of payments developments of the east European countries during the last few years has improved their financial situation. Their rapid capacity to adjust their external accounts has increased the willingness of western banks to lend to them. Consequently, eastern borrowing in the international markets resumed in 1983, albeit at a low rate, and accelerated markedly in 1984.

1.4 APPRAISAL OF THE SHORT-TERM PROSPECTS

A year ago the economic performance in all areas of the ECE region was expected to improve. In fact output expanded over 4 per cent for the region as a whole in 1984 and was even stronger than forecast. Although some slowdown is envisaged for 1985 aggregate growth for the region might still be close to 3 1/2 per cent.

The disparity between rates of growth in *western Europe* and *North America* seems likely to narrow considerably, if not disappear, in 1985. This is mainly due to the deceleration in the United States, which was already apparent in the second half of 1984. In the first quarter of 1985 total output growth in the United States was actually very weak. Although the majority of forecasts in western Europe do not anticipate much change in the overall growth rate, a modest strengthening in economic activity is possible. However, activity in the last months of 1984 and in the early months of 1985 has shown little sign of acceleration. For the *south European countries* some increase in the rate of growth is expected.

For the last few years monetary policies in the *developed market economies* have been set to reduce the rate of inflation mainly by progressively decelerating the rate of growth of the money supply. For 1985, money supply growth targets have been lowered in most countries. Nevertheless, monetary policy appears to be accommodating continued output expansion. While monetary policy has been the prime instrument for bringing down inflation, in most countries, except the United States, fiscal policy has sought to cut budget deficits and to check public spending. Fiscal policy has thus had a restraining influence on economic activity in western Europe, and a further move in this direction is forecast for 1985. In the United States the escalation of the budget deficit has given a strong stimulus to economic activity, which will continue during 1985. This basic difference in the fiscal policy stances of the United States and western Europe is an important factor in the disparity between their growth rates. At the beginning of 1985 there were no indications of major changes in the basic orientation of monetary and fiscal policy. However, in the early months of the year there was mounting pressure for some relaxation in western Europe and increasing anxiety in the United States at the domestic consequences of failure to curb the federal deficit.

There is a risk that normal cyclical factors, strengthened by increasing domestic and external imbalances, might lead, even before the end of the current year, to a recession in the United States. Such an eventuality would undoubtedly have serious repercussions on the rest of the world economy unless other compensatory sources of growth appear. In the west European economies, which are less dependent than other regions on the United States economy, stronger growth than is generally forecast would then be required to counteract the weakening stimulus from the United States. To achieve such growth west European economic policies should be co-ordinated so as to give more support to growth than has been the case in the recent past. In particular, investment in fixed capital should be encouraged.

Following a period of recent acceleration in economic growth in the *centrally planned economies*, annual plans indicate that strategies are designed to stabilize expansion at the rate attained in 1983 and 1984 rather than to attempt any further speeding up of output growth. Nevertheless, the plans indicate somewhat higher growth in eastern Europe and the Soviet Union in 1985.

Although the constraints arising from external balances appear to have eased somewhat, most countries will continue to hold back the rise in 2 domestic demand (NMP used) relative to domestic output (NMP produced). The planned growth should leave more room for increased allocation of resources to investment and hence to reversing the investment slowdown of recent years. There is a pressing need to modernize productive capacities and to achieve faster structural adjustment.

Due to the severe winter, construction and production in several industries in eastern Europe and the Soviet Union actually fell in the first two months of 1985. Some of the countries concerned have already taken measures to make up the losses of output during the rest of the year. These shortfalls in output, as well as strains on energy balances, raise uncertainty as to the feasibility of implementing some of the annual plans for 1985. Nevertheless, for the group as a whole the aggregate growth rate of NMP implied in the plans seems to be still within reach.

After a strong but uneven revival in 1984 the outlook for *world trade* in 1985 is for slower volume growth but for a more balanced distribution among the major economic regions. The more moderate increase in world trade reflects mainly an expected fall in the growth of imports into the United States, which in 1984 was the main stimulus to the expansion of trade. Although no acceleration in the growth of west European imports is foreseen, the relative contribution of developments in this region to the expansion of world trade is likely to be greater in 1985 than in 1984. Given the importance of intra-European trade, import demand in the European countries will be the main determinant of west European exports.

The major part of the European centrally planned economies' trade consists of intra-CMEA area transactions where volume growth was unusually high in 1984. A somewhat smaller rise is likely in 1985. Developments in the world market and in western Europe in particular will have a decisive influence on the centrally planned economies' trade with the market economies in 1985. Since a substantial increase in imports of developed market economies is still foreseen, there will probably be room for further growth in east European exports to the west. Even with reduced export volume growth the countries of eastern Europe should be able to maintain the 1984 pace of import volume growth within the targets set for their external balances. The volume of Soviet imports from the west will be boosted, as it was in the last quarter of 1984, by the need to compensate for the poor grain harvest in 1984. The future development of world energy prices will be an important determinant of the Soviet Union's earnings in 1985.

During recent years the *international debt* situation has posed a serious threat to the stability of the international financial system. However, progress has been made towards a more lasting solution to this problem. Growth in the industrialized countries has enabled the developing debtor countries to expand exports enough to allow the resumption of moderate economic growth in debtor countries and for improvements in their external payments situation. The prospects for 1985 indicate that the debt problem will not improve much further because growth in the industrialized countries and in world trade will decelerate. The international financial system still remains vulnerable to sudden changes in the situation of debtor countries, which require many years to consolidate the progress made so far and to correct existing structural imbalances. The latter needs a resumption of capital inflow into these countries, a requirement that may not be easily met.

Chapter 2

WESTERN EUROPE AND NORTH AMERICA

2.1 RECENT DEVELOPMENTS AND POLICY ISSUES

This section summarizes the main economic developments in 1984 in western Europe and North America; then follows a discussion of policies, the outlook for 1985 and an appraisal of the current economic situation.

(i) An overview of recent developments

The present recovery of the growth of output in the market economies of the ECE region, which began towards the end of 1982, continues to be dominated by developments in the United States, where a large fiscal deficit and sharply rising consumer credit kept domestic demand rising at an annual rate of nearly 11 per cent in the first half of 1984 (in the second half it fell to about 5 per cent). Although domestic output has risen strongly in response to this growth of demand, the United States' balance of payments has moved into considerable deficit and this has been a major factor in stimulating output in the rest of the world, albeit somewhat unevenly.

After growing by nearly 4 per cent in 1983, GNP in the United States continued to grow strongly in the first half of 1984. Growth was in fact unexpectedly strong. Some deceleration had been expected as a result of rising interest rates, but in the first two quarters of 1984 output grew by 10 and 7 per cent respectively (seasonally adjusted annual rates): this was faster than during the first year of the recovery, a pattern which is exceptional in the run of post-war recoveries. The initial (or "flash") estimate of growth in the second quarter was 5.7 per cent (successively revised to 7.1 per cent) but expectations in the financial markets had been nearer 4.5 per cent: the continuing strength of the US economy thus increased fears of "overheating" and interest rates began to rise. In fact the Federal Reserve had already decided to tighten monetary policy at the end of March and by the end of June prime rates had risen to 13 per cent (2 points above their level in January) and stayed there until September. This tightening of monetary conditions contributed to a sharp deceleration of output growth in the third quarter. Stagnant consumption and a deterioration of net exports were the main factors in this slow-down, the sharpness of which was as unexpected as the buoyancy of growth in the first half of the year. The initial estimate of third-quarter growth (3.6 per cent) was generally welcomed as a sign that the economy was settling down to a rate of expansion which was more sustainable than the earlier pace but which would still permit further progress in reducing unemployment. However, there were increasing signs that the slowdown was more severe than suggested by this first estimate and in September there was a marked easing of monetary policy. (The estimate of third quarter growth was eventually revised to 1.6 per cent.) The effects of this relaxation of monetary policy are still unclear but the most recent estimates for the last quarter of 1984 put GNP growth at 4.9 per cent with improvements in private consumption, fixed investment and government spending. For 1984 as a whole United States' GNP is provisionally estimated to have risen by nearly 7 per cent, compared with a little under 4 per cent in 1983 and an official forecast in February 1984 of 5.3 per cent.

The expansion in the United States has been supported by an exceptionally rapid growth of fixed capital investment, particularly in the business sector—its growth has been exceptional not only in relation to the other main components of demand but also to previous post-war recoveries. In the four quarters from 1983(II) to 1984(I) the total volume of gross domestic capital formation was rising at annual rates of more than 20 per cent. Although there was a sharp deceleration from such high rates of growth in the second half of 1984, business fixed investment was still providing strong support to US growth. Investment expenditure on housing flattened out in the second quarter with little change in the rest of the year. Although the performance of fixed investment has been especially prominent, the recovery has been broadly based: private consumption grew strongly (5-8 per cent) in the first two quarters of 1984 and, in contrast to 1983 when there were large cuts in non-defence expenditures, government spending was rising throughout the year. After destocking in 1983, stock accumulation in the business sector increased substantially in 1984, particularly in the first three quarters, and made a significant contribution to output growth. However, much of this increased expenditure has gone into imports and the current account deficit, which has risen from under 1 per cent of GNP at the beginning of 1983 to over 3 per cent in the last quarter of 1984, has become an increasing drag on the growth of domestic output.

Average GDP growth in western Europe in 1984 was about 2.5 per cent, a little better than was forecast at the start of the year but very modest in comparison with the United States' rate of 6.8 per cent (table 2.1.1). France lowered the average rate with expansion of less than 2 per cent while only a handful of the smaller economies grew by more than 3 per cent. Norway and Denmark were the most rapidly expanding economies, with annual growth rates of more than 4 per cent.

The persistent weakness of western Europe in comparison with the United States during the present upturn can be seen clearly in chart 2.1.1 which gives quarterly industrial production figures for both sides of the Atlantic. By the third quarter of 1984 industrial production in North America was 22 per cent above its level in the last quarter of 1982, the trough of the last recession: in western Europe it was only 7 per cent higher. Production in the United States increased in seven successive quarters from the last quarter of 1982, whereas the recovery in Europe has not only

11

TABLE 2.1.1

Main economic developments in western Europe and the United States, 1982-1984

	Western Europe[a]			United States		
	1982	1983	1984	1982	1983	1984
Targets:						
1. GDP growth[b]	0.5	1.2	2.5	−2.1	3.7	6.8
2. Employment growth	−0.8	−0.8	0.1	−0.8	1.3	4.1
3. Unemployment rate[c]	8.4	9.4	9.7	9.5	9.5	7.4
4. Inflation rate[d]	9.3	7.0	5.8	6.1	3.2	4.3
5. Current account/GDP	−0.3	0.3	0.3	−0.3	−1.3	−2.7
6. Misery index (3 + 4)	17.7	16.1	15.7	15.8	12.8	11.5
Instruments:						
7. Budget deficit/GDP[e]	−4.8	−4.8	−4.5	−3.8	−4	−3.2
8. Change in structural budget deficit[f]	0.5	0.5	0.4	−1.3	−0.6	−0.5

Sources: National statistics and OECD, *Economic Outlook*, December 1984.

[a] Thirteen countries (excluding southern Europe).

[b] GNP for the United States.

[c] Per cent of total labour force.

[d] Change in consumer prices.

[e] Eleven west European countries (Ireland and Switzerland excluded).

[f] As per cent of nominal GDP/GNP–11 west European countries.

been weak but also hesitant: in most individual countries output has stagnated or fallen in one or more quarters during this period. By the first quarter of 1984 west European output had regained the average level of 1980 (a year of recession) but there was a setback in the second quarter mainly because of strikes in the Federal Republic of Germany and the United Kingdom (table 2.1.2): output in the Federal Republic of Germany recovered quite sharply in the second half of the year, but in the United Kingdom it continued to be affected by the coal miners' strike (coal usually accounts for about 4 per cent of UK industrial production and the strike is estimated to have lowered the level of industrial production by about 3 1/2 per cent in the second half

CHART 2.1.1.

Industrial production in western Europe and North America, 1980 — 1984 [a]

(1975 = 100)

North America ———   Western Europe ••••••••

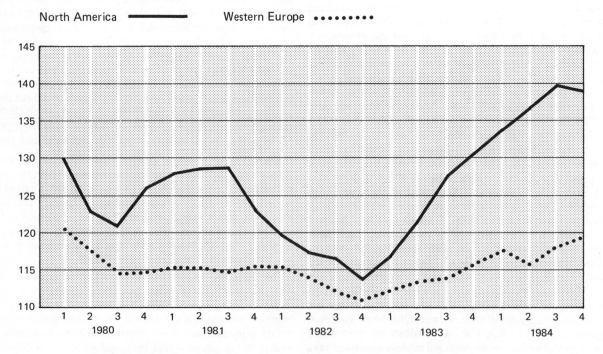

Source: OECD, *Main Economic Indicators,* Paris (monthly).

a Seasonally adjusted; national indices weighted by 1975 shares in total regional output; western Europe = 12 countries

of 1984). In many of the smaller economies industrial production rose quite strongly in the first half of 1984, partly because of a rapid growth of exports.

The recovery of output in the market economies has been largely supported by private consumption, although in 1984 fixed investment and stockbuilding played an increasing role. In the United States private consumption (supported by rising employment and incomes, falling inflation and rising personal debt) increased more in 1984 than in 1983, while for western Europe as a whole the rate of growth was much the same in both years. Growth was also supported by public expenditure in the United States where it accounted for about 10 per cent of the rise in GNP; in most of western Europe the growth of real public expenditure continued to decelerate (it actually fell in Belgium, Ireland and the Netherlands) and provided less than 10 per cent of the total rise in GDP. There were large increases in fixed investment (particularly business investment) in the United States (up 18 per cent after a 10 per cent rise in 1983), the United Kingdom (6 1/2 per cent), and in Denmark (12 per cent). In France investment fell again in 1984 (for the fourth year running) while in the Federal Republic of Germany a small increase for 1984 as a whole reflects both a fall in capital expenditure in the first half of the year, when confidence was seriously affected by the metal-workers' strike, and a deceleration due to the abolition (at the end of 1983) of investment allowances for machinery and equipment which had encouraged a bunching of investment in 1983. In most of the smaller countries fixed investment did better than in 1983 although there was a deceleration in Switzerland and declines in Finland and Ireland. Stockbuilding in western Europe, which was negative in 1983, contributed about one quarter of the rise in GNP; in the United States business inventories rose significantly (with substantial quarter-to-quarter differences) and accounted for somewhat more than a quarter of the GNP rise. There was a marked acceleration in west European exports of goods and services in 1984: their volume rose some 6.5 per cent compared with about 2 per cent in 1983. (The improvement was particularly marked for the four larger economies whose export performance had lagged behind that of the smaller countries in 1983.) Imports also accelerated sharply, but the net balance on goods and services nevertheless contributed about 17 per cent of the increase in GDP in the four large economies and some 30 per cent in the smaller ones. In the United States, the fall in net exports was equivalent to a quarter of the real GNP rise.

The recovery of the last two years has not been accompanied by any upsurge in *inflation* rates, although there were many commentators and officials who argued that any fiscal stimulus such as that experienced in the United States would lead to accelerating inflation. This has not happened and in the major economies consumer price inflation has shown little sign of rising. In the United States the average rate of increase fell from 4.5 per cent in the last quarter of 1982 to about 2.5 per cent in the third quarter of 1983 after which there was a slight increase; however, throughout 1984 the rate has remained between 4 and 4.5 per cent. In western Europe the average rate (for 13 countries) has fallen from over 11 per cent in 1980-1981 to around 5 per cent in the fourth quarter of 1984. The differences among the European countries have narrowed, mainly as a result of a marked deceleration of rates of inflation in those countries where they had still been relatively high in 1983 (Italy and France, for example). Nevertheless, in the last quarter of 1984 inflation in western Europe was on average still higher than in the United States: only in the Federal Republic of Germany, the Netherlands and Switzerland was it lower.

A number of factors appear to have contributed to this relative stability or deceleration of inflation rates. Although the demand for labour has varied widely among different countries, increases

TABLE 2.1.2

Industrial production in western Europe and North America, 1984
(Percentage change over previous quarter, seasonally adjusted)

	I	II	III	IV
France	1.5	−1.5	2.4	−1.5
Germany, Federal Republic of . .	1.2	−4.6	6.1	1.7
Italy	1.1	0.5	1.9	−1.8
United Kingdom	0.1	−2.1	0.3	1.1
Total 4 countries	*1.0*	*−2.4*	*3.3*	*0.2*
Austria	2.1	0.5	2.8	0.9
Belgium	−0.7	6.1	−3.6	..
Finland	0.6	0.8	1.4	3.6
Ireland	2.6	7.5	−3.5	..
Netherlands	4.1	0.3	0.6	−1.3
Norway	0.3	0.3	0.3	4.5
Sweden[a]	1.9	2.8	−0.9	6.1
Switzerland[a]	2.8	−1.2	1.3	..
Total 8 countries	*1.9*	*1.5*	*−*	*..*
Total western Europe	1.2	−1.6	2.6	..
United States	2.7	2.1	1.5	−0.3
Canada	0.6	0.9	3.1	0.2
North America	2.6	2.0	1.7	−0.3

Sources: OECD, *Main Economic Indicators*, Paris; and national sources.
[a] Mining and manufacturing.

in average hourly earnings have moderated or remained stable in most countries. In western Europe increases during 1984 were not very different from those in 1983, and there was a marked deceleration in France, Italy and the Netherlands. In the United States the wage moderation that appeared during the recession has been maintained: even during this last year of rapid growth and falling unemployment, the growth of hourly earnings was no more than in 1983. Labour cost pressures have been considerably eased by the lower rate of nominal wage increases and by further improvements in productivity (although in general the latter rose less sharply than in 1983). In western Europe unit labour costs rose on average by some 4 per cent in 1984 compared with 8 and 6 per cent in 1982 and 1983. In the United States the rise was some 2 1/2 per cent after a sharp deceleration in the second half of 1983. Moderate wage increases, rising productivity and some acceleration in final output prices all allowed profits to improve quite markedly in 1984.

International cost pressures have also weakened during the present recovery although, because of exchange rate changes, the impact of these will have been greater for the United States (and Japan) than for western Europe. Nevertheless the continued weakness of world crude oil prices during the present recovery has been significant, not only for measured inflation rates but also for improving expectations that the recovery could continue without setting off another supply-side shock of the type experienced in the 1970s. In the first quarter of 1984 the average OPEC price was about 10 per cent lower than a year earlier (which in turn was just over 10 per cent below its peak of $36.20 in the first quarter of 1981). For the rest of 1984 the OPEC cartel was trying to defend its $29 a barrel reference price in the face of expanding production from non-OPEC members and falling spot prices. A number of short-run factors contributed to the weakness of oil prices in 1984 but longer-run changes in energy demand are probably beginning to have an impact: energy consumption per unit of GDP in the market economies has been on a falling trend as a result of structural change (away from the more energy intensive sectors such as steel), energy conservation and generally greater fuel efficiency. Within this global decline in the energy-output ratio, there has been a continuing switch away from oil to other fuels.

Other world commodity prices were also weak for most of 1984. Some of the fall in commodity prices may be due to the rise in the dollar exchange rate, but the UNCTAD index in SDR terms has also fallen. A variety of specific reasons may be advanced for this weakness (high interest rates, which discourage restocking; the relatively weak recovery in western Europe which takes a much larger proportion of world imports of primary materials than the United States, etc.) but, as in the case of oil, there does appear to have been some weakening of the relationship between output changes in the developed market economies and the demand for primary commodities (possibly for similar reasons: structural change towards activities with a low raw-material content, such as services and electronics, increased consumption of synthetic substitutes produced in the market economies themselves, and generally greater efficiency in raw material use). However, for all the west European countries this favourable influence of world prices on their domestic inflation rates was attenuated by the depreciation of their currencies against the dollar: for all of them, import prices in dollars fell but in national currency rose, in some cases quite considerably.

The recovery has had a marked effect on *employment and unemployment* only in the United States where the former increased by about 4 per cent in 1984 and the latter fell from 8 per cent of the labour force in the first quarter to around 7 per cent in the fourth quarter. In western Europe unemployment generally remained on a rising trend during 1984 and there was some acceleration in the summer, partly because stronger demand has encouraged re-entries into the labour force. At the end of 1984 total unemployment in western Europe was more than 19 million, or a little over 9.5 per cent of the total labour force. The fall in west European employment came to an end in 1984 and there was some recovery in the second half of the year, mainly in the Federal Republic of Germany, the United Kingdom, and in the Scandinavian countries. But two years of "recovery" in western Europe have so far failed to restore employment (and unemployment) to their pre-recession levels.

International trade and payments in 1984 continued to be dominated by the widening United States' current account deficit, which is estimated to have exceeded $100 billion, more than double the figure for 1983. The main factor behind this deficit is the deteriorating trade account (particularly imports which rose by almost 30 per cent in volume in 1984), although the United States' traditional surplus of investment-income is being eroded by the rapid increase in the flow of net interest paid abroad and the lower dollar value of profits remitted by US companies.

For western Europe as a whole (13 countries excluding southern Europe) the current account surplus of some $11 billion in 1983 increased slightly in 1984. However, this aggregate conceals a diversity of changes in individual countries: improvements in the Federal Republic of Germany, France and the smaller economies were offset by a deterioration in Italy and the United Kingdom. In France the deficit has been reduced considerably as a result of restrictive policies at home and rising exports. In Italy there was a move back to deficit as rising domestic demand led to a sharp rise in imports and in the United Kingdom the coal miners' strike was partly responsible for the current account deterioration. Although strikes also affected the performance of the Federal Republic of Germany in early 1984, there was a sharp improvement in the current account in the last quarter. In most of the smaller economies current accounts improved in 1984, the strongest by far being Norway, the Netherlands and Switzerland with surpluses of between $3 and $4.5 billion.

The principal counterpart of the United States' current account deficit is a massive inflow on the capital account in response to very high *interest rates*. The level and variability of United States' interest rates has been a source of difficulty for other countries ever since October 1979 when US monetary policy began to emphasize money supply targets. Since then prime lending rates have been as high as 20 per cent and stood at 10.75 per cent at the end of 1984, although inflation has fallen from around 14 per cent to about 4 per cent.

In February and March 1984, financial markets were increasingly concerned with the United States' Federal Government and balance of payments deficits and with fears that continuing high rates of growth in the US economy would soon lead to overheating. Short-term rates in the United States began to rise, albeit with fluctuations, but did not automatically affect European rates–indeed the dollar fell in February and March. However, once it became known that the Federal Reserve had decided towards the end of March to tighten monetary policy then foreign sentiment about the dollar improved and the potential linkage between US and European rates was restored.

The rise in United States' interest rates in the first half of 1984 (table 2.1.3) reflected the strong private sector demand for credit and the continuing pressure on the capital markets from the need to finance the federal deficit. Private sector credit demand was also affected by the increasing shift from private consumption to business investment which meant an increase in corporate borrowing. (The latter was also inflated in the first half of the year by a bout of merger activity financed largely by debt issues.) Given the stance of monetary policy, rates rose sharply from mid-March to the end of May. There was then a temporary easing of rates as a result of the need to supply liquidity to a major US bank and of rumours that other US banks were facing liquidity problems: given their large exposure to developing country debt it was feared that a further rise in interest rates would have serious repercussions on the US banking system. However, these fears soon diminished, partly because of increased confidence that the debt problem was under control. With a record increase in consumer credit in June, US rates rose sharply again: on 25 June prime rates, which were 11 per cent at the start of the year, were raised to 13 per cent where they remained throughout the summer.

In September the Federal Reserve eased monetary policy appreciably in response to an unexpectedly sharp deceleration in real output growth: with weaker output and a low inflation rate, there were renewed fears about the impact of high interest rates on the stability of the US financial sector and concern at the effects of the strong dollar on domestic activity. For most of 1984 the growth of the M1 and M2 aggregates had been near the bottom of their set limits: with output growing more slowly and with inflation expected to remain low, the Federal Reserve acted to bring the aggregates nearer the middle of their ranges. Short-term interest rates began to fall throughout the last quarter and the more accommodating stance of policy was underlined at the end of November by a half-point cut in the discount rate to 8.5 per cent, the first cut in this rate since December 1982: a further cut, to 8 per cent, followed on 21 December, the lowest level since October 1978. At the end of 1984 the prime rate had been reduced to 10.75 per cent, a marked fall from the mid-year peak of 13 per cent but not very much below the rate prevailing at the end of 1983. (In January 1985 it fell further, to 10.5 per cent.)

Although west European central banks are clearly aware of the limited scope for insulating European interest rates from those in the United States, nevertheless there was some degree of "decoupling" in 1984. Between January and August (when US rates peaked), commercial bank lending rates (to prime borrowers) in the larger west European economies rose only in the United Kingdom in response to sharp falls in the dollar-sterling exchange rate. In the United Kingdom, where rates have been

TABLE 2.1.3

Selected interest rates, 1982-1984, end of month

	1982 Dec.	1983 Dec.	1984			
			Mar.	June	Sept.	Dec.
A. *Short-term rates*[a]						
United States	7.98	8.94	9.76	9.77	10.60[b]	7.65
France	12.71	12.19	12.54	12.23	11.05	10.69
Germany, Federal Republic of	6.62	6.48	5.86	6.13	5.82	5.83
Italy	19.11	16.95	15.61	14.85	15.40	14.69
United Kingdom	9.72	8.84	8.38	8.86	9.98	11.55
Japan	6.96	6.45	6.41	6.35	6.32	6.33
B. *Long-term rates*[c]						
United States	10.33	11.44	11.90	13.00	12.23[b]	11.21
France	15.71	13.99	13.99	13.68	13.38	11.91
Germany, Federal Republic of	7.9	8.2	7.9	8.1	7.6	7.0
Italy	19.70	17.69	15.69	15.47	15.58	14.53
United Kingdom	10.20	9.90	9.85	10.63	10.04	9.99
Japan	7.50	6.94	6.63	7.12	6.79	6.30

Source: OECD, *Main Economic Indicators*, Paris, February 1985.

[a] Short-dated treasury bills.

[b] August (interim peak for the short-term rate in the United States).

[c] Yields on public sector bonds.

largely determined by market forces, there was some decoupling from US rates in the early part of 1984, but in July a sharp fall in the pound sterling against most other currencies (not just the dollar), combined with the threat of a dock strike, led to a 2 1/2-point rise in base rates to 12 per cent. Rates subsequently fell to 10 1/2 per cent by mid-August and 10 per cent by November. However, in the opening weeks of 1985, the sterling exchange rate again began to fall sharply and the clearing banks raised their base rates to 10 1/2 per cent on January 11 and to 12 per cent on January 14.[2] However, the pressure on sterling persisted with the concern for oil prices and interest rates were raised further, to 14 per cent, at the end of January.

Among the smaller economies in western Europe short-term interest rates tended to remain fairly stable throughout the year, although at relatively high levels. In Norway and Finland tighter monetary policies were accompanied by a reduction in the extent of direct regulation of credit markets: both these countries, with high interest rates and strong exchange rates have attracted foreign capital inflows. Policies have also been tightened in Denmark and Sweden where the current account and foreign debt positions still leave these countries highly vulnerable to movements in international interest rates.

After rising in the first half of 1984 long-term interest rates also began to ease in the second half and, in contrast to short-term rates, were generally lower at the end of the year than in the spring. This flattening of the yield curve, which was very pronounced in the United States and the Federal Republic of Germany, is a sign that there has been a significant weakening of inflationary expectations.

(ii) The stance of economic policies

There were no major changes in the basic orientation of monetary and fiscal policies in the developed market economies in 1984. Particular changes in individual countries have been gen-

---

[2] This second increase was triggered by the temporary reintroduction of Minimum Lending Rate (administered by the Central Bank) at 12 per cent: it is possible that market rates would anyway have risen to this level, but the effect of this move was to remove some of the earlier doubts as to the authorities' attitude towards the decline in the exchange rate.

erally consistent with their medium-term strategies and short-run targets. For the last four years *monetary policies* in western Europe and North America have been set with the basic objective of reducing, and then keeping down, rates of inflation. This has been done mainly by setting targets for a progressive deceleration in the rates of growth of selected monetary aggregates. In the past, cyclical recoveries in output have been frequently accompanied by fast rates of monetary expansion, but in the present recovery the growth of the monetary aggregates has been moderate. As is clear from table 2.1.4 the growth of money stock has decelerated in most countries since 1982 (and in many of them since 1979). The acceleration in the United States in 1983 reflects only partly the easing of policy in 1982: large changes in the financial system had taken place (including the introduction of new types of interest-bearing accounts which households could use for transactions) which inflated aggregates such as M2, and the influence of falling inflationary expectations on the demand for money seems to have justified a once-for-all rise in the money stock. The increase in the demand for the money was also influenced by the lack of confidence engendered by the recession (an increased precautionary demand for money). Given the uncertainties, the Federal Reserve's monetary targets for 1983 were higher and wider than those for 1982, but the targets for 1984 were lower than those for 1983 by 1/2 to 1 percentage point. There was in fact a sharp slowdown in money growth from mid-1983 through mid-1984. For 1985, most of the countries in table 2.1.4 have lowered their targets for the key aggregates by a percentage point or two. Given the slowdown in output growth forecast in many of them, particularly in the United States, monetary policy appears to be accommodating continued expansion. In the last few years, targets have been generally set to allow for real growth and steadily declining rates of inflation over the medium term. The monetary authorities have anyway retained some flexibility in their systems of control by setting targets for a number of aggregates. Morever targets are frequently expressed as ranges and this allows some leeway for supporting output growth since the authorities can aim at different points in the range: the various changes in United States monetary policy in 1984—the tightening in March, the easing in September—fall into this latter category.

In an environment where the overriding objective is to bring

TABLE 2.1.4

Growth of the money stock
(*Yearly averages, annual percentage change*)

	Definition of money stock	1982	1983	1984a
France	M2	11.2	9.0	8.7
Germany, Federal Republic of	M3	6.5	6.7	4.2
Italy	M3	16.2	14.9	12.6
United Kingdom	£M3	11.5	10.8	9.3
Belgium	M2	9.7	5.3	8.6
Denmark	M2	11.0	19.6	13.0
Ireland	M3	13.7	9.0	9.2
Netherlands	M2	7.4	9.9	4.4
United States	M2	9.4	12.4	7.3

Source: Commission of the European Communities, *European Economy*, 22 November 1984, p. 137.

aForecasts by Commission services except United States for which actual growth rates over 12 months to June are shown.

inflation under control and where the prime instrument for doing so is monetary policy, *fiscal policy* is relegated to a subordinate role. However, there are wide differences among countries in their interpretation of the role of fiscal policy although these may be obscured at present because of the apparent uniformity in practice: governments in virtually all the market economies are engaged in attempts to cut public sector deficits and to check the historical, upward trend in public spending. In western Europe governments have been trying to reduce public borrowing requirements in order to support the aims of their monetary policies and to avoid still higher rates of interest for a given stance of monetary policy. More specifically their concern has been that once the upturn in output got under way the expected recovery of investment might be crowded out by the demands of the public sector on domestic savings. At the same time governments have not only been concerned with public sector deficits but also with the *levels* of general government spending: it is felt that these are now so high that they hamper the workings of the market mechanism through their effects on incentives and relative prices in general. However, this general subordination of fiscal to monetary policy does not imply that all west European governments share the same rejection of short-run demand and stabilization policies that has accompanied, at least in principle, monetarist policies in countries such as the United States and the United Kingdom. For some of them, their attempts to reduce borrowing and expenditure levels simply reflects the fact that, in the wake of the two oil shocks, they had reached such excessively high levels that there was virtually no leverage left for discretionary fiscal action: in such cases present fiscal restraint is necessary to re-open the possibility of a more active fiscal policy in the future.

Perhaps the most distinctive approach to macro-economic policy in western Europe, at the present time, is to be found in the Nordic countries. Finland has continued to pursue counter-cyclical demand management policies: government spending was increased in 1982 and 1983, with emphasis on improving supply-side efficiency, but tightened during the upswing in 1984. After the devaluation in 1982 Swedish fiscal policy was used to support an export-led recovery to help improve investment and competitiveness while reducing subsidies to the business sector and expenditures on welfare. Norway cut taxes in 1982 (after the September devaluation) in an attempt to encourage industrial recovery and in the autumn of 1983 presented a moderately expansionary budget for 1984. In all these attempts to find a "middle way" between inflationary expansionism and high rates

of unemployment, wage restraint has made an important contribution. Unwilling to adopt a resigned attitude to the growth of unemployment, the Nordic countries adopted in January 1985 an economic co-operation package centred on regional transport investments—this represents a limited attempt at co-ordinated international action to stimulate growth and cut unemployment.

As can be seen in table 2.1.5, west European fiscal adjustment in the last three years has been significant. The continuing recovery in 1984 helped to check the rise in the actual deficits. But the real impact of the fiscal tightening is to be seen in the move towards surplus of the cyclically adjusted—or structural—deficits: in the last three years this has amounted to about 1.5 per cent of average west European GDP, with a further move in the same direction forecast for 1985. In sharp contrast the United States has moved into structural deficit by some 2.5 per cent of GDP with another large increase expected in 1985.

As already noted above, within the framework of macro-economic policy adopted in the United States since the beginning of 1981, fiscal policy was intended to work on the "supply-side" of the economy by correcting relative price distortions and other disincentives to expanding output. The administration's programme included three successive cuts in personal income tax and large increases in business depreciation allowances, all within a complex set of fiscal reforms. At the same time there were to have been large changes in the structure of Federal expenditure, with defence spending rising in volume and non-defence expenditures falling. After an initial delay, the tax cuts were speedily implemented and defence spending moved ahead and at a slightly faster pace than envisaged at the beginning of 1981. However, the cuts in non-defence expenditure have fallen far short of those planned and instead of a balanced budget in fiscal year 1984, the original plan, the deficit has risen to more than 3 per cent of GNP. Although the size of this nominal deficit in relation to GDP is not very different from those in several other developed market economies, international concern is focused on its structural nature: that is, instead of falling with the revival of output, it has continued to rise.

Given the firm anti-inflationary stance of monetary policy in the United States, the financial balances of the various sectors in the economy have become the main determinants of interest rates. Expectations concerning future government deficits may also play a role in raising interest rates in the United States.

The escalation in the United States' budget deficit has not led to a "crowding out" of private investment nor has it provoked a resurgence in the inflation rate. This is mainly because the high levels of United States' interest rates have pulled in large amounts of capital from abroad (and greatly reduced the flow of American capital overseas). The inflation-reducing effect of this net inflow has been reinforced by weak commodity prices and wage moderation. Meanwhile the very large stimulus from the budget deficit has boosted output which in turn has encouraged productivity growth and investment. Investment might have been inhibited by the exceptionally high levels of real interest rates but this effect was outweighed by the powerful stimulus to output expectations and by the tax concessions to the business sector. (Interest payments were in any case deductible from tax liabilities so that the post-tax rate of interest is generally very much lower than pre-tax nominal rates.)

High and rising US interest rates present the authorities in a number of other countries with a difficult choice: either they allow their own rates to follow suit or they let their national currencies depreciate against the dollar. Higher interest rates may check the growth of investment and endanger an already fragile rate of economic recovery; for countries with a large public debt, they would also make it still more difficult to correct

TABLE 2.1.5

Changes in the actual and structural financial balances of general government, 1982-1985

(Per cent of GDP/GNP, change over the previous year)

	1982		1983		1984[a]		1985[a]	
	A	B	A	B	A	B	A	B
France	−0.8	−0.5	−0.8	−0.3	−0.1	0.7	−0.3	0.1
Germany, Federal Republic of . .	0.4	1.5	0.7	1.4	1.0	0.9	0.9	0.5
Italy	−0.9	0.1	0.9	2.2	−1.7	−0.8	0.4	0.3
United Kingdom	0.7	1.4	−0.9	−1.1	0.2	−0.1	0.2	0.4
Total	*−0.1*	*0.7*	*−0.1*	*0.5*	*0.1*	*0.3*	*0.3*	*0.3*
7 smaller economies[b] . .	−1.1	−0.3	0.3	0.3	1.2	0.6	0.5	−
Total western Europe . .	*−0.3*	*0.5*	*−*	*0.5*	*0.3*	*0.4*	*0.4*	*0.3*
United States	−2.9	−1.3	−0.3	−0.6	0.9	−0.5	−0.4	−1.3

Sources: OECD, *Economic Outlook*, Paris, December 1984. A positive sign indicates a tightening of policy, a negative sign a move towards expansion. European groups weighted by 1982 GDPs.

Note: A−Actual, B−Structural

[a] Forecasts.

[b] Austria, Belgium, Denmark, Finland, Netherlands, Norway and Sweden.

budget deficits. Failure to increase interest rates, however, would accelerate the flow of capital into the United States.

Although European interest rates continue to be heavily influenced by those in the United States, developments in 1984 show that a small area of manoeuvre is possible if domestic circumstances, particularly concerning inflation and the current account, are favourable. Although the Bundesbank intervened on several occasions to check too rapid changes, the depreciation against the dollar did not provoke any other policy reactions in the Federal Republic of Germany: the threat of imported inflation was not regarded as being very serious during 1984 and in any case some of the depreciation against the dollar was offset by weakening primary product prices. The pressure on domestic interest rates was also eased by a reduction in the public sector borrowing requirement. The officially-induced cut in interest rates in France was also helped by sharp reductions in the rate of inflation and in the trade deficit and, in spite of a revival of investment, relatively weak demand from the private sector for credit. Domestic conditions have also been favourable in the United Kingdom: inflation has fallen and remained low, and domestic credit demand was weakening during the year. However, the situation here has been complicated by the weakness of the international oil market. Both in July 1984 and January 1985 the prospect of a renewed fall in oil prices accelerated the fall in the exchange rate to the point where the authorities feared that their anti-inflation objective would be threatened and therefore felt obliged to acquiesce in higher interest rates, however unwelcome from a purely domestic point of view. It is significant that in both instances this official acquiescence appears to have occurred not so much in the face of a drop in the dollar rate but when there was a significant fall against the Deutschmark or in the trade-weighted index. The reason for this reaction, and one which applies to other European countries, appears to be as follows: the depreciation against the dollar is welcome to the west Europeans because it increases their export competitiveness in the buoyant US market and in third countries; at the same time, as long as their currencies fall more or less together against the dollar the inflationary pressures from higher import prices are not very great when world commodity prices are weak and when Europe is not very dependent on the United States for its imports of manufactures. However, the inflationary threat becomes more serious if a west European country's currency starts depreciating against that of one of its major *European* trading partners. As is shown

elsewhere in this *Survey* (see below, section 5.2(ii)), most west European countries do most of their trade with other west European countries and most of this intra-European trade consists of manufactures. Most of these manufactures, in turn, consist of intermediate and capital goods and are often exchanged within highly specialized and interdependent production systems (for example, the European motor car industry). Import demands within such systems are likely to be very inelastic, at least in the short to medium run, and so a sharp fall of one European partner's currency against another is likely to have more serious consequences for the depreciating country's inflation rate than a similar fall against the dollar.

The European Monetary System provides one solution to this problem, but not all European countries are members of the EMS (although some non-members try to keep their exchange rate *vis-à-vis* the Federal Republic of Germany within some target range) and, even for members, persistent depreciation against the dollar will eventually lead to the threat of imported inflation or higher interest rates and greater difficulties in maintaining stable exchange rates within the system. (Although, in 1984, stability of intra-European exchange rates has been helped by the continuing convergence of rates of inflation and money supply growth.)

The central banks have generally been very hesitant to intervene directly in the foreign exchange markets in order to limit the appreciation of the dollar. For some authorities this reflected a belief that their main priority was to establish "sound" domestic policies, especially for money, and when this was achieved the determination of the exchange rate could be left to market forces; others considered that attempts to intervene would be unlikely to have any significant effect on the rise of the dollar and that the main outcome would be a waste of foreign exchange reserves and a risk to domestic monetary restraint. At the Versailles economic summit in 1982 an unsuccessful attempt was made to persuade governments to use their official reserves to check the appreciation of the dollar, although a year later, at the Williamsburg summit, the same seven governments agreed "to improve consultation, policy convergence and international co-operation" with a view to stabilizing the foreign exchange market. Subsequent attempts at intervention, mainly by the Bundesbank in August 1983 and again in September 1984, were not co-ordinated with other central banks and had limited effect. The suggestion that a concerted intervention by the central banks might be sufficient to tip the dollar into a decline, which would then continue under its own momentum, was widely discussed in 1983, but the persistent upward trend in the dollar in 1983 and 1984 made such an idea appear increasingly like wishful thinking. When the pound sterling fell sharply in the summer of 1984 and in January 1985, the UK authorities, as noted above, raised interest rates by 2 and 4 points respectively. However, this last fall in sterling appears to have led to a reassessment of official attitudes towards intervention: the finance ministers of the Group of Five[3] decided at their Washington meeting in January to take a more active and co-ordinated role in the foreign exchange markets. This reaffirmation of the Williamsburg statement was quickly followed by a publicized, and co-ordinated intervention by a number of central banks. There are a number of reasons for this shift in attitudes towards intervention. Although predictions of the imminent fall of the dollar have been repeatedly falsified during the last two years, most western governments believe that such a fall must come eventually and that joint intervention could help to avoid too precipitous a reversal. In the United States the strong dollar has contributed to the maintenance of a low inflation rate, but there is increasing concern at the associated costs of a burgeoning trade deficit and the increasing weakness of many manufacturing industries faced with competition from cheap imports. Western Europe has benefited from its increasing competitiveness *vis-à-vis* the United States (although by no means to the same extent as Japan and other Asian countries) but there are increasing fears that the rising dollar will lead to further restrictions on US imports, a development that would clearly be inimical to Europe's longer-run interest and one which would not be quickly reversed. The effects on west European inflation rates of the rising dollar were offset by lower domestic inflationary pressures in 1984; but the dollar effect could be stronger as the slide in world commodity prices levels off and as the cyclical gains in productivity growth become smaller. West European governments are also anxious to avoid any further rise in interest rates which might weaken the prospects for continued, albeit modest, growth in 1985.[4] Thus this more favourable attitude towards intervention on the foreign exchanges reflects current policy dilemmas and perhaps frustration at not being able to escape from them. Whether this change in attitude will lead to more effectual action remains uncertain: it is widely accepted that the central banks are unlikely to succeed in reversing an underlying trend in a given exchange rate and even the correction of short-run fluctuations may be difficult if there are doubts as to what is the actual trend value. Nevertheless, by the end of 1984 the belief that the value of the dollar is being increasingly inflated by speculative demand and that central bank reserves can be deployed to counter this appears to have gained ground.

(iii) The outlook for 1985

Economic developments in the last two years have been marked by the wide disparity between the rates of growth of output in western Europe and the United States. Although the weaker European performance has been often ascribed, with some justification, to a lack of flexibility in dealing with structural problems, an important factor behind the difference in performance has been the markedly different stance of fiscal policies: as already noted above, these have been very restrictive in

western Europe for the past several years while in the United States they have been highly expansionary. At the beginning of 1985 there are few signs that this contrasting stance of policies will be significantly altered in the course of the year.

In western Europe, governments' budget plans for 1985 generally indicate the continuation of fiscal restraint with targets, often over a two to three-year period, for the reduction of budget deficits in relation to GDP. Only in Norway has a slightly more expansionary stance been adopted for 1985; in Switzerland the expansionary stance of fiscal policy in 1983 and 1984 will be reduced in 1985 (but not eliminated). Fiscal restraint is also accompanied in many cases by fiscal reforms and changes in the structure of taxation. In France and the United Kingdom, for example, income tax cuts have been proposed for 1985 (and for 1986 in the Federal Republic of Germany)—the effects on the budget deficit, however, should be offset by indirect taxes and reduced government expenditure. However the net effects of complicated tax reform packages, such as that introduced in the 1984 budget in the United Kingdom, are often very difficult to predict: this UK budget, although intended to be neutral, was probably slightly expansionary, adding about one quarter of a percentage point to total output.[5] The UK budget for 1985 may also be less restrictive than it appears insofar as the sale of public assets to the private sector is included in the targeted reduction in the borrowing requirement. However, although there is inevitably some margin of error in estimates of the actual outcome, the general intention of fiscal policy in western Europe is to maintain, and indeed intensify, the current restrictive stance. The basic stance and objectives of European monetary policies will also be maintained—the main question here however, is whether they will continue to be more restrictive than warranted by purely domestic considerations. The answer to this will depend largely on the course of interest rates in the United States, which in turn will be influenced in large measure by whether or not significant cuts in the Federal deficit can be achieved. Current prospects for speedy and effective action in this direction do not appear to be very good however. Although the Federal Reserve eased monetary policy in response to the slowdown in output growth in the second half of 1984, it is unlikely that it will do any more than move cautiously within the pre-set limits for monetary growth. Interest rates are therefore likely to remain high. It should be recalled that the Federal Reserve's firm commitment to an anti-inflationary policy stance has been a major factor in maintaining foreign confidence in the dollar and, therefore, in restraining interest rates from rising to even higher levels.

Against this background aggregate GDP growth for the market economies of the ECE region is officially forecast to slow down from about 4.5 per cent in 1984 to about 3 per cent in 1985. The forecast deceleration in growth is due essentially to the United States, the underlying growth rate in western Europe not being expected to change very much (table 2.1.6).

The United States' Administration has recently forecast a growth rate of 4 per cent between the fourth quarters of 1984 and 1985, which is equivalent to a year-on-year increase of some 3.7 per cent. At the same time the rate of inflation (as measured by the GNP deflator) is forecast at 4.3 per cent, slightly higher than in 1984. The forecast for real output growth is only a little more optimistic than most independent forecasts made at the turn of the year: OECD's December forecast was for (year-on-year) growth of 3 per cent and in the United States at the end of 1984 the consensus of professional forecasters was around 3 1/2 per cent. This perspective is based on the less restrictive

---

[3] France, the Federal Republic of Germany, the United Kingdom, the United States and Japan.

[4] The choice is not simply between the risk of higher inflation and higher interest rates: higher interest rates will also affect measured inflation rates, particularly where mortgage costs are included in the consumer price index.

---

[5] NIESR, *National Institute Economic Review*, London, May 1984, p. 6.

stance of monetary policy since last September, continuing reserves of spare capacity in industry and no alarms over the inflation rate. Private consumption and business fixed investment should provide the main supports to growth, although rising at significantly lower rates than in 1984. After rising some 18 per cent in 1984 gross domestic fixed capital formation could slow down to around 6 per cent in 1985, with the deceleration in business fixed investment being somewhat less. The slowdown in output growth in 1985 should entail a marked fall in the growth of imports of goods and services–these increased in volume by nearly 30 per cent in 1984 but this growth rate should slow down by more than a half in 1985. However, export growth is not forecast to accelerate markedly and so there is likely to be some further deterioration in the trade deficit, although not at the rate of the last three years.

TABLE 2.1.6

Annual changes in real GDP, 1983-1985[a]
(*Percentage change over previous year*)

	1983	1984	1985
France	1.0	1.9	1.8
Germany, Federal Republic of[b]	1.3	2.6	2.0
Italy.	−1.2	2.8	2.5
United Kingdom	3.0	2.5	3.5
Total 4 countries	*1.1*	*2.4*	*2.3*
Austria.	2.1	2.4	3.0
Belgium	0.4	1.5	1.5
Denmark	2.0	4.2	2.8
Finland	2.9	3.0	3.5
Ireland.	0.6	3.7	3.0
Netherlands.	0.6	1.5	2.0
Norway	3.2	4.3	0.9
Sweden	2.5	2.7	2.1
Switzerland	0.7	2.4	1.6
Total 9 countries	*1.5*	*2.6*	*2.1*
Total western Europe.	*1.2*	*2.5*	*2.3*
Canada[b]	3.3	4.2	2.8
United States[b]	3.7	6.8	3.9
Total above	*2.4*	*4.6*	*3.1*

Sources: National statistics. For 1984 estimates and 1985 forecasts see Appendix to section 2.2.

[a] At market prices.

[b] GNP.

The slowing down of the United States economy is partly due to normal cyclical factors but it is also influenced by the strength of the dollar. As noted above, a strong dollar and high interest rates have enabled the government to give a large fiscal stimulus to the economy without re-igniting inflation or crowding out private investment. But the balance of advantages has been changing: the rising trade deficit means that an increasing proportion of the stimulus to final demand has been leaking abroad. The lower price of imports holds back the inflation rate but the consequent rise in import penetration holds back the growth of output. However, the immediate outlook for 1985 is for continued growth and only moderate inflation. This prospect is nevertheless subject to a number of uncertainties concerning the dollar, interest rates and the budget deficit which by definition cannot be incorporated into short-run forecasts–these are discussed below.

The less rapid growth rate of the United States economy in 1985 of course means a weaker stimulus to the rest of the world. Domestic demand (excluding stockbuilding) is forecast to pick up a little in western Europe, mainly because of business invest-

ment and private consumption; stockbuilding is likely to be smaller than in 1984, though remaining positive. But with fiscal policies remaining restrictive and external demand weakening, west European GDP growth in 1985 is not forecast to be very different from that in 1984, that is, around 2 1/2 per cent.

Current official forecasts suggest a slowdown in the volume growth of exports of goods and services from about 6 1/2 per cent in 1984 to 5 per cent in 1985, with a larger deceleration (from around 7 to about 4 per cent) for the smaller economies (table 2.1.7). However, the net contribution of the current account to output growth is likely to increase for France and the Federal Republic of Germany (mainly because of a faster deceleration of imports than of exports), while for the nine smaller economies taken together the net contribution is close to zero. However, in looking at the effect of the external account, it should be borne in mind that a higher level of intra-European trade, as is expected in 1985, will have a favourable influence on economic activity in general.

Public expenditure continues to decelerate in western Europe with average growth of about 1 per cent expected in 1985, compared with about 1 1/4 per cent in 1984; in the United States the Administration forecasts real public expenditure growth of nearly 3 per cent between the fourth quarters of 1984 and 1985. Absolute falls in public expenditure are projected in Belgium and Ireland and zero growth in Italy and the Netherlands.

The main support to west European growth in 1985 will therefore be private domestic demand. Consumers' expenditure should rise by nearly 2 per cent on average (compared with 1 per cent in 1984), with an acceleration in France, the Federal Republic of Germany and the United Kingdom. This improvement is due to several factors including better real incomes and proposed (or assumed) cuts in personal income taxes. The modest recovery of gross domestic fixed capital formation in 1984–up by just over 2 per cent on average–is likely to continue at a similar rate in 1985. However, within this aggregate the weakness of the housing and public sectors conceals a more buoyant prospect for business investment.

It should be emphasized that this view of 1985 is subject to considerable uncertainty. Much will depend–as in the last two years–on developments in the United States: the forecast there, of a more subdued but relatively stable development, assumes that there will not be another large rise in interest rates, that the dollar will not continue to rise and that if it falls it will do so gradually. Developments in the early months of 1985 suggest that these assumptions may not be as robust as west European policy makers would like. However, the sources of uncertainty do not arise solely from prospects for the dollar and United States interest rates. The official forecast for the United Kingdom of 3.5 per cent growth in 1985, which is a little higher than the consensus of independent forecasts (about 3 per cent), assumes a recovery from the effects of the coal miners' strike: this accounts for about 1 per cent, so there is really little acceleration in the underlying rate of growth. Another, and now more important, uncertainty in the United Kingdom concerns interest rates: as a result of the fall in the sterling exchange rate in January, interest rates (clearing banks base rates) have risen from 10 to 14 per cent since the beginning of the year. If these are maintained at such levels for any significant length of time–and in the first quarter there was little optimism that they will fall as rapidly as they rose–then the prospects for growth in 1985 could weaken.

The outlook for the Federal Republic of Germany is also clouded by uncertainties with respect to private consumption and business investment. The growth of private consumption in 1984 was actually weaker than in 1983, mainly because of the slow growth of real incomes but also because of uncertainties

TABLE 2.1.7

The growth of GDP and its main components in western Europe, 1983-1985

	Percentage change over previous year			Contribution to the change in GDP[a]		
	1983	1984	1985	1983	1984	1985
A. *Four major European countries*[b]						
Private consumption	1.3	1.1	1.9	0.8	0.7	1.1
Public consumption.	1.5	1.4	1.0	0.3	0.2	0.2
Gross fixed investment	0.6	1.9	1.9	0.1	0.4	0.4
Change in stocks.	..	..	..	−0.1	0.4	−
Exports, goods and services.	1.2	6.4	5.7	0.3	1.8	1.6
Imports, goods and services	1.1	5.6	2.9	−0.3	−1.4	−1.0
GDP at market prices	1.1	2.4	2.3	1.1	2.4	2.3
B. *Total western Europe*[c]						
Private consumption	1.1	1.0	1.7	0.7	0.6	1.0
Public consumption.	1.5	1.3	1.0	0.3	0.2	0.2
Gross fixed investment	0.6	2.2	2.1	0.1	0.4	0.4
Change in stocks.	..	..	..	−0.1	0.5	0.2
Exports, goods and services.	2.3	6.5	5.0	0.7	2.1	1.7
Imports, goods and services	1.5	5.5	3.9	−0.5	−1.7	−1.2
GDP at market prices	1.2	2.5	2.3	1.2	2.5	2.3

Sources: National statistics and official forecasts aggregated by the ECE secretariat.

[a] The component contributions may not always add up to the total GDP change because of rounding.

[b] France, the Federal Republic of Germany (GNP), Italy and the United Kingdom.

[c] Austria, Belgium, Denmark, Finland, Ireland, the Netherlands, Norway, Sweden and Switzerland, plus the four major European economies.

concerning exhaust emission controls on motor cars. This latter uncertainty continues with negative effects on the timing of investment in the motor industry. Within the Federal Republic of Germany there is an important difference of view between the five main forecasting institutes and Council of Economic Advisers (the *Sachverständigenrat*). The former anticipate a slight deceleration of GNP growth in 1985 while the latter forecast an acceleration to 3 per cent. The main difference between the two appears to turn on the prospects for business investment and private consumption. The Council forecasts a growth of 4 per cent in gross domestic fixed capital formation in 1985 based on an improvement in the profitability of investment (real rate of return in fixed relative to financial assets) and the urgent need for modernization in the industrial sector. The Institutes, however, do not see these two forces as being strong enough to produce such a strong increase: profits have improved, but from a very low point. Also it is not clear that the relative real rate of return has switched back in favour of real investment in industry as compared with financial assets. The Council is also more optimistic as regards private consumption in 1985: it forecasts an increase of 2.5 per cent, which is 1 percentage point more than the Institutes. The basic factor making for this difference is the Council's expectation of a stronger increase in the level of employment and, consequently, of disposable income.

(iv) An appraisal of the current economic situation

The official and, indeed, the consensus outlook for 1985, as summarized above, is surrounded by a number of uncertainties which by their very nature are difficult or even impossible to quantify and therefore cannot be properly incorporated into short-run forecasts. In addition, it should be emphasized that business cycle fluctuations are still important for economic developments in the market economies. The business cycle point of view is in fact a good starting-off point for a discussion of short-run prospects.

In the United States the current cyclical upswing is now in its third year. In last year's *Survey*[6] the question was raised as to whether this upswing might be curtailed earlier than in a normal recovery because of the effect of monetary factors on investment. Although the recovery in the United States continued at a much faster pace than forecast in 1984, the sharp slowdown in the second half of the year suggests that this restrictive monetary factor was operative. Since monetary policy was eased fairly quickly in response to this setback, fears of a recession quickly evaporated and activity regained strength towards the end of the year.

Investment in the United States has remained strong as a result of buoyant business expectations and lower effective costs of capital. The Economic Recovery Tax Act of 1981 effectively reduced the average rate of taxation on income from new investments, but at current rates of inflation the corporate tax structure has a marked bias towards equipment rather than structures, and assets with short rather than long lives.[7] This has contributed to the nature of investment in the current investment boom: the emphasis has been on durable equipment and this accounted for about three quarters of total business investment in 1984, an exceptionally high proportion. The more investment shifts towards shorter asset lives the greater is the sensitivity of investment behaviour to changes in output, expectations, confidence, shifts in economic policy and all the other factors which affect business confidence and the willingness to invest.[8] This shift in the structure of investment may also have been influenced by the competitive pressures on US industry deriving from the strong dollar.

It should be stressed that the current investment boom has already been underway for a longer period than usual at the pres-

[6] Economic Commission for Europe, *Economic Survey of Europe in 1983*, United Nations, New York, 1984, pp. 6-7.

[7] See *Economic Report of the President*, Washington, D.C., February 1985, p. 81.

[8] See section 2.2(iii) below.

ent stage of the upswing: this is because it recovered earlier than normal in the recovery, which is possibly a reflection of the pent-up demand for the renewal of equipment which in turn was a result of the length of the previous recession. It cannot be ruled out that the investment boom could continue for some time yet, but normal business cycle behaviour would lead to the expectation of a downturn in 1986 or even in 1985. Output growth has anyway slowed down quite sharply, partly because of the rapidly deteriorating trade balance; with a lag, this should lead to a weakening of investment insofar as changes in output growth affect business expectations. Morever, the factors mentioned above would imply that a weakening of investment intentions could lead to a fall in investment which is much steeper than normal. If these factors are at work then one cannot be sure that the current cyclical upswing will survive 1985.

Among the factors which might lead to such a sharp revision of business confidence, interest rates and the dollar exchange rate seem at present to be the most likely candidates. The upswing in the United States has been exceptional in that it has been accompanied by high real rates of interest and a strongly appreciating dollar: such a combination has enabled a large fiscal stimulus to take effect without boosting inflation or crowding out investment. However, this favourable combination cannot endure indefinitely. During 1983 and 1984 the growing strength of the dollar appears to have been supported by real factors in its favour: large interest rate differentials, a vigorous growth of output and business profits and the general aura of confidence surrounding the American economy particularly against the background of modest growth in the rest of the world. However, the appreciation has continued very rapidly in the opening months of 1985 and there is increasing evidence that the element of speculation has come to dominate the underlying factors, which have in fact been weakening since the middle of 1984. At the beginning of 1984 a majority of analysts expected a fall in the dollar during the year: this expectation was generally based on the analysis of real factors. For some months now there has been a distinct nervousness in the foreign exchange markets as regards the dollar: the market seems to be increasingly conscious of being in the presence of a speculative bubble, where the dollar appears to have acquired a momentum of its own.[9] Another feature of the present situation is the increasing number of expert and official warnings about what is happening in the foreign exchange markets. However, history shows that in speculative booms the speculators are generally immune to such advice.[10] If the present stage of dollar appreciation corresponds to such a speculative boom, then it must contain the seeds of its own destruction: if so, it would be surprising if it were to continue for very much longer. The danger here is that the longer this boom continues, the less likely it becomes that the eventual fall of the dollar will be gradual, which is the assumption (or hope) in the consensus view of likely developments in 1985. When the dollar falls, and particularly if it falls rapidly, a rise in US interest rates appears unavoidable and, as argued above, this could lead to a sharp drop of investment and so to the end of the upswing.

The strength of the dollar in the last two years has significantly benefited west European exports and this has been an element in the European upswing. However, high US interest rates have been a factor in maintaining high rates in western Europe, and these have retarded the European recovery, although between the two elements the net effect has probably been expansionary. If the dollar were to fall sharply, as suggested above, it would

certainly weaken the competitiveness of European industry *vis-à-vis* the United States, but the negative effects of this on west European net exports would not be felt immediately due to lagged reactions in output and trade. In the meantime a lower dollar would have a quicker and beneficial effect on European rates of inflation and this would allow some decoupling of European from United States' interest rates. Since a fall in the dollar would be likely to lead to higher interest rates in the United States, as suggested above, "decoupling" would not necessarily imply a significant fall in European rates. Since higher interest rates are likely to signal the end of the current upswing in the United States, the stimulus to west European exports would disappear. The total effect of such a US slowdown on Europe would be still greater because of its negative effects on the developing countries whose import capacities would be immediately lowered by weaker exports and higher interest rates.

The situation in western Europe has much improved in the last two years: international trade, particularly intra-European trade, has played an important role and business investment, stimulated by higher profits and higher rates of capacity utilization, rose significantly in 1984 and should continue to do so in the current year. The elements of a normal upswing in western Europe therefore exist, but so far they do not appear to be strong enough to raise economic activity above the modest levels of the recent past. Although there have been considerable improvements on the supply side, the long recession of the early 1980s appears to have had a depressing effect on long-run business expectations as to the future of the European economy. Of course the very improvements of the last two years may themselves have a positive effect on these expectations and this might lead to somewhat stronger growth than is currently expected for 1985. However, such a spontaneous improvement would be most unlikely to have a decisive impact on the unemployment problem or to be large enough to offset a weakening of activity in the United States.

One factor behind the weakening of long-run business expectations has been the major change in the stance of fiscal policy in the 1980s. From a macro-economic point of view fiscal policy has been increasingly restrictive as governments have concentrated on cutting budget deficits and reducing expenditure. A consequence of this general approach has been the abandonment of the short-run stabilization objectives of fiscal policy: until the 1970s stabilization policies had helped to create confidence in the prospects of steady growth and this helped to maintain investment. However, there is now widespread pessimism as to the ability of governments to manage their economies in the short run with fiscal policy. But at the present time the concentration on narrow fiscal objectives has led to policies which are so restrictive that they may be restraining the natural cyclical forces working for an upswing in western Europe.

If the United States economy does weaken, as suggested above, then it would be necessary for this restrictive stance of fiscal policy in western Europe to be eased quickly if business confidence and the existing pace of activity is to be preserved. However, any relaxation of fiscal policy would have to be gradual and cautious, because output is already fairly close to the limits of existing production capacity. The main constraint is the capital stock which has been growing very slowly as a result of low rates of net investment. In the present circumstances so-called "classical unemployment" (which is due to an excessive level of real wages) is not a serious problem, at least when considered against the possible scope for expansion allowed by the existing capital stock. The key issue is therefore investment, which is needed both to strengthen the current upswing and to increase productive capacities—without the latter there is little prospect of western Europe returning to anything close to full employment.

---

[9] On the "atmosphere" in the New York foreign exchange market see *Financial Times*, 27 February 1985, p. 5 of the Frankfurt edition.

[10] See Charles P. Kindleberger, *Manias, Panics and Crashes—A History of Financial Crises*, Basic Books, New York, 1978, Chapter 6.

As emphasized already, any relaxation of fiscal policy would have to be made cautiously, but to have any effect on investment expectations it might be useful to accompany such a change with a commitment of governments to longer-run fiscal policy objectives for the stable growth of nominal national incomes.[11] Ad-herence to such objectives could be an important factor in improving business confidence in the possibilities of sustained growth in western Europe. This would now appear to be a critical issue. In the last few years there has been considerable progress in Europe in improving many of the conditions required for higher investment (in particular, higher profits and moderate wage growth), but without expectations of sustained output growth a strong improvement of investment will not occur.

---

[11] This is one element in the New Keynesianism of Professor J. E. Meade. See especially his *Stagflation—Volume 1: Wage Fixing*, George Allen and Unwin, London, 1982.

2.2 THE STRUCTURE OF DEMAND

This section discusses changes in the main components of GDP in 1984 and their likely development in 1985. Two notes discuss, respectively, the determination of household savings in western Europe and the problems involved in trying to assess current levels of capacity utilization.

(i) Private and public consumption

Private consumption has been a major support of the recovery of the last two years in the United States and in the four larger economies of western Europe. In 1983 it accounted for over 80 per cent of GNP growth in the former and for about 70 per cent of GDP growth in the latter; as the recovery broadened, particularly to fixed investment, these proportions fell to around one half and some 30 per cent respectively in 1984. Nevertheless, there are large variations between countries in the growth of private consumption (table 2.2.1). The strong recovery of consumer demand in the United Kingdom, which began in the second quarter of 1982, probably reached its cyclical peak in 1984, although its weakness in the first half of 1984 was partly due to the effects of the coal miners' strike and delays in some public sector wage settlements. The strength of the boom in consumer demand in both the United States and the United Kingdom appears to have been partly due to a pent-up demand for the replacement of consumer durables, which had been delayed because of the exceptional duration of the preceding recession. As the United Kingdom is somewhat ahead of other west European countries, in terms of cyclical timing, a similar pent-up replacement demand might be supposed to exist elsewhere as well. However, real income growth in many other European countries has been more restrained than in the United Kingdom. In the Federal Republic of Germany consumption was boosted in the first quarter of 1984 by wage bonuses (paid to avoid an imminent rise in social security contributions) but then stagnated in the wake of the metal workers' strike which appears to have dented consumer confidence (although a drop in the savings ratio appears to have cushioned the effect of the strike). Another factor was the uncertainty surrounding the proposed legislation on exhaust emissions which depressed the demand for motor cars. Consumption recovered in the third quarter and the prospect is for a continuing steady growth in 1985: this should be supported by a small rise in employment and the continuation of a modest rate of inflation. In France the relatively slower recovery of private consumption reflects the continuing effects of the adjustment policies introduced in March 1983 although households have cushioned the effect on their disposable incomes by reducing their savings ratio. Private consumption in 1985 should accelerate a little, partly in response to cuts in income tax. In Italy, consumer demand, which fell in 1983, recovered quite sharply in 1984 in line with a strong recovery in output and a rise in real disposable income. Although higher interest rates and higher unemployment are negative factors, the growth of consumption is likely to continue at a similar pace (about 2 per cent) in 1985, aided perhaps by a fall in the savings rate.

In contrast to the United States and the four major economies of western Europe, consumption has been, in general, a relatively

TABLE 2.2.1

Changes in the volume of private and public consumption, 1983-1985
(*Percentage change over previous year*)

	Private			Public		
	1983	*1984*	*1985*	*1983*	*1984*	*1985*
France	1.0	0.8	1.5	1.9	1.2	0.6
Germany, Federal Republic of	1.1	0.8	1.5	–	1.9	1.0
Italy.	−0.5	2.0	2.0	2.8	1.0	0.0
United Kingdom	4.0	1.5	3.0	3.0	1.0	2.0
Total 4 countries	*1.3*	*1.1*	*1.9*	*1.5*	*1.4*	*1.0*
Austria.	5.0	−1.0	2.5	2.0	2.0	2.0
Belgium	−1.0	−0.8	−0.7	0.2	−0.3	−0.6
Denmark	1.7	3.0	2.0	–	–	0.7
Finland	2.0	3.0	3.0	3.9	3.5	2.0
Ireland.	−3.5	1.2	2.3	–	−0.5	−0.5
Netherlands.	−0.2	−0.5	0.5	1.0	−1.0	0.0
Norway	1.0	1.0	2.4	3.7	2.6	1.3
Sweden	−1.7	0.8	1.3	0.9	2.3	0.8
Switzerland	1.5	1.5	1.3	4.4	3.4	3.6
Total 9 countries	*0.5*	*0.6*	*1.2*	*1.5*	*1.2*	*0.9*
Total western Europe.	*1.1*	*1.0*	*1.7*	*1.5*	*1.3*	*1.0*
Canada.	3.1	3.8	2.2	0.3	2.3	2.5
United States	4.8	5.3	3.0	−0.3	3.5	5.0
Total above	*3.0*	*3.3*	*2.4*	*0.6*	*2.5*	*3.0*

Sources: National statistics. For 1984 estimates and 1985 forecasts see appendix to this section.

minor support to the recovery in the smaller European countries. On average it accounted for about 20 per cent of GDP growth in 1983 and 12 per cent in 1984. This reflects the export-led nature of the recovery, a fairly usual feature of a cyclical upturn in small open economies, but one which has been reinforced in several of them in the last few years by policies designed to redress domestic imbalances while at the same time improving international competitiveness: thus, on average, private consumption rose by about half of 1 per cent in 1983 and 1984 while the volume of exports of goods and services rose 4 and 7 per cent respectively. The extreme case in 1984 was Austria where consumption fell 1 per cent and export volume rose 18 per cent. In 1985 there should be an acceleration of consumption growth, partly as a lagged response to this external stimulus, and this is likely to account for about one third of the growth in GDP. However, private consumption was not depressed in all the small countries: in Denmark, Finland and Ireland it actually increased more than anywhere else in western Europe.

As a result of pro-cyclical fiscal policies in western Europe *public consumption* has played a relatively small and declining role in supporting total output. In both the larger and the smaller economies it accounted for about a quarter of GDP growth in 1983 and for about 8 per cent in 1984—in 1985 its relative contribution will decline still further, while in the United States its importance will more than double to about one quarter of the forecast rise in GNP. However, public expenditure growth was still quite high in those countries which have continued to implement counter-cyclical fiscal policies—such as Finland, Norway and Sweden (some 4, 3 and 2 per cent growth respectively in 1984) and Switzerland, where an expansionary fiscal policy was introduced in 1983 (speeding up of government equipment orders, increased subsidies for residential construction, and support for industrial restructuring). Apart from Finland in 1984, Switzerland has the fastest growth of public consumption for the 1983-1985 period.

Although public consumption growth rates are generally low and declining, they have nevertheless tended to be higher than forecast or planned—in 1984 this was true of eight of the 13 countries in table 2.2.1. The main reasons for this slippage have been increases in social security spending, a result of rising unemployment, and the rising burden of servicing public sector debt.

(ii) Household savings

The recovery of private consumption during 1983 and 1984 was generally much stronger than expected, particularly in 1983. The reason for this is that there was a large and unexpected fall in household savings, which in turn has been widely explained by the fall in inflation rates. This has meant that households have been able to spend more of their current disposable income and to divert less of it to maintaining the real value of their stock of financial assets. In other words the "inflation tax" on the monetary assets of households (liquid assets multiplied by the inflation rate) has fallen sharply: in the United Kingdom it dropped from 12 per cent of disposable income in the second quarter of 1980 to around 4 per cent in the third quarter of 1983.[12] The fall is also likely to have been affected by greater consumer confidence about economic prospects in general and about inflation and the prospects of becoming unemployed in particular. However, savings behaviour is affected by a number of variables and this section presents a brief discussion of them within a simple analytical framework.

Developments in the savings ratios of households are shown in chart 2.2.1 for nine west European countries and for the United

States for the period 1970 to 1982. The sample of countries is restricted for reasons of data availability.[13] Most of the ratios display a generally downward trend, the main exception being Finland and, in the 1970s, the United Kingdom and Italy. The downward tendency has been quite strong, which might suggest future problems for the financing of investment. Another feature of the ratios is their considerable variability over time. This may be the result of substitution between the savings of the different sectors (households, private business and the public sector). However, an analysis (not presented in this note) of the private sector and the aggregate national savings ratios showed that they were in fact less stable than the household ratio between 1970 and 1984; moreover, the different ratios were only partially correlated: the correlation between the household and private sector ratios was weak and between the household and national savings ratios virtually non-existent. From the viewpoint of policy this presents a problem because it means that focusing on only one ratio can give a misleading view of the overall behaviour of savings in the economy.

The determinants of savings behaviour in the period 1971-1982 were examined with the following savings function:

$$(s/y) = \sum_{i=1}^{10} D_i + b_1(s/y)_{-1} + b_2PCR + b_3YR + b_4DU + b_5RR + b_6GPR,$$

where (s/y) denotes the ratio of household savings to disposable income, PCR the rate of change of consumer prices (the consumption deflator), YR the rate of change of real income, DU the (first) difference in the unemployment rate, RR the *ex post* real rate of interest and, finally, GPR the rate of change of public (i.e. general government) consumption at constant prices. The D_is are the individual country intercepts to be used in the context of pooled cross-country data. Because of the lack of degrees of freedom, pooled data were more or less obligatory and this, in turn, partly dictated the functional form used: for example, it will be noticed that the above equation is completely free of the units of measurement.

The basic story behind this function is that the rate of change of real income has a positive effect on the savings ratio and that changes in the savings ratio show a certain inertia. The first two terms are thus compatible with the standard life-cycle model. As far as the inflation rate variable is concerned, there are many possible channels via which inflation can affect private consumption and saving. The one mentioned at the outset of this section, and which is most often mentioned in this context, is the effect of inflation on households' real balances. Because inflation erodes the real value of assets, households are forced to increase their saving in order to reach or maintain their desired level of real assets. Inflation may also influence saving in other ways, via increased relative price uncertainty or the misperception of relative and absolute prices.[14]

---

[12] NIESR, *National Institute Economic Review*, London, February 1984.

[13] With the exception of France, the Federal Republic of Germany, Italy and Norway the ratios used are net of depreciation. Private consumption includes expenditure on consumer durables. Data are from OECD, *National Accounts*, magnetic tape for the period 1970-1982. The figures for Norway, not shown in the chart but included in the analysis below, are based on A. Cappelen, *Intektsfordeling og Konsum 1962-1978*, Statistisk Sentralbyra, Artikler Nr. 123, 1980.

[14] An extensive survey of these possibilities is given in R. A. Williams, "Household Saving and Consumption in the 1970s" (with comments by K. W. Clements, H. N. Johnston, J. C. Looker and J. W. Nevile), in *Conference in Applied Economic Research*, Reserve Bank of Australia, 1979, pp. 130-192.

CHART 2.2.1.

Households' savings ratios, 1970 — 1984

(Net savings as a percent of disposable income)

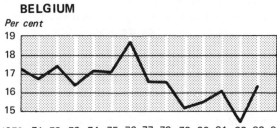

BELGIUM

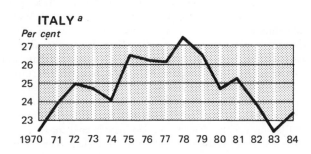

ITALY [a]

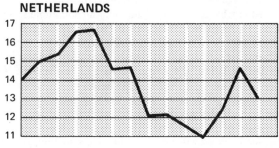

NETHERLANDS

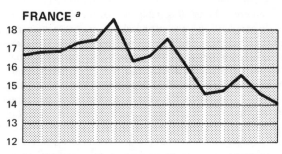

FRANCE [a]

UNITED KINGDOM

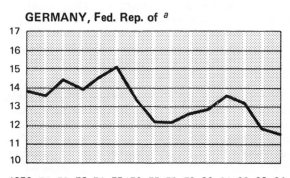

GERMANY, Fed. Rep. of [a]

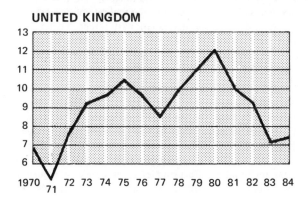

UNITED STATES

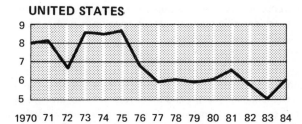

AUSTRIA

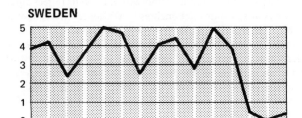

SWEDEN

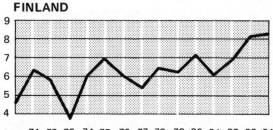

FINLAND

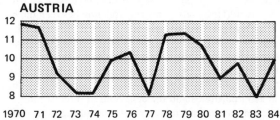

Source: OECD, *National Accounts,* Paris; national statistics.

a Gross savings (includes depreciation).

The unemployment variable, *DU*, in the savings function is a proxy for real income uncertainty which should have a positive effect on household saving; the real rate of interest, *RR*, should also have a positive effect on the assumption that the respective substitution effect outweighs the income effect.

Finally, the growth rate of public consumption, *GPR*, is included in the equation in order to take into account the possible substitution of public for private consumption. The use of this variable is not without problems. Early Keynesian analysis assumed that the savings ratio was relatively stable and that fiscal policies affected consumption only via their effect on current disposable income. This view not only excluded interest rate and wealth effects but also ignored the implications of the intertemporal behaviour of households with respect to consumption and labour supply. The Keynesian view is challenged—at the other extreme—by Barro's "debt neutrality" hypothesis which states that households do not only respond to taxes but also to government deficits, thus implying that there is a more or less perfect substitution between household (or private sector) saving and government saving. Obviously, this latter view makes very strong assumptions about the public's ability to see through the "veil" of government action, and this alone might lead to a questioning of the empirical relevance of the "debt neutrality" hypothesis. But even if this extreme hypothesis is abandoned, by referring to a lack of rationality and foresight on the part of the general public, it might still be doubted whether households totally ignore public consumption. Presumably a part of public consumption is a substitute for private consumption, and it should therefore stimulate household (or private sector) saving.[15] It is also possible for public consumption to be a substitute also for *future* private consumption and therefore it would reduce saving. This would be the case for public pension benefits and the provision of care for the aged. If public consumption depresses savings in the way Feldstein[16] has argued then the sign of the GPR term will be negative.

Before turning to the empirical analysis, it will be useful to make a few comments on the time series for the explanatory variables specified in the savings function given above. First: the rate of inflation and the growth rates of real income and of public consumption behave in very much the same way across countries. However, the unemployment rate and the real rate of interest seem to behave differently. It is evident that these differences are partly due to measurement errors which means that the results of the empirical analysis must be considered with due care. Second: the coefficients of correlation between the household savings ratio and the rate of inflation differ markedly from country to country. This suggests that the impact of inflation on household savings (given a savings model of the type specified above) might differ between countries, reflecting, for example, variations in the degree of indexation, the composition of household asset portfolios and the behaviour of interest rates. And, third: the way interest rates are determined seems to vary considerably between countries and, presumably, over time within each country. This makes it very difficult to assess the impact of interest rates on saving. One practical problem arises from the fact that in some countries, notably Finland and Spain, nominal interest rates have been nearly constant: this creates a difficult multi-collinearity problem which should be kept in mind when interpreting the corresponding estimation results.

Estimation of the savings function was carried out on both pooled cross-country data and on data for individual countries. The estimation was also carried out for the private sector savings ratio and the aggregate national savings ratio, although the results are not detailed here. The idea behind these alternative specifications of the dependent variable is that if there exists perfect, or even considerable, substitution between the three sectoral ratios, then the household savings ratio would not be the relevant concept of savings from the point of view of economic policy.

As mentioned already, individual country data give only very few degrees of freedom to the estimated parameters. Small sample bias is therefore so evident that the focus here is on the results from the pooled data. Estimation was carried out by using both unweighted and weighted data, the weights being the estimates of mid-year population in each country.

The results of the estimation on pooled cross-country data are presented in table 2.2.2. The changes in the household savings ratio, both from country to country and within each country, are explained rather well by the estimating equation. The estimated coefficients are mostly of the expected sign and magnitude indicating that inflation, the rate of change of real income and changes in the unemployment rate all have a positive impact on the household savings ratio. The rather high value on the coefficient of the lagged savings ratio indicates that savings adjust only sluggishly to the optimal level. As far as the real rate of interest and the growth rate of public consumption are concerned, the respective coefficients cannot be precisely estimated; this may reflect both theoretical ambiguity and measurement errors (particularly in the case of the real rate of interest). The results for individual country equations (not reported here) show similar signs and magnitude of the coefficients, although in Austria, Finland, Norway and Italy the estimates were so imprecise that no conclusions could be drawn.

When the function was estimated with the savings ratio for the whole private sector as the dependent variable, the results were very similar to those for the household sector. Thus it appears that the same set of variables can be used to explain changes in both ratios, although the magnitudes of the parameters differ: in the case of the private sector savings ratio, the real income effect is larger, the inflation effect smaller, and the speed of adjustment is lower than for the household ratio. It is, in fact, only in the growth rate of public consumption where there is a significant difference in the two equations: the equation for the private sector savings ratio suggests that this variable may, after all, have a negative impact on saving.

The results with the national savings ratio differed considerably from those with the household and private sector savings ratios, the general flavour of the results suggesting that the "consolidated approach", and other related ideas, do not represent a satisfactory framework. Only the real income growth rate variable and the lagged dependent variable had coefficients of the correct sign and magnitude. Otherwise the results reflect different kinds of spurious relationships.[17] Obviously this cannot be avoided because the national savings ratio cannot be isolated from the general equilibrium framework. This, in turn, raises the question whether it is at all appropriate to use such an abstract and "non-behavioural" concept such as the national savings ratio in an analysis which is intended to serve economic policy.

[15] See L. A. Sjaastad and D. L. Wisecarver, "The Social Cost of Public Finance", *Journal of Political Economy*, 1977, pp. 513-547, which provides a framework for analysing the effects of changes in public consumption.

[16] M. S. Feldstein, "Social Security, Induced Retirement, and Aggregate Capital Accumulation", *Journal of Political Economy*, 1974, pp. 905-926.

[17] A decrease in public saving (i.e. an increase in the public sector deficit) presumably has an impact on the rate of inflation and on interest rates. In turn, an increase in interest rates will lead to a reallocation of resources between consumption and investment.

TABLE 2.2.2

Estimation results of the household savings ratio equation with cross-country data, 1971-1982

	Eq. 1	Eq. 2	Eq. 3	Eq. 4	Eq. 5	Eq. 6
$(s/y)_{-1}$	.551 (8.55)	.551 (8.75)	.581 (8.61)	.487 (6.44)	.485 (6.53)	.476 (6.17)
PCR.	.114 (2.99)	.114 (3.89)	.087 (2.84)	.097 (1.99)	.092 (2.72)	.083 (2.35)
YR	.355 (7.17)	.360 (8.37)	.258 (6.70)	.316 (5.65)	.320 (6.75)	.242 (5.85)
DU	.492 (4.13)	.497 (4.27)		.492 (2.98)	.425 (3.04)	
RR	.002 (0.05)			.009 (0.19)		
GPR.	.007 (0.27)			.010 (0.29)		
100*SEE	.857	.849	.915	.980	.971	1.008
D-W.	1.903	1.911	1.986	1.987	1.995	2.034
Weighting of observations	POP	POP	POP	None	None	None

Note: The numbers in parentheses are *t*-ratios; other symbols are explained in the text. All equations include individual country intercepts which are, however, not displayed. The number of observations is 120. The weighting variable is the estimate of the mid-year population (POP). The Durbin-Watson autocorrelation statistics have been adjusted for the gaps in data when moving from one country to another. Due to the presence of a lagged dependent variable in all estimated equations the Durbin-Watson statistics are biased towards rejecting the hypothesis of autocorrelated residuals.

The results in table 2.2.2 suggest that household savings ratios may continue to fall or to remain at their current low levels in the near future. The growth of real incomes seems likely to improve in 1985 and this should lead to a rise in the ratio, although the improvement in real income is small compared with changes in the period for which the equation was estimated. On the other hand, the rate of inflation has fallen considerably in the last few years and if this continues (or is maintained) savings ratios could fall still further or refrain from rising. Similarly, rates of unemployment are still rising, but at a decreasing pace and this would imply lower uncertainty as to future income on the part of those in work—and this too implies lower savings ratios. Real rates of interest remain high and their future course remains uncertain. Although the effects of real interest rates on household saving are not clear, a fall in interest rates will probably lead to lower household savings ratios. Thus, on balance there would appear to be good reasons for concluding that the large drop in household savings ratios in the last few years will not be reversed in the near future.

(iii) Investment

(a) *Stockbuilding*

With the recovery moving into its second year, stockbuilding accounted for about one quarter of total GDP/GNP growth in 1984 in both western Europe and the United States. In western Europe it added nearly a percentage point to the growth of domestic demand and nearly two points in the United States. In 1983 there had been destocking in most of the smaller European economies as well as in France and Italy: the turnround in the stock cycle was thus sharp in most of these countries. The pace of stockbuilding is forecast to weaken in 1985 although still remaining positive: in both western Europe and in the United States it is expected to provide less than one tenth of the rise in GDP.

(b) *Fixed investment*

The cyclical upturn was increasingly sustained by fixed investment in 1984. This was not unexpected, since it is generally the case that fixed investments do not lead but lag behind the cyclical upswing in production, a reflection *inter alia* of the existence of relatively large margins of spare capacity at the trough of a cycle and the uncertainties of firms about the persistence of the improvement in sales.

In the majority of countries, therefore, the increases in domestic fixed capital formation in 1984 were well above those for 1983. The most conspicuous exceptions were France, with a virtually unchanged investment level (minus 0.1 per cent), Finland and Ireland. In the latter two countries investment declined last year by 1.5 and 2 per cent respectively. In the Federal Republic of Germany there was a significantly smaller increase in 1984 (1.3 per cent) than in 1983 (3.1 per cent). However, this mainly reflects the abolition of the investment subsidy schemes for machinery and equipment at the end of 1983, which led many firms to bring forward their investment expenditures, and the strike in the metal industry at the beginning of the year. Another factor was the sizeable decline of investment by the construction sector following a large fall in the demand for dwellings.

There is quite a lot of variation among the changes in real investment in the individual countries of western Europe and North America. The dominating feature is the investment boom in the United States where, according to preliminary estimates, private sector expenditures rose by 18 per cent last year, after a 10 per cent increase in 1983. This is the highest annual increase in the post-war period but it should be remembered that strong cyclical variations of investment are typical of the US economy. Nevertheless the current investment upswing in the US has been more vigorous than in previous post-war recoveries. The major factors behind this surge were purchases of producers' durable equipment and of non-residential structures. This is in marked contrast to 1983 when the bulk of the increase of 10 per cent was due to the rise in the construction of dwellings (which increased 42 per cent).

In western Europe the underlying rate of increase of total fixed investment was in general still quite moderate: in 1984 the rate of change was on average between 2 and 3 per cent. However, there were some notable exceptions: in the United Kingdom fixed investment has now risen for the third year in succession and

CHART 2.2.2.

**Real GDP, gross domestic fixed capital formation and investment ratios
in western Europe and the United States, 1973–1984**

GDP, GDFCF
Index
1973 = 100

GDP ▬▬▬   GDFCF ▪▪▪▪▪▪▪   GDFCF/GDP ═══════   Investment ratio

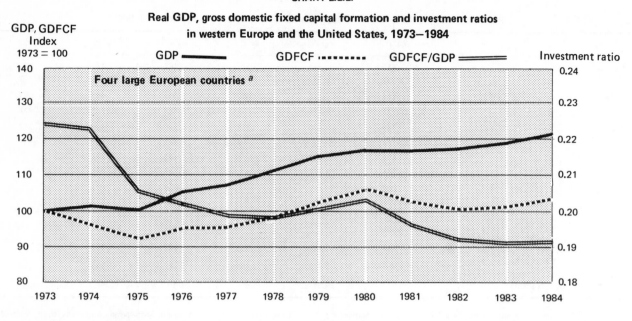

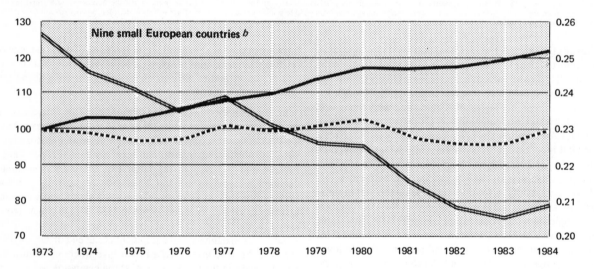

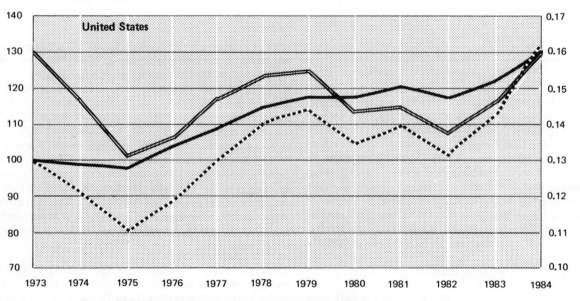

Source: OECD, *National Accounts,* Paris and national statistics.
a France, Germany, Fed. Rep. of, Italy, United Kingdom.
b Austria, Belgium, Denmark, Finland, Ireland, Netherlands, Norway, Sweden, Switzerland.

increased by about 6.5 per cent last year; and in Denmark the estimates available point to growth of well above 10 per cent. In Denmark investment in dwellings was particularly strong with a 20 per cent rise in 1984 (after an increase of 17 per cent in 1983).

From the partial estimates that are available it appears that these increases in total fixed investment would have been somewhat higher in a number of countries had it not been for the further stagnation or decline of public sector investment, a consequence of the restrictive stance of fiscal policy and the continuing efforts to reduce budget deficits by cutting expenditures. Thus business and, in particular, industrial investment—notably in machinery and equipment—has risen considerably in a number of European countries (e.g. Austria, the Netherlands, Sweden and the United Kingdom), and the evidence available from business surveys indicates that expenditure plans announced in late 1983 were generally revised upwards during the course of 1984.

Investment in residential construction generally remained sluggish or even declined. The underlying "natural" strength of developments in the housing market are always difficult to assess because of the various governmental subsidy schemes that are more or less regularly turned off and on. The general effect of these tax schemes is often only to induce investors to alter the timing of their expenditures, thus creating a correspondingly large fall in demand after the subsidy has been suspended. However, the weakness of the housing market also reflects the modest increases in disposable income in the last few years. With declining inflation rates, high real interest rates and increasing regulation investment in housing may have also become less attractive relative to financial assets.

Apart from the more country-specific, investment incentive schemes, there were several general factors in 1984 which help to explain the improved investment performance of the business sector and, in particular, of industry.

First, profit margins improved markedly owing mainly to the modest wage increases and the relatively strong productivity gains of the last few years, which together implied smaller increases in unit labour costs (see also section 2.3(i) and (ii)). This and increased sales have significantly improved the overall cash flow position of firms thus making it easier to finance more investments out of own-funds, as well as facilitating access to external funds.

Second, the increase in production—together with the modest rise in production capacities—has led to higher rates of capacity utilization (see below) and stimulated investment in new equipment and machinery. Moreover, after the relative sluggishness of investment in recent years a backlog of investment demand may have built up, particularly for modernizing production processes and developing new product lines.

Nevertheless, it should be noted that the level of total investment in many countries is still well below or only in the approximate neighbourhood of the levels last reached in 1979, the previous cyclical peak, and it seems that in western Europe there has been a decline in the underlying trend of the investment-output ratio (see chart 2.2.2).

Investment forecasts have often proved to be subject to wide margins of error. From the currently available information it appears that in general public sector investment will continue to stagnate or even decline further in 1985, although there are some exceptions (e.g. Denmark and the Federal Republic of Germany). Also dwellings will not make a significant contribution to investment growth in 1985, but will probably fall in many countries below the levels reached in 1984.

The major driving force of investment in 1985 thus appears to be private non-residential investment and, in particular, industrial expenditures on machinery and equipment. The factors making for the generally sustained or accelerated growth in business investment are basically the same as in 1984, namely, favourable profit margins and still higher rates of capacity utilization. Moreover, it may well be that the increase in production in 1985 will bring many firms into the vicinity of "normal" rates of capacity utilization. Somewhat above these rates, marginal costs of production will probably increase fairly strongly, and it can therefore be expected that capacity-augmenting investments will

TABLE 2.2.3

Changes in real gross domestic fixed capital formation

Country	Average annual rate of growth		Percentage change over previous year			
	1973-1979	1979-1984	1982	1983	1984	1985
France	1.0	−0.1	−0.6	−1.4	−0.1	1.4
Germany, Federal Republic of	0.8	−0.3	−4.7	3.1	1.3	1.5
Italy	−0.5	0.2	−5.2	−5.3	2.2	4.0
United Kingdom	0.1	0.5	6.7	4.0	6.5	2.0
Total 4 countries	*0.6*	*−*	*−1.7*	*0.6*	*1.9*	*1.9*
Austria	1.2	−0.9	−6.8	−1.9	3.0	3.5
Belgium	1.5	−3.5	−1.1	−6.4	3.3	3.0
Denmark	−1.1	−3.0	5.4	3.2	11.9	10.0
Finland	−1.6	3.4	3.5	2.5	−1.5	4.5
Ireland	6.0	−3.3	−6.1	−7.7	−2.0	2.2
Netherlands	1.1	−2.7	−4.2	0.4	2.4	2.3
Norway	2.1	2.3	−10.2	2.8	4.4	−7.1
Sweden	−0.6	0.1	−1.1	1.1	2.4	1.8
Switzerland	−2.9	3.5	−2.7	4.3	3.8	3.4
Total 9 countries	*0.1*	*−0.4*	*−2.8*	*0.4*	*3.2*	*2.5*
Total western Europe	*0.4*	*−0.1*	*−2.0*	*0.6*	*2.2*	*2.1*
Canada	3.2	−0.9	−9.7	−4.9	1.0	2.5
United States	2.3	3.0	−6.8	9.7	18.2	6.0
Total above	*1.3*	*1.1*	*−4.4*	*3.8*	*8.7*	*3.8*

Sources: National statistics. For 1984 estimates and 1985 forecasts see appendix to section 2.2.

gain somewhat in importance. Whether this will also lead to significantly higher levels of employment, however, remains to be seen.

These developments in the business sector are to a large extent offset by changes in private and public sector investment in structures (residential and non-residential), thus pulling down the growth rates for total investment in 1985, as shown in table 2.2.3. It can be seen that for total fixed investment the general feature is for increases of about the same or somewhat below the rates in 1984. The largest change is expected in the United States with private investment expenditure increasing 6 per cent in 1985, a drop of 12 percentage points compared with 1984. This is a normal reaction to the very strong acceleration in 1983-1984 and to the expected slowdown in economic growth. Nevertheless, it is a rate which is still far above the average increase of 2-2.5 per cent forecast for the 13 west European countries.[18]

The question of capacity utilization in manufacturing

A recurring feature of the analysis of the economic situation in the western market economies over the last year or so is the increasing uncertainty about the rate at which the economy, and in particular industry, could grow if all resources were fully utilized. A series describing such potential output can be constructed following a number of different statistical methods, but they all involve, in one way or another, the construction of benchmark estimates of the full employment levels of labour and capital and/or the determination of the trend paths of capital or labour productivity. However, this has proved more and more difficult in recent years, with the consequence that the margins of error associated with such estimates are believed to have become disturbingly large.[19]

This is a matter of concern because measures of potential output and the associated capacity utilization rates occupy an important place in economic analysis and policy formulation. Thus, changes in capacity utilization rates are important in explaining the investment behaviour of firms and in the analysis of changes in prices and productivity. For the economy as a whole, the estimate of potential output is at the basis of calculations of the full-employment budget surplus, which is used for assessing the stance of fiscal policy. In the context of inflation analysis, the growth rate of capacity output together with the actual capacity utilization rate helps to assess how quickly a given increase in demand will move actual output towards the capacity

ceiling and, consequently, how great the risks are that higher demand will generate more inflation.

In a more general way many of these difficulties and uncertainties reflect a lack of understanding of the economic consequences of the two oil price shocks and the causes of the slowdown in productivity growth after 1973; but there is also the increased difficulty of separating structural from cyclical unemployment in the presence of persistently low output growth and a marked change in the age-sex composition of the labour force.

Moreover, as regards manufacturing industry, the question has arisen whether the official capital stock series can still be regarded as a plausible approximation to the economically useful capital stock and–a related issue–whether the relationship between additions to the capital stock and changes in industrial capacity output has altered significantly.

It is now generally accepted that the sharp rise in relative energy prices after 1973 and 1979 reduced (or even eliminated) the profitability of part of the installed stock of equipment, which in turn led to an accelerated rate of scrapping. Moreover, there are other factors which may have increased scrapping rates–and hence shortened the service life of capital goods–such as recent changes in industrial competitiveness and the consequential need for structural adjustment (for example in industries such as steel, shipbuilding, clothing, and textiles) and the persistent slow growth of demand for goods in general which has probably led to a scaling down of medium-term sales expectations and hence levels of planned capacity.

Unfortunately, accelerated scrapping or, more generally, sudden changes in the average length of service life of physical capital goods, cannot be detected simply by inspecting the capital stock series compiled by national statistical offices. The reason is that these series are calculated on the basis of traditional, constant rates of depreciation and retirement.

However, the assumptions made about the economically useful life of capital investments in individual industries is a key element in the compilation of capital stock series. The longer these service lives are the larger, *ceteris paribus*, is the capital stock. From a purely technical viewpoint the useful life of equipment may be extended indefinitely given appropriate repair and maintenance. However, from an economic viewpoint the cost of operating a given machine may become too high relative to the flow of revenues and therefore it will be discarded.

Clearly, any investment undertaken by firms is based on an assumed future stream of income which, in turn, is dependent upon changes in relative prices–for goods and factor inputs–and the overall level of demand. This assumed rate of return is, of course, the major risk or uncertainty surrounding each investment. It therefore follows that the average service life of equipment is itself an uncertain variable, as it depends on the deviations of expected relative price changes from those that are eventually realized. Therefore the exact service life of machinery can only be known *ex post*, that is, after it has been scrapped.

This implies that any capital stock series will provide a reliable approximation to the actual economically useful capital stock only if the assumed average service life of capital goods reflects more or less closely the actual situation in industry.[20]

---

[18] For the Federal Republic of Germany the investment forecast for 1985 is a matter of dispute. The Ifo-Institute has estimated recently that investments in machinery and equipment will increase in real terms by about 5 per cent, mainly as a result of an increase in manufacturing industry of about 10 per cent. This implies, together with the expected decline in expenditures on structures, an increase in total fixed investment of about 1.5 per cent. These figures are roughly in line with the forecasts made by the other economic research institutes. In marked contrast to this, the forecast made by the Council of Economic Advisers (*Sachverständigenrat*) expects an increase in total investment of 4 per cent, reflecting an increase in total expenditure on machinery and equipment by the business sector of 10 per cent and a virtual stagnation for structures. This is generally regarded as too optimistic and the government, in its annual economic report, seems to have opted for a compromise forecast: its projected increase of 5 to 6 per cent at current prices corresponds roughly to a volume increase of 2 to 3 per cent.

[19] For example, the United States Council of Economic Advisers, as from 1982, stopped publishing the official potential output series for the US economy, a series which had occupied an important place in the annual *Economic Report of the President* since the beginning of the 1960s. In the Federal Republic of Germany, the DIW has re-estimated the potential output series for industry in an attempt to account for the apparently changing trends in capital productivity. See R. Pischner, "Zur Neuberechnung des Produktionspotentials im Bergbau und verarbeitenden Gewerbe", in DIW, *Vierteljahresheft*, No. 2-1982, pp. 194-219.

[20] Thus, for example, in the United Kingdom the Central Statistical Office has recently revised its estimates of the United Kingdom capital stock because "discussions with some larger undertakings in a variety of industries have indicated that the lives assumed hitherto for manufacturing plant and building have been unduly long ... The broad effect of these reductions in service life assumptions has been to increase capital consumption and to reduce the estimates of the capital stock." CSO, *National Income and Expenditure* 1983 Edition, p. 114.

A further reason why the use of capital stock data in constructing a potential output series has become more delicate and difficult is the possibility that the effects of investment on capacity have changed. Thus, for example, legislation has imposed more stringent controls on production activities as regards environmental pollution, with the consequence that part of industrial investment is directed towards fulfilling environmental norms and does not necessarily add to productive capacity.[21]

Moreover, the persistent weakness of demand and increasing cost pressures have also reduced the importance of capacity augmentation as a primary investment motive as opposed to rationalization and replacement,[22] although the precise effects may be difficult to separate in practice.[23]

As all the above-mentioned factors lead one to question the series on potential output and the associated capacity utilization rates which are based on statistical estimation methods, it seems more prudent for the time being to base an assessment of changes in capacity utilization on information available from business surveys. At the same time this permits comparison between the capacity output series that is *implied* by the utilization rates and the changes in capital stock and thus to infer whether the latter is still in line with the development of technical capacity in industry. The basic assumption behind this comparison is that respondents to business surveys have a capacity concept in mind that measures the output that can be produced with the available capital stock at a normal level of utiliation, and that this concept is consistent through time.[24]

It should be noted that among the capacity utilization rates and capacity output series compiled in tables 2.2.4 and 2.2.5, the series for the United States is largely but not exclusively based on business survey results (it takes changes in the capital stock, as compiled by the Bureau of Commerce, into account). The series for Canada is not at all based on business surveys but is estimated on the basis of the observed historical minimum values for the capital-output ratios of manufacturing industries. For this reason it is not possible to infer possible divergencies between the development of capital stock and capacity output in Canada.[25]

Recent changes in capacity utilization rates

Capacity utilization rates in manufacturing industry for the most recent years and for 1973 and 1979 are given in table 2.2.4. Their development since 1969 is traced in chart 2.2.3, which at the same time brings out clearly their close association with invest-

ment: higher rates of utilization of resources lead—sometimes with a lag—to accelerated capital formation and vice versa.

Capacity utilization rates in manufacturing industry in 1984 reached levels that in general are well above those in 1983. The overall picture, however, is quite varied. Thus in Belgium and France utilization rates remained at their 1983 levels, whereas in the United Kingdom and the United States they rose by 6 to 6.5 points.[26] For the remaining countries there was, on average, an upward drift of 2 to 3.5 points.

If compared with the utilization rates achieved at the last major cyclical peak, in 1973, the current rates suggest that there is still a large margin of spare capacity in manufacturing industry (see table 2.2.4, column 6). However, it is questionable whether 1973 is the most appropriate year for placing the current situation in perspective. It may be argued that the rates attained in 1973 reflected overheated economies, with firms producing at levels where marginal costs were rising sharply and resources being used beyond their "normal" level of intensity. Such a situation cannot be sustained for long, given the consequential cost pressures and inflationary risks.

It may therefore be more appropriate to compare the current situation with 1979, the last peak before 1984. The results of such a comparison, given in column 7 of table 2.2.4, suggest that two country groups can be distinguished. In the first, utilization rates are still well below those in 1979: this group comprises Austria, France, the Federal Republic of Germany, Canada and the United States. In the other group, manufacturing industry is now operating at rates which are close to those in 1979. In fact, in Sweden[27] and the Netherlands operating rates are now higher than during the previous peak, and in Belgium the rate is the same.

However, the relative speed with which utilization rates have responded to changes in actual production over the last year or so suggests that in France and the Federal Republic of Germany the previous peaks could be reached quickly even with relatively modest rates of ouput growth.

Capacity utilization rates reflect the relative movement of two separate variables, namely production capacity on the one hand and actual output on the other. It is the former which determines the possibility of growth in industry without immediate pressure on costs and prices, and it is therefore of importance to examine more closely the growth of capacity output that is implied by these capacity utilization rates.

Trends in capacity output growth

The changes in capacity output of total manufacturing industry since 1969 are given in table 2.2.5. They show a substantial decline in the growth of potential output in western Europe after 1973, a trend which in general has accelerated since 1979. In fact, between 1979 and 1984 the calculations indicate that capacity output in manufacturing rose by about only 1 per cent a year in Belgium, France, the Federal Republic of Germany and Italy, whereas in the Netherlands and the United Kingdom there was even an absolute decline in potential output. In Canada and the United States there was also a slowdown in capacity output growth although it appears to be less dramatic than in western Europe.

---

[21] For example, a study of the United States finds that the elasticity of capacity in total manufacturing industry with respect to capital stock declined in the 1970s and this is related to the increasing importance of investment in pollution-abatement control equipment, and also to investment in increased occupational safety and health. See: R. F. Rost, "Capacity-Neutral Investments and Capacity Measurement" in *The Journal of Industrial Economics*, vol. XXX, June 1982, No. 4, pp. 391-403.

[22] In the Federal Republic of Germany the Ifo business surveys indicate that the percentage of firms in manufacturing industry which invested primarily in order to increase capacity has declined from about 50 per cent in the period 1960-1964 to about 40 per cent in 1970-1979: the percentage is currently around 25-30 per cent. See *Ifo-Schnelldienst*, No. 13/1981 and No. 19/1984.

[23] For example, this is the case with the capacity effects of the increasing computerisation of production processes and the use of robots.

[24] This may not always be so, however. Thus capacity utilization rates derived from business surveys have been found to have cyclical biases, i.e, in periods of cyclical downswing firms "lose" capacity and in an upswing they "find" capacity. See George L. Perry: "Capacity in Manufacturing", *Brookings Papers on Economic Activity*, No. 3-1973, pp. 701-742.

[25] See G. Schaefer, "Measuring capacity utilization: a technical note", *Bank of Canada Review*, May 1980, pp. 3-13.

[26] The increase in capacity utilization rates in the United Kingdom, estimated by EUROSTAT, seems surprisingly high given the rise in manufacturing output of around 2 1/2 per cent in 1984. These figures imply that potential output fell by roughly 5 per cent in 1984.

[27] As compared with 1980.

CHART 2.2.3.

Capacity utilization and real gross fixed investment in manufacturing industry, 1969 — 1984.

Total investment (1973 = 100) ━━━━━━━━   Capacity utilization or firms ▬▬▬▬▬▬▬

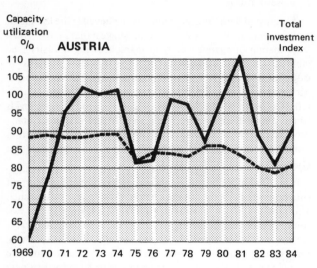

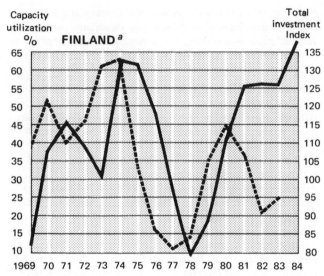

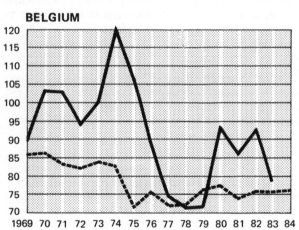

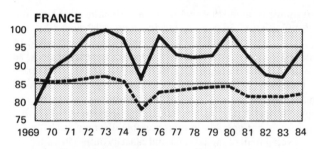

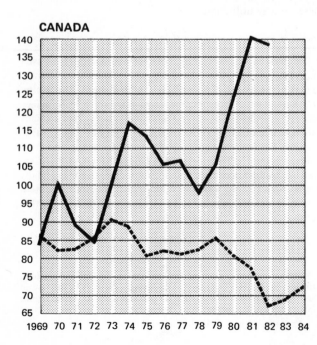

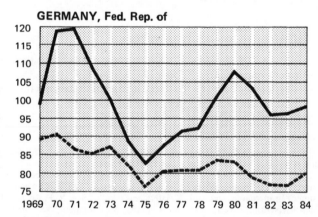

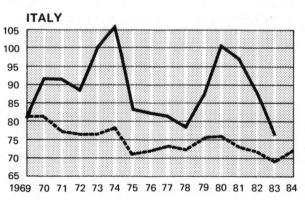

CHART 2.2.3. (Continued)

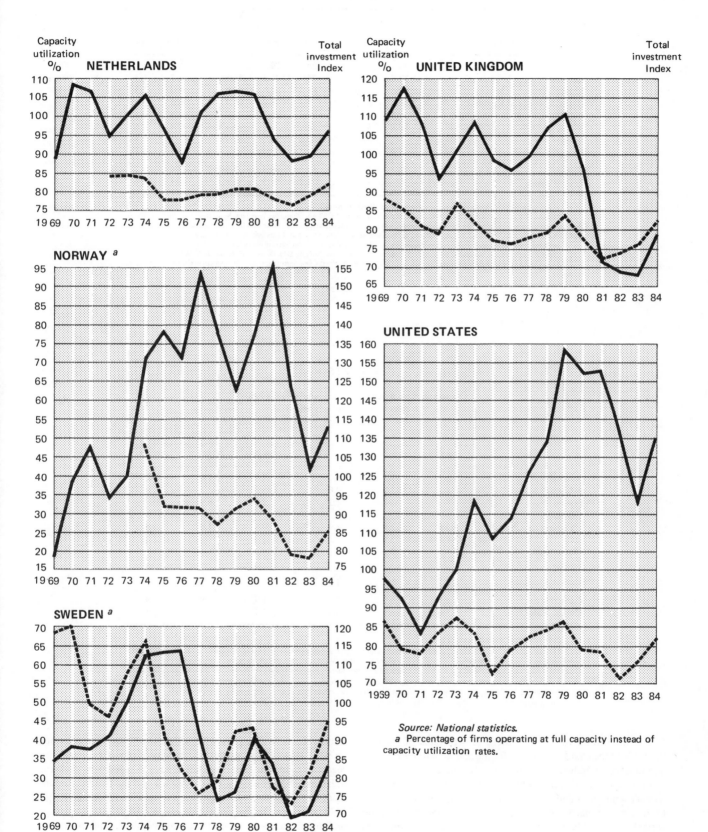

Source: National statistics.
a Percentage of firms operating at full capacity instead of capacity utilization rates.

TABLE 2.2.4

Capacity utilization rates in manufacturing industry[a]
(*Per cent*)

Country	Reference years					Differences	
	1973	1979	1982	1983	1984	1984/73	1984/79
Austria [b]	89	86	80	79	81	−8	−5
Belgium	84.8	76.2	75.8	75.7	76.1	−8.7	−0.1
France	87.6	84.6	81.5	81.5	81.9	−5.7	−2.7
Germany, Federal Republic of . .	87.1	84.2	77.2	76.8	80.3	−6.8	−3.9
Italy	76.5	75.4	71.9	69.9	71.9	−4.6	−3.5
Netherlands	84.8	81.4	76.7	79.4	82.4	−2.4	−1.0
Sweden	..	83.1[c]	80.0	82.2	84.9[d]	..	1.8[e]
United Kingdom	87.9	84.2	74.2	76.4	82.4	−5.5	−1.8
Canada	90.5	85.7	67.0	69.3	72.9[d]	−18.0	−13.2
United States	87.6	86.0	71.1	75.3	81.8	−6.1	−4.5

Sources: Austria: Wifo, *Monatsberichte* various issues (Investitionstest).

Belgium, France, Germany, Netherlands, United Kingdom: EUROSTAT, *European economy*, Supplement B, *Business Survey Results*, various issues. The data do not cover the food, beverages and tobacco industry. Note that the capacity utilization rates for the United Kingdom are EUROSTAT estimates based on business survey data relating to firms operating at full capacity.

Sweden: *Statistics Sweden Statistiska meddelanden*, I 1984:5.5, Industrins kapacitetsutnyttjandet.

Canada: The series is calculated by Statistics Canada and was extracted from OECD, *Main Economic Indicators*.

United States: Federal Reserve Board Series. Data are from the *Business Conditions Digest* (US Department of Commerce), various issues.

[a] Average rates.

[b] Data refer to November.

[c] 1980.

[d] Average of the first three quarters.

[e] 1980-1984.

TABLE 2.2.5

Changes in capacity output[a] in manufacturing industry
(*Average annual rates of growth*)

Country	Annual average rates of growth			Growth elasticities[b]		
	1969-1973	1973-1979	1979-1984	1969-1973	1973-1979	1979-1982
Austria	3.3	3.1	3.7	1.0	1.0	1.2
Belgium	8.1	3.9	0.6	..	..	..
France	6.3	3.7	1.3	1.0	0.9	0.4
Germany, Federal Republic of . .	4.6	2.4	0.9	0.8	1.0	0.8
Italy	7.1	3.0	1.2	..	..	..
Netherlands	..	2.4	−1.0	..	..	..
Sweden	..	..	1.7[c]	..	..	−0.1[c]
United Kingdom	2.7	−	−1.7	0.8	−	−1.5
Canada	4.8	3.7	3.3	1.0	0.9	0.9
United States	3.6	3.1	2.5	1.3	0.8	0.7

Sources: As for tables 2.2.4 and 2.2.6.

[a] For all countries capacity output was obtained by dividing actual real output by the average capacity utilization rate for the corresponding year. Actual output is defined as the real value added of total manufacturing industry (National Accounts series). For the United States the series was calculated on the basis of the Federal Reserve Board's Index of Industrial Production for total manufacturing.

[b] These were calculated as the ratio of the average annual growth rates of capacity output and real capital stock. Original capital stock data (K_t) referring to the end of year t were transformed into mid-year values by means of the formula $K_t = (K_t - K_{t-1})/2$.

[c] 1980-1982.

It is interesting to compare these growth rates of capacity output with the changes recorded for the real capital stock in total manufacturing industry. Unfortunately, there are no capital stock data for some countries listed in the table, and for some for which capital stock data are available (Finland, Norway, Sweden) there are no capacity utilization rates. For Sweden, the latter variable is available only from 1980, but for the remaining cases the comparison is quite instructive. Changes in real gross capital stock are given in table 2.2.6 for nine countries.

In all four European countries for which both capital stock and potential output series are available, the decline in capacity output is everywhere associated with a slowdown in capital stock growth. However, whereas the elasticity of capacity output with regard to capital stock appears not to have changed very much (or to have declined only slightly) in Austria and the Federal Republic of Germany, there is a significant drop of about one half after 1979 in France. In the United Kingdom capacity output growth no longer appears to respond to changes in the capital stock after 1973: in fact the implicit elasticity is even negative after 1979. Although it has not been possible to calculate a capacity output series for Norway and Sweden the development of the capital stock relative to *actual* output is nevertheless somewhat puzzling: the capital stock continued to grow more or less steadily after 1973 whereas output either stagnated or declined. These developments imply that capital productivity declined by 4.4 and 3.3 per cent per annum in Norway and Sweden between 1973 and 1982 (1982 being the last year for which capital stock data are available). In other words, assuming that capital stock is measured correctly, then the apparent capital productivity in 1982 of manufacturing industry in Norway was about 33 percentage points below its 1973 level; for Sweden the corresponding fall is 26 percentage points.

TABLE 2.2.6

Changes in capital stock of total manufacturing industry
(*Average annual rates of growth*)

	1969-1973	1973-1979	1979-1982
Austria.	6.0	3.4	2.7
Finland	6.2	4.0	3.1
France	6.5	4.1	2.8
Germany, Federal Republic of .	6.0	2.3	1.8
Norway	4.1	4.8	3.3
Sweden	4.4	3.7	2.1
United Kingdom	3.2	2.1	0.6
Canada.	4.7	3.9	4.1
United States	2.7	3.8	4.1

Sources:

Austria: F. Hahn, "Neufassung der Wifo-Kapitalstockschaetzung für die Industrie und das Gewerbe nach Branchen", Wifo, *Monatsberichte*8/1983; and direct communication from the Oesterreichisches Institut für Wirtschaftsforschung.

Finland: Economic Planning Centre (TASKU), Helsinki, direct communication.

France: OECD, *Flows and Fixed Capital, 1955-1980*, Paris, 1980, and direct communication from OECD.

Germany, Federal Republic of: Statistisches Bundesamt, *Volkswirtschaftliche Gesamtrechnungen*, Fachserie 18.

Norway: National accounts, Central Bureau of Statistics.

Sweden: *Statistiska meddelanden*, Central Bureau of Statistics.

Canada: *Fixed Capital Flows and Stocks*, Statistics Canada.

United States: *Survey of Current Business*, February 1981, October 1982, August 1983, August 1984.

*Note:*Original end-year capital stock data were transformed into mid-year values by using the formula in footnote b of table 2.2.5.

In the United States there is also a conspicuous change in the relationship between the two variables: indeed, an acceleration in capital stock growth was accompanied by a declining growth rate of capacity output, leading to a drop of the implicit growth elasticity in 1979-1982 by about one half relative to 1969-1973.

The above discussion has focused on a concept of capacity that measures the output that could be produced if the available equipment and labour were used at a normal level of intensity. This is, however, a purely technical measure, as it does not involve any consideration of the costs of production. It might therefore be more useful to have a capacity measure that explicitly incorporates factor costs. Such a concept has for some time been associated with the micro-economic notion of "capacity output", which is defined as that level of output at which the short-run total average cost curve attains its minimum for a given capital stock.[28] This approach clearly emphasizes that capacity is essentially a short-run concept, which is based on the fixity of certain factor inputs. In the long run, when all factor

inputs can be adjusted to changes in demand, there are no capacity limitations. At any given time therefore this optimum level of output is determined by relative factor prices, the available capital stock, and the available technology.

Two specific features of this concept are noteworthy. First, the implied capacity utilization rates can be directly related to the investment behaviour of firms.[29] Thus, if actual output is equal to capacity output, then by definition there is full capacity and if firms expect no change in that level of output there will be neither net investment nor disinvestment. However, if there were a persistent increase in demand such that the actual output produced—for a given capital stock—were higher than the capacity output at which costs are minimized, then the capacity utilization rate would be greater than 1 and firms would invest (i.e. add to their capital stock) in order to produce the higher output at lower unit cost. If, on the contrary, there is a persistent decline in demand, firms will reduce their capacity output in order to move to a lower cost-minimizing level of output.

Second, as capacity output at each point in time is defined for a given constellation of relative factor prices, it is possible in principle to evaluate the impact of changes in the costs of specific factor inputs (for example, labour and energy) on the optimum output level.[30]

Conclusions

To sum up, the official time series of real capital stock appear to have become less reliable as a guide to changes in production capacity in manufacturing industry in a number of countries. The reasons for this are not yet well understood[31] and it has led, for example, the Federal Reserve Board to reduce the weight given to capital stock growth in its recently revised measures of capacity output in US industry.[32] Intuitively, however, this seems to support the argument that the economic disturbances of the 1970s led to a reduction in the general service lives of assets which has not been reflected in measures of the capital stock. If the average service lives of the individual capital vintages have actually become shorter, then this implies that the growth of potential output will react more strongly to changes in investment or, in other words, that capacity output will adjust more rapidly to cyclical fluctuations in demand.[33]

The declining trends in the growth of capacity output are a matter of great concern, for they suggest that the short- to medium-term growth possibilities of west European industry

---

[28] See, for example, J. M. Cassels, "Excess Capacity and Monopolistic Competition", *The Quarterly Journal of Economics*, vol. LI, May 1937, No. 3, pp. 426-443; L. R. Klein, "Some Theoretical Issues in the Measurement of Capacity" in *Econometrica*, vol. 28, No. 2, April 1960, pp. 272-286; G. J. Stigler, *The Theory of Price*, 3rd edition, New York, 1968, pp. 156-158; B. G. Hickman, "On a new method of capacity estimation", in *Journal of the American Statistical Association*, vol. 59, June 1964, No. 306, pp. 529-549.

[29] See E. R. Berndt and C. J. Morrison, "Capacity Utilization Measures: Underlying Economic Theory and an Alternative Approach", in *American Economic Review, Papers and Proceedings*, vol. 72, No. 2, May 1981, pp. 48-52, for an application to US manufacturing industry.

[30] Berndt and Morrison, *loc. cit.* Some preliminary work by the secretariat on these cost-based capacity utilization measures suggests that in the 1970s actual output was generally lower than the level at which costs would be minimized—in other words, there was little or no incentive for firms to invest because the existing capital stock was already larger than that required for minimizing short-run total costs. This result is consistent with the slowdown in technical capacity output, noted above, and with the increased emphasis on investment for rationalization rather than expansion of capacity.

[31] For the United States these changes were discussed for the first time in an article by B. Bosworth "Capital Formation and Economic Policy", in *Brookings Papers on Economic Activity* No. 2-1982, pp. 273-326.

[32] See R. F. Rost "New Federal Reserve Measures of Capacity and Capacity Utilization", in *Federal Reserve Bulletin*, July 1983, pp. 515-521.

[33] See Arthur Boness and Rainer Pischner: "Auswirkungen unterschiedlicher Nutzungsdauern der Investitionen auf das Produktionspotential" in Joachim Frohn and Reiner Staeglin (eds.), *Empirische Wirtschaftsforschung, Konzeptionen, Verfahren und Ergebnisse*, Festschrift für Rolf Krengel, Berlin, 1980, pp. 61-75.

may have been seriously compromised by the low investment activity of recent years. In contrast, the growth of capacity output in the United States has been much faster in the last five years than in all the west European countries in table 2.2.3 except Austria. This, and the fact that the recovery started from relatively low levels of capacity utilization, helps to explain why rapid output growth in the United States has not placed any severe pressure on costs and prices. It is the underlying growth of potential output which determines the overall supply and employment possibilities in an economy and a reversal of the declining trend requires that investment be motivated again by the need to increase capacity. Labour has been losing out in the current recovery since the increase in utilization rates has not lead in general to an increase in employment (the United States is the main exception). For this to occur, output growth would have to be much stronger.

Morever, the additions to capacity that have been made in recent years do not only reflect the modest rates of growth actually experienced and the dominance of rationalization as an investment motive but also the reduced expectations of growth in the future. Since it takes time to add to capacity and given the relatively slow growth of potential output over the last few years, there is a danger that any strong upswing now would propel industry relatively quickly towards the existing capacity ceilings and so lead to a situation where inflationary risks would have to be contained by more restrictive policies and before any significant improvement in employment had been achieved.

However, the continuation of the currently low rates of output growth also imply a bleak outlook for employment: labour therefore risks being caught in a low growth trap where modest increases in production can be supplied simply by productivity growth.

(iv) Foreign demand

There was a marked acceleration in the growth of exports of goods and services from western Europe in 1985 (table 2.2.7): on average they rose by nearly 6 1/2 per cent in volume compared

with a little over 2 per cent in 1983. Performance was also better than forecast at the beginning of 1984 (some 4 1/2 per cent). The improvement in exports was particularly marked in the four larger economies, partly because of the increased demand for investment goods in 1984. In spite of the metal workers' strike in the second quarter, exports from the Federal Republic of Germany also rose more than forecast a year ago.

There was also a resumption of export growth in the United States in 1984: after two years of decline exports rose by some 4.5 per cent. Exports to Canada, Japan and Latin America seem to explain most of this increase.

The strengthening of export growth in 1984 originated in the recovery of import demand in both western Europe and North America. In western Europe import volumes accelerated sharply in response to rising activity, particularly in manufacturing industry: for western Europe as a whole they rose some 5 1/2 per cent in 1984 compared with 1 1/2 per cent in 1983. Imports also rose much faster than expected at the beginning of 1984: although special factors were at work in individual countries (higher energy imports into the United Kingdom as a result of the miners' strike, for example), this was a general phenomenon.

The volume of imports into North America rose at a two-digit rate. In the United States import volumes increased by about 27 per cent, reflecting the rapid growth of domestic demand and losses of competitiveness in the home market.

Western Europe has clearly benefited from this rapid growth of imports into the United States, although intra-west-European trade seems to have played a more important role in the improvement of west European performance. In fact, following the free trade agreements of the 1960s and 1970s, western Europe has become increasingly dependent upon developments inside the region.[34] This is illustrated in table 2.2.8, which provides an estimate of the relative impact of import demand in the United States and in western Europe on the growth of west European

---

[34] See section 5.2.

TABLE 2.2.7

Changes in the volume of exports and imports of goods and services,[a] 1983-1985
(*Annual percentage change*)

	Exports			Imports		
	1983	*1984*	*1985*	*1983*	*1984*	*1985*
France	3.6	4.7	4.1	−0.9	3.0	2.6
Germany, Federal Republic of	−1.3	7.4	6.5	0.5	5.5	4.5
Italy	3.9	6.0	5.0	0.8	7.2	5.0
United Kingdom	1.5	6.5	6.5	5.5	8.5	3.5
Total 4 countries	*1.2*	*6.4*	*5.7*	*1.1*	*5.6*	*3.9*
Austria	6.2	18.3	5.6	9.9	19.1	5.5
Belgium	−	4.8	4.1	−3.0	2.3	2.3
Denmark	3.4	4.8	5.6	0.7	6.9	5.3
Finland	3.6	6.0	5.0	3.8	1.5	5.0
Ireland	10.6	14.2	10.0	3.9	6.8	7.8
Netherlands	0.4	2.4	2.3	4.9	3.5	3.0
Norway	7.0	6.1	−1.4	−1.2	1.6	2.8
Sweden	10.5	7.2	3.6	−	5.7	5.8
Switzerland	0.9	5.2	3.1	4.7	6.5	3.8
Total 9 countries	*4.3*	*6.7*	*3.9*	*2.2*	*5.4*	*3.9*
Total western Europe	*2.3*	*6.5*	*5.0*	*1.5*	*5.5*	*3.9*
Canada	6.4	18.5	5.3	8.1	16.0	4.5
United States	−5.5	4.5	6.5	7.5	27.1	12.5
Total above	*0.8*	*6.8*	*5.4*	*3.1*	*10.6*	*5.9*

Sources: National statistics and official forecasts listed in the appendix to this section.

[a] National accounts basis.

TABLE 2.2.8

**The contribution of intra-regional trade and of exports to the United States
to total volume growth in west European exports of goods, 1984[a]**

Exporters	Impact of west European imports			Impact of United States imports		
	A	B	C	D	E	F
Western Europe	65.6	6.5	4.0	7.6	39.0	3.0
of which:						
France	56.3	6.5	3.5	6.0	40.0	2.5
Germany, Federal Republic of.	63.9	3.5	2.5	7.6	45.0	3.5
Italy	54.7	3.0	2.0	7.7	51.5	4.0
United Kingdom	56.0	6.5	4.5	13.8	18.0	2.5
Austria.	66.7	5.0	3.5	3.0	51.5	1.5
Belgium-Luxembourg	77.7	3.5	2.5	5.1	36.0	2.0
Finland.	55.4	17.5	9.5	4.1	72.0	2.9
Netherlands	77.9	5.5	4.0	5.1	51.5	2.5
Norway.	83.4	8.5	7.0	4.3	35.0	1.5
Sweden.	68.5	9.5	6.5	8.9	47.5	4.0
Switzerland	58.8	7.5	4.5	8.6	27.5	2.5

Sources: ECE secretariat estimates based on data in OECD, *Monthly Statistics of Foreign Trade*, January 1985, and United Nations, *Monthly Bulletin of Statistics*, June 1984.

Note: A—Share of western Europe in exports from the countries indicated in 1983;

B—Percentage change in west European imports from the countries indicated;

C—Percentage point contribution to total growth in exports from the countries indicated;

D—Share of the United States in exports from the countries indicated in 1983;

E—Percentage change in United States' imports from the countries indicated;

F—Percentage point contribution to total growth in exports from the countries indicated.

[a] January-September.

exports of goods in the first three quarters of 1984. West European imports from the region itself increased in volume by about 6.5 per cent, an expansion that contributed 4 percentage points to the export growth of western Europe. Of the countries listed, only Italy and the Federal Republic of Germany gained more from the United States than from western Europe.

Intra-west-European trade was particularly important for the export growth of a number of the smaller countries. On the other hand, imports of the United States from western Europe rose in volume by almost 40 per cent, but this increase contributed only 3 percentage points to the rise in western Europe's total exports. For the Federal Republic of Germany and Italy the impact was above average and also larger than the effect of intra-European trade.

The impact of net foreign demand on domestic output growth was generally positive in 1984 although there were marked differences among individual countries. For the nine smaller economies, net exports accounted on average for about 28 per cent of GDP growth, rather less than the two thirds in 1983 when the recovery was more narrowly based. Nevertheless the continuing process of adjustment via large shifts of resources into the external sector of several of the smaller countries has meant that GDP growth has continued to be dominated by foreign demand (Belgium and Ireland, for example). Among the larger economies net foreign demand provided about a fifth of GDP growth in France and about a third in the Federal Republic of Germany (in the latter this represents a sharp turnround from 1983 when the foreign sector had a negative effect on output growth). In Italy and the United Kingdom the impact of net foreign demand was negative in 1984 though to a much smaller extent than in 1983. In contrast with western Europe, in the United States net foreign demand made a large negative contribution to GDP growth: the nearly 9 per cent growth in domestic demand was lowered by some 2 percentage points.

For 1985 some slowing down in west European export growth is implied in the current forecasts (from 6 1/2 to 5 per cent, on average) with a somewhat sharper deceleration for the smaller economies than for the larger ones. Nevertheless the foreign sector is still expected to contribute significantly to growth in 1985, by about a fifth of the rise in GDP in the four large economies and with a particularly large effect (45 per cent) in the Federal Republic.

In the United States export growth is anticipated to improve further in 1985 mainly under the stimulus of strong import demand in Japan and Latin America. However, the rise in imports is projected to continue to exceed that of exports, entailing another large, negative contribution of net foreign demand to the growth of GDP.

APPENDIX

Sections 2.1 and 2.2 refer frequently to official forecasts of GDP and its components in 1984. Regional aggregates were made by the secretariat on the basis of the dollar values of the relevant variables at 1975 prices and exchange rates. The sources of the various forecasts (and in many cases for estimates of 1984 as a whole) are as follows:

Austria: WIFO *Monatsberichte*, 11/12-1984.

Belgium: *Budget des Recettes et des Dépenses pour l'année budgétaire 1985*, Ministère des Finances, October 1984.

Canada: OECD *Economic Outlook*, December 1984.

Denmark: Ministry of Economic Affairs, press release, February 1985 and Economic Council, *Dansk Økonomi*, November 1984.

Finland: Ministry of Finance—*Kansantalouden Kehitysarvio 1985*, February 1985.

France: *Comptes Prévisionnels de la Nation pour 1984 et principales hypothèses économiques pour 1985*, October 1984.

Germany, Federal Republic of: SBW, *Statisticher Wochendienst 1984*, 17 January 1985 and DIW, *Wochenbericht*, 1-2/1985.

Ireland: The Economic and Social Research Institute, *Quarterly Economic Commentary*, December 1984.

Italy: ISCO, *Rassegna Mensile—Congiuntura Italiana*, October 1984.

Netherlands: Central Planning Bureau, *Macroeconomische Verkenning 1985*, September 1984.

Norway: CBS, *Økonomisk Utsyn*, February 1985 and Ministry of Finance, *Nasjonalbudsjettet 1985*, September 1984.

Sweden: Konjunkturinstitutet: *Preliminär national-budget 1985*: 1 January 1985.

Switzerland: *La Vie Economique — La Conjuncture Suisse en 1984 et les Perspectives pour 1985*, January 1985.

United Kingdom: H.M. Treasury, *Financial Statement and Budget Report 1985-86*, March 1985.

United States: *Economic Report of the President*, February 1985 and OECD *Economic Outlook*, December 1984.

2.3 THE CONDITIONS OF SUPPLY

This section discusses a number of developments on the supply side of the market economies: productivity, costs and prices, and changes in unemployment and employment. The section on costs and prices includes a discussion of profit margins before and after 1973 and that on labour markets pays special attention to the extent that demographic changes have eased or exacerbated employment problems. This last section also includes a discussion of the concept and measurement of full employment.

(i) Labour productivity

Growth rates of labour productivity in 1984 (for the whole economy) do not display any clear pattern across individual countries. In some there was some acceleration (Denmark, Italy, France), in others growth rates remained roughly the same or even declined in comparison with 1983 (notably in the Netherlands, the United Kingdom and in North America). It appears from preliminary data that the generally faster growth of real GDP in 1984 was accompanied by a deceleration in the decline of labour input or even by an absolute increase (notably in Finland, Sweden, the United Kingdom and North America) thus making for some slowing down in the rate of productivity growth. The most striking examples of such a slowdown are the United Kingdom and the United States. In fact in the latter real GDP increased by of 3.7 per cent in 1983 and productivity by 3 per cent; in 1984 the increase in real GNP of 6.8 per cent was accompanied by an increase in persons engaged of roughly 4.5 per cent, implying a fall in productivity growth.

In a somewhat longer-term perspective the increase in labour productivity over the period 1979-1984 does not in general compare favourably with that in earlier periods (see table 2.3.1).

In fact, the rates of growth for 1960-1973 are in most countries still much higher than current rates of increase; and only in six of the 15 countries listed in table 2.3.1 is the average rate of change in 1979-1984 higher than the average rate for 1973-1979.

More or less rapid increases in labour productivity during periods of economic upswing are a familar fact and *inter alia* can be explained by labour-hoarding[35] and the more efficient use of resources as rates of capacity utilization increase.

However, the years after 1979, notably from 1981 to 1983, appear to be atypical in that relatively rapid increases in productivity growth in several countries have been associated less with higher output growth than with considerable reductions in the levels of employment. This seems to be mainly a consequence of both the process of rationalization and structural adjustment that has been going on for quite some time and the sluggish growth of demand.

This development, in general, is much more accentuated in manufacturing industry (table 2.3.2). It can be seen from a comparison of tables 2.3.2 and 2.3.1 that productivity growth in manufacturing has been traditionally faster than in the economy as a whole. There was a marked acceleration of productivity growth in manufacturing industry after the cyclical trough in 1982. In some countries (Austria, Belgium, the United Kingdom) this acceleration had occurred earlier.

---

[35] See, for example, Walter Y. Oi: "Labour as a Quasi-Fixed Factor", *The Journal of Political Economy*, vol. LXX, December 1962, No. 6, pp. 538-555.

TABLE 2.3.1

Changes in labour productivity:[a] total economy

Country	Average annual rates of growth			Year-to-year changes				
	1960-1973	1973-1979	1979-1984	1980	1981	1982	1983	1984[b]
France	4.7	2.9	1.7	1.1	1.0	1.9	1.5	3.0
Germany, Federal Republic of .	4.4	3.0	1.7	0.9	0.6	0.7	3.1	3.0
Italy	5.8	1.8	0.8	3.2	−0.3	−0.1	−1.3	3.0
United Kingdom	2.8	1.2	2.0	−1.9	3.0	3.3	4.2	1.5
Austria. . . . . . . - . . .	5.2[c]	2.5	2.1	2.8	−0.2	2.2	3.3	2.5
Belgium	4.1	2.2	1.9	3.4	0.9	2.4	1.4	1.0
Denmark	3.3	1.5	2.0	0.7	0.5	2.9	1.9	4.0
Finland	5.0	2.8	2.2	2.7	1.0	2.2	2.6	2.5
Ireland.	4.4	4.3	2.9	1.5	3.9	2.4	2.6	4.0
Netherlands.	4.1	2.2	1.2	0.1	0.8	0.8	2.7	1.5
Norway	3.4	3.7	2.3	2.5	0.4	1.4	3.3	4.0
Sweden	2.9[d]	0.8	1.2	0.2	−0.2	1.3	2.7	2.0
Switzerland	3.1	0.9	1.4	2.7	0.2	−0.4	2.0	2.5
Canada.	2.6	0.3	0.3	−1.9	0.5	−1.2	2.4	2.0
United States	2.1	0.6	1.1	−0.7	1.6	−0.4	3.0	2.5

Source: National statistics and secretariat estimates.

[a] Real GDP per person employed. For the Netherlands and Norway employment is measured in terms of man-years and for the United States the number of persons engaged was used.

[b] Estimates rounded to the nearest 0.5 percentage point.

[c] 1964-1973.

[d] 1963-1973.

TABLE 2.3.2

Changes in labour productivity:[a] total manufacturing industry

Country	Average annual rates of growth			Year-to-year changes				
	1960-1973	1973-1979	1979-1984	1980	1981	1982	1983	1984[b]
France	6.2	4.2	3.0	1.9	1.8	2.3	3.7	5.5
Germany, Federal Republic of .	5.0	3.5	2.1	–	0.6	0.6	5.3	4.0
Italy[c]	6.4	2.5	2.4	4.1	0.6	0.1	−0.7	8.0
United Kingdom	3.6	0.8	2.9	−3.7	3.0	5.4	6.8	3.5
Austria[d]	6.0[e]	3.5	3.3	2.4	0.6	3.7	4.4	5.5
Belgium	6.2	5.5	3.3[f]	1.2	3.1	4.2	4.8	..
Finland	4.2	3.0	4.4	3.7	3.2	2.9	5.6	6.5
Netherlands[d, g].	6.4	3.8	3.1	−0.2	0.8	0.5	6.9	8.0
Norway[g]	3.5	0.5	1.8	−0.8	0.3	1.8	4.5	3.5
Sweden	5.3[h]	1.0	3.6	0.1	−0.7	3.2	9.4	6.0
Switzerland	4.2	2.0	2.2	3.5	−1.5	0.8	2.9	5.3
Canada.	4.0	1.5	2.5	−4.6	0.9	−3.4	8.4	12.0
United States[i]	3.5	1.2	3.0	−0.7	2.8	1.1	7.2	5.0

Source: National statistics and secretariat estimates.

[a] Real value added per person employed.

[b] Estimates rounded to the nearest 0.5 percentage point.

[c] Manufacturing including fuel and power products.

[d] Manufacturing and mining.

[e] 1964-1973.

[f] 1979-1983.

[g] Real value added per man-year.

[h] 1963-1973.

[i] Real value added per person engaged. Persons engaged = full-time equivalent employees plus self-employed.

A characteristic feature of productivity developments after 1979 has been not so much the support from output growth but the impact of the reduction of labour inputs in industry. Thus in all countries (except Finland) the average annual rates of decline of employment in 1979-1984 were higher than in 1973-1979, whereas the average growth rate of production was in general significantly smaller.

The decline of employment in manufacturing industry over the last few years or so decelerated in most countries in 1984 as a result of the stronger growth of output. (Only in Sweden and the United States was there actually an increase in employment–the first since 1979.) It may well be that this labour shedding, which has been substantial in a number of countries, has now reached its limit for prevailing levels of output. If this is so, any further sustained improvement in the growth of labour productivity can only be brought about by generally higher rates of output growth. So far the apparent deviation in recent years from previous historical relationships between output growth and productivity changes was probably only temporary: this "break" can be seen most clearly in the United Kingdom where the very rapid increases in labour productivity in 1982 and 1983 resulted from an absolute decline in output and an even larger absolute decline in employment. It seems reasonable to assume that productivity gains from such a combination of falling output and employment cannot be maintained over a long period. In fact, they are more likely to represent a once-and-for-all shift in productivity levels. Recent developments in western Europe and North America do not in any case undermine the hypothesis that a return to the high productivity growth rates of the 1960s and early 1970s will only be possible as the result of a marked improvement in output growth.

(ii) Costs, factor incomes and prices

During 1984 cost pressures weakened and domestic inflation rates fell. These favourable cost and price developments paved the way for a more dynamic profit performance and improved economic activity.

Input costs in national currencies in western Europe accelerated in 1984 largely due to the appreciating US dollar. However this upward cost pressure was largely offset by developments in unit labour costs. The growth rate of unit labour costs declined strongly in 1984 due to a combination of rising productivity and decelerating average earnings. Therefore, despite a further fall in price inflation, profit margins continued to widen and this, combined with better output performance, led to buoyant profits. In addition, the rates of return on capital further recovered during 1984, as a result of higher capacity utilization during the year. However, the extent to which this higher profitability will influence investment and future employment, given prevailing interest rates, is not yet clear.

In the United States, contrary to many expectations, inflation did not accelerate despite a strong fiscal stimulus. This was a consequence of a further moderation in labour costs and cheaper input prices which were partly due to the strong dollar. A further improvement in profit margins combined with strong output growth pushed profits up sharply.

This section reviews recent changes in material input prices, labour costs, profit margins and price inflation. A note at the end of the section examines the behaviour of profit margins in manufacturing industry during the 1960-1983 period. Emphasis is placed on differences between pre- and post-1973 behaviour in the countries of western Europe and North America.

(a) *Input costs*

During the current recovery of output growth, *primary commodity prices* have moved in a somewhat unusual manner. Non-oil commodity prices, after reaching a low point at the end of 1982, recovered considerably through 1983 and most of the first half of 1984. However, contrary to expectations, they fell significantly after reaching a peak in mid-May. The HWWA index of market prices (in US dollars)[36] of non-energy commodities rose by 1.9 per cent in 1984, compared with 4.4 per cent in 1983, but the index in 1984 was still 15 per cent below its record level in 1980. Price movements, however, differed considerably in the first and second halves of 1984: they increased in the first and second quarters by 12.9 and 7.4 per cent respectively; in the third quarter, however, they fell by 3.5 per cent and in the final quarter there was a further decline of 8.0 per cent.[37] This fall in non-oil commodity prices is partly due to changes in the exchange rate of the US dollar; but even in SDRs, the same trends occur, although the changes are more moderate. These price developments basically reflect ample supplies and weak demand. Stock releases, the strained financial circumstances of some producers and a reduction of acreage restrictions in the United States are among the main factors behind the increase in supplies. While the demand for manufactures has increased more than expected during the present upswing, demand for primary commodities has been relatively weak partly because of the dominance of the recovery by the United States, which is not as important as an importer of primary products as western Europe. Also high interest rates have slowed the pace of rebuilding stocks of primary commodities.

World energy prices remained weak in 1984, the HWWA energy index falling by 3 per cent during 1984. Although the OPEC price for crude oil remained (officially) unchanged throughout 1984 an increasing proportion of world trade in oil has been conducted on the spot market where dollar prices in the third quarter of 1984 were nearly 10 per cent lower than a year earlier. Despite the recovery in activity in the market economies the demand for crude oil remained weak: this is partly the result of long-run shifts in the pattern of demand away from oil- and energy-intensive activities and of energy-conservation efforts which have been increasing since 1979. In western Europe demand for oil has also been restrained by the fact that the appreciation of the dollar has meant sharply rising prices for crude oil in terms of national currency.[38] Increases in energy taxation, especially for gasoline, in most west European countries has added to this rise in prices. During 1984, therefore, western Europe did not benefit as did the United States from the impact of lower oil prices on the rate of domestic inflation.[39] However, the higher oil prices in western Europe will have helped to maintain efforts to raise energy efficiency and to substitute alternative energy sources for oil, and in the longer run this will strengthen Europe's ability to maintain lower inflation rates in the face of any renewed attempts by the OPEC cartel to secure large increases in the price of oil.

Changes in *intermediate goods prices* in western Europe and North America are shown in part B of table 2.3.3. These prices are in national currencies and the coverage of goods is more comprehensive than the primary commodities index discussed above. The deceleration in the annual rate of growth of inter-mediate goods prices in 1982 and 1983 came to a halt in 1984. They accelerated in all the west European countries except Norway and Sweden. In North America there was a marked acceleration in the United States, but not in Canada. However, despite the much stronger recovery of demand in the United States, the increase in US input prices was about one third of the average European rate, due in part to the appreciation of the dollar.

(b) *Earnings and unit labour costs*

The decline in the rate of increase in *average hourly earnings* continued in 1984 in western Europe, although with less momentum than in 1983. The weighted average rise in west European manufacturing industry in 1984 was around 7 per cent, about 1 point less than in 1983 and 3.5 percentage points less than in 1982 (table 2.3.4). Comparing the first three quarters of 1984 with those of 1983, the growth of nominal earnings slowed down in all the west European countries except Austria and the United Kingdom where there was no change.

The growth of earnings is still high in a number of countries (Italy, France, the United Kingdom, Ireland, and the Nordic countries except Denmark). However, there has been a marked deceleration in France and Italy and in some of the smaller economies. Rates of growth nevertheless have remained fairly stable in the United Kingdom and Ireland while in Norway and, particularly, Sweden there has been a marked acceleration during the course of 1984.

After falling sharply in 1983, the growth of nominal earnings in the United States in 1984 stabilized at around 4 per cent, much less than in most west European countries (only in the Netherlands, the Federal Republic of Germany and Switzerland was the increase less than in the United States).

During 1984 *average real earnings*[40] in west European manufacturing industry continued to grow by around 1 per cent (weighted average). However, in most of the small countries real wages fell significantly during 1984. The largest decline was in the Netherlands (2.2 per cent), where despite a low rate of inflation, a sharp deceleration in nominal earnings growth rate pushed real earnings to well below their levels at the end of the 1970s. Among the four major west European economies real wages grew strongly only in the United Kingdom (by just under 4 per cent), the result of a relatively high rate of nominal earnings growth (9 per cent, the third highest in the region) and a relatively modest inflation rate (5 per cent). There was virtually no real earnings growth in the Federal Republic of Germany and only modest increases (around 0.5 per cent) in Italy and France.

In the United States, real earnings fell slightly due to a modest acceleration in prices and no change in the growth of nominal earnings. After a sharp deterioration during 1983, real earnings in Canada recovered somewhat, the result of higher nominal earnings and lower inflation.

Thus, in most countries real wages, which started to fall in 1981 and stabilized somewhat in 1982 and 1983 thanks to the sharp fall in inflation rates, deteriorated further in 1984. At the end of 1984 the average level of real wages in manufacturing industry was lower than in 1980 in nine of the 13 west European countries (chart 2.3.1). On the other hand real earnings in 1984 were higher than in 1980 in the United Kingdom, Italy, France and Finland. The largest gain was in the United Kingdom where an average manufacturing worker's real earnings in 1984 were 12 per cent

---

[36] The HWWA (Hamburg) index weights world market prices by the relevant shares in total imports of western industrialized countries in 1974-1976.

[37] For further discussion of world commodity prices see section 5.1(i).

[38] Because the ECU has depreciated sharply against the dollar since mid-1983, the average west European price of crude oil imports (in ECUs) in September 1984 was 15 per cent higher than in mid-1983. This rise occurred despite the fact that the official dollar price of oil remained unchanged over the same period and spot prices fell.

[39] During the 12 months to September 1984, retail energy prices in the United States rose by around 1 per cent and by about 5 to 6 per cent in western Europe. But because the energy component of the consumer price index ranges only from 5 to 7 per cent of the total in western Europe, its direct effect on overall inflation rates was not large.

[40] Average growth rates of hourly earnings (table 2.3.4) deflated by the consumer price index (table 2.3.10)

TABLE 2.3.3

Changes in the prices of raw materials and intermediate goods
(*Percentage change over corresponding period of previous year*)

	1981	1982	1983	1984	1984 Q1	1984 Q2	1984 Q3	1984 Q4
A. *World market price of raw materials* (in US dollars)								
All items								
Including energy	6.5	−5.0	−8.4	−2.1	−6.8	1.8	−0.8	−1.9
Excluding energy	−13.9	−13.3	4.4	1.9	12.9	7.4	−3.5	−8.0
Food	−16.2	−15.9	10.1	5.1	21.6	15.3	−3.6	−9.6
Industrial materials	−12.4	−11.4	0.8	−0.4	7.2	2.2	−3.5	−6.8
Energy	13.6	−2.9	−11.5	−3.1	−11.4	0.1	−	−
B. *National intermediate goods prices* (in national currency)								
France	11.0	11.1	11.1	13.3	15.6	14.4	12.8	10.4
Germany, Federal Republic of .	11.6	3.4	−0.1	5.0 N	4.6	5.5	4.6	4.9 N
Italy	17.5	12.9	8.0	11.3 O	11.1	12.2	11.1	10.3 O
United Kingdom	9.2	7.3	6.9	8.1	7.2	8.6	7.5	9.2
Unweighted average of 4 . . .	*12.3*	*8.7*	*6.5*	*9.6 O*	*9.6*	*10.2*	*9.0*	*9.4 O*
Austria	15.2	3.9	−1.1	4.8	3.1	5.7	5.0	5.5
Belgium	8.3	8.6	5.7	10.8 N	12.8	12.4	9.3	7.2 N
Denmark	18.1	10.2	4.6	7.5	8.1	9.8	6.4	6.1
Finland	12.1	5.7	3.8	6.0	4.7	6.5	6.4	6.6
Ireland	12.6	7.9	6.9	. .	7.6	7.5	6.7	6.8 O
Netherlands	20.0	4.7	−1.5	7.7 O	7.4	8.7	7.3	6.9 O
Norway	17.7	6.6	7.5	8.3	7.7	8.8	8.4	8.5
Sweden	11.0	13.7	11.3	7.2	8.7	8.1	6.1	6.1
Switzerland	6.2	2.3	−0.7	3.4	2.9	3.5	3.4	3.6
Unweighted average of 9 . . .	*13.5*	*7.1*	*4.1*	*7.0 **	*7.0*	*7.9*	*6.5*	*6.8 O*
Unweighted average of 13 . . .	*13.1*	*7.6*	*4.8*	*7.8 **	*7.8*	*8.6*	*7.3*	*7.6 O*
Canada	19.2	8.3	5.3	2.7 O	3.9	3.3	1.8	0.6 O
United States	7.7	1.3	1.2	2.9	3.5	3.9	2.5	1.5

Source: National statistics. For definitions of national indices see *Economic Survey of Europe in 1982*, p. 32, except for Sweden – where the domestic supply price index is an aggregate (made by the secretariat) of the following price series: paper and cardboard; chemical, petroleum, rubber and plastic products; non-metallic minerals; basic metals; metal products (other than machinery and equipment).

Note: O = January-October or October. N = January-November or October + November.

higher than four years earlier. In North America real wages suffered less than in most of western Europe.

The growth of *unit labour costs* (for the whole economy) continued to decelerate strongly in 1984 (table 2.3.5). In western Europe they increased by about 4 per cent (weighted average), one third less than in 1983 and almost half the 1982 rate. There are, however, large inter-country differences: they actually fell in the Netherlands and elsewhere ranged from 1 per cent growth in the Federal Republic of Germany and Switzerland to 8 per cent in Italy. They accelerated slightly only in the United Kingdom and Sweden, in the former mostly due to the fast growth of earnings per worker, in the latter largely because of falling productivity.

The deceleration in unit labour costs in 1984 in western Europe, as in 1983, was due to a combination of rising productivity and decelerating average earnings. However, in 1984 the favourable effect of lower earnings growth was generally stronger than that of productivity growth except in France, Italy and Denmark where productivity growth (for the total economy) accelerated strongly: in France this was mainly due to declining employment and in the others to strongly accelerating output growth.

Unit labour costs in North America had fallen much more strongly than in western Europe during 1983. In 1984 they continued to decelerate sharply in Canada (due to rising productivity growth) but levelled off at their 1983 growth rate in the United States. In the United States this loss of downward momentum was due to a significant productivity slowdown combined with stable earnings growth.

The *real product wage* in 1984 fell in all west European countries except the United Kingdom, where it increased by about 2 per cent due to the acceleration of unit labour costs. Unit labour costs also accelerated in Sweden but due to a higher inflation rate the real product wage fell although at a slower rate than in 1983. In the United States real product wages continued to fall at the same rate as in 1983. The general fall in real product wages indicates the important role played by the moderation of wage costs and productivity gains in the improvement of profit margins during the 1983-1984 upturn. Real product wages were also falling during 1982, but then it was largely due to higher inflation rates rather than an easing of labour costs.

Wage costs are only part of total labour costs. The growth of *non-wage labour costs*[41] has been rapid in recent years and they now account for almost half of total labour costs in many west European countries. Table 2.3.6 shows that the share of non-wage costs in total labour costs rose everywhere during the 1971-1981 decade: within western Europe it was only in Denmark and the United Kingdom that their share was less than one third in 1981. In Austria, Belgium, France, the Federal Republic of Germany, Italy and the Netherlands, non-wage costs were almost half of total labour costs. In the United States and Canada the share of non-wage labour costs was well below the west European

---

[41] Non-wage labour costs include employer's costs for employee benefits such as paid leave, severance pay, health and life insurance, pension and saving plans, social security, unemployment insurance, workers' compensation etc.

TABLE 2.3.4

Annual and quarterly changes in average hourly earnings in manufacturing industry

(Percentage change over corresponding period of previous year)

	1982	1983	1984*	1984 Q1	1984 Q2	1984 Q3	1984 Q4
France[a]	15.2	11.2	8.5	10.0	8.3	7.6	..
Germany, Federal Republic of[b]	4.9	3.3	2.5	2.9	1.7	2.5	..
Italy[c]	17.2	15.3	11.5	13.6	12.3	..	..
United Kingdom[d]	11.2	9.0	9.0	9.5	8.1	8.8	..
Unweighted average of 4	12.1	9.7	8.0	9.0	7.6	..	..
Weighted average of 4	11.1	8.9	7.5	8.3	6.9	..	..
Austria.	6.1	4.5	4.5	5.7	4.8	3.4	..
Belgium[e]	7.4	5.9	4.5	5.4	4.5	4.5	..
Denmark[f].	10.0	6.6	4.5	4.1	5.4	4.5	..
Finland	10.5	9.6	9.0	9.6	9.9*	..	..
Ireland[g]	14.4	10.3	10.0	12.1	11.7*	..	..
Netherlands[c]	7.2	2.2	1.0	0.7	0.7	1.1	..
Norway[h]	10.2	8.4	8.0	7.5	7.8	9.0*	..
Sweden[f]	7.9	7.9	7.0	3.1	6.4	9.7	..
Switzerland[i,j]	5.9	3,7	2.0	2.3	1.6	1.6	..
Unweighted average of 9	8.8	6.6	5.5	5.6	5.9	..	..
Weighted average of 9	7.9	5.8	5.0	4.5	4.8	..	..
Unweighted average of 13	9.9	7.5	6.5	6.7	6.4	..	..
Weighted average of 13.	10.5	8.3	7.0	7.5	6.5	..	..
Canada.	11.8	3.5[k]	5.0	3.8[k]	6.1	5.9	..
United States	6.3	4.0	4.0	4.1	4.0	3.8	..

Source: National statistics, and OECD, *Main Economic Indicators*, Paris.

[a] Wage rates. Quarterly data, referring to the beginning of January, April, July and October respectively. Annual figures are obtained by averaging the five observations from January of one year to January of the following year.

[b] Quarterly data, referring to January, April, July and October.

[c] Wage rates.

[d] Weekly earnings of all employees, Great Britain.

[e] Industry, adult male workers.

[f] Including mining.

[g] Quarterly data referring to March, June, September and December.

[h] Males ony.

[i] Series currently under revision.

[j] Data refer to workers who had accidents during the relevant period.

[k] OECD estimate.

TABLE 2.3.5

Growth of unit labour costs[a] and real product wages[b] for the whole economy

(Percentage change over previous year)

	Unit labour costs 1982	Unit labour costs 1983	Unit labour costs 1984[c]	Real product wages 1982	Real product wages 1983	Real product wages 1984
France	12.2	8.7	4.5	−0.2	−0.1	−2.5
Germany, Federal Republic of	3.3	0.7	1.0	−1.3	−2.4	−0.8
Italy	17.5	16.5	8.0	−0.3	1.3	−2.4
United Kingdom	4.7	4.5	5.0	−2.2	−0.6	2.1
Unweighted average of 4	9.4	7.6	4.5	−1.0	−0.5	−0.9
Weighted average of 4	8.3	6.3	4.0	−1.0	−0.8	−0.9
Austria.	3.8	2.2	3.0	−2.7	−1.5	−1.3
Belgium	5.0	4.9	..	−2.0	−0.9	..
Denmark	9.2	5.7	3.5	−1.9	−2.2	−3.2
Finland	8.1	7.1	7.0	−0.9	−1.8	−0.5
Ireland	11.6	7.1	5.5	−3.2	−3.2	−2.5
Netherlands	4.5	0.4	−1.5	−1.5	−1.5	−4.1
Norway	10.4	5.0	..	0.5	−2.0	..
Sweden	4.9	5.4	6.0	−3.4	−3.7	−1.9
Switzerland	8.6	3.9	1.0	1.2	0.6	−1.9
Unweighted average of 9	7.3	4.6	3.5*	−1.5	−1.8	−2.5*
Weighted average of 9	6.3	3.9	3.0*	−1.2	−1.3	−2.0*
Unweighted average of 13	8.0	5.5	4.0*	−1.4	−1.5	−2.0*
Weighted average of 13.	7.8	5.7	4.0*	−1.0	−1.0	−1.5*
Canada.	12.4	2.2	1.0	1.9	−3.1	..
United States	7.9	2.7	2.5	1.8	−1.1	−1.2

Source: National statistics.

[a] Compensation of employees per unit of real GDP or GNP.

[b] Growth of unit labour costs for the whole economy deflated by the GDP deflator.

[c] Preliminary figures and secretariat estimates rounded to the nearest 0.5 percentage point.

CHART 2.3.1.

**Indices of nominal and real^a earnings in 1984 in west European
and North American manufacturing industry**

(1980 = 100)

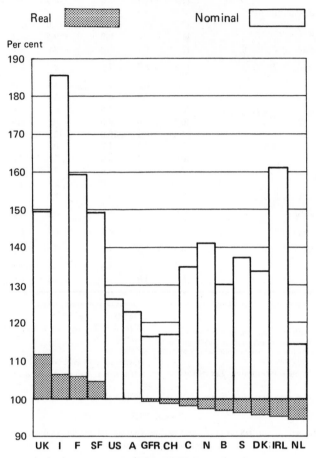

Real   Nominal

Source: As for tables 2.3.4. and 2.3.10.

a Real earnings are estimated by deflating nominal
earnings by the consumer price index.

TABLE 2.3.6

**Share of non-wage labour costs in total labour costs in manufacturing,
1971-1981**

(Percentages)

	1971	1981
Austria	43.2	47.1
Belgium	38.7	44.4
Denmark	14.5	20.6
Finland	23.1	36.7
France	40.1	44.4
Germany, Federal Republic of	33.8	43.5
Italy	47.6	46.2
Netherlands	40.8	43.8
Norway	26.5	33.0
Sweden	22.5	40.1
United Kingdom^a	17.4	27.0
Canada	16.7	22.5
United States	21.3	27.0

Source: Based on inforation in: Swedish Employers' Confederation, *Wages and total labour costs for workers—International Survey 1971-1981*, Stockholm 1984.

^aGreat Britain.

average. (By far the lowest share of the non-wage element, among the developed market economies, was in Japan where in 1981 it was only 16 per cent.)

(c) *Final output prices*

Final output prices (table 2.3.7) generally rose faster in 1984 than in 1983. They decelerated further only in France, Italy and Sweden, which nevertheless had the highest growth rates in 1984. The smallest increases were in the United States (2.1 per cent), the Federal Republic of Germany and Switzerland (around 3 per cent).

The increase in output prices was higher than that for input prices only in Sweden, Canada and Finland (by around 1.5 points in each case). Elsewhere input prices rose more than final output prices, the largest differences being in Belgium (8 points) and France (5.5 points). These differences between input and output prices imply that if unit labour costs had not strongly moderated during 1984, profit margins would have been severely squeezed in many of the countries of the region.

TABLE 2.3.7

Changes in final output prices of manufacturing industry
(Percentage change over corresponding period of previous year)

	1981	1982	1983	1984[a]	Q1	Q2	1984 Q3	1984 Q4[a]
France	12.8	11.5	8.9	7.6	8.7	7.7	7.0	7.1
Germany, Federal Republic of . .	6.0	4.8	1.5	2.8	3.0	3.2	2.6	2.5
Italy	16.3	14.8	11.8	10.1[O]	10.7	10.7	9.5	8.6[O]
United Kingdom	9.5	7.8	5.4	6.1	6.0	6.3	6.1	6.2
Unweighted average of 4	11.1	9.7	6.9	6.7[O]	7.1	7.0	6.3	6.1[O]
Austria	8.1	3.1	0.6	3.8	3.6	4.8	3.6	3.3[N]
Belgium	6.6	6.9	3.2	3.6[N]	3.4	3.9	3.4	3.5[O]
Denmark	13.3	10.6	5.9	7.5	8.3	9.9	6.6..	5.9[N]
Finland	10.8	6.9	6.2	7.0	6.1	7.1	7.4	7.2
Ireland	16.7	11.9	6.5	7.7[O]	7.8	8.3	7.1	6.9[O]
Netherlands	9.2	6.6	1.8	4.3[O]	4.4	4.8	3.9	4.1[O]
Norway	9.9	7.0	5.6	6.2	6.3	6.9	6.7	6.9
Sweden	10.0	12.0	11.0	8.9	9.4	9.7	8.4	7.9
Switzerland	5.6	3.7	1.1	3.0	2.9	3.3	2.9	2.7
Unweighted average of 9	10.0	7.6	4.7	5.9[O]	5.8	6.5	5.6	5.3[O]
Unweighted average of 13	10.4	8.3	5.4	6.2[O]	6.2	6.7	5.8	5.6[O]
Canada	10.2	6.0	3.5	4.1[N]	4.5	4.2	3.8	3.9[N]
United States	9.2	4.0	1.6	2.1	2.4	2.5	1.9	1.7

Sources: National statistics. For definitions of national indices see *Economic Survey of Europe in 1982*, p. 33, except for the United States–Producer price index; Total finished goods.

[a] O = January-October or October. N = January-November or October + November.

TABLE 2.3.8

Growth of profit margins in manufacturing industry,[a] 1982-1984
(Percentage change over corresponding period of previous year)

	1982	1983	1984[b]	1984 Q1	1984 Q2	1984 Q3
Finland	14.2	22.1	15	18.9	9.0	18.1
France	25.4	18.2	1	2.6	−6.4	7.1
Germany, Federal Republic of	4.5	16.0	5	13.9	−3.3	4.9
Italy	18.3	21.4	15	12.2	16.3	15.2
Sweden	12.2	43.7	56	69.4	59.9	38.4
United Kingdom	20.0	1.0	−8	−4.5	−9.4	−11.8
Canada	−23.0	..	32	32.1	29.0	35.1
United States	18.7	30.6	9	16.9	4.2	4.3

Sources: See Appendix to this section.

[a] Operating surplus per unit of gross output.

[b] Average of first three quarters rounded to the nearest whole number.

(d) *Profit margins*

Profit margins (profits per unit of manufacturing gross output), which were squeezed during most of the period between 1973 and 1981, recovered strongly in 1982 in most west European countries, and continued to improve in the United States.[42] This recovery in margins accelerated strongly in 1983 and continued, but at a less rapid pace in 1984 (table 2.3.8).

The recovery of margins in 1982 was due to the weakening of both unit labour costs and the prices of materials inputs. In 1983, despite a significant slowdown in the growth of final output prices, profit margins rose strongly because of a further decline in the growth of input prices and of unit labour costs. It was only in the United Kingdom and, to a much lesser extent, in France that

profit margins were under pressure in 1983. However, profit shares (the share of operating surplus in value added) and total profits in the United Kingdom manufacturing sector increased significantly during 1983 due to a large increase in output.

In 1984 the growth of profit margins decelerated everywhere except in Sweden and Canada.[43] Such a deceleration is normal given the high growth rates in 1983 and the fact that the cyclical recovery was moving into its second year. Another factor was the appreciation of the US dollar *vis-à-vis* the European currencies which led to higher input prices during 1984. In Sweden the faster growth of profit margins in 1984 was due to the large difference between output and input prices–more than 1.5 points (tables 2.3.3 and 2.3.7)–and the absence of any rise in unit labour costs in manufacturing (mainly due to strong productivity

---

[42] Long-term movements (1960-1983) in profit margins are studied in section 2.3(ii)(g). The methodology used here for estimating profit margins is described in this section.

[43] Data on margins are not available for Canada in 1983 due to a break in the earnings series but, given a significant improvement in productivity, margins are likely to have recovered from their decline in 1982.

CHART 2.3.2.

**Percentage distribution of the contribution of domestic costs and import prices
to the total rise in final output prices[a] 1980 — 1984**

(Percentages)

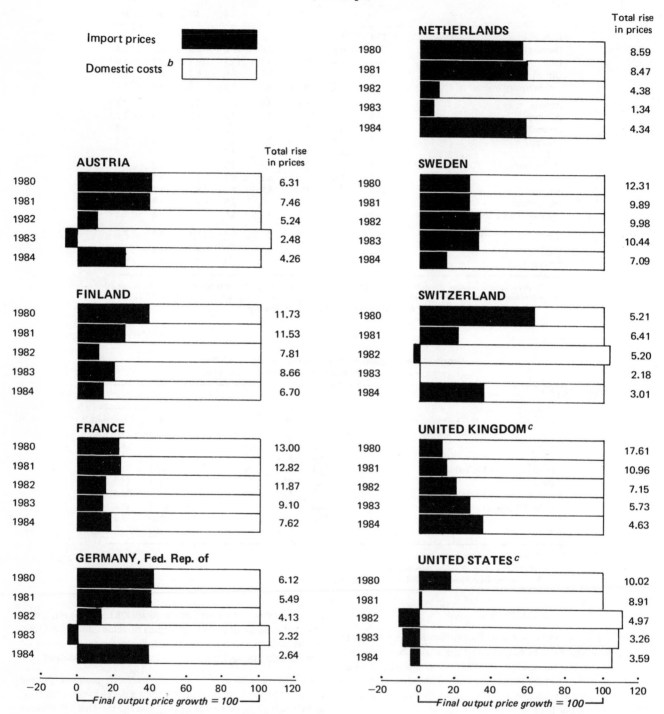

Source: National statistics.

a Market prices of home produced and imported goods and services available for private and public consumption, investment and export (i.e. the implicit deflator of total final expenditure).
b Incomes from employment plus gross profits and other trading income and usually self-employment income;(before provision for depreciation)plus net taxes on expenditure per unit of final expenditure.
c January-September 1984 over January-September 1983.

gains).[44] The same factors were behind the faster growth of margins in Canada in 1984.

Profit margins were badly affected during the second quarter of 1984 by output losses in the Federal Republic of Germany (the seven-week metal workers' strike) and price freezes in France. In the United Kingdom margins declined in the first three quarters of 1984 due to a sharp deceleration in productivity growth, stable earnings growth and a narrowing of the input-output price differential.[45]

In the United States profit margins also rose less in 1984 than in 1983; however, while in western Europe this was partly due to the effect of dollar appreciation on input prices, in the United States it was almost entirely due to a sharp fall in productivity growth.

Despite the general slowdown in margins, profit shares increased during 1984, in some countries more than in 1983 due to faster output growth. The extreme case was Italy where although the increase of profit margins in 1984 was one third less than in 1983, profit shares grew by almost 20 per cent (5 points higher than in 1983). Profit shares also grew faster than in 1983 in Finland, France and Canada. In the United States there was a sharp slowdown in the improvement of profit shares in 1984, but total profits still increased faster than in many west European countries due to the much better growth of output.

(e) *Cost components of inflation*

As shown above, the increase in domestic costs and prices weakened in 1984 in both western Europe and the United States. Unit labour costs continued to decelerate except in Finland, Sweden and the United Kingdom (table 2.3.5). Profit margins, which had improved markedly in most countries in 1983, continued to grow in 1984, although in general at a slower rate (table 2.3.8). The relatively weaker growth of domestic costs, however, was accompanied in western Europe by rising import prices in national currencies. Thus, while the lower pressure from domestic costs (especially wages) accounted for a large proportion of the fall in the overall rate of inflation, import prices continued to provide a significant offset to this improvement, because of changes in exchange rates. In the United States, however, domestic cost pressures were accompanied by lower import prices.

Some idea of the relative importance of domestic costs and import prices can be obtained by breaking down the rise in the price of total final expenditure into these two separate components: this is shown in chart 2.3.2.

The contribution of domestic costs, namely the sum of unit wage costs, other factor incomes and net taxes on expenditure, declined in all countries in 1984 except Finland and Sweden. Nevertheless, the domestic cost component still accounted for more than 80 per cent of the rise in prices in France, more than 70 per cent in Austria and more than 60 per cent in the Federal Republic of Germany, Switzerland and the United Kingdom. It

was only in the Netherlands that domestic costs accounted for less than half of the inflation rate. In the United States, however, the domestic contribution was higher than the inflation rate itself, as import prices pulled down the inflation rate.

Table 2.3.9 disaggregates the contribution of imports to the rise in prices into its dollar price and exchange rate components. For the fourth year running the change in the dollar price of imports fell significantly for all the west European countries in 1984, mainly because of the drop in prices for oil and non-oil commodities. The favourable effect of lower dollar prices, however, was largely offset by the continuing appreciation of the US dollar. In the Federal Republic of Germany, the Netherlands and Switzerland, the contribution of exchange rate depreciation to the increase in final output prices was significantly larger than that of all the domestic components. Hence, as table 2.3.9 indicates, in the absence of exchange rate changes, the rise of final output prices in five of the west European countries included in the table would have been significantly lower than in the United States.

The breakdown of the rise in the total final expenditure price into its components is essentially an accounting exercise which cannot itself say anything about the causes of inflation. However, the relative importance of the various factors suggested by this breakdown is supported by the results of a more econometric approach. A previous issue of this Survey contained an analysis in which year-to-year changes in consumer prices, for a pooled time-series, cross-section sample of 13 west European countries, were related to changes in consumer prices in the previous year (a proxy for the wage-price spiral), import prices (exchange rate and dollar price components), M1 money stock (as a proxy for demand pressure) and output relative to its trend (as a measure of the rate of capacity utilization).[46] The results obtained from this equation when it was refitted to the data up to 1983 indicates the following: the equation predicts a price change of 6.2 per cent in 1984 which is virtually the same as the actual outcome, with about 70 per cent of the total change in consumer prices due to the weakening of the wage-price spiral in the previous period, 16 per cent due to stronger demand, and the remainder (about 14 per cent) due to higher import prices in national currencies. There was virtually no rise in prices attributable to the level of capacity utilization. Dividing the contribution of import prices into the exchange rate and dollar import price components, exchange rates alone contributed 1.5 points to the total price change (i.e. about 25 per cent) while import prices in dollars pulled down the rise in consumer prices by 0.7 points (or about 11 per cent). Comparing 1984 with 1983, the rate of change of prices was nearly 1 percentage point less in 1984 for the weighted average of the 13 west European countries. According to the estimating equation, this deceleration was due mainly to the impact of steadily diminishing inflation in the previous year and slower growth in the money stock. However, import costs contributed more strongly to the increase in consumer prices in 1984 than in 1983.

(f) *Consumer prices*

Consumer price inflation continued to fall during 1984 and reached its lowest rate since 1971. The weighted average rate of increase for western Europe fell from 7 per cent in 1983 to 6 per cent in 1984 (table 2.3.10). In the United States the inflation rate, which has fallen much faster than in western Europe since the second oil shock and which in 1983 was at its lowest since 1968,

---

[44] Unit labour costs for the Swedish economy as a whole increased by 6 per cent in 1984. This contrast with the manufacturing sector appears to be due to the various supports to employment which are concentrated mainly in the public sector.

[45] "During 1984 cost pressures in the United Kingdom increased largely due to a 3 per cent earnings drift reflecting increases over time, concentrated in the latter part of 1983 ... and sterling's depreciation which contributed to a 9 per cent rise in manufacturing inputs. ... Some of these cost rises have been absorbed in profit margins in expectation of some recovery in the exchange rate which would reduce the sterling cost of inputs from abroad. At the same time, however, manufacturers took advantage of sterling's depreciation to increase their profit margins on exports sales.": Bank of England, *Quarterly Bulletin*, London, December 1984.

[46] *Economic Survey of Europe in 1981*, United Nations, New York, 1982, pp. 40-43.

Table 2.3.9

Contribution of import prices to the rise in final output prices, 1980-1984

(Percentage change over previous year)

| | | | of which due to: | |
| | | | | of which: |
	Rise in final output prices[a]	Import prices in national currency	Import prices in US dollars	Change in exchange rate
Austria				
1980	6.31	2.58	3.58	−1.00
1981	7.46	2.96	−3.05	6.01
1982	5.24	0.56	−1.46	2.01
1983	2.48	−0.15	−1.56	1.41
1984	4.26	1.11	−1.50	2.61
Finland				
1980	11.73	4.61	5.82	−1.21
1981	11.53	3.03	−0.81	3.83
1982	7.81	0.90	−1.74	2.64
1983	8.66	1.71	−1.65	3.36
1984	6.70	0.93	−0.56	1.50
France				
1980	13.00	2.91	3.04	−0.14
1981	12.82	2.98	−1.83	4.81
1982	11.87	1.83	−1.84	3.68
1983	9.10	1.21	−1.66	2.87
1984	7.62	1.39	−0.96	2.34
Germany, Federal Republic of				
1980	6.12	2.58	2.78	−0.20
1981	5.49	2.22	−2.63	4.86
1982	4.13	0.53	−1.13	1.66
1983	2.32	−0.11	−1.29	1.18
1984	2.64	1.02	−1.15	2.17
Netherlands				
1980	8.59	4.81	5.15	−0.34
1981	8.47	4.98	−3.07	8.06
1982	4.38	0.44	−1.90	2.34
1983	1.34	0.10	−2.15	2.25
1984	4.34	2.53	−1.16	3.70
Sweden				
1980	12.31	3.39	3.76	−0.37
1981	9.89	2.74	−1.68	4.42
1982	9.98	3.27	−1.85	5.12
1983	10.44	3.35	−1.70	5.05
1984	7.09	1.02	−1.60	1.63
Switzerland				
1980	5.21	3.32	3.09	0.23
1981	6.41	1.36	−3.06	4.42
1982	5.20	−0.16	−1.06	0.90
1983	2.18	−	−0.85	0.85
1984	3.01	1.05	−1.50	2.56
United Kingdom				
1980	17.61	2.14	4.44	−2.30
1981	10.96	1.67	−1.12	2.78
1982	7.15	1.47	−1.35	2.82
1983	5.73	1.62	−1.20	2.83
1984[b]	4.63	1.62	−0.19	1.81
United States				
1980	10.02	1.76	1.76	−
1981	8.91	0.16	0.16	−
1982	4.97	−0.51	−0.51	−
1983	3.26	−0.27	−0.27	−
1984[b]	3.59	−0.17	−0.17	−

Source: National statistics and IMF, *International Financial Statistics,* Washington, D.C.

[a] Market prices of home produced and imported goods and services available for private and public consumption, investment and export (i.e. the implicit deflator of total final expenditure).

[b] January-September 1984 over January-September 1983.

increased from 3.2 per cent in 1983 to 4.3 per cent in 1984. Despite the further strengthening of the dollar vis-à-vis the European currencies, the difference between the rates in western Europe and the United States narrowed.

The annual inflation rate fell in all west European countries except Austria, where there was a sharp acceleration, the Netherlands, Switzerland and the United Kingdom. The acceleration in Austria is due to increases in value added tax, higher public charges and tariffs, and a large devaluation of the schilling against the dollar. Inter-country differences in the rates of inflation narrowed significantly in 1984.[47] The largest decelerations were in Italy, the Federal Republic of Germany, and Norway, where inflation rates were one fourth less than in 1983.

In 1984 much of the deceleration in the rate of inflation occurred in the second half of the year. During the first quarter the stickiness in the consumer price index was almost entirely due to retail food prices which increased twice as much as the overall rise in consumer prices. Retail energy prices also recovered somewhat and this pattern continued into the second quarter. Beginning in June, the general weakening in commodity prices, which had started in May, began to feed through to retail prices. In addition, the moderation in unit labour costs, which had already been exerting downward pressure on prices for several quarters, gained further momentum. During the third quarter there was a general, and in some countries a very strong, price deceleration which continued until the end of the year.

At the beginning of the present upswing there was general concern that strengthening demand would revitalize inflation. However, while the present upswing has raised labour productivity and profit margins, wage moderation has continued, and this has further reduced the rise in unit labour costs and prices. Furthermore, the present upswing has not greatly strengthened the demand for primary commodities.

Inflation rates in 1985 are likely to remain at the relatively low rates achieved in the second half of 1984: domestic and international cost pressures are not expected to change very much and in several countries governments are trying to improve the situation still further with specific measures to contain prices and incomes. They are doing so at a time when labour markets are still very weak and recent wage settlements have shown continuing restraint. In most countries automatic indexation of wages has been abandoned and in the rest is being modified so as to support the governments' lower inflation targets (Italy, for example). Unions are also more easily and frequently agreeing than in the past to ease their demands for wage increases and other benefits; in some countries they have settled for increases in take-home pay via lower income taxes (for example, in France).

There has been a marked recovery in profit margins but they are still far from being an element of inflationary pressure. The recent improvement of margins has been mainly due to moderation in the costs of production rather than accelerating prices. Since in most countries these costs may continue to moderate in 1985, profit margins may widen further without any inflationary risk. Given this easing of domestic inflationary pressures and little likelihood of supply shortages in world commodity markets, the downward trend of inflation rates should continue in 1985.

[47] The standard deviation of the average west European rate of consumer price inflation shown in table 2.3.10 fell from 3.5 points in the third quarter of 1983 to 2.3 points in the third quarter of 1984.

TABLE 2.3.10

Annual and quarterly changes in consumer prices
(*Percentage change over corresponding period of previous year*)

	1982	1983	1984[a]	1984			
				Q1	Q2	Q3	Q4
France	11.8	9.6	7.4	8.8	7.8	7.3	6.8
Germany, Federal Republic of	5.3	3.3	2.4	2.9	2.8	1.8	2.1
Italy	16.5	14.7	10.8	12.1	11.4	10.5	9.4
United Kingdom	8.6	4.6	5.0	5.2	5.1	4.7	4.8
Total of 4							
Unweighted average	10.5	8.0	6.4	7.2	6.8	6.1	5.8
Weighted average	9.8	7.4	5.8	6.7	6.2	5.5	5.3
Austria	5.4	3.3	5.6	5.7	6.0	5.7	5.2
Belgium	8.7	7.7	6.3	7.0	7.1	5.8	5.5
Denmark	10.1	6.9	6.3	6.3	6.6	6.4	5.8
Finland	9.6	8.3	7.1	8.2	7.3	6.6	6.3
Ireland[a]	17.1	10.4	8.6	10.2	9.7	8.0	6.7
Netherlands	5.9	2.8	3.3	3.6	3.8	2.9	2.9
Norway	11.3	8.4	6.2	6.5	6.5	6.1	6.0
Sweden	8.6	9.0	8.0	8.3	8.6	7.6	7.6
Switzerland	5.6	3.0	3.0	2.9	2.9	2.8	3.0
Total of 9							
Unweighted average	9.2	6.6	6.1	6.5	6.5	5.8	5.5
Weighted average	7.9	5.9	5.5	5.8	5.9	5.2	5.0
Total of 13							
Unweighted average	9.6	7.1	6.2	6.7	6.6	5.9	5.6
Weighted average	9.3	7.0	5.8	6.5	6.2	5.4	5.2
Canada	10.8	5.8	4.4	5.2	4.6	3.9	3.7
United States	6.1	3.2	4.3	4.5	4.3	4.2	4.1

Source: National statistics.

[a] February, May, August, November and averages thereof.

Profit margins in manufacturing industry, 1960-1983

This note examines the behaviour of profit margins (profits per unit of gross output) with emphasis on the periods before and after 1973. The different effects on margins of the two oil shocks of the 1970s are brought out in the data, as are the contrasting developments in western Europe and the United States.

The measure of profit margins used here is based on the elementary accounting identity which makes the value of gross output equal to the sum of the wage bill, total material input costs and gross operating surplus. This identity allows the change in profit margins to be derived as a residual from changes in other unit costs and final prices, given that the shares of the various components in total gross output are available. Although it is not without problems[48] the method provides a relatively easy way of establishing changes in profit margins and, in conjunction with additional data on output, changes in total profits. The method is also useful for short-run analysis of profits: it is based on price and wage data which are generally more widely available on a quarterly basis than are national accounts, and even where the latter are available they usually appear with a longer time lag than the series on prices and wages. Moreover, quarterly national accounts are typically subject to large revisions and so it is useful to have an alternative estimate of changes in such sensitive variables as profits and profit margins.

The basic series for unit costs of production (material inputs and labour), final output prices and profit margins are shown in chart 2.3.3. As regards the trends in profit margins, there are two main differences between the period before the first oil shock (1960-1972) and the period following it (1973-1983).

First, the average level of profit margins was in general higher during the pre-1973 period than in the post-1973 period. Despite the general and strong improvement of margins in 1982 and 1983, their levels generally remained well below those of the early 1970s. The exceptions are Finland, France, and the United States, where they quickly resumed an upward trend after the first recession.

Second, before 1973 profit margins in most countries had followed closely price and cost changes, but after 1973 margins tended to fluctuate strongly and to diverge widely from movements in prices and costs.

These differences between the pre- and post-1973 periods help to explain the lower rates of profitability in the period following the first oil shock.[49] During the 1960s and the early 1970s manufacturing output increased steadily (with a brief exception in the late 1960s), accompanied by slowly but steadily growing profit margins. Total profits and profit shares increased during this period. After 1973, however, lower profit margins combined with weak or falling output reduced total profits and profit shares to unprecedented levels.

After 1973 there have been two recessions, differing in duration and other characteristics. Profits and profitability declined during both recessions: however, their rates of fall and the factors behind them were different.

The first recession can be described as a period of high unit costs of production. Raw material prices (oil and non-oil)

---

[48] The methodology is discussed in the Appendix to this note.

[49] While the growth rates of profit shares and rates of return are in general strongly correlated and profit shares therefore can be used as a proxy for profitability, profit margins and profit shares are not necessarily related, because the profit share is an aggregate measure while the margin is a unit measure.

CHART 2.3.3.

**Patterns of annual change in profit margins, output prices and unit production costs
in manufacturing industry, 1960-1983**

(Indices 1970 = 100)

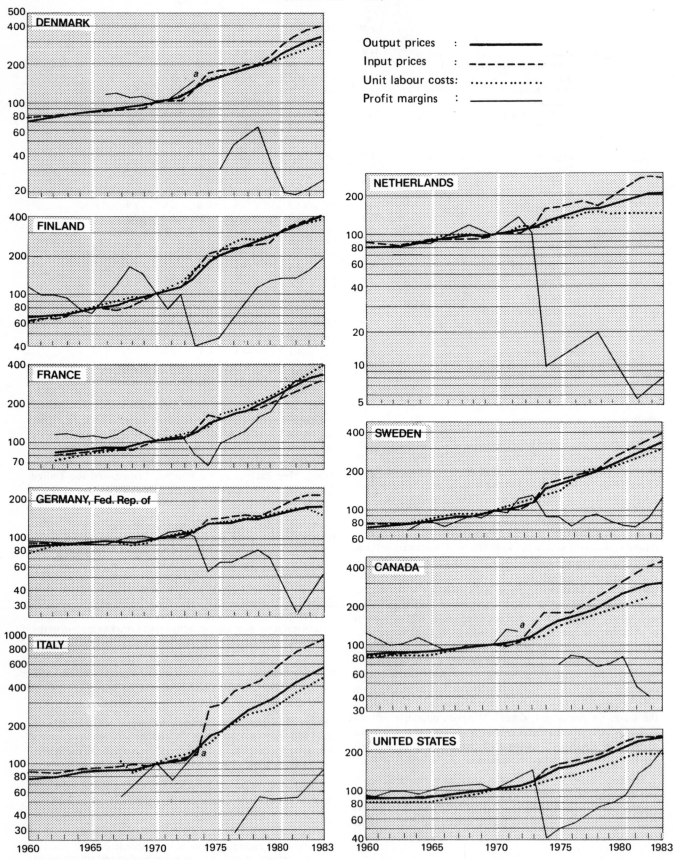

Output prices   : ———————
Input prices   : – – – – – –
Unit labour costs: ·············
Profit margins   : ———————

Source: See appendix to this note.

a The broken series indicate financial losses, that is, negative profit margins.

increased sharply. Unit labour costs reached unprecedented levels due to falling output combined with wage rigidity and relatively stable employment. These sharp increases in the unit costs of production reduced profit margins despite accelerating final output prices. In turn, falling profit margins (in some cases financial losses) combined with lower production levels caused profit shares to shrink acutely. Despite its severity, the first recession was rather short: in general (except in the Nordic countries which lagged behind the rest of Europe) it ran from the second quarter of 1974 to the second quarter of 1975.

The recession following the second oil shock was much longer, lasting for almost three years. A severe squeeze on profit margins, such as occurred during the first recession, was avoided in North America and in most west European countries thanks to weaker prices for non-oil materials (there was even a sharp fall in 1982) and some deceleration in unit labour costs. The length of the second recession and the weakness of demand had cumulative effects on production and capacity utilization and thus on profits and profitability. Nevertheless, profit shares fell less than in the first recession thanks to the relatively better performance of profit margins. This may be seen in table 2.3.11 where the trough levels of profit shares are given. Out of ten countries, in only two did profit shares in the second recession fall below their lowest level in the first: in France profit shares fell more or less continuously from 1974 and in the Federal Republic of Germany the underlying long-run decline[50] continued between the two recessions. In the United States profit shares in the two recessions were almost the same.

TABLE 2.3.11

Comparison of trough levels of profit shares during the two recessions of the post-1973 period

(Per cent of value added)

	First recession	Second recession
Denmark	21.4 (1974)	23.5 (1979)
Finland	30.3 (1977)	34.3 (1982)
France	32.4 (1975)	29.7 (1982)
Germany, Federal Republic of	29.1 (1975)	25.6 (1981)
Italy	28.3 (1975)	35.6 (1981)
Netherlands	37.7 (1975)	no trough
Norway	23.7 (1978)	26.1 (1982)
Sweden	14.5 (1977)	20.6 (1981)
United Kingdom	17.3 (1975)	20.0 (1980)
Canada.	30.2 (1977)	31.9 (1982)
United States	22.4 (1974)	21.8 (1980)

Source: National accounts statistics.

Profit margins did not fall during the second recession as severely as in the first. During the first there were three countries, namely Denmark, Italy and Canada, where heavy financial losses (i.e. negative profit margins) were recorded. During the second recession it was only in the Federal Republic of Germany and the Netherlands that profit margins were lower than during the first recession. In these two countries the recovery of margins between the two recessions was not strong and at the same time they had the lowest inflation rates. Hence the increase in input prices was largely at the expense of wages and profit margins.

In Finland and France profit margins were not squeezed during the second recession. While in Finland margins somewhat stabilized, in France they increased and added to the

inflationary pressure. As a result, profit margins in these countries in 1983 were at their highest level since 1970: in France they were almost three times higher and in Finland they were more than double. In contrast, profit margins in the Federal Republic of Germany in 1983 were half of their 1970 levels and in the Netherlands about one tenth.

In the United States inflation rates accelerated less than in the majority of west European countries but, contrary to the west European and Canadian experience, input prices also accelerated at a much slower pace, which was partly due to the strong dollar during most of the period. Moreover, almost all of this rise in input prices was passed on to the general price level without a reduction in profit margins. In addition, unit labour costs rose less than final output prices, which provided further scope for higher margins. Thus, while the squeeze on profit margins was a universal phenomenon during the first recession, it was not so during the second.

Another difference between the two recessions was that profit margins started to recover only at the end of the first recession while they recovered strongly well before the end of the second. Moreover, at the end of the first recession the recovery in margins was accompanied by rising output and so profit shares also improved. However, during the second recession the recovery in profit margins was not accompanied by output growth and so they did not translate into higher profitability. In fact, while profit margins, which reached their lowest levels in 1981 in most of western Europe, recovered strongly in 1982, profit shares were still stagnating or falling (except in the Federal Republic of Germany, Italy and Sweden) due to weak demand and output. In 1983 profit margins tended to increase further but in some countries at a slower pace than in 1982. Profit shares, however, generally recovered in 1983 except in Italy and in France. These recent developments in profit margins are examined in more detail above (2.3(ii)(d)).

APPENDIX

The estimation of changes in profit margins from cost and price data

The derivation of the growth rate of profit margins in manufacturing industry from the definition of gross output is as follows:

GO = Gross output (in current prices)

I = Total expenditure on material inputs

P = Gross operating surplus

WS = Compensation of employees

pp = Change in final output prices

pi = Change in material input prices (proxy for changes in unit material input costs)

pm = Change in profit margins (profits per unit of gross output)

q = Change in gross output (in constant prices)

ULC = Change in unit labour costs

Dots over a variable signify growth rates

$$GO = I + P + WS \qquad \ldots(1)$$

and

$$\dot{GO} = (I/GO)\,\dot{I} + (P/GO)\,\dot{P} + (WS/GO)\,\dot{WS} \qquad \ldots(2)$$

that is,

$$pp + q = (I/GO)(pi + q) + (P/GO)(pm + q) + (WS/GO)(ULC + q)$$
$$= q\,(I/GO + P/GO + WS/GO) + (I/GO)pi + (P/GO)pm + (WS/GO)ULC$$

---

[50] See *Economic Survey of Europe in 1983* for a discussion of long-term falling trends in profit shares.

Since

$$I/GO + P/GO + WS/GO = 1$$

$$pp = (I/GO)pi + (P/GO)pm + (WS/GO)ULC$$

and

$$pm = \frac{pp - ((I/GO)pi + (WS/GO)ULC)}{(P/GO)} \qquad ...(3)$$

Apart from the weights (i.e. *I/GO*, *WS/GO* and *P/GO*), all variables in equation (3) are readily available on a quarterly basis. However, the data to construct the weights are available, in most cases, only from the national accounts on an annual basis, and usually with a publication lag of one year or more.

Obtaining a plausible set of weights for equation (3) required the construction of comparable time series on gross output, total material input expenditure, total wage bill, and profits. This was a complicated exercise insofar as the industrial census and national accounts data often differ considerably. National accounts were used for value added (compensation of employees plus operating surplus). Material input expenditures, when not available directly from the national accounts, were estimated on the basis of the share of value added in gross output in the industrial censuses if value added according to both sources was more or less identical or differed only because of the incomplete coverage of enterprises in the industrial censuses.[51] The price series for inputs and final output are those regularly published in this *Survey* (see tables 2.3.3 and 2.3.7 above).

Austria, Belgium, Ireland, Switzerland, Norway and the United Kingdom are excluded from the estimates because of lack of data (or lack of consistent data). For Austria and Switzerland value added data and for Ireland and Belgium gross output data are not available. For the United Kingdom the problem is that there are two value added series (national accounts and census of production, both at factor cost) which give very different figures for operating surplus (e.g. profit shares in 1975 were 19 per cent according to the national accounts and 34 per cent according to the production census). This is not a problem exclusive to the United Kingdom. However, for other countries gross output and input expenditures were available in the national accounts, whereas in the United Kingdom the only source for these aggregates is the production census.

(iii) Employment and unemployment

(a) *Current developments*

In 1984 changes in the labour markets of the market economies in the ECE region were relatively favourable. Employment rose substantially and unemployment declined for the first time since 1979. Although after the sharp drop in 1982 employment had already shown some signs of recovery in 1983, the increase was only marginal. The rise was much more marked between 1983 and 1984: the number of jobs rose by close to 4.8 million (2 per cent), a number well in excess of the estimated increase of the labour force of about 3.0 million. As a result, the annual average number of unemployed fell, by about 1.8 million (or 9 per cent) between 1983 and 1984. These improvements, however, reflect principally the favourable developments in North America and conceal a continuing stagnation in western Europe.

Labour markets in 1984 thus continued to be marked, as in 1983, by the contrast between rapid recovery in North America, especially in the United States, and the absence of clear signs of improvement in western Europe. Data for 1984 confirm the emergence, already noted in 1983, of different patterns in the two regions: a rapid expansion of employment and large reductions in unemployment in North America and the persistence of serious employment and unemployment problems in western Europe.

Between 1983 and 1984 employment in North America, in terms of annual changes, is estimated to have increased by more than 4 per cent. The average annual number of unemployed, which had reached its highest level of the recession in 1983, was reduced by one fifth. The unemployment rate, also in terms of annual averages, declined by two percentage points to about 7.2 per cent.[52] The differences between North America and western Europe are striking. Employment levels in western Europe have not exhibited any of the dynamism found in North America. Even if allowance is made for the fact that employment in western Europe fell to its lowest average level a year later (1983) than in North America, there was at best only a marginal increase between 1983 and 1984. The continuing stagnation of employment in western Europe was associated with a further worsening of unemployment: between mid-1983 and mid-1984 the number of unemployed rose by a further 5 per cent and the unemploy-

The large differences between western Europe and North America, and especially the United States, as regards the evolution of labour markets since the beginning of the recession in 1979 are illustrated by the following indicators:

TABLE 2.3.12

Labour market changes, 1979-1984
(*Annual averages*)

	Western Europe	North America	United States
Working age population (thousands)	9,200	9,700	8,500
Labour force (thousands)	3,900	9,900	8,700
Total employed (thousands) . . .	−2,200	7,100	6,500
Unemployed (thousands).	6,100	2,800	2,200
Unemployment rate (percentage of total labour force)	+4.5	+1.7	+1.5

Source: National statistics.

The differences between the two regions as far as employment and unemployment are concerned reflect different factors, including the growth of the working age population, labour force participation and employment. Although the working age population in western Europe and in North America has increased by about the same amount since 1979, the underlying trends in the two regions have moved in opposite directions. Whereas the

---

[51] Gross output, operating surplus and compensation of employees are mainly taken from the national accounts. However, for Italy use was made of United Nations, *Yearbook of Industrial Statistics* (various issues), New York, and other national publications on industrial statistics. For the United States, figures on gross output were taken from E. R. Berndt, B. C. Field (eds.), *Modeling and Measuring Natural Resource Substitution*, Cambridge, Massachusetts (MIT), 1981.

[52] These unemployment rates have been calculated on the basis of the total estimated labour force. They may therefore be lower than those obtained on the basis of narrower definitions of the labour force (civilian labour force, the working population excluding the self-employed) or on the basis of the number of those covered by employment or social insurance schemes. Nevertheless, taking into account the variations in national practice, the estimates on the whole seem to be consistent. In addition, it should be noted that the unemployment rates used here are annual averages. At times of rapidly changing unemployment, annual averages may substantially diverge from the unemployment rates observed at the end of the year or from quarterly or monthly estimates.

growth of the working age population in North America slowed down in the latter half of the 1970s and the early 1980s, in western Europe it was rising. In 1982 the annual increase of the working age population was 1.1 per cent in both regions, but in the case of western Europe it had risen from about 0.4 per cent in 1975, while in North America the rate had dropped from 1.9 per cent in the same year. As a result the potential expansion of the labour force in North America in the critical years from 1979 to 1982 was checked by this demographic slowdown, while in western Europe the demographic trends exacerbated existing pressures in the labour market. Further comparisons show that rather than changes in the rate of increase of total population, it was differences in the growth of the population of working age which were responsible for these contrasting trends. In 1980-1984 the growth rate of the total population of western Europe was somewhat higher than in 1975-1979 (0.4 and 0.2 per cent per year, respectively), but not enough to account for the substantially higher growth of the working age population. In North America the growth of total population was virtually unchanged between these two periods and thus had no effect on the declining growth rate of the population of working age.

The slowdown in the growth of the working age population in North America since the late 1970s has been mainly due to the cumulative effect of the declining number of teenagers of working age, who belonged to the smaller generations born after the fertility decline of the early 1960s. The number of those aged 15-19 years started to fall in 1979 and by 1984 had dropped by 3 million, or more than one eighth of the 1979 total. In addition, although the 20-24 year age group did not start to decline in absolute terms until 1983, the growth in this age group fell by two thirds between 1979 and 1984. As a result the number of potential young entrants into the labour force, which during 1975-1979 had increased by about 1 per cent per year, declined from 1979 through 1984 by 6.5 per cent or in absolute terms by about 2.4 million. Although the same basic tendencies are found in western Europe, the later onset of the fertility decline in the 1960s in most of the countries concerned implied continuing, albeit declining, increases in the 15-19 year age group and a high growth rate (about 1.5 per cent annually) through 1984 in the 20-24 year group.

The implications of these different developments in labour supply in western Europe and North America are important, as can be illustrated by applying constant 1980 age-specific participation rates (which happen to be practically the same in both regions) to the subsequent population in the 15-19 and 20-24 year age groups. According to these calculations the economically active population in the younger age groups would have increased in western Europe by about 1.6 million, which represents more than 40 per cent of the actual increase in the total labour force between 1979 and 1984. In North America the labour force in the younger age groups would have declined by about 950,000, which represents about 10 per cent of the actual growth in the labour force. In terms of annual averages western Europe should have created every year close to 325,000 jobs to match the increase in the number of young workers, whereas in North America the younger generations required about 190,000 fewer jobs each year.

These demographic trends were largely responsible for the difference in labour market behaviour between western Europe and North America since 1979. Traditionally, labour force growth in North America has been significantly higher than in western Europe and the much larger increase since 1979 suggests the continuation of this trend. Although in both regions labour force growth slowed down in 1981 and 1982, the worst years of the recession, the difference in growth rates has remained substantial: the annual growth rate of 1.6 per cent between 1979 and 1984

in North America was nearly three times higher than the 0.6 per cent rate in western Europe. A second major difference between the two regions is that whereas in western Europe the growth rate in the 1979-1984 period was the same as the average rate in 1970-1979, in North America the average 1979-1984 rate was significantly lower than that in 1970-1979, when the labour force increased at an average of 2.5 per cent annually.

This deceleration was in large part due to the decline in the number of teenagers of working age. If the number of workers under 25 years of age in North America had increased in the last five years at the same rate as between 1975 and 1979, then the total labour force between 1979 and 1984 would have increased at about the same pace as in 1970-1979. On the supply side demographic developments thus considerably eased the adjustment to changing demand conditions in the North American labour market. The favourable effect of a slowdown in labour force growth was further reinforced by the fact that it occurred in the younger age groups, which as a rule are disprportionately affected by a depressed demand for labour. In contrast there were no such beneficial effects in western Europe, where on average, labour force growth has not slowed down since the beginning of the recession and where, moreover, the increase in young workers has represented a comparatively high share of total labour force growth.

Apart from changes in the age structure, migration is another factor which can have a significant effect on labour supply, as was the case during the 1973/74 recession. Even though the fall in the proportion of foreign workers in the recent recession did not reach the same dimensions as in the preceding one, the impact of changes in the number of foreign workers on labour supply has nevertheless been important in several countries. This reflects the fact that changes in migration need not be very large in order to affect labour force growth in countries where the growth of the domestic labour force is low. Under such conditions a turnround in international migration from a moderate positive balance to one that is negative may have a substantial effect on the expansion of the labour force.

The importance of this factor can be gauged from estimates of the domestic and foreign components of labour force change in Austria, the Federal Republic of Germany and Switzerland. All three countries are characterized by a slow "natural growth" of the labour force and by continued, but moderate, inflows of foreign workers prior to and during the early years of the recession, followed by a turnround in immigration. Table 2.3.13 shows the components of average annual labour force changes in two periods. The first period refers to the years in the late 1970s during which the number of foreign workers increased; the second period includes the following year or years during which the number of foreign workers fell. The lower panel shows the differences between the two periods in the composition of changes in the total labour force.

Although these figures should be considered only as orders of magnitude, the impact of changes in the number of foreign workers on labour supply seems to be clear, particularly in the case of Austria and the Federal Republic of Germany. In the former, the switch from an annual positive balance to a negative one accounted for two thirds of the fall in the average annual growth of the labour force between 1979-1981 and 1981-1983. In the Federal Republic of Germany nearly four fifths of the decline in labour force growth was due to a similar shift from positive to negative immigration balances. In Switzerland the reversal in labour force growth, from an average annual increase to a fall between 1982 and 1983 mainly reflects the turnround in domestic labour force growth. Even so, the change from a positive to a negative migration balance still represents more than two fifths of the deceleration in labour force growth.

Although supply factors contributed significantly to the different labour market developments in western Europe and in North America, the major difference between the two regions has been the strength of demand for labour. Already by the third quarter of 1983 total employment in the United States had surpassed the pre-recession level of the second quarter of 1981. The increasing demand for labour in the United States is also evident from a number of other labour market indicators. The number of vacancies, as reflected in indices of "help-wanted advertising", which had dropped by 40 points between 1980 and mid-1982, had returned to its 1980 level by the beginning of 1984. The number of workers on part-time schedules for economic reasons, that is those involuntarily working less than full-time, declined in the first half of 1984 to about 5.5 million, more than 1 million below the highest level during the recession. The working week in manufacturing reached about 40.5 hours in mid-1984, a level approaching that of the mid-1960s and considered high by recent standards. Finally, a significant decline, from more than 1.8 million in the fourth quarter of 1982 to about 1.3 million in the second quarter of 1984, is estimated to have occurred in the number of discouraged workers, i.e. those who want to work but have dropped out of the labour force because they think they will be unable to find employment.

TABLE 2.3.13

Components of average annual labour force changes
(Thousands)

Country	Period	Total	Domestic labour force	Foreign
		Average annual change		
	First period			
Austria	1979-1981	11.5	9.0	2.5
Germany, Federal Republic of .	1978-1980	250.0	165.0	85.0
Switzerland	1978-1980	22.0	6.0	16.0
	Second period			
Austria	1981-1983	−10.5	2.0	−12.5
Germany, Federal Republic of .	1980-1983	85.0	130.0	−45.0
Switzerland	1982-1983	−24.0	−19.5	−4.5
	Difference in labour force change between periods			
Austria		−22.0	−7.0	−15.0
Germany, Federal Republic of .		−165.0	−35.0	−130.0
Switzerland		−46.0	−25.5	−20.5

Source: National statistics.

The decline in unemployment is another sign of the strength of the recovery. The average unemployment rate of 7.2 per cent in 1984 was only moderately above pre-recession levels and close to current estimates of the "natural rate of unemployment" for the United States (see (b) below). Moreover, the unemployment rate for men, which during recessions tends to increase more rapidly than that for women, had been higher than that for women in 1982 and 1983, but in 1984 fell below the level for women in conformity with the usual cyclical pattern.

The recovery in the United States is distinguished not only by its strength but, more important from the viewpoint of employment and unemployment, by its speed. In the United States the upturn in employment and the fall in unemployment were clearly more rapid than in western Europe. Between the fourth quarter of 1982 and the second quarter of 1984, employment in the United States increased by more than 6 per cent. This is an exceptionally rapid increase, even for the United States: a recov-

ery of such magnitude in the course of the six quarters following the trough of a recession is unprecedented since the 1953/54 recession. The reduction in the number of unemployed by more than one quarter during the same period is also uncommon: larger declines over a similar time span occurred only in the recoveries of the late 1940s and early 1950s.[53]

One major reason for the faster employment recovery in North America since 1982 is the much more rapid growth of output than in western Europe. Average annual growth of GDP over the last two years has been of the order of 5 per cent, which compares with a growth of about 2 per cent in western Europe. A second factor is the lower rate of productivity increase in North America than in Europe. The data in table 2.3.14 show the degree of difference in this respect between the two regions:

TABLE 2.3.14

Average annual growth rates of GDP, employment and productivity, selected periods
(Per cent)

Period	Western Europe			North America		
	GDP[a]	Employment	Productivity	GDP[a]	Employment	Productivity
1970-1974 .	3.7	0.4	3.3	3.8	2.2	1.6
1975-1979 .	3.4	0.5	2.9	4.5	3.4	1.1
1979-1984 .	1.1	−0.4	1.5	2.0	1.3	0.7
1982-1984 .	1.9	−0.3	2.2	5.1	2.7	2.4

Source: National statistics.
[a] At constant 1975 rates of exchange.

These estimates clearly show the relative roles of employment and productivity increases in the two regions. Quarterly data for selected countries on GDP and employment, covering the period following the recovery of GDP from its lowest level in the recent recession, appear to confirm the continuation of the different regional patterns:

TABLE 2.3.15

Average annual growth rates[a] of GDP, employment and productivity, selected countries
(Per cent)

Country	Period (year, quarter)	GDP	Employment	Productivity
Germany, Federal Republic of .	82.4-84.2	1.4	−0.9	2.3
United Kingdom . . .	81.4-83.4	3.2	0.4	3.6
Canada	82.4-84.2	5.7	2.7	3.0
United States	82.3-84.2	6.1	3.2	2.9

Source: National statistics.
[a] Quarterly data at annual rates.

Another related factor is the greater importance and more rapid growth of service sector employment in North America as compared with western Europe. To the extent that employment in the service sector is less sensitive to cyclical variations, the higher proportions of the labour force in services in North America would create an additional buffer against unemployment. Differences in this respect between western Europe and North America are still significant. In North America the service sector presently accounts for about 70 per cent of total employment, while in western Europe the proportion is about 58 per cent. The continuing expansion of service sector employment in

---

[53] Richard M. Devens, "Employment in the First Half: Robust Recovery Continues", in *Monthly Labour Review*, August 1984, pp. 3-7.

North America, by about 3.9 million jobs between 1979 and 1982, prevented a decline of total employment in this period and in fact more than offset the loss of some 2.8 million jobs in other sectors. In the same period service employment in western Europe also continued to grow but an increase of 2.5 million jobs was insufficient to compensate for the disappearance of 4 million jobs in other sectors.

A number of other factors may have a more or less significant impact on the employment and unemployment differences between the regions. In the case of North America, the decline in the relative importance of the younger generations, which are normally characterized by above-average unemployment, is estimated to have reduced the unemployment rate by as much as 0.4 per cent over the twelve months following the trough of the cycle.[54] In the case of the European countries of immigration, the departure of foreign workers and the halt to further immigration may have had a significant effect on unemployment. If the migrant workers who actually left had stayed, the unemployment rates in Austria and the Federal Republic of Germany would have been, respectively, 0.7 and 0.5 per cent higher than they

Although the divergence between western Europe and North America is perhaps the most striking feature of labour market developments in the market economies of the ECE region, substantial inter-country variations are also to be found within western Europe. Estimates for 1984 confirm that for the majority of countries in western Europe, there was a slight improvement in comparison with the sharp deterioration in employment and unemployment between 1979 and 1982. Employment, after several years of stagnation or decline, either started to grow or declined less than before, while unemployment in most countries rose less or even declined in some countries. Labour force growth, which in 1982 and 1983 had been low in many countries, began to pick up, as is frequently the case after the worst of the recession is over. The improvements, however, are only modest and in the large majority of countries cannot be taken as representing or even heralding a phase of significant recovery of either employment or unemployment.

The changes in individual countries varied considerably. Between 1983 and 1984 only the Nordic group of countries showed a persistent improvement. In each of these countries employment increased (by between 0.4 and 1.3 per cent) while unemployment fell somewhat in Norway and Sweden. The unemployment decline in these two countries, however, may be the result of a slowdown in labour force growth. Moreover, it should be noted that in Sweden public works projects and other employment promotion measures have been implemented to prevent the growth of unemployment. Finland, where the unemployment rate appears to have stabilized in recent years at between 5 and 6 per cent, occupies an intermediate position between the more and less favourably situated countries. According to available estimates, employment expanded rapidly in the Netherlands and the United Kingdom between 1983 and 1984, but so did the labour force and consequently unemployment in these countries tended to increase further in 1984. Employment continued to fall in Belgium, France, the Federal Republic of Germany, Ireland, Italy and Switzerland. The magnitude of job losses in Ireland appears to have been substantial (more than 1 per cent) and, despite a slowdown in labour force growth, unemployment increased sharply. In France a moderate decrease in employment (a little over 0.5 per cent) combined with an apparent turnround from negative to positive labour force growth led to a significant increase in the number of

unemployed. Employment fell marginally in Italy but as the labour force continued to increase at a moderately high rate (close to 1 per cent), the number of unemployed rose substantially. In the Federal Republic of Germany and Switzerland further increases in unemployment were held in check by a fall in the labour force. Finally, in Austria neither the labour force nor employment changed very much between 1983 and 1984 and as a result unemployment remained more or less unchanged.

As in the United States, employment has risen in Canada since 1982 and unemployment has fallen since 1983. The pace of change, however, has been much slower than in the United States. Average annual employment increased by less than 1 per cent between 1982 and 1983 and by about 2.5 per cent in 1984. However, with a high rate of labour force growth (1.7 per cent a year between 1983 and 1984) the reduction of the unemployment rate in the course of 1984 was only modest (from around 11.9 to 11.2 per cent of the labour force).

Considering that the economic recovery which has been under way for some time now has, with few exceptions, failed to produce a sustained growth in employment and a significant decline in unemployment, unemployment is emerging as a critical issue for policy making in the ECE region. Even taking into account the fact that the economic recovery so far has been comparatively weak in western Europe, and that employment usually reacts with a lag to more favourable economic conditions, the lack of progress in reducing unemployment is a major source of concern in many countries. The effectiveness of policies to reduce unemployment, however, will largely depend on the extent to which this is possible without creating a new inflationary spiral. The following section discusses this question by reviewing what is known about the so-called full employment rate of unemployment.

(b) *Estimating the rate of full employment: policy issues and empirical evidence*

Introduction

As inflation has fallen and attention is shifting to the reduction of high unemployment, one of the major questions being asked is how far can the unemployment rate fall before labour shortages appear, pressures for higher wages mount and a resurgence of inflation occurs? Embodied in this hypothetical rate of unemployment is the concept of full employment, which has preoccupied economists and government planners charged with the formulation and implementation of labour market policies. For a number of years this concept served as a yardstick against which the actual rate of unemployment could be compared. However, in the more inflationary environment of the 1970s, it ceased to provide a guide for policy because for many governments the need to check accelerating inflation became the overriding concern. Concomitant with rising unemployment, however, has been an upward drift in the estimates of the full employment rate of unemployment, resulting in a growing divergence between the actual and optimum rates of unemployment. The question of full employment is also important when viewed in terms of the impact on employment of current and future trends in the growth of output. Does the evolution in technological and structural processes (new technologies, declining industries) imply a lower growth of labour demand for a given rate of output growth than in the past? In this context the effect of demographic changes on labour force structure also has ramifications for full employment.

The importance of studying the question of full employment is underscored by the long standing commitment of a number of governments towards achieving this goal. Greatly influenced by

[54] *Economic Report of the President*, February 1984, p. 187.

CHART 2.3.4.

Unemployment rates in selected countries, 1970 — 1984

(Percent of total labour force)

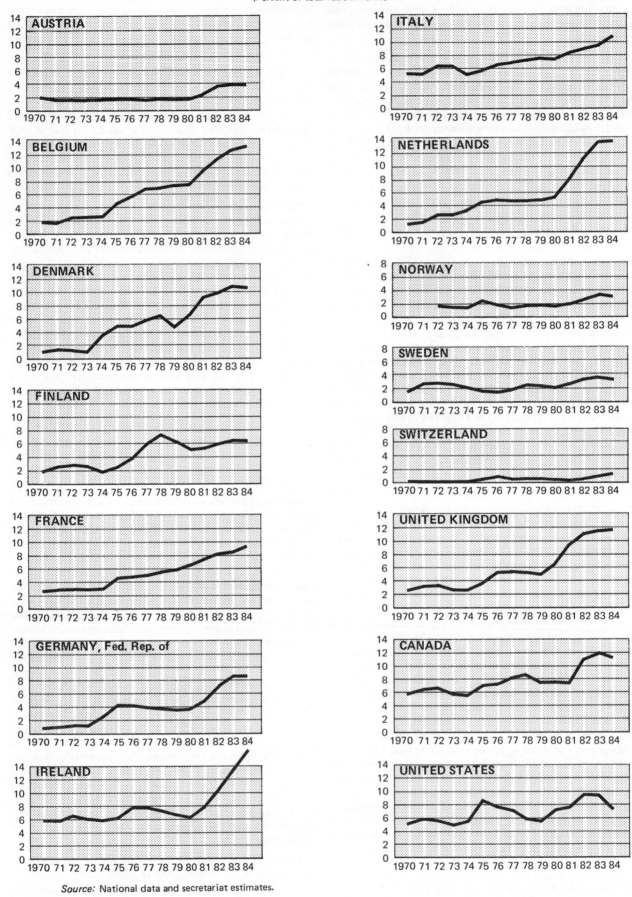

Source: National data and secretariat estimates.

considerations of social policy, the full employment concept has its roots in the years immediately preceding and following the Second World War. The White Paper on Employment Policy issued by the British Government in 1944 was the first formal acceptance by a government of a responsibility to maintain a high and stable level of employment. In 1945 the Government of Canada followed suit with a similar declaration, while in the United States the Employment Act of 1946 made full employment an official goal of the government.

The following discussion reviews briefly a few of the theoretical and methodological issues surrounding the estimation of full employment, supplemented by a compilation of various full employment estimates. On the basis of these estimates and some existing analytic studies, conclusions are provided in the form of implications for macro-economic and labour market policies.

During the 1950s and 1960s there were few obstacles to the pursuit of full employment as a policy goal. Rapid economic growth accompanied by a steadily increasing demand for labour, particularly in the west European market economies, led to labour shortages and unprecedentedly high levels of employment that approached or even exceeded full employment goals. This situation changed radically with the 1974/75 recession and the subsequent slowdown in the growth of labour demand: unemployment began to climb, accelerating rapidly by the end of the 1970s and the beginning of the 1980s. The achievement of the socio-economic goal of full employment was no longer so easy in the presence of the major imbalances, both domestic and external, which appeared at this time.

Labour market analysis, in attempting to explain the causes of unemployment, has traditionally been characterized by two conflicting theoretical approaches. One is based on a Keynesian analysis in which insufficient aggregate demand is considered as the main determinant of unemployment. The analytic framework is based on a disaggregation of total unemployment into demand-deficient, frictional and structural components. In the other approach (classical unemployment), a general equilibrium model is constructed to understand labour market behaviour. The explanation of unemployment focuses on the disequilibrium brought about by the distortion of incentives. Excessive real wages as a result of such factors as exorbitant union demands or overly generous unemployment schemes are viewed as the major cause of unemployment. Thus, within this framework of classical unemployment, treating unemployment with Keynesian policies to boost demand will provoke inflation without appreciably lowering unemployment.

Defining full employment

The tendency in the last two decades has been to link the pursuit of full employment with the acceleration of inflation, although the precise relationship between unemployment and inflation is unclear. The trade-off between unemployment and inflation, normally quantified in terms of a Phillips curve, has as one of its postulates the existence of a particular unemployment rate or full employment rate of unemployment at which the inflation rate can be expected to neither accelerate or decelerate. The full employment rate of unemployment is an elusive concept. As the definition determines to a certain degree the estimation method utilized, rather than vice versa, it is useful to identify first some of the more frequently encountered definitions. While the relationship between the rate of unemployment and that of inflation provides the theoretical underpinnings for one definition of full employment, namely, the NAIRU, there are others. The following is a sample of full employment definitions that have been drawn from recent literature on the subject—although the

basic approaches may differ, the definitions are not necessarily contradictory.

— *The non-accelerating inflation rate of unemployment (NAIRU)* is the unemployment rate at which the rate of inflation remains constant. It is based on the statistical relationship that emerges if changes in the growth of aggregate demand are the predominant factor accounting for economic fluctuations. The majority of full employment estimates are derived from this concept.[55]

— *The natural rate* is that rate to which the economy gravitates in the long run if left alone and can be viewed as the behavioural explanation of the NAIRU. Deviations from the natural rate are temporary and are automatically reversed when price anticipations catch up with actual price movements. Thus, there is only a short-run trade-off between inflation and unemployment and in the long-run the Phillips curve is vertical.[56]

— *The equilibrium rate* is the rate at which inflows into and out of unemployment are equal. It is based upon a model in which a large number of firms face exogenous variations in output price. Workers move from one firm to another in response to wage differentials and while moving they are unemployed. In equilibrium there exists an average output price that remains fixed. Business cycles are thus assumed to exist for individual firms, but not for the economy as a whole.[57]

— *The frictional unemployment rate* describes some minimal amount of unemployment due to functional turnover and search periods, that is, people "between" jobs. It represents the lower bound or floor of unemployment and can be considered as the socially optimum unemployment rate. Shifts of employment demand between sectors of the economy necessitate continuous labour reallocation and as it requires time for workers to find new jobs, some unemployment is unavoidable.[58]

— *The cyclical unemployment rate* (Keynesian unemployment) is the rate due to fluctuations in the business cycle. It is associated with a shortfall in aggregate demand and is typically matched by a corresponding drop in capacity utilization. It is more variable than other forms of unemployment.[59]

— *The voluntary unemployment rate* results when all workers who desire to work are employed. Because of the difficulties in distinquishing empirically between voluntary and involuntary unemployment, no generally accepted measure exists. Among the various elements that have been identified as indicative of voluntary unemployment and which underly classical unemployment are excessive wage expectations, inactive job search, unrealistic job aspirations, and a preference for short-time or casual work.[60]

[55] D. Grubb, R. Jackman, R. Layard, "Causes of the Current Stagflation", *Review of Economic Studies*, 49, 1982, pp. 707-730.

[56] The terms NAIRU and natural rate are often used interchangeably, creating some confusion between them. A few studies consider the distinction between the two rates to be fundamental. The natural rate is the level of demand that does not add to inflation, while the non-inflationary rate is the rate required to avoid inflation in the presence of exogenous shocks. See Otto Eckstein, *Core Inflation*, Prentice-Hall, Inc., Englewood Cliffs, New Jersey, 1981.

[57] S. Nickell, "The Determinants of Equilibrium Unemployment in Britain", *Economic Journal*, 92, September 1982, pp. 553-575.

[58] M. Reder, "The Theory of Frictional Unemployment", *Economica*, Vol. 36, 1969, pp. 1-28. Even in periods of stable aggregate employment, continuous labour reallocation within the United States results in almost 5 per cent of workers shifting from one job to another every month. See, D. Lilien, "Sectoral Shifts and Cyclical Unemployment", *Journal of Political Economy*, vol. 90, No. 4, 1982, pp. 777-794.

[59] J. M. Keynes, *The General Theory of Employment, Interest and Money*, Macmillan, London, 1936.

[60] D. Worswick (ed.), *The Concept and Measurement of Involuntary Unemployment*, Allen and Unwin, London, 1976.

TABLE 2.3.16

TABLE 2.3.16

Estimates of the full employment rate of unemployment

| Country | Full employment, unemployment rate | | | Actual unemployment rate | Unemployment gap |
	NAIRU	Full capacity[a]	Other		
Finland					
1970-1974	3.4	. .	. .	2.1	−1.3
1975	3.1	. .	. .	2.2	−0.9
1980	4.9	. .	. .	4.7	−0.2
1982	6.5	. .	2.5[b]	5.9	−0.6, 3.4
France					
1974	. .	2.5	. .	2.8	0.3
1975	. .	2.8	. .	4.1	1.3
1976	. .	3.4	. .	4.4	1.0
1976-1980	5.3	. .	. .	5.3	0.0
1981-1983	6.9	. .	. .	8.0	1.1
Germany, Federal Republic of					
1965-1973	1.6	. .	. .	1.1	−0.5
1974	. .	1.8	. .	2.1	0.3
1974-1981	4.3	. .	. .	3.6	−0.7
1975	. .	3.0	. .	4.0	1.0
1976	. .	3.5	. .	4.0	0.5
1976-1980	3.7	. .	. .	3.6	−0.1
1981-1983	5.3	. .	. .	6.5	1.2
Ireland					
1979	. .	. .	4.6[b]	7.9	3.3
Italy					
1974	. .	5.8	. .	5.3	−0.5
1975	. .	6.4	. .	5.8	−0.6
1976	. .	6.8	. .	6.6	−0.2
1976-1981	8.9	. .	. .	7.4	−1.5
1981-1983	7.1	. .	. .	9.0	1.9
Netherlands					
1975	. .	2.5	. .	3.2	0.7
1975	. .	2.9	. .	4.5	1.6
1976	. .	3.5	. .	4.9	1.4
			. .		
United Kingdom					
1966-1970	2.2	. .	. .	1.8	−0.4
1970s	4.0	. .	. .	3.7	−0.3
1971-1975	4.0	. .	. .	2.9	−1.1
1973	. .	. .	2.3[c]	2.3	0.0
1974	. .	2.1	. .	2.3	0.2
1975	. .	2.7	. .	3.6	0.9
1976	. .	3.3	. .	5.0	1.7
1976-1980	5.5	. .	. .	5.3	−0.2
1979	. .	. .	5.8[d]	6.2	0.4
1980	. .	. .	7.3[e]	6.2	−1.1
1981-1983	9.0	. .	. .	10.6	1.6
Canada					
1973	6.4	. .	. .	5.5	−0.9
1974	6.5	5.2	. .	5.3	−1.2, 0.1
1975	6.6	5.8	. .	6.9	0.3, 1.1
1976	6.5	6.5	. .	7.1	0.6
1977	6.7	. .	. .	8.1	1.4
1978	6.6	. .	. .	8.3	1.7
1979	6.2	. .	. .	7.4	1.2
1980	6.3	. .	. .	7.5	1.2
United States					
1974	. .	4.9	. .	5.5	0.6
1975	. .	5.1	. .	8.3	3.2
1976	. .	5.5	. .	7.5	2.0

TABLE 2.3.16 (*continued*)

Estimates of the full employment rate of unemployment

	Full employment, unemployment rate			Actual unemployment rate	Unemployment gap
Country	NAIRU	Full capacity[a]	Other		
United States (*continued*)					
1979	5.1, 7.2	..	..	5.7	0.6, −1.5
1980	6.5	..	..	7.0	0.5
1983	7.7	..	4.0[b]	9,5	1.8, 5.5
1984	6.0-6.5	..	..	7.2	1.2-0.7

Sources : Full employment, unemployment rates: W. Franz, "The Past Decade's Natural Rate and the Dynamics of German Unemployment", *European Economic Review*, vol. 21, No. 1/2, March/April 1983, pp. 51-76; *Economic Report of the President*, Washington, D.C., 1983; "Jobs For the Boys and their Dads", *The Economist*, 26 May 1984, p. 38; Otto Eckstein, *Core Inflation*, Prentice-Hall, Inc., 1979, Englewood Cliffs, New Jersey; S. F. Kaliski, "Why Must Unemployment Remain so High", *Canadian Public Policy*, vol. X, No. 2, June 1984, pp. 127-141; R. Layard, G. Basevi, O. Blanchard, W. Buiter, R. Dornbusch, *Europe: The Case for Unsustainable Growth*, Centre for European Policy Studies, Paper No. 8/9, Brussels, 1984; David Metcalf, "The Measurement of Employment and Unemployment", *National Institute Economic Review*, Number 109, August 1984; P. Minford, "Labour Market Equilibrium in an Open Economy", *Oxford Economic Papers, 1983*, vol. 35, No. 4, pp. 531-568; S. Nickell, "The Determinants of Equilibrium Unemployment in Britain", *Economic Journal*, September 1982; OECD, *A Medium Term Strategy for Employment and Manpower Policies*, Paris, 1978; J. Paunio and A. Suvanto, "Wage Inflation Expectations and Indexation", *Journal of Monetary Economics*, vol. 8, 1981; M. Ross and B. Walsh, *Regional Policy and the Full Employment Target*, The Economic and Social Research Institute, Policy Studies, No. 1, Dublin, 1979; M. Scott with R. Laslett, *Can We Get Back to Full Employment?*, MacMillan Press, London 1978; M. Sumner and R. Ward, "The Reappearing Phillips Curve", *Oxford Economic Papers*, 35(4), 1983; A. Tanskanen, "Kilpailukyky ja työllisyys Suomessa", *Finnish Economic Journal*, 4/84; *U.S. News and World Report*, "From High Unemployment to a Labor Shortage", 17 September 1984, p. 56. Actual unemployment rates: National statistics, *OECD Labour Force Statistics*, Paris, various issues; secretariat estimates.

[a] Rate at full capacity of existing capital stock, calculated from equation containing estimates of labour supply and capital stock.

[b] Government goal.

[c] Based on estimate of induced unemployment.

[d] Equilibrium male rate calculated from equations estimating unemployment inflows and outflows.

[e] Long-run rate calculated from four equation system using unemployment, real wages output and real exchange rate.

— *The optimal wage-fixing rate of unemployment* results if, against a background of a steady growth in the total money demand for labour services, the principle of wage-fixing institutions in each sector of the economy is the promotion of employment in that sector. This is a variant of the NAIRU, the difference being the assumption of employment maximization as an objective rather than wage maximization.[61]

Estimating full employment: some methodological and theoretical considerations

Inter-country comparisons of full employment estimates are extremely hazardous, given the variety of definitions, assumptions and estimation methods employed. One might reasonably focus in greater detail on a particular country, however, in order to understand better some of the mechanics involved in full employment estimates. As estimates for the United Kingdom encompass a wide spectrum of definitions and estimation methods, they can be considered as representative of the techniques employed in other countries as well.

As is shown in table 2.3.16, the estimate of full employment in the 1970s in the United Kingdom is a NAIRU calculated from a Phillips curve augmented by price and tax change expectations. The 1973 rate is based on estiates of labour supply, both in terms of quantity and skill levels, and of the unemployment induced by unemployment benefits: the two are then added to the average unemployment rate for the 1948-1966 period. The estimates for 1974, 1975 and 1976 are defined as unemployment rates at full capacity use of the existing capital stock and are calculated from equations which include labour supply (including the impact of sex-age changes, labour turnover and hoarding, unemployment compensation, and migration) and capital stock as explanatory variables. A model based on equations containing variables that influence flows into and out of unemployment, such as trade union bargaining power, the replacement rate of income and

deviations of output from trend, were the basis for the 1979 equilibrium rate estimate (the impact of inflation was considered to be of only secondary importance). The 1980 long-run rate is the result of a four-equation system in which unemployment, unionization, real wages, output and the real exchange rate are among the determinants. The 1966-1970, 1971-1975, 1976-1980 and 1981-1983 estimates of NAIRUs are calculated from wage equations incorporating real wages, unemployment and a trend variable and is the average of four alternative estimates, with differing assumptions concerning the error term in the wage equation and the rate of real wage growth.

The various approaches to full employment estimation have been criticized on numerous theoretical grounds. Disaggregating unemployment into its components is a difficult and controversial exercise requiring a substantial amount of highly reliable data on both unemployment and vacancies. One methodological problem in calculating frictional unemployment is that the estimates are highly sensitive to the degree of disaggregation.[62] Voluntary unemployment, because of the myriad definitions used to distinquish it from involuntary unemployment, as well as the numerous methods by which it has been quantified, make it an extremely difficult concept to support empirically.[63]

The Phillips curve approach has come under attack because of perceived weaknesses in some of its assumptions. For example, it is felt that the estimates arising from this model are neither measuring labour market structure nor providing explanatory

---

[61] J. E. Meade, *Stagflation: Wage-Fixing*, vol. 1, George Allen and Unwin, London, 1982.

[62] For a more extensive discussion of the difficulties inherent in this approach see, for example, J. Creedy, *The Economics of Unemployment in Britain*, Butterworth and Co., London, 1981, G. Standing "The Notion of Structural Unemployment", *International Labour Review*, vol. 122, No. 2, March-April 1983, pp. 137-153; K. G. Abraham, "Structural/Frictional vs. Demand Deficient Unemployment", *American Economic Review*, vol. 73, No. 4, September 1983, pp. 708-723.

[63] This issue is treated in depth in G. Standing, "The Notion of Voluntary Unemployment", *International Labour Review*, vol. 120, No. 5, September-October 1981, pp. 563-578; O. Ashenfelter, "The Withering Away of a Full Employment Goal", *Canadian Public Policy*, vol. IX, No. 1, 1983. pp. 114-125.

variables for the nature of unemployment.[64] Another weakness is the prediction, based on models of the United States, that profit rates vary inversely with the unemployment rate, which contradicts actual profit data for the United States.[65]

Empirical evidence

Against this background of some qualitative aspects of full employment, it is useful at this juncture to look at the results of a few studies that have attempted to quantify the concept. In presenting full employment estimates for various countries, table 2.3.16 is intended only to illustrate the previous discussion without in any way claiming to be an exhaustive inventory of such estimates.[66] The full employment unemployment rates have been categorized according to whether the NAIRU, full capacity utilization of the capital stock or some other method is the basis of the estimation. In addition, actual unemployment rates have been included in the adjoining column to facilitate a comparison of the two. The "unemployment gap", is the difference between the full employment and actual unemployment rates.

Despite the diversity of definitions and methodologies, two features are readily apparent in table 2.3.16. The most striking is that full employment unemployment rates have risen over time in countries for which a long time series is available. The second is the substantial divergence which now exists between the full unemployment rate of unemployment and the actual rate. As indicated by the "unemployment gap", since 1980 or 1981 actual unemployment has exceeded the full unemployment rate by at least 1 per cent in seven countries. An additional feature of the unemployment gap worth noting are those instances when actual unemployment rates fell below full employment and appear in the table as negative values. In the Federal Republic of Germany, Finland, the United Kingdom, Canada and the United States these negative gaps cropped up at various times in the late 1960s and early 1970s, implying that wage inflation may have been increasing or that real wage growth had been excessive.[67] This could in part be explained as a manifestation of rising demand pressure which in turn fuelled inflation and inflationary expectations.[68]

---

[64] See for example, A. P. Thirlwall, "What are Estimates of the Natural Rate of Unemployment Measuring?", *Oxford Bulletin of Economics and Statistics*, vol. 45, No.2, May 1983.

[65] R. Cherry, "What is So Natural About the Natural Rate of Unemployment?", *Journal of Economic Issues*, vol. XV, No. 3, September 1981, pp. 729-743 .

[66] The table does not include full employment estimates for Austria, Norway, Sweden and Switzerland, since these countries have enjoyed extremely low levels of unemployment for the last three decades and can be considered as having managed to maintain full employment. Even as unemployment has climbed steeply in the rest of western Europe and North America since the mid-1970s, the rate of unemployment, conventionally measured, which peaked in 1983 in these four countries, was only 3.9 per cent in Austria, 3.3 per cent in Norway, 3.5 per cent in Sweden and 0.9 per cent in Switzerland. These relatively low rates of unemployment are partly due to a number of special factors, such as the repatriation of large numbers of immigrant workers (Austria and Switzerland) and government schemes designed to provide employment (Sweden).

[67] Because of the lack of comparability of unemployment data over time in Italy, the negative unemployment gap for Italy may be a statistical fluke, rather than a reflection of labour market conditions.

[68] As was already pointed out, some work has been undertaken to distinquish between the full employment and natural rates of unemployment. The estimates for the United States in 1979 of a full employment rate of 7.2 per cent and a natural rate of 5.1 per cent are products of this type of analysis. The explanation for the difference is the following: if unemployment is at the natural rate, but there are shocks to the system, there will be accelerating inflation. In order that inflation should not increase in the presence of exogenous shocks, the rate of full employment must exceed that of natural unemployment. See, O. Eckstein, *op. cit.* p. 11.

Explaining the rise in full employment rates of unemployment

The empirical evidence contained in table 2.3.16 suggesting a rise in the full employment rate of unemployment, raises a number of issues relevant to labour market policies. The substantial and growing gap between the actual unemployment rate and the full employment rate of unemployment implies that there is room for Keynesian demand-boosting policies. Given the excess of unemployment over the full employment rate, such policies could lower the level of unemployment to that of the NAIRU without the risk of setting off a new round of inflation. While broad-based macro-economic policies can eliminate demand-deficient Keynesian unemployment, thus closing the gap between actual unemployment and the NAIRU, this represents a potential drop in the unemployment rate of only about 1 to 2 per cent in individual countries. Furthermore, classical unemployment, a consequence of a too high real wage, would not be resolved by this type of policy. With additional measures designed to attack various institutional rigidities, however, the NAIRU could be pushed down to a level closer to what might be considered optimal from a policy point of view. In more concrete terms, this entails identifying and analysing those factors that are responsible for the growth of the NAIRU, and then making the necessary adjustments to labour market behaviour.

Providing causal explanations for the upward shift in the NAIRU has been the objective of a number of studies. Some of the analytical efforts have tried to explain the worsening trade-off between unemployment and inflation by identifying the distorting influences on labour market adjustments. Among the adverse factors cited are:

(1) The substantial increase in labour supply and the changing demographic composition of the labour force, particularly the growing share of young and female workers.

(2) The emergence of skill shortages as a result of barriers to skill acquisition, occupational mobility, vocational training, the reclassification of jobs and the declining propensity of workers to move from one region to another.

(3) The implementation of minimum wage laws and their dampening effect on the recruitment of young and unskilled workers.

(4) The role of unemployment compensation and other welfare support schemes in stimulating voluntary unemployment by raising the reservation wage and prolonging job search.

(5) Unionization and improvements in job security provisions (such as protection from unjust dismissal, extension of the period of notice and the increase in the size of severance payments) which limit the firm's flexibility in responding to changing demand conditions.

(6) The growth in non-wage labour costs such as employer expenditures for social security and health insurance.

According to another point of view inflationary momentum, reflecting real wage bargaining, formal wage indexation, restoration of wage differentials and anticipation of future inflation, which had built up in the 1970s due to exogenous price and wage shocks, was superimposed on pent-up demand pressures. The combined effects produced an outward shift of the Phillips curve, so that a given rate of unemployment was associated with a higher rate of inflation.

Recently a substantial body of research has been accumulated, based on comparative analyses of a large sample of countries in Western Europe and North America.[69] Most of these studies

---

[69] D. Grubb, R. Jackman, R. Layard, "Wage Rigidity and Unemployment in OECD Countries", *European Economic Review*, vol. 21, No. 1/2,

however, are inconclusive in determining the link between real wage costs and unemployment. Some studies found no link whatsoever.[70] Others agree that real wage developments contributed to aggravating the unemployment problem after 1973, but estimates of the size of the impact vary widely. While real wage elasticity with respect to employment demand in some studies is estimated at between −0.1 and −0.2, the majority of estimates are in the range of −0.3 to −0.5.[71] Such orders of magnitude imply that, *ceteris paribus*, a 10 per cent reduction in real wages would only lead to a 3-5 per cent increase in employment. One recent study undertook to disaggregate the NAIRU for eight countries between 1957 and 1982.[72] It concluded that the increase in the NAIRU since the 1970s was the result of additional inflationary pressures divided, more or less equally, between higher relative import prices, lower productivity growth and the time trend.

An appropriate full employment goal

One of the primary objectives of accurately identifying a full employment rate of unemployment is the formulation and implementation of a full employment target[73]. From the mid-1940s to the early 1970s the countries of Western Europe and Northern America experienced a unique period of sustained economic growth. In such a climate there emerged a strong consensus that a priority of government should be the attainment of full employment. However, beginning in the mid-1970s there has been a weakening of the commitment to full employment.[74]

A situation marked by rising unemployment, coupled with accelerating inflation led to stringent monetary policies to combat inflation. With the advent of Philipps curve analyses of the labour market there has been a shift from the view of full employment as a paramount objective of economic and social policy to one emphasizing its inflationary aspects. The current use of the NAIRU as the definition of full employment implies that the proper role of government is to undertake policies ensuring a steady non-accelerating rate of inflation. The advantage of this approach is that it permits two policy objectives to be pursued jointly, that of lowering unemployment while simultaneously controlling inflation. However, there is no reason to assume that the NAIRU coincides with a socially optimal level of unemployment. From a societal point of view even a level of unemployment reduced to the NAIRU may still be unacceptable.[75]

The quantification of full employment can provide important inputs into macro-economic policy formulation and implementation if based on explicit definitions, assumptions and estimation procedures. On the other hand, if based on a less than robust analysis it can lead to a further erosion of a full employment goal. Despite the widespread use of the NAIRU as a measure of full employment there is a great deal of uncertainty concerning the relationship between inflation and unemployment and the factors contributing to the growth of the NAIRU. While disproportionate increases in labour costs lead to a deterioration in the cost structure of firms, boosting inflation and accelerating capital labour substitution, it is difficult to distinguish between the impact of real wage costs and fluctuations in aggregate demand on unemployment. Quite likely wage moderation in the presence of demand weakness may only have a small positive influence on the level of employment if not accompanied by expansionary fiscal policies. Policy makers whose objective is the elimination of pockets of unemployment need to address the issues of separating the various causes of unemployment. If, for example, youths continue to suffer primarily from structural unemployment when full employment is attained, broadbased fiscal priming measures may only result in inflation. Labour market policies which alleviate a specific cause of unemployment can more effectively eliminate these pockets of unemployment.

March/April 1983 pp. 11-39; R. Layard, G. Basevi, O. Blanchard, W. Buiter and R. Dornbusch, *Europe: The Case for Unsustainable Growth*, Centre for European Policy Studies, Brussels, 1984; J. Artus, "The Disequilibrium Real Wage Rate Hypothesis: An Empirical Evaluation", *International Monetary Fund Staff Papers*, vol. 31, No. 2, June 1984, pp. 240-302.

[70] P. Geary and J. Kennan, "The Employment-Real Wage Relationship: An International Study", *Journal of Political Economy*, vol. 90, August 1982.

[71] In a study restricted to male employees in Great Britain, the elasticity of employment with respect to the real wage was calculated to be as high as around −0.9 for this subgroup of the labour force. The severe shortfall in aggregate demand experienced by Great Britain in the period 1980-1983 was cited as the most important factor for the large discrepancy between the NAIRU and actual rates of unemployment. See R. Layard and S. Nickell, "The Causes of British Unemployment" *National Institute Economic Review*, No. 111, February 1985, pp. 62-91.

[72] D. Grubb, R. Layard, and J. Symons, "Wages, Unemployment, and Incomes Policy", in M. Emerson (ed.), *Europe's Stagflation*, Clarendon Press, Oxford, 1984.

[73] Despite serious measurement problems, an attempt has been made to quantify the macro-economic costs of not achieving full employment. The amount of unrealised value-added due to unemployment exceeding the full employment unemployment rate was approximated by taking the recorded average labour productivity multiplied by the difference between the actual level of unemployment and the full employment level. Full employment was assumed to be the average unemployment rate prevailing in the 1960s. On this basis the "static" costs of unemployment in terms of foregone output amounted to $340 billion in 1981 for all the OECD countries (this includes Australia, New Zealand and Japan). OECD, *The Challenge of Unemployment, A Report to Labour Ministers*, Paris, 1982.

[74] Recently a number of articles have discussed the apparent reluctance on the part of governments to promote full employment. For example, see W. Albeda, "Reflections on the Future Full Employment", *Labour and Society*, (Part I) vol. 7, No. 4, October-December 1982, (Part II) vol. 8, No. 1, January-March 1983; J. Meade, "A New Keynesian Approach to Full Employment", *Lloyds Bank, Review*, No. 150, October 1983; "Towards Fuller Employment", *The Economist*, 28 July, 1984.

[75] The Full Employment and Balanced Growth Act of 1978, more commonly known as the Humphrey-Hawkins Act, established a 4 per cent rate of unemployment in the United States as the official government definition of full employment—a target that most economists view as attainable only during an extreme economic boom. The unlikelihood of unemployment falling to 4 per cent was officially acknowledged in *Economic Report of the President*, Submitted to the Congress, February 1984, which, in reporting the Administration's economic assumptions for 1984-1989, provides a revised timetable for progress towards the employment goals of the Employment Act. According to the timetable, the unemployment rate is projected to fall to 5.7 per cent by 1989. This represents an additional 1.7 per cent of unemployment, in excess of what is mandated by the Employment Act. For a discussion of the political developments leading up to the enactment of the Act, see H. Ginsburg, *Full Employment and Public Policy: The United States and Sweden*, Lexington Books, Lexington, 1983.

Chapter 3

SOUTHERN EUROPE

After growing by barely 0.6 per cent in 1983, total output in southern Europe[76] increased by 2.7 per cent in 1984; there was a recovery or a mild acceleration in the rate of economic activity in all countries except Portugal. In contrast to 1983, GDP growth in southern Europe in 1984 was slightly above that of the more industrialized countries of western Europe (chart 3.1.1). An

---

[76] Southern Europe here refers to Greece, Portugal, Spain, Turkey and Yugoslavia.

outstanding feature of developments in southern Europe has been the persistent fall in capital formation in all countries except Turkey. Not only has investment fluctuated more than in the rest of western Europe (see chart 3.1.1) but its influence on growth continued to be negative in 1983 and 1984: last year fixed capital formation in the region fell by about 6 per cent (see also chart 3.1.2). This downward trend, which has lasted since 1979, is particularly serious because of its effects on growth prospects.

Although the volume of imports increased faster than in 1983,

CHART 3.1.1.
Average rates of change in GDP and its components in southern and western Europe, 1970-1984

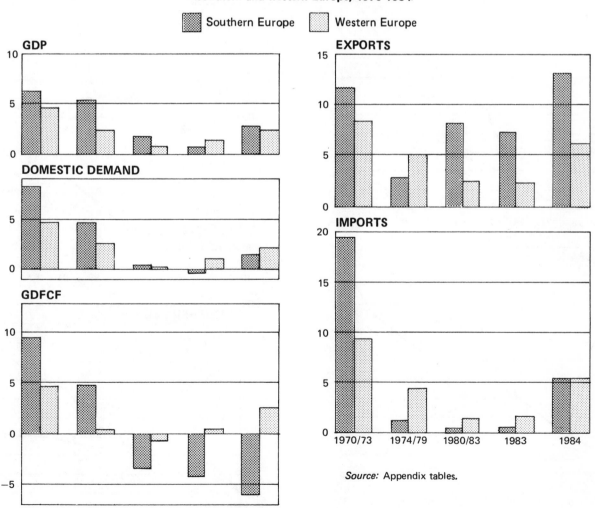

Source: Appendix tables.

CHART 3.1.2

Indices of gross domestic product, gross fixed capital formation and exports of goods and services, 1975-1984

(1975 = 100)

GDP: — — — — — — —
GFCF: —————————
Exports: ████████

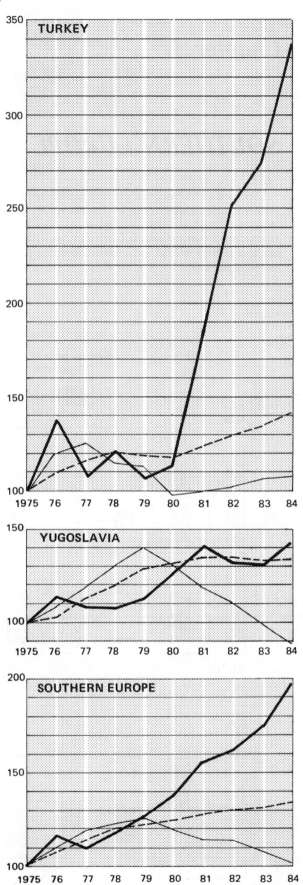

Source: Appendix tables.

a more rapid increase in exports in 1984 led to a considerable reduction in the combined current account deficit of these countries, from some $7.4 billion in 1983 to about $1 billion in 1984. The improvement in the current account stemmed mostly from commodity trade: the services account was less satisfactory in spite of a good year for tourism.

Inflationary pressures increased in 1984: a modest deceleration of prices in Spain and Greece were more than offset by a renewed acceleration in the other three. Except for Portugal, where it changed little, unemployment increased everywhere in 1984. Unemployment remains a serious problem in southern Europe particularly in Spain and Turkey where unemployment rates are above or around 20 per cent of the active population.

According to official forecasts the south European countries should expand in 1985 at a higher rate than in 1984 (by roughly 3.5 to 4 per cent). The differences between the individual rates of growth of output is also expected to become smaller as lagging countries recover more rapidly than the others.

The main support to growth in 1985 will come from domestic demand since a relative weakening of exports is expected. The improvement in domestic demand is expected to come from investment and, though with less dynamism, from private consumption. This pattern of recovery may lead to a widening of the current account deficit, but this should not be an increased constraint on policy in 1985.

Inflation and unemployment remain considerable problems. Although inflationary pressures might be reduced slightly in 1985, particularly in those countries with high rates of inflation in 1984, the inflation rates in relation to the more industrialized western countries will still remain very high and require continued policy efforts to reduce them. As for unemployment, the expected increases in output are not yet large enough (given existing productivity trends) to allow any significant reduction in the coming year.

The first section of this chapter summarizes the economic effects and policy changes brought about by the oil price shocks of the early 1970s, since these provide an essential perspective for the discussion of more recent changes. This section is followed by an account of recent output and demand developments. Subsequent sections deal with recent developments in inflation, the labour market, trade and payments, and foreign debt. Finally, there is a short note on the particular problems of Yugoslavia.

3.1 POLICIES AND POLICY ISSUES

(i) Medium-term adjustments

The recent evolution of the south European economies is in great part determined by the timing of their policies of adjustment to the first and second oil shocks. Past *Surveys* have given country-specific accounts of the policy measures taken after the first oil shock, but a common point to be stressed is that the adjustment measures were taken considerably later than in the more industrialized countries of western Europe. Comparing 1974-1979 with 1970-1973, it can be seen that the decline in the growth of output was considerable in southern Europe (chart 3.1.3) but nevertheless remained higher than in western Europe. In the first period total domestic demand increased in all five countries (including Yugoslavia) faster than output, but in the second period total output (except in Yugoslavia) increased more rapidly than domestic demand as a result of the effort to displace resources abroad. In Greece demand-restraining policies had been introduced already in 1973 (aimed at checking an excessive housebuilding boom) and so a sharp decline in domestic demand had preceded the effects of the first oil price shock; but thereafter policies remained relatively easy until the end of the decade. Adjustment policies were introduced in Spain, Turkey and Portugal in 1977-1978.

The second oil shock caught the south European countries at very different stages of expansion and policy stance. In 1980 severely restrictive policies were also introduced in Turkey and Yugoslavia but there was a mild stimulus in Greece, Portugal and Spain. In 1982 Portugal and Spain were forced to adopt harsh adjustment policies. Taking the five countries together, the years 1980-1983 are characterized by a further deceleration of output growth, from over 6 per cent in 1970-1973 and 5 per cent in 1974-1979 to less than 2 per cent in 1980-1983, and by an even more radical decline in the growth of total domestic demand, from 8 per cent in 1970-1973 to less than 5 per cent in 1974-1979 and to less than one half of 1 per cent in 1980-1983. The adjustment was particularly severe in Yugoslavia where domestic demand declined during this period at a rate of 1.3 per cent per annum (it started to recover only in 1984).

The component of domestic demand which was more severely affected by the restrictive policies of the late 1970s and early 1980s was investment. After 1980 the contraction of investment and domestic demand was more severe than in the rest of western Europe.

Chart 3.1.2 shows the evolution of GDP, investment and exports. For the region as a whole 1979 is the year in which external demand started to expand faster than output and investment started to fall. Nevertheless the timing of the "investment crisis" varies considerably among countries: the downturn is in 1980 in Greece, 1983 in Portugal, 1978 in Turkey (where contrary to the other countries the trend is slightly upwards in the early 1980s) and 1980 in Yugoslavia. Spain is a case apart insofar as capital formation has been on a virtually uninterrupted downward trend since 1975. The widening gap between the growth of total output and external demand is also shown very clearly in chart 3.1.2.

The great vulnerability of the south European countries to the two major oil shocks of the 1970s was due to a variety of factors,[77]

but among the most prominent were their structural trade deficits and their relatively high dependence on energy imports. These factors made adjustment to the new situation much more difficult than for the industrially advanced western countries, as is illustrated by the fact that while for the latter a 5 per cent growth of their 1978 commodity exports would have been enough to eliminate their combined current balance, the south European countries would have needed almost a doubling of their commodity exports.

These initial constraints have in turn led to others such as the high level of foreign debt and large public sector borrowing requirements.

The foreign debt constraint[78] has lately been tightening and derives from the increase in long and short-term capital borrowing from abroad, which rose from some $25 billion in 1975 to over $96 billion at the end of 1984. Because most of this foreign debt is denominated in US dollars, against which their currencies have depreciated sharply during the last six years, and average interest charges have increased rapidly, there has been a sharp and unexpected increase in the financial costs of domestic borrowers and a further strain on an already deteriorating current balance. From 1975 to 1983 the increase in southern Europe's current account expenditure due to increases in average interest rates was about $5.5 billion, which was equivalent to about three quarters of their combined current account deficit in 1983.

(ii) Recent developments by country

Economic policy in *Greece* has maintained, in contrast to other south European countries, a relatively easy stance in spite of moves (starting in mid-1982) to stop the rising trend in public sector borrowing and to check an excessive growth of real wages. There were various attempts to tighten monetary and credit policies during 1982-1984, but in spite of these M3 continued to increase more rapidly than monetary GNP in 1984 and real interest rates remained negative (although less so than in the past). (The 1983-1987 economic and social development plan proposed raising real interest rates to positive levels.) Nevertheless, the gap between inflation and interest rates is closing and recent data (for October 1984) show that short-term interest rates were nearly equal to the rate of inflation. The maintenance of a high level of employment continues to be an important policy target and in September 1984 measures to limit labour-shedding in medium and large-sized enterprises were reinforced.[79] Nevertheless the initial plan of creating 270,000 new jobs by 1987 has been reduced to 150,000. Also in contrast with policies in other southern countries is the fact that the public sector (including public enterprises) is to continue to play an increasing and stimulative role in the economy. The 1983-1987 plan announced the adoption of a "supply side" policy geared to development. In most western countries the "supply side" emphasis is normally associated with an enhancement of the role of the private sector and a vigorous rejection of the economic role of the state but in Greece, strategies aimed at increasing productivity and economic

---

[77] For a discussion of these factors see *Economic Survey of Europe in 1982*, United Nations, New York, 1983.

[78] See also section 3.6 below.

[79] Measures were also taken to subsidize tourist enterprises which remain open during the "low" season.

CHART 3.1.3.
Average rates of change in GDP and its components in south European countries, 1970-1984
(Percentages)

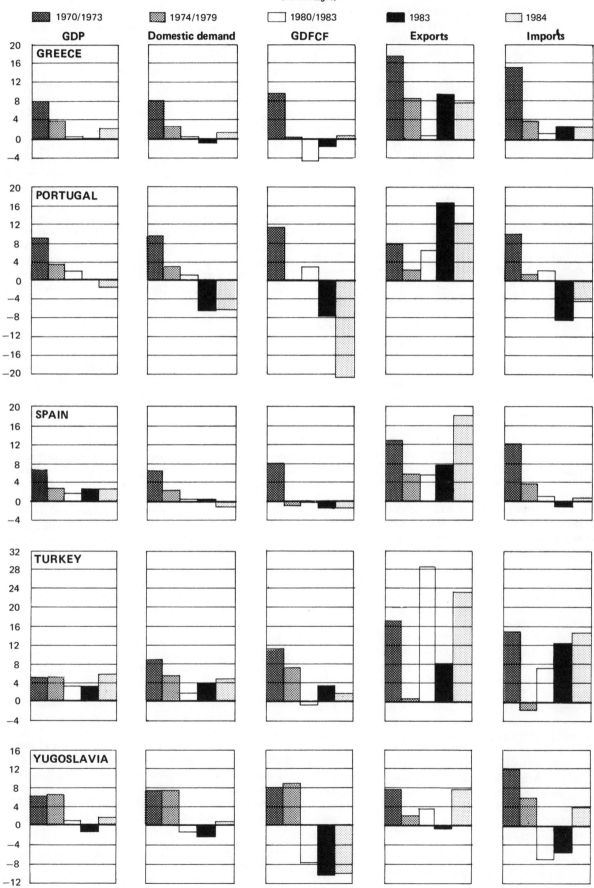

Source : Appendix tables.

efficiency in general are combined with an increasing role for the public sector, particularly in "high-risk" areas which private capital tends to avoid. The contrast between the economic policies of Greece and those of other south European countries is also reflected in the greater use of direct controls to fight growing economic imbalances (for example, the increase in excise duties on certain imports to limit their growth) and a reluctance to reduce the extent of administered prices in the public sector.

Economic policies are expected to remain basically unchanged in 1985. The 1985 budget envisages a nominal increase in expenditure of 27 per cent and in receipts of nearly 30 per cent, which would leave the state deficit virtually unchanged at a little more than 10 per cent of GDP. As in other south European countries, the interest charges on the state debt will increase particularly rapidly (by 46 per cent). Inflationary pressures are expected to ease slightly. The target rate of increase in consumer prices for 1985 is put at 16 per cent (December to December). This target is the same as that for 1984 which was exceeded by two points. The current balance is expected to remain at the same level as in 1984 and total demand growth to accelerate slightly, led by foreign demand, public sector consumption and investment. Private investment is likely to remain sluggish and private consumption to grow at the same moderate rate as in 1984. The targets most open to doubt are those for inflation and employment: labour costs will probably continue to increase rapidly (an increase in public sector salaries of nearly 25 per cent is foreseen which will have obvious repercussion on the private sector) and past exchange rate depreciations (18 per cent in 1983 and 14 per cent through November 1984) may ensure that imported inflation will remain strong in 1984. As for employment, the weakness of private investment and the attempt to limit the increase in the public sector deficit may result instead in an increase in unemployment.

Developments in *Portugal* in 1984 continued to be determined by the restrictive economic policy adopted in 1983. In 1982 the current account deficit was $3.2 billion (13.5 per cent of GDP), compared with a virtually balanced account in 1979. This sharp deterioration resulted from both domestic and external factors. Domestically, there was no adjustment to the second oil price shock and, up to 1982, demand continued to increase at rates well above those prevailing in the more industrialized countries. But the situation was aggravated by sluggish or falling foreign demand, a rise in world interest rates and the appreciation of the US dollar. In early 1983 the country faced significant external financing difficulties, resulting in sizeable losses of official reserves. The improvement of the external position therefore became the main policy objective. By mid-1983, the government embarked on a stabilization programme supported by a stand-by arrangement with the IMF. The programme was intended to reduce the current account deficit to 9 per cent of GDP in 1983 and 6 per cent in 1984. The strategy, designed to cut domestic demand and promote foreign exchange earnings, included: (a) a 12 per cent devaluation of the escudo in June 1983, followed by a continuation of the policy of a "crawling peg" depreciation against a basket of currencies; (b) increased interest rates (in August 1983); (c) tax increases equivalent to about 1 per cent of GDP, sharp increases in administered prices of essential goods and of public services, and cuts in the public investment programme; (d) a reduction in the deficits of public sector enterprises; and (e) a marked deceleration in the growth of total liquidity in the economy.

During 1984, monetary and fiscal policies remained fairly tight, although some indicators suggest some relaxation: the import surcharge that had been raised to 30 per cent in 1983 was rolled back to 10 per cent and external credit expanded again, as new,

large loans were obtained in July and August 1984. The outcome of these policies was a substantial drop in the external deficit as well as a reduction in the public sector deficit.

The current account deficit was $1.6 billion (7 per cent of GDP) in 1983 and is estimated to have been about $700 million (or 2 per cent of GDP) in 1984. The public sector deficit fell from 22 to 15 per cent of GDP between 1982 and 1983 but in 1984 there seems to have been no further significant change. However, unemployment rose (by at least 1 percentage point) and the rate of inflation increased from 25 per cent in 1983 to about 30 per cent in 1984, partly due to the reduction of state subsidies to essential goods and services.

Economic policy in 1985 may be somewhat less restrictive than in 1984 and credit is expected to grow more than in 1984. Domestic demand is expected to improve, due to a small rise in both fixed investment and private consumption. Some reconstitution of stocks might also contribute to GDP growth. As a result domestic demand is expected to increase by 3 per cent, the first rise since 1982. Export demand is likely to remain lively, but as import demand is also expected to recover the foreign sector is not expected to give a significant contribution to GDP growth. Consumer price inflation is expected to slow down to an annual rate of about 20 per cent. The unemployment rate will probably stabilize at around 10 per cent and the balance on current account is forecast to be in deficit by about $1 billion, or 5 per cent of GDP.

In *Spain*, policies to keep the cash deficit of the central government at a little more than 5 per cent of GDP and to enforce strict control over monetary aggregates have been successful. However there has been some relaxation insofar as interest rates in the money market at the end of 1984 were some 8 points below the levels of a year earlier.

Economic policies for 1985 assume a growth of GDP of 3 per cent, due mainly—and in sharp contrast with 1984—to an expansion of domestic demand of 2.4 per cent, a further improvement (equivalent to 0.6 per cent of GDP) in the external sector, and a continued reduction in the rate of inflation. Growth in 1985 should thus be sustained by consumption and investment. According to official forecasts, nominal disposable incomes should increase in 1985 by 9.2 per cent or 1.2 per cent in real terms. Gross domestic fixed capital formation should increase by 4.2 per cent, supported by a continued increase in the financial surplus of enterprises (resulting from the wage moderation agreements signed in October)[80] and from a decline in the real interest rate from 3.5 per cent in 1984 to 2 per cent in 1985. Although monetary targets for 1985 have not been announced it is clear that the intention of Spanish policy-makers is to ease monetary policies. Fiscal policy, however, will remain restrictive as the reduction of the public sector deficit is still a major priority.[81]

Austere fiscal policies in 1985 will be combined with a sustained effort at structural reform of both the public and private sectors. The introduction of better management methods, increases in administered prices and the closing of inefficient plants had already led to a substantial decline in the 1984 operating deficit of the large state industrial holding company, INI (National Institute of Industry), and a plan to close the most uneconomic railway lines in the national network is being implemented. Policies towards the private sector have included incen-

---

[80] The largest trade unions organization has however not signed this tripartite agreement.

[81] Ministerio de Economía y Hacienda: *Programa económico a medio plazo 1984/87.* "Evolución general y proyecciones de la economía española", and "Reformas estructurales e institucionales".

tives to industrial branches (such as shipbuilding or steel) to reduce capacity and employment: it has been estimated that the necessary reductions in the "labour surplus" branches have already reached 76 per cent of the target set. It is expected that part of the employment losses of the first stage of industrial restructuring will be offset by new jobs in the "ZURs" (zones of urgent re-industrialization), in which subsidies may cover up to 30 per cent of investment, and by the intensification of efforts to attract foreign direct capital investment (which increased rapidly in 1984).

The medium-term (1984-1987) economic programme for the structural reform of the economy does not set employment targets but only alternative employment scenarios depending on the evolution of output and productivity trends, the results of which are rather pessimistic since substantial employment creation would require considerably higher rates of output growth than in the recent past and lower rates of labour productivity growth.

Economic developments in *Turkey* in recent years have been greatly influenced by the introduction of an economic stabilization plan in early 1980,[82] supported by a three-year stand-by agreement with the IMF (approved in June 1980) which gave priority to the correction of a critical external imbalance and the strengthening of the market mechanism as the means of achieving a more efficient distribution of resources.

After declining in 1980, GNP increased by over 4 per cent in both 1981 and 1982. Inflation fell from over 100 per cent in 1980 to below 30 per cent in 1982, and the current account deficit was reduced from 6.2 per cent of GNP in 1980 to 2.2 per cent in 1982. The shift of resources abroad implied that real total domestic demand remained weak, declining in 1980 and growing by less than 3 per cent in 1982. Exports (of goods and services), boosted by devaluation, expanded in volume by 62 per cent in 1981 and by 36 per cent in 1982. In these two years, the foreign balance contributed 2.4 and 1.7 percentage points respectively, to the growth of GNP. With exchange rate and interest rate adjustments encouraging workers' remittances, and despite a further deterioration in the terms of trade and a 12 per cent increase in the volume of imported goods, the current account deficit was reduced to 3.9 per cent of GNP in 1981 and to 2.3 per cent in 1982.

At the beginning of 1983, Turkey had eliminated virtually all external debt arrears incurred before 1980 and enjoyed renewed creditworthiness in the international capital markets, but it was felt that the healthy external position needed to be consolidated in view of the still large requirements for servicing the foreign debt. On the domestic side, demand pressures were more under control but inflation, although on a downward trend, was still quite high and the moderate output growth achieved was proving insufficient to reduce unemployment. During 1983 the economy suffered serious setbacks in respect of inflation and the balance of payments, mainly because the authorities hesitated to tighten

monetary and fiscal policies. The growth of real GNP decelerated to 3.2 per cent reflecting a bad harvest and lower export growth. An acceleration in the growth rate of final domestic demand (to 4.2 per cent) was led by private consumption which quickly responded to an increase in real disposable income. There was a sharp increase in imports, a decline in workers' remittances (discouraged by falling domestic real interest rates), and the current account deficit increased to 4.3 per cent of GNP. Fixed investment decelerated as public fixed investment growth was reduced because of budgetary restraint. Inflation started to pick up, especially towards the end of the year, when wholesale prices were 40 per cent higher than 12 months earlier.

In November 1983 the new administration embarked on a new stabilization programme. At the government's request the existing stand-by arrangement with the IMF was cancelled in April 1984 and replaced by a new one lasting for a year. The principal elements of this programme were: (i) a sharp reduction in lending by the Central Bank leading to a return to positive real interest rates; (ii) a substantial reduction in the budget deficit and in budgetary transfers to the State Economic Enterprises (SEEs); (iii) structural adjustments, including reorganization of SEEs' operations with more emphasis on efficient management and flexible pricing policies; (iv) liberalization of the external sector and the introduction of a flexible exchange rate policy to promote efficient resource allocation and competitiveness.

Economic policy is likely to remain restrictive in 1985, with emphasis on reducing further the current external deficit and lowering domestic inflation. In 1985 GNP is expected to increase by 5 per cent and total domestic demand by 4 per cent. Gross fixed investment is expected to grow by 6 per cent (private investment growing by 7 per cent) and be the most dynamic component of domestic demand. However, given the fairly low levels of capacity utilization and the restrictive policy stance, the target for gross fixed capital formation may be optimistic. The current account deficit is forecast to narrow slightly, influenced by export-promoting fiscal and monetary policies. Inflationary pressures from import prices will continue due to the depreciation of the lira, while wage costs are difficult to forecast given the present high levels of inflation and the limited success of wage guidelines in the past. According to the 1985 annual plan, the increase in consumer prices is expected to decelerate rapidly, to 35 per cent for the year as a whole.

Recent economic policies in *Yugoslavia* have been largely determined by the stabilization measures taken from 1981 onwards which were aimed essentially at restoring external balance. The policies followed have succeeded in the attainment of this objective but at a high social cost of declining consumption and rising unemployment. The recent aggravation of inflationary pressures will continue to call (as in 1984) for policies of restraint combined with other measures designed to improve the productive and allocative efficiency of the economy. In 1985, led by exports, output growth is forecast to accelerate to more than 3 per cent; employment is expected to grow slightly and inflation to decline. (See below for a separate note on Yugoslavia.)

---

[82] See, *Economic Survey of Europe in 1980* and *Economic Survey of Europe in 1981.*

3.2 RECENT CHANGES IN OUTPUT AND DEMAND

The principal features of recent developments in output and demand are found in most of the countries of southern Europe: these are the strong contribution of exports to growth during 1983-1984, the weakness of investment (which fell 10 per cent during the last two years) and, on the output side (table 3.2.1), higher agricultural output in 1984 and low levels of construction (negatively influenced by low demand and rising real interest rates).

Following three years of virtual stagnation economic activity seems to have recovered moderately in *Greece* in 1984. Available output data cover mostly the first half of the year but it seems clear that the agricultural sector has improved, confirming the usual two-year cyclical pattern. During the first half of the year

agricultural output increased by over 8 per cent and partial indicators show that this favourable trend might have continued, although perhaps less strongly, during the second half of the year, when the main harvests are gathered. The recovery of industrial production, which started slowly in the third quarter of 1982, seems to have continued steadily and perhaps accelerated in the second half of the year. Industrial output increased during the first half by nearly 2 per cent but manufacturing proper increased very little (by less than 1 per cent). Construction activity expanded during the first half of the year by over 2 per cent, a slow-down on 1983. The dwelling sector has been adversely influenced by rising interest rates and by rapidly rising costs, while public works and "other building" fared considerably better. The service sectors seem to have increased roughly in line

TABLE 3.2.1

Annual changes in output in the south European countries
(*Annual percentage changes, at constant prices*)

	1970-1973	1974-1979	1980	1981	1982	1983	1984
Greece[a]							
Gross domestic product at factor cost . . .	8.4	3.7	2.1	−0.2	−	0.3	2.5
of which:							
Agriculture	4.5	1.0	12.8	−1.6	3.2	−6.0	8.7
Industry	13.1	4.7	0.7	−1.1	−3.0	0.2	1.2
Construction	7.3	0.5	−13.6	−8.3	−8.0	4.5	2.0
Services	8.0	4.8	2.3	1.5	1.4	1.6	2.0
Portugal[b]							
Gross domestic product at factor cost . . .	9.2	2.9	4.1	0.8	3.5	−	−1.6
of which:							
Agriculture	1.7	−1.0	0.4	−13.2	8.0	−4.0	6.0
Industry	10.5	3.0	3.9	1.3	3.6	1.4	−2.0
Construction	10.5	0.8	7.9	4.0	2.0	−3.0	−8.0
Services	10.5	4.5	5.0	4.0	3.4	−0.4	−1.7
Spain[c]							
Gross domestic product at factor cost . . .	6.8	2.7	1.5	−0.3	1.2	2.0	2.5
of which:							
Agriculture	3.4	1.6	8.8	−10.1	1.9	4.0	7.8
Industry	9.9	2.6	0.4	0.5	−0.5	2.5	3.0
Construction	4.1	−2.3	−1.7	−2.5	2.5	−0.5	−4.0
Services	6.0	3.8	1.2	1.4	2.2	1.6	2.5
Turkey							
Gross domestic product at factor cost . . .	6.1	5.9	−1.0	4.7	4.3	3.8	5.8
of which:							
Agriculture	1.2	5.5	1.7	0.1	6.4	−0.3	4.1
Industry	7.9	6.4	−5.9	7.6	4.6	7.6	8.9
Construction	4.6	6.1	0.8	0.4	0.5	0.6	0.3
Services	8.7	5.8	−0.2	5.6	3.3	4.0	5.7
Yugoslavia							
Gross domestic product[d] at factor cost . .	5.7	6.3	2.2	1.4	0.7	−1.3	1.7
of which:							
Agriculture	4.5	2.4	−	1.4	7.5	−1.5	1.2
Industry	7.4	7.9	4.2	4.2	0.1	1.3	5.8
Construction	1.1	8.6	−	−4.6	−7.8	−13.7	−9.6

Sources: National Accounts of OECD Countries; OECD *Economic Surveys;* ECE secretariat estimates; and Greece—Bank of Greece, *Monthly Statistical Bulletin.* Portugal—Banco de Portugal , *Relatório do conselho da administraço,* annual issues. DCP, *Grandes Opçoes para 1985* and direct communication to ECE secretariat. Spain—INE, *Contabilidad Nacional de España,* annual issues. Turkey—Ministry of Finance, *Yillik Ekonomik Rapor,* annual issues. Ministry of Commerce, *Konjunktür 1978 and 1979-80.* T.C. *Resmî Gazete,* 11 December 1976.

[a] Data by sectors cover only the first half of 1984.

[b] 1980-1984 at market prices.

[c] Except for agriculture, sectors are secretariat estimates.

[d] Yugoslav definition, i.e. excluding non-material services and including turnover tax.

with the economy as a whole, mainly because 1984 was a good year for tourism.

After a very large fall in 1983, total domestic demand probably increased slightly in Greece in 1984. The increase stems from small improvements in the growth of private consumption and, possibly, of public demand, and also from a slight upturn in gross fixed capital formation after four years of decline. The increase in private consumption has been influenced by increases in real earnings and redistributive policy measures.[83]

Gross fixed capital formation increased, but this was mainly due to the public sector since private residential and business investment continued to fall. New incentives to productive investment, reinforcing those of the 1982 law, were introduced in September but obviously these can only yield results in 1985. According to latest (OECD) estimates, the most rapidly growing component of demand in 1984 (as in 1983) was exports of goods and services (which rose by 8 per cent). Domestic demand has nevertheless been negatively influenced by increasing interest payments abroad and a sharp decline of worker remittances: these two factors combined have brought about a sizeable decline in net factor income from abroad.[84]

According to recent estimates [85] GDP in *Portugal* in 1984 fell by 1.6 per cent following zero growth in 1983. The influence of restrictive policies, which prevailed in 1983, seems to have weakened during the second half of 1984. As in the rest of southern Europe, growth in 1984 was helped by good harvests. Industrial output was hit by a large (6.6 per cent) decline in total domestic demand which could only be partly offset by buoyant foreign demand. Following closely the movement of demand, the industrial production index shows that branches producing investment goods were those most affected by the deep recession.

As the result of a sharp drop in real disposable income (in turn the result of the stringent policies introduced in late 1983),[86] total domestic demand continued to fall in 1984 (the cumulative decline in the last two years being over 13 per cent). Of the various components of domestic demand only government consumption increased in 1984, but by considerably less than in 1983. Private consumption fell due to a sharp decline in real wages. Fixed investment fell in 1984 by 20 per cent and private investment by 25 per cent. (The decline affected all categories of investment goods with machinery particularly hard hit.) Destocking also depressed the growth of total demand but by proportionately much less than in 1983. Foreign demand was the most rapidly expanding sector of final demand in 1984 but whereas in 1983 it had prevented a fall in GDP this was not possible with its more moderate rate of expansion in 1984.

There was a mild recovery in *Spain* in 1984. The current account deficit was eliminated, inflation fell and there was progress in limiting the public sector deficit. However, labour market conditions deteriorated further and productive investment failed to revive. On the basis of preliminary estimates, GDP is expected to have grown by 2.5 per cent, only slightly more than in 1983.

As in the other south European countries, agricultural output contributed to the growth of incomes and total output. For the first time in many years there was a small agricultural trade surplus during the first nine months of 1984.

The evolution of industrial output is more uncertain. The index of industrial production, increased by only 1.3 per cent (January-October) but other indicators (industrial consumption of electricity, steel production, order books) point to an increase of nearly 3 per cent. The decline in the construction sector intensified in 1984 and most indicators point to a fall in output of about 5 per cent. Finally the output of the service sectors may have increased roughly in line with GDP: it was a good year for tourism and there was continued expansion in the public services.

Changes in the components of demand in 1984 have been estimated on the basis of the (fairly similar) forecasts of the Bank of Spain and the Ministry of economy and finance.[87]

Private consumption probably fell by about 1 per cent in 1984. This is obviously due to the decline in nominal and real wages and salaries, and a 2.5 per cent drop in employment. Public consumption probably continued to increase although at a slightly lower rate than in 1983; it was the only component of final domestic demand to increase.

Gross fixed capital formation continued to fall for the third consecutive year, thus prolonging the downward trend which has lasted since 1975 and reduced the levels of investment to almost 15 per cent below those in 1974. The fall in fixed investment in 1984 was due to private investment since public investment stagnated. Investment in plant fell rapidly (by 4 to 5 per cent), but investments in machinery may have increased slightly (from 1 to 2 per cent). Stock changes are uncertain: according to official sources they declined in 1984, but the improvement in agricultural output, as well as the actual October data for industrial stocks, point in the other direction.

The available estimates point to a contraction of domestic demand of around 1 per cent in 1984, which is more than offset by an exceptional growth of foreign demand. Exports of goods and services may have increased in real terms by 16 to 18 per cent and the net contribution of the external sector to growth in 1984 appears to have been equivalent to about 3 percentage points of GDP in 1983. As a result the domestic saving ratio increased considerably and exceeded the gross national investment ratio.

The increase in national savings is due in great part to the prolongation and intensification of policies favouring the recovery of the gross operating profits of enterprises: these may have increased their share of GDP by about 1.2 percentage points. Insofar as this redistribution of income corresponded with an ex-ante target, as is the case in Spain, economic policies might be regarded as being successful, but the question still remains open as to whether these policies are most appropriate to the economic and social structure of Spain.[88]

---

[83] Industrial workers' hourly earnings at the end of the second quarter of 1984 were over 28 per cent higher than a year earlier and average monthly earnings of employees 22 per cent; the equivalent period increase in the consumer price index was 19 per cent. Earnings in the retail sector increased even faster and only construction workers' monthly earnings seem to have lagged much behind consumer prices. The policies of wage indexation, in force since 1982, which foresaw full maintenance of real earnings for only the lowest paid workers seem to have been only partially enforced. Retail sales, in volume, confirm the recovery of consumer demand since the index increased by 4 and 3 per cent during the first and second quarters of 1984 over the same quarters of the previous year.

[84] In an attempt to stop the decline in remittances, higher interest rates were introduced in November 1984 in order to attract greater deposits by emigrant workers.

[85] By the Central Planning Department.

[86] Introduced in close co-operation with, and embodied in a letter of intent to, the IMF of September 1983; subsequently revised by a new policy statement in July 1984.

---

[87] Banco de España: *Boletin Económico:* October 1984 and Ministerio de Economia y Hacienda, *Nota Economica,* January 1985. After this chapter was completed a new estimate, of 2 per cent GDP growth in 1984, was released by the Spanish National Institute of Statistics (March 1985).

[88] The implicit model in this set of policies has been recently challenged by an econometric study carried out under the aegis of the Center of Studies and Planning (Barcelona) by Professors Garrido, Sanromá and Trillén.

Output growth accelerated in *Turkey* in 1984 thanks to good export growth and increased agricultural output. Output in all sectors exceeded the target growth rates for the year as a whole. The only sector where growth decelerated was construction.

Total domestic demand, which had recovered strongly in 1983, accelerated slightly in 1984. While the rise in public consumption was faster than in 1983, private consumption grew at the same pace (by about 5 per cent). Private consumption and investment were again the most dynamic components of domestic demand. Most of the private investment was concentrated in the export-oriented industries and in agriculture. For the first time since 1980, public investments fell in 1984 as the result of efforts to reduce the public sector's share of manufacturing. The growth of public sector investment has in fact decelerated continuously since 1981. Foreign demand also contributed significantly to the growth of GNP in 1984 (more than 1 percentage point) due to sharp export growth.

After four years of declining growth rates and a minor contraction of output in 1983, there was a revival of economic activity in *Yugoslavia* in 1984 discussed more fully below. The growth in output was sustained by external demand with exports increasing by almost 13 per cent in volume. There was a particularly sharp decline in investment which has now fallen for five consecutive years. Total domestic demand however is thought to have stagnated due to restocking. On the output side the export-led recovery was mostly reflected in a growth of industrial output (by almost 6 per cent). Agricultural output recovered slightly but the construction sector followed the trend of investment demand and sharply declined.

Data on *industrial capacity utilization* for south European countries are less reliable than for the advanced industrial countries. The large number of small semi-artisanal industrial enterprises is either insufficiently covered by the enquiries or insufficiently represented in the results due to low response rates. Capacity margins seem nevertheless to remain wide and hence capacity constraints have not impeded output growth in any of the southern countries. For *Portugal*, capacity utilization data show a virtually uninterrupted fall since the second quarter of 1980. Latest data (for the second quarter of 1984) show a rate of 75 per cent. Capacity utilization, lowest in the investment goods industries, thus followed slack investment demand, but a small recovery seems to have taken place among intermediate goods producers.

For *Spain* seasonally-adjusted data on capacity utilization show a clear downward trend, with minor fluctuations, since the second quarter of 1982. The overall trend is largely determined by the precipitous fall in the capacity utilization rate in the investment goods industries (from 84 per cent in the last quarter of 1982 to 70 in the same period of 1984). A minor recovery appears to have occurred in the consumer goods industries in 1984.

In *Turkey* the main data available on capacity utilization are quarterly figures published by the Istanbul Chamber of Industry. Although available time series are not fully comparable, the data show a rapidly rising trend from a low point of 45 per cent in 1979 to 73 per cent in the first quarter of 1984. Three sectors continued to register low ratios: forestry products, capital goods, and machinery and basic metals. The highest rates were in food and textiles, both branches operating at around 75 per cent of capacity. The rising trend probably continued throughout 1984—particularly in exporting branches.

3.3 PRICES AND INCOMES

Inflationary pressures in the southern European countries continued at high levels in 1984 and worsened during the year in three of them (Portugal, Turkey and Yugoslavia). The weighted average rate of increase in consumer prices in the five south European countries accelerated from 21 per cent in 1983 to over 25 per cent in 1984, compared with a deceleration from 7 to less than 6 per cent in the more industrialized countries of western Europe. The acceleration of inflation in southern Europe in 1984 is disquieting since it took place in a year in which agricultural supplies improved, and in which the depreciation of national currencies in the exchange markets was smaller (except for Turkey) than in 1983. Due to the normal lags, the currency depreciation element of imported inflation moderated in the second half of the year.

Inflationary pressures decelerated slightly in *Greece* though they still remained high (table 3.3.1). The slowdown partly resulted from a lower rate of effective exchange rate depreciation, and also to the restraining effect of wage indexation on wage costs. Other factors seemingly did not alter much in 1984. Inflation is expected to decelerate further in 1985 if these influences persist; it is expected to fall to 16 per cent—2 percentage points below its 1984 level.

The inflation rate in *Portugal* accelerated in 1983 and 1984. The movement was particularly strong in the second half of 1983, and in the first quarter of 1984 it reached an annual rate of 34 per cent. This resulted mainly from increases in administered prices and a sizeable devaluation of the escudo. Inflation slowed down in the second half of 1984 and during the last quarter of the year declined to an annual rate of 26 per cent. For the year as a whole inflation was about 30 per cent.

Import prices contributed over a quarter of the inflation in 1983. This can be attributed entirely to the depreciation of the escudo, since dollar import prices fell (the depreciation of the escudo on its own accounted for as much as 37 per cent of the rise in consumer prices in 1983). Factor incomes other than wages contributed about one third and labour costs were responsible for some 29 per cent. The remaining 11 per cent was accounted for by rising indirect taxes. The escudo depreciated less in 1984 than in 1983. As nominal wages rose less in 1984 than in 1983, their contribution to inflation was also probably smaller than in the previous year. Therefore, the acceleration of the inflation rate in 1984 was due to non-wage incomes—particularly the rising enterprise surplus—and by higher net indirect taxes resulting from cuts in state subsidies.

TABLE 3.3.1

Annual price change in southern Europe
(Percentages)

	1970-1973	1974-1979	1980	1981	1982	1983	1984
Greece							
GDP deflator (at market prices)	7.9	15.5	17.7	19.3	24.6	19.8	18.0
Wholesale prices: Total	9.1	16.4	28.4	25.9	16.0	19.8	21.6
Consumer prices: Total	6.5	16.2	24.9	24.5	21.0	20.5	18.5
Food	8.4	16.7	27.6	30.1	21.1	18.1	18.3
Portugal							
GDP deflator (at market prices)	6.1	20.1	19.4	18.3	22.2	23.4	26.6
Wholesale prices: Total	5.6	25.1	6.5	21.5	19.1	25.0	29.0
Consumer prices: Total	8.7	23.7	16.6	20.0	22.4	25.5	29.5
Food	8.2	27.0	10.4	19.5	24.1	25.1	33.0
Spain							
GDP deflator (at market prices)	8.8	18.3	13.9	13.6	13.7	11.8	10.5
Wholesale prices: Total[a]	..	14.7[b]	17.4	15.7	12.2	14.2	13.2
Consumer prices: Total	8.4	18.4	15.5	14.6	14.4	12.2	11.3
Food	8.3	17.2	9.1	13.6	15.0	10.7	12.5
Turkey							
GDP deflator (at market prices)	16.9	33.4	102.3	42.0	28.0	28.3	43.9
Wholesale prices: Total	15.3	32.7	107.2	36.8	25.2	30.6	52.0
Consumer prices: (Total	13.5	31.4	116.6	35.9	27.1	28.0	..
Old series:[c] (Food	13.2	32.3	106.7	40.7	29.0	29.6	..
New series:[d] (Total	..	..	..	..	..	31.4	48.4
(Food	..	..	..	..	..	26.1	57.1
Yugoslavia							
GDP deflator (at market prices)	13.3	16.5	30.0	40.1	31.7	40.4	52.0
Cost of living	..	..	30.3	40.7	31.7	40.9	53.4

Sources: For GDP deflator, as for table 3.2.1. For wholesale and consumer prices, ILO *Monthly Memorandum on Consumer Prices Indices*; OECD *Press Release*, mid-February 1985; and Greece—Bank of Greece, *Monthly Statistical Bulletin*; Portugal—Instituto nacional de estatistica, *Boletim mensual de estatistica*; Banco de Portugal, *Boletim trimestral*; DCP direct communication to ECE secretariat; Spain—Instituto nacionál de estadistica, *Boletín mensuál de estadistica, indice de precis industriales indice de precios de consumo*; Turkey—State Institute of Statistics, *Toptan Esya ve Tüketici Fiyatlari Aylik Indeks Biilteni*; Yugoslavia, *Statistical Yearbook 1982* and subsequent issues.

[a] Index of industrial prices.

[b] 1975-1979.

[c] Ankara.

[d] Total urban areas.

73

Since 1982, the rise in nominal wages has clearly fallen behind the inflation rate, entailing a sharp deterioration in real wages. In 1983 they declined by nearly 6 per cent and, probably, by 12 per cent in 1984.

All available indicators point to a further but minor deceleration of price increases in *Spain* during 1984. The consumer price index, which grew at an annual rate of 13 per cent in the first quarter, decelerated to a year-on-year rate of less than 10 per cent in the last quarter of 1984. The distribution of inflationary pressure among its various cost elements changed considerably between 1983 and 1984. Unit wage costs and import prices, which had accounted for 33 and 37 per cent respectively of the price increase in 1983, contributed 21 and 18 per cent respectively in 1984. The effect of indirect taxation on the other hand increased from 6 to 9 per cent. The role of the gross enterprise surplus rose from 31 per cent in 1983 to 51 per cent in 1984 and was the main factor underlying the price increase in the latter year. Unit labour costs are estimated to have increased by 5.5 per cent in 1984 compared with 10 per cent in 1983, while import prices, which increased by 20 per cent in 1983, rose by 10 per cent in 1984. The medium-term programme foresees some further deceleration of inflation in 1985. This is likely to be concentrated in the second half of the year since many administered prices were increased during the first quarter of 1985.

Inflation in *Turkey* accelerated to a very high rate in 1984 (44 per cent as measured by the GDP deflator). Data on the different cost elements underlying price changes are scanty. However, unlike other countries of the group, the import price element probably continued to exert an increasing influence in spite of the relatively closed character of the Turkish economy.[89] The effect of net indirect taxes should also have acted in the same direction; many of the administered prices for primary products and basic services sold by the public sector were increased in an attempt to restrict the growth of the budget deficit while avoiding tax increases. Data on wages and salaries, although their coverage is very limited, point clearly to a big decline in real earnings.

Based on data which are very limited in coverage,[90] the average daily wages of insured workers increased by about 37 and 40 per cent in 1983 and 1984 respectively. Thus, while real wages improved in 1983 after deteriorating since 1980, they fell sharply, by about 10 per cent, in 1984.

In *Yugoslavia* inflationary pressures accelerated during 1983 and 1984 and prices rose at very high rates. Unlike the other southern countries, every major cost element including import prices contributed to the acceleration. Non-wage labour costs seem to have increased somewhat more rapidly than wage costs per unit of output. The incomes policies introduced in 1980 and 1981 have thus yielded disappointingly small results.[91]

---

[89] The Turkish lira was devalued by 34 per cent *vis-à-vis* the dollar in 1983 (end December 1982/83) and by 36.4 per cent in 1984, but no data on the effective rates of lira depreciation are available.

[90] The main wage and salary data are published by the Social Insurance Institute which is restricted to workers covered by the Social Insurance System. They account for only about 12 per cent of total employment and 30 per cent of employment in the non-agricultural sector.

[91] See section below on Yugoslavia for a discussion of structural aspects of this problem. See also OECD, *Economic Survey, Yugoslavia*, Paris, December 1984.

3.4 EMPLOYMENT AND UNEMPLOYMENT

The coverage of employment statistics differs substantially between countries in southern Europe; even within individual countries, changes in definitions and methodology are frequent and mar the comparability of time series. Moreover "informal" labour markets, underemployment and segmentation in these countries are much more extensive than in the industrially advanced western countries. Thus comparisons of absolute levels of employment and unemployment among countries is risky and the data available can only be used to illustrate trends over time in an individual country—or, at best, to give rough orders of magnitude between countries (see table 3.4.1).[92]

In *Greece* available data for 1984 show that, despite increases in public sector employment and the maintenance of employment in medium and large manufacturing enterprises, unemployment continued to increase. The Labour Force Employment Organization index for August 1984 was nearly 29 per cent above its year-earlier level, and it has been officially estimated that the real unemployment ratio could have reached about 8 per cent of the active population by mid-year.

Labour market trends in *Portugal* continued to be unfavourable in 1984. Employment declined significantly in 1983, particularly in the second half of the year, and the fall continued in the first quarter of 1984. Data for the second quarter suggest that employment stabilized in all sectors except construction, where the number of workers continued to fall. By mid-1984, employment in manufacturing and in services was 2-3 per cent below the mid-1983 level. Full-year estimates which refer to employment in all sectors and includes a 2 per cent drop in agricultural employment, put total employment at some 1 per cent below the 1983 level. Agricultural employment already fell sharply in 1983 (by almost 9 per cent), but this may partly be explained by unfavourable weather conditions as output also decreased substantially. In manufacturing, the impact of restrictive policies seems to have been felt in 1983 when employment declined 3 per cent. The fall could be around 1 per cent in 1984. Thus manufacturing employment declined, by somewhat less than the average in both years, in line with relatively more dynamic performance of the exporting branches.

Unemployment is estimated to have risen in 1983 and the unemployment rate increased by 1 percentage point. However, comparisons between 1983 and 1984 are difficult to make because a broader concept of "unemployed" was used in the Employment Survey of 1983. On the new definition, unemployment was somewhat above 10 per cent in 1983 and is likely to have remained at about the same level in 1984. The rate of unemployment is, however, much higher among women (15 per cent) and, particularly, among young people (24 per cent).

Demand for labour in *Spain* was particularly unfavourable in 1984. According to latest data, which refer to an inquiry conducted in the last quarter of 1984, unemployment increased by 435,000 persons to reach nearly 2.9 million persons or 21.7 per cent of the active population. This increase is however partly spurious and results from differences in the statistical treatment

---

[92] The data given in table 3.4.1 are based on national definitions. They differ in several cases from those given in appendix table A.12 which are taken from international sources which attempt to apply a standard definition to all countries.

TABLE 3.4.1

Unemployment rates in south European countries
(Per cent of total labour force)

	1983	1984
Greece	7.8	8.3 *
Portugal	10.3	10.4 *
Spain		
Registered unemployment	17.7	19.7
Active population enquiry	18.4	21.7
Turkey		
Excluding disguised unemployment in agriculture	15.8	17*
Including disguised unemployment in agriculture	19.4	21*
Yugoslavia	9.0	9.5

Source: National statistics.

of people working under "communal employment programmes" (these were previously considered as employed but are now considered as unemployed). Taking this into account, unemployment may have increased by 315,000 persons in 1984, reaching a rate of 20.7 per cent of the active population by the end of the year. On the same definition, there would have been a fall in employment of 297,000 persons. The effect of unemployment in discouraging the search for work intensified in 1984 as the active population remained stagnant (increasing by 0.1 per cent) in spite of an increase in the working age population of nearly 200,000 persons. This contrasts with the increase of 122,000 persons (0.8 per cent) in the active population in 1983. The decrease in employment in 1984 was thus bigger than in the previous record year of 1981, when employment fell by 309,000. The change in numbers registered as unemployed moved roughly parallel to that of the inquiry-based data referred to above. Registered unemployment increased by 262,000 during 1984 giving a total of over 2.6 million persons. The inquiry data show that the main employment loss was concentrated among private sector wage and salary earners, the number of which decreased in 1984 by 297,000 persons. The loss among salaried employees in 1984 was exceeded only in 1979 (when there was a decrease of 324,000) and public sector salaried employment also fell in 1984. As in west European countries, unemployment rates in Spain were particularly high for women (24 per cent at the end of the third quarter of 1984) and for young workers (16 to 24 years of age) among which the unemployment rate reached 47 per cent in the same period.

Although the rate of increase in the civilian labour force of *Turkey* decreased in 1983 and 1984 as compared to 1982 (2.3 per cent annually as compared with a 2.6 per cent increase in 1982) the labour market continues to be characterized by excess supply due to rapid population growth. Other structural factors which tend to intensify existing labour market imbalances are the still very high rates of decline in agricultural employment (which still accounts for roughly 58 per cent of total employment) and the loss of emigration outlets. Although no accurate information on labour market trends is available, it has been officially estimated that the unemployment rate (excluding an approximation for disguised agricultural unemployment) increased from 15.8 per cent in 1983 to about 17 per cent in 1984.

In *Yugoslavia* the unemployment rate continued to rise in 1984 but, contrary to general experience in the other south European countries, employment also increased in response to rising in economic activity. It is generally agreed that registered unemployment in Yugoslavia overstates (by about a quarter) the actual number of those really unemployed if account is taken of employed people seeking to change jobs. If this is taken into account the unemployment rate would fall to 7.3 per cent of the active population.

3.5 TRADE AND PAYMENTS

The evolution of the external sector was particularly favourable in the south European countries during 1984. According to preliminary estimates the combined current account deficit of the five major countries decreased from about $7.4 billion in 1983 to about $1 billion in 1984. The regional current balance is greatly influenced by Spain, which achieved a swing of nearly $4.5 billion over the two years, but the current positions of Portugal, Turkey and Yugoslavia also significantly improved. In Greece changes were apparently marginal (table 3.5.1).

Most of the improvement in the combined current balance in 1984 arose from the $5.5 billion reduction in the trade deficit. This followed a $4.6 billion fall in 1983. Most of the improvement in 1984 reflected higher exports, but the surplus on net services and transfers also contributed. The region's trade deficit fell from over $30 billion in 1980 to less than $13 billion in 1984.

Although data on the external transactions of *Greece*—particularly its trade data—are not always easy to interpret,[93] it seems unlikely that there was any big change in the current balance in 1984. The January-November cash payments data show a minor increase (of $100 million) in the current deficit. This must result entirely from a decline in the net surplus on services since the

trade deficit declined slightly. Customs-based trade data for January-September show an 18 per cent increase in the current drachma value of imports and a 50 per cent rise in the value of exports. This corresponds to volume increases of 3 and 27 per cent respectively. The growth of exports to the United States and EFTA countries was particularly buoyant while the increase in imports reflected mostly higher purchases from industrially advanced west European countries.

The recent evolution of trade and payments in *Portugal* has been largely conditioned by the goals agreed with the IMF: to reduce the current account deficit from of 13.5 per cent of GDP in 1982 (equivalent to $3.2 billion) to 9 and 6 per cent respectively in 1983 and 1984.

In fact the deficit fell to 4 per cent of GDP ($1.6 billion) as early as 1983, and to about 2 per cent in 1984 (about $0.7 billion). The improvement in 1983 originated mostly in changes in the trade balance. The volume of exports rose rapidly (by 20 per cent) and imports declined. Following an effective devaluation of 20 per cent, Portugal made important market gains in OPEC countries and also in its more traditional west European markets.

In 1984, export growth appears to have been less buoyant and the share of growth due to increasing competitiveness was less important than in 1983. Data on commodity exports for January-October indicate a value change similar to 1983. Given the bigger export price increases, volume growth is, however, likely to have been smaller than in 1983 (about 15 per cent). On the other hand, world imports rose more rapidly in 1984 (by some 11 per cent

---

[93] See OECD, *Economic Surveys 1983-1984, Greece*, Paris, November 1983. The main difficulties derive from the fact that national accounts data on net borrowing from the rest of the world cannot be reconciled with balance of payments data. Morever transaction- and settlement-based external accounts differ widely, while price and volume trade indices seem inadequate.

TABLE 3.5.1

South European countries: selected balance of payments data
(Millions of US dollars)

	1980	1981	1982	1983	1984*
Greece					
Current balance	−2 209	−2 408	−1 892	−1 878	−1 900
Trade balance	−5 557	−5 377	−4 769	−4 294	−4 200
Service and transfers (net)	3 348	2 969	2 877	2 416	2 300
Portugal					
Current balance	−1 064	−2 605	−3 250	−1 620	−700
Trade balance	−4 029	−5 060	−4 862	−3 056	−2 200
Service and transfers (net)	2 965	2 455	1 612	1 436	1 500
Spain					
Current balance	−5 173	−4 989	−4 240	−2 480	1 995
Trade balance	−11 728	−10 113	−9 250	−7 387	−4 018
Service and transfers (net)	6 555	5 124	5 010	4 908	6 013
Turkey					
Current balance	−3 233	−1 908	−790	−1 747	−1 000
Trade balance	−4 010	−3 113	−1 991	−2 348	−1 650
Service and transfers (net)	777	1 205	1 201	603	650
Yugoslavia					
Current balance	−2 316	−961	−475	275	504
Trade balance	−4 890	−3 165	−2 024	−1 231	−700
Service and transfers (net)	2 573	2 205	1 549	1 507	1 204
Southern Europe					
Current balance	−13 995	−12 871	−10 647	−7 450	−1 100
Trade balance	−30 214	−26 828	−22 896	−18 320	−12 770
Service and transfers (net)	16 218	13 958	12 249	10 870	11 670

Source: IMF, *Balance of Payments Statistics*, vol. 35, and national sources as given in table 3.2.1.

against 2 per cent in 1983). Therefore, the growth in Portugal's exports seems to have owed most to the revival of foreign demand in 1984, rather than to market gains as in the previous year.

In both 1983 and 1984 exports of consumer goods (textiles, shoes) and metals rose particularly fast. On the import side, machinery fell sharply due to the depressed state of domestic productive investment.

Data for the first three quarters of 1984 show a marked increase in net tourist receipts (nearly 30 per cent in dollars) which contrasts with a decline in 1983 (3 per cent), and virtual stagnation in unrequited transfers (overwhelmingly emigrants' remittances) after several years of steady decline.

Forecasts for 1985 anticipate some increase in the current account deficit. Though exports are expected to remain lively, imports are projected to increase even faster as the growth of domestic demand resumes. The balance on services and incomes is likely to show a deficit similar to 1984. A further but small decline in emigrants' remittances is also expected. The likely rise in the current account deficit will thus mainly reflect the anticipated widening of the trade gap. The current account deficit is projected to reach $970 million, equivalent to 5 per cent of projected GDP.

As already noted the improvement of trade and payments in *Spain* was very marked in 1984. GDP thus grew moderately despite declining domestic demand. The estimated contribution of trade to GDP growth was about 2 percentage points and the improvement in net exports of services accounted for a further 1 per cent. Preliminary (transactions-based) data released at the end of January 1985 show that exports increased by almost 20 per cent (to $3,950 million) while the trade deficit fell (by $4,250 million). Tourist receipts increased rapidly (by $1 billion) and as a result the current balance closed with a surplus of $2 billion. This compares with a deficit of nearly $2.5 billion in 1983. Cash transactions data show that emigrants' remittances fell and that the fall in the long-term net capital inflow was due entirely to anticipated debt repayment.

Customs-based data for 1984 show a 20 per cent increase in the dollar value of exports and a 1 per cent fall in imports. As a result the trade deficit, at $5.2 billion, was 45 per cent lower than in 1983. The volume of commodity exports is estimated to have increased by 18.5 per cent and of imports by 1 per cent. The commodity pattern of exports stayed fairly constant. This implies important market-share gains, since demand in Spain's export markets increased by only 7 per cent in 1984. Exports to the industrially advanced western countries (the United States, the United Kingdom and Italy) rose fastest, but exports to de-

veloping countries virtually stagnated in real terms due to a decline in exports to OPEC countries.

Recent estimates suggest an improvement in the external sector of *Turkey* in 1984. The current deficit decreased by some $800 million, or from a $1.7 billion deficit in 1983 to one of less than $1 billion in 1984.[94] The improvement in the current balance derives mostly from the decline in the trade deficit. Export growth resumed in response to monetary and fiscal stimuli. Their current dollar value is expected to be over 22 per cent higher than in 1983. The dollar value of imports rose by less than 6 per cent. The estimates suggest that the net invisible surplus improved slightly due to lower interest payments and that a minor recovery in remittances offset a fall in net receipts from tourism.[95] Trade data for the period January-October however throw some doubt on the extent of the improvement in the trade balance. In this period, when the import regime was liberalized and administrative procedures simplified, imports increased at a rate of over 15 per cent and the customs-based trade deficit decreased by only $131 million. This seems low compared with the estimated decrease for the year of $757 million.

A breakdown by commodity groups shows a rapid loss of the share of agricultural goods in total exports due to a small fall in absolute current dollar values (January-September 1984 data). The main changes in the geographical distribution of trade flows were the lower share of Middle Eastern countries (particularly in Turkish exports) and, following the world wide trend, the increasing share of the industrially advanced countries both as suppliers and markets for Turkey.

Payments data for *Yugoslavia* show a further increase in the current account surplus. The improvement is especially significant since it derives mostly from transactions with the convertible currency area. It stemmed wholly from commodity trade, the volume of exports increasing by nearly 13 per cent while imports remained at the same level as in 1983. The balance on services deteriorated mainly because of higher interest payments.

---

[94] Data in table 3.5.1 are adjusted where necessary to ensure conformity with the definitions of the IMF's balance of payments manual. The main difference from the original data given by the State Planning Organization (SPO) is that the trade balance given in table 3.5.1 is on a uniform *f.o.b.* basis. A further adjustment had to be made because freight charges by national carriers, contrary to standard practice, are included in payments for freight in the SPO data.

[95] The recovery in remittances can be traced to the narrowing of differentials between the official and the free market rates of exchange for the Turkish lira.

3.6 FOREIGN DEBT

The vulnerability of the south European countries to the oil shocks of the 1970s was discussed above, as was the delay with which economic policies responded to the crisis. A consequence of both factors was a rapid deterioration in their current accounts and a rapid accumulation of foreign debt. Benefiting from the recycling of oil revenues, these countries were able in fact to finance their deficits with private capital inflows obtained on relatively favourable terms. Thus in the wake of the first oil shock the foreign debt of southern Europe rose from $25 billion to $61 billion. The need to redress this situation was recognized in southern Europe before the second shock of 1979, but such a change was made more difficult by the fact that this second shock was followed by a significant shift in the macro-economic policies of the major market economies and by the most severe recession of the post-war period. With rising interest rates and falling demand for their exports many debtor countries found themselves with serious problems in servicing their accumulated debt.

The *total foreign debt* of the south European countries is now very large.[96] At the end of 1984 it amounted to $97 billion which compares with a total of some $880 billion for all the developing countries.[97] Between 1975 and 1983 south European debt grew by some 17 per cent a year, at roughly the same pace as that for the developing countries.

This rate of increase exceeded considerably that for the increase in the dollar value of total south European current account receipts for the same period (11.4 per cent a year) and even more so the rate of volume growth of their combined GNP (5 per cent a year). Debt service (on medium- and long-term debt) increased at a faster rate (21 per cent a year) than total debt due to rising interest rates and the shortening of debt maturities as debt was rolled over.

Taking the five countries together a clear pattern emerges in the development of total debt with a rapid acceleration of indebtedness in the period 1975-1977, a slowdown in 1978-1979, a new and ephemeral acceleration in 1980 (resulting from the increase in the current deficit after the 1979-1980 rise in oil prices), and a sharp deceleration in the years 1981-1984.

---

[96] The data given here for the south European countries are always on a *gross* basis. The distinction between gross and net is of little relevance in the cases of Greece, Portugal and Turkey; for Yugoslavia the difference is of roughly 10 per cent. In the case of Spain the difference is very large as in mid-1984 the loans of the Spanish banking system to foreign countries were $13 billion compared with a gross debt of less than $31 billion. Note that the difference between gross and net here is not reserves, as is sometimes the case in other publications.

[97] Spain is included in the latter total.

TABLE 3.6.1

Foreign debt and debt service indicators in southern Europe, 1975-1984

	1975	1976	1977	1978	1979	1980	1981	1982	1983	1984*
Gross foreign debt in billions of US dollars										
Greece	3.4	3.4	4.0	4.5	4.9	6.4	7.5	8.3	9.5	9.6
Portugal	2.3	2.9	4.4	5.4	7.3	8.9	11.0	13.7	14.4	14.9
Spain	8.5	11.2	15.1	17.4	19.5	23.7	27.2	28.8	29.5	30.2
Turkey[a]	4.7	7.3	11.2	14.4	14.2	16.2	16.8	17.6	18.4	20.8
Yugoslavia[a]	6.6	7.9	9.5	11.8	15.2	18.9	21.1	20.3	20.6	20.8
Five countries combined . .	25.1	32.7	44.3	53.6	61.1	74.1	83.6	88.7	92.4	96.3
Total gross foreign debt as percentage of GDP at current prices and exchange rates										
Greece	15	15	15	14	13	16	20	22	27	29
Portugal	16	19	27	30	36	36	46	58	68	77
Spain	8	10	13	12	10	11	14	16	19	20
Turkey	13	18	23	27	20	28	29	33	36	46
Yugoslavia	20	21	21	22	22	27	31	33	45	50
Five countries combined . .	12	15	17	18	16	18	22	25	30	33
Total gross foreign debt as percentage of current account receipts[b]										
Greece	69	67	69	65	55	68	71	87	99	100
Portugal	56	80	94	96	93	90	118	158	158	165
Spain	55	70	81	72	61	65	75	79	84	78
Turkey	136	198	327	362	294	277	199	173	190	191
Yugoslavia	82	87	92	100	109	104	105	103	122	117
Five countries combined . .	71	87	103	102	90	93	99	105	115	111
Service payments on medium- and long-term debt as percentage of current account receipts[b]										
Greece	15	16	15	14	13	14	17	18	22	22
Portugal	11*	15*	13*	15	16	15	20	27	27	27
Spain	11	13	16	23	17	15	19	19	21	20
Turkey	10	13	13	12	15	19	16	20	21	24
Yugoslavia	16	15	16	16	20	18	19	18	28	27
Five countries combined . .	12	14	15	19	17	16	18	20	22	23

Sources: National statistics; ECE secretariat estimates; OECD, *National Accounts, Main Aggregates*, Volume I; OECD, *Endettement extérieur des pays en développement*; IMF, *International Financial Statistics*.

[a] Including IMF.

[b] Including transfers.

Total indebtedness grew by some 33 per cent a year between 1975 and 1977, but this slowed to 19 per cent between 1977 and 1980, and to only 7 per cent for 1980-1984. Except for Greece most countries follow this average pattern fairly closely.

The foreign debt position of individual countries, shown in table 3.6.1, varies considerably. Thus, while for the five countries taken together, the ratio of debt to GDP trebled from 12 per cent in 1975 to 33 per cent in 1984, the deviations from these averages are very large. The share of gross foreign debt in GDP rose fairly steadily in all countries. The increase was particularly large in Portugal, Turkey and Yugoslavia and much more moderate in Greece and Spain.

The *sources of supply* of this foreign debt and changes in its structure were also similar in these countries with the conspicuous exception of Turkey.

The main common feature is the growing importance of international private banking as a source of credit. For the five countries taken together about 70 per cent of the increase in debt consists of gross liabilities to BIS reporting banks. If Turkey is excluded the increase in gross assets of BIS reporting banks *vis-à-vis* the other four countries would account for over 80 per cent of the increase in their debt. The increase in gross assets of the BIS reporting banks *vis-à-vis* southern Europe was very large during the period 1975-1980; it then decelerated, later coming to a virtual standstill in 1983, but in 1984 increased again slightly. OECD data on medium and long term debt (MLTD) by source of origin, covering only the period 1975-1982, confirms the rising share of private markets, particularly of commercial bank loans, in the growth of total MLTD [98] of these countries. A corollary of the growing importance of private sources as suppliers has been a declining share of debt granted under liberal conditions.

The OECD source excludes Spain, but national sources of Spain show the same trends insofar as the share of official multilateral credits in total debt (including short term) fell from 26 per cent in 1975 to 8 per cent in 1982. The share in total debt of foreign credits channelled through national banks or obtained directly from foreign banks and foreign credit institutions rose from 67 per cent in 1975 to 88 per cent in 1982.

Foreign suppliers' credit has always remained low in Spain (less than 2 per cent of total debt) and the main difference between Spain and the other southern countries is the much greater resort to foreign bond issues. Thus in the period 1975-1983 out of south European bond issues (in OECD capital markets) totalling $5.7 billion nearly, 83 per cent were issued by Spain.[99]

The institutional classification of *foreign borrowing by type of borrower* differs greatly from country to country and does not lend itself to standardized presentation. The position in individual countries appears to be as follows:

In *Greece*, public sector borrowing abroad (including publicly guaranteed private debt) accounted in 1982 for 74 per cent of total debt. Within the public sector, the element, which has absorbed the foreign debt fastest, has been "public entities" which increased their share of total public foreign debt from 34 per cent in 1977 to 36 per cent in 1982.

In *Portugal*, the sector which has been mostly responsible for the increase in the level of foreign debt has been the state enter-

prise sector, which has increased its foreign debt from less than $2.0 billion in 1978 to $7.6 billion in the second quarter of 1984. This represents roughly 60 per cent of the increase in total foreign debt during the same period. A large share of the increase in state enterprise debt has been short term and, in the second quarter of 1984, the state enterprise sector was holding over 85 per cent of Portugal's total short term debt. Short-term lending became a prominent feature of financial markets in the early 1980s. In Portugal this form of external finance increased rapidly in 1980-1982; in 1983 short-term debt declined but increased again in 1984.

In *Spain*, the relative importance of private and public sector borrowers has remained remarkably stable during the period 1975-1983. The share of the public sector—in a wide sense (i.e. covering public enterprise)—in total foreign borrowing was 46.3 per cent at the end of 1975 and 47.0 per cent at the end of the third quarter of 1983. Within the public sector, the direct foreign debt of state and local corporations fell slightly in relative importance, while that of official credit institutions rose from 2.5 to 7 per cent. The state debt fell from 14.0 per cent of the total at the end of 1975 to 12.4 per cent in the third quarter of 1983. The share of the public enterprise sector in total foreign debt has remained between 24 and 27 per cent. Within the private sector there has been decreases in short term private debt from 4.4 in 1975 to 0.5 per cent in 1983, and in medium and long term debt with state guarantees (from 9.1 to 6.6 per cent). The main beneficiaries of private state-guaranteed debt were firms building motor roads.[100]

The institutional distribution of the foreign debt of *Turkey* stands in great contrast to that of the other south European countries in that multilateral and concessional debt is still very large (and it is mostly used by or channelled through the public sector for development purposes) and the share of commercial bank loans, although increasing rapidly in recent years, is still relatively low. The distribution of foreign debt between the public and private sectors largely reflects the maturity structure of the toal debt as the private sector has virtually no direct access to medium- and long-term loans (i.e. loans for three years and over). The two debt rescheduling agreements of 1979 and that of 1982 converted a substantial amount of convertible Turkish lira deposits into longer term commercial bank loans held by foreign commercial banking creditors. As a result the share of "short" term loans held by the private non-bank sector fell from 38 per cent of the total debt in 1978 to 6.5 per cent in 1982.

Information about *Yugoslavia* is scanty and its special institutional structure makes detailed comparison with other countries difficult. Foreign credits are mostly administered through the federal banking system and are used for both commercial and development purposes. The most clear trend since the early 1970s is the increasing share of private non-guaranteed debt which has risen from about 60 per cent in 1975 to about two thirds of the total foreign debt in 1983.

Debt service payments rose considerably in 1975-1978 and in 1980-1983. In the first of these periods the increase in the debt service burden was mainly due to the growth in total debt; in the second it mostly reflected the rise in interest rates. The ratio of debt service to current account receipts increased, for the whole region, from 12 per cent in 1975 to 22 per cent in 1983. In 1983, the ratios ranged from 21 per cent in Spain and Turkey to 28 per cent in Yugoslavia. In 1984 there were no significant changes except for a deterioration in the debt service burden of Turkey.

---

[98] For the period 1975-1982 the increase in Bank loans accounted for 68 per cent of the increase in MLTD for Greece, 62 per cent for Portugal, 31 per cent for Turkey and 51 per cent for Yugoslavia. For Spain national sources put the ratio at over 95 per cent of the increase total debt (1975-1984).

[99] Source OECD, *Financial Market Trends*: March 1984 and OECD *Financial Statistics Monthly*, September 1984.

---

[100] Spanish foreign debt is very concentrated. In the private sector about 50 enterprises absorb some 80 per cent of external borrowing. See, D. de la Dehesa: "Perspectivas a medio plazo del endeudamiento exterior de España", *Información Comercial Española*. December 1983.

3.7 GROWTH UNDER EXTERNAL CONSTRAINTS AND STRUCTURAL IMBALANCES: YUGOSLAVIA

After four years of successively declining growth rates, from 7 per cent growth in 1979 to a contraction of more than 1 per cent in 1983, the social product of Yugoslavia—roughly comparable to gross national product—increased by some 2 per cent in 1984.[101] On the supply side there was a rise in the volume of industrial output of almost 6 per cent and a similar increase in the transport sector; agricultural output grew only 1 per cent and output in the construction sector fell by almost 10 per cent. On the demand side, exports increased by almost 13 per cent in volume and there was some increase in stocks; however, final domestic demand continued to contract at a similar rate to that in 1983, namely, some 3 per cent. External adjustment has remained the priority of economic policy. The trade deficit was 20 per cent lower than in 1983 and is now less than a quarter of the record level of $7.2 billion in 1979. Thanks to a large surplus on the services account, the current account was in surplus for the second year running, and in fact was almost double that in 1983. In convertible currency transactions the adjustment was even greater: the surplus on current account almost tripled in 1984 to reach some $865 million. This helped to stabilize the total foreign debt and to reduce the debt in convertible currencies (which accounts for more than 90 per cent of the total), but the debt servicing ratio remained high.

---

[101] The data in this section, unless otherwise stated, are based on the Federal Statistical Office of Yugoslavia, *Saopštenje*, vol. XXVIII, No. 568, 25 December 1984; *Statistički godišnjak Jugoslavije* and *Indeks*; National Bank of Yugoslavia, *Godišnji izveštaj*, 1983, and *Bilten*; and documents published in *Službeni list Jugoslavije*, vol. LX, No. 71, 31 December 1984.

Economic performance was boosted by expanding international trade and better-than-expected agricultural output. Had the changes in the economic system and economic policies envisaged in the long-term programme of economic stabilization been followed consistently, both external and internal performance would have been significantly better. Thus, improvements in the foreign sector are still compromised by serious domestic problems: falling real wages and rising unemployment and a record inflation rate of more than 50 per cent (in terms of the GNP deflator). Economic policy is now aiming to strengthen the improvement in the foreign sector and to check the unfavourable domestic trends. Progress towards both objectives depends largely on whether the changes proposed in the comprehensive stabilization programme can be implemented faster and more consistently.

In this section four items will be discussed: (i) recent domestic developments, (ii) adjustment in the foreign sector, (iii) foreign trade and structural imbalances and (iv) development prospects.

(i) Recent domestic developments

Besides adjustment problems in the foreign sector, which are discussed below, the main underlying problems of the Yugoslav economy in recent years have been the sharp fall in output growth, increasing unemployment, decreasing labour productivity and high inflation. Against this background, the economic objectives set at the end of 1983 were an increase in social product of some 2 per cent and a rise of 2 per cent in employment; inflation was to be checked and further declines in labour pro-

TABLE 3.7.1

Yugoslavia: volume growth of demand and output

	1983		Annual percentage change					
	Billion current dinars	Percentage shares	1979	1980	1981	1982	1983	1984
Final domestic demand . . .	3 487	85.8	5.9	0.0	−4.3	−1.9	−3.6	−3.0
Private consumption . . .	2 100	51.7	5.2	0.7	−1.0	−0.1	−0.6	−1.0
Collective consumption . .	352	8.7	7.9	2.7	−2.9	−1.0	1.0	−1.6
Gross fixed investment . .	1 035	25.4	6.4	−1.7	−9.8	−5.7	−10.2	−10.0
Total domestic demand . . .	4 064	100.0	9.7	1.3	−1.1	−1.7	−2.6	−
Changes in stocks	577	14.2	4.3	1.4	3.0	−	0.6	2.5
Statistical discrepancies . . .	−1	−	−0.7	−4.4	−1.4	1.6	0.1	1
Foreign balance (goods and services). . . .	9	..	−2.4	5.3	4.0	0.9	1.2	2.3
Social product	4 072	100.0	7.0	2.2	1.4	0.7	1.3	1.7
Agriculture and fishery[a] . .	664	16.3	5.7	0.0	1.4	7.5	1.5	1.2
Industry[a]	1 739	42.7	7.0	4.2	4.2	0.1	1.3	5.8
Construction[a]	346	8.5	9.6	0.0	−4.6	−7.8	−13.7	−9.6
Transport[a]	318	7.8	4.1	4.0	−1.8	−2.9	2.2	5.1
Industrial output per worker .	..	..	4.2	1.9	1.6	−3.1	1.3	2.8

Source: National statistics and direct communication to ECE.

[a] Index of physical volume output.

TABLE 3.7.2

Yugoslavia: employment

	End-1982 (thousands)	Percentage shares	Annual percentage change					
			1979	1980	1981	1982	1983	1984
Total population	22 635	..	0.9	0.6	0.7	0.8	0.7	0.7
Population of working age . .	14 731	..	1.5	0.7	0.6	0.5	0.9	..
Total labour force (active population)	9 974	100.0	1.1	1.1	1.0	1.1	1.1	1.2
Employment outside agriculture	6 104	60.3	4.4	3.3	2.9	2.3	1.9	2.0
Employment in agriculture[a] .	2 239	23.4	−5.5	−3.5	−3.4	−3.0	−2.4	−4.7*
Employment abroad	760	7.6	−1.3	−2.5	−	−1.3	−*	−2.0*
Registered unemployed . . .	862	8.7	3.7	3.0	3.0	6.6	5.6	6.8
Vacancies.	71	..	11.1	−2.5	−1.3	−7.8	2.8	4.1

Source: As for table 3.7.1.

[a] Calculated as residual between total labour force and other relevant items.

ductivity and real wages avoided.[102] Judged against these aims economic policy was only partially successful..

On the positive side there was a significant recovery of *economic growth* from the deepest recession experienced in Yugoslavia since the war (table 3.7.1). Social product grew by 2 per cent in 1984 and industrial output, after stagnation in 1982 and growth of 1 per cent in 1983, rose by 6 per cent. There was also some increase in overall labour productivity (almost 3 per cent in industry and 6 per cent in agriculture).

Employment developments (table 3.7.2) were less favourable. In spite of a relatively slow growth of the total labour force in recent years and a 2 per cent growth of employment outside agriculture, the overall situation has deteriorated. The number of registered unemployed increased by 7 per cent in 1984 and at the end of the year represented 9 per cent of the total labour force. Although not all of the registered unemployed are effectively unemployed,[103] these are the highest figures ever recorded in post-war Yugoslavia.

[102] "Resolution on Socio-Economic Policy of the Socialist Federal Republic of Yugoslavia in 1984", *Službeni list Jugoslavije* (Yugoslav Official Register), vol. XXXIX, No. 70, 30 December 1983.

[103] Yugoslav statistical sources treat private farmers and other self-employed persons as unemployed as soon as they register with an employment bureau. According to OECD "about one fourth of registered job-seekers are actually employed but wish to change jobs". OECD, Economic Survey *Yugoslavia*, 1984/1985, Paris, December 1984, p. 58.

From both the economic and social viewpoints, it is important to note that the number of unqualified job-seekers has been declining slightly since 1981, while the number of qualified ones increased on average by more than 12 per cent between 1981 and 1984. At the same time the number of first-time job-seekers in 1984 was more than 70 per cent of all the registered unemployed.[104] Unemployment has also been exacerbated by the return of many Yugoslav workers previously employed abroad.

Progress in reducing cost pressures and the rate of *inflation* has been very limited (table 3.7.3). Indeed, after a slowdown in 1982, when the rise in the GNP price deflator was some 32 per cent, the inflation rate increased to 40 per cent in 1983 and 52 per cent in 1984, the highest rate of inflation in the last 40 years.[105] *Import prices* had a substantial direct influence on the inflation rate in 1979-1981 and later on via successive devaluation of the national currency, but domestic factors have clearly dominated. Monetary policy has been continuously restrictive, with money supply (M1) growth substantially lower than that of social product at current prices (table 3.7.4). Although domestic demand has declined in real terms in each of the last four years, the growth of

[104] All figures calculated on the basis of the *Saopštenje* ... , p. 11.

[105] In their anti-inflation programme adopted in 1982 the authorities had anticipated a deceleration in the rate of inflation from 40 per cent at the end of 1982 to 15 per cent at the end of 1984. See *Dokumenti Komisije*, Beograd, Centar za radničko samoupravljanje, 1982, p. 73.

TABLE 3.7.3

Yugoslavia: wages, costs and prices [a]
(*Annual percentage change*)

	1979	1980	1981	1982	1983	1984
Real wages	0.1	−7.0	−5.0	−3.3	−10.0	−8.0
Nominal wages.	20.5	20.5	33.6	27.4	26.0	41.0
GNP price deflator	20.7	30.0	40.1	31.7	40.4	52.0
Wages costs per unit of output	16.3	17.5	31.1	24.1	30.4	41.0
Industrial producer prices	13.2	27.2	44.7	25.0	32.0	56.9
Agricultural producer prices	25.6	35.6	52.9	34.9	45.6	49.0
Export prices[b]	14.9	19.3	8.5	7.2	−2.3	−4.8
Import prices[b]	19.3	19.6	10.4	2.0	−0.4	3.4
Retail prices	22.0	30.0	46.0	29.5	39.1	56.8
Cost of living	20.4	30.3	40.7	31.7	40.9	53.4

Source: As for table 3.7.1.

[a] Wage data refer to the whole economy.

[b] In US dollars.

TABLE 3.7.4

Yugoslavia: money supply and consolidated budgets

	1979	1980	1981	1982	1983[a]	1984
	Billion current dinars					
						a
Money supply (MI)	375.2	461.7	584.3	739.8	888.6	1 190.1
Bank credits	1 209.1	1 564.3	1 919.2	2 370.0	3 176.0	4 477.1
Foreign exchange transactions . .	−110.5	−255.1	−365.8	−587.9	−1 197.2	−1 983.2
Non-monetary—deposits[a' b] . . .	−568.3	−769.0	−1 030.4	−1 386.7	−2 038.7	−2 740.5
Budget expenditures	425.3	523.2	707.4	891.7	1 172.6	1 358.6
	Annual percentage change					
						c
Money supply (MI)	19.0	23.1	26.6	26.6	20.1	37.1
Bank credits	27.0	29.4	22.7	23.5	34.0	47.0
Foreign exchange transactions . .	−243.2	−130.9	−43.4	−60.7	−103.6	−76.1
Non-monetary deposits[a' b] . . .	−26.1	−35.3	−34.0	−34.6	−47.0	−40.9
Budget expenditures	25.7	23.0	35.2	26.1	31.5	45.3
						d
Social product at current prices . .	29.2	33.3	42.2	32.5	39.0	54.6

Source: Godišnji izveštaj 1983 (Annual Report 1983), National Bank of Yugoslavia, Belgrade, 1984, p. 23 and direct communication to ECE secretariat.

[a] January-November, 1984.

[b] Minus sign indicates a *rise* in deposits and *decrease* in money supply.

[c] November 1984/November 1983.

[d] 1984/83.

nominal wages and unit labour costs has remained very high (tables 3.7.1 and 3.7.3). In the face of such pressures the various price policies implemented in recent years (including three temporary price freezes) were mostly ineffective. Direct price controls were gradually abandoned from mid-1984 and this move is expected to lead to a better balance between demand and supply in the medium and long term. In the short term, however, the abolition of price controls led to an acceleration of price increases in the autumn of 1984 and the beginning of 1985. Against this background of spiralling nominal wages and inflation, *real wages* continued to contract for the fifth successive year: in 1984 they had fallen to some 70 per cent of their level in 1979.

(ii) Adjustment in the foreign sector

Since 1980, the main determinant of macro-economic policy in Yugoslavia has been the need for adjustment in the foreign sector. In many respects the actual adjustment has been considerable (table 3.7.5).

After reaching a record level of more than $7.2 billion in 1979, the *foreign trade deficit* was reduced to less than one quarter in 1984. The adjustment has not fallen only or mostly on imports. The value of imports fell nearly 20 per cent between 1980 and 1984, while export values rose more than 50 per cent between 1979 and 1984. At the same time Yugoslavia's terms of trade deteriorated continuously (except in 1982), with an overall

TABLE 3.7.5

Yugoslavia: balance of payments and foreign debt, total

	1979	1980	1981	1982	1983[a]	1984
	Annual percentage change					
Volume growth						
Exports	4.3	10.7	12.2	6.4	2.3	12.7
Imports	18.0	−10.1	−5.3	−10.0	4.8	−0.2
Terms of trade	−2.4	−0.4	−1.7	5.1	−1.9	−7.9
	Million current US dollars					
Trade balance	−7 225	−6 086	−4 323	−3 093	−2 240	−1 739
Exports	6 794	8 978	10 205	10 241	9 914	10 254
Imports	14 019	15 064	14 528	13 334	12 154	11 993
Balance on services						
and transfers	3 564	3 795	3 377	2 629	2 514	2 243
Remittances	1 710	1 539	2 443	1 944	1 705	1 789
Tourism	1 183	1 515	1 073	844	929	998
Transportation	731	832	899	855	714	750
Interest	−633	−1 084	−1 621	−1 773	−1 532	−1 638
Other	573	993	583	759	698	344
Balance on current account	−3 661	−2 291	−946	−464	274	504
Capital account	2 200	2 100	600	−888	−31	32
Change in reserves[a]	1 461	191	346	1 352	−245	−536
Gross foreign debt	..	..	..	..	20 501	20 533
Net foreign debt	16 811	18 911	19 511	18 623	18 653	18 583

Source: As for table 3.7.1.

[a] Minus sign indicates a *rise* in reserves.

decline of about 9 per cent between 1978 and 1984. The volume of exports in 1984 was about 34 per cent higher than in 1979 while the volume of imports was 20 per cent lower.

The adjustment in terms of *convertible currency transactions* (table 3.7.6) was even larger than the overall adjustment. The value of Yugoslav exports in convertible currency has grown by about 40 per cent between 1979 and 1984, while imports fell by some 30 per cent. The trade deficit in 1984 was only 18 per cent of that in 1979. With a decreasing but still substantial surplus on services and transfers, the huge current account deficit of some $3.3 billion in 1979 has been eliminated and in 1984 was in surplus for the second year running. This is a significant adjustment and has helped to keep the level of gross foreign debt in convertible currencies unchanged since 1981 and even to reduce it somewhat in 1983 and 1984. However, due to high interest rates and the unfavourable maturity structure of the debt, the *debt servicing ratio* has continued to grow and in 1984 was about 37 per cent.

(iii) Foreign trade and structural imbalances

Throughout the 1970s and early 1980s, Yugoslavia always had a large surplus on the services and transfers account, and this partly offset the deficit in merchandise trade. However, from 1970 merchandise imports started to expand faster than exports and the export-import ratio fell from around 70 per cent to only 48 per cent in 1979, one of the lowest ever recorded. Among the reasons for this growing imbalance, the most prominent is the role played by structural imbalances. These reflect a lack of effective macro-economic development policy.

In fact, balanced economic growth can be achieved in various ways which can be grouped around two main approaches. In the centrally planned economies, overall balance is maintained mostly by means of directive planning based on sets of material balances drawn up at a greater or lesser degree of aggregation. These are used to harmonize developments in different branches in terms of physical units, calculated according to inter-sectoral (input-output) relations in the form of "technical coefficients". In market economies, in particular in "open" market economies, developments in different branches are reconciled by market forces—both within the national market and, via exports and imports, on the international market. Faster growth of some

branches within the national economy in the latter case thus comes about either through the faster growth of vertically connected branches via market forces or through larger imports of inputs which are not produced domestically in sufficient quantities. To provide a balanced overall economic development, of course, a corresponding expansion of exports by other sectors is needed.

In the first decade of its post-war development, Yugoslavia relied mainly on the first method of co-ordination. The material balance system was implemented by directive planning. At the end of the 1950s, the second method based on market forces and the orientation of investments by means of financial mechanisms was applied. Where necessary, imports compensated for shortfalls in production in individual branches. At the end of the 1960s and in particular through the 1970s, however, both approaches lost ground. In fact, the country entered a phase in which there was no effective mechanism to bring about macro-economic structural adjustments. Yugoslavia has thus become increasingly import-dependent in many sectors. Since in general export-oriented growth weakened, and the country in many respects proved to be inward- rather than outward-looking, economic development became increasingly vulnerable both to internal bottlenecks and to constraints in the foreign trade sector.

The lack of necessary macro-economic co-ordination may be illustrated by developments in the main output sectors. Throughout the 1960s and 1970s industrial output expanded on average by 6.2 per cent, while that of agriculture by only 2.3 per cent and forestry by 1.5 per cent.[106] This implies lagging production not only of foodstuffs but also of many raw materials. Within industry itself, structural imbalances were also very sharp: there were large variations in the relative growth of output in branches which are linked by inter-sectoral flows. Imbalanced expansion of processing industries as compared with the production of raw materials led to the country being heavily dependent on imports even for products where there were significant national resources. Imports of energy and raw materials grew persistently and in 1979 had reached almost 64 per cent of the total.[107]

---

[106] Calculated on the basis of *Statistički godišnjak 1981*, p. 157.

[107] *Saopštenje*, No. 415, Belgrade, 23 December 1983, p. 22.

TABLE 3.7.6

Yugoslavia: balance of payments and foreign debt, convertible currency transactions
Million current US dollars

	1979	1980	1981	1982	1983	1984
Trade balance	−6 570	−5 665	−4 880	−3 781	−1 798	−1 171
Exports.	4 766	5 656	5 720	5 854	6 271	6 588
Imports.	11 338	11 321	10 600	9 635	8 069	7 759
Balance on services and transfers .	3 266	3 462	3 059	2 361	2 097	2 036
Remittances	..	1 527*	2 430	1 927	1 671	1 757
Tourism	..	1 488*	1 038	801	879	954
Transportation	..	729	758	742	622	680
Interest.	..	−1 051	−1 590	−1 733	−1 489	−1 595
Other	..	769	423	624	414	240
Balance on current account. . . .	−3 304	−2 203	−1 821	−1 420	299	865
Capital account	1 843	2 012	1 475	58	54	329
Changes in reserves[a]	1 461	191	346	1 352	245	536
Gross foreign debt	15 317	17 329	18 804	18 862	18 808	18 479
Convertible debt service ratio[b,c].	..	..	24.8	27.0	34.2	37.0

Source: As for table 3.7.1.

[a] Minus sign indicates a *rise* in reserves.

[b] Ratio of total convertible debt service to all convertible currency receipts.

[c] Includes medium- and long-term debt.

From this point of view, Yugoslav stabilization policy needed to achieve much more than a reduction in domestic demand and an expansion of exports. It required a substantial restructuring of the national economy in line with its natural resource endowment and comparative advantages. The possibilities for such a restructuring have so far been very limited, as it is generally the case that weak output growth does not provide a favourable environment for large structural adjustments. In fact, in 1984 national production of energy and industrial raw materials was almost 15 per cent higher than in 1979: industrial production in general and equipment and consumer goods in particular, were 16-17 per cent higher.[108] Hence the gap between the growth of manufactures and raw materials and energy production has narrowed, but large differences in the levels of output nevertheless remain. To overcome existing imbalances, the share of energy and raw materials in total imports increased to 83 per cent in 1984.[109] But even this was not enough to remove all the bottlenecks that had accumulated and many branches are still working at 60-70 per cent of their capacities.

Low capacity utilization, coupled with rigid cost levels (partly reflecting the costs of servicing credits, but also the difficulties of reallocating labour within the Yugoslav economic system) highlights the nature of Yugoslav inflation which tends to move inversely with the growth of output (chart 3.7.1). The same factors explain why after 1980—when imbalances in the domestic output structure could no longer be offset by imports—there was no trade-off between unemployment and inflation. In fact inflation and unemployment grew at the same time (chart 3.7.2). Thus, in spite of an unquestionable adjustment in the foreign sector, economic policy in Yugoslavia has not yet achieved a comparable degree of domestic stabilization in line with the programme adopted in mid-1983.

---

[108] *Saopštenje* (Communiqué), No. 568, 25 December 1984, p. 13.
[109] *Ibid.*, p. 20.

(iv) Development prospects

Given the complex constraints on growth discussed above, the implementation of the long-term stabilization programme (and, therefore, sustained economic recovery) requires several essential conditions to be met of which the main ones are as follows:

— medium-term rescheduling of the foreign loans due for repayment in the second half of the 1980s: the annual arrangements of the three last years did not give enough breathing space to tackle the crucial problems of structural imbalance;

— a mechanism for securing a rational allocation of national income between wages and net capital formation;

— concentration of the available investment resources so as to eliminate the main bottlenecks, particularly in the supply of energy and a number of critical raw materials required for both industry and agriculture;

— changes in current economic policy which would maintain progress towards possible real interest and realistic foreign exchange rates and towards a more realistic and more consistent system of relative prices (as compared with those of the 1970s and early 1980s, which were largely responsible for the structural imbalances within the country);

— a medium- and long-term development policy which would seek a consistent specialization among all the federal units according to comparative advantages;

— changes in the economic system which would provide more room for the effective operation of market forces and far more efficient macro-economic policy-making including country-wide planning.

The Yugoslav authorities have already undertaken steps to create these conditions. At the end of 1984 the Yugoslav authorities proposed a multi-year rescheduling of the country's foreign debt: this is now under consideration.

Considerable efforts are being made to remove energy and raw materials bottlenecks and production of electricity, coal, pig iron,

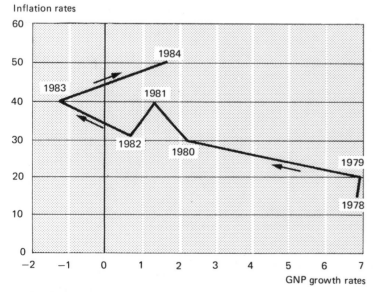

CHART 3.7.1

Gross national product and inflation

(Annual percentage change)

Source: National statistics.

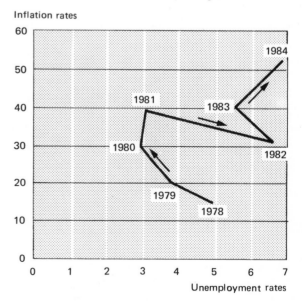

CHART 3.7.2

Unemployment and inflation

(Annual percentage change)

Source: National statistics.

steel and aluminium, etc., improved significantly in 1984. Since April 1984 substantive changes have been made in interest rate policy and these are expected to yield results during the first half of 1985. There have been a number of measures of price liberalization and the policy of continuously adjusting the exchange rate to the rate of internal inflation has been strictly followed. Other measures have sought to improve the efficiency of the national banking system, to achieve more realistic pricing of both factor inputs and outputs of enterprises, to enlarge the scope for foreign participation and investment in the Yugoslav economy, and to reform the foreign exchange system which has been blamed as a major source of allocational inefficiency.

Against this background of wide-ranging policy measures, the Yugoslav authorities envisage a growth rate of social product of more than 3 per cent in 1985 (more than 4 per cent for industry and 2.5 per cent for agriculture). There should be some increase in employment and a 1.5 per cent growth of labour productivity. Exports should reach some $12 billion (12 per cent increase as compared with 1984, including 15 per cent growth in convertible currency receipts), while invisibles should increase to $3.7 billion. With stagnant public consumption and stable real incomes, there should be a surplus on current account of $900 million. With rescheduling of part of the maturing debt, this should allow regular debt servicing and a reduction in the total foreign debt by some $400 million.

Given the progress made in 1984, these forecasts are not out of reach, but neither can they be taken for granted. The adjustments so far have been achieved at a high price in terms of unemployment, falling real incomes and so forth, and many Yugoslav commentators doubt whether there is very much room left for manoeuvre. But as international conditions in 1985 are not expected to differ substantially from those in 1984, a comprehensive improvement in economic development in Yugoslavia, as in previous years, will have to depend largely on more consistent and more substantial changes in macro-economic policy and in the economic system.

Chapter 4

EASTERN EUROPE AND THE SOVIET UNION

4.1 GENERAL DEVELOPMENTS

Aggregate net material product (NMP)—the usual measure of national output in the centrally planned economies—increased by some 3 1/2 per cent in eastern Europe and the Soviet Union in 1984. This compares with 4 per cent recorded in 1983. The upturn in economic growth which started in 1983 thus continued, though somewhat more slowly. The overall change recorded for the region in 1984 conceals a noticeable difference in the pace of economic growth in eastern Europe compared with the Soviet Union. In eastern Europe the expansion of net material product (NMP) produced picked up from almost 4 per cent in 1983 to more than 5 per cent in 1984. In the Soviet Union, the growth of net material product used for domestic consumption and accumulation weakened from 3 1/2 per cent in 1983 to 2 1/2 per cent in 1984. Growth of Soviet NMP produced in 1984 moderated from 4 to an estimated 3 per cent. Soviet performance was affected by a contraction in crop production which led to stagnation of total gross agricultural output in 1984. In eastern Europe, agricultural output surged by almost 7 per cent over its 1983 level—which was itself the highest ever achieved by the six countries as a whole. This gave an important boost to the acceleration of NMP growth. Industrial expansion in 1984 was higher than in 1983 in both eastern Europe and the Soviet Union—particularly in the former. Aggregated annual plan targets for 1985 call for NMP growth of over 4 per cent in the region as a whole—somewhat less than that in the Soviet Union—and of almost 5 per cent in eastern Europe.

Developments in 1984 and those anticipated in the annual plans for 1985 confirm that the centrally planned economies of eastern Europe and the Soviet Union are currently aiming to stabilize medium-term growth at rates similar to 1983-1984. This objective is to be combined with the attainment of higher overall efficiency, a priority which overrides the acceleration of economic growth. Nevertheless, the transition to an "intensive" (i.e. resource efficient) path of economic growth appeared to be much more complex than envisaged. National policy documents now claim that the countries of the region are in fact only at the first stage of a comprehensive intensification of economic and social development. Statements on the economic strategy to be followed in the five-year plans for 1986-1990 and long-term plans to 1995 or 2000 emphasize that a transformation of the patterns of growth will be required in the second half of the 1980s.

Both supply and demand factors contributed to changes in the pace of economic growth in the region. On the supply side, the acceleration in economic growth was assisted by the removal of the bottlenecks which braked performance in 1979-1982. This was coupled with greater efficiency in the use of many material

inputs, in some countries in particular. However, factor productivity other than labour productivity lagged behind expectations. Indeed, capital productivity continues to decline. During the last two years significant changes also occurred on the demand side. This is especially true for investment expenditures in eastern Europe: they contracted in 1980-1982 but expanded by 2 per cent in 1983 and by an estimated 3 1/2 per cent in 1984. The same is true for the Soviet Union where investment growth averaging 3 per cent in 1980-1982 was followed by a jump of almost 6 per cent in 1983 and an additional 2 per cent in 1984. Thanks to the acceleration in output growth, consumption also expanded in most countries, with some variation in growth rates between personal (private) and social (public) consumption. Nevertheless, resources for domestic use (net material product used for domestic consumption and accumulation) continued to lag behind NMP produced. This highlights the fact that the fastest rising demand component remained exports, the expansion of which outstripped the growth of output. Increased surpluses on the balance of trade eased debt servicing problems in those countries which had them. After several years of a virtual freeze, some new credit lines were opened in 1984 by financial institutions in the market economies in favour of the centrally planned countries of the region.

With regard to individual countries it is noteworthy that the deceleration of output growth in Bulgaria, which due to the bad harvest in 1983 persisted through that year, was checked in 1984. Poland recorded NMP growth of more than 5 per cent for the second year running and is thus gradually returning to a normal development path.[110] Developments in this country nevertheless still merit attention. NMP produced in Poland in 1984 attained only roughly the 1975 level and external financial constraints still pose a considerable challenge. The German Democratic Republic and Romania recorded the highest growth rates among the seven economies of the region, but NMP growth in 1984 also accelerated in Czechoslovakia and Hungary. This was so particularly in the latter country in which output virtually stagnated in 1983.

In the rest of this section, the main themes underlining the general developments summarized above are presented under te following headings: (i) the pace of recent and medium-term growth; (ii) patterns of economic growth; (iii) factor inputs and

---

[110] For this reason the group "eastern Europe excluding Poland", contained in tables in the last three *Surveys*, is omitted in this edition.

efficiency; (iv) foreign economic relations; (v) resources for domestic use; and (vi) policy objectives for 1985.

(i) The pace of recent and medium-term growth

Economic developments in the region in 1983-1984 may be viewed from four different aspects: against the background of the decelerating trends recorded in the second half of the 1970s and at the beginning of the 1980s; of the average paces of growth laid down in the five-year plans for 1981-1985; of the relationship between the annual and five-year plans and also the likelihood of implementing the latter (table 4.1.1, appendix table B.1 and chart 4.1.1).

Chart 4.1.1A clearly indicates the basic features of *recent economic developments* and their role in the years 1980-1984. Aggregated NMP changes for both eastern Europe alone and including the Soviet Union suggest that the decelerating trend in the region was checked as early as 1981. However, some other evidence suggests that the forces responsible for the deceleration in economic growth were not in fact overcome until 1982.

In the first place, it is important to note that NMP produced in eastern Europe in 1982 virtually stagnated. The change in the aggregate NMP growth rate of the six countries concerned from negative to slightly positive in that year resulted mainly from the smaller absolute decline in Polish NMP (a fall of 5 1/2 per cent in 1982 as compared with a 12 per cent decline in 1981). In fact, the combined NMP growth rate of the five other east European countries in 1982 (just over 2 per cent) was still lower than that in 1981 (just under 3 per cent). On the other hand, changes in Soviet NMP growth rates, due to wide fluctuations in agricultural output, do not necessarily indicate changes in the underlying development trend. Indeed, chart 4.1.1B and Appendix table B.13 clearly show that a substantial recovery in agricultural growth—from a 1 per cent decline in 1981 to a 5 1/2 per cent rise in 1982—masked a continuing slowdown in Soviet industrial production. A clear reversal of the underlying trend of decelerating growth, which characterized the second half of the 1970s and the beginning of the 1980s, could only be achieved by a change in the trend of industrial growth—by far the largest sectoral contributor to the country's NMP growth in most years. Chart 4.1.1C and Appendix table B.11 show that this reversal did not occur until 1983. Thus the years 1983-1984 appear to be the turning point for NMP growth in the region as a whole.[111]

Developments in 1983-1984 can also be assessed *relative to the average annual NMP growth rates as envisaged by the five-year plans* for 1981-1985 (table 4.1.1 and chart 4.1.2). The relationships between average annual NMP growth rates laid down in the five-year plans and the annual NMP growth rates actually recorded by most countries suggest that the period 1981-1984 could be divided into two. The transitional year between the two sub-periods is either 1982 or, in some countries, 1983. In the first sub-period, annual NMP growth rates in some countries were below the average targets of the five-year plans, while in the second they exceeded them. This was the case in Czechoslovakia and Poland (the three-year plan in Poland is taken as a substitute for the five-year plan here). However, this pattern is not so clear cut in the other countries. In Bulgaria, in spite of the deceleration which lasted through 1983, actual NMP growth rates in 1981-1984 were above the average annual NMP growth rate envisaged by the five-year plan in all years but 1983. In the Soviet Union, where the annual NMP target within the five-year plan itself is broken into

---

[111] This was pointed out also by the *Financial Times*, 12 November 1984, p. 7: "The most noticeable feature of developments in Comecon recently has been the general economic upturn, beginning in 1983 and apparently continuing into this year."

CHART 4.1.1.

Net material product and sectoral gross output

(Annual percentage change)

Eastern Europe — ·— ·— ·—
Soviet Union ············
Eastern Europe
and Soviet Union ————

A. NET MATERIAL PRODUCT

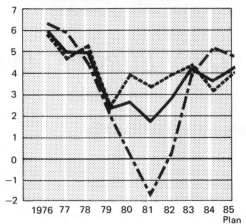

B. GROSS AGRICULTURAL OUTPUT

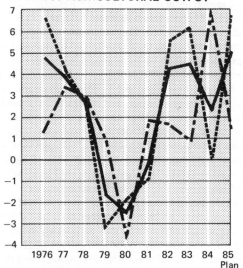

C. GROSS INDUSTRIAL OUTPUT

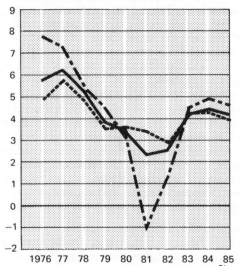

Source: National statistics.

TABLE 4.1.1

Net material product
(*Annual percentage change*)

	1976-1980	1981	1982	1983	1984	Plan 1985	Plan 1981-1985	Plan 1981-1985[a]	1981-1985[b]
Bulgaria	6.1	5.0	4.2	3.0	4.6*	4.1	3.7	4.1	4.2
Czechoslovakia	3.7	0.1	0.2	2.3	3.0	3.0	1.6-2.2	1.9	1.7
German Democratic Republic .	4.2	4.8	2.6	4.4	5.5	4.4	5.1	4.6	4.3
Hungary	2.8	2.5	2.6	0.3	2.8-3.0	2.3-2.8	2.7-3.2	1.8	2.2
Poland	1.2	−12.0	−5.5	6.0	5.1	3-3.5	3.5-5.6[c]	2.7	4.7*[d]
Romania	7.3	2.2	2.7	3.7	7.7	10.0	7.5	6.9	5.2
Eastern Europe	3.9	−1.9	0.1	3.9	5.1	4.8	3.3	. .	2.4
Soviet Union	4.3	3.3	3.9	4.2	3.0*	4.0*	3.8*	3.8*	3.7
	3.8[e]	3.2[e]	3.6[e]	3.6[e]	2.6[e]	3.5[e]	3.4[e]	3.3[e]	3.3[e]
Eastern Europe and the Soviet Union	4.2	1.7	2.8	4.1	3.6	4.2	3.7*	. .	3.3

Source: National statistics, plan and plan fulfilment reports.

[a] Five-year growth rate implied by the annual plans 1981-1985.

[b] Implied by actual growth rates 1981-1984 and annual growth rate planned for 1985.

[c] Three-year plan 1983-1985.

[d] Implied by actual growth rates 1983-1984 and annual growth rate planned for 1985.

[e] Net material product used for domestic consumption and accumulation.

NMP objectives for individual years, actual NMP growth was below the average five-year target in 1981, above it in 1982-1983 but below it in 1984.

In the German Democratic Republic, and especially in Romania, actual NMP growth mostly remained below the average annual rate envisaged by the five-year plan. In fact, NMP growth in both countries in 1984 rose slightly above the average five-year target for the first time in the current quinquennium. In Hungary actual NMP growth rates remained below the average annual five-year plan objectives in all years since 1980. Indeed, only the highest (3 per cent) annual NMP growth rate attained during 1981-1984 approached the average growth objective retained in the five-year plan (2.7-3.2 per cent).

The *relationship between annual and five-year plans* is also of interest. In all countries of the region the five-year plans are the main planning instruments. Annual plans are considered to embody the tactical initiatives needed to implement the five-year plan strategy. Hence, it is recognized that annual plans may respond to changing circumstances and even depart from the path laid down in the five-year plans. Such departures are, however, expected to be temporary. Any deviation of annual plans over several years from the general line determined by the five-year plan is usually described as an adjustment or refinement of the five-year plan. It can, however, constitute more than that.

An analysis of such deviations (chart 4.1.2) suggests several conclusions. First, the similarity between the growth curves of annual plan targets and of actual growth rates in most countries indicates that the authorities were already aware of growth constraints at the beginning of the 1980s (table 4.1.1 and chart 4.1.2). The lag of actual NMP growth rates at the beginning of the period compared with plans could indicate that the strength of these constraints were underestimated when the five-year plans were prepared. In contrast, when the adjustment policy began, policy-makers tended to take a cautious stance in framing annual plan targets. This is indicated by the fact that actual NMP growth rates in the second half of the quinquennium were above the annual plan targets.

Second, a comparison of the average annual NMP growth rates of the five-year plans for the period 1981-1985 and the combined annual NMP targets contained in the annual plans for the same period shows the relationship between the two kinds of plan. Three main situations can be identified. Taking into account the good performance in 1981-1982, the Bulgarian annual plans upgraded the five-year NMP target from 3.7 per cent foreseen in the five-year plan to more than 4 per cent implied by the corresponding annual plans. The relationship between the two sets of targets is somewhat different in the Soviet Union and Czechoslovakia. The combined targets for net material product used for domestic consumption and accumulation contained in the last five annual plans of the Soviet Union imply virtually the same average annual rate (3.3 per cent) as that incorporated in the five-year plan (3.4 per cent). The average annual NMP produced growth rate implied by annual plans of Czechoslovakia (1.9 per cent) falls within the margin envisaged by the five-year plan (1.6-2.2 per cent). Finally, in the German Democratic Republic, Hungary, Poland and Romania, the combined NMP targets of successive annual plans indicate some scaling down relative to the NMP growth targets envisaged in their corresponding five-year plans (three-year plan 1983-1985 in the case of Poland). However, since the difference between the two sets of five-year average NMP growth rates ranges from 1/2 to less than 1 percentage point, it can be concluded that in those cases also the annual plans remained within the limits of adjustment and refinement of the medium-term plans.

Finally, actual NMP growth rates recorded in 1981-1984 can be combined with the NMP growth rate targeted for 1985 in order to assess *potential overall implementation of the five-year plans.* A comparison between implied five-year performance and the average NMP growth rates of the five-year plans can then be made. The exercise suggests that, if actual NMP growth in 1985 develops according to the annual plan for that year, Bulgaria will achieve faster economic development than envisaged in its five-year plan. For the Soviet Union, the average growth rate of NMP used for domestic consumption and accumulation would virtually coincide with its five-year plan. In Czechoslovakia,

CHART 4.1.2.

Net material product

(Annual percentage change)

Actual growth ———   Five-year plans ----------   Annual plans —·—·—

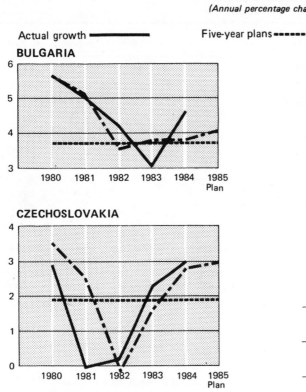

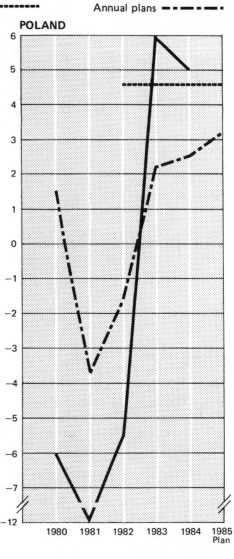

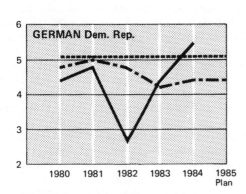

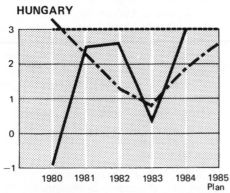

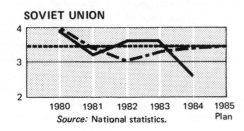

Source: National statistics.

actual performance on the same assumption will be slightly above the lower margin of the rate envisaged in the five-year plan. The likely outcome for Poland is similar relative to its three-year plan for 1983-1985. In the three remaining countries, even if NMP growth rates envisaged by the annual plan for 1985 are achieved, average annual NMP growth rates will lag behind the five-year plan targets by about one sixth in the case of the German Democratic Republic, one quarter in Hungary and by about one third in Romania. However, it should be mentioned that both the five-year and the annual 1985 objectives for Romania are the most ambitious of the region.

(ii) Patterns of economic growth

As already shown in section (i), industry and agriculture play different roles in determining the pace of economic growth of the centrally planned economies. Industry, as the biggest sector, determines medium- and long-term rates of growth while agriculture is the main contributor to short-term fluctuations. The comparisons between the roles of the two sectors in output changes presented earlier were, nevertheless, indicative rather than conclusive. This is because the changes in gross output of industry and agriculture were compared with overall net material product. Moreover, no other sector was considered.

To provide a more reliable comparison between total and sectoral outputs and thus to highlight patterns of economic growth, total gross output and the sectoral gross outputs of industry, agriculture and construction are presented in table 4.1.2 and chart 4.1.3. Some significant features of the gross output indicator should, however, first be pointed out.

First, it should be kept in mind that gross output as defined in the seven countries of the region includes not only fixed capital costs as in gross national product (GNP) in the System of National Accounts (SNA system) of output measurement, but also the intermediate consumption of material goods and services. This is so for both total output (usually referred to as gross social or gross material product) and sectoral output. This implies that gross output contains an element of double counting of items which are produced in one sector and processed in another. Comparisons between total and sectoral gross output therefore contain the implicit assumption that the degree of double counting is similar at both national and sectoral level, and also over time. Both assumptions may be questioned over long time periods, but in the short to medium term they can be taken as realistic. In any case changes in the gross output of industry, agriculture and, in some countries, also construction, regularly published in plan fulfilment reports issued at the beginning of

TABLE 4.1.2

Gross material product by sector
(Annual percentage change)

	1976-1980	1980	1981	1982	1983	1984	Plan 1985
Bulgaria							
GMP total	5.9	6.0	5.9	3.3	3.6	4.7*	4.7*
Industry	6.0	4.2	4.9	4.6	3.9	4.6	5.2
Agriculture	2.1	−4.6	5.9	5.2	−7.2	6.8	3.2
Construction	5.9	3.6	5.9	3.0	3.1	3.6	..
Czechoslovakia							
GMP total	3.7	2.9	0.3	0.9	2.9	3.2*	1.8*
Industry	4.7	3.5	2.1	1.1	2.8	3.9	3.0
Agriculture	1.6	4.8	−2.5	4.5	4.2	3.6	−1.1
Construction	3.0	1.9	−1.8	−3.8	2.8	1.7	1.2
German Democratic Republic							
GMP total	4.3	4.1	3.7	0.3	2.6	4.4*	3.5*
Industry	5.0	4.7	4.7	3.2	4.2	4.2	3.8
Agriculture	1.3	0.7*	1.6*	−4.0*	4.1*	8.5*	−1.0*
Construction	3.3	1.4	4.1	3.0	2.9	2.5	3.4
Hungary							
GMP total	3.4	−0.6	2.8	2.5	0.9	2.1*	2.5*
Industry	3.4	−1.7	2.4	2.5	1.4	3	3.0
Agriculture	2.9	4.6	2.0	7.3	−2.7	2.5-3.0	1.0
Construction	2.4	−3.0	−0.2	0.5	−3.4	−(4-5)	1.0-2.0
Poland							
GMP total	1.2	−5.9	−12.1	−5.6	5.9	5.5*	2.9*
Industry	4.7	0.0	−10.9	−2.2	6.4	5.3	4.0-4.5
Agriculture	0.5	−10.7	3.8	−2.8	3.3	5.7	−(0.8)-1.4
Construction	−0.5	−10.0	−21.0	−6.1	6.4	6.9	..
Romania							
GMP total	6.8	3.4	0.4	2.5	3.0	7.8*	7.4*
Industry	9.5	6.5	2.6	1.1	4.7	6.7	6.0-6.0
Agriculture	4.9	−4.3	−0.9	7.6	−1.6	13.3	6.0-6.8
Construction	5.8	−0.8	−4.8	1.0	..	..	..
Soviet Union							
GMP total	4.2	3.6	3.2	3.4	4.2	3.3*	4.3*
Industry	4.5	3.6	3.4	2.9	4.2	4.2	3.9
Agriculture	1.7	−1.9	−1.0	5.5	6.1	0.0	5.8
Construction	2.6	1.2	2.0	2.8	..	3.0	..

Source: National statistics; *Statisticheskii ezhegodnik stran-chlenov SEV 1983* (CMEA Statistical Yearbook 1983), pp. 17-24; plans and plan fulfilment reports.

CHART 4.1.3.

Patterns of economic growth

(Indices, 1978 = 100)

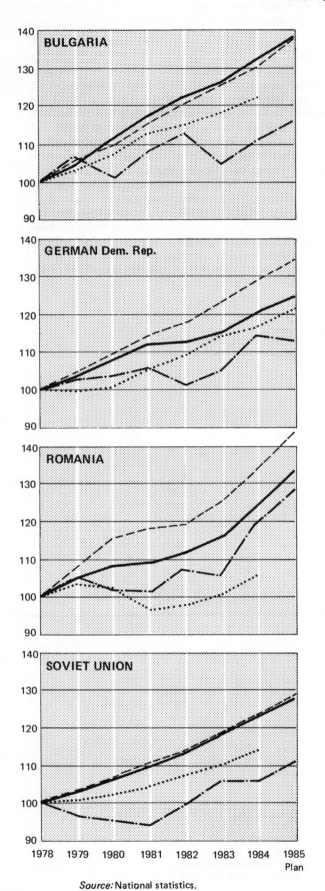

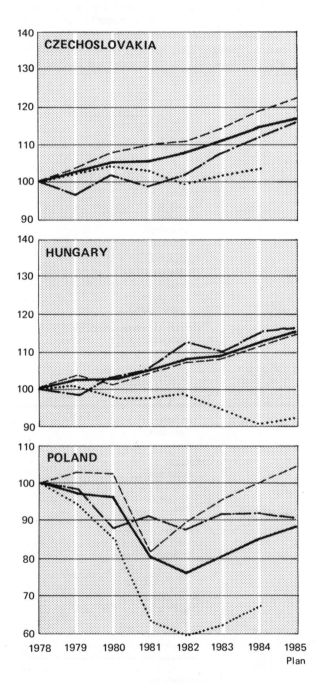

Total ————————

Industry – – – – – – –

Agriculture – · – · – · – · –

Construction ··················

Source: National statistics.

each year to summarize performance in the previous year, are the only output indicators available.

Another problem with gross output as a measurement of national and sectoral output stems from the fact that plan fulfilment reports issued at the beginning of each year on developments in the preceding year do not usually contain any information on change in aggregate gross output. This is available only later on, in either national or CMEA statistical yearbooks. Changes in the pattern of economic growth in 1984 can therefore be assessed either by comparing overall net total output and sectoral gross output, or by estimating total gross output. In most previous *Surveys* the first approach was used. In this sub-section, however, the second approach will be attempted.

To provide a more consistent inter-country comparison, changes in total gross output are calculated on the basis of indices regularly published for all countries of the region, except Poland, in the statistical yearbooks of the Council of Mutual Economic Assistance (CMEA). For Poland national figures are used for total gross output, and also for sectoral gross outputs. Where changes in gross output of construction for 1984 or even 1983 have not yet been reported in national sources, they were estimated on the basis of reported or estimated changes in investment and in particular on the share of construction work in total investment.

It is clear from the data assembled in this way that changes in *total gross output* closely follow both the direction and the size of changes in *industrial gross output* (table 4.1.2 and chart 4.1.3). This reflects the high share of industry in total national production.[112] Nevertheless, the relationship between changes in total and industrial gross outputs are not the same in all countries. They are virtually parallel in Bulgaria, Hungary and the Soviet Union; they diverge somewhat, but are still very close in Czechoslovakia, and diverge more widely in the German Democratic Republic, Poland and Romania. On the other hand, it is noteworthy that in six out of the seven countries in 1978-1984 the indices of industrial gross output shown in chart 4.1.3 were higher than those of total gross output—except in Bulgaria after 1979. The annual changes in *agricultural gross output* shown in table 4.1.2 and the indices in chart 4.1.3 demonstrate that changes in this sector were much larger than in industry. They were very volatile in some countries. In spite of the relatively low shares of agriculture in total national production,[113] therefore, this volatility caused considerable fluctuations in the total output of individual countries—for instance in the German Democratic Republic in 1982 and in the Soviet Union in 1984.

Over the medium term, however, it seems that agriculture consistently played an influential role—particularly, in different ways, in Hungary, Poland and the Soviet Union. In *Hungary* agriculture was the fastest expanding sector and it has pulled overall growth upward since 1979. Even in the short run, falls in Hungary's agricultural production should be interpreted, bearing in mind the unusually strong rise in output in 1982, as fluctuations around the post-1979 trend. Hungarian agriculture thus mitigated the decelerating trend of output from the end of the 1970s to the beginning of the 1980s. At the same time, it provided

sizeable export surpluses. In *Poland* agriculture has played a different but nevertheless positive role in the medium-term growth of Polish output. Imported agricultural inputs were cut back sharply in 1979 and 1980, and gross agricultural output in Poland fell by 12 per cent in those years. It subsequently fluctuated around this lower level, while industrial output continued to fall throughout 1982. Its below average import dependence, and also institutional factors, made Polish agriculture more resistent to output-inhibiting constraints than any other sector. Total gross output thus fell by less than it might have done otherwise.

In the *Soviet Union*, agriculture had a quite different and indeed substantial growth-inhibiting influence. The fall of agricultural output in three consecutive years (1979-1981) reinforced other growth constraints which were at their strongest at that time. The gross output and net material product growth rates recorded in 1979 were the lowest of the post-war period, and mainly reflected the decline in agricultural output. In 1984, zero growth of gross agricultural output again depressed the gross and net material product growth rates, and halted the acceleration which had begun in 1983. An exceptional sequence of unfavourable climatic conditions, particularly in 1979-1982, largely explains Soviet agricultural performance. However, the country's size, as well as its geographical and climatic variety, suggests that weather is not the only explanation.[114] Soviet commentators have themselves pointed out that "normal" climatic conditions (i.e. the most frequent or average conditions) should be distinguished from desired or optimal weather. Policy now leans towards concentration of production on land where the effect of weather can to some extent be controlled, rather than towards further extension of agricultural land. This would provide a more stable basis for Soviet agricultural output, in particular grain production. A decree issued in October 1984 focuses directly on this objective, and other steps to improve agricultural performance have been undertaken.

Finally, it should be mentined that the data presented suggest that *construction* was not an important determinant of overall growth performance in any of the countries of the region (see also chart 4.1.3). Indeed, gross output of construction fell by much more than agriculture and industry in Poland, and declined or remained stable in three other countries in which total gross output decelerated strongly (Czechoslovakia, Hungary and Romania). In Bulgaria and the Soviet Union, construction output rose but at a much slower pace than in industry. These developments are not unexpected, since variations in economic growth tend to affect construction more than any other sector. The revival of construction output in 1983-1984, when the pace of economic activity turned upwards in all countries but Hungary, confirms this. The continuing decline in Hungarian construction output can also be interpreted in terms of the emphasis placed on using existing capacities more efficiently and limiting new starts. However, the steep decline in the Hungarian accumulation ratio[115] may also indicate that net capital formation in Hungary

---

[112] In NMP terms, the share of industry in national output ranged over the region between 44.2 per cent for Hungary and 68.7 per cent for the German Democratic Republic in 1980, and between 45.3 per cent and 68.5 per cent for the same two countries in 1983. *Statisticheskii ezhegodnik stran-chlenov SEV 1984* (CMEA Statistical Yearbook 1984), Moscow, 1984, p. 39.

[113] These ranged between 8.4 per cent in the German Democratic Republic and 17.0 per cent in Bulgaria in 1980, and 7.8 per cent in the German Democratic Republic and 20.3 per cent in the Soviet Union in 1983 (NMP terms), *ibid.*

[114] In commentaries on crop results in 1984, it was stated: "The sector [agriculture] is not developing steadily. During the years of the 10th five-year plan fluctuations in grain production reached 58 million tonnes. This year too the drought did considerable damage. There is a great diversity in yields, sometimes even on neighbouring farms. Skill and zonal agricultural techniques, tried and tested in practice, are not skilfully brought into play everywhere against bad weather. As a rule, it is because of poor organisation that crop rotation and new varieties are introduced only slowly and the schedules for carrying out operations are violated." *Pravda*, 26 November 1984.

[115] In Hungary the share of accumulation (net capital formation) in domestically used NMP was 27.7 per cent in 1975. It declined progressively to only 12.8 per cent in 1983—by far the lowest of the seven countries of the region. See *Statisticheskii ezhegodnik stran-chlenov SEV 1984*, (CMEA Statistical Yearbook 1984), Moscow, 1984, p. 40.

CHART 4.1.4.

Net material product, fixed assets and capital productivity

(Indices, 1980 = 100)

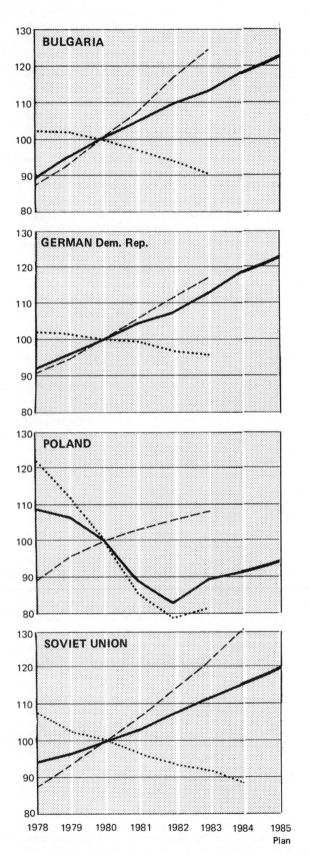

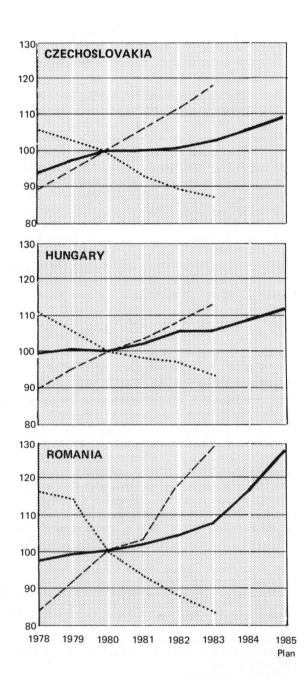

Net material product ———

Fixed assets – – –

Net material product/fixed assets ··········

Source: National statistics.

has fallen below the level necessary to provide balanced economic growth in the future. Any further contraction of construction activity could brake the structural changes necessary to consolidate growth potential under the changed condition of recent years.

(iii) Factor inputs and efficiency

Employment and labour productivity, as well as fixed assets and capital productivity, have been regularly analysed in previous issues of the *Economic Survey of Europe*. At the beginning of 1985, no statistical data on employment in the material sphere were available for most countries of the region in 1984, but information to hand did not suggest any great changes from previous years. It is thus likely that labour productivity continued to grow at rates close to that of NMP or perhaps even higher—for instance in Hungary. Similarly, it can be assumed that capital productivity continued to decline in most countries (chart 4.1.4). Because of recent slowdowns in the growth of fixed assets, however, it is likely that rate of decline of capital productivity moderated. In Poland, where exceptionally low investment slowed down the growth of fixed assets to the point that in 1983 they grew significantly slower than NMP produced, capital productivity in 1984, as well as in 1983, probably rose.

Both labour and capital productivity are discussed in some detail in the sections on agriculture (section 4.2 below) and industry (section 4.3 below). For this reason, this sub-section will focus mainly on material inputs and investment.

(a) *Material inputs and material intensity*

Direct, fully accessible information on material input use is only available by calculating the relationships between output and consumption of individual items (such as electricity, coal, oil, steel, etc.). As shown in a previous edition of this publication,[116] and also in section 4.3 below, several individual material inputs did constrain growth in 1980-1982. The subsequent expansion of output by the respective branches eased bottlenecks while the main production aggregates also expanded at faster rates. The use of such partial indicators is inadequate for an assessment of the relationship between material inputs and the growth of the economy as a whole. There is, however, no physical unit which can be used as a common denominator for all material inputs. Their global role can therefore only be analysed indirectly.

One approach is to compare the growth of gross material product, usually referred to as gross social product, and of net material product. As already mentioned in sub-section 4.1(ii), gross social product is defined as the gross value of the national output of all material sphere sectors.[117] It includes both fixed capital costs (depreciation) and the intermediate consumption of material goods and services. Taking into account that, due to the vertical (sectoral) linkages between economic units, the goods produced in some enterprises are processed in others, gross output clearly includes a significant degree of double counting.[118] This varies from country to country, depending on the extent of vertical integration of economic activities as well as on other

institutional structures.[119] Such differences make it impossible to compare levels of gross output of different countries, but the relationships over time between gross social product and net material product can provide meaningful information.

The ratio of gross social product to net material product, which can be derived in volume terms for all countries of the region, can therefore be taken as an approximate measurement of the material intensity of net material product. The differences between gross social product and net material product include depreciation charges in addition to the value of intermediate material goods and services. This somewhat distorts the result. The distortion remains however within tolerable limits, first because depreciation charges in all countries account for less than 10 per cent of net material product; and second because the ratio of depreciation charges to net material product does not change significantly over time. Its effects will therefore be ignored hereafter.[120]

Ratios of gross social product to net material are presented both for recent years and also for the period 1960-1980 (table 4.1.3).[121]

The figures presented in the table show clearly that during the 1960s growth was based upon an "extensive" rather than on a resource-efficient growth strategy in eastern Europe and the Soviet Union.[122] In fact, in all east European countries except Hungary, gross material product grew by 1-1 1/2 per cent per year faster than NMP. In the Soviet Union, however, gross material product grew somewhat slower than NMP, and material intensity declined. Among other things, this was probably a result of the economic reforms introduced in 1965. In 1971-1975, the ratio of gross to net material product remained virtually unchanged in all east European countries but Poland (where it rose), and Romania (where it declined). NMP growth rates in that period were

---

[116] *Economic Survey of Europe in 1983*, pp. 111-112.

[117] Aggregate social product appears to be a synonym for (gross) social product. It is similarly defined by Academician A. Anchishkin, *National Economic Planning*, Moscow, Progress Publishers, 1980, p. 246.

[118] This is also pointed out in *Basic Principles of the System of Balances of the National Economy*, Series F, No. 17, United Nations, New York, 1971, p. 13, where gross social product is termed as "the global product": "The inclusion of material inputs in the global product means that the value of the product contains an element of duplication."

[119] For example, at current prices the gross social product of Bulgaria in 1983 was 68,782 million leva while net material product amounted to 23,479 leva or 34.1 per cent of the former. In the same year, the gross social product of the Soviet Union (at current prices) was 1,293.9 billion roubles while net material product totalled 548.1 billion roubles or 42.4 per cent of the former. *Statisticheski godishnik na NR B'lgaria* (Statistical Yearbook of Bulgaria), Sofia, 1984, p. 12-13 and *Narodnoe khoziaistvo SSSR v 1983 g.* (Statistical Yearbook of the USSR in 1983), Moscow, 1984, pp. 47 and 407.

A more precise indication of the extent of double counting could be obtained by adding depreciation charges (4-7 per cent of the gross material product) to net material product, but these are not available for all the countries at constant prices. Further to this, it should be noted that comparison between gross and net output within an individual country is feasible as long as gross and net output continue to be identified and measured in enterprises and other economic agents which remain at the same level of organizational subordination over the time period to be examined.

[120] To avoid possible methodological inconsistencies, the calculations are based on data in CMEA statistical yearbooks.

[121] The stability of *annual* changes in the ratio provides implicit confirmation of its reliability, and of its relative freedom from possible breaks in the relationship indicated above. Further indirect confirmation arises from the conclusions they suggest. For instance, the ratio declined fastest in the German Democratic Republic whose successful performance in reducing material inputs per unit of output is frequently taken as a model for other countries of the region.

[122] The still prevailing extensive character of the overall development path in the Soviet Union was also emphasized by Academician A. Aganbeg'ian, Director of the Institute of Economics and Organisation of Industrial Production of the Siberian Department of the USSR Academy of Sciences: "So far approximately two thirds of the country's national economic development has been effected by enlisting additional production resources, that is, extensively. Here the integral (or aggregate) indicator of social production efficiency growth—including the degree to which fixed capital, capital investment, fuel, raw material and manpower are used—increases by approximately 1.5 per cent per year. Of course, this figure satisfied no-one." A. Aganbeg'ian, "Experiment and Self-Financing (Khozraschet)", *Trud*, 28 August 1984.

TABLE 4.1.3

Gross material output to net material output ratio[a]

(Annual percentage changes)

	1961-1970	1971-1975	1976-1980	1981-1984	1981	1982	1983	1984[b]	1961-1984
Bulgaria	1.3	−0.1	−0.2	0.1	0.7	−0.8	0.5	0.1	0.5
Czechoslovakia	0.8	0.2	–	0.6	–	1.1	0.5	0.2	0.5
German Democratic Republic .	1.1	0.2	0.2	−1.5	−1.3	−2.0	−1.7	−1.1	0.3
Hungary	0.4	−0.1	0.6	–	0.2	0.2	0.3	−0.8	0.3
Poland	1.6	1.7	–	−0.6	0.1	−3.3	0.5	0.5	0.5
Romania	0.7	−0.7	−0.2	−0.6	−1.6	–	−0.9	–	–
Soviet Union	−0.2	0.6	−0.2	–	–	−0.5	–	0.3	–

Source: Calculated on the basis *Statisticheskii ezhegodnik stran-chlenov SEV 1984* (CMEA Statistical Yearbook 1984), Moscow 1984, pp. 17-24.

[a] Calculated from the ratio of the index of gross material output divided by the index of net material output.

[b] Estimates.

accompanied by import expansion in the countries concerned. This helped to prevent bottlenecks, which in fact appeared in the late 1970s as inputs were cut back. In the Soviet Union some deterioration in the ratio took place in 1971-1975. As Soviet import dependence is relatively low this cannot be explained in terms of foreign balance constraints. The temporary decline in efficiency therefore could be attributed to a deceleration in the pace of economic reforms. In 1976-1980, further improvements occurred in all the east European countries but the German Democratic Republic and Hungary. In the latter case the rather strong deceleration in NMP growth in 1978-1980 could partly explain the increase in the gross to net output ratio. There was also some decline in material intensity in the Soviet Union in 1976-1980. Finally, almost all countries experienced either unchanged or declining material intensity in 1981-1984: the exception was Czechoslovakia, due to slow NMP growth. Altogether, as for the *direction of changes*, all countries have moved towards more efficient use of material inputs. As already mentioned, the most striking improvements in this respect were achieved by the German Democratic Republic.

With regard to the *degree of change*, developments were much less satisfactory. In fact, the last column of the table indicates that material intensity as described by ratio of gross to net material product has hardly declined over almost a quarter of a century. Indeed, even if allowance is made for somewhat higher depreciation charges in recent years, and for the fact that changes in the degree of vertical integration have contributed to changes in the difference between gross and net output, the data nevertheless indicate no significant decrease in material inputs per unit of output in most countries until recently. Moreover, those recorded recently, except in the German Democratic Republic, did not significantly change *overall material intensity*. Of course this is not to deny that in some sectors—as, for instance, in industry (see section 4.3 below)—material intensity may meanwhile have declined, at least in some countries.[123] It simply takes into account overall changes in gross-to-net output ratios.[124]

Two other points should be taken into account in interpreting these findings. First, the overall level of material intensity in

most countries of the region is still very high judged by contemporary technological standards—about 40 per cent higher than in the most developed market economies according to some experts.[125] Second, even in the Soviet Union—and still more in eastern Europe—energy and raw material production cannot in future rise at previous rates. Development of the remaining deposits of these resources will entail higher exploration and transport costs. Thus, increasing scarcity and higher costs of developing new energy and raw material resources can be only partly offset by improved use of existing technologies in the short- to medium-term. In the longer term they can only be solved by large-scale introduction of new technologies, accompanied by far-reaching changes in the structure of output and resource use.[126] The achievement of lasting economies of energy and raw

---

[123] According to M. R. Eidel'man, *Statistika obshchestvennogo produkta i natsionalnogo dokhoda v SSSR*, Moscow, Statistika, 1980, p. 8, in the Soviet Union, ever since the 1960s, "...the size of the increment in national income [NMP] in all branches of material production except in agriculture in all periods outstripped the size of the increment in social product. In agriculture there were opposite tendencies in the same periods. Only in years with good harvests (1966, 1970 and 1973) were the sizes of the increments in net output in agriculture higher than those in gross output."

[124] As for the Soviet Union, it is interesting to note that the faster growth of gross relative to net output began in the 1970s, while in the three previous decades the contrary relationship prevailed: "The pace of growth of national income [NMP] as compared with 1940 outstripped that of social product, which was determined by a decrease in the share of productive material costs in the total social product. In certain periods, in particular in the last two quinquennia [1971-1975 and 1976-1980], the tendency was in the reverse direction; it was caused by the expansion of fixed investments and by the renewal of fixed assets, in particular in agriculture, and also by structural shifts in the national economy." M. R. Eidel'man, *op. cit.*, pp. 7 and 8.

[125] This was pointed out, among others, by Academician O. Bogomolov, Director of the Institute of Economics of the World Socialist System of the Acedemy of Sciences of the USSR: "according to our analysis we [CMEA countries] consumme 40 per cent more of raw materials and energy per unit of net material product than on the average in the most developed western countries." *Borba*, Belgrade, 26 July 1984, p. 6.

Similar comments may be found in the daily newspapers of the countries concerned. In the editorial published in *Pravda*, 8 August 1983, p. 1, for instance, it was stated in respect of the Soviet Union that: "On the whole, the situation in the utilization of material resources has remained unfavourable. In comparison with the best world indicators, we still consume more energy and raw materials per unit of national income [NMP]."

[126] On the basis of comparisons between long-term economic developments in all the countries concerned but Romania, the Czechoslovak economist A. Nešporová stated: "Empirical estimates have led to the conclusion that the more developed an economy is, while at the same time having only limited or zero supplementary resource increments in the available resources at its disposal, the more the substitution rate among productive factors declines and approaches fixed proportions. The summary efficiency of productive factors in the studied period [1960-1980] has grown relatively very slowly. Unless a substantial increase in the efficiency of production due to technical progress and adequate changes in the economic mechanism occurs, any single productive factor limited can act as a barrier to economic growth." A. Nešporová, "Komparace dlouhodobého ekonomického růstu šesti socialistických zemí" (A comparison of long-term economic growth in six socialist countries), *Politická ekonomie*, Prague, vol. XXXII, 1984, No. 10, p. 1048.

materials per unit of output is thus highly dependent on the volume of investment, structural changes and comprehensive efficiency adjustments in the overall system of planning and economic management. So far these have lagged behind requirements.[127]

(b) *Investment and output/investment ratio*

In almost the whole post-war period economic growth in the centrally planned economies of eastern Europe and the Soviet Union was based mostly on the creation of huge new production capacity. In addition to the maximum mobilization of manpower, and ever increasing energy and raw material supplies, this required rapid investment expansion[128] and therefore high rates of accumulation in domestically used net material product.[129] This entailed, among other things, slower growth in the standard of living as compared with growth of NMP produced. In the second half of the 1970s, most of the countries concerned found that this type of development—usually referred to as "extensive" growth—could not be continued. Hence, as pointed out in many national statements and explicitly or implicitly in the five-year plans for 1981-1985, the transition to an "intensive" (i.e. resource efficient) development process was declared to be the central feature of the new development strategy. In the long run this should leave room for faster growth of total consumption relative to total domestically used net material product, i.e. the share of accumulation in the latter should decline. This is often referred to as socially (i.e. standard of living, welfare) oriented growth. On the other hand, this assumes that further growth of NMP produced can be achieved with relatively lower investment growth. Accordingly, in the five-year plans for 1981-1985, differences in the growth rates of the two aggregates have been very marked in Romania and substantial in most other countries. Five-year plan strategies specified no growth in investment in the

German Democratic Republic and Hungary and even indicated a decline in its level in Czechoslovakia and also in Poland (in the latter case, relative to the provisions of the three-year plan 1983-1985). Comparisons between planned and actual growth of NMP and investment (table 4.1.4) suggest several conclusions.

First, overall economic growth in most countries of the region indicates that the relationship between NMP growth and gross investment growth is rather stable and, therefore, cannot be changed in the short- or even in the medium-term without effects on output growth. This general observation is apparent, if to a differing extent in the various countries concerned. If developments in 1985 are as specified in the annual plan for that year, NMP in Bulgaria in 1981-1985 will grow slightly faster than laid down in the five-year plan and so will gross investment. The average ratio of NMP growth to investment growth for the quinquennium as a whole will remain unchanged. In Czechoslovakia, investment fell within the limits set by the five-year plan, but NMP growth only attained the lower point of the target range. Output per unit of investment thus rose more slowly than expected. In the German Democratic Republic, investment will probably be marginally lower, instead of marginally higher as planned. NMP growth will be about one sixth lower than targeted by the five-year plan. A marked decline will be recorded in Hungarian investment in 1981-1985, compared with the no-growth plan objective, but actual NMP growth for the quinquennium will be about three quarters of the rate implied by the mid-point of the target range of the five-year plan. Nevertheless, it should be stressed that in both Hungary and the German Democratic Republic, NMP will grow faster than investment, i.e. output growth will be considerably less investment-intensive compared with the previous quinquennium. To halt the decline in NMP recorded in 1979-1982 and push the NMP growth rate up to 5 per cent, Poland has had to expand investment by some 6 per cent annually, as compared with a decline of about 6 1/2 per cent laid down in its three-year plan for 1983-1985. In Romania investment expanded considerably less than foreseen by the five-year plan, but so did NMP produced. Furthermore the NMP to gross investment ratio increased markedly. Finally, in the Soviet Union it proved necessary to expand investment at almost twice the rate envisaged in the five-year plan in order to obtain the expected NMP produced growth of some 4 per cent annually. The NMP/gross investment ratio in fact remained unchanged.

The above review of changes in factor inputs and efficiency suggests the following tentative conclusions. *First*, the acceleration in economic growth recorded in 1983-1984 was obtained mainly by removing critical bottlenecks in energy and raw material supplies. The overall level of efficiency of energy and raw material utilization—despite some improvements in recent years—remained virtually unchanged in most countries. *Secondly*, present levels of efficiency in the use of energy and raw materials can only be improved by the introduction of new technologies in many sectors and by significant structural changes.[130] The contribution of changes in economic management, so far

---

[127] Assessments of this kind may be found in political statements of the countries concerned:

In mid-1983, the late Mr. Y. Andropov, at that time General Secretary of the CPSU Central Committee and President of the Presidium of the USSR Supreme Soviet, stated: "Above all, we cannot be satisfied with the pace of the transfer of the economy to the lines of intensive development. The reasons are different. It seems that in looking for ways to resolve new tasks we were not vigorous enough, that not infrequently we resorted to half measures and could not overcome the accumulated inertia fast enough. Now, we must make up for what we have lost. This will demand, among other things, changes in planning, management and the economic mechanism. And we are obliged to make such changes in order to enter the new five-year period so to say fully armed." Quoted according to *Press Bulletin*, Geneva Permanent Mission of the Soviet Union, No. 147 (595), August 1983, p. 2.

One year later a similar statement was made by Mr. M. Jakeš, member of the Presidium and Secretary of the Central Committee of the Communist Party of Czechoslovakia: "In management and decision-making practice the extensive approach has survived. The current mechansim of management is not creating sufficiently effective pressure towards innovation in production and production programmes, improving quality and in this way achieving high productivity." *Rudé právo*, 17 June 1984, p. 3.

[128] According to a recent CMEA secretariat review of long-term economic development within the organisation, the NMP of the CMEA countries increased by 80 per cent in 1971-1983, while the total volume of capital investment increased by 84 per cent. This confirms the close relationship between investment and growth in all the CMEA countries. *Social and Economic Achievements of the CMEA countries over 1971-1983*, Moscow, CMEA secretariat, July 1984, pp. 2 and 3.

[129] The share of accumulation in domestically used NMP ranged between 24 per cent in Hungary and almost 30 per cent in the Soviet Union in 1970 and between 22 per cent in the German Democratic Republic and as much as 34 per cent in Poland in 1975. *Statisticheskii ezhegodnik stran-chlenov SEV 1984*— (CMEA Statistical Yearbook 1984), Moscow 1984, p. 40.

[130] The importance of such changes was emphasized by Mr. M. S. Gorbachev, Secretary General of the CPSU: "The improvement of the economic apparatus and of the entire system of economic management, and the implementation of a number of structural shifts in production, are on the agenda. The solution of these tasks necessitates the faster development of science and technlogy and the introduction of their achievements into practice. To increase the pace of scientific and technical progress is an imperative command of the times. Something else is equally important—to make efficient and thrifty use of everthing that already exists." *Pravda*, 21 February 1985, p. 2.

TABLE 4.1.4

Gross investment and net material product
(*Annual percentage change*)

	1976-1980	1981	1982	1983	1984	1985 plan	1981-1985[a] implied	1981-1985 plan
Bulgaria								
Net material product	6.1	5.0	4.2	3.0	4.6*	4.1	4.2	3.7
Gross investment	4.0	10.5	3.6	0.7	—*	6.1*	4.1	3.6
NMP/gross investment ratio .	2.0	−5.0	0.6	2.3	4.6	−1.9	0.1	0.1
Czechoslovakia								
Net material product	3.7	−0.1	0.2	2.3	3.0	3.0	1.7	1.6-2.2
Gross investment	3.5	−4.6	2.3	0.6	1.5*	2.0	−0.6	−(2.1-0)
NMP/gross investment ratio .	0.2	4.8	2.6	1.7	1.5	1.0	2.3	3.8-4.4
German Democratic Republic								
Net material product	4.2	4.8	2.6	4.4	5.5	4.4	4.3	5.1
Gross investment	3.4	2.8	−5.1	–	—*	—*	−0.5	−0.5
NMP/gross investment ratio . .	0.8	1.9	8.2	4.4	5.5	4.4	4.8	4.6
Hungary								
Net material product	2.8	2.5	2.6	0.3	2.8-3.0	2.3-2.8	2.2	2.7-3.1
Gross investment	2.2	−4.3	−1.6	−3.7	−(6-7)	1.1	−3.0	–
NMP/gross investment ratio .	0.6	7.1	4.3	4.2	8.2-8.4	1.3-1.8	5.0	2.2-2.6
Poland								
Net material product	1.2	−12.0	−5.5	6.0	5.0	3.0-3.5	4.7[b]	3.5-5.6[c]
Gross investment	−3.0	−22.4	−12.1	9.4	8	–	5.7[b]	6.4*[c]
NMP/gross investment ratio .	4.3	13.4	7.5	−3.1	−2.8	3.0-3.5	−1.0[b]	10.6-12.8[c]
Romania								
Net material product	7.3	2.2	2.7	3.7	7.7	10.0	5.2	7.1
Gross investment	8.5	−7.1	−3.1	2.5	6.1	8.3	2.3	5.2
NMP/gross investment ratio .	−1.1	10.0	6.0	1.3	1.5	1.6	2.8	1.8
Soviet Union								
Net material product	4.3	3.3	3.9	4.2	3.0	4.0	3.8	4.0*
Gross investment	3.4	3.8	3.5	5.8	2	3.4	3.9	2.0
NMP/gross investment ratio .	0.9	−0.5	0.3	−1.4	1.0	1.6	–	2.0

Sources: National statistics, plans and plan fulfilment reports.
[a] Implied by actual growth rates 1981-1984 and annual growth rate planned for 1985.
[b] Three-year plan 1983-1985.
[c] Implied by actual growth rates 1983-1984 and annual growth rate planned for 1985.

insufficient and in fact marginal,[131] could in this respect play a decisive role—in particular, incentives to stimulate enterprises themselves to reduce energy and raw material inputs per unit of output.[132] *Thirdly*, experience suggests that dynamic structural

[131] The limited and in fact inadequate extent of changes in econmic systems and policies introduced in the centrally planned economies so far, and the necessity for more comprehensive changes, was stressed by Mr. K. I. Mikul'ski, Deputy Director of the Institute of Economics of the World Socialist Economic System of the USSR Academy of Sciences. His report at the international symposium on problems of the pace of economic growth in the CMEA-member countries in conditions of transition to the intensive path of economic development, held in Moscow in October 1984, included the comment that: "One must not claim that the new tendency—the tendency to improve the pace of production in the USSR and other socialist countries—has yet acquired a stable character, or that it now determines long-term economic change in the economies. So far it has been based mostly on mobilization by administrative methods, of reserves which lie on the surface and less on steering (*ovladeniem*) by levers of long-term significance: stimulation of workers to more efficient use of working time and material resources, rational restructuring of production structures, accelerated scientific and technical progress and increased efficiency of countries' participation in the international division of labour." K. I. Mikul'skii: *Aktual'nye problemy analiza tempov ekonomicheskogo rosta na sovremennom etape razvitiia sotsialisticheskoi ekonomiki* (Current Problems of the Analysis of the Pace of Economic Growth at the Contemporary Stage of Development of the Socialist Economies), Moscow, 1984, pp. 6-7.

[132] On the basis of a comparative analysis of the long-term pace and proportions of economic growth in the countries concerned, the Czechoslovak economist R. Vintrová came to similar conclusions: "The

changes are only possible when national output is expanding. To attain the necessary structural changes, the centrally planned economies will have to ensure overall economic growth of at least 3-4 per cent per year on average. *Fourthly*, overall economic growth in this range would require investment at similar or only slightly lower rates if structural changes involving investment in capital-intensive branches such as energy, extractive industry, infrastructural projects, etc., are to be implemented. *Fifthly*, the investment expenditure necessary to provide these structural changes and to ensure buoyant economic growth will require net fixed capital formation to grow at rates similar to those of NMP produced.

Since shifts of resources away from domestic demand to improve trade balances will probably have to continue, accumulation may have to grow somewhat faster than consumption unless depreciation rates are considerably increased.

outlooks for further economic development depend upon how successful we shall be in preparing the more extensive modernization of the economy, deeper structural changes and the reconstruction of the economic mechanism which would make it possible to more fully utilize qualitative forms of intensification, i.e. above all scientific and technological development and social factors, which will increase the production capability of resources and their ability to satisfy requirements". R. Vintrová, "Tempa a proporce reprodukce v ekonomické strategii socialistických zemí" (The Rates and Proportions of Reproduction in the Economic Strategy of the Socialist countries), *Politická ekonomie*, Prague, vol. XXXII, 1984, No. 10), p. 1032.

Finally, it should also be pointed out that a reorientation towards faster economic growth and structural change opens the way to, and also requires, a more differentiated pattern of specialization, within and among all countries of the region, and also between them and other countries. This has already been pointed out at the CMEA summit meeting held in mid-1984, where a further, broader and deeper division of labour between member countries was agreed to be a common need.[133] The need for greater mutual trade than in previous years was also stressed at this meeting. But if the strategy described is incorporated in the next set of five-year plans, and if it receives a positive reaction on the part of the developed market economies, it will also open many opportunities for east-west trade, as well as for technical co-operation, financial and other arrangements.[134]

[133] "...The participants in the conference noted that there still exist considerable reserves for expanding mutual co-operation, deepening specialization of production and co-prduction, increasing mutual trade in the interest of more effective utilization of productive, scientific and technlogical potential of the fraternal countries and raising the living standards of their peoples." *Summit Economic Conference of the CMEA Member Countries*, Moscow, CMEA Secretariat, 1984, p. 11.

[134] The insufficient level of trade between CMEA and EEC member countries was pointed out by E. Kemenes; "CMEA in the European Economy", *Marketing in Hungary*, Quarterly Market Research Review of the Hungarian Chamber of Commerce, 1984, No. 2, p. 21: "The countries of CMEA and of the Common Market produce together half of the world's industrial output, but their mutual trade only accounts for 4 per cent of world trade. Since two halves of the same continent are at issue, this low share is unrealistic on economico-geographical considerations alone."

(iv) Foreign economic relations

The foreign economic relations of the centrally planned economies progressed in line with the objectives incorporated in the five-year plans. These laid down that foreign trade should grow faster than output, that exports should grow faster than imports and that intra-CMEA trade links should be strengthened. They also called for surpluses on the trade and current account balances in convertible currencies and a reduction of the trade deficits of the east European countries with the Soviet Union.

Table 4.1.5 presents foreign trade values of eastern Europe and the Soviet Union in terms of foreign trade turnover (exports plus imports), exports and imports and also export/import ratios. Due to the appreciation of the US dollar in which current-value annual changes are shown, the table does not give precise information on volume changes—a subject dealt with in chapter 5. The figures it contains nevertheless allow certain conclusions to be drawn. In current US dollars, the *foreign trade turnover* of the centrally planned economies virtually stagnated in 1984. This reflected a small decline in the trade turnover of the Soviet Union and an increase of some 2 per cent for the six east European countries. However, if the appreciation of the US dollar is taken into account, these figures mask increased foreign trade volumes for eastern Europe in particular and also for the Soviet Union. The east European countries' exports increased more than their imports, while Soviet export growth was accompanied by some decline in imports (in current dollars). Hence, the *export/import ratios* of both eastern Europe and the Soviet Union improved further in 1984 for the fourth successive year. Foreign trade adjustments did not follow the same path in all countries. Adjust-

TABLE 4.1.5

Foreign trade of eastern Europe and the Soviet Union

(Annual percentage change and ratios in current dollars)

	Bulgaria	Czechoslovakia	German Democratic Republic	Hungary	Poland	Romania	Eastern Europe	Soviet Union	Eastern Europe and Soviet Union
Foreign trade turnover									
1979	15.2	12.9	12.4	16.3	14.6	21.9	15.0	18.8	16.7
1980	15.4	9.7	16.4	7.1	7.0	19.2	12.2	18.4	15.0
1981	7.2	−1.8	10.0	0.5	−20.3	−9.9	−3.1	5.2	0.8
1982	6.9	5.1	4.8	−1.0	−5.1	−16.8	−0.1	7.9	3.9
1983	6.3	5.7	8.1	−2.3	3.3	−3.5	4.1	4.2	4.2
1984	4.5	4.4*	1.9*	−3.1*	1.0*	0.6*	2.0*	−0.7*	0.6*
Exports									
1979	18.9	12.3	13.5	24.9	17.7	20.8	17.1	23.6	20.1
1980	17.2	13.1	14.9	8.6	5.0	17.3	12.2	18.2	15.1
1981	3.0	−0.1	14.7	1.4	−21.9	−1.9	−1.2	3.8	1.2
1982	7.0	4.9	9.5	1.5	6.0	−9.5	4.0	9.6	6.9
1983	6.1	5.5	9.4	−1.0	3.2	0.4	5.0	5.1	5.0
1984	5.8	4.2*	0.7*	−1.7	1.4	3.4*	2.2*	0.2*	1.4*
Imports									
1979	11.7	13.3	11.3	9.4	11.8	22.9	13.1	13.9	13.5
1980	13.6	6.6	17.7	5.8	8.9	20.9	12.2	18.6	15.0
1981	11.7	−3.4	5.8	−0.2	−18.8	−16.8	−4.8	6.8	0.3
1982	6.8	5.4	0.1	−3.2	−14.9	−24.2	−4.1	6.2	0.9
1983	6.5	5.9	6.6	−3.5	3.4	−8.9	3.1	3.3	3.2
1984	3.1	4.6*	3.4*	−5.0	0.6	−3.1*	1.9*	−1.6*	0.1*
Export/Import ratios									
1979	104.1	92.6	92.9	91.3	92.4	89.1	93.3	112.0	101.4
1980	107.5	98.3	90.7	93.7	89.0	86.4	93.2	111.6	101.4
1981	99.0	101.6	98.4	95.3	85.6	101.8	96.7	108.5	102.3
1982	99.1	101.2	107.7	99.9	109.5	121.6	105.9	112.0	109.0
1983	98.8	111.8	110.5	102.5	109.3	133.0	107.8	113.9	110.9
1984	101.3	100.4	107.7*	106.0	110.2	141.9*	108.1*	116.1	112.1*

Source: National statistics, plan fulfilment reports and ECE secretariat estimates.

ment policies applied by Hungary in particular were somewhat different from the other countries. Imports declined by more than exports, providing another surplus on the balance of foreign trade. In Bulgaria, the export/import ratio was lower than unity in 1981-1983 but rose above unity in 1984. There was also a noticeable decline in Czechoslovakia's export/import ratio in 1984.

Table 4.1.6 shows the *regional orientation of foreign trade* of the seven countries of the region. It should be noted that in spite of virtual stagnation in current dollar terms, the volume of trade of the seven countries with the developed market economies increased in both 1983 and 1984. This rise was particularly evident for eastern Europe in 1984. Trade with developing countries lagged behind, in particular in the foreign trade turnover of the Soviet Union. A development which is somewhat masked by the data because of the exchange rate effect is the continuous growth of intra-regional trade in both volume and value (in rouble terms). This partly reflected pressure to bring about fast adjustment in the region's foreign trade with the convertible currency area at the beginning of the 1980s. It also arises from a deliberate policy reorientation of the countries in the region, in response to the volatility of changes in world trade flows and in their terms of trade. Larger-scale, intra-regional co-operation is now under consideration for incorporation in the five-year plans for 1986-1990.[135] However, the regional trade pattern of individual east European countries already varies considerably as can be seen by a comparison between Bulgaria and Romania which have respect-ively the most and least CMEA-oriented trade pattern of the six countries.[136]

Movements in the *foreign trade balances* of eastern Europe and of the Soviet Union indicate three main conclusions (table 4.1.7 and Appendix table C.3). First, the overall balance of trade of the seven countries jointly shifted from a deficit in 1978 to a first surplus in 1979. It continuously improved in the following years, to reach an estimated $19 billion surplus in 1984. The Soviet balance of trade had already been positive for several years. Eastern Europe's surplus was the third in consecutive years and, at almost $7 billion, was somewhat higher than in 1983. The surplus of some $4 1/2 billion on trade with the developed market economies in 1983 almost doubled in 1984, with eastern Europe and the Soviet Union accounting for virtually the same shares. This is a considerable change for both. The Soviet Union in particular had either usually balanced, or recorded deficits on, its trade with the developed market economies in recent years. The surplus on trade with the developing countries declined for both eastern Europe and the Soviet Union. This reflected sluggish demand for imports in the developing countries concerned, which arose because of the adjustment policies they introduced to cope with the debt servicing problems experienced in the last few years. Finally, significant changes occurred in the balance of the rouble-denominated trade of eastern Europe with the Soviet Union. East European deficits contracted in 1982-1983, but rose again in 1984 to about 1 billion roubles—the same as in 1982. This

---

[135] For decisions of the Summit and recent CMEA activities linked with it see *Summit Economic Conference of the CMEA Member Countries*, Moscow, CMEA secretariat, 1984 and *Survey of CMEA Activities between the 37th and 39th Meetings of the Session of the Council* Moscow, CMEA Secretariat, 1984.

[136] Based on the rouble value of total east European foreign trade turnover, the share of the trade with other CMEA countries for eastern Europe was 61.1 per cent in 1983, while those of individual east European countries ranged between 47.7 per cent for Romania and 76.8 per cent for Bulgaria. The share of eastern Europe in total Soviet trade on the same basis was 51.2 per cent in the same year. Calculated on the basis of *Statisticheskii ezhegodnik stran-chlenov SEV 1983* (CMEA Statistical Yearbook 1983), Moscow, 1984, pp. 295 and 297.

TABLE 4.1.6

Foreign trade turnover of eastern Europe and the Soviet Union by selected regions
(*Annual percentage change in current dollars terms*)

	Bulgaria	Czechoslovakia	German Democratic Republic	Hungary	Poland	Romania	Eastern Europe	Soviet Union	Eastern Europe and Soviet Union
With developed market economies									
1979	38.5	20.2	28.5	17.3	9.6	23.0	19.5	35.9	26.9
1980	27.3	14.7	22.9	11.8	7.4	8.6	13.5	23.9	18.6
1981	8.7	−11.1	14.1	−4.7	−33.0	−10.2	−9.2	1.0	−4.0
1982	−10.4	−7.5	3.6	−6.6	−18.8	−29.1	−10.5	5.7	−1.9
1983	−7.4	−4.6	12.8	−0.8	−0.4	−6.2	−1.6	−0.6	−0.3
1984	−2.6	−2.2*	−	0.3	5.9	25.4*	3.9*	−3.9*	−0.5*
With developing economies									
1979	17.8	8.2	12.7	16.9	41.2	45.9	28.0	15.2	21.0
1980	36.5	22.5	36.4	20.2	29.2	45.4	34.3	27.5	30.7
1981	34.0	−	−11.3	−0.2	−27.5	5.0	−1.6	24.0	11.4
1982	12.9	−6.0	23.6	14.3	−14.1	−15.5	−2.8	1.7	−0.3
1983	−11.8	8.0	0.2	7.6	4.6	−10.1	−2.7	2.5	0.3
1984	17.7	−1.7*	1.1*	12.8	0.5	1.6*	1.4	−10.3*	−5.5
With European CMEA countries									
1979	11.4	10.4	7.4	16.0	14.3	9.3	11.1	11.0	11.0
1980	11.0	6.7	10.9	1.9	4.1	15.6	8.1	12.2	9.7
1981	3.7	0.5	11.1	3.6	−10.5	−18.1	−0.1	2.4	0.9
1982	10.8	9.5	4.3	−	−32.4	−7.1	−1.6	10.3	3.3
1983	12.1	8.8	6.9	−5.7	5.3	6.1	6.8	9.5	7.9
1984	3.7	7.1*	2.9*	−4.2	−2.5	−18.9*	1.2*	2.5*	1.8*

Source: As for table 4.1.5.

mainly reflected the effects of higher world oil prices on the five-year moving average-based prices applied in intra-CMEA trade. Since energy-saving measures are high on the policy agenda of all east European countries, this could prove to be only a temporary deviation from the policy objective of balancing trade between eastern Europe as a whole and the Soviet Union.

(v) Resources for domestic use

The volume and pace of growth of national output is the principal determinant of the volume and pace of domestic utilization. However, in the short and even in the medium term, net material product used for domestic consumption and accumulation (net capital formation), hereafter referred to as resources for domestic use or NMP used, may be bigger or smaller than NMP produced. Any differences represent mainly the balance of trade outcome. A surplus on balance of trade means that domestic utilization is lower than NMP produced, while a deficit implies the opposite. Changes in NMP produced and NMP used, and also changes in the allocation of NMP used to consumption and accumulation, are shown in table 4.1.8, and also appendix tables B.1 and B.2.

The necessity of achieving growing balance of trade surpluses implied that the *volume of resources for domestic use* (the NMP used) in most east European countries grew slower, and sometimes markedly slower, than NMP produced. This was particularly noticeable for Czechoslovakia and for the German Democratic Republic in 1981-1983, and in Hungary since 1972. In all three countries, in fact, NMP used fell in absolute terms in one or more years. In Poland the decline in the level of NMP used started as early as the second half of the 1970s and lasted until 1982 inclusively. This was partly attributable to adjustments in the foreign sector and also to falls in the level of NMP produced. Bulgaria and the Soviet Union are in fact the only countries of the region where there was no contraction in resources for domestic use. Even so, NMP used in Bulgaria has grown considerably slower than NMP produced since 1982. The smallest difference between the two was recorded in the Soviet Union, where NMP used is the main output indicator in both five-year and annual plans. In the first four years of the current quinquennium, Soviet NMP produced expanded by an annual average of 3 1/2 per cent, while NMP used grew at about 3 per cent annually. The only exception to the above general trend in the relationship between NMP used and NMP produced was Poland in 1983-1984, when both expanded at similar rates. This was due to a reversal in the sharp contractions in NMP used in the three previous years. NMP used was almost 25 per cent lower in 1982 than in 1979. Romania publishes no annual data on NMP used.

An important feature of overall economic strategy in the five-year plans 1981-1985 was slower investment growth as discussed in sub-section (iii) above. This had significant consequences for the *allocation of NMP used*. Columns (2), (3) and (6) of table 4.1.8 clearly show that in most cases total domestic consumption expanded considerably faster than accumulation (net capital formation). In fact accumulation contracted in several years in all east European countries, and also in the Soviet Union in 1980. The contraction was particularly big in Poland, the level of accumulation in 1983 falling to about 48 per cent of its 1979 figure. In Hungary, a similar decline reduced accumulation levels in 1984 to about 57 per cent of the 1979 volume. Furthermore, accumulation also declined in both countries in 1976-1980—especially in Poland. Reductions were also considerable in Czechoslovakia, where the accumulation level in 1983 was only 70 per cent of the 1980 figure. Among the east European countries, the fall was the least in Bulgaria. In the Soviet Union there has been no contraction in accumulation during the current five-year period.

The factors underlying the changes described in the allocation of resources for domestic use were: the deceleration in the growth of NMP produced and increasing surpluses on balances of trade. The changes also reflected a deliberate policy orientation which gave priority to consumption rather than to accumulation. As indicated above (sub-section (ii)), slowly growing or even falling accumulation affected NMP growth to a great or lesser extent because of its close association with investment. Once the deceleration of NMP growth itself was checked, the fall in accumulation levels in most countries slowed down or was even reversed. The latter was especially noticeable for the Soviet Union, where the growth of accumulation surpassed consumption growth by a wide margin in 1983-1984. It was also true in Poland in 1983-1984.

Columns (4) and (5) of table 4.1.8 present changes in the *allocation of total consumption between personal and social (public) consumption*. Personal and social consumption data are also shown in chart 4.1.5, together with accumulation. The table and the chart show that during the 1980s, the countries of the region did not follow identical policies with regard to the allocation of consumption resources. Three different sets of policies can be identified.

In Bulgaria, both personal and social consumption expanded—the latter by considerably more than the former. In Czechoslovakia, social consumption grew considerably since 1980, while personal consumption fluctuated at around the level attained in 1979. In both countries, these outcomes are in line with the traditional consumption policies of the centrally planned econ-

TABLE 4.1.7

Foreign trade balances of eastern Europe and the Soviet Union by selected regions
(*Billion US dollars or roubles*)

	Eastern Europe	Soviet Union	Eastern Europe and the Soviet Union
Total (billion US dollars)			
1980	−5.8	8.0	2.2
1981	−2.6	6.2	3.6
1982	4.4	9.3	13.7
1983	6.0	11.2	17.1
1984[a]	6.8*	12.7*	19.5*
With developed market economies (billion US dollars)			
1980	−3.8	0.2	−3.6
1981	−2.9	−1.2	−4.1
1982	1.3	−0.1	1.2
1983	3.2	1.3	4.5
1984[a]	4.8*	4.3*	9.1*
With developing countries (billion US dollars)			
1980	−0.4	2.7	2.3
1981	3.4	1.2	4.6
1982	3.9	4.8	8.7
1983	3.0	4.5	7.5
1984[a]	2.6*	3.3*	5.9*
With the Soviet Union (billion roubles)			
1980	−1.3	..	..
1981	−2.3	..	..
1982	−1.1	..	..
1983	−0.4	..	..
1984[a]	−1.0*	..	..

Source: As for table 4.1.5.

[a] Preliminary estimates.

TABLE 4.1.8

NMP produced and NMP used

(*Annual percentage change*)

Country and period	NMP produced (1)	NMP used^a (2)	Consumption			Accumulation		
			Total (3)	Personal^b (4)	Social^c (5)	Total (6)	Net fixed capital formation (7)	Changes in stocks (8)
Bulgaria								
1976-1980	6.1	2.8	4.0	4.1	5.2	0.1	2.4	5.3
1980	5.7	5.1	3.6	3.7	12.5	9.5	−42.6	459.3
1981	5.0	7.7	5.3	5.0	5.4	14.8	..	..
1982	4.2	1.9	3.7	3.6	6.7	−3.3	..	..
1983	3.0	1.2	2.9	2.5	2.5	−3.6	..	..
1984	4.6	..	..	..	..	..	..	..
Czechoslovakia								
1976-1980	3.7	2.2	2.5	1.7	4.8	0.9	0.4	2.6
1980	2.9	2.7	1.0	−0.1	3.7	8.2	5.9	12.6
1981	−0.1	−3.4	2.6	1.7	4.9	−21.7	11.1	−83.5
1982	0.2	−1.6	−1.1	−2.3	1.8	−3.6	−25.3	275.6
1983	2.3	0.7	2.7	2.2	3.3	−7.2	..	..
1984	3.0	..	2.4*	2.0	5.0	..	..	..
German Democratic Republic								
1976-1980	4.2	3.7	3.8	3.9	3.1	3.6	3.4	6.7
1980	4.4	5.0	2.9	3.4	−1.2	12.4	..	..
1981	4.8	1.1	2.7	2.8	2.7	−3.3	..	..
1982	2.5	−3.2	1.3	1.4	0.3	−20.1	..	..
1983	4.4	0.4	0.9	1.4	−2.3	−1.9	..	..
1984	5.5	..	..	..	..	..	..	..
Hungary								
1976-1980	2.8	1.7	3.0	2.6	5.9	−2.9	−1.8	−8.7
1980	−0.9	−1.7	0.2	0.2	0.1	−8.7	−6.9	−19.5
1981	2.5	0.7	3.0	3.0	3.0	−8.6	−15.5	37.6
1982	2.6	−1.1	1.4	1.4	1.3	−12.4	−15.7	1.4
1983	0.3	−2.7	0.6	0.5	2.0	−20.4	15.3	−142.9
1984	2.8-3.0	−	..	..	..	−(8-9)	..	..
Poland								
1976-1980	1.2	−0.2	4.5	4.3	5.2	−11.8	−9.2	−29.0
1980	−6.0	−6.0	2.1	2.3	1.2	−29.6	−25.4	−61.3
1981	−12.0	−10.5	−4.6	4.1	−8.1	−27.6	−24.2	−69.5
1982	−5.5	−10.5	−11.5	−14.6	11.5	−6.6	−19.9	400.0
1983	6.0	5.4	5.6	6.2	1.9	4.9	9.5	17.6
1984	5.0	5.0	..	5.0	..	..	..	..
Soviet Union								
1976-1980	4.3	3.8	4.5*	..	..	1.6*	..	..
1980	3.9	3.9	6.0	..	..	−0.6	..	..
1981	3.3	3.2	4.0	..	..	0.9	..	..
1982	3.9	3.6	1.2	..	..	11.0	..	..
1983	4.2	3.6	2.9	..	..	5.8	..	..
1984	3.0	2.6	..	..	..	..	..	..

Sources: National statistics and plan fulfilment reports.

a NMP used for net capital formation and consumption.

b Volume of consumer goods supplied to the population.

c Consumption of material goods in institutions providing amenities and social welfare services.

omies, which call for faster growth of social (public) as distinct from personal (private) consumption.[137]

In the three remaining reporting countries of eastern Europe, however, this orientation does not seem to have been retained recently. In fact, it seems that such a policy has definite limits, beyond which it may compromise the principle of distribution of the wage fund (earnings) in accordance with work performed. This has always been a basic tenet of income distribution in the

[137] However, judging by the presentation of the five-year plan of Czechoslovakia for the 1981-1985 period by Mr. S. Potáč to the Federal Parliament of Czechoslovakia, *Rudé právo*, 16 December 1981, p. 3, personal consumption was expected to grow faster than social consumption.

centrally planned economies. Hence in Hungary, personal and social consumption expanded at almost parallel rates since 1979, and personal consumption tended to grow slightly faster. There was a similar tendency in Poland, where personal consumption and social consumption tended to grow and contract simultaneously until recently. However, growth rates of personal consumption and general consumption differed considerably from each other in 1981-1983. In Hungary the relationship between the two consumption categories can be partly explained in terms of general development theory which indicate that personal, i.e. private, consumption—similarly to wages in market economies—is the most resistant to downward changes, both in cases of deceleration and, especially, in cases of contraction in overall consumption.

CHART 4.1.5.

Allocation of national income for domestic use

(Indices, 1979 = 100)

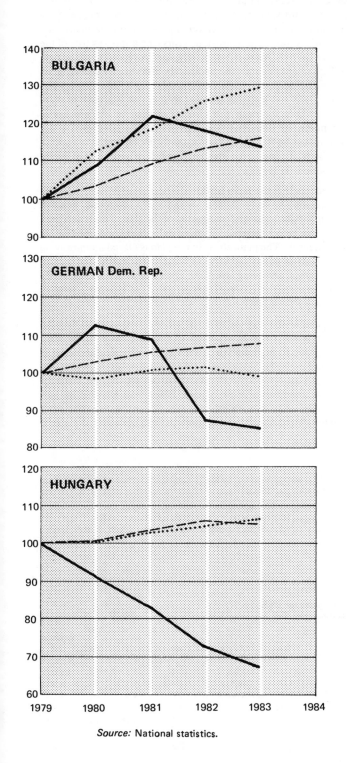

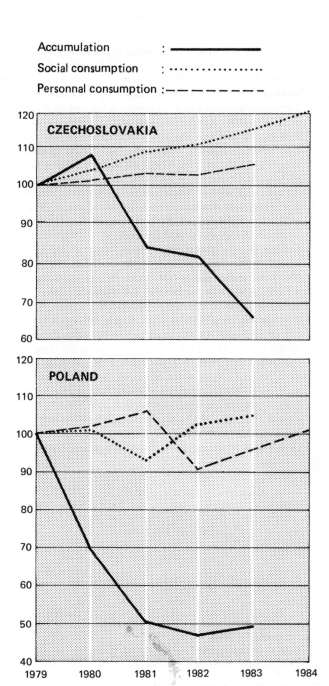

Source: National statistics.

Finally, the NMP deceleration in the German Democratic Republic which lasted until 1982 was very slow and in fact the slowest of all the countries of the region. Nevertheless, social consumption in that country since 1980 has fluctuated around the level attained in 1979, whereas personal consumption has continuously expanded at rates higher than total consumption. On this basis, it can be seen that there was a clear turnround in policy determining the relative growth rates of the two kinds of consumption in the German Democratic Republic. This reflected in particular efforts to boost economies of factor inputs, especially energy and raw materials, by linking overall income distribution more closely with performance. This is much easier to achieve via wage and salary adjustments than through social consumption funds.

Neither Romania nor the Soviet Union report figures on annual changes in personal and social consumption and recent development in this respect cannot be assessed.

(vi) Policy objectives for 1985

Various aspects of short- and medium-term policy orientation have been already discussed in previous sub-sections. In this one only a summary of the main policy objectives revealed by annual plans for 1985 will be given.[138]

The general impression conveyed by the annual plans of the east European countries and the Soviet Union is of increasing confidence that the decelerating trend of growth has ended and that a period of more normal economic conditions is to come. At the same time, almost all plans point out the twofold importance of the year 1985. It is the final year of the current five-year planning period, and also the base year for the five-year plans for 1986-1990. As already mentioned in sub-section (i) above, the majority of the countries concerned will not achieve the NMP growth rate envisaged for 1981-1985. But all of them claim that the basic objectives of the plans can and will be achieved. Against this background, the annual plans for 1985 (table 4.1.9) contain indications which suggest that in the case of most east European countries, NMP growth will fall between performance in 1984 and the average annual growth rates for the whole period envisaged by the five-year plans. In the case of the Soviet Union, the annual growth rate of NMP used targeted in the annual plan for 1985 is virtually the same as that included in the five-year plan, but it is markedly higher than in 1984. Hence, because of the high weighting of the Soviet Union in the region as a whole, overall economic growth in the seven countries concerned in 1985 is expected to be somewhat higher than in 1984 (about 4 per cent as compared with 3 1/2 per cent). This is virtually the same as in 1983. It confirms that overall medium-term strategy is to stabilize economic expansion at the rate already attained rather than to attempt any significant acceleration. Finally, the faster growth of exports than imports envisaged by most of the annual plans indicates that NMP for domestic use will continue to grow slower than NMP produced, particularly in some countries.

In *Bulgaria*, the annual plan for 1985 foresees NMP growth of 4 per cent. This is half of 1 percentage point less than in 1984 but higher by almost the same amount than average annual NMP growth rate retained in the five-year plan. Some novelties characterize the Bulgarian plan. On the formal side, the draft annual plan was not submitted to a Central Committee plenum of the Bulgarian Communist Party on the eve of the parliamentary session, as was usual in previous years (the same was true of the Soviet Union). More substantively, the presentation of the plan to Parliament included the phrase "the 1985 State Plan is characterized by numerous features distinguishing it from the previous years plans and bringing it closer to the new approach to planning". This approach will also be applied in the process of compiling and implementing plans at the enterprise level, and it will further be "totally and consistently implemented in compiling the Ninth Five-Year Plan and the future long-term plans for the period up to 2000"[139]

It seems that the main feature of the new approach is greater participation by sectoral, regional and micro-economic agents in the preparation and implementation of the plan. This is designed to ensure better material, financial and other conditions for its fulfilment.[140] The main stress in the plan is placed on improving the quality of goods and services, fostering scientific and technical progress, achieving structural change and on making better use of investment resources. Investment is to increase considerably faster than NMP itself.

As employment in the material sphere is expected to decline, labour productivity is expected to increase faster than NMP itself. Due to high growth in 1984, gross agricultural output is targeted to rise half as fast as in 1985. Industrial gross production growth is expected to accelerate. As usual, provision is made for foreign trade turnover to increase faster than national output. The share of trade with other socialist countries is expected to reach its highest ever level of more than 82 per cent (63 per cent

---

[139] This was pointed out by Mr. S. Bonev, Chairman of the State Planning Committee, *Rabotnichesko delo*, 27 November 1984, p. 2.

[140] "Protocols were signed for the first time between ministries, departments, *okrug* (district) people's councils and enterprises for creating the necessary conditions to guarantee the implementation of state tasks"; *ibid.*

---

[138] A short review of annual plans of all the CMEA-member countries is given in *Ekonomicheskaia gazeta* Nos. 1 and 2, January 1985.

TABLE 4.1.9

Selected indicators of annual plans for 1985

	Bulgaria	Czecho-slovakia	German Democratic Republic	Hungary	Poland	Romania	Soviet Union	Byelo-russian SSR	Ukrainian SSR
Net material product	4.1	3.0	4.4	2.3-2.8	3.0-3.5	10.0	3.5[a]	3.8	3.6
Agriculture (gross product)	3.2	−1.1	−1.0*	1.0	(−0.8)-1.4	6.0-6.8	5.8	3.5	6.3
Industry (gross product)	5.2	3.0	3.8	3.0	4.0-4.5	7.5	3.9	4.1	3.1
Construction	..	1.2	3.4	1.0-2.0	..	..	..	..	..
Employment in the material sphere	−0.2*	0.4*	..	..	..	..	0.4[b]	0.4[b]	0.2[b]
Labour productivity	4.3	2.6*	..	..	..	..	..	..	3.7
Gross investment	6.1*	2.0	−*	1	−	8.3	3.4	5.6	3.0
Gross incremental capital output ratio	..	..	..	..	..	..	..	..	..
Foreign trade turnover	4.5	4.7[c]	8.0..	..	..	..	..	..	..
Exports	..	..	..	..	..	..	..	..	..
Imports	..	..	..	..	..	..	..	..	..
Real incomes per capita	3.0	..	..	1.5-2.0	..	3.3	3.3	3.3	3.0
Retail trade turnover	4.5	4	4.0	2	..	..	5.2	4.3	5.1

Source: National plans.

[a] NMP used for domestic consumption and accumulation.

[b] Workers and employees only.

[c] With socialist countries.

with the Soviet Union alone). Three quarters of domestically used NMP will be allocated to consumption. A 3 per cent rise in real incomes is expected in 1985.

In *Czechoslovakia* the annual plan for 1985[141] foresees NMP growth at 3 per cent. This is the same as attained in 1984 and is considerably higher than the average for 1981-1984. It is also higher than the annual average expected under the five-year plan. This implies that the main factors which constrained the economy in the early 1980s have been largely eased and that the country now counts on a continuation of economic growth at the rates recently attained. However, the Czechoslovak authorities note that the presence of substantial differences in performance between individual factories, enterprises, co-operative and other economic units indicate the existence of untapped possibilities.[142] Against this background, the NMP growth rate mentioned will have to be achieved with the same gross industrial output growth and a small contraction in agricultural output. This implies that considerable savings will have to be achieved in primary energy consumption per unit of output (3 per cent) and many other material inputs (rolled steel by 3 per cent, copper by 4 per cent, cement by 3 per cent, etc.). At the same time, labour productivity is expected to provide for almost 90 per cent of NMP growth, since employment in the material sphere will hardly grow. Foreign trade turnover, in particular with socialist countries, is expected to grow faster than national output. The expected trade surplus will restrict the expansion of NMP for domestic utilization to three quarters of the growth rate of NMP produced. Nevertheless, there will be room for a 2 per cent rise in personal consumption and also of gross investment. Social consumption is planned to expand somewhat faster—by more than 5 per cent. The 4 per cent planned nominal growth of retail trade turnover compared with a 2 per cent increase in personal consumption—indicates a certain increase in the consumer price index.

In the *German Democratic Republic* the annual plan for 1985[143] calls for NMP growth of 4 1/2 per cent, slightly below the 5 per cent average annual rate incorporated in the current five-year plan. This is nearly the same as growth attained in 1984 (5 1/2 per cent) and virtually the same as already achieved in 1981-1984 (4.3 per cent, the highest among the seven countries concerned).

As in some other countries, the German Democratic Republic plan expects a slower growth of gross industrial output than of NMP produced. There may also be some contraction in agricultural output following the extraordinarily strong expansion of almost 9 per cent in 1984. The stress on energy and raw materials savings in which the German Democratic Republic has already achieved well-known successes will continue. Policy is now also specifically emphasizing improvements in the use of fixed assets and a reversal of the long-term decline in capital productivity.[144]

Foreign trade turnover is set to expand considerably faster than national output (8 per cent). Resources for domestic use will probably lag behind NMP produced. No figure was mentioned in the plan for investment and consumption growth in real terms. But the 4 per cent target for retail trade turnover growth suggests that total consumption may increase more than in 1983, the last reported year, when it rose by 1 per cent.

Further adjustments in the foreign sector—which are common to all east European countries—remain the basic priority in the annual plan of *Hungary* for 1985.[145] Taking into account this and NMP growth in 1984, the plan includes several crucial objectives. First, exports are to increase by 5-6 per cent and imports by only 2-3 per cent. This should bring about a convertible currency surplus on the balance of trade of $600-700 million, which would ensure normal debt servicing and also further reductions of Hungary's foreign indebtedness. Second, energy and raw material consumption per unit of output is to be considerably reduced—particularly in industry. If this is achieved, the plan expects, third, that NMP produced will grow by about 2-3 per cent, as in 1984. This is the same as the average annual NMP growth rate envisaged by the five-year plan. Fourth, resources for domestic use could also increase to some extent—for the first time after three years of stagnation or contraction. Thus, for the first time in several years, the plan suggests that investments will be able to increase. Real wages would stabilize at the current level and real incomes increase by 1 1/2 to 2 per cent. Retail trade turnover could also expand at a similar rate. The leading sector of NMP growth will remain industry, where expansion is planned at 3 per cent. Construction is targeted to grow by 1-2 per cent and agriculture by 1 per cent. In conclusion, a further impetus is to be given to the economic reform introduced in the late 1960s and which continued, if with some hesitations in the early 1970s. This brought Hungary a reputation as the most reform-oriented centrally planned economy in eastern Europe. A further set of both micro- and macro-economic changes will carry the process several stages further in 1985. New initiatives range from the introduction of the self-management principle in the election of enterprise management through changes in the taxation and financial requirements.

The annual plan of *Poland* assumes a continuation in 1985 of the developments recorded in the previous two years.[146] Furthermore, if the 3 to 3 1/2 per cent planned increase in NMP produced—based on 4 to 4 1/2 per cent increase in gross industrial output and preservation of the 1984 level of agricultural output—is achieved, then overall economic growth in Poland in 1983-1985 will have been somewhat above the mid-point of the range envisaged by the three-year plan of the country for those years.

---

[141] For presentation of the plan see S. Potáč, *Rudé právo*, 6 December 1984.

[142] "Despite a certain improvement, the technical-economic standard of a number of products and the level of social labour productivity still lag behind current possibilities. It must be said, in general, that considerable untapped possibilities exist in our economic, research and development potentials, as well as in the utilisation of manpower. These are not our only problems and shortcomings, and they are not new either ... The majority of shortcomings stem from the still unsatisfactory quality of management, planning and control, a quality which far from corresponds to the exacting nature of the tasks." This was pointed out by Mr. S. Potáč, Chairman of the State Planning Committee, *ibid.*, p. 3.

[143] For the text of the plan and its presentation by Mr. W. Stoph, Prime Minister of the German Democratic Republic, see *Neues Deutschland*, 1-2 December 1984. Both were also published in No. 4/1984 of *Documents on the policy of the German Democratic Republic*, Panorama DDR, Berlin, 1984.

[144] This was pointed out by Mr. W. Stoph: "The 1985 national economic plan provides for the strict pursuit of modernization as the principal form of renewing our fixed assets. In raising their technological level and efficiency, increased emphasis will have to be given to combining preventive maintenance with performance-boosting general overhauls and provision of new equipment.": *op. cit.*, p. 15.

[145] *Népszabadság*, 23 December 1984 (Government's final version of the plan), and also *Népszabadság*, 13 December 1984, *Magyar Hirlap*, 20 December 1984, and *Figyelö*, 3 January 1985 (presentation of the plan).

[146] As in 1983, the preparation of the annual plan of Poland was carried out in two phases. The draft plan for 1985 was prepared in July 1984 and offered for broad national discussion. This led to certain changes in the plan which, though smaller than for the 1984 plan, were still considerable. The final version was passed in December 1984. For details on the evolution of the plan see *Rzeczpospolita*, 26 July 1984; *Zycie Gospodarcze*, No. 31, 29 July 1984; *Rzeczpospolita*, 30 November 1984 and also *Trybuna Ludu*, 21 December 1984.

Nevertheless, NMP produced in Poland in 1985 will still be 12 per cent lower than in 1978.

Many external and internal imbalances remain in spite of vigorus remedial action. This background determines the main plan priorities. Further export expansion will, if successful, bring about a considerable surplus within the convertible currency area, while a deficit with CMEA partners would remain. The plan also aims to restore supply/demand balance in the domestic market and reduce inflation to the one-digit level. In recent years the growth of NMP produced has substantially exceeded the growth of NMP used for domestic consumption and accumulation. The Polish plan for 1985 indicates that the gap between the two will remain unchanged and in fact that both aggregates will expand in parallel. If achieved, this would leave room for a 3 per cent increase in domestic consumptions, while fixed investment outlays would stay at the 1984 level. The bulk of the expected increase in accumulation will thus be available for stockbuilding; the reconstruction of reserves is necessary for the smooth functioning of the economy. To attain the prescribed objectives, further economies in the use of energy and raw materials will be needed. Two thirds of the increment in industrial output in fact is scheduled to be achieved by lowering inputs per unit of output. Similarly, the whole of the NMP increment is to be achieved through productivity, since the number of people on the point of attaining working age is not sufficient to bring about any rise in the material sphere labour force.

In sum, the objectives laid down by the plan are within reach but circumstances do not allow them to be taken for granted. Thus, a varied set of measures have been promulgated to ensure their implementation. They range from a closer linkage of wages with labour productivity to government guarantees of supplies to those firms willing to give a commitment to produce priority goods needed for export or for the domestic market. However, in the medium and long term, Polish economic development will depend substantially on the management of its huge foreign debt, and the restoration of normal economic relations with governments and business circles in the developed market economies. At the beginning of 1985 prospects for this seem considerably better than a year ago.[147]

In *Romania*, the key priorities of the annual plan for 1985 are "to accelerate the economic growth rate compared with first years of the current five-year plan; to develop and modernize industry; to steadily increase agricultural yields; to expand activities in other economic branches; to extend the country's participation in the international division of labour; and to enhance strongly qualitative aspects in all fields".[148] These are not easy tasks to achieve in a period of one year. Both five-year and annual plans for Romania have for many years been the most amibitious of all countries of the region, and the annual plan for 1985 is no exception. Following an average NMP growth rate of somewhat less than 3 per cent in 1981-1983, reported NMP produced growth rate in 1984 surged to some 7 1/2 per cent. For the first time in the current quinquennium the NMP growth in 1984 corresponded with the rates envisaged by the five-year plan. The annual plan for 1985 calls for a further acceleration: NMP is to grow by 10 per cent. The year 1976 was the last when growth at such a high rate was recorded (appendix table B.1). This sharp acceleration is to be based on substantial cuts in energy and raw material costs: gross social product is scheduled to expand 3 percentage points slower than NMP, and the planned 7 1/2 per cent rise of gross

industrial output is expected to be accompanied by a 13 1/2 per cent rise in net industrial output. For industry this implies a reduction in energy and raw material inputs per unit of output of more than 5 per cent.[149] The reduction in material inputs implied for agriculture is similar to that for overall output. At the same time, labour productivity is planned to provide for five sixths of NMP growth. Foreign trade value (turnover) is expected to increase by 15 per cent and to lead to a further sizeable surplus on the balance of trade. Resources for domestic use will lag considerably behind NMP produced. Within NMP used accumulation will be granted priority, and gross investment is expected to increase by more than 8 per cent. Consumption will increase much more slowly. Real incomes per capita are nonetheless planned to rise by more than 3 per cent. Finally, it should be mentioned that, in November 1984, Romania issued guidelines on the five-year plan for 1986-1990. This calls for a further acceleration in economic growth compared with the recent past.

The annual plan of the *Soviet Union* has already been referred to several times when comparing developments in the Soviet Union and eastern Europe. Only its main features will be described here. According to one published statement: "The 1985 plan is geared towards stepping up intensification, improving the technical standard of production, the dynamic and balanced development of the economy and making maximum use of productive and scientific and technical potential and internal economic reserves."[150] This is in line with previous findings on factor inputs and efficiency in their use (sub-section (iii) above). To encourage better use of existing potential, 21 more all-union and republican ministries and consumer service enterprises in many provinces will be harnessed to work according to the methods used under the economic experiment introduced at the beginning of 1984.[151] This has already brought about significant changes. Special policies will be applied in agriculture. The area of reclaimed land will be enlarged. Its better use is necessary to reduce year-to-year production fluctuations, in particular crop production. Gross agricultural output is expected to rise by 6 per cent. This, with a planned 4 per cent increase in gross industrial production, should bring about a 3 1/2 per cent expansion in resources for domestic use, as compared with an estimated 4 per cent growth of NMP produced. Almost 90 per cent of NMP growth is expected to be provided by labour productivity increases. Foreign trade turnover should expand faster than national output. As gross investment and real income per capita are envisaged to grow at rates similar to that of NMP used, the allocation of resources for domestic use will be similar to that in previous years (one quarter for accumulation, three quarters for consumption). This is in line with the overall allocation pattern envisaged in the current five-year plan. The roughly 5 per cent increment planned in retail trade turnover refers to increment in nominal terms. The preparation of the next five-year plan has already started and a long-term plan of overall social and economic development up to the year 2000 is well under way.

[147] For a western assessment of the issue see e.g., "Talking again with Poland", *Financial Times*, 6 August 1984, p. 8.

[148] This was pointed out in the presentation of the plan to the national parliament, by Mr. S. Birlea, *Scinteia*, 13 December 1984.

[149] Article 4 of the final text of the plan, among others, requires that the Council of Ministers, together with other organs, ensure "primary utilization of domestic resources and the reduction of imports to the absolute minimum", *Scinteia*, 13 December 1984.

[150] This was pointed out by Mr. N.K. Baibakov, Deputy Chairman of the USSR Council of Ministers and Chairman of the State Planning Committee, in his presentation of the plan to the Supreme Soviet. See *Pravda*, 28 November 1984.

[151] Soviet economic management reforms introduced since January 1984 were also favourably assessed in the international press. See e.g., D. Buchan, "Management reforms pay off in higher Soviet production", *Financial Times*, 3 October 1984, p. 2.

TABLE 4.1.10

**Net material product and sectoral gross output in the
Byelorussian SSR and the Ukrainian SSR**

(*Annual percentage changes*)

| | Net material product | | Gross output | | | |
| | | | Agriculture[a] | | Industry | |
	Plan	Actual	Plan	Actual	Plan	Actual
Byelorussian SSR						
1976-1980	6.0	5.2	2.3	1.5	7.4	7.2
1981	3.9	5.0	18.9	12.9	4.1	5.0
1982	4.2	2.2	9.3	−4.2	4.3	4.7
1983	3.8	7.0	12.0	9.3	3.4	5.0
1984	3.9	5.0	3.4	5.2	4.1	5.6
1985	3.8	..	3.5	..	4.1	..
1981-1985	4.3	..	2.1	..	5.1	..
Ukrainian SSR						
1976-1980	4.9	3.4	2.5	1.6	5.9	3.9
1981	3.8	2.7	16.9	0.8	3.5	2.8
1982	3.6	3.5	..	6.9	4.0	2.9
1983	3.0	4.0	10.2	2.6	2.8	4.4
1984	3.4	4.3	1.8	3.2	3.1	4.0
1985	3.6	..	6.3	..	3.1	..
1981-1985	3.6	..	2.3	..	4.2	..

Source: National statistics, plans and plan fulfilment reports.

[a] For five-year period, average annual percentage changes are calculated on the basis of annual averages relative to the annual averages for the previous five-year period total.

Recent developments and policy objectives for 1985 in the *Byelorussian and Ukrainian Soviet Socialist Republics* are shown in table 4.1.10.

The beginning of the 1980s in *Byelorussian SSR*—as in the Soviet Union as a whole—was marked by some slowdown in the pace of economic growth. In the first four years of the five-year plan, agricultural production fluctuated substantially. In fact, the lowest growth rate of NMP produced—about 2 per cent in 1982—reflected mainly a sharp, 4 per cent contraction in gross agricultural output in that year. However, the growth of gross industrial production was rather stable, around 5 per cent annually. This helped to boost NMP in the Republic by more than 12 per cent in 1983-1984, compared with only about 7 per cent in the two previous years.[152] Average annual NMP growth in the first four years of the quinquennium thus achieved an average of almost 5 per cent annually, which is above the rate envisaged by the five-year plan. Following a rather good performance in 1983-1984, the annual plan of the Republic envisages a somewhat slower expansion in 1985.[153] However, if achieved, the average growth over the whole five-year period will be faster than originally expected.

Special attention is being paid to the quality of production, and in 1984 one quarter of total industrial production was granted the Soviet seal of quality. This was one result of the "complex programme" to ensure continuous improvement in the quality of national production.[154] The development of efficiency was also helped by changes in overall management within the framework of the economic experiment introduced on 1 January 1984. The

experience of the Republic indicates that such developments should, however, occur at a faster rate and more consistently.[155]

Overall development in the *Ukrainian SSR* in the four years since 1980 was marked by stable improvement in the main economic indicators. No stagnation or contraction in agricultural output took place in those years. The lowest growth rate of NMP produced, 2 1/2 per cent, was recorded in 1981, after which it accelerated in three consecutive years to 4 1/2 per cent in 1984.[156] A similar development in gross industrial production occurred. The upturn in economic growth in 1983-1984 compared with the two previous years ensured almost the same pace of overall expansion for 1981-1984 as had been envisaged by the five-year plan (3.6 per cent). The NMP growth target for 1985 is the same[157], indicating that the Republic's five-year plan target for NMP will be achieved. Targets for 1985 include a 3 per cent increment in industrial and a more than 6 per cent rise in gross agricultural production. Emphasis has been placed on "development of branches determining an accelerated rate of implementation of the achievements of science and technology into the national economy, on timely fulfilment of target-oriented scientific and technical programmes, on an enlargement of the scale of implementation of resource-saving technologies, and on substantial improvement of final work outcomes".[158] Increasing

---

[152] For more details about recent developments in the Republic, and especially in 1984, see *Sel'skaia gazeta*, 31 January 1985.

[153] Annual plans for 1985, and also the budget for the same year, were published in *Sovietskaia Bielorussiia*, 8 December 1984. For presentation of the plan by A. A. Reut, Chairman of the State Planning Committee of Byelorussia, see *Sovietskaia Bielorussiia*, 7 December 1983.

[154] P. Yanus, "Attestat na perspektivnost'", *Sotsialisticheskaia industriia*, 23 November 1984, p. 3.

[155] This was pointed out by Mr. G. Serov, Deputy Chairman of the State Planning Committee of Byelorussia: "When enlarging the economic experiment it is necessary to depart more decisively from the orientation towards gross output (*val*). Such an orientation allows the achievement of high performance indicators on a formal basis only." G. Serov, "Bez ogliadki na privichnoe", *Sotsialisticheskaia industriia*, 2 October 1984, p. 2.

[156] Plan fulfilment report was issued in *Pravda Ukrainy*, 29 January 1985, pp. 1 and 2.

[157] The laws on the state plan and the state budget of the Ukrainian SSR were published in *Pravda Ukrainy*, 7 December 1984.

[158] This was pointed out by Mr. V. A. Masol, Chairman of the State Planning Committee of the Ukraine, in the presentation of the annual plan for 1985 to the Supreme Soviet of Ukraine, *ibid.*, p. 2.

labour productivity is to account for the whole increment in NMP produced in 1985. The experience of the Dniepropetrovsk Combine in reducing and more efficiently using available manpower acquired support throughout the Soviet Union and was singled out in a special decree of the Central Committee of CPSU.[159]

The economic experiments implemented in some branches since January 1984 were found to give positive results. They are

[159] *Ekonomicheskaia gazeta*, No. 47, November 1984, p. 3.

expected to be introduced on a wider basis in 1985.[160] Special attention is to be paid to closer linkage of economic enterprises and organisations in various economic sectors in order to provide more balanced development and to better satisfy demand.

[160] In an interview to *Izvestiia*, 26 August 1984, p. 2, Mr. I. I. Lukinov, Director of the Institute of Economics of the Academy of Sciences of the Ukrainian SSR stated: "... There has not so far been full clarity with regard to the practical implementation of rights in the area of independent planning of enterprises and of the incentive factors."

4.2 AGRICULTURE

Recent developments in agricultural production and inputs in eastern Europe and the Soviet Union, together with some policy innovations, are reviewed in this section. Sub-section (i) deals with gross agricultural output in 1984 against the background of performance in previous years and of the five-year plan targets. In sub-section (ii) factor inputs and productivity changes are described. Trends in the crop and the livestock branches of agriculture are summarized in sub-sections (iii) and (iv). Finally, sub-section (v) reviews recent policy measures affecting agriculture.

(i) Growth of agricultural output

Gross agricultural output in the east European countries reached a record level in 1984. The 7 per cent rise was more than three times higher than planned (table 4.2.1 and appendix table B.13). Bulgaria, the German Democratic Republic, Poland and Romania recorded the fastest annual rise of any year of the current five-year plan. Czechoslovakia registered its third consecutive rise in output. In most countries of eastern Europe below-plan shortfalls in 1983 were generally made good, and output growth accelerated for the six countries together.

Nevertheless, the fact that each country fell short of its agricultural output target in at least one year of the current five-year plan period makes it questionable whether the overall expansion planned for 1981-1985 compared with 1976-1980 will be achieved. If the annual targets for 1985 are added to the results for 1981-1984, gross agricultural output in 1985 will range between 8-15 per cent higher than in 1980 in most countries. This will, at least, ensure an acceleration in the average annual growth rate of gross agricultural output in 1981-1985 compared with 1976-1980 in the German Democratic Republic and fulfilment of the plan target in Hungary, but not in the other countries.

There was no increase in Soviet gross agricultural output in 1984. More buoyant growth in 1982 and 1983, in which agriculture recovered from three previous consecutive years of production shortfalls, was halted in 1984; bad weather retarded overall performance for the fourth year in a six-year period. If the target for 1985 is implemented, gross agricultural output will none the less rise more than 3 per cent higher than in 1980 and ensure the same average annual growth rate as in the preceding five-year period.

Crop production was the main component of changes in agricultural output in 1984. A late spring, which delayed crop growing by three to four weeks, was followed by favourable weather throughout eastern Europe. Irrigation measures taken to safeguard crops after the dry summers of 1982 and 1983 also contributed. The main cultivation operations were completed on time. *Grain output* achieved record levels in five out of the six east European countries, Bulgaria's harvest falling slightly below the previous best result of 1982. The harvest of *non-grain crops* was also higher than in 1983. The delayed winter in 1984 reduced losses of potatoes and sugar beet. The weather also favoured raw fodder production and extended the grazing period for cattle. As a result, the output and productivity of the livestock branch progressed and surpassed the 1983 results in all countries, and plans were more than fulfilled in some.

The performance of the livestock branch, which generally fluctuates less than crop output, was the main factor in maintaining gross agricultural output in the Soviet Union at its 1983 level. A higher carry-over of feed stocks partly reflected a jump in feed grain imports and helped to offset a sharp decline in crop production. Crop damage during the winter could not be made good by resowing in the spring. Most crops, especially grain, suffered from drought in the summer. Thus there was a growing disparity between crop and livestock output in the Soviet Union, where feed shortages are regularly compensated by imports. In eastern Europe, on the other hand, progress in the livestock branch is conditional on domestic crop performance. The harvests of 1984 improved domestic supplies of raw materials and foodstuffs for 1984/85 in most countries. The room for manoeuvre of traditional net exporters of agricultural products such as Bulgaria, Hungary and Romania increased, while net importers such as Czechoslovakia and the German Democratic Republic may be able to reduce their import volume. Poland's grain imports will probably stay at the 1983 level and possibilities of compensating wheat import requirements by exports of rye have improved. Early purchases of grain indicate a record level of grain imports by the Soviet Union in 1984/85.

(ii) Agricultural inputs and productivity

(*a*) No big changes in the *agricultural land area* or its cropping structure were reported for 1984. Indeed the area has remained constant over the last few years in almost all countries of eastern Europe (table 4.2.2). Romania, which follows a policy of steady expansion of the arable area, is the exception. Czechoslovakia and Hungary have halted the decline in area which occurred every year in the preceding five-year period. The cropping structure has changed in favour of grain since 1981, reflecting in most countries measures to encourage higher grain output. They included the expansion of grain sowings within an unchanged arable area. In contrast, the area of land under grain in the Soviet Union has decreased and at an accelerating rate in recent years compared with 1976-1980. This probably reflects two developments: the withdrawal of certain particularly low-yielding areas from grain cultivation, and changes in land use following winter damage in particular years (e.g. resowing with green maize instead of maize grown to full maturity).[161] The last argument in particular seems to account for the sharp decrease in the grain area in the Ukrainian SSR in 1983.

(*b*) Declining trends in *agricultural employment* in many countries followed past trends until 1983. In *Bulgaria*, the release of agricultural labour to industry and other sectors accelerated in 1983 (table 4.2.3 and appendix table B.14). Bulgarian farm workers account for more than 20 per cent of the total economically active population. However, their average age is high and rising. Thus the rural exodus, despite the large size of the remaining work force, needs to be offset by increasing supplies of productivity-enhancing material inputs and by continuous modernization of equipment. The fast increases in capital intensity in recent years bear witness to this approach. *Labour productivity* has, in fact, registered high growth rates but it fell sharply in 1983 as a result of the decline in agricultural output in that year. Improved output performance in 1984 was accompanied by a rise in labour productivity which will probably equal the improvement in 1982.

---

[161] Reported land use is based on *harvested* rather than on sown area.

TABLE 4.2.1

Gross agricultural production
(*Annual percentage change*)

Country	1976-1980	1981	1982	1983	1984 Plan	1984 Actual	1985 Plan	1981-1985 Plan
Bulgaria								
Total	2.1	5.9	5.2	−7.2	3.1	6.8	3.2	3.4
Crop	0.7	10.2	7.9	−17.4	..	13.9	..	..
Animal	4.0	2.2	2.6	3.0	..	1.1	..	..
Czechoslovakia								
Total	1.5	−2.5	4.4	4.2	—	3.6	−1.1	1.4-1.9
Crop	1.3	−5.3	13.8	2.8	5.2	4.2	..	..
Animal	2.1	−0.5	−2.0	5.4	−3.9	3.2	..	..
German Democratic Republic								
Total	1.2	1.6	−4.0	4.1	6.4[a]	8.5	−1.9*	1.1
Crop	0.1	1.9	1.7	1.2	8.4[a]	13.9	−4.6[a]	..
Animal	2.0	1.5	−7.4	6.0	5.1[a]	5.1	—*	..
Hungary								
Total	2.9	2.0	7.3	−2.7	3.4-4.1	2.5-3.0	1.0	2.3-2.8
Crop	1.8	1.6	9.4	−7.5	9.8	4	2.0	3.0-3.4
Animal	4.1	2.4	5.3	2.2	..	1	—	1.6-2.3
Poland								
Total	0.6	3.8	−2.8	3.3	1.5-2.0	5.7	(−0.8)-1.4	2.2*
Crop	−0.3	18.9	−2.5	5.9	1.4-2.4	7.6	(−0.5-3.5)	..
Animal	1.7	−8.9	−3.2	0.4	1.5	3.4	2.4-3.6	..
Romania								
Total	4.8	−0.9	7.6	−1.6	5.4-6.0	13.3	6.0-6.8	4.5-5.0
Crop	3.8	0.6	12.8	−5.2	..	..	..	..
Animal	6.3	−2.8	0.2	3.7	..	..	..	..
Eastern Europe								
Total	1.9	1.8	1.6	0.8	2.2	6.9	1.4	2.9
Crop	0.9	6.7	5.0	−1.0	..	..	..	..
Animal	3.0	−2.9	−1.5	3.0	..	..	..	..
Soviet Union								
Total	1.7	−1.0	5.5	6.1	6.4	—	6.7	2.5
Crop	1.9	−2.4	9.2	5.9	..	..	..	3.2
Animal	1.6	0.1	2.6	6.3	..	..	..	2.5
Byelorussian SSR								
Total	1.5	12.9	−4.2	11.0	3.4	5.2	3.5	2.1
Crop	1.1	33.1	−15.5	18.7	..	..	..	..
Animal	1.8	−0.1	5.3	6.8	..	..	..	..
Ukrainian SSR								
Total	1.6	0.8	6.9	2.6	1.8	3.2	6.3	2.3
Crop	1.4	1.8	13.7	−2.8	..	..	..	..
Animal	1.7	−0.1	1.3	7.6	..	..	..	..
Eastern Europe and the Soviet Union								
Total	1.7	−0.1	4.2	4.3	5.0	2.2	5.0	2.6
Crop	1.4	0.5	7.8	3.6	..	..	..	..
Animal	2.1	−1.0	2.6	6.3	..	..	..	..

Sources: Statisticheskii ezhegodnik stran-chlenov SEV 1984 (CMEA Statistical Yearbook 1984) Moscow, 1984, p. 157; national plans and plan fulfilment reports.

[a] Calculated on the basis of indicated change in physical terms.

In *Czechoslovakia*, where agricultural employment stabilized at the beginning of the current five-year period, the outflow resumed thereafter, and in 1983 it rose to the same average annual rate of decrease as during the preceding five-year period. The unbroken three-year period of rising output since 1982, together with a notable rise in agricultural fixed assets, led to high labour productivity growth, and an increase of 4-5 per cent can be assumed for 1984.

The *German Democratic Republic* halted the outflow of labour from agriculture after 1980. The declared policy of stabilizing employment levels by stressing the labour-intensive livestock branch contributed to the retention of workers, and hence to improvements in the age structure of the agricultural labour force. The price which had to be paid was stagnating labour productivity over 1981-1983, but good output performance was registered by the livestock branch despite a setback in crop production in 1983. The big turnround in 1984 vindicated this policy: labour productivity probably increased by 7-8 per cent in that year.

TABLE 4.2.2

Arable land area
(*Annual percentage change*)

	Total				of which under grain			
	1980/1975	1981	1982	1983	1980/1975	1981	1982	1983
Bulgaria	—	0.9	0.2	−0.2	−1.4	1.6	2.7	—
Czechoslovakia	−0.4	—	—	−0.1	−0.9	−0.9	−0.9	−1.3
German Democratic Republic. .	0.3	−0.4	−0.2	0.1	−1.1	−1.6	1.3	0.9
Hungary	−0.4	0.1	−0.2	—	−1.5	−3.5	3.2	0.7
Poland	−0.2	0.1	0.3	−0.4	−0.1	0.5	2.3	0.8
Romania	0.2	0.2	0.2	0.3	0.7	1.1	−6.5	—
Soviet Union	0.1	0.1	—	0.1	−0.2	−0.8	−2.0	−1.8
Byelorussian SSR.	0.2	—	—	—	−3.8	−3.9	−2.3	−1.0
Ukrainian SSR.	0.1	—	—	—	−0.1	1.2	−0.2	−7.7

Source: Statisticheskii ezhogednik stran-chlenov SEV 1984 (CMEA Statistical Yearbook 1984), Moscow, 1984, p. 162; *Narodnoye khoziaistvo USSR v 1983 godu* (Statistical Yearbook of the USSR), Moscow, 1984, p. 227.

Agricultural employment in *Hungary* fluctuates considerably more than in other countries. The declining trend of the agricultural labour force was actually reversed at the end of the 1970s. In 1981, the workforce grew by more than 4 per cent but after 1982 the decline resumed. The decision to permit the establishment of small-scale private operations in the industrial and service sectors of the economy has attracted employees from state and cooperative agricultural activity.[162] In the long run this could have favourable effects on productivity in the economy as a whole, given that agricultural employment still acounts for more than 20 per cent of the total labour force. The question is whether negative consequences for agriculture can be avoided in the short run. The high rates of growth of capital intensity since 1981 seem to reflect awareness of this problem.

Changes in agricultural employment in *Poland* were influenced by the economic and social disturbances at the beginning of the 1980s. Interest in agricultural work has been revitalized by changes in agricultural policy, and this has led to improvements in the age structure of the farm labour force.[163] Nevertheless, there is still an outflow of workers according to data for 1982-1983. In spite of agriculture's large and increasing share of total investment outlays, the recent decline in overall investment spending suggests strongly that in the medium-term agricultural output gains will continue to depend on labour-intensive operations in the overwhelmingly small-scale, privately owned agricultural sector. A high share of the total labour force will continue to be employed in agriculture during the next years—it is currently still nearly 30 per cent.

In *Romania* the long-term falling trend of agricultural employment was halted in 1983. Data for 1984 are not yet available and it is thus not known whether 1983 was an exceptional case or

[162] In 1984, around 20,000 co-operative members moved away from agricultural occupations. *Magyar Nemzet*, 3 January 1985.

[163] See *Economic Survey of Europe 1983*, p. 130.

TABLE 4.2.3

Employment, labour productivity and capital intensity
(*Annual percentage change*)

	Employment[a]				Labour productivity[b]				Capital intensity[c]			
	1980/1975	1981	1982	1983	1980/1975	1981	1982	1983	1980/1975	1981	1982	1983
Bulgaria	−2.7	−1.5	−2.8	−3.1	3.7	7.5	8.2	−4.2	8.3	−0.1	8.3	8.6
Czechoslovakia	−1.4	—	−0.8	−1.4	3.4	−2.5	5.2	5.7	8.1	6.1	6.1	6.4
German Democratic Republic. .	−0.3	0.4	0.6	1.5	3.8	1.2	−4.6	2.6	5.5	4.5	4.3	3.2
Hungary	−0.5	4.4	0.4	−1.0	2.9	−2.3	6.9	−1.7	6.0	−0.1	3.9	5.1*
Poland	0.5	1.1	−0.5	−0.5	−2.2	2.9	−2.3	3.8	6.2	2.9	2.4	2.5
Romania	−4.4	−2.7	−1.0	0.2	8.6	1.8	8.6	−1.8	12.4	11.8	11.2	9.7
Soviet Union	−0.8	−0.4	0.1	0.2	2.3	−0.6	5.4	5.9	8.2	7.1	7.0	6.4

Sources: Statisticheskii ezhegodnik stran-chlenov SEV 1984 (CMEA Statistical Yearbook 1984), Moscow, 1984, pp. 43, 157, 363-366; national statistics.

[a] Annual average.

[b] Gross output per employee.

[c] Fixed assets per employee.

TABLE 4.2.4

Investment, fixed assets and capital productivity
(*Annual percentage change*)

	Investments				Fixed assets				Capital productivity [a]			
	1980⁄1975	1981	1982	1983	1980⁄1975	1981	1982	1983	1980⁄1975	1981	1982	1983
Bulgaria	1.3	10.7	−18.6	1.6	5.4	−2.3	5.3	5.2	−4.3	8.4	−0.1	−11.8
Czechoslovakia	0.7	5.0	4.6	12.6	6.6	6.1	5.3	4.9	−4.5	−8.1	−0.9	−0.7
German Democratic Republic. .	−0.4	2.9	−7.6	−9.3	5.2	4.9	4.9	4.7	−3.9	−3.1	−8.5	−0.6
Hungary	−0.5	8.0	−1.0	−15.4	5.5	4.3	4.3	4.0*	−2.8	−2.2	2.9	−6.4*
Poland	−0.5	−12.5	−15.3	5.6	6.7	4.0	1.9	2.0	−7.9	−0.2	−4.6	1.2
Romania	7.5	10.0	−1.8	8.6	7.5	8.8	10.1	9.9	−3.4	−8.9	−2.4	−10.5
Soviet Union	2.9	2.6	1.6	3.5	7.3	6.7	7.1	6.6	−5.3	−7.2	−1.5	−0.5

Sources: Statisticheskii ezhegodnik stran-chlenov SEV 1984 (CMEA Statistical Yearbook 1984), Moscow, 1984, pp. 43, 135, 137; national statistics.

[a] Gross agricultural output per unit of fixed assets.

whether a point of stabilization has been reached. Variations in output and labour productivity were wider than in most other countries. The growth rates of capital intensity decelerated, but they are still considerably higher than in the other countries of the region. They reflect efforts to make good the low level of mechanization achieved in the past.

The fall in agricultural employment has also apparently been arrested in the *Soviet Union*. Since 1981, the agricultural labour force stabilized as a result of the food programme currently being implemented.[164] The productivity potential of the Soviet agricultural labour force under relatively normal weather conditions has been sustained by high growth rates in capital intensity. Labour productivity thus rose at high rates in 1982-1983. The shortfall of crop production per worker in 1984 may be balanced by productivity gains in the livestock branch, resulting in zero growth of productivity in 1984 for agriculture as a whole.

(*c*) Changes in *agricultural investment* during the current five-year plan reflect widely different priorities in individual countries. Year-to-year fluctuations have been considerable—particularly in Bulgaria and Romania in 1981-1983 (table 4.2.4 and appendix table B.14). Both countries reported further increases in supplies of machinery and equipment in 1984. Czechoslovakia, Poland and the Soviet Union recently accelerated the growth of agricultural investments. In Czechoslovakia, effort is concentrated on the replacement of outdated equipment. Poland is making efforts to increase supplies of machinery which correspond to the needs of its predominantly small-scale agricultural structure. The Soviet Union is implementing a food programme which provides for improved supply of machinery and spare parts, cooling and storage equipment and processing units for first stage processing of products within the agricultural sector itself.

In the German Democratic Republic and Hungary, agricultural investments declined in absolute terms in recent years. Agriculture in both countries is characterized by high machinery and equipment levels, and current policy is focused on putting them to better use rather than expanding their quantity. In 1984, the German Democratic Republic stabilized the level of investments in agriculture at around the 1983 level.

(*d*) The stock of *fixed assets* in agriculture grew remarkably in most countries, although growth rates in 1981-1983 were lower than the yearly average of 1976-1980 except in Romania, where they accelerated. *Capital productivity* since the early 1970s fell in all countries, and continued to decline at faster rates in 1981-1983 than in 1976-1980 in all countries but Poland. The generally still insufficient return on high capital inputs is a problem with complex causes. Among these are shortcomings in the level and structure of current inputs, especially fertilizers, and the lack of certain categories of machinery. Moreover, despite high overall levels of mechanisation of cultivation and harvesting, machinery is not always well adapted to local soil conditions. These shortcomings have had consequences ranging from decreasing soil fertility to failures in adjusting crop structures and shielding the harvest from bad weather. It can be assumed that the capital productivity decline decelerated in 1984 in most countries due to substantial output increases.

(iii) Crop production

In 1984 the countries of the southern part of the region (Bulgaria, Hungary and Romania) aimed to repeat the good results achieved in 1982 and to recover from the fall in crop production in 1983. The other countries of the region increased output at levels higher than in the preceding year. Results surpassed expectations in 1984, except in the Soviet Union (table 4.2.5). The main factor contributing to success in eastern Europe was *grain*. For the first time, output approached 100 million tonnes in eastern Europe as a whole—slightly below the combined plan targets of the six countries for the final year of the current five-year plan and 25 per cent higher than the annual average of harvests in 1976-1980 (appendix table B.18). All east European countries achieved record or, in the case of Bulgaria, near-record grain harvests.

The upswing of Soviet grain production in 1982 and 1983 was halted in 1984. No output data for 1984 have been published, continuing a black-out since the year 1980, but it has been confirmed that there was a substantial grain shortfall.[165] The volume of output has been estimated at about 170 million tonnes.[166] Drought affected autumn-sown crops, while hot, dry winds damaged spring-sown coarse grains. Soviet agriculture's

---

[164] A food programme of the Soviet Union for the period ending in 1990 was adopted in 1982 by the Central Committee of the CPSU. For further details, see *Economic Survey of Europe 1982*, p. 146.

[165] *Pravda*, 24 October 1984.

[166] FAO, *Monthly Bulletin of Statistics*, vol. 7, October 1984.

TABLE 4.2.5

Crop and grain production and grain yields
(*Annual percentage change*)

	Crop production					Grain production					Grain yield per hectare				
	1980	*1981*	*1982*	*1983*	*1984*	*1980*	*1981*	*1982*	*1983*	*1984*	*1980*	*1981*	*1982*	*1983*	*1984*
Bulgaria	0.8	10.2	7.9	−17.4	13.9	1.3	10.8	17.9	−20.5	16.3	1.3	9.1	14.7	−20.6	17.5*
Czechoslovakia . .	1.0	−5.3	13.8	2.8	4.2	1.6	−12.2	9.3	7.9	6.7*	1.6	−11.5	10.4	9.4	8.0
German Democratic Republic	−	1.9	1.7	1.2	13.9	0.8	−7.8	13.1	0.4	13.3	−0.2	−6.4	11.6	−0.5	14.8
Hungary	2.1	1.6	9.4	−7.5	4.0	2.1	−8.0	15.7	−7.6	12.8*	3.5	−5.1	12.5	−8.3	13.0*
Poland	−0.2	18.9	−2.5	5.9	7.6	−1.5	7.5	7.3	4.7	10.9	−0.5	6.9	4.9	3.9	9.1
Romania	3.8	0.6	12.8	−5.2	..	5.4	−1.1	12.3	−12.9	20.4	4.5	−3.2	20.0*	−14.0*	19.0*
Soviet Union . . .	1.9	−2.4	9.2	5.9	..	2.5	−15.4	11.9*	11.7*	−15.0*	1.7	−14.8	11.8	12.0	−10.0*

Sources: Statisticheskii ezhegodnik stran-chlenov SEV 1984 (CMEA Statistical Yearbook 1984), Moscow, 1984, pp. 157-158, 175, 181, and plan fulfilment reports.

vulnerability to weather conditions is still very high and possibilities for limiting such damage are not comprehensively used. Even so, many examples are reported of farms which yielded good results even under difficult conditions.[167]

Since the grain area in the region as a whole has not changed much, the volume of output is primarily determined by yields. There is also a close connection between grain and total crop production. This varies between countries in accordance with the varying share of grain in total arable output. Grain is highest relative to total crop output in Bulgaria, Hungary and Romania, and is lower in Czechoslovakia, the German Democratic Republic, Poland and the Soviet Union.

Grain in fact varied between 40 and 70 per cent of total arable output in the seven countries of the region in 1981-1983. An overview of annual changes in non-grain crop production up to 1983 is given in table 4.2.6. The data reported above indicate positive changes in most countries in 1984.

Detailed data for *non-grain crops* in 1984 are not yet available. The reported output of potatoes, sugar beet and other crops in 1984 indicate satisfactory to good results. Bulgaria did not achieve its plan targets in some crops but surpassed the results achieved in 1976-1980 in most cases by 6-14 per cent. Czechoslovakia recorded higher production of potatoes, sugar beet and green maize than in 1983. In the German Democratic Republic,

[167] *Pravda*, 26 November 1984.

where—as in Czechoslovakia—potato and sugar beet yields have stagnated at low levels over a long period, better results were recorded in 1984. Yields increased by more than 30 and 15 per cent respectively. Pastures and meadows yielded record amounts of fodder. In Hungary, only the fruit and grape harvest fell short of output in 1983. Poland reported higher output than in 1983 for most crops, though sugar beet production fell slightly. Romania's production of potatoes, sugar beet and vegetables was considerably higher than in 1983. In the Soviet Union, output of potatoes increased slightly and sugar beet by 4 per cent. Raw cotton production, which varied between 9-10 million tonnes for several years, decreased to 8.6 million tonnes in 1984. This was anticipated in view of cold spring weather, which necessitated the replanting of large areas in the southern republics of the Soviet Union.

(iv) Livestock and livestock output

Limited preliminary information for 1984 indicates that the livestock sector improved its performance in all countries. Even countries with unsatisfactory crop production in 1983 managed to hold their herds stable and raise output per animal (table 4.2.7 and appendix table B.9). The structure of herds changed little. In *Bulgaria*, the number of cattle, cows and pigs decreased slightly in 1983 in favour of sheep, goats and poultry. The process of restructuring was pursued as planned in *Czechoslovakia*. Final data for 1983 show an increase in cattle and a decrease in pig

TABLE 4.2.6

Non-grain crop production [a]

	Annual percentage change				Percentage share in total crop output			
	1976-1980	*1981*	*1982*	*1983*	*1976-1980*	*1981*	*1982*	*1983*
Bulgaria	1.0	6.2	9.9	−13.0	36.1	34.6	33.0	35.0
Czechoslovakia	0.5	−0.1	5.2	4.1	46.6	49.4	48.4	47.5
German Democratic Republic . .	0.4	7.1	−11.9	2.9	52.9	56.2	50.0	49.1
Hungary	3.8	4.3	4.8	−11.9	32.2	34.8	32.5	31.5
Poland	0.2	37.4	−17.9	7.0	60.0	61.1	54.6	55.1
Romania	3.3	−1.9	20.2	..	36.5	34.8	36.3	..
Soviet Union	1.9	−4.5	11.4	6.0	45.8	50.6*	50.5*	49.2*

Sources: Statisticheskii ezhegodnik stran-chlenov SEV, 1984 (CMEA Statistical Yearbook 1984), Moscow, 1984, pp. 157-158, 175, and 181; plan fulfilment reports.

[a] Based on physical terms (grain units). Data may not cover all crops and slight deviations from national calculations are therefore possible.

TABLE 4.2.7

Livestock and livestock output
(Annual percentage change)

	Livestock[a]				Meat production				Milk producction				Eggs			
	1976-1980	1981	1982	1983	1976-1980	1981	1982	1983	1976-1980	1981	1982	1983	1976-1980	1981	1982	1983
Bulgaria	2.3	0.6	0.4	0.1	3.5	1.7	1.6	3.7	4.2	3.6	5.5	4.5	5.8	−0.4	2.4	6.6
Czechoslovakia .	1.4	−1.5	−	6.1	2.1	1.8	−7.4	5.2	1.4	0.1	2.2	9.5	1.7	1.4	1.2	4.0
German Democratic Republic	1.2	0.9	−3.3	−0.6	0.7	5.2	−8.1	2.1	−0.4	−1.4	−5.2	6.5	1.8	2.8	0.5	2.7
Hungary	1.4	1.4	3.7	2.0	2.0	0.8	7.2	5.8	6.9	5.3	2.3	2.6	1.8	0.2	−0.8	1.9
Poland	−0.7[b]	−1.9[b]	−4.4[b]	−4.5[b]	0.5	−19.6	2.1	−3.1	0.1	−7.0	−0.3	5.3	2.1	−1.0	−13.4	0.1
Romania	2.9	4.4	0.1	8.8	5.2	1.0	..	..	3.6	−7.9	−5.8	10.2	5.3	3.5	2.1	5.1
Soviet Union . . .	1.2	1.0	1.7	2.0	0.1	0.8	1.1	7.0	−	−2.2	2.4	5.9	3.2	4.2	2.5	3.6

Source: Statisticheskii ezhegodnik stran-chlenov SEV 1984 (CMEA Statistical Yearbook 1984), Moscow, 1984, pp. 187-189 and 194-195.

[a] Conventional units in terms of cows. Conversion ratios: cattle (other than cows) 0.6; pigs 0.3; sheep and goats 0.1; horses 1.0; poultry 0.02. Source: *Spravochnik po planirovaniiu sel'skogo khoziaistva*, Kolos, Moscow, 1974, p. 151.

[b] Excluding goats.

stock. Good results in crop farming paved the way for better results in the livestock sector than were planned for l984. Developments in the *German Democratic Republic* were similar. The share of cows in the national livestock herds (expressed in livestock units) fell but was offset by productivity gains. *Hungary*'s cattle stock, including cows, fell by small amounts in 1983 but rose again in 1984. There was a considerable increase in the pig herd. In *Poland*, the decreasing trend in herd sizes which prevailed during recent years was stopped in 1984: cattle numbers stabilized and the pig herd was partially rebuilt. Nevertheless, the process of full recovery in livestock will take some time. Available data on livestock development in *Romania* for 1983 indicate a sharp increase in animal numbers. Underlying an increase in total livestock of around 9 per cent in conventional units, there was an increase of more than 13 per cent in the cattle and pig population. The number of sheep increased by 9 per cent and goats by 33 per cent. In the *Soviet Union*, measures to implement the food programme seem to be paying off more quickly in the livestock than in the crop sector. The output of all livestock products has increased in recent years including 1984. The state plan for the procurement of livestock products was surpassed.

(v) Agricultural policy

A wide range of agricultural policy measures promulgated in 1984 included some dealing with short-term objectives as well as directives and orientations of a longer-term character. Among the former are price changes for several inputs (machinery, mineral fertilizer, etc.). Higher contract purchasing prices have been offered to eliminate subsidies and to stimulate the output of certain products in Hungary, Poland and Romania. Hungary has encouraged irrigation by abolishing water charges. Romania decreased the rate of interest paid on credits granted to machine-tractor stations, co-operatives and their members and to private farmers.

In some countries, outlines of medium- and long-term agricultural development strategies have been introduced or prepared. In *Czechoslovakia* a long-term programme for the development

of agriculture and the food branches to 1995 was adopted.[168] It will be a basic document in preparing the five-year plan for 1986-1990. Key points of the programme are scientifically based improvements in diet, and further steps towards self-sufficiency in agricultural products. The *German Democratic Republic* introduced a comprehensive agricultural price reform in 1984, which abolished state subsidies on industrial inputs to agriculture and raised agricultural procurement prices by 50-70 per cent. It aims to achieve better balance between crop and livestock production, to ensure the creation of financial resources by agricultural co-operatives themselves and to stimulate efficiency. Output results for 1984 have been interpreted as a first indication of the efficacy of this approach.[169] In *Poland* three important laws have been passed which will become operative in 1985 and which will also influence future agricultural development.[170] The scope of regional authorities in decision-making and financing has been enlarged, which may result in a smoother adaptation of policies to regional and local conditions than before. In October 1984, the Communist Party of the *Soviet Union* devoted a Central Committee session to agricultural problems. After a critical analysis of results achieved relative to the decision adopted at the plenary session in May 1965, a new resolution has been passed to supplement the existing Food Programme by measures to improve the quality and productivity of land.[171]

---

[168] *Rudé právo*, 4 October 1984.

[169] E. Höfner, Minister of Finance: "Experiences from the agricultural price reform convincingly confirm that its application increases the material interest of the agricultural co-operatives and state farms, co-operative peasants and farm workers in raising production and lowering the production input." *Neues Deutschland*, 1/2 December 1984.

[170] Law on the people's councils; the regional self-government law; the new budget law.

[171] Long-term programme for land improvement and for enhancing efficiency in the use of improved land in order to achieve a steady increase in the country's food reserves. *Pravda*, 24 October 1984.

4.3 INDUSTRY

The upturn in industrial growth which started in 1983 continued in 1984 at a rate of 4 1/2 per cent for the east European countries and the Soviet Union as a whole. The plan target of 4 per cent was thus overfulfilled. Various factors contributed to the upswing in industrial growth, mainly the removal of supply constraints. One explanatory factor for the east European countries was the development of foreign trade; increased imports in 1983 and 1984, made possible by a revival of exports, were generally concentrated in intermediate products. The easing of bottlenecks due to higher imports and the expansion of domestic output facilitated the implementation of policies to raise efficiency and encouraged a shift towards a more intensive industrial growth pattern. Accelerated industrial output growth was accompanied by a strong revival of industrial labour productivity. Progress was also achieved in reducing fuel, energy and material consumption per unit of industrial output. The decline of industrial capital productivity slowed down. Nevertheless progress so far achieved in reducing the material intensity of industrial production and in halting the fall in capital productivity is judged to be slow.

The forces which shaped industrial growth in the last two years are expected to continue exerting a positive influence on industrial performance in 1985. Plans for that year envisage a 4 per cent growth of industrial output for the region as a whole. Industrial policy continues to stress a speed-up of scientific and technical progress and further development of the international division of labour—mainly oriented towards closer co-operation between CMEA countries.

In sub-section (i) the changes in industrial production in 1984 are assessed, together with the factors which contributed to the upswing in industrial growth. Developments in labour produc-

tivity, material intensity and capital productivity are examined in sub-sections (ii), (iii) and (iv). The relationship between foreign trade and industry is discussed in sub-section (v). Sub-section (vi) presents industrial branch developments. An overview of the main policy objectives for 1985 in the region as a whole and by country is given in sub-section (vii).

(i) Growth of industrial output

Joint east European and Soviet industrial performance in 1984 was the best in the current quinquennium. Industrial output expanded at a rate of 4.4 per cent—the highest since 1979 for the region as a whole. Industrial growth in 1984 also exceeded the plan target for that year.

Despite differences in the industrial performance of individual countries, output growth rates in 1984 were higher than or the same as in 1983 in all countries of the region but Poland. They ranged between 3 per cent in Hungary and almost 7 per cent in Romania (table 4.3.1). Comparison of individual countries' planned and actual performance thus suggests that industrial growth expectations for 1984 materialized.

The factors which contributed to industrial expansion in 1983, analyzed in the previous edition of this publication,[172] continued to play a role in 1984. Factors helping to remove supply constraints were particularly important, notably:

— the expansion of production in industrial branches where slow growth gave rise to bottlenecks in previous years (fuel and energy, metallurgy and chemicals);

---

[172] *Economic Survey of Europe in 1983*, p. 145.

TABLE 4.3.1

Industrial output growth
(*Average annual percentage change*)

	1976-1980 actual	1981	1982	1983	1984 Actual	1984 Plan	1985 plan	1981-1985 implied[a]	1981-1985 plan
Bulgaria	6.0	4.9	4.6	3.9	4.6	5.0	5.2	4.6	5.1
Czechoslovakia	4.7	2.1	1.1	2.8	3.9	2.9	3.0	2.6	2.7-3.4
German Democratic Republic[b]	5.0	4.7	3.1	4.1	4.2	3.6	3.8	4.0	5.1
Hungary	3.4	2.4	2.5	1.4	3.0	1.5-2.0	3.0	2.5	3.5-4.0
Poland	4.7	−10.8	−2.1	6.4	5.3	4.5	4.0-4.5	5.2-5.4[c]	3.8-5.4[d]
Romania[e]	9.5	2.6	1.1	4.7	6.7	6.7	7.5	4.5	7.6
Eastern Europe	5.6	−0.6	1.2	4.4	4.9	4.3	4.6	2.9	3.7-3.8
Soviet Union	4.5	3.4	2.9	4.2	4.2	3.8	3.9	3.7	4.7
Eastern Europe and the Soviet Union	4.8	2.2	2.4	4.3	4.4	4.0	4.1	3.5	4.4

Source: National statistics, plans and plan fulfilment reports.

[a] Average annual industrial growth in 1981-1984 and annual growth rate planned for 1985.

[b] Marketable production.

[c] Average annual industrial growth in 1983-1984 and annual growth rate planned for 1985.

[d] Three-year plan 1983-1985.

[e] Since 1981, marketable production.

—favourable developments in agriculture where three successive years of good agricultural performance in most countries substantially improved the supply of industrial inputs of agricultural origin;

— higher imports by the east European countries in 1984;

— the reduction of fuels, energy, raw materials and other inputs per unit of industrial output. The last factor reinforced those mentioned above (see the more detailed analysis in sub-section (iii)).

Two periods of industrial development can be distinguished in the last four years. In the first (1981-1982) a marked slowdown in gross industrial output growth occurred—to an average rate of only 2.3 per cent annually. The slowdown was more pronounced in the six east European countries than in the Soviet Union. Poland contributed substantially to this development. In 1983-1984 a marked upswing in industrial growth took place. Aggregate gross industrial output in the seven countries together grew by an annual rate of 4.4 per cent—almost twice as high as in the preceding two years. Industrial growth performance improved substantially in eastern Europe—from a very low 0.3 per cent annually in 1981-1982 to a 4.6 per cent average in 1983-1984. The corresponding figures for the Soviet Union were 3.2 and 4.2 per cent. Differences in industrial growth between countries in 1981-1984 can be seen in chart 4.3.1.

The expansionary forces behind the marked upswing in industrial growth in the last two years varied between countries. Perhaps the two most important elements were, as indicated above, the removal of supply constraints and reductions in the material costs of output. Some analysts emphasize the high dependence of industrial output growth on fuel, energy and raw material supplies which were in short supply at the beginning of the 1980s.[173] Slow adjustment to new conditions also contributed to decelerating industrial growth rates. Industrial policy stressed the removal of supply/demand imbalances. Efforts to economize on scarce production factors brought positive results and a significant upturn of industrial growth in 1983-1984.

The developments which shaped industrial growth in the last two years are expected to stimulate industrial performance in 1985, though to a varying degree in different countries. The *annual plans for 1985* indicate that aggregate industrial output for the seven countries of the region will grow by 4.1 per cent, slightly below the pace of the last two years. Thus industrial strategy in the region appears designed to stabilize rather than accelerate industrial growth on a year-to-year basis. This policy can be explained partly by the marked improvement in efficiency in the last two years which exhausted to a certain extent some more easily activated short-term factors, but also by persisting uncertainties and limited factor input growth. Information on expected fuel and energy supplies in 1985 indicates that primary energy consumption in most east European countries will only slightly exceed the 1984 level. More stringent fuel and energy savings per unit of industrial output are thus likely to be required than in previous years. Manpower will also be limited. Possibilities for increasing imports will depend on export performance. Thus the attainment of planned industrial output targets in 1985 will require further improvements in the efficiency with which all factor inputs are used. Special prominence is therefore given to

the basic factors determining efficiency growth: scientific and technical progress, improvements in management and planning and human factors.[174]

The CMEA economic summit conference held in June 1984 adopted measures to strengthen the intensification process on the basis of international co-operation.[175] They are mostly of a long-term character. It was decided to formulate a comprehensive programme of scientific and technical progress for the next 15-20 years. Decisive importance is attached to electronics, automation, the nuclear power industry, the developments of new materials and production techniques and biotechnology. Closer co-operation in agricultural production and in the processing of agricultural produce will also be promoted. Co-operation in solving problems of fuel, energy and raw material production and of rational resource use were also agreed. Altogether an acceleration of the transition to intensive economic development ranks among the most important tasks of the CMEA countries.

(ii) Industrial employment and labour productivity

Despite a marked upturn in industrial growth, aggregate industrial employment in the region as a whole increased slowly—by 0.5 and an estimated 0.3 per cent in 1983 and 1984 respectively. Decelerating *industrial employment* growth has been apparent since 1977, but it was very noticeable in the last three years. The rise in employment slowed from 1.3 per cent annually in 1976-1980 to only 0.4 per cent in 1982-1984. However, inter-country differences were significant, ranging from absolute declines in Hungary and Poland to rises of approximately a 1/2 per cent in Czechoslovakia, the German Democratic Republic and the Soviet Union. Up to 1983, in contrast, relatively large increases compared with other countries were recorded in Bulgaria and Romania (table 4.3.2). Nevertheless, the plan fulfilment reports of Bulgaria and Romania for 1984 indicate a substantial slowdown of industrial employment growth in those countries too.

Several factors contributed to the declining trend in industrial employment growth. Demographic factors were responsible for the slowdown in the growth of the active population attaining working age. The previous steady declines in the economically active population in agriculture were halted in some countries at the beginning of the 1980s (German Democratic Republic and Hungary in 1981 and 1982, Romania in 1983 and the Soviet Union in 1982 and 1983). Such changes substantially reduced the reservoir of manpower available for redeployment in industry. Growing demand for labour in the non-material sphere intensified this constraint.

Full employment is a priority policy objective in the centrally planned economies. This is reflected in the slow adjustment of employment to output changes: in periods of slow industrial growth the labour force does not usually constitute a limiting factor. But in periods of substantial upturns in industrial growth, as in 1983-1984, some industrial manpower shortages have been reported. However, as has often been pointed out,[176] manpower

[173] R. Vintrová points out that the role of growth factors changes over time and that under present conditions output growth rates depend above all on the more efficient use of energy and other scarce resources. See her article "Tempa a proporce reprodukce v ekonomické strategii socialistických zemí" (Rates and proportions of reproduction in the economic strategy of the socialist countries), *Politická ekonomie*, No. 10, 1984, pp. 1017-1026.

[174] Academician V. Afanasyev stresses three basic factors of intensification—scientific and technical progress, improvement of the economic mechanism and of the entire system of economic management and better development of the labour force's education and skills. Special importance is attached to improving the economic mechanism and the system of management, *Pravda*, 11 January 1985.

[175] Statement on the main directions for the further development and deepening of economic, scientific and technical co-operation between CMEA member countries, *Pravda*, 16 June 1984.

[176] See, *inter alia*, V.A. Sidorov: "The effectiveness of labour and the quality of training of blue-collar workers", *Problems of Economics*, vol. XXV, No. 3, July 1982, or L. Kalinová: *Máme nedostatek pracovních sil?* (Are we short of labour?), Svoboda, Prague, 1979.

CHART 4.3.1.

Growth of gross industrial output
(Annual percentage change)

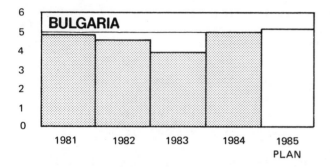

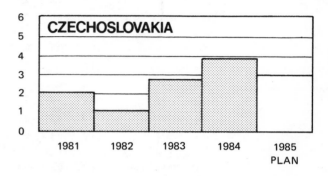

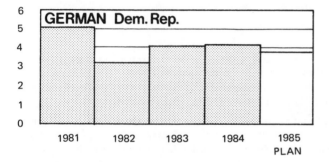

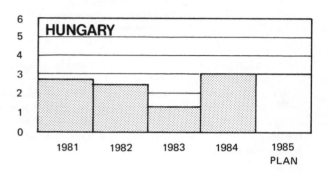

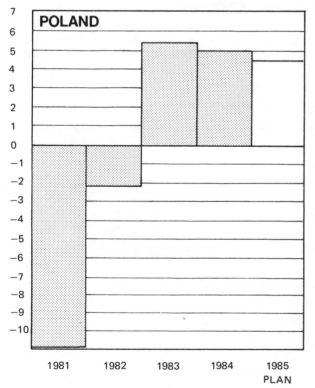

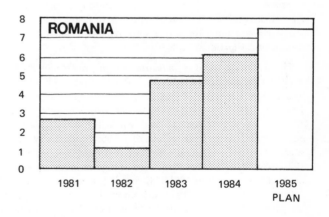

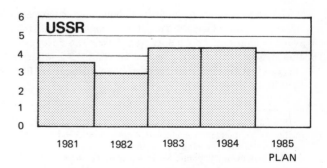

Source : National statistical yearbooks.

TABLE 4.3.2

Industrial employment and labour productivity growth
(*Average annual percentage change*)

	Industrial employment					Industrial labour productivity[a]				
	1986 1980	1981	1982	1983	1984	1976 1980	1981	1982	1983	1984
Bulgaria	1.3	2.8	2.4	1.4	0.5*	4.6	2.0	2.1	2.4	4.1*
Czechoslovakia . . .	0.5	0.6	0.4	0.5	0.6	4.2	1.5	0.7	2.3	3.3
German Democratic Republic	0.6	0.5	0.3	0.3	0.4	4.3	4.2	2.9	3.9	3.8*
Hungary	−1.6	−2.4	−2.2	−2.1	−	5.1	5.0	4.9	3.6	3.0*
Poland	0.2	−0.2	−4.7	−0.1	−0.5	4.5	−10.6	2.7	6.5	5.8
Romania	3.5	2.0	2.1	1.7	−*	5.8	0.5	−1.0	3.0	6.7*
Eastern Europe. . .	0.8	0.5	−0.9	0.4	0.1*	4.7	−1.1	2.1	4.0	4.8*
Soviet Union	1.6	0.9	1.0	0.6	0.4	2.8	2.5	1.9	3.6	3.8
Eastern Europe and the Soviet Union .	1.3	0.8	0.4	0.5	0.3*	3.4	1.4	2.0	3.7	4.1*

Source: National statistics and plan fulfilment reports.

Note: Due to differences in coverage of industrial employment, figures in this table may differ slightly from officially reported data.

[a] Gross industrial output per employee.

shortages can be compensated by improvements in the quality, organization and deployment of the work force. It is commonly believed that while labour resources are limited, the raising of labour productivity levels can provide an important boost to industrial growth potential. A number of measures adopted in the field of labour organization, incentives, education and training are thus important elements in policies designed to increase productivity. Some countries introduced in recent years the "brigade" system of labour organization. Wage reforms and improved manpower planning have also brought some results. Czechoslovakia and the Soviet Union have begun to introduce long-term education reforms to improve professional qualifications and vocational skills.[177]

The declining trend in *industrial labour productivity* growth, which became apparent in the second half of the 1970s and continued at the beginning of the 1980s, was reversed in the course of 1983 and 1984. This upturn reflected the substantial acceleration of industrial growth and a slowdown in the rise of industrial employment. Aggregate industrial labour productivity in the seven countries combined rose at annual rates of 4 per cent in 1983-1984. This is more than twice as high as industrial labour productivity growth in 1981-1982 and is also above the annual average reached in 1976-1980. Labour productivity performance improved in the last two years in all countries of the region except Hungary (table 4.3.2).

The strong revival of industrial labour productivity growth reflects a variety of factors, most of them connected with the upswing in industrial growth discussed above. The close relationship between the two is apparent in chart 4.3.2, which also suggests that the upturn was more pronounced in eastern Europe than in the Soviet Union.

Numerous policy measures were taken to increase labour productivity, notably in the sphere of labour organization and discipline, the accelerated adoption of science and technology and in improving planning and incentive systems.[178]

Labour productivity's contribution to industrial output growth in 1984 rose in Bulgaria, Czechoslovakia, Poland and the Soviet Union. It remained at high levels in the German Democratic Republic and Hungary. In the region as a whole, there was a significant rise in the contribution of labour productivity to total industrial output growth (table 4.3.3).

Only scarce data are available on industrial employment and labour productivity growth plans for 1985. Estimates derived from published figures on gross industrial output and labour

TABLE 4.3.3

Contribution of labour productivity to the growth of industrial output
(*Percentage shares*)

	1976-1980	1981	1982	1983	1984
Bulgaria	78	37	48	64	89
Czechoslovakia	89	71	64	82	85
German Democratic Republic	86	89	91	95	90
Hungary	147	179	196	257	100
Poland	96	..	..	102	111
Romania	61	19	..	62	100
Eastern Europe. . . .	84	..	175	91	98
Soviet Union	62	73	65	86	93
Eastern Europe and the Soviet Union . . .	71	64	83	86	93

Sources: As for table 4.3.2.

Note: Due to differences in coverage and methodologies applied, figures in this table may differ slightly from officially reported data. When industrial employment decreases in absolute terms, the proportion of output growth accounted for by rising labour productivity is more than 100 per cent.

[177] Improved organization and planning in the allocation and use of qualified personnel together with better motivation of labour are stressed as main directions for effective utilization of labour potential in the German Democratic Republic. See H. Koziolek, G. Pietrzynski: "Ökonomische Strategie: Anforderungen an die Entwicklung und rationelle Nutzung des gesellschaftlichen Arbeitsvermögens in den Kombinaten der DDR" (Economic strategy: requirements for the development and rational use of national labour power in the combines of the German Democratic Republic), *Wirtschaftswissenschaft*, No. 4, 1984, p. 493.

[178] Some of these measures were discussed in the *Economic Survey of Europe in 1983*, p. 146.

CHART 4.3.2.

Industrial output, employment and labour productivity growth

(Index number, 1975 = 100)

Gross industrial output ━━━━━━━━   Industrial labour productivity ▬▬▬▬▬   Industrial employment ⋯⋯⋯⋯⋯

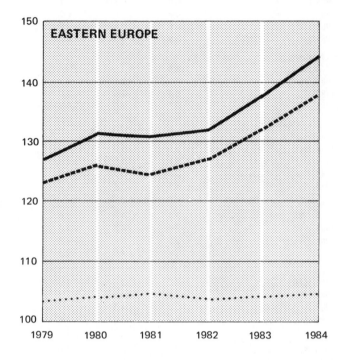

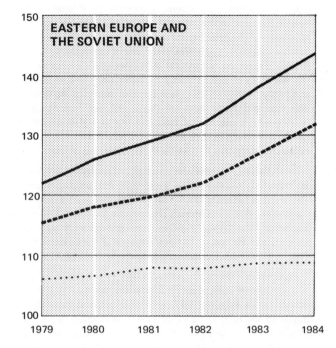

Source : National statistical yearbooks and ECE estimates.

productivity growth planned for that year suggest that industrial employment will grow only modestly and that labour productivity growth will stabilize at around the 4 per cent rate already attained. As a result, the share of industrial output increases accounted for by labour productivity growth in the region as a whole will come close to 95 per cent.

(iii) Material intensity of industrial production

The efficiency of material input and particularly energy use is an important component of intensification policies. Indeed this element of factor productivity is of the utmost importance given continuing constraints of supplies of fuel, energy, raw and other materials. Greater efficiency in material input use (lower energy- and material-intensity of production) helps to make more economic use of scarce production factors. Reduction of the energy and material intensity of production is thus an important determinant of future industrial growth and explains the importance attached to this aspect of efficiency in both industrial policy and economic analysis.

Indicators of primary energy resources are given in table 4.3.4. The close relationship between energy consumption and industrial growth was analysed in the previous edition of this publication.[179] In 1983, eastern Europe and the Soviet Union recorded a rise of more than 2 per cent in primary energy production, with above average performance in Romania and the Soviet Union. In 1984 it increased by 3 per cent, with a marked upturn in Bulgaria, the German Democratic Republic and the Soviet Union. The region as a whole is a net exporter of fuel and energy. However,

[179] *Op. cit.*, p. 148.

increments in primary energy production will in future be lower than in the past due to higher extraction costs. Transport costs are also rising because of the greater distances between new deposits and the main consuming areas. Hence, energy and other material input savings per unit of output are to be higher than in the past. Progress in this respect will be decisive in achieving sustained industrial growth.

TABLE 4.3.4

Primary energy production
(Average annual percentage change)

	1976-1980	1981	1982	1983	1984
Bulgaria	2.1	−1.2	9.4	1.7	3.9
Czechoslovakia	1.3	−0.5	1.1	1.5	1.1
German Democratic Republic	1.2	3.6	3.2	1.7	7.1
Hungary	1.5	−0.3	3.9	−1.5	2.4
Poland	2.0	−14.2	13.9	1.7	2.0
Romania	0.4	4.2	0.2	3.5	1.4
Eastern Europe. . . .	1.4	−4.2	6.3	1.9	2.8
Soviet Union	4.2	1.8	2.8	2.3	3.0
Eastern Europe and the Soviet Union . . .	3.6	0.6	3.4	2.2	3.0

Source: CMEA statistical yearbooks, national yearbooks and plan fulfilment reports.

Note: Data on primary energy production calculated by the ECE secretariat in standard coal equivalent (coefficients vary across countries). Figures for 1984 based on national plan fulfilment reports and ECE estimates.

The energy and material intensity of industrial production is excessive by international standards throughout the region. Some countries have adopted national programmes to promote the rational use of energy and other material resources. Systems of planning have been improved by applying consumption norms for the use of main material inputs.[180]

Analysis of progress in reducing the material intensity of industrial production faces a number of statistical and methodological problems. Traditional comparisons of gross and net output changes, which roughly indicate changes in the overall efficiency of material input use, are not always consistent with data on reported economies in the use of selected commodities (mostly expressed in physical terms per unit of output). This inconsistency is caused partly by differences in data coverage, and partly by the fact that the volume of intermediate consumption (the difference between gross and net output) may be influenced not only by real variations in material inputs used but also by other factors such as changes in the degree of integration between enterprises and shifts in the structure of output.

Nevertheless, the material intensity of industrial production, as reflected in changes in gross and net industrial output, improved in 1983—the latest year for which data are available—in Czechoslovakia, the German Democratic Republic, Poland and Romania. The highest material input savings were reported by Bulgaria and Hungary. The performance of the Soviet Union in 1983 in this respect deteriorated markedly (table 4.3.5).

Progress in 1984 can be judged only on the basis of the partial and not always comparable information reported by individual countries. In *Bulgaria* and *Czechoslovakia* the share of material inputs in the total value of industrial production decreased by almost 1 percentage point. Nevertheless, in Czechoslovakia the plan targets for material input saving were not fully implemented. The *German Democratic Republic* reported the best performance in this respect so far as can be assessed from a comparison of net and gross output (8 and 4 per cent respectively). The consumption of important fuel, energy, raw and other materials per unit of industrial output fell by 5 per cent. In *Hungary* some economies in material inputs per unit of output were reported at national level, but efficiency in energy use deteriorated. In *Poland* only moderate results were reported, and the material intensity of industrial production is still judged excessive. In *Romania* net output growth surpassed the growth of marketable output (8 and 7 per cent respectively) but plan targets were not met. In the *Soviet Union* the objectives for material input savings were reached. In general, the material intensity of industrial production in 1984 tended to fall, but progress in the majority of countries is judged as slow and inadequate.

(iv) Industrial fixed assets and capital productivity

Industrial fixed assets grew rapidly in the 1970s as a whole throughout the region, average annual rates ranging between 6 per cent in Czechoslovakia and 12 per cent in Romania. In the second half of the decade, despite some deceleration in all countries of the region except Czechoslovakia, high rates within a range of 5 per cent in the German Democratic Republic to 10 per

---

[180] The importance of norms and normatives in promoting higher efficiency in the utilization of material inputs is stressed in the article by G. Ritzschke: "Zur Anwendung der Massstäbe für die umfassende intensiv erweiterte Reproduktion in der Effektivitätsplanung" (On the application of measures for overall intensive reproduction in planning efficiency), *Wirtschaftswissenschaft*, No. 2, 1984. An overall assessment of measures taken to reduce the material intensity of production in the CMEA countries is given by I. Oleinik in his article "Opyt stran SEV v ekonomii materialnykh resursov" (Experience of the CMEA countries in savings of material resources), *Voprosy ekonomiki*, No. 5, 1984.

TABLE 4.3.5

Material intensity of industrial production
(*Average annual percentage change*)

	Gross output	Net output	Implied material intensity[a]
Bulgaria			
1976-1980	6.0	6.8	−0.8
1981	4.8	5.0	−0.2
1982	4.6	9.8	−4.7
1983	3.9	8.5	−4.2
Czechoslovakia[b]			
1976-1980	3.5	3.5	−
1981	−	−0.1	0.1
1982	0.4	−1.6	2.0
1983	2.3	1.6	0.7
German Democratic Republic[b]			
1976-1980	5.0	5.0	−
1981	4.7	5.5	−0.8
1982	3.2	3.5	−0.3
1983	4.1	5.4	−1.2
Hungary[b]			
1976-1980	3.4	4.0	−0.6
1981	2.4	4.8	−2.3
1982	2.5	5.4	−2.8
1983	1.4	4.0	−2.5
Poland			
1976-1980	4.7	2.6	2.0
1981	−10.8	−14.6	4.4
1982	−2.1	−4.5	2.5
1983	6.4	5.8	0.6
Romania[b]			
1976-1980	7.3	8.4	−1.0
1981	1.6	3.9	−2.2
1982	1.3	1.8	−0.5
1983	4.7	6.1	−1.3
Soviet Union			
1976-1980	4.5	4.9	−0.4
1981	3.4	3.5	−0.1
1982	2.9	3.2	−0.3
1983	4.2	3.1	−1.1

Sources: National statistics and CMEA statistical yearbooks.

[a] Calculated from the ratio of gross output index to net output index.

[b] Based on national accounts statistics.

cent annually in Romania were maintained (table 4.3.6). In 1981-1983, country differences persisted. In Bulgaria and the German Democratic Republic industrial fixed assets growth accelerated, while in other countries they slowed down—markedly so in Hungary and Poland. Further deceleration will probably continue in the foreseeable future due to investment declines in recent years, and given the time lag between investment starts and the entry into service of new fixed assets (see also section 4(ii) below).

High rates of growth of fixed assets were considered in the past to be a decisive factor in industrial growth, especially in periods of relatively abundant energy and other material inputs and fast employment growth. The marked slowdowns in the supply of fuel, energy, raw and other material input supplies and in industrial employment growth (see sub-sections (ii) and (iii) above) considerably modified the role previously attributed to fixed assets. Their quantitative growth was no longer adequate to sustain industrial growth, which began to depend more and more on the achievement of important qualitative changes in their composition. The importance of fixed assets in industrial expansion is now considered to be a function of the scientific and technical progress which they incorporate. As noted earlier, debate

TABLE 4.3.6

Industrial fixed assets and capital productivity growth

(*Average annual percentage change*)

	Industrial fixed assets				Industrial capital productivity[a]			
	1976 1980	1981	1982	1983	1976- 1980	1981	1982	1983
Bulgaria	7.9	8.1	9.8	7.5	−1.8	−3.0	−4.7	−3.3
Czechoslovakia	6.1	6.7	5.2	4.9	−1.3	−4.3	−3.9	−2.0
German Democratic Republic. .	5.5	6.0	6.2	5.6	−0.5	−1.2	−2.8	−1.4
Hungary	7.5	4.3	4.9	..	−3.8	−1.4	−2.3	..
Poland	8.5	3.4	2.4	2.8	−3.5	−13.7	−4.4	3.5
Romania	10.2	9.1	9.5	9.4	−0.6	−6.0	−7.7	−4.2
Soviet Union	7.5	7.0	6.9	6.9	−2.8	−3.4	−3.7	−2.5

Source: As for table 4.3.2.

[a] Industrial gross output–fixed assets ratio.

focuses on the degree to which they contribute to economies of such scarce production factors as labour and material inputs. Many countries have reported that progress in making the transition to this "intensive" type of fixed assets is rather slow and that growth still follows the "extensive" path.[181] Certainly, economic development so far has been accompanied by capital productivity declines. The growing importance of this topic has become apparent as economic research in this field intensifies.[182]

In 1983 the declines in capital productivity slowed down in all countries for which data are available (table 4.3.6). The improvement was predicted in the last edition of this publication.[183] In some countries this reflected a deceleration of industrial fixed assets growth in 1983 and marked upturns in industrial output growth (in Czechoslovakia and the German Democratic Republic). In Romania and the Soviet Union, high rates of industrial fixed asset growth in 1983, though slightly lower than in 1976-1980, were accompanied by slower declines in capital productivity; these were largely attributable to the sharp acceleration in gross industrial output growth. In Bulgaria a slowdown in industrial fixed assets growth contributed to a deceleration of the capital productivity decline. This may have continued in 1984 in line with improved output performance (sub-section (i) above), together with a probable further slowdown in industrial fixed asset growth. However, there is some evidence to assume that the rises in fixed assets themselves, and hence the capital productivity decline noted above, may be overstated due to valuation problems.[184]

An important component of measures to improve capital productivity is related to improving investment efficiency by allocating a larger share of expenditure to the reconstruction and modernization of fixed assets. Essentially this means raising the technical level of existing production facilities rather than constructing new ones. In some countries, capacity utilization

norms have been set. An increasing role for wage incentives is also foreseen—higher pay for second and third shift working, an extension of enterprises' own financing of fixed capital formation, etc. Incentives to encourage the faster retirement of obsolete equipment have also been proposed.

(v) Industrial growth and foreign trade

The interdependence of industrial growth and foreign trade has become more apparent in recent years, when world trade disturbances influenced the industrial performance of the east European countries. Foreign trade turnover rose at faster rates than industrial output in the 1970s (average annual rates of 7 and 6 per cent respectively) in the region as a whole. Industrial expansion thus became more dependent on foreign trade than in the past. Input-output tables illustrate the high import-intensity of some industrial branches.[185] Similarly, the share of gross industrial output exported is also high in several branches.

[184] Some economists believe that the statistical time series on fixed assets changes do not reflect actual trend changes due to methods of calculating price changes (based on representative samples) and difficulties in properly evaluating new types of machines, equipment, buildings and structures. Attempts have been made to approximate the real changes in fixed assets by reported changes in capacities in physical units. However, this method cannot be considered satisfactory since it takes into account only capacities reported for a selection of product groups. Thus they refer to potential production only of key machinery and equipment within a given product range, rather than total fixed assets employed for the products within that range. There is some evidence to suggest that fixed assets changes, as reported in national statistics, are overestimated. If so, the extent of capital productivity declines would be less than reported. However, this hypothesis requires further research. See for example V. K. Fal'tsman: "Moshchnostnoi ekvivalent osnovnykh fondov" (Capacity equivalent of fixed assets), *Voprosy ekonomiki*, No. 8, 1980 and K. K. Valtukh: "Investitsionnii kompleks i intensifikatsiia proizvodstva" (The investment complex and the intensification of production), *EKO*, No. 3, 1982, pp. 4-31.

V. Krasovskii shows a discrepancy in the valuation of new fixed assets put into operation and old fixed assets. Moreover, worn-out equipment is often retained in service. Both factors contribute to the high published growth rates of the volume of fixed assets. See his article "Intensifikatsiia ekonomiki i fondoëmkost' proizvodstva" (Intensification of the economy and capital productivity), *Voprosy ekonomiki*, No. 5, 1984.

[185] For example in Czechoslovakia the share of imported material inputs in total intermediate consumption (excluding depreciation charges) reached 47 per cent in fuels, 34 per cent in non-ferrous metallurgy, 26 per cent in chemicals, 20 per cent in textiles and footwear, 11 per cent in engineering in 1977. (*Statistická ročenka ČSSR 1980*, Prague, SNTL, pp. 128-129).

[181] One Soviet author views the principal cause of low investment efficiency and declining capital productivity as insufficient linkage between investment and scientific and technical progress. See V. I. Kushkin: "Razvitie proizvodstvennogo apparata i investitsionnye protsessy" (Development of production and investment processes), *EKO*, No. 11, 1984, p. 71.

[182] Various authors have suggested that low fixed asset utilization rates and slow modernization are the main contributors to declining capital productivity. See V. Krasovskii and L. Fridman: "Fondootdacha: faktory rosta" (Capital productivity: factors of growth), *Ekonomicheskaia gazeta*, No. 38, 1984, p. 11.

[183] *Economic Survey of Europe in 1983*, p. 147.

Aggregate import volume data and industrial output indices also show a high degree of interdependence:[186] in 1976-1980, the import elasticity of industrial output growth was unity in eastern Europe and the Soviet Union combined. At the beginning of the 1980s, elasticity coefficients declined sharply, especially in 1981. This was reflected in growing tightness in material input supplies, and imbalances between industrial supplier and user branches. They recovered again to almost 1 in 1982 and 1983. The years 1981-1982 can be considered exceptional because the east European countries had to adjust to markedly worse external conditions at the same time as reducing foreign indebtedness. This resulted in absolute declines in eastern Europe's total import volumes in 1981 and 1982 (6 1/2 and 4 1/2 per cent respectively—see appendix table B.15). These developments contributed to the slowdown of industrial growth noted in sub-section (i) above. However, the effects varied according to country. Drastic import cuts occurred in 1981 and 1982 in Poland and Romania, where the fall in industrial output growth was particularly marked. The steep decline in Polish industrial output and import levels was also connected with social and economic disturbances, but a gradual consolidation started in the second half of 1982. Of the seven countries, only Bulgaria and the Soviet Union succeeded in increasing import volumes in both 1981 and 1982—perhaps one reason for their above-average industrial growth compared with the other countries of the region.

The upswing in industrial growth in 1983 was accompanied by an import revival (4 per cent in volume terms) for the region as a whole. Import increases were significant in Bulgaria, the German Democratic Republic, Hungary and Poland. In Romania, absolute declines continued but at substantially lower rates. Import growth decelerated in the Soviet Union and Czechoslovakia.

Available data for 1984 indicate further import growth. Marked increases were recorded in imports from the developed market economies, which had fallen for the six east European countries taken together in three consecutive years (1980-1982). A recovery began in the second half of 1983 and gathered pace in 1984. The Soviet Union recorded a slowdown in the growth of imports from non-socialist countries. Increased imports throughout the region in 1983 and 1984 were generally concentrated in the fuel, raw material and semi-manufacture categories. They are likely to have eased material input shortages and thus contributed to the upturn in industrial growth noted in both years (for a recent analysis of international trade, see chapter 5 below).

Industrial performance was influenced not only by imports but also by the changes in exports. Export promotion has a dual effect on industrial growth. First, it provides the resources to finance increased imports and to expand production in the relatively import-dependent branches. Second, it stimulates production growth in export-oriented branches. Since industrial goods predominate in the export structure of the centrally planned economies of eastern Europe and the Soviet Union there is also an important link between industrial output and export changes.

A marked deceleration of the region's export volumes at the beginning of the 1980s (from an annual average of almost 6 per

cent in 1976-1980 to only 2 per cent annually in 1980 and 1981) was reflected in a slowdown of industrial growth. The export revival in 1983 and 1984 contributed to the upswing in industrial output growth. The major part of the European centrally planned economies' trade consists of intra-CMEA area trade, where growth in volume terms increased substantially in 1984. Of the factors influencing export potential, the most frequently stressed are: faster adjustment to changed external conditions, improvements in the quality and technical level of exports, increased specialization and faster changes in the structure of output for export.

(vi) Industrial output performance by branch

Industrial output structures have been affected by a range of factors on the supply as well as on the demand side. At the beginning of the 1980s, the structures of industrial output had to adapt to changed internal and external conditions, in particular to supply constraints of domestic and foreign origin and to slack demand for exports and for investment goods. The growing requirements of scientific and technical progress and foreign trade—particularly intra-CMEA trade—were also important influences on the performance of individual branches.

The increased momentum of industrial output growth in 1983 and 1984 affected some branches more than others. Most of the increment in 1983 and 1984 was accounted for by rises in engineering production, metallurgy and chemicals. Shifts in the structure of output in 1983 and 1984 appear to have taken place on a bigger scale than in the earlier years of the 1980s.

The growth of *engineering and metal working* accelerated in 1983, and recorded the highest rates of any branch in all countries of the region except Hungary (table 4.3.7). For 1984, partial data indicate that this continued. The plans for 1985 confirm that engineering is given growth priority. Engineering and the electro-technical sub-branches produce equipment required for both technical innovation and consumer durables, demand for which is growing at high rates. Morever, increased intra-CMEA product specialization and co-operation to promote intensification affects the engineering branch in particular. The 39th session of the CMEA in October 1984[187] confirmed that the main elements of this strategy relate to electronics, comprehensive automation (including flexible automated production units), nuclear power, new types of materials and production techniques, robotics[188] and biotechnology. Efforts are being made to ensure that the quality of engineering products approaches world levels and to improve supplies of machinery components and spare parts.

Metallurgy production recovered in 1983 in all the countries of the region except Hungary and Romania. Bulgaria and Poland recorded very high output increases. In the Soviet Union, metallurgy output rose by 4 per cent. For 1984 only a few data are available but they indicate that metallurgical output expanded even more rapidly than planned in Czechoslovakia, Hungary and the Soviet Union.

The *chemical industry* generally performed well in 1983. In Bulgaria, Czechoslovakia, Poland and the Soviet Union rates of growth were above the industrial average. Partial information

[186] The lack of fully adequate trade statistics make it difficult to separate out imports of material inputs for industry (which is relevant for the analysis of the dependence of industrial growth on imports) from total import volumes. Data in CMEA statistical yearbooks show a very big and growing share of those commodity groups which constitute material inputs for industrial production (within a range of 50-70 per cent of total imports). The analysis is thus based on the assumption that changes in total import volumes do not differ strongly from changes in material input imports.

[187] See *Ekonomicheskaia gazeta*, No. 46, November 1984, pp. 7-9.

[188] According to O. Rybakov the total number of robots in the CMEA countries is expected to reach 200,000 units in 1990. See his article "Dolgovremennaia strategiia uglubleniia sotsialisticheskoi ekonomicheskoi integratsii stran-chlenov SEV" (Long-term strategy of deepening the socialist economic integration of the CMEA countries), *Planovoe khoziiaistvo*, No. 8, 1984, p. 78.

confirms that this movement continued into 1984 in several countries. The expansion of the chemical industry has been based on product diversification and on adaptation of output to reflect the availability of petrochemical feed stocks.

The expansion of *fuel and energy* in the region was strong, particularly given the natural constraints on output growth. Primary energy production grew by 2 and 3 per cent in 1983 and 1984 respectively. Industrial policy is, at the same time, directed towards lowering fuel and energy consumption per unit of output. These objectives have been enshrined for the CMEA countries as a whole in the long-term comprehensive programme for fuel, energy and raw materials, which was adopted at the 37th session of the CMEA held in October 1983.

The *light and food industries* continued to improve supplies to domestic markets and foreign trade in 1984. The expansion of these branches was dependent on agricultural performance and on the availability of imported material inputs. The modernization of fixed assets in the consumer goods branches was frequently stressed in connection with output growth. Output performance of the light and food industries differs by country, but is generally below the average for the industry as a whole. Shortages of some consumer goods and quality problems were reported by some countries. A greater degree of international co-operation in these branches is expected to stimulate the quality and broaden the assortment of goods offered.

Differences in the rates of growth of *producer goods* ("group A") and *consumer goods* ("group B") industries tended to narrow in 1983 (table 4.3.8). In Hungary and the Soviet Union, the growth of consumer goods was even higher than for producer goods. This tendency may well continue in future since demand for the output of the producer goods branches is likely to be constrained most by economies in the use of material inputs which they produce. However, the structure of domestic output does not necessarily coincide in this respect with the structure of consumption. Some countries are sizeable exporters of food and other consumer goods, while importing in their place substantial

TABLE 4.3.7

Gross industrial output by major branches
(*Annual percentage change*)

	Industry total	Electricity and heating	Fuel	Metallurgy	Engineering and metal working	Chemicals and rubber	Construction materials	Light industry	Food processing
Bulgaria				a					
1976-1980	6.0	7.5	..	6.9	9.4	8.9	8.4	4.0	4.1
1981	4.9	6.7	..	6.4	5.3	4.3	3.8	5.4	8.4
1982	4.6	9.2	..	−1.4	5.5	6.4	2.7	3.6	4.1
1983	3.9	−4.2	..	6.7	6.0	5.9	4.6	2.6	1.1
Czechoslovakia									
1976-1980	4.7	4.8	2.6	2.8	6.7	5.8	4.4	4.2	2.7
1981	2.1	1.1	−0.5	0.7	4.2	1.7	1.8	2.1	1.3
1982	1.1	1.3	−1.5	−1.0	3.2	1.1	−1.7	2.2	−0.6
1983	2.8	2.0	0.7	0.8	5.0	3.5	0.3	1.5	2.6
German Democratic Republic								b	
1976-1980	5.0	5.9	3.6	3.9	7.0	4.9	2.3	4.2	2.8
1981	4.7	3.0	2.7	6.8	7.8	2.5	−	2.6	2.3
1982	3.2	1.2	8.5	2.4	4.8	5.6	−3.1	2.5	−0.4
1983	4.1	5.1	2.4	3.0	5.1	3.0	2.1	4.6	3.6
Hungary [c]									
1976-1980	3.4	6.0	0.6	1.6	3.3	6.5	4.3	2.1	3.4
1981	2.4	3.4	−2.8	−1.6	5.7	3.1	0.2	3.1	3.0
1982	2.5	1.9	2.7	1.5	4.4	1.9	1.0	−1.2	4.3
1983	1.4	2.8	−2.1	−1.5	1.2	1.4	1.2	1.0	1.5
Poland								d	
1976-1980	4.7	5.4	2.5	3.3	7.0	4.3	1.2	3.4	2.4
1981	−10.8	−6.1	−12.7	−13.2	−12.0	−11.4	−17.6	−10.1	−8.6
1982	−2.1	0.6	9.2	−7.1	−0.9	0.1	1.8	−7.1	−5.6
1983	6.4	8.4	3.5	6.7	6.9	8.1	5.1	3.9	5.8
Romania									
1976-1980	9.5	4.6	3.9	8.1	12.6	9.6	12.8	8.8	6.0
1981	2.6	4.1	−1.3	3.6	2.2	3.9	−0.2	5.3	−1.0
1982	1.1	−1.1	−2.6	−1.0	3.5	1.4	2.0	2.4	−2.2
1983	4.7	3.0	8.2	1.1	4.9	5.3	2.2	4.2	5.4
Soviet Union				a					
1976-1980	4.5	5.1	3.0	1.9	8.2	5.7	1.9	3.4	1.4
1981	3.4	2.2	1.9	0.5	5.9	5.9	1.9	3.0	2.1
1982	2.9	3.3	1.3	1.4	4.8	3.0	1.9	−	3.5
1983	4.2	2.6	1.9	3.9	6.3	5.5	4.8	1.0	5.7

Source: National statistics and CMEA statistical yearbooks.

[a] Excluding non-ferrous metallurgy.

[b] Excluding textiles.

[c] Branch data refer to state and co-operative industry only.

[d] Excluding wood and paper.

volumes of producer goods. The methodology of measuring the producer and consumer goods components of industrial output may also play an important role.[189]

(vii) Main policy objectives for 1985

Intensification strategies laid down in the five-year plans for 1981-1985 in all countries of the region and reiterated in their annual plans have not been fully implemented. Improvements can however be observed during the last two years. The plans for 1985 have a twofold significance in this respect. *First,* they stress the need to retain and consolidate improvements already made and so contribute to the fulfilment of the five-year plans for the 1981-1985 period. *Secondly,* 1985 is a transitional year between two five-year plans. Successful implementation of the plan targets will thus create a solid basis for the transition to a predominantly intensive industrial growth which is expected to be a central feature of the five-year plans to 1990.

Common features with regard to industrial policy, as contained in the plans for 1985, may be summarized as follows:

— faster adjustment of industrial production to changing demand and supply, which is to be promoted by improved management and planning, and by investment policies oriented towards the reconstruction and modernization of existing enterprises rather than new starts;

— continued promotion of export-oriented branches, notably in manufacturing (engineering, electro-technical industry, chemicals and light industry) is expected to improve their export performance;

— improvements in the quality of industrial products rank among the main objectives of industrial policy and are closely linked with the two previously mentioned objectives;

— reductions in fuel, energy, raw and other material inputs per unit of output at a faster rate than before are to offset continued shortages in these items;

— labour productivity increases are to come very close to industrial output growth due to limited labour supply.

Among the means which are to lead to the fulfilment of the above objectives, scientific and technical progress is to bear the main burden. Co-operation between the CMEA countries on the basis of the guidelines agreed and the priorities set at the economic summit in June 1984 and at the 39th session of the CMEA in October 1984 is to work to the same end.

These common elements are emphasized to a differing degree in different countries. *Bulgaria* recorded the most stable and also the highest rates of industrial growth in the region in the course of the current five-year plan. The targeted 5 per cent increase in industrial output for 1984 was almost reached and the plan for 1985 retains the same objective. Priorities established in previous annual plans are unchanged, and fast growth is expected in the engineering, electronics, automation technique and microprocessor branches. Total engineering output is to rise by almost 12 per cent and branches contributing to technical progress by even more. In the energy sector, electricity generation is to increase by a little less than the industrial average, but a considerable rise is envisaged for coal production. Chemical production is expected to grow by more than 6 per cent and light industry by slightly less than the industrial average.

Industrial policy stresses unit cost reduction, and special stress is also laid on product quality.[190] The national party conference in Sofia in March 1984,[191] was devoted entirely to the attainment of quality improvements. Several measures were taken to modify the management and planning system, notably with regard to incentive systems (profit is henceforth to be the main criterion for evaluating enterprise performance), management responsibilities, labour organisation and discipline. A comprehensive long-term programme of quality improvement was adopted.

In *Czechoslovakia* the plan for 1985 envisages 3 per cent industrial growth, slightly less than in 1984. Efforts to reduce material inputs per unit of output suggest that the rise in net output may be higher.

Engineering is expected to occupy the key position in Czechoslovak industrial development, its output rising twice as fast as the industry average. The most dynamic branch however is the electrotechnical industry, where output is planned to rise by 10 per cent. The priority accorded to selected engineering and electrotechnical branches is incorporated in special "state target-oriented programmes", where production is to rise by 14 per cent. Wood-processing and chemicals are to grow by slightly more and light industry by slightly less than the industrial average. Neither

---

[189] An industrial enterprise which produces both A and B group products is classified as belonging to group A or group B according to the predominant end-use of its output.

[190] A national programme for the intensive exploitation of energy and raw materials and quality improvement was examined in the article by T. Bozhinov, Deputy Premier and Minister of Energy and Raw Material Management, "Tsialosten podkhod" (A comprehensive approach) in *Rabotnichesko delo*, 16 May 1984.

[191] *Rabotnichesko delo*, 23 March 1984.

TABLE 4.3.8

Producer and consumer goods in total industrial output
(Percentage shares)

	Producer goods				Consumer goods			
	1980	1981	1982	1983	1980	1981	1982	1983
Bulgaria	62.0	65.2	61.4	61.9	38.0	34.8	38.6	38.1
Czechoslovakia	68.2	68.1	68.2	68.4	31.8	31.9	31.8	31.6
German Democratic Republic. .	66.4	66.5	66.7	66.8	33.6	33.5	33.3	33.2
Hungary	64.5	63.7	63.4	63.0	35.5	36.3	36.6	37.0
Poland	63.7	62.5	63.0	63.2	36.3	37.5	37.0	36.8
Romania	74.3	73.1	76.3	76.4	25.7	26.9	23.7	23.6
Soviet Union	73.8	73.7	75.1	74.9	26.2	26.3	24.9	25.1

Source: Statisticheskii ezhegodnik stran-chlenov SEV 1984, (CMEA Statistical Yearbook 1984) Moscow, 1984, p. 58.

metallurgy nor primary energy consumption are expected to rise above the 1984 level, and energy savings per unit of industrial output are to accelerate. The structure of energy consumption will shift towards gas and nuclear energy, while the share of coal and oil is to decrease. Nuclear electricity generation is planned to rise to more than 13 per cent of total electricity production.

Persistent shortfalls in efficiency growth,[192] despite improvements recorded in the course of the last two years, have stimulated further measures to accelerate scientific and technical progress. The improved system of management and planning, already outlined by government decree,[193] will be introduced in 1986—at the beginning of the eighth five-year plan covering 1986-1990.

The *German Democratic Republic* has obtained impressive results in implementing intensification policies since 1980. Energy, raw and other material inputs consumed per unit of output fell at an average annual rate of almost 6 per cent in 1981-1984. Primary energy consumption has scarcely risen since 1980, yet relatively high rates of industrial growth (about 4 per cent annually) were maintained up to 1984. The 1985 plan in this respect is again very demanding, calling for substantially higher growth of net industrial output compared with marketable production (the targeted output increases are 8 and 4 per cent respectively). Production costs in industry are to decrease by almost 3 per cent.

Emphasis is placed on the electrical engineering and electronics branches and on the manufacture of robots. Rapid expansion of production in these branches, as well as machine tools and metal-working machinery, reflect efforts to boost the share of high-technology products suitable for export. Thus, electronics and electrical engineering output is to rise twice as fast as industry as a whole. Above-average growth rates are also envisaged for machine tools and metal-working machinery and for general and agricultural engineering and vehicles. Chemical production is scheduled to grow by about the same as total industry, but the share of highly refined products will rise. Energy and material-intensive branches such as coal, energy and metallurgy are expected to grow slightly slowly, and light industry slightly faster than the industrial average.

The central feature of intensification strategy in the German Democratic Republic is material input savings, but quality improvements are also stressed. The plan expects that one third of the yearly output of the combines will consist of new products, while the output of high-quality goods will rise by 20 per cent.

Hungary envisages a 3 per cent increase of gross industrial output in 1985—the same as in 1984. The basic aim of industrial policy is to speed up technological progress and raise the competitivity of industrial products on world markets. Rapid growth of microelectronics, computers, robots and telecommunications will contribute to this end. The pharmaceutical, as well as the aluminium and vehicles industries, are also given high growth priority. Structural change is to accelerate in line with changing demand and will be promoted by further economic reform. Central macro-economic management will be improved by

enlarging the role and scope of economic regulators which are to be applied uniformly in all enterprises. At the enterprise level the board of directors or—in small firms—the director himself will be elected by the employees. These are considered the basic conditions on the management and planning side for ensuring the "renewal" of Hungarian industry.

Fuel and energy savings are another priority policy objective. Coal extraction is planned at about the same level as in preceding years. Coal and electricity output lag behind industrial needs, and Hungary has worked out a long-term programme for fuel and energy production and savings. Energy consumption is expected to increase by a maximum of 1 per cent a year. Electricity generated at the Paks nuclear power station is henceforth expected to play an important role in the Hungarian energy balance.

Export promotion is one of the basic objectives of Hungarian industrial policy. Export deliveries are to grow by 5-6 per cent. This concerns mainly the engineering, chemical and light industries for which both production and exports are to grow faster than the industrial average.

The 1985 planned industrial target for *Poland* is 4 to 4 1/2 per cent. Taking into account the somewhat higher industrial output rises in 1983 and 1984, the fulfilment of the three-year national socio-economic plan for 1983-1985 seems attainable.

Industrial policy for 1985 sets the following priorities:

— fuel, energy and other material input savings should accelerate, yielding a 3 percentage point decrease per unit of industrial output;

— the targeted rise in industrial output should be met exclusively by labour productivity growth;

— the expansion of export-oriented branches is to be promoted—notably the engineering and electro-technical branches;

— the supply and quality of consumer goods, especially non-food items, is to be improved;

— the expected higher-than-average growth for chemicals, light industry and electrical engineering should lead to more balanced growth, notably by reducing the share of the metallurgical, food, fuel and energy branches in total output.

The attainment of the 1984 industrial output targets of *Romania* (nearly 7 per cent) was a big improvement on performance in 1981 and 1982, when output growth was very low by historical standards. The rate of increase accelerated in 1983 and the upturn is expected to continue into 1985. The plan's ambitious 7 1/2 per cent target is to be ensured by a more pronounced change in output structures and by accelerated product innovation. Almost half of manufacturing output is to consist of new and updated products.

A central feature of the plan is the drive to achieve significant savings in material inputs. Net and gross industrial output growth targets are 13 1/2 and 7 1/2 per cent respectively. A new standardization bill was adopted to encourage lower fuel, energy, raw and other material input consumption by setting consumption norms and improving product quality. A central council for standardization, norm-setting and quality was set up.

A long-term programme of output quality improvement was adopted. This is designed to ensure that the share of technically high-quality products in total industrial output will increase substantially.[194]

The engineering and chemical branches are selected for fastest growth. In the energy sector, the 1985 plan provides for the

---

[192] "The present state of scientific and technical development and innovation activity does not fully meet our requirements. The destination of produced goods is not always in line with plan. Beside this, there are problems in investment and foreign trade." Speech of L. Štrougal, Czechoslovak Prime Minister at the 39th Session of the CMEA in Havana, *Rudé právo*, 30 October 1984, p. 6.

[193] Published as the supplement to *Hospodářské noviny*, No. 42 and 43, 1984.

[194] See *Revista Economica*, No. 16-17, 20 and 27 April 1984.

extraction of 64 million tons of coal, 12.6 million tons of oil and 33 cu m of natural gas. The first two represent increases of 45 and 10 per cent respectively, though natural gas output is not expected to rise above the 1983 level. Electricity generation in 1985 will rise at the same rate as total industrial output and metallurgy (steel) by somewhat more. Industrial policy also aims at improving supplies of consumer goods, mainly food for domestic consumption.

The plan for 1985 presupposes marked improvements in efficiency indicators. Industrial labour productivity is expected to intensification of industrial production and improved technical levels and output quality.[195] Gross industrial output is to grow by almost 4 per cent, slightly above the average annual rate of the preceding four years but slower than in 1983 and 1984. Above-average growth rates are foreseen for engineering, chemicals, and consumer goods.

Engineering is seen as playing the decisive role in retooling the national economy and in accelerating scientific and technical progress. The faster introduction of electronics and automation equipment and industrial robots is envisaged.[196]

The expansion of the fuel and energy branches is to continue. Coal and oil production are scheduled to grow less than the industry-wide average rate. Gas and electricity generation are to increase by 8 and 4 per cent respectively and nuclear electricity is to increase its share in energy output, as provided for in the long-term energy programme up to the year 2000.[197] Fuel and energy export objectives highlight the importance of energy savings. Special emphasis is laid on savings of motor fuel. Primary energy consumption is planned to increase at a lower rate than in previous years.

In metallurgy, structural change in favour of high-quality metals and the size and specification range of rolled products is to be promoted. Savings of metal are to be accelerated (engineering is expected to reduce consumption of ferrous metals per unit of output by almost 4 per cent).

In the consumer goods branches, attention is concentrated on quality improvement and broadening the assortment. Consumer goods production is to grow slightly faster than the production of producer goods.

The plan for 1985 presupposes marked improvements in efficiency indicators. Industrial labour productivity is expected to increase by almost 4 per cent, and the contribution of labour productivity to total industrial growth is expected to reach 95 per cent—the highest ever attained. Two nation-wide programmes for reducing manual labour are being drawn up. The first is designed to reduce the share of manual labour in all sectors of the economy, while the second is directed to improving mechanization and automation in loading, hoisting, transport and storage. Growing attention is devoted to the material intensity of industrial production. The production costs [198] of industrial output are to decline by almost 1 per cent, which is substantially more than achieved in previous years.

---

[195] K. Chernenko, former Head of State of USSR and the Secretary-General of the CPSU, stated that the intensification process on the basis of scientific and technical progress and improvement of the forms and methods of socialist economic management is dictated not only by a shortage of resources, but by the necessity to attain a qualitatively new level of the national economy. *Kommunist*, No. 18, December 1984.

[196] The output of industrial robots will rise by 14 per cent to 14,300 units.

[197] See *Economic Survey of Europe in 1983*, p. 149.

---

[198] The value of industrial enterprises' current outlays on industrial output; includes the value of intermediate consumption (fuel, energy, raw and other material inputs), depreciation of fixed assets, and wages. Decreases in production costs are calculated in relation to marketable industrial production.

4.4 INVESTMENT

The first sub-section summarizes developments in investment in 1981-1985. Policies during the current five-year plan period as they have developed since 1976-1980, and progress in the intensification of the investment sector in response to changed internal and external conditions are outlined in sub-section (ii). Sub-section (iii) focuses on performance in the construction sector. In sub-section (iv), changes in the structure of investment within the total economy, the material sphere and industry are presented, and their relationship to changes in output structure are discussed. In conclusion, sub-section (v) examines present investment levels relative to long-term trends for each country, and the synchronization of investment fluctuations between the various countries of the region.

(i) Investment outcomes, 1981-1984

Gross fixed capital formation in 1981-1984 followed the path of reduced growth foreseen in the medium-term plans for the current five years. Slow or declining growth, especially in eastern Europe in 1981-1982, was followed by some recovery in the last two years. Investment, which developed at widely different rates in individual countries, rose by 2 1/2 per cent in the region in 1984–well down on the increases recorded in 1983 (table 4.4.1 and chart 4.4.1). It also grew slightly below the rate indicated by an aggregation of the seven countries' plan targets for the year.

Most of this shortfall in 1984 resulted from below-plan performance in the Soviet Union, where investment growth was much less than half the 1983 outcome and only just over half the plan target. Eastern Europe's investment, in contrast, rose twice as fast as in 1983 and well above the modest objective retained for 1984.

Even within eastern Europe performance was mixed. Most of the increase resulted from a considerable and above-plan jump in Polish investment. This brought Polish investment to about two thirds its level in the last "normal" year of 1978. It was also 20 per cent below its already reduced 1980 total. Investment growth was also high in Romania, sharply reinforcing the upturn which began in 1983. But while investment was buoyant in these two countries in 1984, and indeed more than expectedly so if the outcomes are compared with the modest objectives for the year, scarcely any growth took place in the other four countries of eastern Europe. In Czechoslovakia, the small rise was slightly higher than planned. In Hungary a further decline, though less than the reduction planned, continued a record of falling investment unbroken since 1980. In Bulgaria and the German Democratic Republic, planned rises of about 4 per cent were followed by little or no growth at all.

This patchy performance had one common feature: the *investment ratio* (ratio of gross fixed capital formation to NMP produced) continued to fall in all countries but one (table 4.4.2). The exception was Poland, where a 5 percentage point decline in the ratio compared with 1976-1980, which had reduced it to the lowest in the region in 1983, was reversed in 1984. In most countries the investment ratio remained, as in 1981-1983, below the level implied by the five-year plans. Exceptions are Bulgaria, Czechoslovakia and the Soviet Union, where investment growth has either been higher than planned or has fallen below targets by less than NMP. The investment costs of growth, as measured by the *incremental investment-output ratio* (IIOR—the investment ratio divided by NMP growth) has declined substantially from the high levels recorded in some countries in the late 1970s and

TABLE 4.4.1

Gross fixed capital formation, 1976-1985
(Annual percentage changes)[a]

	1976-1980	1981	1982	1983	1984	Plan 1985	Plan 1981-1985
Bulgaria	4.1	10.5	3.6	0.7	—*	6.1[b]	0.9
Czechoslovakia	4.1	−4.6	−2.3	0.6	1.5*	2	−1.7
German Democratic Republic.	4.7	2.8	−5.1	−	—*	—*	0.7
Hungary	3.8	−4.3	−1.6	−3.7	−(6-7)	1.1	−
Poland	−0.4	−22.4	−12.1	9.4	8	−	..
Romania	9.7	−7.1	−3.1	2.5	6.1	8.3	4.4
Total eastern Europe	4.1	−7.2	4.4	1.9	3.5	3.4	1.4[c]
Soviet Union	3.9	3.8	3.5	5.8	2	3.4	1.6
Total eastern Europe and the Soviet Union	4.0	0.4	1.3	4.7	2.4	3.4	1.5[c]

Source: National statistics, plan documents and plan fulfilment reports.

Note: Data for Bulgaria and the German Democratic Republic are at 1980 prices, for Czechoslovakia at 1977 prices, for Hungary and Romania at 1981 prices, for Poland at 1982 prices, and for the Soviet Union at (assumed) 1976 prices. These prices bases are adhered to in all following tables except where otherwise stated.

[a] Both actual and planned figures for five-year periods shown are geometrical average rates based on the final year of the previous five-year period. Hence they differ from those shown in table 4.1.4 and in appendix table B.8. Where five-year plan targets were not broken down for individual years, investment growth over 1981-1985 was calculated by assuming constant annual rates over the period.

[b] At current prices.

[c] Excluding Poland.

127

CHART 4.4.1.

Changes in level of NMP, gross fixed capital formation, and investment ratio

(Indices 1973-1977 = 100)

Net material product
Actual
Five-year plan

Gross fixed investment
Actual
Five-year plan

Investment ratio
Actual
Five-year plan

HUNGARY

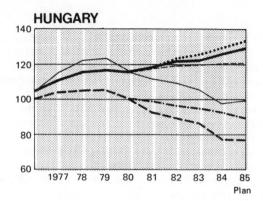

BULGARIA

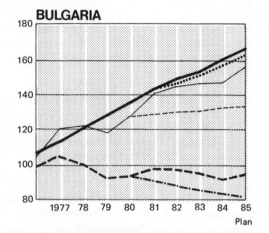

POLAND

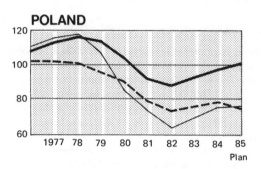

CZECHOSLOVAKIA

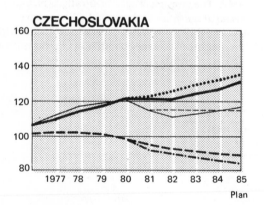

ROMANIA

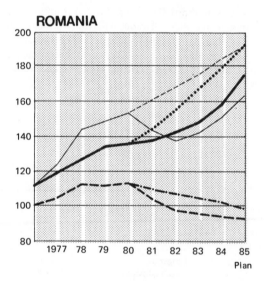

GERMAN, Dem. Rep.

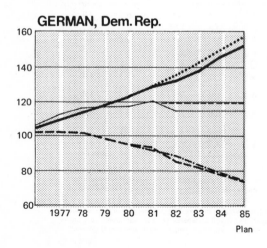

USSR

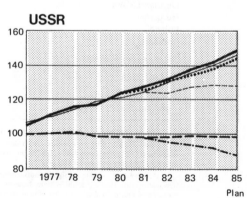

Source: National statistics.

TABLE 4.4.2

Investment ratios and incremental investment-output ratios (IIORs)

						Plan	
	1976-1980	1981	1982	1983	1984	1985	1981-1985
Investment ratios [a]							
Bulgaria	35.4	35.7	35.4	34.6	33.1	33.8	31.2
Czechoslovakia.	33.7	31.6	30.8	30.3	29.8	29.6	29.4
German Democratic Republic	30.7	28.6	26.4	25.3	24.0	23.0	25.8
Hungary	37.2	33.7	32.3	31.0	28.2	27.7	33.2
Poland	30.7	24.8	23.1	23.8	24.5	23.7	..
Romania	41.1	39.2	36.9	36.4	35.9	35.3	39.9
Soviet Union	30.3	29.9	29.7	30.2	29.9	29.6	28.4
IIORs [b]							
Bulgaria	5.7	7.1	8.4	11.5	7.2	8.2	8.4
Czechoslovakia.	8.6	−284	131	12.5	9.9	9.9	12.9
German Democratic Republic	7.5	5.9	10.2	5.7	4.4	5.2	5.2
Hungary	9.9	13.4	12.2	103	9.7	10.9	11.4
Poland	10.1	−2.1	−4.2	4.0	4.9	7.3	..
Romania	4.9	18.8	13.3	9.4	4.7	3.5	5.6
Soviet Union	6.4	9.1	7.4	7.2	9.9	6.6	8.8

Source: As for table 4.4.1.

[a] Gross fixed capital formation as a percentage of NMP produced.

[b] Investment ratio divided by annual rates of growth of NMP (based on geometrical average rates of growth of NMP over five-year periods).

early 1980s. By 1984, it was below the level implied by the five-year targets in all countries but the Soviet Union.

The common objective in the five-year plans of all countries of the region was to reduce the rate of growth of investment and investment ratios. This was achieved, and in most countries more than achieved, in 1981-1984 as a whole. The objective reflected first and foremost the need to shift resources away from domestic uses and in favour of improving the foreign balances. The degree to which this affected investment depended on the severity of constraints affecting individual countries—both internal resource and production, factor availabilities—and external factors such as debt repayment and servicing commitments, changing export competitivity, changes in fuel and raw material import prices etc. (see sub-section (ii) below). The Soviet Union's limited degree of dependence on foreign trade, its manageable level of indebtedness relative to export earnings, and above all its position as a fuel and raw material exporter, gave it more room for manoeuvre than the other countries of the region. In contrast, Poland, following a sustained period of overcommitment of internal and, especially, of foreign financial resources to investment in the mid-1970s, was the country where investment cutbacks were the biggest.

As will be argued in sub-section (ii) below, the need for far-reaching adjustment in response to domestic and past foreign trade imbalances now calls for a vigorous policy of structural change in all countries. The fact that resources were not freely available in 1981-1984 to increase investment for this purpose thus imposed new imperatives. The first was to ensure that the more restricted quantity of investment funds was used to the best possible advantage. The second was to concentrate investment on the re-equipment of the economy with labour- and other resource-saving technology, and on the reduction of the investment and capital costs of growth. These objectives continue to enjoy prominence in the annual plans for 1985 in all countries.

As shown in sub-section (v) below, investment growth is running well below the trend of performance in 1950-1980. There

has also been a decline in the underlying trend of investment ratios, which represents a very marked break in the long-term trend. The general decline in these ratios points up a continuing feature of overall resource allocation policy since the late years of the 1970s and of the five-year plan targets themselves: the priority accorded to maintaining the share of current consumption in an already slower-growing total of resources available for domestic use.

Changes in the relationship between actual and planned NMP growth and actual and planned investment suggest that the resumption of higher and stable investment increments in the near future will depend on an upturn in overall output growth. Actual performance relative to the NMP and investment targets for recent years laid down in the five-year plans for 1981-1985 is consistent with the hypothesis that investment is currently seen to some extent as a residual, for allocation after a certain quantity of resources has been set aside for the reduction of trade debts and to finance "social and personal" (i.e. government and private) consumption. Thus the share of investment in total demand tends to increase where growth performance exceeds plans, and to decline when growth is lower than planned. For 1981-1984, two countries (Bulgaria and the Soviet Union) overfulfilled or came very close to fulfilling the five-year targets for NMP, and investment plans were overfulfilled by 11 and 5 per cent respectively. In the same four years, NMP shortfalls ranging from 2-9 per cent occurred in four of the remaining five countries for which five-year plan data are available. In three of these four countries, investment targets were underfulfilled by between 3 and 18 per cent. Czechoslovakia was a partial exception in that its investments have fallen only fractionally below target, whereas its NMP fell somewhat below the mid-point of its planned range.

Investment prospects for 1985 can be set against a background of improving growth performance in eastern Europe as a whole. Yet mixed performance by country suggests that conditions for a resumption of stable investment growth have not yet been fully achieved. In the Soviet Union, growth of NMP in 1981-1984 was affected by a series of poor harvests and reinforced by lower prices for fuel exports in the last 18 months. Thus more real resources are being diverted to maintaining the surplus on external trade. Nevertheless, both eastern Europe and the Soviet Union plan on a further acceleration of output growth in 1985. The aggregated 1985 plan targets indicate expectations of 3 1/2 per cent investment growth in the six east European countries as well as in the Soviet Union and hence for the region as a whole. But in four countries, investment targets are in the 0-2 per cent range. Bulgaria and Romania expect more buoyant rises, but part of the Bulgarian increment probably includes a price element—the published target is based on value data.

A degree of flexibility appears to be built into the targets, however. For the region as a whole, the above-plan investment performance of 1984 reflected above-plan NMP performance. Since, as noted in a preceding paragraph, planning strategy appears to be to allocate a high share of any above-plan resource increase to investment purposes, investment growth outcomes for 1985 may vary substantially from the targets. Good perform-ance in 1985 could lay the foundations for a resumption of investment growth more closely in line with, or exceeding, output growth. Most countries have now completed the some-times drastic balance of payments readjustments which became necessary after the late 1970s. There should now be more room to mobilize growth resources, and hence to reverse the invest-ment slowdown of recent years. As discussed in sub-section (iii) below, this is now a pressing need given the effects of the slow-down on the age structure of fixed assets at a time when faster structural adjustment is needed to consolidate future output and export prospects.

(ii) Investment policies, 1976-1985

In this sub-section, investment policies during the current and previous five-year plan periods are examined. It first summarizes the build-up of internal and external constraints on economic development as they have affected overall resource availabilities and, second, examines progress in the intensification of the investment process.

During the 1970s, the emphasis of planning policy changed from the objective of growth based largely on the deployment of increasing quantities of factor inputs to a much more cost-conscious effort to combine growth with a reduction in the unit costs of production (the "intensification" policy). While this policy was not new, the pressures to implement it became acute in the second half of the 1970s as unfavourable internal and external pressures converged. In fact, the investment sector has carried a particularly heavy burden of the readjustment efforts to which these pressures gave rise.

(a) Changes in *overall economic conditions* were far from uniform in all the seven countries of the region. Even where conditions were similar in several countries, they did not affect all of them in the same way or to the same extent. This was true with regard to both internal and external events. But sufficient common elements exist to account for a similarity of general policy approaches as well as some of their specific features. For instance, the exhaustion of easily accessible fuel and raw ma-terials in the western part of the Soviet Union has entailed more costly development of resources in Siberia and the Far East. The cost and price of the Soviet Union's own fuel and raw materials thus parallels the higher import cost of these items experienced in the east European countries. Difficulties have been ex-perienced by almost all the countries concerned in competing on

world export markets for manufactures.[199] These difficulties were connected with the assortment of goods available for export and also with their quality and design. Additionally, certain shortcomings in the supply of goods for domestic consumption, notably food but also some other consumer goods, have been recognized and are now the object of both national and intra-CMEA initiatives.

Whatever their cause, internal and external constraints have entailed for all the countries concerned, with the exception of the German Democratic Republic, a period of historically low and below-trend rates of output growth. The need to divert resources to the foreign balance either to service debt or to offset terms of trade losses, or both, has superimposed on this an even slower growth of resources available for domestic use. Under these circumstances, the choice has been made to maintain levels of government and private consumption to the extent possible at the expense of investment. Even in Poland, consumption as a whole has declined by less than accumulation. This policy has acted not only directly on investment allocations, but also in-directly through sharp cuts in the growth rates, and, in several countries, in the levels of investment goods imports. As reported in previous editions of this publication, the slowdown in such imports from outside the CMEA area was much bigger than the slowdown in investments.[200] Since this class of imports was undertaken in the first place as one means of improving access to modern technology, its sharp contraction probably postponed developments in this direction relative to planners' longer-term expectations.

Given the choice to maintain government and private consumption levels, a central dilemmma remains for the bodies currently engaged in the preparation of the five-year plans for the period 1986-1990—and one already experienced during the prep-aration of the five-year plan for the current period. All the con-straints on growth, however they differ and whatever their impact on any one country, require for their removal changes in the structure of output and foreign trade. The dilemma, therefore, is this: how to achieve the pressing need for structural change in final output—changes in the assortment of goods produced at the quality and in the quantities necessary to meet current and future levels of foreign and domestic demand—at a time when slower growth in the availability of domestic production factors, higher production costs, current foreign debt repayment and servicing commitments and export constraints are limiting the expansion of investment expenditures. Improvement in the various and important input-saving provisions of the "intensification" poli-cies is currently being pursued throughout the region. But this alone cannot solve structural problems. Slower output and resource growth experienced in the current five-year plan period have themselves impeded structural adjustment. In particular, a vigorous policy of structural change cannot easily be carried through with stagnant or even declining investment levels.

(b) In the present climate of slower resource growth, the *in-tensification of the investment process*—a prominent feature of economic policies since the late 1960s—can be viewed as a policy option with the dual role of making a virtue out of necessity. Investment activity is unique in that it is not only itself subject to the requirements of the intensification process; it is also the prime mover in ensuring that decisions to improve production efficiency in other spheres are transmitted rapidly via adequate supplies of new machinery and equipment. This has particular importance with regard to cutting the current excessively high

---

[199] See *Economic Bulletin for Europe*, vol. 35, No. 4, Pergamon Press for the United Nations, December 1983, pp. 441-500.

[200] See *Economic Survey for Europe in 1982*, table 3.6.22, p. 221.

levels of fuel and other material inputs per unit of output. Thus, the intensification of the investment process, especially under conditions of below-plan and below-trend investment, is a precondition of success in the intensification of other sectors. It also offers, for a while at least, a way of offsetting the quantitative reduction in investment resources.

The central feature of the intensification of investment activity itself is the need to cut *gestation periods* and hence improve the speed with which up-to-date equipment is brought into operation. Success in the medium term can actually raise the increment of capital stock, irrespective of fluctuations in current investment performance. It is thus a top priority objective at the present time. It involves the co-ordination of a complex of operations to ensure that construction work is carried out in a timely manner and that operations are not impeded by shortages of building materials or by late delivery of machinery and equipment. The process stretches back therefore to the activity and efficiency of the construction sector itself, and further to investment goods manufacturers and importers.

The slowdown in investment growth itself should, by relieving pressure on the enterprises responsible for construction activity, have contributed to improvements in the investment process in recent years. One of the basic indicators of lead times is the change in the *ratio between the annual value of fixed capital brought into operation and of investment* (table 4.4.3). In almost all countries this ratio improved by between 1 and 9 percentage points between 1976-1980 and 1981-1983. The exception is Poland, where it fell between the two sub-periods by 5 percentage points. In Czechoslovakia, relatively slow progress since 1980 has not yet returned the ratio to the levels of the early 1970s. Much of the improvement in the other countries during the current five-year plan period can probably be attributed to reductions in starts due to the slowdown in the growth of investment (investment is the denominator of the ratio). However, since the ratio for the whole economy and for most individual sectors rarely exceeds 100 per cent, it is clear that the stock of unfinished investment continues to rise—even if at slower rates. The failure to reduce the investment backlog is not easy to explain, given the investment cutback and the high priority given to this objective in economic policy statements and plan directives.[201]

Reductions in the stock of *unfinished construction* can be achieved in two ways: by restricting new starts on one hand, and by hastening the completion of existing projects on the other. A generally recognised though indirect indicator of progress in either respect is the change in the share of machinery and equipment, as distinct from construction, in total investment expenditures (table 4.4.4). The importance of this indicator is that it provides an indirect measure of the success of policies to concentrate resources on finishing projects in hand. The final stage of the investment process is machinery- and equipment-intensive, whereas the initial stage of a new project is construction-intensive. The importance attached to this indicator arises from the fact that machinery is also considered as the "active component" of investment, the key element in increasing output capacity.

In fact only Bulgaria, and to a much smaller extent the German Democratic Republic, show increases in the *share of machinery*

[201] A possible explanation is suggested by a Hungarian economist: "... curbing investments may also mean simply expending lesser sums on them, without actually reducing (or even increasing) new starts and thus adding to commitments. This leads to a deconcentration of projects, even more projects are launched but are carried on more sluggishly. Gestation times lengthen and the tied up stock measured in unit years may increase indeed very sharply." A. Bródy: "About Investment Cycles and their Attenuation", *Acta Oeconomica*, Volume 31 (1-2), Budapest, 1984, p. 44.

TABLE 4.4.3

Fixed capital brought into operation
(Per cent of gross fixed capital formation)

	Total economy	Industry	Total economy	Industry	Total economy	Industry
	Bulgaria[a]		*Czechoslovakia*		*German Democratic Republic*	
1976-1980	90.1	83.8	94.2	93.9	92.5	89.9
1980	88.3	95.1	97.4	94.7	94.1	92.5
1981	87.3	78.1	96.9	99.1	93.8	90.7
1982	94.7	96.7	91.7	90.5	105.9	105.9
1983	92.8	87.2	97.2	97.8	90.3	78.4
	Hungary		*Poland*		*Romania*	
1976-1980	89.1	84.2	83.9	83.1	83.7	81.4
1980	94.1	87.4	81.4	76.6	88.4	80.8
1981	94.0	90.7	89.8	78.9	89.4	85.6
1982	92.1	84.4	71.2	70.0	93.7	95.6
1983	102.3	106.2	81.8	73.5	96.7	96.4
	Soviet Union					
1976-1980	93.0	90.0				
1980	98.7	99.9				
1981	95.6	92.7				
1982	97.0	95.5				
1983	97.3	94.4				

Source: National statistics.

[a] Current prices.

and equipment in total investment between 1976-1980 and 1981-1983. In Czechoslovakia, Hungary and Romania, changes have been positive but small, or even negative, and the indicator fell very sharply in Poland. In the Soviet Union—where investment growth was highest in the region—performance with respect to this indicator in 1983 was roughly in line with the annual provision of the five-year plan for that year, though a subsequent upward revision seems not to have been attained. The fact that this indicator moved only slowly, and in some cases not at all, in the direction required provides further indirect evidence either that the number of new project starts may have been higher, or more probably, the number of completions smaller, than originally expected during the current five-year plan period. The former would perhaps be surprising, given the small increases and sometimes declines in investment levels recorded in eastern Europe. The problem probably lies in difficulties in completing existing projects. In many cases, slow progress may reflect shortages of investment goods—and in particular of the machinery and equipment needed for installation in existing and in new plant.

Output of the engineering industries continued to grow more rapidly than investment in machinery and equipment since 1980—as throughout the 1970s. However, since the engineering industry produces many products other than investment goods, this relationship is inconclusive. What can be demonstrated is that the supply of imported investment goods, particularly from the industrialized market economies, has been cut back in the east European countries by considerably more than investment itself. Since imported goods are by definition not easily substitutable, and may also be key components of a particular installation, the cutbacks in imports mentioned may have had disproportionate effects in delaying the completion of projects. In the Soviet Union the situation is somewhat different: investment goods imports from the OECD area were restrained—and in volume terms reduced—for several years after the peak of 1978. However, it has partly compensated this by imports of investment goods from the east European countries in recent years. Moreover, imports of investment goods from the OECD area

132   Eastern Europe and the Soviet Union

TABLE 4.4.4

Gross fixed capital formation: selected indicators

(Annual percentage changes and per cent of total)

	1976-1980	1980	1981	1982	1983	1984
Bulgaria						
Machinery and equipment investment	1.5	6.9	20.8	7.6	0.8	..
− per cent of total	32.3	30.6	33.5	34.8	34.8	..
Engineering output	9.1	5.3	7.1	8.2	9.4	9.8
Machinery and equipment imports[a]	6.4	7.3	13.9	11.4	10.2	..
− from OECD area[b]	−4.8	34.2	47.7	−7.0	3.9	..
Construction investment	5.3	8.2	5.6	1.7	0.8	..
Czechoslovakia						
Machinery and equipment investment	5.9	2.8	−7.5	0.7	−0.6	..
− per cent of total	43.5	44.9	43.1	44.4	44.2	..
Engineering output	6.7	4.6	4.3	3.2	5.0	6.5
Machinery and equipment imports[a]	11.7	8.0	−0.1	4.5	9.8	..
− from OECD area[b]	6.0	−	−24.0	−2.9	−10.9	..
Construction investment	1.9	1.7	−0.5	−4.6	0.6	..
German Democratic Republic						
Machinery and equipment investment	3.0	0.6	7.0	−8.8	5.9	..
− per cent of total	47.0	47.0	49.0	47.1	49.9	..
Engineering output	6.9	7.6	7.6	4.9	5.6	..
Machinery and equipment imports[c]	12.6	3.9	10.5	5.3	0.9	..
− from OECD area[b]	9.3	−31.3	22.7	−12.3	15.2	..
Construction investment	3.9	−	−1.1	−1.7	−5.3	..
Hungary						
Machinery and equipment investment	−8.6	−16.1	−4.2	9.9	0.3	..
− per cent of total	42.9	40.1	41.4	43.9	43.4	..
Engineering output	3.1	−5.8	5.8	4.6	1.2	..
Machinery and equipment imports[d]	−3.6	−3.6	−3.6	1.6	1.2	..
− from OECD area[b]	12.5	−5.3	4.5	−4.2	−21.8	..
Construction investment	−3.1	−8.2	−9.4	−0.4	2.4	..
Poland						
Machinery and equipment investment	−2.0	−5.1	−22.9	−26.7	6.1	..
− per cent of total	36.8	36.8	36.6	30.5	29.6	..
Engineering output	6.9	0.3	−12.1	−0.9	6.9	..
Machinery and equipment imports[a]	6.1	−0.7	−15.1	−20.1	−1.2	..
− from OECD area[b]	−6.2	6.0	−53.1	−34.2	1.6	..
Construction investment	−2.9	−16.1	−22.0	−3.7	10.8	..
Romania						
Machinery and equipment investment	11.6	5.7	−10.1	−1.6	3.7[a]	..
− per cent of total	45.3	47.2	45.7	43.2	42.0[a]	..
Engineering output	12.6	10.1	2.2	3.5	5.5	..
Machinery and equipment imports[a]	13.7	−7.1	..	−14.6	15.8	..
− from OECD area[b]	4.8	−25.9	−50.2	−46.4	−40.5	..
Construction investment	6.1	0.7	−4.5	8.8	8.9[a]	..
Soviet Union						
Machinery and equipment investment	6.5	5.2	5.1	4.7	6.8	..
− per cent of total	36.2	38.0	38.5	38.9	39.3	..
Engineering output	8.2	6.2	5.9	4.8	6.3	7.0
Machinery and equipment imports[c]	13.4	4.7	5.6	22.0	17.3	..
− from OECD area[b]	3.1	−12.7	−1.8	29.5	4.2	..
Construction investment	1.8	0.6	3.0	2.9	5.0	..

Source: National statistics; OECD technology transfer data base.

Note: Figures for 1976-1980 are average annual compound growth rates.

[a] Current prices, national currencies.

[b] Current dollar prices, investment goods only (see UN Broad Economic Classification) plus large diameter steel pipes, structural parts and railway track components.

[c] Current prices, transferable roubles.

[d] Constant prices.

also rose very sharply in value (by nearly 30 per cent) in 1982 and also increased in 1983 (though they declined again in the first half of 1984).

(iii) Recent developments in the construction sector

The construction sector remains a key component of the investment process. Since it has not been examined in detail in this publication for some years, its performance in 1981-1983 relative to the five-year plan period 1976-1980 is summarized in the following paragraphs.

Notwithstanding efforts to reduce the construction component of investment, it still accounts for about half, and in some countries a much higher share, of investment expenditures. The sector's main performance indicators are shown in table 4.4.5.

TABLE 4.4.5

The construction sector
(*Annual percentage change*)

	1976-1980	1980	1981	1982	1983	1984
Bulgaria						
Gross output[a]	5.9	3.6	5.9	3.0	3.1	3.6
Net output[a]	4.5	4.2	8.3	7.0	2.8	..
Labour productivity[b]	3.7	4.8	6.6	6.4	1.5	..
Capital productivity[c]	−4.3	−2.2	3.1	−1.0	−10.2	..
Fixed assets change per unit change in labour productivity	5.4	1.7	−1.5	1.6	12.8	..
Output of construction materials.	7.5	4.2	4.0	2.6	4.6	..
Czechoslovakia						
Gross output[a]	3.0	1.9	−1.8	−3.8	2.8	1.7
Net output[a]	1.9	3.9	2.2	−2.9	0.8	..
Labour productivity[b]	0.8	3.5	3.7	−2.2	0.5	..
Capital productivity[c]	−5.7	−3.2	−2.3	−7.2	−3.0	..
Fixed assets change per unit change in labour productivity	7.2	3.6	0.8	6.9	3.4	..
Output of construction materials.	4.3	4.0	1.8	−1.7	0.3	1.3
German Democratic Republic						
Gross output[a]	3.3	1.4	4.1	3.0	2.9	2.5
Net output[a]	2.7	2.3	5.1	0.2	4.6	..
Labour productivity[b]	1.8	2.1	5.6	1.3	5.8	..
Capital productivity[c]	−5.0	−5.1	−1.0	−4.5	0.1	..
Fixed assets change per unit change in labour productivity	6.1	5.6	0.5	3.6	−1.2	..
Output of construction materials.	2.3	−0.6	−0.6	−3.2	2.6	..
Hungary						
Gross output[a]	2.4	−3.0	−0.2	0.5	−3.4*	−(4−5)*
Net output[a]	4.4	−2.9	1.7	0.1	..	..
Labour productivity[b]	5.8	−0.2	4.5	2.6	..	..
Capital productivity[c]	−5.8	−9.3	−2.6	−1.0	..	..
Fixed assets change per unit change in labour productivity	4.7	7.3	−0.1	−1.5	..	..
Output of construction materials.	4.9	1.6	1.0	0.8	1.2	..
Poland						
Gross output[a]	−0.5	−10.0	−21.0	−6.1	6.4	6.9
Net output[a]	−5.4	−21.7	−25.1	−8.4	7.7	..
Labour productivity[b]	−4.3	−19.5	−22.3	−2.4	9.0	..
Capital productivity[c]	−15.1	−26.3	−26.3	−8.7	6.2	..
Fixed assets change per unit change in labour productivity	16.5	32.0	30.7	2.8	−6.9	..
Output of construction materials.	1.2	−0.9	−17.6	1.8	5.1	..
Romania						
Gross output[a]	5.8	−0.8	−4.8	1.0	..	..
Net output[a]	6.3	−	−3.1	1.1	8.9	..
Labour productivity[b]	5.4	9.2	4.2	0.4	10.6	..
Capital productivity[c]	−6.8	−3.6	−10.7	−5.5	2.1	..
Fixed assets change per unit change in labour productivity	8.1	−5.0	4.2	6.5	−3.5	..
Output of construction materials.	12.8	4.6	−	1.7	2.7	..
Soviet Union						
Gross output[a]	2.6	1.2	1.8	1.9	3.9	3.0
Net output[a]	3.2	3.8	2.5	2.5	4.2	..
Labour productivity[b]	1.9	3.0	2.0	2.5	4.0	..
Capital productivity[c]	−5.7	−1.9	−6.0	−6.8	−3.2	..
Fixed assets change per unit change change in labour productivity	7.4	2.7	6.9	7.3	3.4	..
Output of construction materials.	1.9	1.3	1.9	1.9	4.9	2.0

Source: National statistics.

[a] National accounts definition.

[b] Net output per worker.

[c] Net output per unit of fixed assets.

Output has clearly been affected by slower overall and investment growth. Its share of net material product has fallen in all countries of the region since 1980. Its labour force and its share of material sphere fixed assets, in contrast with developments between 1975 and 1980, have also declined. The data on labour and capital productivity in the construction sector however show better performance than the material sphere total from 1980 to 1983. Though actual increases in labour productivity decelerated in some countries—but by less than for the material sphere as a whole—they actually speeded up in others. Construction was virtually the only sector where this occurred. Capital productivity continued to decline between 1980 and 1983, but at much slower rates than in the late 1970s in all countries.

By 1983 the sector accounted for about 9 per cent of the labour force in the material sphere, but somewhat more than this in Czechoslovakia and the Soviet Union (12-13 per cent).[202] In all countries but Bulgaria, the share of construction in the total material sphere labour force declined and in all but the Soviet Union it fell in absolute terms over the same period. In a majority of countries this represented a strong reinforcement of a decelerating growth trend already apparent in 1975-1980.

The construction work force is still underendowed with fixed capital relative to other sectors. Its share of fixed assets amounts to between 2 and 6 per cent of the material sphere total. Labour productivity levels are somewhat below the average for the total of material sphere activity in most, but not all countries. The improvement in labour productivity in 1980-1983 compared with other sectors, as distinct from its slow growth relative to other sectors in 1976-1980, owed a great deal to reductions in the work force already noted. It may also owe something to the fact that construction's share of investment had risen in the latter half of the 1970s and available fixed assets also increased at fast rates.[203] However, this was accompanied by a much faster capital productivity decline than for the material sphere as a whole. The rise in fixed assets per unit growth of labour productivity was thus also very high relative to other sectors in all countries during the second half of the 1970s. Construction's share of material sphere investment expenditures also declined in 1980-1983. As a result of this and of labour shedding, the fixed asset "cost" of labour productivity increases slowed down very considerably in most countries—it even declined in some—in 1981-1983, and in this respect it outperformed virtually all other material sphere activities.

The fact that labour productivity gains have tended to be very costly in terms of increases in fixed assets in the construction sector, which was the case not only in 1976-1980 but also earlier in 1971-1975, suggests two possibilities. The first is that productivity levels in the sector cannot be raised simply by improving the admittedly low *level* of capital intensity per worker. The recent fall in construction employment in most countries mentioned above strongly suggests that there has been a substantial level of overmanning in this sector and that the redeployment of labour away from it has benefited its performance more than has increasing the industry's capital stocks. A range of other factors contributed to the poor labour productivity growth performance

throughout the 1970s, such as material supply shortages, problems arising from management of the sites affected, shortcomings in planning and preparatory work. The slowdown in the demand for construction work has probably eased problems of this kind, though a comparison of building materials output and changes in the construction sector's output suggest that some tightness in supply persists in Romania and the Soviet Union.

(iv) Sectoral and industrial branch investment allocations

Changes in the allocation of investment between end-users have been noticeable since 1975, and, especially, since the late 1970s. This is not apparent in some countries at the level of main sectors of the economy, but even in those countries there has been considerable variation within industry (tables 4.4.6 and 4.4.7).

(a) Between the first half of the 1970s and the early 1980s, the *share of the material sphere in total investment* stayed fairly stable in most countries. The exceptions are Czechoslovakia where it rose sharply, and Poland where it fell even more sharply. In Czechoslovakia, a big share of the shift in resources to the material sphere was taken up by the construction sector up to 1980. In Poland, the shift away from the material sphere occurred at the expense of industry—the only country of the region where this happened. In all other countries, investment allocations *within the material sphere* were dominated quantitatively by industry, which accounted for between 45 and 70 per cent of the material sphere total throughout the period since 1970.[204] In most countries, industry's share also remained fairly stable. The exceptions are Bulgaria and the German Democratic Republic, where the sector's share of the material sphere allocations rose very sharply, and Poland where, as mentioned, its share fell.

The movements in these three countries reflected changes in the share of agriculture—the second biggest sectoral investor in all countries of the region. While agriculture's share remained constant in most countries, it fell in Bulgaria and the German Democratic Republic. In Poland, it rose considerably over the period.

The other sector to register noticeable change was construction. In most countries its share rose in the second half of the 1970s, but fell back in 1980-1983. The exceptions were Bulgaria, where its share did not rise until 1981-1983, the German Democratic Republic where its share fell steadily, and the Soviet Union where its share remained constant throughout.

If the special circumstances prevailing in Poland are excluded, the relative stability of overall investment patterns in most countries brings out two features of the economies of the region. First, among the more developed economies, only the German Democratic Republic has been able to direct resources continuously away from agriculture to consolidate its industrial investment. The same is true of Bulgaria among the less developed economies of the region. The need to maintain the share of agricultural investment at levels no less than 20-30 per cent of total allocations to the material sphere appears to be a major constraint on industrial development in other countries of the region—and especially in Poland. It is this element which is also

---

[202] This is due in large part to the exclusion of passenger transport from the material sphere in these two countries, which tends to inflate the shares of all other material sphere sectors relative to the other five countries.

[203] Fixed assets per construction employee in 1975-1980 rose by 8.3, 6.9, 7.1, 12.3, 12.5, 13.1 and 8.1 per cent annually in Bulgaria, Czechoslovakia, the German Democratic Republic, Hungary, Poland, Romania and the Soviet Union respectively, whereas they rose for the material sphere as a whole by 8.1, 5.8, 4.9, 6.5, 7.4, 10.0 and 6.3 per cent respectively in the same period.

[204] In 1983, industry's share of *total* investment (i.e. including the non-material sphere) in the seven countries was as follows (*in per cent*): Bulgaria 43, Czechoslovakia 41, the German Democratic Republic 58, Hungary 31, Poland 28, Romania 49, and the Soviet Union 35. However, these shares are affected *inter alia* by price policies. It is unlikely for instance that industry would account for such a low share of investment in the Soviet Union, or for such a high share in Bulgaria and Romania, if common pricing criteria were applied in all countries.

TABLE 4.4.6

Gross fixed investment by sector in 1975, 1980 and 1983
(Percentage shares)

	1971-1975	1976-1980	1981-1983
Bulgaria			
Material sphere = 100			
— Industry	55.4	56.4	60.2
— Construction	4.6	3.8	4.0
— Agriculture	20.5	18.1	14.9
— Transport and communications	15.2	16.5	15.8
— Trade etc..	4.1	4.6	4.5
— Other	0.2	0.6	0.7
Total economy = 100			
— Non-material sphere	27.6	27.8	28.2
Czechoslovakia			
Material sphere = 100			
— Industry	58.0	58.4	58.3
— Construction	6.2	7.9	9.6
— Agriculture	18.4	17.7	18.8
— Transport and communications[a]	9.4	9.1	7.6
— Trade etc..	7.5	6.5	5.3
— Other	0.4	0.5	0.3
Total economy = 100			
— Non-material sphere	37.8	35.1	31.7
German Democratic Republic			
Material sphere = 100			
— Industry	64.2	65.3	72.1
— Construction	3.5	4.2	2.3
— Agriculture	15.3	13.4	12.0
— Transport and communications	11.4	11.3	9.9
— Trade etc..	4.4	4.6	3.2
— Other	1.2	1.2	0.8
Total economy = 100			
— Non-material sphere	20.6	21.9	21.9
Hungary			
Material sphere = 100			
— Industry	44.6	47.7	45.5
— Construction	3.2	3.7	2.4
— Agriculture	21.9	18.9	20.1
— Transport and communications	17.5	16.6	16.5
— Trade etc..	5.5	5.7	6.6
— Other	7.4	7.4	8.8
Total economy = 100			
— Non-material sphere	29.4	27.9	29.7
Poland			
Material sphere = 100			
— Industry	52.1	49.7	44.3
— Construction	5.9	6.5	3.5
— Agriculture	22.7	24.6	30.0
— Transport and communications	13.1	11.5	10.1
— Trade etc..	3.3	2.7	3.7
— Other	2.8	5.0	8.5
Total economy = 100			
— Non-material sphere	26.8	28.5	35.0
Romania			
Material sphere = 100			
— Industry	59.4	59.6	59.1
— Construction	4.8	7.0	4.5
— Agriculture	18.7	17.0	19.6
— Transport and communications	12.3	12.9	14.0
— Trade etc. ⎱	4.7	3.5	2.8
— Other ⎰			
Total economy = 100			
— Non-material sphere	19.9	18.9	17.2
Soviet Union			
Material sphere = 100			
— Industry	48.3	47.6	47.9
— Construction	5.3	5.4	5.3
— Agriculture	27.8	27.5	26.4

TABLE 4.4.6 *(continued)*

	1971-1975	1976-1980	1981-1983
Soviet Union (continued)			
— Transport and communications[a]	15.0	16.1	16.5
— Trade etc. ⎱	3.6	3.4	3.8
— Other ⎰			
Total economy = 100			
— Non-material sphere	27.7	25.8	25.9

Source: National statistics.

[a]Unlike other countries, passenger transport and communications are included in the non-material sphere by Czechoslovakia and the Soviet Union.

conditioning the stable, and in some countries even the declining, share of the non-material sphere in total investment. As noted in section 4.6, there are objective reasons why allocations to the non-material sphere should increase faster than the average for the economy as a whole. Such an increment was discernible, apart from the special case of Poland, only in Bulgaria and the German Democratic Republic—precisely the two countries where agriculture's share of investment has fallen.

(*b*) These considerations are noteworthy given movements within *industrial investment* over the same period. Such changes have been characterized for the region as a whole by very large shifts in allocations towards the fuel and, to a lesser extent, the energy branches. Both—especially energy—are highly capital-intensive relative to output. Gross output per unit of fixed assets currently ranges between 20-35 per cent of the all-industry average for energy and between 30 and 70-80 per cent for fuel. By 1983, only Bulgaria and the German Democratic Republic allocated less than 30 per cent of their total industrial investment to the combined fuel-energy branches. The other five countries allocated between 32 and 40 per cent, compared with a range for these five of 23-28 per cent in 1971-1975, and 25-30 per cent in 1976-1980.

It was noted in a previous edition of this publication that up to 1979: "For the area as a whole, there is little sign of a major sustained resource transfer into fuels and energy in recent years".[205] In fact, the shift did not occur until 1980 or later in most countries, but its suddenness clearly compounded the effects of its size.

It is noteworthy that both Bulgaria and the German Democratic Republic are again exceptions to the general trend of investment in the region, though for different reasons. Bulgaria benefits as far as fuel is concerned from its closeness to the Soviet Union—the main supplier of the region's oil and gas. The case of the German Democratic Republic is different. It took decisions in the 1960s to restrain the growth of its dependence on imported fuels in favour of developing lignite production. Both countries have thus succeeded in shielding their industry and investment patterns from the sudden readjustments which had to be undertaken in the other countries of the region in the late 1970s and afterwards. The German Democratic Republic has also carried through vigorous fuel and energy conservation measures, and indeed devotes a substantial part of its investment effort to this purpose.[206]

---

[205] *Economic Survey of Europe in 1979*, p. 194.

[206] For 1984 the German Democratic Republic, which has achieved a particularly high concentration of resources on such measures, announced that 57 per cent of its industrial investment was devoted to rationalization of existing production. *Neues Deutschland*, 19/20 January 1985, p. 4.

TABLE 4.4.7

Industrial gross fixed investment by branch in 1975, 1980 and 1983

(Per cent of total industrial investment)

	Energy	Fuel	Metallurgy	Engineering	Chemicals	Construction materials	Wood, paper	Textiles	Other light[a]	Food	Other	Total
Bulgaria[b]												
1975	13.2	6.0	4.2	20.1	13.2	7.9	4.7	5.8	3.9	12.5	8.5	100.0
1980	13.8	9.5	6.3	26.3	9.4	8.3	3.5	2.0	1.4	8.2	11.4	100.0
1983	13.6	7.9*	6.0	36.2	8.5	4.0	3.4	1.9	1.4	5.8	11.5*	100.0
Czechoslovakia												
1975	14.1	9.2	8.6	21.3	9.1	6.0	5.3	4.3	3.8	7.7	10.6	100.0
1980	15.3	12.8	9.1	22.4	6.4	4.3	8.4	3.6	3.5	7.0	7.1	100.0
1983	15.4	16.6	8.4	21.7	6.8	3.1	5.4	2.6	3.6	7.2	9.2	100.0
German Democratic Republic												
1975	24.4		5.9	22.7	16.6	4.2	..	4.1	8.9	7.9	5.5	100.0
1980	22.8		10.7	25.0	18.1	3.6	..	2.9	6.1	5.4	5.3	100.0
1983	22.9		12.0	26.1	17.3	2.3	..	2.6	6.7	5.4	4.7	100.0
Hungary		c										
1975	14.1	10.6	6.5	16.5	20.2	6.6	4.0	4.4	3.5	12.5	1.1	100.0
1980	19.7	14.1	12.0	17.3	11.3	4.9	1.5	2.4	3.1	12.4	1.2	100.0
1983	21.6	16.7	8.3	15.9	15.3	3.7	3.0	2.2	2.4	10.1	0.9	100.0
Poland												
1975	8.0	12.3	16.6	24.2	9.1	6.6	4.6	4.7	2.4	11.2	0.4	100.0
1980	15.1	22.0	10.9	22.4	9.5	2.9	3.5	2.4	2.2	8.7	0.3	100.0
1983	16.5	21.0	5.2	23.2	10.2	3.1	3.1	2.5	3.1	12.2	0.7	100.0
Romania												
1975	14.2	14.4	14.1	18.6	14.6	4.6	5.0	3.3	1.7	6.7	2.9	100.0
1980	11.0	13.4	14.1	28.4	13.9	4.2	3.0	3.9	1.4	4.5	2.2	100.0
1983	20.2	19.8	10.6	19.9	11.4	2.1	3.9	2.0	1.0	7.2	2.0	100.0
Soviet Union												
1975	9.2	18.6	6.5	25.1	9.6	4.4	4.6	2.8	1.3	7.2	10.8	100.0
1980	9.5	23.1	5.9	25.0	8.4	4.0	3.8	3.0	0.8	6.5	10.1	100.0
1983	8.6	26.3	6.1	24.8	7.6	3.7	3.6*	2.8*	0.7*	6.1	9.7*	100.0

Source: National statistics.

[a] In the Soviet Union other light industry covers clothing, leather, footwear and furs only. In the other countries, it also includes printing (except Bulgaria), glass and ceramics plus, in the German Democratic Republic, wood and paper.

[b] Current prices.

[c] Includes mining of all kinds.

In the other five countries, the effects of such a large shift of resources have been felt mainly by the textile, light and food industry branches, and also in some countries by the chemical industry. In general, it has had the least influence on engineering. So far, no country but Poland has registered declining levels of investment in this branch. But the engineering branch has also suffered, and only in Bulgaria and the German Democratic Republic has the previous long-term trend increase in its share of industrial investment continued. This is likely to have important consequences for the future since the engineering branch is the main supplier of technology, via investment goods, to other branches. Its performance is thus a vital element in plans for the intensification of investment and of the economy as a whole.

(c) In this part of the sub-section, an attempt is made to assess *developments in the rate of structural change* in investment by country and over time.

Structural change indices, in the form of "similarity indices" measuring the degree of difference in the structure of investment, were first calculated (table 4.4.8).[207] This approach has its limits since it summarizes movements between main sectors and branches only, whereas structural change may also have taken place at sub-branch levels. Bearing this in mind, the rates of

change presented indicate that the pace of structural change as a whole accelerated over the successive sub-periods reviewed: 1970-1975, 1975-1980 and 1980-1983. This was so for the material sphere as a whole, and also for industry. The fastest rates of change were recorded in Bulgarian and Romanian industry, and

[207] Structural change means the change over time in the percentage share of individual sectors relative to the material sphere total, and in individual industrial branches relative to the total for industry. The index of structural change (similarity index) is not an index in the usual sense of the word. It is calculated as half the sum of changes (irrespective of sign) in shares of all sectors or branches between a base year and subsequent years, viz.

$$0.5 \sum | a_{in} - a_{io} |$$

where a_{in}, a_{io}, are percentage shares of sector or branch i in total (i.e. material sphere or industry) in year n and in the base year o, respectively. The index for each year was first calculated relative to the year 1970 and showed a generally uninterrupted trend away from the structural pattern in that year. Average rates of change for sub-periods shown in table 4.4.8 were calculated between the final year of the sub-period and the final year of the preceding sub-period. See also *Economic Survey of Europe in 1980*, p. 189 and footnote.

in the Polish material sphere. The slowest rates were recorded for the material spheres of Hungary and the Soviet Union. In Bulgaria, and to some extent in Hungary, the degree of change was probably affected by the often substantial year-to-year changes which are associated with the effects of a few large projects in the smaller economies of the region. This "lumpiness" is a characteristic of Bulgarian investment patterns, but may affect in principle the reliability of the index between two individual years in any country, and in the smaller countries of eastern Europe in particular.

TABLE 4.4.8

Structural change in investment, 1970-1983
(*Average annual percentage change*)[a]

	Material sphere			Industry		
	1970-1975	1975-1980	1980-1983	1970-1975	1975-1980	1980-1983
Bulgaria	1.7	1.1	1.3	1.6	3.4	3.4
Czechoslovakia . .	0.8	1.4	1.5	1.8	2.0	2.3
German Democratic Republic	0.6	1.5	2.0	2.1	1.8	1.5[b]
Hungary	1.3	0.9	1.7[b]	2.3	3.3	4.0[b]
Poland	1.5	1.5	3.0	2.6	3.7	2.7
Romania	0.7	0.7	1.5	1.2	2.2	6.8
Soviet Union . . .	0.7	0.2	0.5	1.0	1.0	1.6[b]

Source: ECE secretariat calculations based on national statistics.

Note: Based on a 6-sector (5 in Romania and the Soviet Union) breakdown for the material sphere, and an 11-branch breakdown (10 in the German Democratic Republic) for industry.

[a] Average annual change in the similarity index between years indicated.

[b] 1980-1982.

In contrast with investment, structural change in output as measured by the same technique shows evidence of a deceleration between 1970-1975 and 1975-1980, and between 1980-1983 and the latter period, except in Poland (industry) and Hungary (both industry and the material sphere). Output patterns do not depend, in the short run at least, exclusively on changes in investment: factors both external and internal can also play a role. Capacity utilization rates may change due to supply shortages, and the pattern of potential output itself can change as a result of differences in the rate of retirement of fixed assets between sectors or branches. Material sphere output patterns may be determined largely by agricultural output fluctuations. Shortages of inputs, which affect some sectors and branches more than others, have also made contributions to structural change in most east European countries in 1981-1983—notably in those countries where NMP or industrial growth decelerated to low rates or where actual declines in output took place.[208]

(*d*) Some attempts were made to establish the timing of *structural change in output relative to investment* by running regressions of changes in the share of individual sectors and branches in total material sphere and industrial output respectively, against changes in sector and branch shares of investment. No significant results were obtained. This probably reflects differences in sectoral and branch gestation periods—which can vary from a relatively short time in some to several years in others where very large complex installations are required (energy, chemicals). There is thus no direct evidence of why sector/

branch shifts in investment have been accompanied by a deceleration in the rate of change in the structure of output.

In industry in particular, the shift to the capital-intensive fuel and energy branches might be expected *a priori* to have contributed to this slowdown. This is not, however borne out by the facts. In the short term, and *ceteris paribus* (i.e. assuming no change in capacity utilization rates, labour force deployment and policy towards enterprise closures, etc.), the main contributor to changes in output structures in the short term is the structure of fixed assets. These are of course ultimately affected by changes in the structure of investment but only after a lag. The contribution of changes in the structure of fixed assets relative to growth has not in fact been very large in most countries of the region during 1970-1983 as a whole, particularly in industry. Five countries (excluding the German Democratic Republic and Romania) publish fixed asset data by industrial branch. Secretariat calculations suggest that over the sub-periods 1970-1975, 1975-1980 and 1980-1983 the effect of changes in the structure of fixed assets on the growth of industrial output was rather small. This component, small but positive in all countries at the beginning of the 1970s, generally exerted a downward influence on growth in 1980-1983, but it was still only small.[209]

The slowdown in the pace of structural change in output mentioned earlier suggests that adjustment policies, which have been vigorous at the level of investment—or at least industrial investment—are not fully effective in terms of final results. As already mentioned, the effect of lags between investment and fixed asset structural changes presupposes that the pace of structural change in output will be slower over a given period than the pace of structural change in investment. What is surprising is that, whereas the latter is accelerating, the former has slowed down. This suggests two possibilities, which are not mutually exclusive: first, that the *ceteris paribus* assumption above be discarded, and due weight given to the differing degree to which different types of industrial activity have been affected first by supply constraints and hence variations in capacity utilization rates. Such effects are likely to have been substantial in the 1980-1983 period of slow output growth and large scale internal and external adjustment. They cannot however be quantified. The second possibility is that for various reasons the structure of fixed assets has not responded as fast as it should to changes in the structure of investment expenditures. It can be argued that one reason for this is that the rate of retirement of obsolete equipment has slowed down. This may be connected with efforts by enterprises to maintain productive capacity, in the absence of adequate investment, by extending the life of existing fixed assets , i.e. by cutting retirement rates (table 4.4.9). In other words, the share of certain output lines, though not being encouraged by new investment, is not falling as rapidly as it should.

Retirement rates tend to be low in the region. Only in Bulgaria do they rise much above 2 per cent, whereas rates in the other countries vary around 1-2 per cent.[210] They have risen only in Bulgaria (industry) and in Hungary (material sphere and

---

[208] Declining NMP levels were recorded in Czechoslovakia in 1981, Hungary in 1980 and Poland in 1979-1982 inclusive, while industrial production levels declined in Czechoslovakia in 1981 and 1982, Hungary in 1980 and Poland in 1980-1982 inclusive.

[209] The data on which this statement is based, not tabulated here, are part of longer-term research being carried out by the ECE secretariat.

[210] According to a recent Soviet publication, the norms for fixed asset retirement in industry needs to rise to 2.5-3.5 per cent annually, see A. Malygin: "*Nazrevshie voprosy planirovaniya vosproizvodstva osnovnykh fondov*" (Imminent problems in planning the reproduction of fixed assets), *Planovoye Khoziaistvo*, No. 8, 1984, Ekonomika, Moscow 1984, p. 66. Successive editions of *Narodnoye Khozyaistvo SSSR* (the Soviet statistical yearbook) show industrial fixed asset retirement rates of 1.6 per cent in 1975 falling to 1.3 per cent at the beginning of 1983. Similarly, data for Czechoslovakia show a fall in the retirement rate of machinery and equipment from 1.5 to 1.4 between 1975 and 1983—see *Statistická ročenka ČSSR 1984*, Prague, 1984, pp. 230 and 248.

TABLE 4.4.9

Apparent retirement rates of fixed assets, 1971-1983

(Percentage shares) [a]

	Material sphere			Industry		
	1971-1975	1976-1980	1981-1983	1971-1975	1976-1980	1981-1983
Bulgaria	3.3	3.2	3.2	4.2	4.9	4.3
Czechoslovakia . .	1.6	1.4	0.9	1.4	1.2	0.5
German Democratic						
Republic	1.9	1.9	0.8	1.4[b]	2.1[b]	1.0[b]
Hungary	1.2	1.9	1.8[c]	2.0	2.5	2.3[c]
Poland	1.2	0.5	1.2	1.7	1.0	1.0
Romania	2.1	3.5	1.1	1.3[b]	3.3[b]	0.7[b]
Soviet Union . . .	2.4	2.5	1.7	2.9	2.4	1.9

Source: ECE secretariat calculations based on national statistics.

[a] Investment minus absolute increment of fixed assets (both expressed in constant price monetary units) as a percentage of fixed assets in the periods shown.

[b] National accounts basis.

[c] 1981-1982.

TABLE 4.4.10

Share of fixed assets under five years old, 1975-1983 [a]

(Percentage shares)

	Material sphere			Industry		
	1975	1980	1983	1975	1980	1983
Bulgaria	48.6	45.8	42.7	52.8	51.8	49.6
Czechoslovakia . .	31.5	32.3	28.9	29.8	31.0	27.9
German Democratic						
Republic	33.3	32.0	28.0	33.6[b]	32.9[b]	30.6[b]
Hungary	31.7	32.5	29.8[c]	41.1	41.3	36.5[c]
Poland	36.2	33.7	21.9	44.8	37.8	22.7
Romania	51.2	53.2	44.3	51.0[b]	52.8[b]	44.1[b]
Soviet Union . . .	44.3	40.9	37.0	45.2	41.1	37.2

Source: ECE secretariat calculations based on national statistics.

[a] Cumulated investment over the previous five years as a share of fixed assets in years shown.

[b] National accounts basis.

[c] 1982.

industry) while in the other countries already low rates have declined further. The fall was substantial in most cases in 1981-1983 compared with 1971-1975, despite some acceleration in 1976-1980.

The decline from the late 1970s onwards compared with the higher rates recorded in 1976-1980—both for industry and for the material sphere as a whole—suggests a connection with the investment deceleration. The retention in service of old plant in order to compensate slower growth of new equipment could also have been a factor in the accelerated rate of decline in capital productivity recorded in most countries. By definition, those assets whose working life was prolonged tend to consist of obsolete equipment with a lower productivity level.

A concomitant of the extension of the working life of fixed assets noted above and stagnating investment is a deterioration in the age structure of the capital stock. Full data are available only for Czechoslovakia, but a comparison of investment cumulated over five-year periods and compared with fixed assets in the final year of successive periods shows sharp declines of fixed assets under five years old over time in most countries (table 4.4.10). In 1975, the final year of the last five-year plan period to achieve consistently rising investment ratios relative to NMP in the region, the share of fixed assets under five years old amounted to between 32 and 51 per cent in the material sphere, and between 30 and 53 per cent in industry. By 1983, these shares had fallen to a range of 22-44 per cent, and 28-50 per cent respectively. Moreover, the share fell much more in some countries than these ranges suggest—particularly in Poland and the Soviet Union.

The slowdown in the structural change of output despite an acceleration, noted earlier, of structural change in investment since 1970, cannot yet be conclusively explained on the data available. The foregoing assessment however suggests some possible causes. First, progress in reducing lead times, as described in sub-section (ii) above, has been unsatisfactory, and has not provided a counterbalance to slower investment growth. Second, the fall in retirement rates which accompanied slower investment growth has reinforced the effects of the investment slowdown. These two factors have led to a deterioration in the age structure of fixed assets in use, hence maintaining output of certain product lines despite investment cutbacks. This is perhaps one reason for the negative effects of structural changes in fixed assets on output growth in recent years, even though they are small relative to total output growth.

While the precise link between structural changes in investment, fixed assets and output cannot be traced with any precision, the above discussion highlights some of the likely impediments to such change under conditions of decelerating or declining investment. Given the imperatives for structural change which changed economic conditions have imposed, these questions need urgent attention. Emphasis in plans, documents and policy statements continues to be placed on the key objective of reducing investment lead times in order to maximize and accelerate the effect of new investment on output. This is expected to go hand in hand with qualitative improvements in the capital stock based on new technology. It is however clear that the recent slowdown in investment has complicated the solution of these problems too: there has been no consistent fall in the volume of unfinished investment in any country. Plans for 1985 show full awareness of the current investment needs of the economy. Some upward trend in the volume of capital outlays is now discernible, though still at a low overall rate. The reversal of the current five-year-long investment slowdown in most countries is thus likely to be a central issue in the preparation of the forthcoming five-year plans for 1986-1990.

(v) Trends and fluctuations in investment growth

(a) As already noted in sub-section (i) above, investment plans for 1981-1985 were set at lower levels than in the previous quinquennium in most east European countries and in the Soviet Union. In fact, the growth rates recorded for 1981-1984 reflect a clear-cut check in the underlying upward trend that can be observed for gross investment since the 1950s. The only exceptions to this pattern in the period 1981-1984 are Bulgaria and the Soviet Union. However, even in these two countries the actual annual change in the recent period clearly fell below the longer-run trends observed over the previous three decennia (table 4.4.11).

It can be seen that, after accelerating very rapidly in the 1950s, investment activity decelerated abruptly in the first half of the 1960s, though it maintained on average relatively high growth rates in the 1960s and the 1970s compared with the whole 34-year period. Indeed, the rates for the 1970s as a whole conceal a sharp deceleration that occurred in nearly all countries in the second half of the decade. This holds notably for Poland, where the average annual growth rate dropped from an annual average increase of 18 per cent in 1971-1975 to an annual decline of 3 per cent in 1976-1980.

TABLE 4.4.11

Gross fixed investments in eastern Europe at constant prices
(Average annual percentage change)[a]

	1951-1955	1956-1960	1961-1965	1966-1970	1971-1975	1976-1980	1981-1984[b]
Bulgaria	12.8	17.1	7.9	12.5	8.6	4.0	3.6
Czechoslovakia	9.6	13.3	2.0	7.2	8.2	3.5	−1.2
German Democratic Republic.	17.8	14.9	4.8	10.0	4.8	3.4	−0.7
Hungary	1.3	13.0	5.6	10.6	6.9	2.2	−4.1
Poland	11.1	9.0	6.7	8.1	17.5	−3.0	−5.3
Romania	18.3	13.7	11.3	11.2	11.5	8.5	−0.6
Total, eastern Europe	11.6	12.7	6.0	9.5	10.8	2.7	−1.6
Soviet Union	12.3	13.1	6.2	7.5	7.0	3.4	3.8
Total, eastern Europe and the Soviet Union .	12.1	13.0	6.2	8.1	8.1	3.2	2.2

Source: National statistics. Weights are derived from data on CMEA studies of relative per capita levels of investments in benchmark years in the first half of the 1960s, population, and changes in the variable between 1965 and 1975. For per capita data, see Ia.Ia. Kotkovskii *et al, Sopostavleniia urovnei ekonomicheskogo razvitiia sotsialisticheskikh stran* (Moscow: *Ekonomika*, 1965); O. Rybakov "Vyravnivanie urovnei ekonomicheskogo razvitiia sotsialisticheskikh stran", *Voprosy ekonomiki*, 1967, No. 1, pp. 106-116.

[a] Average annual percentage changes between the final year of the period shown and the final year of the previous period.

[b] 1984 data are provisional.

A strong deceleration of investment growth had already occurred over the period 1961-1965 relative to 1956-1960 in all countries but Poland and Romania. However, the current swing seems to be more persistent and is unique, from a historical perspective, in that several countries recorded absolute declines in investment levels at the same time—sometimes for several years successively—from the late 1970s. Moreover, it represents a far-reaching modification of an important element of growth strategy. The long-term plans of all countries of the region in virtually all past periods were characterized by investment-led growth. This strategy has been in abeyance since the late 1970s in all countries of eastern Europe and, though to a less marked extent, also in the Soviet Union.

This change in economic policy priorities can best be illustrated by the development of investment relative to total output. Clearly, part of the investment slowdown is simply a consequence of declining rates of output growth but a noticeable general feature in recent years is the trendwise lag of investment relative to output. This has led to sharp falls in the investment ratios of the eastern European countries in particular.[211]

As can be seen from chart 4.4.2 and table 4.4.12, the investment ratios showed an upward trend from the 1950s onward. In Bulgaria and the German Democratic Republic, this ratio started to level off in the late 1960s and early 1970s, respectively. In contrast, the investment ratio continued its relatively rapid upward path until the year 1975 or so in the four remaining eastern European countries. In six countries, however, the trend values declined from after the peak reached around the years 1976-1978. Indeed the values recorded at the end of the observation period are about the same as those prevailing around 1970.

It can also be seen from chart 4.4.2 that the Soviet investment ratio has been remarkably stable since about 1960. From 1960 to the peak year of 1976/1977 it increased from 28.7 to 30.0 per cent, and now stands only just below the 1975 level.

(b) The foregoing illustrates that the basic pattern of changes in investment trends in all six eastern European countries is rather similar. There are, however, marked differences among the individual countries regarding the degree of acceleration or deceleration of the underlying growth rates. This sub-section focuses on the extent to which *cyclical* fluctuations of investment around the trend in an individual country are associated with similar *concurrent* movements in the rest of the region, i.e. whether or not the individual countries investment cycles are synchronous with the rest of the region. The analysis of fluctuations in the economic activity of centrally planned economies

[211] Output is measured in terms of net material product. As noted in sub-section (i) above, the investment ratio is calculated as the share of gross fixed investment in NMP produced.

TABLE 4.4.12

Trends in investment ratios[a]
(Percentages)

	1955	1960	1965	1970	1975	Peak[b]	1980	1982
Bulgaria	20.8	27.1	32.7	36.3	36.6	36.9	35.3	35.0
Czechoslovakia	23.4	28.1	28.3	29.8	33.2	33.8	32.7	31.2
German Democratic Republic. . .	17.6	22.4	24.6	29.8	30.7	30.9	29.1	26.7
Hungary	22.9	26.3	30.7	34.7	36.1	37.4	35.6	32.3
Poland	19.7	21.4	22.6	25.1	33.0	33.2	27.2	24.9
Romania	24.3	29.2	33.7	37.7	38.1	40.5	39.7	36.9
Soviet Union	24.9	28.7	28.7	28.9	29.7	30.0	29.5	29.4

Source: National statistics.

Note: The price bases used differ in some cases from those shown in table 4.4.2.

[a] Gross fixed investment as a percentage of NMP produced shown as centred five-year moving averages.

[b] Bulgaria: 1976; Czechoslovakia: 1977; German Democratic Republic: 1977; Hungary: 1977; Poland: 1976; Romania: 1978; Soviet Union: 1976-1977.

CHART 4.4.2

Investment ratios,[a] 1950-1984

(in percentage)

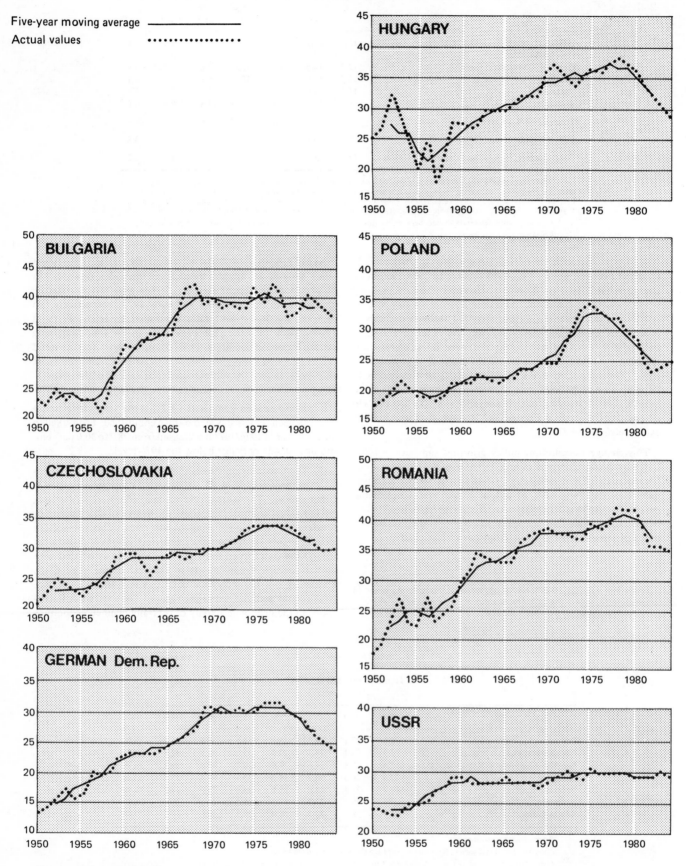

Five-year moving average ———————

Actual values ·····················

Source: As for table 4.4.12

a Gross fixed investments/net material product

CHART 4.4.3

Synchronization of investment fluctuations in Eastern Europe, 1952—1982

(Percentage deviation from trend)

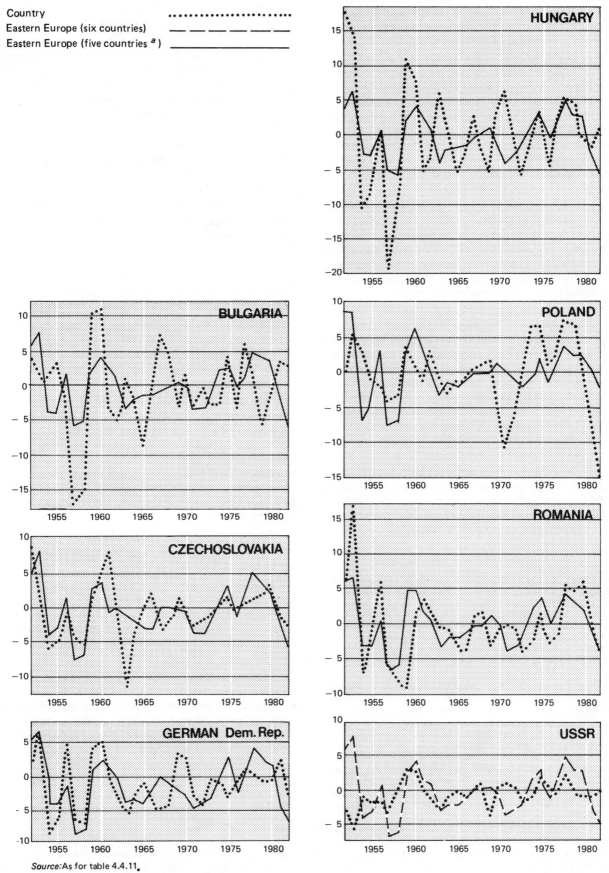

Source: As for table 4.4.11.

a Eastern Europe excluding the country of reference.

has by now a long tradition.[212] Much of this literature reflects the view that investment policies are country-specific–due for instance to the different importance of agriculture and some other activities at different times and in different countries, or because average gestation periods vary between countries due to different investment structures. In the following paragraphs, an attempt is made to identify and where possible measure the degree of synchronization between the countries of the region.

The trend of investment was defined as a centred five-year moving average of the original annual data for 1950 to 1984, and the cycle is accordingly measured as the deviation of the actual values from this trend.[213] For each of the six east European countries, the annual percentage deviations from the trend for the years 1952 to 1982 were then regressed on the cyclical values measured in the same way for the weighted regional aggregate of the five remaining countries.[214] Finally, eastern Europe as a whole was compared with the Soviet Union using the same method.

In order to examine whether the association between the cycle of an individual country and the region was stable over time, the estimation was also carried out for two sub-periods, namely 1952-1970 on the one hand and 1971-1982 on the other. This choice of sub-periods allows, incidentally, separate analysis of the period of region-wide harmonization of five-year planning which was introduced in 1971 and strengthened thereafter.

The results obtained for the whole period 1952-1982 and for the two sub-periods retained are given in table 4.4.13. The results suggest that the cyclical association has in general not been stable over time. Hence the following remarks are limited to differences between the two sub-periods. First, it can be seen that over the period 1952-1970 there was a statistically significant association of concurrent (i.e. unlagged) cyclical investment movements in each of the six east European countries with the rest of the region.[215] In contrast, no significant relationship could be detected between the investment cycles of eastern Europe as a whole and the Soviet Union.

It is striking that for the second period examined (1971-1982) a statistically significant synchronization with the region was only found for three out of six countries, namely Czechoslovakia, Romania and, perhaps somewhat surprisingly, Poland (see also chart 4.4.3).[216] And, as in the previous case, there was again no

significant association between the investment cycle of the six east European countries as a group and of the Soviet Union.

It is furthermore interesting to note that, for Czechoslovakia and Romania, a statistical test designed to expose any difference in the estimated relationships for the two periods depicted in table 4.4.13 is not statistically significant, i.e. the relationship is stable over the whole period 1952-1982.[217]

It is recalled that the above analysis does not focus on changes in investment themselves but rather on the concurrent association of cyclical deviations from the underlying trend. The results therefore suggest that this association was for various reasons much more pervasive for the period 1952-1970 that for the years thereafter.[218]

It would be interesting as a further step to examine in more detail the determinants of the investment fluctuations in individual countries, notably their quantitative relationship with major domestic and international macro-economic variables. This, however, is beyond the scope of the present note.

The main findings of this sub-section can therefore be briefly summarized as follows: compared to the long-term trend there was a significant, but not entirely unprecedented, deceleration in investment activity over the last few years. Morever, investment activity showed a marked deceleration relative to total NMP, a trend which led to sharp falls in the investment ratios in some countries.

The synchronization of investment cycles was found to be much stronger before than after 1970. More research on an individual country basis is called for however in order to shed more light on the determinants of fluctuations and cycles in investment activity.

(c) The following *statistical note* briefly describes the main data series used in parts (a) and (b) of this sub-section. The exercise was carried out using published long-term series on gross fixed capital formation and net material product at constant prices. Where no such series were published for the entire period, available absolute figures or indices were linked using the "chain" method. An attempt was made to use time series giving the broadest possible coverage. The following specific points should be noted:

— the constant price base years used for investment are fairly recent, (except for the Soviet Union where it is unspecified) but vary by country from 1977 to 1982;

— the data for the early 1950s are significantly less reliable and less accurate than for later years. Retrospective long-term annual figures on a standard price or classification basis in absolute terms, or with an accuracy of one significant decimal in the case of indices, have not been published by all countries and gaps remain;

— a further problem should be mentioned, though its effects can only be guessed at. The estimation of price changes in order to obtain volume data is particularly difficult in the investment sector. At least in one case, for which a detailed methodology of the methods applied was published, it appears that the official statistics include part of changes in nominal values in volume

---

[212] See e.g. George J. Staller, "Fluctuations in Economic Activity: Planned and Free Market Economies", *American Economic Review*, June 1964, pp. 385-395; Alexander Bajt, "Fluctuations and Trends in Growth Rates in Socialist Countries", *Ekonomska analiza*, No. 3-4, 1969. A recent extensive discussion of investment cycles can be found in T. Bauer: *Tervgazdaság, beruházás, ciklusok* (Planned Economy, Investments, Cycles), Közgazdasàgi ès Jogi Könyvkiadó, Budapest, 1981. See also the same author: "Investment Cycles in Planned Economies", *Acta Oeconomica*, vol. 21, No. 3, 1978.

[213] Note that the method of centred moving averages eliminates the first two and the last two years, so that the cycle can only be analysed for the period 1952-1982.

[214] The annual time-series model estimated was:
$C_{j,t} = a + b\, C_{r,t} + e_t$ where $C_{j,t}$ and $C_{r,t}$ denote the percentage deviations of investment from the trend in country j and the region (excluding country j and the Soviet Union) respectively, in year t. The variable e_t is the disturbance term. The coefficients a and b were estimated using the method of ordinary least squares. The estimated coefficient b indicates the change in the percentage deviation from trend in country j that is associated with a one percentage point change in the deviation from trend in the region.

[215] It should be noted, however, that the cyclical association of Poland with the rest of the region was rather weak.

[216] Alternative estimations made indicate that these findings are not sensitive to the impact of the specific Polish investment cycle on the corresponding regional aggregates.

[217] The stability of the estimated relationship was examined with the Chow-Test. See G. C. Chow: "Tests of Equality between Sets of Coefficients in Two Linear Regressions", *Econometrica*, vol. 28, July 1960, pp. 591-605.

[218] See also J. Goldmann, "Fluctuations and Trends in the Rate of Economic Growth in Some Socialist Countries", *Economics of Planning*, 1964, No. 2, pp. 88-98, who found a degree of synchronization for the 1950s.

TABLE 4.4.13

Synchronization of investment fluctuations in eastern Europe, 1952-1982
(*Regression equation:* $C_{j,t}$: $a + b\ C_{r,t} + e$)

Country	1952-1982				1952-1970				1971-1982			
	Estimates				Estimates				Estimates			
	a	b	R^2	SEE	a	b	R^2	SEE	a	b	R^2	SEE
Bulgaria . . .	−0.42 (0.41)	0.66 (2.19)**	0.14	5.75	−0.54 (−0.37)	1.09 (2.64)**	0.29	6.36	−0.07 (−0.07)	−0.15 (−0.46)	0.02	3.76
Czechoslovakia	0.13 (0.23)	0.69 (4.26)*	0.38	3.15	0.11 (0.12)	0.78 (3.10)*	0.36	4.03	0.20 (0.97)	0.50 (7.48)*	0.85	0.73
German Democratic Republic	0.17 (0.30)	0.61 (3.93)*	0.35	3.02	0.24 (0.31)	0.86 (4.11)*	0.50	3.32	0.17 (0.34)	0.13 (0.85)	0.07	1.75
Hungary . . .	0.29 (0.27)	1.43 (4.19)*	0.38	5.94	0.09 (0.06)	2.08 (4.65)*	0.56	6.19	0.83 (0.76)	0.29 (0.82)	0.06	3.78
Poland	−0.53 (−0.59)	0.46 (1.89)***	0.11	4.98	−0.30 (−0.53)	0.26 (2.07)***	0.20	2.43	−1.33 (−0.70)	2.65 (2.44)**	0.37	6.54
Romania . . .	−0.20 (−0.28)	0.91 (4.19)*	0.38	4.05	−0.27 (−0.25)	1.01 (3.31)*	0.39	4.72	−0.07 (−0.08)	0.68 (2.39)**	0.36	2.97
Soviet Union .	−0.50 (−1.57)	0.02 (0.16)	−	1.78	−0.85 (−1.81)	−0.03 (−0.26)	−	2.04	0.02 (0.06)	0.12 (0.98)	0.09	1.21

Source: Data used were taken from national statistics—see statistical note, para. (*c*), p. 142.

Note: The abbreviations are as follows. $C_{j,t}$ = annual percentage deviation of gross fixed investments from the trend; $C_{r,t}$ = annual percentage deviation of the regional aggregate from the regional trend, excluding country *j* and the Soviet Union, *e* = error term. Figures in brackets are *t*-test statistics. SEE = standard error of estimates. For definition of trend see text. The asterisks *, ** and *** indicate a significant coefficient at the 1 per cent, 5 per cent and 10 per cent levels of significance respectively (two-tailed test).

changes.[219] It is reasonable to assume that whenever the officially acknowledged price rises are already quite significant (Hungary and Poland are the obvious examples), then the probability of an upward bias in the volume estimates increases;[220]

— for aggregating individual country figures, the secretariat's own weighting system was used as explained in the footnote to table 4.4.11. However, the results of the synchronization exercise are not very sensitive to changes in weights. Even when all countries are equally weighted, the synchronization effect is still clearly discernible.

[219] L. Drechsler, "A gazdasági eredmények mérésének problémái", (The problems of measuring economic results), *Országos Tervhivatal Tervgazdasági Intézet*, Manuscript, Budapest, 1983 pp. 119-134. For the methodological description, see J. Nagy and P. Pukli: "A beruházási költségek vizsgálata statisztikai módszerekkel" (The analysis of investment costs with statistical methods), *Statisztikai Szemle*, January 1974.

[220] An overview of published implicit investment price deflators by

sectors and by industrial branches for the 1970-1981 period can be found in *Economic Survey of Europe in 1982*, p. 178. For Hungary, ECE secretariat calculations indicate that the annual investment price rise between 1950 and 1981 averaged 2.7 per cent. This compares with a rise in the officially published cost-of-living index of 3.4 annually over the same period.

4.5 CONSUMER INCOMES AND SUPPLIES

Though there were variations in individual years, real incomes per head of the population—the most aggregated indicator of living standards—increased in all east European countries and in the Soviet Union during 1981-1984. Nevertheless, rates of growth were below the average achieved in the previous quinquennium. The slowdown was anticipated in the five-year plans of the countries concerned and reflected the deceleration of NMP growth which began at the end of the 1970s. Economic policies throughout the region included measures aimed to improve wage systems. These were oriented in particular to achieve closer linkage between the growth of average wages and the growth of labour productivity. At the same time considerable efforts were made to improve the supply of consumer goods, both in volume and quality. In 1983-1984 there was an upward change in real income growth and consumption in most countries of the region. This was made possible by an upturn in the growth of NMP and a corresponding growth of money incomes, decelerating consumer price rises and the expansion of retail trade. In most countries concerned, incomes originating in the social consumption funds tended to grow faster than wages and wage-like incomes, though there were some exceptions.

The issues underlying the developments summarized above are reviewed in more detail in the rest of this section. Sub-section (i) describes changes in the allocation of national income. In sub-section (ii), incomes and income policies are discussed. Sub-section (iii) outlines the development of consumer prices and price policies. Retail trade turnover and housing construction are summarized in sub-section (iv), while sub-section (v) presents recent changes in savings deposits.

(i) Allocation of national income

There were no big changes in the long-term allocation trend of net material product (NMP) used for consumption and accumulation in the countries of the region.[221] In fact, with some fluctuation in individual years, the share of social (public) and personal (private) consumption in NMP used tended to increase, in line with the economic strategy retained for the current five-year period (table 4.5.1 and appendix table B.2).

Nevertheless, movements in the allocation of national income have not been uniform. In all countries but Czechoslovakia in 1982 and Poland in 1981-1982, and despite some variations in individual years, the level of consumption rose in 1981-1984. At the same time, in Czechoslovakia, the German Democratic Republic, Poland and Romania before 1983 and in Hungary during the whole period, there was a marked decrease in the share of accumulation in NMP used. Furthermore, aggregate accumulation in eastern Europe has contracted ever since 1979. In contrast, there has been no decline in the level of accumulation in the Soviet Union since 1981.

The allocation of national income in most east European countries was influenced by the need to shift resources in favour of the foreign balance in order to service convertible currency debt. Within consumption as a whole, there was considerable inter-country variation in the trend of personal as compared with social consumption. Personal consumption developed faster than social consumption in the German Democratic Republic, Poland and probably in Romania during the period 1981-1984. These movements reversed the relationship which prevailed in the

TABLE 4.5.1

Allocation of national income
(*Percentage share*)

| Period | Consumption | | | Accumulation total |
	Total	Personal	Social	
Bulgaria				
1976-1980	74.4	..	..	25.6
1981	73.1	..	..	26.9
1982	74.2	..	..	25.8
1983	75.9	..	..	24.1
Czechoslovakia				
1976-1980	74.3	54.3	20.0	25.7
1981	79.9	57.6	22.3	20.1
1982	79.6	57.2	22.4	20.4
1983	80.6	57.7	22.9	19.4
German Democratic Republic				
1976-1980	77.0	64.0	13.0	23.0
1981	78.3	65.7	12.5	21.7
1982	82.0	69.0	13.0	18.0
1983	82.4	69.7	12.7	17.6
1984*	82.4	69.7	12.7	17.6
Hungary				
1976-1980	76.4	66.6	9.8	23.6
1981	82.2	71.1	11.1	17.8
1982	84.2	72.8	11.9	15.8
1983	87.2	75.3	11.8	12.9
1984*	88.2	76.0	12.0	11.8
Poland				
1976-1980	71.6	60.0	11.6	28.4
1981	90.1	77.6	12.5	9.9
1982	73.7	62.5	11.2	26.3
1983	76.1	64.4	11.7	23.9
1984	78.2	65.6	12.6	21.8
Romania*				
1976-1980	63.7	..	..	36.3
1981	65.0	..	..	35.0
1982	66.0	..	..	34.0
1983	67.2	..	..	32.8
1984	68.2	..	..	31.8
Soviet Union				
1976-1980	74.1	..	..	25.9
1981	76.4	..	..	23.6
1982	73.8	..	..	26.2
1983	73.2	..	..	26.8
1984	75.0	..	..	25.0

Sources: National statistics, plans and plan-fulfilment reports, *Statisticheskii ezhegodnik stran-chlenov SEV,* (CMEA statistical yearbook), various issues.

---

[221] The only exception was Poland, where an abrupt decrease in the share of accumulation in five successive years, from 34.7 per cent in 1976 to only 9.8 per cent in 1981 reflected an exceptional deceleration in economic growth, accompanied by a sharp contraction of net material product in 1979-1982. *Statisticheskii ezhegodnik stran-chlenov SEV 1981,* (CMEA Statistical Yearbook 1981), Moscow, 1981, p. 46: *ibid,* 1982, p. 42.

TABLE 4.5.2

Real incomes, real wages
(*Annual percentage change*)

	Real incomes per head of population	Real wages per wage or salary earner
Bulgaria		
1976-1980	2.6	0.5
1981	5.8	4.7
1982	4.1	2.2
1983	2.8	1.0
1984	2.7	..
Plan 1985	3.0	..
Plan 1981-1985	2.8	..
Czechoslovakia		
1976-1980	1.3	0.7
1981	1.6	0.8
1982	−0.7	−2.5
1983	1.7	1.0
1984	1.3	0.8*
Plan 1985	..	..
German Democratic Republic		
1976-1980	4.5	2.7
1981	4.0	2.2
1982	3.3	1.9
1983	2.3	1.3
1984	4.0	..
Plan 1985	..	..
Plan 1981-1985	3.9-4.2	..
Hungary		
1976-1980	1.8	0.7
1981	2.9	1.1
1982	0.9	0.7
1983	1.1	−3.2
1984	1.0	−2.3
1984	1.0	−2.3
Plan 1985	1.5-2.0	−
Plan 1981-1985	1.1-1.4	..
Poland		
1976-1980	2.9	2.1
1981	3.3	2.3
1982	−18.0	−24.9
1983	0.4	1.1
1984	..	3.6
Romania		
1976-1980	5.1	5.2
1981	1.5	1.0
1982	..	7.7*
1983	..	−2.1*
1984	..	6.0 a
Plan 1981-1985	3.5	2.9
Soviet Union		b
1976-1980	3.4	3.0
1981	3.3	2.1
1982	0.1	2.8
1983	2.0	2.6
1984	3.0	2.5
Plan 1985	3.3	3.0
Plan 1981-1985	3.1	..
Byelorussian SSR		b
1976-1980	3.6	3.7
1981	4.7	2.1
1982	0.5	2.8
1983	4.1	1.8
1984	3.5	3.2
Plan 1985	3.3	2.9
Plan 1981-1985	3.1	2.6
Ukrainian SSR		b
1976-1980	3.2	3.0
1981	5.0	1.8
1982	0.6	2.8

TABLE 4.5.2 (*continued*)

	Real incomes per head of population	Real wages per wage or salary earner
Ukrainian SSR (*continued*)		
1983	1.7	1.8
1984	2.0	1.6
Plan 1985	3.0	..
Plan 1981-1985	3.2	2.3

Sources: As for table 4.5.1.
a 1984 to 1980.
b Average nominal wage.

previous five-year period except in the German Democratic Republic. In Bulgaria and Czechoslovakia, social consumption has tended to rise faster than personal consumption over several recent years, as also in the Soviet Union.

The deceleration in the rate of growth of social consumption and its falling share of national income was not accompanied by any contraction in the level of social consumption in most of the countries concerned. In fact, social consumption in the German Democratic Republic and also Poland has fallen only once during the last four years (see section 4.1 and table 4.1.8 above).

(ii) Incomes and income policy

Real incomes per capita in 1984 grew considerably in the German Democratic Republic, the Soviet Union, Bulgaria and, according to estimates, in Romania (table 4.5.2). In other countries they increased more modestly, and at rates similar to 1983. A comparison of the annual plans for 1984 with actual changes in individual countries indicates that targets for 1984 were attained in most of them.

The rise in real incomes per head of the population in all countries of the region in 1981-1984 was below the rates recorded in the previous five-year period. In fact, the five-year plans of all countries except Bulgaria envisaged a slight deceleration in rates of growth, which varied from 0 to 1 1/2 percentage points. This was one consequence of slower overall economic growth and of adjustments to changed economic conditions. The slowdown in real income growth in the initial years of the period under review was checked in 1983 in Czechoslovakia, Poland and the Soviet Union. It was reversed later on in the German Democratic Republic and the Soviet Union in 1984.

The growth of *real wages and salaries* ran basically parallel to the pattern of changes in real incomes per capita. The rate of growth was, however, below the rise in real incomes, as the latter include incomes originating from social consumption funds (pensions, etc.) which grew rather faster than real wages.

The contraction in the growth of real wages and salaries in Czechoslovakia and Poland observed at the beginning of the 1980s was checked in 1983. The contraction in Hungary and, according to estimates based on real income growth, the deceleration in Bulgaria, continued through 1984. Furthermore, in Hungary, Poland and Romania real wages and salaries fell in absolute terms in one or more years.

The plan targets for real income growth in 1985 are available only for some countries. The pattern of growth of real wages and retail prices, as well as the acceleration in overall economic growth, give grounds for concluding that in 1985 growth of real income per capita could be higher than the annual average achieved in 1981-1984 in all countries of the region (except Bulgaria) and higher than the average targets for five-year plans.

Money incomes are the largest component of total incomes (about 80 per cent) (table 4.5.3). Money incomes grew at widely varying rates between countries, which mainly reflect differences in the role of prices in economic policy. Thus rates of growth of money incomes in Bulgaria, Czechoslovakia, the German Democratic Republic and the Soviet Union have been lower than in Hungary, Poland and Romania, since the first group of countries tend to maintain stable or only slowly increasing consumer goods prices. Except for Poland, money incomes rose in most countries in the current quinquennium at rates very similar to those of the preceding one. This reflected various factors. On the one hand there was an almost continuous increase in the contribution of labour productivity to NMP growth. However in some countries increasing money incomes also reflect the considerable rise in consumer prices (Poland, Hungary). At the same time there was a fall in the rate of increase of money income in Poland (from 65 per cent in 1982 to about 20 per cent in 1983-1984). This reflected improvements in the supply of consumer goods and particularly foodstuffs and a deceleration in consumer price rises, all of which indicate some stabilization of economic developments.

A faster increase in *agricultural incomes* compared with the growth of wages and wage-like incomes is also a fairly general trend in the countries under review. The policy of accelerated growth of agricultural incomes, which was accompanied by contractions in agricultural employment, aimed to stabilize the number of farmers and achieve faster growth of agricultural production and labour productivity. Nevertheless the level of nominal wages in agriculture is lower than in other branches of the economy.

Pensions and social benefits have also tended to rise faster than total money incomes, though not in Romania, in most years.

The growth of average *nominal wages and salaries* in 1984 (table 4.5.4) generally developed in line with the planned targets for that year and at rates similar to 1983 in most countries. The exceptions are Poland and Romania. In Poland the rate of growth of monthly wages fell in line with the further stabilization of the overall economic situation. In Romania, higher growth of wages compensated price increases. In fact, average monthly wages rose during the period from June 1983 to August 1984 in all branches of the national economy.

A faster increase in wages in those branches which determine the pace of progress in science and technology, as well as in agriculture, is a feature of wage policy in all countries. Furthermore, in Hungary, Poland, Czechoslovakia and Romania wages increased at a faster rate in industries and enterprises producing export goods.

Improvement in the *system of labour remuneration* in general, and notably the increasing incentive role of wages, is expected to make possible a closer linkage between the growth of wages and labour productivity. It involves wider differentiation of earnings in accordance with performance and is expected also to bring about a more direct relationship between the growth of wage funds and the profitability of enterprises in general. It is also intended to promote increased initiative at the level of enterprise management.

In *Czechoslovakia*, the improvement of the labour remuneration system is an integral part of overall changes in the system of management and planning of the economy introduced since 1981. The process was carried out in two phases. In the first, in order to more closely link remuneration with the work performed, a new set of labour norms was introduced. In the second, incentive systems of labour remuneration to improve work performance are to be introduced from 1985.[222]

In *Hungary* during 1983-1984 experimental wage regulation schemes were introduced in a large number of industrial and construction firms, as well as in some agricultural co-operatives, in order to create a more direct relationship between enterprise profitability and personal incomes. In the framework of a general reform package, from 1985 onwards the total wage bill, and not only the increment as was previously the case, is subject to tax. This implies that from the point of view of the enterprises' tax obligations there is no longer a "guaranteed" average wage level.

In *Poland* a new wage system was designed in 1984 to tighten the relationship between production norms and labour remuneration, to improve the employment structure.

In *Romania* a programme to improve wage systems was adopted in 1983.[223] Its starting point is the need for labour productivity to grow faster than wages. An increase in the incentive fund, a wider spread of piece-rate pay for all categories of employed workers, including managers, and the introduction of special incentives for organizations and enterprises engaged in foreign trade, are the other main elements of the system.

In the *Soviet Union*, special attention was paid in 1983 and 1984 to the relationship between labour productivity growth and average wages—both in the economy as a whole and in different branches. In 1983 the rise in average wages for each 1 per cent increment in overall labour productivity was 0.7 per cent. Due to different growth conditions this varied from 0.47 per cent in industry to 0.88 per cent in agriculture, 0.77 per cent in construction and 0.54 per cent in railway transport. In agriculture the coefficient was higher in 1984 than in 1983, due to stagnation in output. In other branches of the economy the ratio remained about the same or fell. For 1985 the relationship between growth of wages and labour productivity is planned at 0.49 per cent in industry and 0.66 per cent in construction.[224]

Incomes originating in the *social consumption fund* influenced real incomes in the economies of the region. In fact, during the deceleration of real wages in the early 1980s in Czechoslovakia, Hungary, Poland and Romania, incomes originating in the social consumption funds ensured a further rise in real incomes in all countries and in all years except Czechoslovakia and Poland in 1982 (table 4.5.5). The prevailing tendency during 1981-1984 was an acceleration in the growth of nominal incomes originating from social consumption funds relative to nominal wages. In Czechoslovakia and Hungary, differences between the growth of these two indicators in nominal terms widened faster than in the Soviet Union (chart 4.5.1).

Changes in 1984 did not markedly affect the structure of the social consumption funds. In 1984, pensions and other social benefits rose and continuous attention was paid to improving the quality of education, health services, housing conditions, etc., in all countries under review. Special attention in some countries was paid to certain aspects of family policy, notably those which encourage the birthrate.

In *Bulgaria*, 30-year loans of 15,000 leva (the equivalent of six years average wages) are now granted without a preliminary deposit to newly-wed couples to buy or build a dwelling. If and

---

[222] "Program zvýšení ekonomické účinnosti mzdove soustavy" (Programme of increasing the economic efficiency of the wage system), supplement to *Hospodářské noviny*, No. 17, 1984. See also *Rudé právo*, 2 April 1984.

[223] *Romania libera*, 2 July 1983.

[224] U. Belik, "Final year of the quinquennium", *Economicheskaia gazeta*, No. 1, Moscow, 1985.

TABLE 4.5.3

Money incomes
(Average annual percentage change)

Country and period	Total money income	Wage and income of wage character	Income from agriculture	Pensions and social benefits	
				Total	Pensions
Bulgaria	*				
1976-1980	6.8	7.3	9.0	9.2	10.9
1981	6.0	6.5	6.8	4.6	6.8
1982	4.2	3.5	2.8	6.9	9.7
1983	3.2	2.8	..	4.4	6.1
Czechoslovakia					
1976-1980	4.1	4.0	1.6	5.7	6.2
1981	2.6	2.6	2.3	1.9	3.3
1982	4.3	3.3	6.2	8.2	7.9
1983	3.1	2.7	5.9	3.6	3.8
1984	2.6	..	..	..	..
Plan 1985	3.8	..	..	..	..
German Democratic Republic					a
1976-1980	3.8	2.8	..	7.2	6.6
1981	3.1	2.4	..	10.6	0.7
1982	2.8	1.9	..	4.8	2.9
1983	2.3	1.3	..	1.5	0.1
1984	3.9	..	..	..	..
Plan 1985	4.0	..	..	..	..
Hungary		b			
1976-1980	8.4	7.5	8.4	12.9	15.6
1981	8.1	4.4	11.0	8.4	9.3
1982	7.3	5.0	11.3	8.5	12.9
1983	8.5	3.0	8.5*	9.1	10.0
1984*	9.0	5.1	5.0	12.1	..
Poland					
1976-1980	11.1	9.7	10.8	19.6	19.7
1981	31.1	27.0	109.0	31.9	28.7
1982	64.9	44.0	35.4	107.1	43.2
1983	23.0	26.1	..	24.0	..
1984	19.6	..	..	..	..
Romania		c	d		
1976-1980	9.7	10.3	10.3	6.8	5.4
1981	5.5	5.9	8.6	3.4	2.9
1982	10.9	9.6	12.7	17.7	11.7
1983	5.1	3.6	..	..	7.2
1984	5.5	..	..	..	..
Soviet Union	*				
1976-1980	4.9	5.0	3.2	5.5	6.4
1981	3.7	3.5	1.6	5.4	6.3
1982	4.3	3.9	4.7	6.1	6.8
1983	4.4	3.5	9.5	7.3	5.8
1984	..	2.9*	..	..	..

Sources: As for table 4.5.1.

a Pensions and social insurance.

b Wages only (excluding wages paid by agricultural co-operatives).

c Net money income, excluding peasant income.

d Socialist sector only.

when a second child is born within four years after the first, 3,000 leva of the loan is remitted—and also a further 4,000 leva if a third child is born. Young families are also entitled to a second loan to furnish their homes which can amount to 5,000 leva. The repayment term is 10 years. This loan is also remitted when children are born—50 per cent when the second child is born and 100 per cent of the remaining sum outstanding when the third child is born.[225]

In *Czechoslovakia* an increase of 240 crowns per year and per child in family allowances will be paid from January 1985. This represents about 8 per cent of the average monthly wage. After six months' maternity leave on full pay, mothers will receive 600 crowns a month (about 20 per cent of the average wage) until the child is 12 months old.

In order to protect the interests of low-income families, as well as to induce young parents to have at least two children, in *Hungary* there are special fringe benefits and loan facilities which are intended to compensate them for general price rises. As of 1 March 1985 a child-care payment has been introduced and will be paid until the child is one year old. This payment may be up to 80 per cent of the nation-wide average wage.[226]

[225] *Rabotnichesko delo*, 28 May 1984.

[226] *Népszabadság*, 19 January 1985.

TABLE 4.5.4

Average monthly nominal wages

	Average monthly wages and salaries in national currency units in 1984	Annual percentage changes				
		1976-1980	1981	1982	1983	1984
Bulgaria	206	4.9	5.2	2.5	1.9	2.2*
Czechoslovakia[a]	2 836	2.8	1.5	2.3	1.9	1.7
German Democratic Republic .	1 082[b]	3.0	2.4	1.9	1.3	..
Hungary[a]	5 510	6.2	6.4	6.7	4.9	5.8
Poland[a]	16 900	8.0	27.4	51.0	25.1	20.2
Romania	2 925	4.3	4.6	7.9	3.0	12.5
Soviet Union	185[c]	3.0	2.1	2.8	2.6	2.5

Sources: As for table 4.5.1.

[a] Socialist sector of the national economy (excluding agricultural co-operatives).

[b] 1983.

[c] 260 roubles if payment and benefits from social funds are included.

In the *German Democratic Republic* maternity leave for working mothers was extended from 12 to 18 months upon the birth of a third child. Various other privileges and priorities already given to families with four children were extended to those with three.

In all countries of the region social welfare policies played an active role in overall adjustment policies. Among other things, these included compensation for the increase in retail prices of goods and services through regular increases in pensions. In the

Soviet Union there was a considerable expansion in the network of educational, health and cultural institutions and an improvement in socio-cultural facilities. An important event of 1984 was the implementation of the first stages of a reform in general and vocational education. The principal objective of the reform is to raise the level of general and vocational education.[227] The reform

[227] G. Aliev, *Pravda*, 13 April 1984.

TABLE 4.5.5

Social consumption fund

(Share in total income of population and percentage structure)

Country and period	Social consumption fund to total incomes of population (per cent)	Pensions and social benefits	Education[a] and culture	Health	Housing subsidies	Other
Bulgaria						
1975	34.3	44.1	22.6	14.4	0.1	18.8
1980	35.8	45.8	21.8	15.0	0.8	16.6
1982	35.8	43.5	23.2	16.8	0.9	15.6
1983	..	43.9	23.0	16.7	0.9	15.6
Czechoslovakia						
1975	36.6	48.3	20.9	15.2	4.1	11.5
1980	38.4	49.7	20.7	15.7	4.1	9.8
1982	40.1	49.1	20.6	15.7	3.9	10.7
1983	40.3	49.2	20.7	15.8	4.0	10.3
German Democratic Republic						
1975	32.9	38.7	24.7	15.8	7.9	12.9
1980	33.6	37.1	21.7	17.8	11.5	11.8
1982	34.6	34.5	23.8	18.1	12.9	10.7
1983	35.0	33.2	23.6	19.0	13.6	10.6
Hungary						
1975	27.2	56.0	21.3	14.6	2.4	5.7
1980	31.9	58.2	20.7	13.8	1.8	5.5
1982	33.0	56.8	21.5	14.8	1.5	5.4
1983	33.1	56.7	21.8	14.8	1.3	5.4
Poland						
1975	18.9	39.8	27.0	26.9	3.9	2.4
1980	21.3	44.8	20.8	25.7	6.1	2.6
1982	26.3	32.6	17.0	18.3	6.5	25.6
1983	26.6	39.0	18.7	19.3	6.6	16.4
Soviet Union						
1975	38.7	37.3	27.9	14.3	5.4	15.1
1980	39.6	37.9	27.0	14.7	5.9	14.5
1982	40.1	38.6	26.5	14.5	6.1	14.3
1983	40.3	39.5	25.8	14.2	6.2	14.3

Sources: As for table 4.5.1, *Statisticheskii ezhegodnik stran-chlenov SEV, 1984* (CMEA Statistical Yearbook 1984) Moscow, 1984, p. 41.

[a] Including student grants.

CHART 4.5.1.
Nominal incomes of the population
(Indices 1975 = 100)

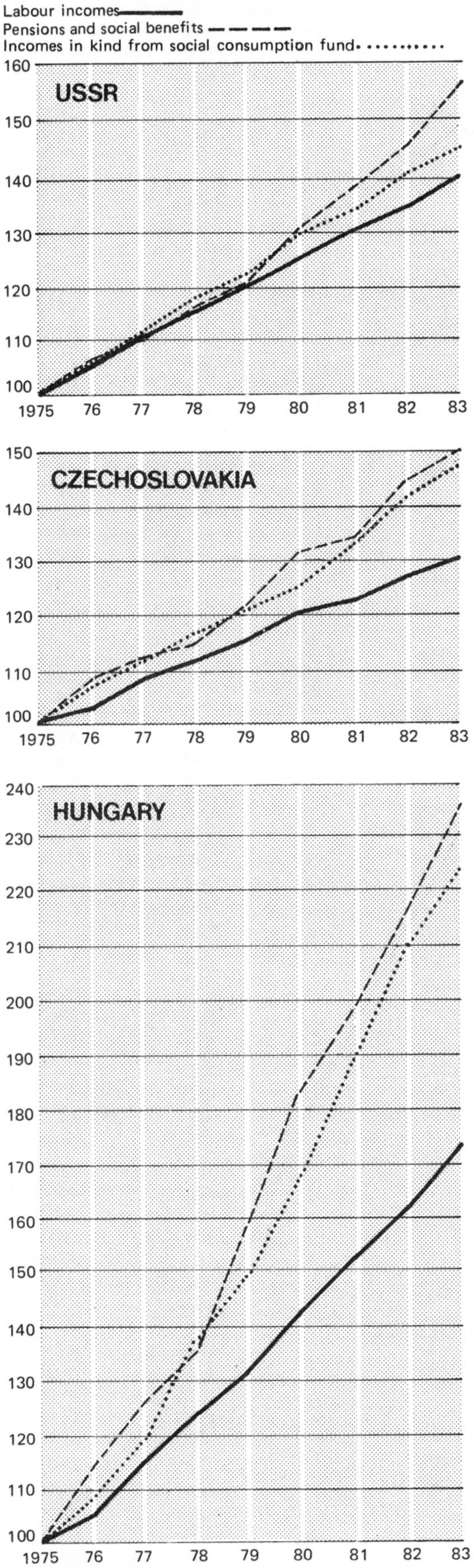

Labour incomes ——————
Pensions and social benefits — — — —
Incomes in kind from social consumption fund • • • • • • • • • •

USSR

(chart with y-axis 100 to 160, x-axis 1975, 76, 77, 78, 79, 80, 81, 82, 83)

CZECHOSLOVAKIA

(chart with y-axis 100 to 150, x-axis 1975, 76, 77, 78, 79, 80, 81, 82, 83)

HUNGARY

(chart with y-axis 100 to 240, x-axis 1975, 76, 77, 78, 79, 80, 81, 82, 83)

Source : National statistics.

will be spread over a number of years. Eleven billion roubles each year (about 3 per cent of the state budget) is envisaged for its implementation, which includes rises in teachers' salaries.

(iii) Consumer prices and price policies

Consumer prices in the centrally planned economies of eastern Europe and the Soviet Union are playing an increasing role in balancing supply and demand for goods and services and also in shaping real incomes. Changes in consumer prices are determined both by overall economic development and by social policy. The general tendency seen in recent years continued in 1984 (table 4.5.6).

In Hungary, Poland and probably Romania the requirements of economic policy to balance supply and demand largely determined increases in consumer prices in 1982 and 1983. The process was also affected by the need to ensure correspondence between consumer prices and production costs. State subsidies on the production of some consumer goods were also removed. Economic policy in Hungary at present is oriented to curtail state support through price subsidies.

In Hungary the faster rise in consumer prices during 1981-1984 was envisaged in national plans if at a somewhat lower pace than actually recorded. In Poland a significant improvement in overall economic performance brought about sharp reductions in the annual rate of growth of consumer price rises—from about 110 per cent in 1982 to 13 per cent in 1984. In 1984 the increase was 2-3 percentage points lower than planned for that year.

Bulgaria, Czechoslovakia, the German Democratic Republic and the Soviet Union form a group of countries in which economic policy is oriented to maintain stable or only slowly increasing consumer price levels. Nevertheless, increases in the retail prices of meat and meat products in Czechoslovakia were announced in 1982, and in Bulgaria in 1983, following an increase in procurement prices for animal products. In order to adjust demand and supply, retail prices of beer and non-alcoholic beverages were increased in Czechoslovakia late in 1984. The new prices should also eliminate or reduce state subsidies for the latter. Temporary increases in consumer prices for seasonal products such as vegetables, fruits, etc., have also taken place in most countries. On the other hand reductions in the prices of some industrial consumer goods also occurred.

Retail price policy in the countries mentioned, in particular in the German Democratic Republic, is supported by state subsidies which compensate for increases in production costs. In the Soviet Union the same policy is applied primarily for basic food products—bread, milk, meat and also for children's footwear and clothing. By 1983 state price subsidies for meat and milk products alone were equal to 40 billion roubles[228] (about 7 per cent of NMP or 13 per cent of the retail trade turnover). A fall in the aggregate retail price index in 1984 resulted from a sharp decrease (about 40 per cent) in the retail prices of some non-food products.

In Hungary, Czechoslovakia and Poland, a rise in the retail prices of some consumer goods can probably be expected in the coming years following the projected increase in wholesale prices for some imported goods and also for raw materials, fuel and energy.[229]

---

[228] This was stated by Mr. N. Glushkov, Chairman of the State Price Committee of the USSR, *Pravda*, 1 September 1984.

[229] *Rudé právo*, 13 October 1984; M. Sabolčík, "Rationalization of the price system in the years 1984-1985", *Czechoslovak Economic Digest*, Prague, No. 6, 1984.

TABLE 4.5.6

Consumer price index
(*Average annual percentage change*)

Country and year	Total	Food	Non-food	Services
Bulgaria				
1976-1980	4.0	6.2	2.4	..
1981	0.5	0.3	0.7	..
1982	0.3	0.6	0.1	..
1983	1.2	2.6	0.1	..
Czechoslovakia				
1976-1980	2.1	1.2	2.8	2.6
1981	0.8	—	1.5	0.7
1982	5.1	9.4	1.5	0.3
1983	0.9	0.6	1.1	1.0
1984	0.9	..	..	..
German Democratic Republic				
1976-1980	0.1	—	—	—
1981	0.3	—	—	—
1982	—	—	—	—
1983	—	—	—	—
Hungary		a		
1976-1980	6.3	8.5	5.9	4.0
1981	4.6	3.4	9.0	6.5
1982	6.9	4.8	6.4	7.2
1983	7.3	5.1	9.3	10.1
1984	8.5	..	..	..
Poland		b		
1976-1980	6.5	7.9	6.5	7.9
1981	18.4	14.6	10.9	27.1
1982	109.4	162.8	85.6	102.1
1983	21.9	13.1	22.3	26.3
1984	13.0	..	..	..
Romania				
1976-1980	1.4	1.0	..	1.6
1981	2.0	1.7	1.9	3.1
1982	16.9 c	..	..	..
1983	5.2 c	..	..	..
1984	0.2*	..	..	..
Soviet Union		a		
1976-1980	0.7	0.4	1.0	..
1981	1.0	0.2	1.0	..
1982	3.8	0.4	2.9	..
1983	—	0.2	—	..
1984	−3.4*	..	..	..

Sources: As for table 4.5.1.

a Excluding alcoholic beverages and tobacco.

b Socialist sector.

c IMF *International Financial Statistics*, December 1984, p. 387.

(iv) Retail trade turnover, housing construction

In the majority of countries, retail trade turnover (table 4.5.7 and Appendix table B.4) rose substantially faster in 1984 than in previous years and was in general in line with the planned targets. A slowdown in the rate of growth prevailed in the initial years of the current five-year period in all countries. Contractions in retail trade in Czechoslovakia and Romania in 1982 and in Poland in 1981-1982 reflected changes in domestic production and limitations on imports of food and non-food goods. This movement halted in 1983. Since then, supplies of foodstuffs and industrial goods improved in most of the countries reviewed. In Poland, rationing was removed on many consumer goods but not on meat or meat products.

A phenomenon common to all countries was the faster increase in retail trade in non-food products compared with food. This reflected a rise in household expenditures on industrial consumer goods (primarily consumer durables).

TABLE 4.5.7

Turnover of retail trade and services
(*Average annual percentage change*)

Years	Total	Food	Non-food	Services
Bulgaria				
1976-1980	3.9	2.4	4.7	..
1981	4.6	4.8	4.5	..
1982	4.5	2.6	6.1	..
1983	2.4	1.5	3.1	..
1984	4.6	..	..	9.3
1985 plan	4.5	..	..	..
1981-1985 plan	3.9	..	6.2	8.5
Czechoslovakia				
1976-1980	1.7	2.3	1.2	5.5
1981	1.5	2.5	0.6	2.6
1982	−2.7	−5.2	−0.2	3.5
1983	2.2	0.9	3.6	2.2
1984	2.2*	2.8 a	3.3 a	1.8
1985 plan a	4.2	..	..	..
German Democratic Republic				
1976-1980	4.1	3.4	4.8	..
1981	2.5	2.9	2.1	..
1982	1.3	2.1	—	8.8
1983	0.7	2.1	−0.6	2.0
1984	4.1	4.1	5.0	2.3
1985 plan a	4.0	..	..	..
1981-1985 plan	3.7	..	..	..
Hungary		b		
1976-1980	2.6	0.5	3.2	3.6
1981	3.2	2.7	4.0	3.8
1982	1.2	0.4	1.6	4.2
1983	0.3	1.5	0.4	4.5
1984	0.2	—	0.9	..
1985 plan	2.0	0.5-0.8	3.0	..
Poland		b		
1976-1980	3.3	3.4	3.7	7.3
1981	−4.6	−8.1	7.5	0.4
1982	−17.4	−14.3	−25.2	−10.9
1983	8.1	2.7	15.4	8.0
1984	6.0	2.0	8.0	4.0
1985 plan	4-4.4	1.8—2.1	5.8-6.1	5.6
Romania				
1976-1980	7.9	7.4	8.4	11.4
1981	4.2	2.4	6.4	..
1982	−2.5*	21.1 a	4.5 a	7.6 a
1983	0.5*	3.3 a	7.2 a	9.1 a
1984	4.8	..	..	..
1985 plan	1.0-1.5 a	..	..	15.0
1981-1985 plan	4.8	..	4.8	12.0
Soviet Union				
1976-1980	4.5	3.5	5.4	7.5
1981	4.3	1.8	6.9	6.2
1982	0.3	0.6	—	4.7
1983	2.7	2.5	3.0	6.0
1984	4.2	..	..	..
1985 plan	5.2	..	..	6.0
1981-1985 plan	4.2	..	..	7.6
Byelorussian SSR				
1976-1980	4.7	4.1	5.0	7.7
1981	4.0	1.6	6.7	6.7
1982	−1.4	0.8	−6.3	5.3
1983	4.4	3.9	4.8	7.0
1984	5.2	..	..	..
1985 plan	4.3	..	..	..
1981-1985 plan	3.1	..	..	7.0
Ukrainian SSR				
1976-1980	4.1	3.1	5.0	8.4
1981	3.3	1.3	5.0	4.7
1982	0.2	−0.1	0.5	3.7

TABLE 4.5.7 *(continued)*

Years	Total	Food	Non-food	Services
1983	2.9	2.0	3.8	6.4
1984	4.2	..	..	..
1985 plan	5.1	..	..	..
1981-1985 plan	3.9	..	..	7.9

Sources: As for table 4.5.1.

[a] At current prices.

[b] Excluding alcoholic beverages and tobacco.

The plans for 1985 in all countries envisage higher rates of growth of retail trade compared with five-year plan target averages. Much attention is to be paid to development of services in rural areas. However, even if annual plans for 1985 are fulfilled, average annual growth rates of retail trade over the five years will lag behind five-year plan targets in the German Democratic Republic and the Soviet Union; there will be a substantial lag in Romania. On the same assumption, growth rates will exceed the five-year targets in Bulgaria. Neither the Hungarian five-year plan nor the Polish three-year plan (1983-1985) contained targets for retail trade growth.

National statistical reports on economic development in 1984 pointed out that the supply of certain high quality consumer goods was inadequate. In Czechoslovakia, demand for some types of textiles, clothing and footwear were not fully met. In Hungary seasonal shortages of fruits and vegetables led to price increases of up to 80 per cent on an annual basis. To help improve the situation, attention is paid in the national economic plans to the development of the consumer goods-producing

TABLE 4.5.8

New dwellings constructed

Country and period	New dwellings (thousands)				New units per 100,000 inhabitants	Average size of dwellings in square metres
	Total	State	Co-operative	Private		
Bulgaria						
1976-1980	351.8	..	..		800	60.7
1981	71.4	34.5	36.9		803	61.7
1982	68.2	30.3	37.9		770	62.9
1983	69.7	30.5	39.2		780	64.1
1984	67.9	..	..		..	..
Czechoslovakia						
1976-1980	648.2	264.6	197.9	185.7	860	..
1981	95.4	32.4	33.6	29.4	623	74.1
1982	101.8	29.7	42.0	30.1	663	75.5
1983	95.7	21.7	45.0	29.0	620	75.3
1984	91.0	18.4	43.5	29.1	..	..
German Democratic Republic	[a]		[b]		[a]	
1976-1980	..	290.3	..	71.6	..	61.8
1981	185.4	62.9	59.7	21.5	1 110	61.8
1982	187.0	62.5	64.6	18.3	1 120	61.0
1983	197.2	61.6	74.6	18.5	1 180	61.7
1984	207.0	..	85.3	13.5	..	..
Hungary						
1976-1980	452.7	162.2	290.5		837	66
1981	77.0	22.8	57.2		722	69.6
1982	75.6	19.1	56.5		706	70.4
1983	74.2	16.3	58.0		695	73.2
1984	70.4	9.9	60.5		..	..
Poland						
1976-1980	1 308.3	245	724.2	339.1	749	62
1981	187.0	32.0	109.0	46.0	519	63.9
1982	185.3	31.5	97.8	56.0	509	66.7
1983	195.5	34.7	103.0	57.8	540	66.9
1984	196.0	140.9 [c]		55.1	..	..
Romania		[c]				
1976-1980	840.6	755.3		85.3	770	..
1981	161.4	150.5		10.9	720	56.6
1982	161.2	150.1		11.1	720	59.2
1983	146.7	135.4		11.3	650	..
1984	131.9	122.5		9.4	..	..
Soviet Union		[c]				
1976-1980	10 241	8 388		1 853	784	51.2
1981	1 997	1 646		351	746	53.3
1982	2 003	1 652		351	742	53.9
1983	2 030	1 675		355	750	55.4
1984	2 081	..		..	..	..

Sources: As for table 4.5.1.

[a] Including modernized dwellings.

[b] Modernized dwellings.

[c] State and co-operative.

TABLE 4.5.9

Changes in savings deposits and money incomes
(Average annual percentage change)

	Savings deposits				Money incomes	
	1971- 1983	1971- 1975	1976- 1980	1981- 1983	1971- 1983	1981- 1983
Bulgaria	9.6	14.3	6.3	7.5	..	..
Czechosolvakia	8.8	12.8	6.0	7.0	4.4	1.9
German Democratic Republic.	6.1	7.7	5.8	4.2	4.3	2.7
Hungary	12.6	14.1	12.3	10.7	8.4	7.9
Poland	18.6	21.4	10.3	29.0	17.9	38.5
Soviet Union	11.2	14.3	11.4	6.0	5.3*	4.1*

Sources: Statisticheskii ezhegodnik stran-chlenov SEV (CMEA statistical yearbook) and national statistical yearbooks for the corresponding years.

branches. Accordingly, production of group B industrial branches (consumer goods) has expanded at higher rates than group A branches (producer goods) in Hungary and the Soviet Union.

Co-operation among the centrally planned economies of eastern Europe and the Soviet Union within the CMEA is also contributing to the development of consumer goods production. Long-term programmes of co-operation among the CMEA member-countries adopted in 1979 in the field of consumer goods production were designed to increase mutual trade and total supplies of different types of consumer goods. The XXXVII session of CMEA adopted a set of complex measures in October 1983 to expand co-operation in the output of food products. The decisions of the Summit Conference of the CMEA member states in 1984 also envisage greater co-operation, *inter alia*, in the consumer goods sector.[230]

---

[230] "To ensure a better supply to the population of high-quality consumer goods the CMEA member states will take joint measures to strengthen the raw material basis for their production, to carry out the technical refitting and modernization of the corresponding branches of industry, to increase substantially the output of these products for mutual delivery, to expand joint production of consumer durables and to increase the exchange of high-quality consumer goods". Statement on the basic guidelines for the further development and deepening of economic, scientific and technical cooperation of CMEA member states, *Pravda*, 16 June 1984.

In 1984 there were no big changes as compared with the post-1980 trend in *housing construction* in individual countries (table 4.5.8). In the German Democratic Republic, Poland and the Soviet Union the volume of housing construction continued to increase, whereas in Bulgaria, Czechoslovakia, Hungary and Romania there was some decline. A feature of recent years has been a shift in all countries towards the construction of larger dwellings, and housing construction has thus been more buoyant than the data on the number of completions suggest.

Housing construction is financed from two sources—from the state and from employer-enterprises on the one hand and from personal savings and mortgage loans in the case of co-operative and private housing construction on the other. In the Soviet Union, the German Democratic Republic and Bulgaria, the state is the main supplier of new dwellings. Its share in the total ranges between 80 per cent in the Soviet Union and close to 50 per cent in the other two countries. The state's share is higher in the German Democratic Republic if dwellings modernized at state expense are included. In Czechoslovakia, Hungary and probably Romania the share of state-constructed dwellings is about 20 per cent.

A notable feature in practically all countries is the increase in the share of housing construction financed from personal savings and mortgage loans. According to the 1985 plan targets in the Soviet Union, the number of houses financed in this way should increase by about 20 per cent.

TABLE 4.5.10

Changes in deposit accounts and savings deposits

	Number of deposits accounts (million)		Average size of deposits account (n.c.u)		Savings deposits (billions of n.c.u.)	
	1970	1980	1970	1980	1970	1980
Bulgaria	7.9	8.8	494	1 170	..	..
Urban	4.9	6.1	..	..	..	..
Rural	2.9	2.7	..	..	..	..
Czechoslovakia	13.6	18.1	4 698	8 613	..	..
Hungary	..	..	..	..	42.1	145.3
Budapest	..	..	..	..	15.8	45.6
Provinces	..	..	..	..	26.3	99.7
Soviet Union	80.1	142.1	583	1 103	46.6	156.7
Urban	58.9	106.6	..	..	34.1	114.4
Rural	21.2	35.2	..	..	12.5	42.1

Sources: National statistics.

(v) Personal monetary savings deposits

In the centrally planned economies of eastern Europe and the Soviet Union, personal monetary savings of the population represent a part of money incomes which is not used for current consumption of goods and services. Most of these savings are deposited in savings banks and other financial institutions.[231]

The principal characteristic of total monetary savings during the 1970s and early in the 1980s in the countries reviewed is their continous fast growth. Savings deposits, the major part of monetary savings of the population, rose in absolute terms by between twofold in the German Democratic Republic and ninefold in

---

[231] For a detailed analysis of the nature of monetary savings of the population see, U. Belugin "O sotsialno-ekonomicheskoi prirode denezhnikh sberezhenii", *Dengi i kredit*, No. 3, 1983, p. 68; A. Shokhin, "Denezhnye sberezhenia", *Ekonomicheskaia gazeta*, No. 35, 1981: I. Kacharov, "Socialno-ekonomicheska spestovanost i effektivnost", *Finansy i kredit*, Sofia, No. 2, 1977, pp. 26-27.

Poland. Despite inter-country differences, a common feature is that they grew faster than money incomes. On the other hand, their rates of growth in the second half of the 1970s were lower than in the first. In the early 1980s, the deceleration continued in the German Democratic Republic, Hungary and the Soviet Union, but was reversed in the other countries concerned (table 4.5.9).

The absolute increase in savings deposits was accompanied by an increase in the number of deposit accounts and in their average size. Available data suggest that in Czechoslovakia the number of deposit accounts rose by one third and the average size of account by about 80 per cent; in the Soviet Union the corresponding increments were 80 and 90 per cent. In Bulgaria, the number of deposit accounts grew by only 10 per cent but there was a substantial increase in the average size of accounts, which rose by one and a half times. Available information also suggests that, in some countries of the region, the size of personal savings deposits rose faster in rural than in urban areas (table 4.5.10).

4.6 RECENT DEVELOPMENTS IN THE NON-MATERIAL SPHERE

A fundamental feature of economic theory and policy in the centrally planned economies is the distinction between the sphere of material production and the non-productive sphere, usually referred to as the material and the non-material spheres of the economies concerned.[232] Since no aggregated statistical series are available on output changes in the latter, previous editions of the *Economic Survey of Europe* have paid systematic attention only to the material sphere. The non-material sphere has been discussed in the main only as an explanatory factor for changes in material sphere, notably on the input side.

There are several reasons why somewhat greater attention needs to be paid to the non-material sphere. *First,* since economic theory in the centrally planned economies maintains that the non-material sphere does not contribute to the increase of national output measured by net material product, decisions on the allocation of factor inputs and national income used for domestic consumption and accumulation between the material and the non-material spheres have always been a delicate issue. Moreover, the outcomes of such decisions have not been systematically monitored. *Secondly,* the conditions of decelerating overall economic growth which prevailed in the centrally planned economies from the end of the 1970s and in the early 1980s, complicated resource allocation between the material and the non-material spheres. *Finally,* due to the special social welfare criteria according to which the non-material sphere is judged, its economic significance remains little-known and often underestimated.

A specific reason for this study is that, because of differences in approaches to economics in general, developments in this sector have been monitored less attentively than in the market economies.

The basic objective of this section, therefore, is to highlight recent developments in the non-material sphere. A more far-reaching analysis in the form of a special study could be undertaken at another time.

The section is divided into four parts: (i) basic characteristics of the non-material sphere; (ii) factor inputs; (iii) indicators of non-material sphere services; (iv) a tentative assessment of the economic significance of the non-material sphere, followed by some general conclusions.

(i) Basic features of the non-material sphere

(*a*) The distinction between the material and the non-material spheres is deeply rooted in the general economic theory of centrally planned economies and is based on the different nature of the work performed in each.[233] Within the material sphere,

work performed creates new value. This is incorporated in material goods and services which make up domestic material output and national wealth. Within the non-material sphere, however, no such new value is created. Therefore the work performed does not contribute directly to domestic material output and national wealth.[234] Accordingly, the non-material sphere is defined as "a complex of branches of national economy which do not participate in the production of the national income".[235] Understood in this way the non-material sphere presents a contrast with material production, which is usually defined as "the aggregate of all the national sectors engaged in producing material goods and services of a productive nature".[236]

(*b*) While usually treated as clear and logical, the definition of the non-material sphere mentioned above has the fundamental weakness that it is *negative.* It defines the non-material sphere on the basis of the features it does *not* possess. To some extent this definition leaves the non-material sphere to be determined as the residual between the total national economy and the material sphere, the latter being defined *positively.* Moreover, the contrasting nature of the two spheres implied by their very definitions gives the impression that the non-material sphere consists only in the consumption of, rather than making any direct contribution to, the national output. To that extent its outcomes might be considered as less important for economic and social development than those of the material sphere, given that the latter is viewed essentially as the only value-creating component.

To avoid such an interpretation, the non-material sphere needs to be defined positively and in accordance with its own characteristics. Definitions of this kind, usually descriptive rather than analytical, can be found mostly in articles and monographs devoted to the non-material sphere itself. According to

---

[232] In centrally planned countries, the terms "productive" and "non-productive" sphere are used. In this section the terms "material sphere" and "non-material sphere" are employed for the sake of easier comprehension since the adjectives "productive" and "non-productive", as used in the economic literature outside these countries, normally refer to a distinction of a different nature.

[233] While in contemporary literature these distinctions are usually referred to only in the centrally planned economies, they go back to the foundation of political economy: "There is one sort of labour which adds to the value of the subject upon which it is bestowed; there is another which has no such effect. The former, as it produces a value, may be called productive; the latter, unproductive labour." A. Smith, *The Wealth of Nations,* Book 1, Penguin Books, Bungay, Suffolk, 1974, pp. 429 and 430.

[234] Statements of this kind can be found in most textbooks on political economy in the centrally planned economies, as, for example, in Bulgaria, Czechoslovakia and the German Democratic Republic:
"The only source of national income is the labour of productive workers or of workers employed in material production ... The non-productive sphere does not directly create national income ... The expenditures of this sphere are covered by national income created in the productive sphere." *Politicheska ikonomiia* (Political Economy), Sofia, Partizdat, 1973, pp. 206 and 207.
"The social product as a sum of material use-values is created by labour in the material sphere, i.e. by productive labour. The theory of productive and non-productive labour divides social production activity (*společenskou výrobní činnost*) into two big spheres: the sphere of material production and the sphere of non-material production. The basic criterion for allocation of any production activity (*vyrobné cinnosti*) is whether the useful results of this activity exist or do not exist in the form of material goods (services) which are able to satisfy social needs." *Politická ekonomie socialismus* (Political Economy of Socialism), Prague, Svoboda, 1980, pp. 316 and 317.
"Aggregate social product arises as a result of the productive labour of society in the sectors of material production." *Politische Ökonomie des Sozialismus und ihre Anwendung in der DDR* (Political Economy of Socialism and its Application in the GDR), Berlin, Dietz Verlag, 1969.

[235] *Ekonomicheskaia entsiklopediia: Politicheskaia ekonomiia* (Economic Encyclopaedia of Political Economy), Izdanie "Sovetskaia entsiklopediia", vol. 3, Moscow, 1979, p. 89.

[236] A. Anchishkin, *National Economic Planning* (published in English), Progress Publishers, Moscow, 1980, p. 238. A similar definition ("aggregate of all branches which produce material goods that satisfy the material and intellectual needs of man, both personal and social") is contained in *Ekonomicheskaia entsiklopediia: Politicheskaia ekonomiia,* vol. 4, Izdanie "Sovetskaia entsiklopediia", Moscow, 1980, p. 87.

such definitions, the non-material sphere is "a source of goods of a specific kind, appearing in the following concrete forms: knowledge, management decisions, training, education, health, culture".[237] A closer analysis of various kinds of activities usually identified as taking place in the non-material sphere suggests the following main features:

(1) The produce of the non-material sphere consists mostly of services, while the produce of the material sphere consists of both with a prevailing share of goods;

(2) Services provided by the non-material sphere appear in most cases during the course of the activities by which they are provided. They do not usually take any material form but rather directly affect various aspects of the lives and activities of their recipients;

(3) In cases when the outcome of a non-material activity manifests itself in material form (a sculpture, a painting, a book, etc.), the object in which it is materialized is in essence an intellectual product, unique and independent of the material form it takes.

Understood in this way, the non-material sphere is in no way antithetical to the material sphere but is rather its complement. This has considerable significance for the balanced development both of individuals in society and of society as a whole. However, this has not always been fully appreciated in either the economic theory or in the economic policies of the centrally planned economies.

(c) The *list of activities belonging to the non-material sphere* is usually based on a combination of the definitions of the material and non-material spheres. Some activities can easily be classified in this way but in many cases neither definition is fully adequate since some activities fall on the borderline between the two spheres. Such problems are therefore usually solved empirically, and national classifications may then contain a certain conventional element justified simply by convenience.

According to the standard Material Product System of national accounting (MPS), the breakdowns of the material and the non-material spheres include:[238]

Material sphere	*Non-material sphere*
1. Industry[239]	1. Housing, communal services and public utilities[242]
2. Construction	2. Education, culture and art
3. Agriculture	3. Health services, social security and sports
4. Forestry	4. Science and scientific services
5. Transport[240]	5. Finance, credit and insurance
6. Communications[240]	6. General government
7. Distributive trades	7. Other branches of the non-material sphere
8. Other branches of material production[241]	

The classification systems of individual centrally planned economies include, as already mentioned, some differences with regard to particular activities on the margin between material production and the non-material sphere. Some of the differences can be seen in table 4.6.1, in which material production activities

are defined as those contributing to national (material) output and non-material activities as those which do not. For comparison the table also shows how various activities in the two spheres of the economy are classified in some countries which are not centrally planned.

While they are important when precise comparisons between individual countries are made, differences in the various national classifications will be ignored hereafter. Nevertheless, it should be noted that the main classification difference between countries is that in Czechoslovakia and the Soviet Union passenger transport and communications servicing the population are included in the non-material sphere, whereas in the other countries of eastern Europe it is classified within the material sphere. In fact, apart from the data on employment and investment, most of the tables which follow are based on CMEA statistical sources, where a number of problems of this kind have been resolved by adopting a standard classification system.[243]

(d) Finally, it should also be mentioned that the terms "non-material sphere" and "the service sector", or infrastructure, as referred to in some sources, while sometimes used as synonyms, in fact differ. For instance, the Soviet Union includes under non-material services "education, health care, culture, sport, science and scientific services, municipal amenities, transport and communications serving the population and enterprises of the non-material sphere, as well as defence, management and certain other forms of non-productive activity".[244] The "service sector" however excludes from this list science and scientific services, management and defence, and includes retail trade, public catering and productive everyday repair and other services (*proizvodstvennye bytovye uslugi*) which belong to the material sphere in the Soviet Union.[245] While not identical, such differences also exist between the "service sector" as defined above and the non-material sphere as defined in the statistical practice of most of the east European centrally planned economies.

(ii) Factor inputs in the non-material sphere

In this section the changing shares of the main factor inputs allocated to the non-material sphere in the total factor allocations of the centrally planned economies are discussed.

[237] E. Agabab'ian, "Nematerial'naia sfera ekonomiki v usloviiakh razvitogo sotsialisma" (The non-material sphere under the conditions of advanced socialism), *Voprosy ekonomiki*, Moscow, 1982, No. 8, p. 118.

[238] *Basic Principles of the System of Balances of the National Economy*, Department of Economic and Social Affairs, Studies in Methods, Series F, No. 17, United Nations, New York, 1971, pp. 5 and 6.

[239] Including dyeing, cleaning and waterworks.

[240] Only goods transport and communication serving branches of material production belong to the material sphere. However, for practical reasons and for reasons of ensuring comparability of data, all transport and communication are included in the material sphere in the tables presented in this section.

[241] Other branches of material production include publishing houses, motion-picture studios, organization for state procurement and primary processing of scrap metal and other salvage, the collection of forest products, wild plants and fruits, private fishing, hunting and trapping and cottage industries and also telegraphic agencies, press agencies and designing organizations, except those serving construction. See *Basic principles* ..., pp. 5 and 52.

[242] Including laundries.

[243] In particular, all transport and communications are included in the material sphere, as is also the practice of the CMEA statistical services (see table 4.6.1).

[244] A. Anchishkin (ed.), *op. cit.*, p. 238.

[245] V. M. Rutgaizer, *Resursy razvitiia neproizvodstvennoi sfery* (Development resources of the non-productive sphere), Izdatel'stvo "Mysl'", Moscow 1975, p. 14.

TABLE 4.6.1

Activities which contribute (+) and activities which do not contribute (−) to national output according to methodologies applied in different countries

	CMEA method-ology	Czecho-slovakia	Hungary	Poland	USSR	Yugo-slavia	Denmark	France	USA, Great Britain, Netherlands
Extractive industry . . .	+	+	+	+	+	+	+	+	+
Manufacturing industry .	+	+	+	+	+	+	+	+	+
Electricity production . .	+	+	+	+	+	+	+	+	+
Gas production	+	+	+	+	+	+	+	+	+
Agriculture	+	+	+	+	+	+	+	+	+
Forestry	+	+	+	+	+	+	+	+	+
Fishery.	+	+	+	+	+	+	+	+	+
Hunting	+	+	+	+	+	+	+	+	+
Construction	+	+	+	+	+	+	+[a]	+	+[a]
Medical services	−	−	−	−	−	−	+	+	+
Freight services	+	+	+	+	+	+	+	+	+
Passenger transport . . .	+	−	+	+	−	+	+	+	+
Communication servicing production	+	+	+	+	+	+	+	+	+
Communication servicing population	+	−	+	+	−	+	+	+	+
Wholesale trade	+	+	+	+	+	+	+	+	+
Retail trade	+	+	+	+	+	−	+	+	+
Insurance.	−	−	−	−	−	−	+	−	+
Real estate operations . .	−	−	−	−	−	−	+	+	+
Housing	−	−	−	−	−	−	+	+	+
Government adminis-tration	−	−	−	−	−	−	+	−	+
Education	−	−	−	−	−	−	+	+[b]	+
Health insurance	−	−	−	−	−	−	+	+	+
Rest and recreation . . .	−	−	−	−	−	−	+	+	+
Hotels	−	−	−	−	−	+	+	+	+
Restaurants	+	+	+	+	+	+	+	+	+
Laundries.	+	−	+	+	−	−	+	+	+
Hairdressing.	−	−	−	−	−	−	+	+	+
Other personal services .	−	−	−	−	−	−	+	+	+
Religious institutions . .	−	−	−	−	−	−	+	−	+
Protection and tutelage .	−	−	−	−	−	−	+	−	+
Legal services	−	−	−	−	−	+	+	+	+

Source: E. S. Kudrova, *Statistika natsionalnogo dokhoda evropeiskikh sotsiialisticheskikh stran* (Statistics of National Income of the European Socialist Countries), Statistika, Moscow, 1969, pp. 9-10.

[a] Excluding private non-commercial construction.

[b] Only private institutions.

(a) Table 4.6.2 illustrates changes in *non-material sphere employment* in eastern Europe and the Soviet Union. The table suggests three main conclusions. *First*, the share of employment in the non-material sphere in total employment at the beginning of the review period (in 1971-1975) varied substantially, from roughly one eighth in Romania to more than one fifth in

TABLE 4.6.2

Employment in the non-material sphere
(Percentage shares in total employment)

	1971-1975	1976	1977	1978	1979	1980	1981	1982	1983
Bulgaria	14.5	16.3	16.3	16.5	16.5	17.0	17.1	17.2	17.2
Czechoslovakia	21.5	22.2	22.6	22.9	23.2	23.6	23.9	24.2	24.1
German Democratic Republic	17.9	18.5	18.7	18.9	19.1	19.3	19.5	19.8	20.0
Hungary	15.7	17.1	17.2	17.5	18.0	18.4	18.3	19.3	19.7
Poland	13.9	14.0	14.1	14.3	14.5	14.7	15.2	15.2	15.6
Romania	12.1	13.6	13.0	13.5	13.7	13.5	13.8	13.8	13.7
Soviet Union	23.8	24.6	25.1	25.6	25.9	26.1	26.3	26.5	26.6

Source: National statistics.

Czechoslovakia and the Soviet Union. The ranking of the countries in this respect generally coincides with their overall level of economic development. Thus, the share is higher in the more developed and lower in the less developed countries.[246] In Czechoslovakia and the Soviet Union, higher than average shares of employment in the non-material sphere reflect also the fact that passenger transport is included in this sphere, whereas in the other countries of the region it is classified within the material sphere. However, in the Soviet Union the share of employment in the non-material sphere was perhaps somewhat higher than might be expected from its relative level of economic development within the region. *Secondly*, from 1976 onwards, there was a steady increase in the share of the non-material sphere in total employment in almost every year in all countries of the region. *Finally*, a comparison of differences in the material sphere's share at the beginning and at the end of the period indicates that the rate of employment growth in the non-material sphere relative to the pace of growth in the material sphere was highest in Hungary and lowest in the Soviet Union. Nevertheless, such differences in relative growth rates so far have not changed the country-ranking based on shares of employment in the non-material sphere between 1971-1975 and 1983.

(*b*) Changes in *investment in the non-material sphere* shown in table 4.6.3 differ significantly from those in employment. At the beginning of the review period, the shares of the non-material sphere in total gross fixed investment of the countries concerned varied between one fifth and somewhat below two fifths, i.e. relatively more than differences between employment shares.

In 1976-1983 developments in investment shares were not uniform in all seven countries. There was a clear decrease in the share of the non-material sphere in total investment in Czechoslovakia and Romania and a somewhat less pronounced fall in the Soviet Union. Changes in different directions occurred in individual years in Bulgaria, the German Democratic Republic and Hungary, but in all of them the non-material sphere's share in 1983 was higher than in 1971-1975. The only country in which the share of investments in the non-material sphere grew continuously between 1976 and 1983 was Poland; in the latter year, this share was by far the highest in the region. Since investment in that country contracted regularly between 1979 and 1982

inclusive, investment in the non-material sphere seems to have been particularly resistant to downward pressure. Altogether, intercountry differences in shares in 1983 were similar to those in 1971-1975.

(*c*) Changes in *the non-material sphere's share of fixed assets* diverged more widely than those of investment relative to employment (table 4.6.4).

The data suggest several conclusions. *First*, at the beginning of the review period, the non-material sphere's share of fixed assets in all the countries of the region was substantially higher than in the case of employment. This partly reflects the inclusion of housing in non-material sphere fixed assets, and indicates that capital intensity in the non-material sphere as a whole was on average higher than in the material sphere. *Secondly*, differences in the shares of fixed assets in the non-material sphere in individual countries varied substantially, ranging from 31 per cent in Romania to 46 per cent in the German Democratic Republic in 1970. *Thirdly*, since 1970, and disregarding oscillations in individual years, there has been a clear decreasing trend in the share of the non-material sphere in total fixed assets in all countries but Poland. This has been much more pronounced than in the case of investment. Though the share of the non-material sphere in total Polish fixed assets seems to have risen since 1980, this appears to reflect mainly changes in the relative prices between the material and non-material spheres following the big upward revaluation of fixed asset prices in 1982. In fact, estimates based on constant prices suggest that the share fell by 8 per cent between 1970 and 1983.[247]

Finally, it is also important to note that for the region as a whole, the shares of the non-material sphere in total fixed assets diverged much less at the end of the review period than at its beginning. In fact, leaving aside Poland, the shares clustered fairly narrowly around one third of total fixed assets by 1983.

(*d*) The changes in the factor inputs described above can be assessed in two basic ways. The first refers back to generally accepted theory on the development of the *primary, secondary*

---

[246] According to ECE estimates for 1973, per capita gross domestic product measured in 1973 US dollars amounted to $2,082 in Romania, $2,433 in Hungary, $2,482 in Poland, $2,507 in Bulgaria, $2,766 in the Soviet Union, $3,117 in Czechoslovaia and $3,301 in the German Democratic Republic. *Economic Bulletin for Europe*, vol. 31, No. 2, United Nations, New York, 1980, p. 31.

[247] Past editions of the CMEA statistical yearbook (*Statisticheskii ezhegodnik stran-chlenov SEV 1981*, Moscow, 1981, p. 51, *Statisticheskii ezhegodnik stran-chlenov SEV 1982*, Moscow, 1982, p. 45) clearly used different price-base years for Poland compared with later editions. According to them, the share of the fixed assets in the non-material sphere in Poland fell continuously throughout the 1970s and into the early 1980s—from 45 per cent in 1970 to 37 per cent in 1981. New figures for 1975 and 1980 onwards appeared for the first time in *Statisticheskii ezhegodnik stran-chlenov SEV 1983*, (CMEA Statistical Yearbook 1983) Moscow, 1983, p. 45, but they cannot be directly linked to the former series.

TABLE 4.6.3

Investment in the non-material sphere
(*Percentage shares in total investment*)

	1971-1975	1976	1977	1978	1979	1980	1981	1982	1983
Bulgaria	27.6	28.6	27.3	27.5	27.0	28.6	27.4	28.0	29.3
Czechoslovakia	37.8	36.4	35.9	35.5	34.2	33.5	31.8	31.7	31.6
German Democratic Republic	20.6	20.9	21.8	22.6	22.6	21.8	22.1	22.0	21.6
Hungary	29.4	28.7	27.8	26.7	27.5	29.1	29.0	29.3	30.9
Poland	26.8	25.5	26.5	27.4	31.7	32.2	33.2	35.6	36.3
Romania	19.9	20.5	19.2	18.4	18.6	18.2	17.8	17.8	15.9
Soviet Union	27.7	26.1	26.2	25.5	25.6	25.5	25.6	25.9	26.2

Source: National statistics.

TABLE 4.6.4

Fixed assets in the non-material sphere
(Percentage shares in total fixed assets)

	1970	1975	1980	1981	1982	1983
Bulgaria	35.6	32.4	32.0	32.0	31.8	31.9
Czechoslovakia .	34.5	34.4	33.4	32.9	32.8	32.7
German Democratic Republic . . .	45.9	41.2	37.9	37.2	36.5	35.8
Hungary	39.9	37.4	35.6[a]	34.4	34.4	34.5
Poland	45.3	38.9	41.4	41.4	41.7	49.4
Romania	31.5	27.9	24.2	23.9	23.4	..
Soviet Union . .	38.3	35.9	34.0	33.6	33.3	33.0

Source: Statisticheskii ezhegodnik stran-chlenov SEV 1984, (CMEA Statistical Yearbook 1984) Moscow, 1984, p. 43.

[a] In terms of the price series used after 1980, this figure is 34.4.

and tertiary sectors. These suggest that the mature stage of industrialization is followed by faster development of the tertiary sector relative to both the primary and secondary sectors.[248] Since the non-material sphere falls entirely into the tertiary sector (though it does not coincide with it), it could be expected that, at the present stage of development of the centrally-planned economies of the region, it would have begun to absorb a growing share of all factor inputs. At the least, it should not be lagging behind.

The other yardstick is based on the *specific development features of the non-material sphere*, which originate in the tendency to aim for continuous improvement in the quality of services rather than constraining the use of factor inputs. Three considerations appear highly relevant. *First*, labour inputs play a key role in most non-material activities, as within it the intellectual and often creative component dominate physical and routine work. Therefore, increases in capital intensity in these activities do not aim to, and do not bring about, savings in manpower comparable to those attainable from the same source in the material sphere. *Secondly*, the overall tendency to faster growth of non-material services relative to the material sphere, even if accompanied by unchanged capital intensity levels relative to the material sphere, suggests that both gross investment and fixed capital expenditure in the non-material sphere should grow by at least the same rates as in the material sphere. If they do not, then the capital intensity of non-material sphere activities will grow less than the average for the economy as a whole, or even contract. *Finally*, development of non-material activities, unlike those in the material sphere, does not necessarily imply any decrease in material inputs per unit of the services provided. Indeed unit material costs in the non-material sphere have a tendency to increase as the level and quality of services (health care, education, etc.) improves.[249] Altogether, this interpretation

of non-material sphere development also suggests that, under normal conditions, the pace of factor inputs in the non-material sphere (employment, gross investment, fixed assets) should expand at rates higher than the average for the economy as a whole.

Viewed in this general way, changes actually observed in the shares of the non-material sphere in the totals of the various factor inputs in the east European countries and the Soviet Union indicate the presence of a definite imbalance.[250] Labour inputs grew almost continuously faster in the non-material than in the material sphere. While gross fixed investment did not show any clear trends, fixed assets in the non-material sphere generally grew more slowly than in the material sphere. Hence, with a few exceptions in individual years for some countries, the growth of capital intensity in the non-material sphere lagged, in some countries substantially, behind that in the material sphere (table 4.6.5). Since these trends are not reflected in any document on longer-term development policy, its roots probably lie in the general development features of the region, in particular in the second half of the 1970s and the beginning of the 1980s.

Since these developments in the supply of basic factors to the non-material sphere can hardly be explained in terms of its own internal requirements, they appear to have taken place in response to developments in the material sphere—primarily the decelerating trends of output growth and, above all, to declining capital productivity of the material sphere itself. In other words, smaller increments in the resources available for investment which resulted from decelerating NMP growth, together with falling capital productivity in the material sphere itself, made necessary an increase in the share of the material sphere in total investment and ultimately in fixed assets. Domestic analyses of recent developments arrive at similar conclusions.[251]

Taking into account the substantially different and to some extent unexpected economic events which marked the end of the 1970s and the beginning of the 1980s, the lags in non-material sphere development described above could be considered as a deviation from the long-term development orientation expressed in policy documents. If it continues, however, it may result in substantial problems—not only for the non-material services provided to the people but also for the material sphere itself. Econmic and social development is heavily dependent on services originating in the non-material sphere—not only technical progress and the development of the qualifications of the work force, particularly specialist and managerial skills, but also the public health and welfare of the community as a whole.

---

[248] The different roles of the three sectors, primary, secondary and tertiary, at different stages of economic development were already described by A. G. B. Fisher, *The Clash of Progress and Security*, MacMillan & Co., Ltd., London, 1935, pp. 13-43. This was further elaborated by the same author in "Production, Primary, Secondary and Tertiary", *Economic Record* vol. XV, No. 28, June 1939 and later on especially by C. Clark, *The Conditions of Economic Progress*, London, MacMillan, 1940 and S. Kuznets, *Modern Economic Growth—Rate, Structure and Spread*, Yale University Press, New Haven and London, 1966.

[249] This specific feature of the non-material sphere is frequently referred to by most specialists, e.g. V. M. Rutgaizer, *op. cit.*, p. 13: "In most kinds of activities which belong to the non-productive sphere, raising the level of consumption of materials is a pre-condition for raising the quality of services, a factor which contributes to more efficient functioning of the corresponding non-productive branches."

[250] A warning that any lag in development of the non-material sphere as compared with the material one may have negative effects on overall developments was pointed out by the Hungarian economist A. Bródy as early as 1969: "The rate of development of housing, passenger transport and services in general, but also that of education and health, permanently and significantly lags behind the rate of development of other sectors of the economy. This neglect has by now already had a hampering effect on the overall pace of development, though ostensibly this neglect was planned in order to accelerate growth by concentrating on the development of industry and other 'productive' branches". A. Bródy, *Ertèk ès ujratermelès* (Value and reproduction), Budapest, Akademiai Kiado, 1969, p. 357.

[251] According to Soviet sources this also explains longer term developments in the non-material sphere of the Soviet Union since 1960: "A certain deterioration in the capital productivity of the fixed assets in the productive sphere, which had to be compensated by a relative rise in the shares of productive gross investment, was reflected in the structure of utilization of the national income of the Soviet Union. The share of allocations to non-productive fixed assets in the accumulation fund in 1960 was estimated at 25.1 per cent (at current prices), in 1970 at 22.6 per cent and in 1973 at 23.7 per cent". V. M. Rutgaizer, *op. cit.*, p. 10. As noted earlier (in footnote 232) "productive sphere" means what is here termed the "material sphere" of the economy.

TABLE 4.6.5

Capital intensity[a]
(Annual percentage change)

	1971-1975	1976	1977	1978	1979	1980	1981	1982	1983
Bulgaria									
Total.	7.2	7.2	9.7	7.0	6.0	6.7	4.4	7.0	7.4
Material sphere	8.9	7.8	10.4	7.8	6.4	8.1	4.0	7.8	7.1
Non-material sphere. . .	1.5	3.5	8.3	4.8	5.2	2.0	5.1	5.7	7.9
Czechoslovakia									
Total.	5.0	5.9	4.8	4.7	4.5	4.4	4.9	4.4	3.8
Material sphere	5.4	6.7	5.8	5.5	5.4	5.5	6.2	4.9	4.2
Non-material sphere. . .	3.6	3.7	2.1	2.6	2.1	1.2	1.9	3.0	3.0
German Democratic Republic									
Total.	3.7	3.5	3.4	3.5	3.5	3.8	3.9	3.7	3.3
Material sphere	5.8	5.0	4.8	4.7	4.5	5.6	5.2	5.3	4.7
Non-material sphere. . .	−0.1	0.9	0.7	1.2	1.1	0.5	0.9	0.3	0.2
Hungary									
Total.	5.5	5.6	5.5	5.3	5.7	6.4	4.1	4.0	. .
Material sphere	6.4	6.6	6.0	6.2	6.7	6.9	4.0	5.2	. .
Non-material sphere. . .	2.1	1.6	4.0	2.5	1.9	4.1	4.8	−1.3	. .
Poland									
Total.	2.8	6.1	5.5	5.9	4.6	3.9	2.4	5.0	2.3
Material sphere	5.7	9.5	8.2	8.3	5.8	5.2	3.2	4.9	2.8
Non-material sphere. . .	−0.5	1.7	2.3	2.3	2.1	1.0	−0.9	4.9	−0.3
Romania									
Total.	8.9	8.7	9.7	8.6	8.2	8.1	7.9	8.1	8.1
Material sphere	11.6	11.7	10.1	10.6	9.1	8.7	8.9	8.9	8.7
Non-material sphere. . .	2.0	−2.1	11.6	1.0	5.2	7.3	4.0	5.6	6.6
Soviet Union									
Total.	5.9	5.3	5.3	5.3	5.3	5.1	5.3	4.6	6.5
Material sphere	7.1	6.5	6.1	6.2	6.4	6.2	6.2	6.0	6.4
Non-material sphere. . .	3.1	3.6	3.3	2.8	2.6	2.5	3.2	4.0	4.0

Source: National statistics.

[a] Fixed assets per employee.

(iii) Indicators of non-material sphere services

For well-known reasons, it is difficult to aggregate non-material sphere activities. They are not only extremely varied in nature—which is also true for material activities—but they cannot easily be valued in terms of their worth to the individual receiving them; or in terms of their worth to society. Finally, it should be mentioned that due to the very distinction made between the non-material and the material spheres, there are divergencies between economic theory and economic practice in the centrally planned economies with regard to the role of prices in measuring the value of output of the non-material sphere.

Hence, output of the non-material sphere can be measured only *indirectly* and even so only at the level of individual activities. In fact, three measurements of this kind are most frequently encountered in statistical sources and economic literature. The first is based on the measurement of the *volume of potential services* quantified according to a relevant output parameter factor. This measurement is usually applied to health services,

TABLE 4.6.6

Number of doctors, including dentists, per 10,000 of the population

	1970	1975	1980	1981	1982	1983	1983-1970 (per cent)
Bulgaria	22.2	25.7	30.0	30.4	31.7	32.9	148.2
Czechoslovakia	23.1	27.0	32.4	33.2	34.1	34.8	150.6
German Democratic Republic.	20.3	23.6	26.1	26.7	27.5	28.2	138.9
Hungary	22.0	24.9	28.1	28.8	29.5	30.0	136.4
Poland	19.3	21.7	22.5	22.7	23.1	23.5	121.2
Romania	14.7	15.9	17.9	18.5	19.5	19.7	134.0
Soviet Union[a]	27.4	32.7	37.5	38.5	39.5	40.4	147.4

Source: Statisticheskii ezhegodnik stran-chlenov SEV 1981 (CMEA Statistical Yearbook 1981), Moscow, 1981, p. 444; *ibid.*, 1983, pp. 421 and 467; *ibid.*, 1984, p. 405.

[a] Including dentists with special vocational training.

TABLE 4.6.7

Hospital beds per 10,000 of the population

	1970	1975	1980	1981	1982	1983	1983-1970 (per cent)
Bulgaria	77.1	85.8	90.8	90.7	91.0	91.1	118.2
Czechoslovakia	99.9	98.7	99.8	99.9	100.0	101.0	101.1
German Democratic Republic	111.0	108.0	103.0	102.0	103.0	102.0	91.9
Hungary	78.6	80.9	84.2	85.4	86.4	87.1	110.8
Poland	74.1	74.7	71.6	71.3	70.5	70.1	94.7
Romania	80.8	89.4	89.6	89.2	89.3	89.4	110.6
Soviet Union	109.0	118.0	125.0	126.0	127.0	128.0	117.4

Source: Statisticheskii ezhegodnik stran-chlenov SEV 1981, (CMEA Statistical Yearbook 1981) Moscow 1981, p. 443; *ibid.,* 1983, p. 421; *ibid.,* 1984, p. 405.

where the volume of potential services is usually expressed by the average number of doctors or the number of hospital beds per 10,000 of the population. The second kind is based on some *conventional measurement of the volume of services themselves,* for instance, the number of recipients. This type of measurement is usually applied when dealing for example with education, and is expressed by the number of those receiving education or a similar service per 10,000 of the population. The third kind of measurement is still more indirect, since the service is assessed according to its influence on the length or quality of human life or on the standard of living etc. Various *demographic indicators* rank among most frequent indirect measurement of the output, or at least of the end result, of certain branches of the non-material sphere.

The purpose of this section is to summarize some indicators of the "output" of the non-material sphere. Since, as noted, few systematic aggregated data are available, a number of partial measurements of non-material sphere activities will be presented, chosen mainly because of the availability of comparable time series for all the countries concerned.

(*a*) Table 4.6.6 shows the development of *health services* in terms of the number of doctors (including dentists) per 10,000 of the population.

The table suggests three main conclusions. In 1970, the number of doctors in most countries of the region calculated on this basis averaged about 20. Romania lagged behind this average by somewhat more than one quarter. The Soviet Union was about one third higher. Between 1970 and 1983, the number of doctors per 10,000 inhabitants increased in all the countries concerned but at different rates. By 1983 the number had risen by one half compared with 1970 in Bulgaria, Czechoslovakia and the Soviet Union, by about one third in the German Democratic Republic, Hungary and Romania and by one fifth in Poland.

Poland, and especially Romania, lagged significantly behind the regional average while the Soviet Union remained markedly above it. Altogether, the figures indicate a significant rise in the volume of health care available.[252]

A somewhat different picture emerges from table 4.6.7 which shows *the number of hospital beds* per 10,000 of the population.

The table indicates substantial inter-country variations at the beginning of the period. The average number of beds per 10,000 inhabitants in Poland was only two thirds of that in the German Democratic Republic. A much more striking observation is the quite divergent inter-country variations between 1970 and 1983. While the average number of hospital beds per 10,000 inhabitants stayed virtually constant in Czechoslovakia, it rose markedly in Hungary and Romania and even more quickly in the Soviet Union and Bulgaria. In contrast, the indicator declined markedly in Poland and the German Democratic Republic. Thus, initial inter-country variations widened. The figure for Poland in 1983 was only 55 per cent of that for the Soviet Union. A comparison of changes in the number of doctors and the number of hospital beds per 10,000 inhabitants also indicates another feature common to all the countries concerned—the number of doctors grew substantially faster than the number of hospital beds. This can be partly explained in terms of the growth of preventive as distinct from curative medicine. But the growing discrepancy between the two, especially when the ageing of the population is taken into account, may also indicate a tendency to promote "extensive" rather than "intensive" development of the health services.

[252] Besides the rise in the volume of health care, all countries aim at improvement in its quality which has also been promoted through special programmes of co-operation within CMEA. For details see *Multilateral Scientific and Technological Cooperation among the CMEA Member Countries,* CMEA Secretariat, Moscow 1982, pp. 167-174.

TABLE 4.6.8

Children in pre-school establishments per 10,000 children of pre-school age

	1970	1975	1980	1981	1982	1983
Bulgaria	4 095	4 672	5 089	5 136	5 248	5 257
Czechoslovakia	3 466	3 607	4 969	5 230	5 487	5 707
German Democratic Republic	5 045	7 204	7 896	8 031	8 129	8 224
Hungary	3 710	4 750	5 959	6 198	6 335	6 513
Poland	1 879	2 610	2 935	2 848	2 825	2 847
Romania	1 855	3 761	4 268	4 297	4 258	..
Soviet Union	3 141	3 759	4 459	4 553	5 487	5 707

Source: Statisticheskii ezhegodnik stran-chlenov SEV 1981 (CMEA Statistical Yearbook 1981), Moscow, 1981, p. 422; *ibid.,* 1983, p. 400; *ibid.,* 1984, p. 384.

TABLE 4.6.9

Numbers receiving education per 1,000 of the population[a]

	1970-1971	1975-1976	1977-1978	1980-1981	1981-1982	1982-1983	1983-1984
Bulgaria	181	173	171	163	164	166	169
Czechoslovakia	198	189	191	197	199	199	199
German Democratic Republic.	200	202	199	184	177	171	167
Hungary	171	162	161	164	168	171	174
Poland	242	219	208	193	187	184	184
Romania	193	201	209	209	208	208	208
Soviet Union	248	234	224	216	214	213	209

Source: Calculated on the basis Statisticheskii ezhegodnik stran-chlenov SEV 1981 (CMEA Statistical Yearbook 1981), Moscow 1981, pp. 8 and 423-427; ibid, 1984, pp. 8 and 385-389.

[a] Students in general educational establishments, vocational schools, specialized secondary schools and higher educational establishments (including universities).

(b) Tables 4.6.8 and 4.6.9 illustrate some aspects of *education,* the potential output of which is measured by the number of recipients of various kinds.

Table 4.6.8 confirms that all the centrally planned economies of the region continue to give priority attention to the provision of *pre-school facilities.* Indeed, the service is an important precondition of the high participation rates of women in the work force which characterizes all countries of the region.

The table shows that as early as 1970, the number of children attending pre-school establishments varied between two out of ten of pre-school age children in Poland and Romania and five out of ten in the German Democratic Republic. Between that year and 1983, this ratio increased in all the countries and has now reached five or more in all countries but Poland and Romania. By far the most advanced country in this respect at both the beginning and the end of the period was the German Democratic Republic.[253] By 1983, an average four out of five children of pre-school age attended such institutions in that country.

The number of people receiving education is another indicator of services originating in the non-material sphere. Table 4.6.9 shows that it was rather high in 1970/1971, ranging between 171 (Hungary) and 248 (the Soviet Union) per 1,000 of the population. This reflects among other things free education at all levels in the countries reviewed. During the 1970s there was some decline in the numbers concerned in all countries except Romania.[254] This can be mainly explained by changes in the age structure of the population, i.e. the declining share of the school-age generations. From 1980/1981 the number of people receiving education per 1,000 of the population increased somewhat in two countries and remained fairly stable in the others. Finally it is also noteworthy that the differences between individual countries in 1983/1984 were smaller than in 1970/1971.

(c) Some indications of the non-material services, especially health and social security services, can also be derived from the demographic indicators presented in tables 4.6.10-4.6.13. These indicators are presented as five-year averages from 1960-1965 onwards.

The first set of important changes can be seen with regard to *infant mortality* (table 4.6.10). In the first half of the 1960s, infant mortality in eastern Europe varied substantially between countries, ranging from 23 per thousand live births in Czechoslovakia to 60 per thousand in Romania. Over the following 20 years, all countries of the region took measures to decrease infant mortality and all succeeded in doing so. However, average infant mortality estimates for the current quinquennium indicate that results were not uniform. By far the most successful country in this respect was the German Democratic Republic, which cut infant mortality to virtually one third of the 1960-1965 average.[255] In most other countries, infant mortality fell below half the rates registered in 1960-1965. Altogether, significant gains were made.

TABLE 4.6.10

Infant mortality per 1,000 births

	1960-1965	1965-1970	1970-1975	1975-1980	1980-1985
Bulgaria	36	31	26	22	20
Czechoslovakia	23	23	21	19	16
German Democratic Republic	31	21	17	13	12
Hungary	44	36	34	27	21
Poland	51	36	27	23	21
Romania	60	52	40	31	26
Eastern Europe.	44	36	28	23	20
Soviet Union	32	26	26	29	25

Source: Population Division, Department of International Economic and Social Affairs of the United Nations Secretariat.

These and other demographic changes can be understood as an indirect reflection of activity in the non-material and material spheres. Data on *life expectancy at birth* (table 4.6.11) are shown for the east European countries individually and as a group. Similar data have not been published by the Soviet Union in recent years.

---

[253] However, it is worth noting that, according to national sources "the number of crèche places is constantly rising for the demand from parents still exceeds availability". *The German Democratic Republic* (in English), Berlin, Panorama, 1981, p.202.

[254] The difference between Romania and other countries originates partly in the fact that the number of those reported as attending special secondary schools in 1977/1978 as compared with 1976/1977 increased by 58 per cent—*Statisticheskii ezhegodnik stran-chlenov SEV 1981* (CMEA Statistical Yearbook 1981), Moscow 1981, p. 425. This suggests some statistical or classification discrepancies.

[255] According to national sources "This advance is to a large extent attributable to intensive pre-natal care as well as improved obstetric and paediatric care". *The German Democratic Republic, op. cit.,* p. 267.

TABLE 4.6.11

Life expectancy at birth
(*Years*)

	1960-1965	1966-1970	1970-1975	1975-1980	1980-1985
Bulgaria	70.0	70.8	71.0	71.5	72.3
Czechoslovakia	70.3	70.1	70.0	70.5	71.6
German Democratic Republic	70.3	71.3	71.2	71.6	72.7
Hungary	68.7	69.2	69.7	69.9	71.2
Poland	68.3	69.9	70.6	70.9	72.0
Romania	66.8	68.4	69.0	69.8	70.9
Eastern Europe	68.8	69.8	70.2	70.6	71.7

Source: As for table 4.6.10.

These data suggest two main conclusions. At the beginning of the period, life expectancy at birth between individual east European countries varied very little (by about three years). The table shows that life expectancy increased in all east European countries over the last quarter of a century by an average of about three years.

The life expectancy data discussed above are further illuminated by data on *life expectancy at birth by sex.* These show a significant and still rising difference between male and female life expectancy (table 4.6.12). The difference apparent at the beginning of the review period ranged between four and five years in all the countries concerned. This is of course a common feature in all countries. But over the following quarter of a century, the differences between male and female life expectancy continued to grow. There are a few striking features. On one hand, differences in male-female life expectancies in some of the countries concerned, especially in eastern Europe, widened considerably between 1960-1965 and the current quinquennium. On the other hand the inter-country difference between the male and female life expectancy gap was quite small at the beginning of the period. But by 1980-1985, estimates suggest that the substantial increase recorded is reaching almost four years (the

margin between 5.4 years in Bulgaria and 8.9 years in the Soviet Union).

Finally, probably the most striking feature is the fact that the difference between male and female life expectancies in some countries in individual periods (Czechoslovakia in 1965-1975; the German Democratic Republic in 1971-1975; Hungary, Poland and the Soviet Union in 1975-1980) widened in part because of a temporary contraction in male life expectancy.[256] This was particularly important for the Soviet Union, where male life expectancy remained unchanged in 1960-1975, dropped slightly in 1976-1980 and recovered during the current period. The exact reasons for such contractions can only be guessed at. One possible explanation is the so-called "war-generation effect", which indicates that people especially affected by the last war tend to experience high mortality when they reach late middle or early old age.

However, to the extent that they arise from the same causes as in other countries (professional, family and other social stresses, loneliness, alcoholism, etc.) this may indicate that some aspects of the health and social security services were not sufficiently and properly prepared to face such problems, especially those affecting the elderly.[257] This seems, judging by the rise in the inter-country margin of difference, to have been the case in some countries more than in others.

---

[256] This phenomenon was also noticed by the World Health Organization. See for example A. Lopez: "Recent trends in life expectancy in the developed countries". *WHO Chronicle*, vol. 36, No. 6, WHO, Geneva, 1982, pp. 234-235.

[257] In one way or another this was also reflected in the five-year plans of the countries concerned for the 1981-1985 period. In the chapter on health and social care of the Hungarian five-year plan, it was stated for instance that: "Social care of the aged group shall intensify. The forms of family-based care must be widened; so must the day-care institutions located in the dwelling areas, further the network of social-working and social homes for the aged." "Act on the Sixth Five-Year Plan of the National Economy", *Hungaropress Economic Information*, Budapest, Hungarian Chamber of Commerce, 1980, No. 21-22, p. 8.

TABLE 4.6.12

Life expectancy at birth by sex
(*Years*)

		1960-1965	1966-1970	1970-1975	1975-1980	1980-1985
Bulgaria	Male	68.2	68.8	68.7	68.7	69.7
	Female	71.9	73.0	73.5	73.8	75.1
Czechoslovakia	Male	67.5	66.9	66.6	67.0	68.2
	Female	73.2	73.4	73.5	73.8	75.1
German Democratic Republic	Male	67.9	68.8	68.6	68.8	69.8
	Female	72.9	74.0	73.9	74.6	75.7
Hungary	Male	66.4	66.7	66.8	66.7	68.0
	Female	71.1	71.9	72.7	73.3	74.2
Poland	Male	65.8	66.9	67.1	67.0	68.2
	Female	71.0	73.0	74.3	75.0	76.0
Romania	Male	65.0	66.4	66.8	67.5	68.5
	Female	68.7	70.6	71.3	72.2	73.6
Eastern Europe	Male	66.5	67.2	67.3	67.4	68.5
	Female	71.3	72.5	73.2	74.0	75.1
Soviet Union	Male	65.5	65.5	65.5	65.0	66.5
	Female	73.2	74.0	74.3	74.3	75.4

Source: As for table 4.6.10.

When it is recalled that output in the material sphere (NMP) in the review period expanded, it seems that the health and some other services originating in the non-material sphere need further strengthening.[258] Comments published from time to time in the socio-economic literature and in policy documents in the east European countries can be interpreted as direct confirmation of such a conclusion.[259]

(iv) The economic significance of the non-material sphere

A question of special importance is the economic significance of the non-material sphere relative to the material sphere. An assessment faces several problems. On the one hand, some statements in general economic texts on the centrally planned economies claim that the economic relations formed within the non-material sphere cannot, by their very nature, be considered the same as those in the material sphere. Some scholars of the countries concerned even claim that they fall outside the science of political economy.[260] On the other hand, other theoretical works do not deny the economic nature of relations within the non-material sphere, but claim that non-material output cannot be measured in value terms[261] and are therefore not in principle comparable with the output of the material sphere. Neither approach is widespread and they are usually criticized and rejected by experts in questions concerning the non-material sphere.[262]

Even if the principal arguments against measuring non-material sphere output in value terms are rejected, there remain other problems if the purpose is to compare its economic significance relative to material sphere output. Three of them seem particularly important. First, many non-material sphere services are provided free and therefore not priced. Second, the prices of paid services are not determined in the same way as prices in the material sphere.

Finally, it should be mentioned that, aside from differences in approaches to economic theory, the economic policies in differ-

ent centrally planned economies do not exhibit the same attitude towards price formation in the non-material sphere. It is thus likely that the figures available are not fully comparable.

While not minimizing the difficulties mentioned above, the economic significance of the non-material sphere in the centrally planned economies will be illustrated by two cases, drawing on estimates for two countries only: the Soviet Union and Hungary.

In the *Soviet Union*, the economic significance of the non-material sphere is usually assessed according to the value of paid and free services. The value of paid services (housing, entertainment, municipal services, passenger transport and communications for the population) is determined by multiplying the volume of services by the corresponding average tariff per unit of service provided. The value of free services (public education, public health services, etc.) is determined on the basis of outlays by the state, collective farms and other organizations.[263]

The value of services provided by the non-material sphere, determined in this way, can be considered as output of the non-material sphere in a conventional sense and, as such, it can be added to output of the material sphere. Table 4.6.13 illustrates the result for the Soviet Union. The material and non-material spheres are expressed both in gross terms (including intermediate consumption of goods and services) and in net terms (net of both intermediate consumption of goods and services and depreciation charges).

TABLE 4.6.13

Soviet Union: output of the material and non-material spheres
(Billion roubles at current prices)

	1970	1975	1980	1983
Gross social product[a]	643.5	862.6	1078.5	1293.5
Conventional gross output of the non-material sphere[a, b] . .	52.8	70.6	92.3	95.3
Conventional total gross output[a]	696.3	933.2	1170.8	1388.8
Percentage share of the non-material sphere in total conventional gross output . .	7.6	7.6	7.9	7.4
Net material product (NMP) . .	289.9	363.3	462.2	548.1
Conventional net output of the non-material sphere[c] . . .	25.6	37.6	49.5	53.6
Conventional total net output . .	315.5	400.9	511.7	601.7
Percentage share of the non-material sphere in the total conventional net output . . .	8.1	9.4	9.7	8.9

Source: ECE secretariat, based on *Narodnoe khoziaistvo SSSR v 1983 g.* (Statistical Yearbook of the USSR 1983), Moscow, 1984, pp. 47, 385, 393, 407. V.N. Kirichenko, *op. cit.*, p. 207.

[a] Including intermediate consumption of goods and services.

[b] Paid and free services of the non-material sphere to the population only.

[c] Wages and salaries of employees in the non-material sphere.

The data in the table indicate that over 1970-1983, the non-material sphere of the Soviet Union accounted for 7-8 per cent of the total conventional gross output of the country (i.e. the sum of gross material product and conventionally determined gross output of the non-material sphere, including intermediate consumption).[264] On the net output basis shown, the share of the

[258] As for the Soviet Union, a similar conclusion was made by Mr. M. S. Gorbachev, Secretary General of the CPSU: "Public health, for example, affects everyone's interests. A truly democratic system of health care has been created in our country. At the same time, one cannot help seeing that medical service does not meet today's requirements in all respects. Party and Soviet agencies must pay greater attention to the work of public health institutions". *Pravda*, 11 December 1984, p. 2.

[259] In 1982 Mr. T. Zhivkov, Head of State of Bulgaria and General Secretary of the CPB, while admitting achievements of health services in Bulgaria, stated: "If we are to examine things more closely and weigh the end results of the medical services as regards improvement of health, the lengthening of life expectancy, etc., we shall see that there are still a number of serious shortcomings in the medical services and that we can aim much higher in this field. Work on the medical front should be decisively improved in order to solve the problems which concern millions of people. These are the problems of prevention, diagnosis, treatment and rehabilitation, the standard of the medical services, etc." T. Zhivkov, *Present-Day Bulgaria—Problems, Guidelines, Solutions* (in English), Sofia Press, Sofia, 1982, pp. 58-59.

[260] Such a point of view is expressed, for example, in N.A. Tsagolov (ed.), *Kurs politicheskoi ekonomii* (Textbook on political economy), tom I, Moscow, 1973, p. 56.

[261] A similar point of view was expressed as follows: "Attempts to assign a monetary value (*dat' denezhnuiu otsenku*) to services of branches of the non-material sphere such as health care, education, etc., from our point of view cannot bring about positive solutions", V. E. Kozak, *Proizvoditel'nyi i neproizvoditel'nyi trud* (Productive and non-productive labour), Kiev, Naukova dumka, 1971, p. 162.

[262] A criticism of both the above concepts is given by V. M. Rutgaizer, *op. cit.*, pp. 3-15; V.N. Kirichenko (ed.), *Sotsial'nye problemy v perspektivnom planirovanii* (Social Problems in Prospective Planning), Ekonomika, Moscow, 1982, pp. 19-216 and T. I. Kor'iagina, *Mezhotraslevye sviazy sfery bytovogo obsluzhivaniia* (Intersectoral links of the sphere of everyday services), Moscow, Legkaia i pishchevaia promyshlennost, 1983, pp. 5-19.

[263] *Metodicheskie ukazaniia k razrabotke gosudarstvennykh planov razvitiia narodnogo khoziaistva SSSR*, (Methodological instructions for elaboration of state plans of development of the national economy of the Soviet Union), Ekonomika, Moscow, 1974, pp. 487-489.

[264] Similar findings relating to the share of the non-material sphere in total gross national production of goods and services are presented in V. N. Kirichenko (ed), *op. cit.*, p. 206.

TABLE 4.6.14

Hungary: output of the material and non-material spheres
(Billion forints at 1981 prices)

	1975	1976	1977	1978	1979	1980	1981	1982
Gross social product[a]	1522.1	1574.3	1686.0	1773.0	1812.3	1800.7	1851.9	1899.1
Conventional gross output of the non-material sphere[a, b] .	154.8	162.9	170.2	184.5	194.1	199.8	211.2	218.8
Conventional total gross output[a].	1676.9	1737.2	1856.2	1957.5	2006.4	2000.5	2063.1	2117.9
Percentage share of the non-material sphere in total conventional gross output .	9.2	9.4	9.2	9.4	9.7	10.0	10.2	10.3
Net material product	520.3	535.9	574.0	596.8	603.8	598.4	613.5	629.7
Conventional net output of the non-material sphere .	60.0	62.4	64.5	69.9	67.8	71.5	74.1	75.6
Conventional total net output	580.3	598.3	638.5	666.7	671.6	669.9	687.6	705.3
Percentage share of the non-material sphere in total net output	10.3	10.4	10.1	10.5	10.1	10.7	10.8	10.7

Source: ECE secretariat, based on *Népgazdasági mérlegek 1970-1977*, Budapest, 1977, pp. 31, 34 and *ibid.*, 1975-1982, Budapest 1984, pp. 15 and 18-21.

[a] Including intermediate consumption of goods and services.

[b] Personal and economic services, health, social and cultural services and also public administration and other services.

non-material sphere in the total is somewhat higher, reflecting the lower material intensity of the non-material sphere. Even so, the share of the latter in total output as defined remains at the level of 8-10 per cent.

Hungary reports basic figures on the value of non-material services on a regular basis. For the sake of comparison, in table 4.6.14 they are presented in the same gross and net terms as for the Soviet Union. Although the underlying methodology is different from the one used for the Soviet Union, the share of the non-material sphere is virtually the same as in the Soviet case: 9-10 per cent of gross output and 10-11 per cent of net output.

In the Soviet case, the low share of the non-material sphere in total national output can be partly explained by the fact that non-material sphere output is limited to the provision of paid and free services to the population. It seems, nevertheless, that the methods usually applied to calculate the economic significance of the non-material sphere substantially underestimate it. This conclusion can be drawn on both theoretical and empirical grounds. On one hand, statements based on the statistical methodology of the centrally planned economies suggest that the calculation of national output according to the SNA concept in the developed market economies "overstates" their national output relative to the MPS system by 20-25 per cent, due precisely to the inclusion of non-material sphere.[265] If so, this means that the share of the non-material sphere in total national output (i.e. including the non-material sphere) should be roughly 17-20 per cent, (i.e. 20/120 to 25/125) if it is assumed that at the beginning of the 1980s the centrally planned economies concerned were at an overall level economic development comparable with that of developed market economies in the mid-1960s. If their general level of development was higher than that, the share of the non-material sphere in national output should be even higher.

Moreover the fact that in 1970-1983 the share of the non-material sphere in total Soviet employment ranged between 22

---

[265] A. I. Petrov (ed.), *Kurs ekonomicheskoi statistiki* (Handbook of Economic Statistics), Moscow, Statistika, 1967, p. 181.

and 27 per cent (table 4.6.2), in fixed assets between 38 and 33 per cent (table 4.6.4) and in total net output only between 8 and 10 per cent (table 4.6.13) strongly suggests an undervaluation of the non-material sphere. This may result, in particular, from price formation policies. The fact that virtually the same relative size of the material and non-material spheres is found in Hungary suggests that the same may be the case in most other centrally planned economies concerned.

Available information suggest that economic policy towards the non-material sphere in most centrally planned economies has two important features. First, except for Hungary, the average level of wages in the non-material sphere is lower than in the material sphere (table 4.6.15). The difference is substantial in the Soviet Union, but less so in Czechoslovakia at the other end of the range. The nature of non-material activities (education, health services, science and scientific service management etc.) suggests that average skill levels in the non-material sphere must be markedly or substantially higher than the average for the material sphere, so that "real" wage differentials may be more even than they appear at first sight. Second, because of the theoretically determined view of the role of non-material services described in the first sub-section above, only the wages of the labour force are employed when calculating the value of output or determining the rise of output. The implicit assumption here is that labour inputs in the non-material sphere do not create any surplus above wages, or any operational surplus. Accordingly, valuation of the services supplied by the non-material sphere does not include any return on fixed assets employed in this sphere, even if they are significant in both absolute and relative terms as, for example, in the housing sector. Furthermore, for some non-material services, valuation does not even include depreciation charges in some countries.

Thus the interpretation of the non-material sphere as "non-productive" as against the material sphere as "productive" has direct consequences in estimating the economic significance of the non-material sphere. Many commentaries on the nature of non-material services hold that such consequences have negative effects both from the point of view of non-material services themselves and development of the national economies as a

TABLE 4.6.15

Average monthly wages
(*National currencies*)

	1970	1975	1980	1981	1982	1983	1983-1970 indices
Czechoslovakia[a]							
Material sphere	1958	2327	2685	2730	2799	2859	146.0
Non-material sphere.	1868	2225	2496	2528	2565	2590	138.7
Non-material/material sphere, percentages.	95.4	95.6	93.0	92.6	91.6	90.6	..
Hungary							b
Material sphere	..	3014	4037	4315	5545	4759	157.9
Non-material sphere.	..	3076	4265	4479	4774	4977	161.8
Non-material/material sphere, percentages.	..	102.0	105.6	103.8	104.9	104.6	..
Soviet Union							
Material sphere	126.4	153.5	178.0	182.5	188.0	192.1	152.0
Non-material sphere.	126.4	153.5	178.0	182.5	188.0	192.1	152.0
Non-material/material sphere, percentages.	77.4	79.5	79.4	78.5	77.4	76.4	..

Sources: Statistická ročenka ČSSR 1977 (Statistical Yearbook of Czechoslovakia 1977), p. 187; *ibid.*, 1984, p. 191, *Statisztikai évkonyv 1983* (Statistical Yearbook of Hungary 1983), p. 57; *ibid.*, 1984, p. 57, *Narodnoe khoziaistvo SSSR v 1983 godu* (Statistical Yearbook of the USSR 1983), pp. 385 and 393.

[a] Socialist sector only (excluding agricultural co-operatives).

[b] 1983/85.

whole.[266] Indeed, both experts on the non-material sphere[267] and many policy documents in the countries concerned repeatedly stress the role played by many non-material services in recent economic and overall developments.[268]

---

[266] This was pointed out by T. I. Kor'iagina, *op. cit.*, p. 10: "In branches of the non-material sphere, conditions of price formation and economic management have been applied which differ from those in the branches of the material sphere. Among other things, capital intensity is not taken into account in determining profit norms and prices. As a rule there are no charges on fixed assets and no turnover tax; prices do not provide for sufficient profitability of activities to make possible the participation of branches and associations in financing their expanded reproduction; the wage system does not ensure the dependence of wages on performance; the level of wages is considerably lower than in the branches of the material sphere, and, furthermore, the difference between the two is increasing; in the planning of wage increases, material sphere branches have been given priority, etc. Thus considerations of the non-productive character of work in the non-material sphere of the national economy, which at first glance have a purely theoretical nature, acquire a shade of meaning which is far from harmless (*priobretaiut daleko ne bezobidnyi ottenok*). Non-productive work retains in full the status of second-rank work as far as its significance in the national economy is concerned."

[267] For example E. Agabab'ian, *op. cit.*, p. 120: "Being a source of specific use values, independently of the character and the direction of their utilization, the non-material sphere plays a role of a growth catalyst of the main productive force of society, and acts as a pre-condition of the qualitative transformation of the whole system of its productive forces."

[268] Two examples of this are as follows: "The results of scientific and technical development and their application have not yet met the requirements of the national economy. We did not succeed in reaching a substantial acceleration of the research-development-production-utilization cycles and there is significant potential for improvement of the technical standard and quality of our output." *Hlavní směry hospodářského a sociálního rozvoje ČSSR na léta 1981-1985* (Main Directions of Economic and Social Development of Czechoslovakia in 1981-1985), Supplement to *Rudé právo*, February 1981, p. 3. "There exists a 'no-man's land' between the scientific elaborations, the things created at the scientific research institutes, the design and technology bureaux and their implementation. This 'no-man's land' is there because there is no economic mechanism

Taking into account all the considerations presented so far, it seems that the centrally planned economies, within the general policy of emphasizing intensive (i.e. resource efficient) use of factor inputs, are rightly paying special attention to the development of the non-material sphere. Policy documents lay down requirements ranging from calls to improve the work of individual branches of the non-material sphere (the health services, education, science and implementation of its outcomes) etc.,[269] via the better linkages with related branches of the material sphere, to the reconsideration of priorities in the broadest sense.[270] It can be assumed that in one way or another these ideas will be reflected in the five-year plans for the 1986-1990 period and in the long-term development programmes to 1995 or 2000.

---

for the introduction of scientific achievements in material production and in the other spheres as well... There is not a system, covering the entire cycle of intrduction—from the signing of the agreement to the mastering of the new technlogy and the realization of production." T. Zhivkov, *op. cit.*, p. 75.

[269] A requirement of this kind was mentioned explicitly in respect of education by Mr. N. Ceausescu, Head of State and General Secretary of the CPR, at the recently-held XIII Congress of the Communist Party of Romania: "We must continuously improve and raise the general level of education, securing highly trained staff, with vast professional technical and scientific knowledge in all fields". *Congressul al XIII—Lea All P.C.R.* (XIII Congress of CPR), in English, Romania, Documents-Events, 19 November 1984, p. 25.

In the Soviet Union and some east European countries comprehensive reforms of the school system are underway.

[270] The need for such a reconsideration was referred to directly by Mr. T. Zhivkov, *op. cit.*, pp. 57-58: "The services are acquiring a decisive significance for the biological development of man, for sustaining his vitality, his working capacities, for promoting his social and cultural development and so forth. There is nothing to fear if we are to slow down the development of some other sectors in order to concentrate our efforts here, because in this way we shall be able to create better conditions for life and work."

Chapter 5

INTERNATIONAL TRADE AND PAYMENTS

5.1 THE REBOUND IN WORLD TRADE AND FINANCIAL MARKETS

World trade rose much more rapidly in 1984 than was expected one year ago. The fast expansion in trade flows was accompanied by a rebound in international financial markets and some easing in the external balance of debtor countries.

These developments are examined below. Sub-section (i) summarizes the recent changes in trade, sub-section (ii) reviews developments in financial markets and the debt situation.

(i) Main features of the trade recovery

Following a 1-2 per cent increase in 1983, the volume of world trade rose at an annual rate of about 8 per cent in 1984. Much of this increase may be attributed to the import boom in the United States. But, given the great importance of western Europe in world trade, a considerable stimulus came also from the nearly 6 per cent growth in imports into this region. There was also a resumption of import growth in the non-oil developing countries. The effects of the recovery in the United States' import demand were spread unevenly over the various regions: the impact was above average in Canada, Japan and south-east Asia, while it was comparatively smaller in the European economies due to the low intensity of trade between Europe and the United States. For western Europe, the impact of the rise in its own imports was probably more significant than the effect of the recovery in North America. Prices of internationally traded goods declined further in dollar terms, owing to the continued appreciation of this currency, the weakening of primary commodity prices and the slowdown of inflation in most industrialized countries. Changes in the regional pattern of current account balances followed the 1983 path: the deficit of the United States widened considerably, the surplus of Japan increased further and that of western Europe improved slightly. The deficits of OPEC and of the non-oil developing countries shrank, but in the latter the improvement was less spectacular than in the previous year. This section reviews these aspects in some detail, with special emphasis on the impact of the recovery in the United States. The section ends with an appraisal and outlook for world trade in 1985.

(a) The uneven revival of world trade

The *volume* of world trade rose at an annual rate of some 8 per cent in 1984, following 1-2 per cent growth in 1983 (table 5.1.1). About half of the increase was accounted for by the rise in the United States' imports, but the increase in west European import demand also made a significant contribution.

Among the developed market economies, the *volume of exports* grew fastest in Japan, but it also rose rather rapidly in North America, owing to the dynamism of the trade between Canada and the United States. Actually, despite the loss of competitiveness resulting from the appreciation of the dollar, United States' exports grew nearly as much as those from Europe.

TABLE 5.1.1

World trade: recent changes in volumes and unit values (in US dollar terms), 1982-1984

(Percentage changes from the previous year)

	1982	1983	1984
TRADE VOLUMES			
Exports			
Developed market economies	−1.0	2.0	8.0
Developing market economies[a] . . .	−9.3	−1.4	7.5
European centrally planned economies	5.1	5.7	5.0
Total above	−2.4	1.5	7.5
Imports			
Developed market economies	−	2.1	10.5
Developing market economies[a] . . .	−4.2	−4.4	4.0
European centrally planned economies	2.2	3.7	5.0
Total above	−0.6	0.9	8.5
UNIT VALUES			
Exports			
Developed market economies	−4.2	−4.3	−3.0
Developing market economies[a] . . .	−5.3	−6.6	−1.5
European centrally planned economies	3.5	1.2	1.5
Total above	−3.8	−4.4	−2.2
Imports			
Developed market economies	−6.1	−4.3	−2.0
Developing market economies[a] . . .	−3.2	−3.2	−2.0
European centrally planned economies	4.7	1.3	1.5
Total above	−4.5	−3.6	−1.7
TERMS OF TRADE			
Developed market economies	2.0	1.0	−1.0
Developing market economies	−2.1	−3.5	0.5
European centrally planned economies	−1.1	−0.1	−

Source: United Nations, *Monthly Bulletin of Statistics*, October 1984. For 1984 and for the centrally planned economies, ECE secretariat estimates based on national and international sources.

[a] Secretariat estimate, based on IMF, *World Economic Outlook* (Revised), September 1984.

166

In the European centrally planned economies, the increase in exports was somewhat below the average: this largely reflects a relatively modest rise in the volume of Soviet exports, which in turn was due to a sharp fall in exports to the developing countries. East European exports to the developed and developing market economies continued to expand at some 10 per cent, an especially high rate given that these exports are concentrated on the less buoyant west European market. Trade among the centrally planned economies appears to have accelerated, particularly among the east European countries.

Exports from the developing countries increased at about the same rate as world trade. The strong recovery in North America and Japan provided a significant stimulus to their exports, as many developing countries conduct a relatively high proportion of their external trade with those countries. However, there were considerable differences among the various developing countries in the extent to which they benefited from that recovery. Trade in oil picked up and exports from the OPEC are estimated to have increased slightly in 1984. In the non-oil developing countries, export growth appears to have been stronger than expected, though most of this growth is accounted for by the exporters of manufactures.

Changes in *import volume* differed substantially between the various regions. Imports into North America surged far above their pre-recession peak: in 1984 their volume was almost 30 per cent above their level in 1983. Imports into Japan also rose considerably, while in Europe they increased at a much slower pace— by some 6 per cent in the European market economies and by some 5 per cent in the centrally planned economies. However, this growth in European import demand was an important factor in the revival of European trade, given the high intensity of trade inside the region.

Following two years of import cuts, the non-oil developing countries were able to raise their import volumes in 1984, though the increase remained moderate. Furthermore, the durability of this recovery is uncertain since the import capacity of these countries continues to be restrained by their financial commitments. On the other hand, imports into the OPEC group fell again in 1984, but by much less than in 1983 when some OPEC members faced serious debt service problems.

World trade *prices*, in dollar terms, tended to fall again in 1984 (table 5.1.2). This is partly a result of the persistent appreciation of the United States currency, but other factors have also contributed. Prices of manufactures fell for the fourth consecutive year, a decline that also reflects the lowering of inflation rates in the developed market economies and an intense competition on world markets.

Oil prices decreased further: although the OPEC official price remained unchanged in 1984, spot prices fell through the summer and autumn. One reason for this fall was the erosion of price differentials between the light crude oil (as produced in the North Sea and by Nigeria) and the heavy crudes. This is because the worldwide upgrading of oil refineries has meant that greater quantities of high quality products (e.g. petrol) can now be obtained from the cheaper crudes. But the steady decline in spot prices is mainly a result of excess supply and competition among oil producers.

Primary commodity prices rose considerably in 1983 and in the first five months of 1984, owing to unfavourable weather conditions and to some stock building. With respect to food, the United States' acreage restrictions also contributed to drive up the prices in 1983. But since the end of May 1984, the market prices of primary products have fallen continuously. In many commodity markets there was a situation of excess supply as the

economic recovery had a larger impact on trade in manufactures than on primary products. The price fall was particularly sharp for food, vegetable oil and seeds, as the easing of previous acreage restrictions contributed to the rise in supplies. The prices of industrial materials also fell because of excess supply: anticipating a strong recovery in demand, many producers raised their output and built up stocks. On average, in 1984, the prices of the principal commodities exported by developing countries were just 1 per cent above their average level in 1983.

TABLE 5.1.2

Changes in trade prices (in US dollar terms), by major commodity groups, 1981-1984

(Percentage change from the previous year)

	1981	1982	1983	1984 Jan.-Sept.
Manufactures[a]	−6	−2	−4	−3
Fuels and related products[b] . . .	9	−6	−11	−5
Non-oil commodities[c]	−16	−16	6	1[d]
of which:				
Food and tropical beverages . .	−19	−17	5	1
Oilseeds and oils	−4	−22	22	35
Agricultural raw materials . .	−13	−14	7	−2
Minerals, ores and metals. . .	−14	−11	−	−6

Source: United Nations, *Monthly Bulletin of Statistics*, December 1984; NIESR, *National Institute Economic Review*, No. 109, November 1984; and UNCTAD, *Monthly Commodity Price Bulletin*, vol. IV, No. 12, January 1985.

[a] Export unit value index for manufactures of developed market economies.

[b] Unit value of the developed market economies' imports of mineral fuels and related materials.

[c] Combined index of market prices of principal commodity exports of developing countries.

[d] Full year for total and for each commodity group.

The export prices of the developed market economies declined further in 1984 and their *terms of trade* deteriorated (table 5.1.1). In the European centrally planned economies, changes in the unit values of trade reflect both current world market price movements and changes in intra-CMEA prices which adjust with a lag to the former. A feature of the latter was that the relative price of fuels was still rising in trade among CMEA countries in 1983 and 1984. As a result, the overall terms of trade of the Soviet Union continued to improve, while those of the east European countries have declined again.

The export prices of the non-oil developing countries may have fallen somewhat, but as import prices dropped more, their terms of trade improved moderately. The oil exporters suffered a further deterioration in their terms of trade.

The main change in the global pattern of *current account balances* is the widening of the United States' deficit, from some $42 billion in 1983 to probably more than $100 billion in 1984. This is partly reflected in a sharp increase in the Japanese surplus, which reached $36 billion at the end of the year. The surplus in the current account of western Europe may have increased somewhat, mainly owing to a significant reduction of the deficit of southern Europe. As a whole, the developed market economies probably ended 1984 with a deficit of almost $70 billion, which compares with a $25 billion deficit in 1983 (chart 5.1.1). However, the current account situation of these countries is likely to be more favourable than shown by the official data, given an apparent under-recording of investment income, receipts from transport services and remittances in some countries.[271] The European centrally planned economies' current

---

[271] See OECD, *Economic Outlook, Occasional Studies*, July 1984 and IMF, *World Economic Outlook*, April 1983.

account with the market economies moved into surplus in 1982 and improved further in 1983, to $8 billion. Further improvement is estimated for 1984, mainly on the strength of larger current-account surpluses of the east European countries.

The current account of the OPEC group has been in deficit since 1982. The deficit was some $17 billion in 1983, and is likely to have been just slightly smaller in 1984: a revival of oil exports was expected to reduce it but the price decline nearly offset the volume growth.[272] Under-recording of receipts on invisible transactions also appears to have occurred in some OPEC member countries. Therefore, the combined deficit of the OPEC countries is probably smaller than the one registered.

In the non-oil developing countries the current account deficit has been considerably reduced, from more than $80 billion in 1981. Most of the adjustment occurred in 1982 and 1983, when the current account deficit was reduced to some $43 billion. In 1984 progress was less spectacular and the deficit is expected to be $35 to 40 billion: while the trade deficit is likely to have been half of the 1983 deficit, this has been partly offset by growing interest payments and a decrease in the surplus on services and transfers.

(b) *The impact of the recovery in the United States*

An important feature of international trade at present is the spreading of the economic recovery in the United States. Imports into this country grew at remarkable rates in 1983/84 and this boosted the exports of other regions. On the other hand, the upswing in the economy of the United States has been accompanied by a strong and steady appreciation of the dollar which, in turn, has had some effects on trade: it has increased the export competitiveness of other countries, but it has also been translated, outside the United States, into higher import prices and a weaker demand for the primary commodities, including oil, that are quoted in dollars.

The upswing in United States' imports: its effect on other regions

Imports into the United States rose substantially in 1983 and 1984: in 1983, they increased 12 per cent in volume and in January-September 1984, on an annual basis, they grew three times as much (table 5.1.3). This import boom derives from an income-induced increase in domestic demand and from a deterioration of the United States' competitive position in the home market.

At an early stage of the recovery, imports of raw materials (other than fuels) rose at a relatively rapid pace. This was probably a result of some stockbuilding and a growth in output corresponding to an increased use of existing production capacity. As output expanded further, investment growth accelerated and imports of capital goods became the fastest growing category. Thus, the industrialized countries are likely to have benefited more from that import growth in 1984 than in 1983, when the developing countries were relatively more favoured.

In chart 5.1.2 the product specialization of various regions' exports to the United States is plotted against the growth of the United States' imports of the same products. The coefficient of product specialization is defined as the ratio between the share of a given product in one region's exports to the United States and the share of the same product in the United States' total imports. A ratio larger (smaller) than 1—to the right (left) of the vertical dotted line in the chart—indicates that the share of the product in the region's exports is bigger (smaller) than the share of that

---

[272] OPEC Secretariat: direct information to the ECE secretariat.

CHART 5.1.1.

Balance of payments on current account, 1980–1984

(Billion US dollars)

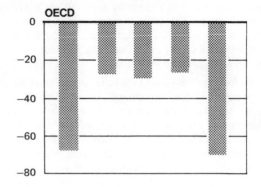

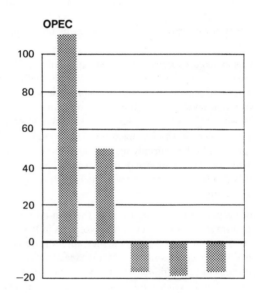

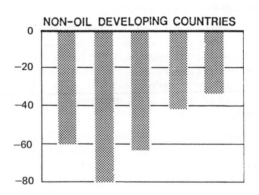

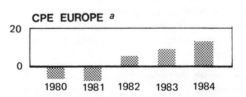

Source: ECE secretariat estimates, based on information published by the OECD, *Economic Outlook* (36), December 1984, the IMF, *International Financial Statistics,* January 1985.
a With the market economies.

TABLE 5.1.3

Volume growth in United States' imports by type of product, 1983 and 1984
(*Percentage change from the same period in the previous year*)

	1983	1984			
		I	*II*	*III*	*Jan.-Sept.*
Total	11.5	37.8	27.6	37.5	34.3
Food and beverages.	6.9	14.4	7.9	16.9	13.1
Industrial supplies, other than petroleum	16.0	35.3	20.2	29.2	28.2
Petroleum and products	−2.0	37.8	14.6	−3.4	16.3
Investment goods, other than autos	7.9	54.3	46.6	59.3	53.4
Autos	19.1	38.2	30.6	43.7	37.5
Consumer goods, other than food and autos	12.8	36.5	27.1	41.5	35.0
Other goods.	3.4	23.1	6.9	16.1	15.4

Source: US Department of Commerce, *Survey of Current Business*, September and October 1984.

product in the United States' total imports. The horizontal dotted line indicates the average growth rate of United States' imports in 1983-1984. Thus, the dotted lines divide the chart into four zones, the "favourable" ones being shaded. Over the last two years, the product mix of the United States' imports was particularly favourable to Japan and to the developing countries in south-east Asia. The products in which exports from Japan and south-east Asia were most "specialized" were those for which United States' import demand was growing faster. West European exports benefited from the fast growth in United States' imports of manufactures in 1984, but over the two years 1983-1984 the average import growth of the products in which western Europe had the highest specialization was very much in line with the average growth of United States' imports.[273] On the other hand, those products making up most of Latin American exports to the United States—primary commodities and fuels—

were those for which United States' import demand was growing most slowly. This applies particularly to 1984 and may explain the low growth, in relative terms, of Latin American exports to the United States in this year.

An estimation of the direct impact of the United States' recovery on world exports by regions is shown in the last two columns of table 5.1.4. The same table also shows the share of the United States in exports from the various regions and the growth of the United States imports from these regions.

In 1983, the recovery in the United States had the largest impact on Latin America and south-east Asia: first because imports from these areas rose at a relatively fast pace, and secondly because the United States is an important market for both regions. In the first three quarters of 1984 the largest impact was on Japan, Canada and the developing countries in south-east Asia. West European exports to the United States rose by nearly 35 per cent, but the impact of this growth on the region's total exports was comparatively less important, due to the relatively

[273] See section 5.2(ii) below.

TABLE 5.1.4

The direct impact of the United States' recovery on world exports, by regions, 1983 and 1984
(*Percentage changes from previous year, in current prices*)

	Percentage share of the US in exports from		US imports from		Change in total exports due to rise in exports to US[a]	
	1982	*1983*	*1983*	*1984 Jan.-Sept.*	*1983*	*1984 Jan.-Sept.*
Western Europe	6.8	7.6	3.3	35.3	0.2	2.7
Canada.	17.1	20.6	12.3	30.0	2.1	6.2
Japan	26.4	29.5	9.1	47.8	2.4	14.1
Other DME[b]	9.4	13.0	−2.2	23.0	−0.2	3.0
Eastern Europe and USSR	0.6	0.9	26.9	55.7	0.2	0.5
OPEC	11.5	10.8	−21.0	13.9	−2.4	1.5
Non-oil developing countries:						
Latin America[c].	31.1	33.5	10.9	16.2	3.4	5.4
Africa[d]	20.7	18.7	−4.5	19.2	−0.9	3.6
South East Asia	20.3	23.9	18.6	38.7	3.8	9.2
WORLD.	12.5	14.0	5.9	31.4	0.7	4.4

Source: Based on United Nations, *Monthly Bulletin of Statistics*, December 1983 and December 1984 and IMF, *Direction of Trade Statistics*, January 1985.

[a] Percentage change from previous year in the different countries' export values (in US dollars): hypothetical growth determined by the increase in United States' imports.

[b] South Africa, Australia and New Zealand.

[c] Including Venezuela.

[d] Including OPEC members.

CHART 5.1.2.

Product specialization ratio in the regions' exports to the United States and growth in US imports, 1983 — 1984

PC Primary commodities
E   Energy products
IS Iron and steel
CH Chemicals
M   Machinery
A   Autos
OT Office and telecommunication
    apparatus
CG Consumer goods

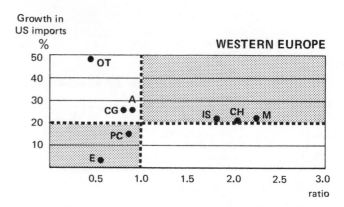

WESTERN EUROPE

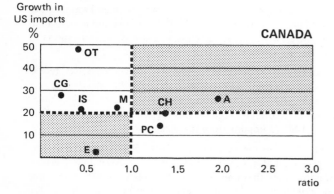

CANADA

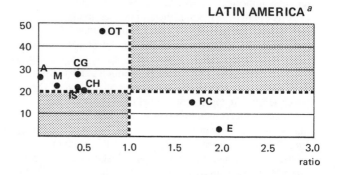

LATIN AMERICA [a]

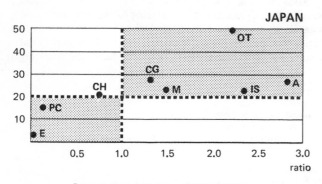

JAPAN

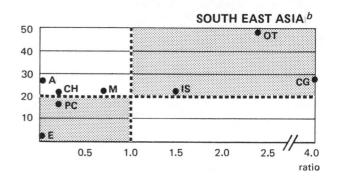

SOUTH EAST ASIA [b]

Source: United Nations, COMTRADE tape.

Note: The product specialization is defined as the ratio between the share of a given product in a region's exports to the United States and the share of the same product in US imports. The ratio equals 1.0 (vertical line) whenever the share of the product is the same in exports to the US and in US imports. The ratios refer to 1982. The horizontal line (20%) indicates the average growth in US imports in 1983 — 1984.
a Argentina, Mexico, Brazil and Venezuela.
b Hong Kong, Republic of Korea, Singapore and Taiwan.

small share of the United States in west European exports.[274] In fact, the effect on western Europe's exports of the 6 per cent growth in the region's own import demand was probably larger. For the European centrally planned economies, a rise of nearly 56 per cent in exports to the United States contributed only half a percentage point to the areas's total export growth.

The extent to which the various regions have shared in the recovery of the United States' imports is also reflected in the trade balances of the United States with the different regions.

The increase in the deficit was particularly striking with respect to trade with the industrial countries, especially with Japan and western Europe (table 5.1.5). This is partly due to the strong rise in imports of investment goods. Imports of consumer goods also rose above average, contributing to a significant increase in the United States' trade deficit with other Asian countries. The deficit *vis-à-vis* OPEC also widened, due to an increase—the first since 1980—in oil imports from OPEC member countries.

The trade deficit of the United States is likely to have increased from some $36 billion in 1982 to about $123 billion in 1984. This was mainly a result of the surge in imports, though in 1983 it was also due to a decrease in exports, reflecting the impact of a

---

274 See section 5.2 below.

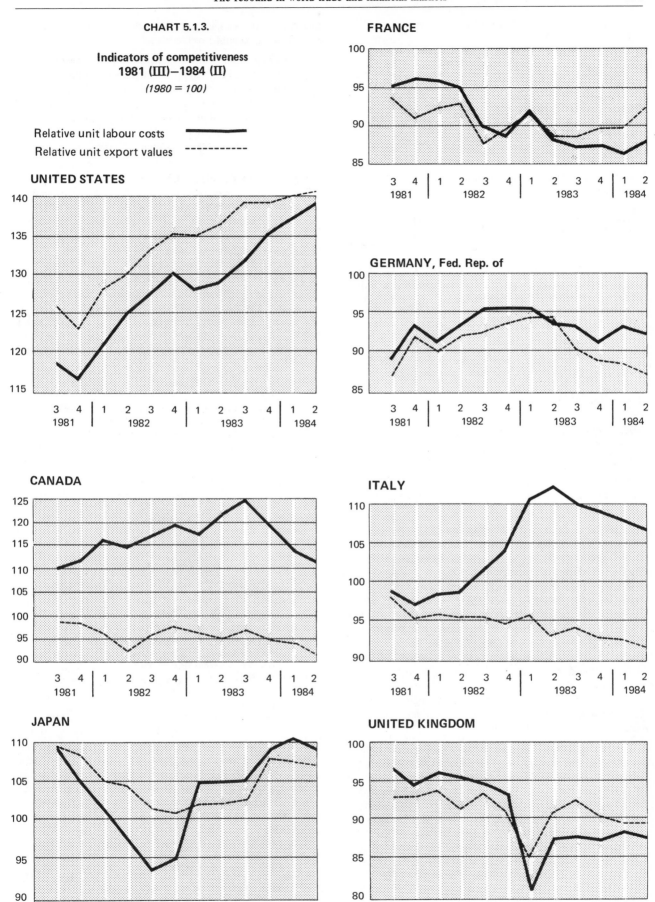

CHART 5.1.3.

Indicators of competitiveness
1981 (III)–1984 (II)

(1980 = 100)

Relative unit labour costs ————
Relative unit export values - - - - - -

UNITED STATES

FRANCE

CANADA

GERMANY, Fed. Rep. of

JAPAN

ITALY

UNITED KINGDOM

Source: IMF, *International Financial Statistics,* January 1985.

TABLE 5.1.5

United States' trade balance by trading partner
(Millions of US dollars)

	1983	1984
Developed market economies	−33 750	−71 600
Western Europe	982	−14 400
Canada	−14 300	−20 400
Japan	−21 700	−36 800
Other countries	1 268	2 356
European centrally planned economies	1 547	2 080
Developing countries	−35 889	−51 704
Latin America [a]	−14 047	−15 036
Asia [b]	−11 460	−20 100
Africa [b]	−346	−480
OPEC	−10 036	−16 088
Total	−68 092	−123 304

Source: US Department of Commerce, *Survey of Current Business*, September 1984 and US Mission in Geneva, *Daily Bulletin*, 31 January 1985.

[a] Excluding Venezuela.

[b] Excluding OPEC members.

decline of imports into Latin America and a loss in the United States' competitiveness. In 1984 there was a significant growth of United States' exports (6 to 7 per cent, in volume), but the rise in imports was five times as large.

Some trade effects of the strong dollar

The firm appreciation of the dollar influenced world trade in two main ways: through the loss in the United States' competitiveness and through the effect on import prices, outside the United States, of commodities priced in dollars in international markets.

In the home market, the deterioration of the United States' competitive position contributed to the import surge discussed above. In foreign markets it enlarged the export possibilities of the United States' major competitors. Chart 5.1.3 depicts relative unit labour costs and relative unit export values for the United States and other major industrial countries. Between 1980 and mid-1984, the United States' relative export unit values rose by about 40 per cent, while those of its European competitors and of Canada fell by some 10 per cent. In Japan, owing to the appreciation of the yen, relative unit values increased 7 per cent in the same period. Measured in terms of relative unit labour costs, competitive positions changed in much the same way: the exceptions are Canada and Italy, where relative unit labour costs increased significantly to mid-1983 and then declined, though remaining above their 1980 levels.

This decline in the United States' competitiveness is probably an important explanatory factor for its losses of market share in 1982-1984. It may also explain the gains of other exporters. In 1983-1984, Japan recorded large share gains. This increase in the Japanese share of the world market, which occurred at a time of a deterioration in its competitive position, is likely to have been much influenced by the rise in Japan's share of the North American market, where Japanese products continued to be competitive *vis-à-vis* domestically produced goods. Japanese exports were also favoured by the product pattern of the United States' import demand (chart 5.1.2). Exports to the United States probably accounted also for the significant share gain in the world market of other south-east Asian countries, especially in 1983-1984. The share of western Europe in world exports rose in 1982, remained unchanged in 1983 and declined in 1984. This decline, which does not seem to be explained by losses in cost/

price competitiveness, is probably a reflection of the 1984 strikes in the Federal Republic of Germany.

The soaring value of the dollar also influenced world trade through its price effects, namely the increase in national currency prices of dollar-priced commodities. In the last few years, however, these effects have been mitigated by the decline in commodity prices in dollar terms.[275] This was especially the case of non-oil commodity prices, which have fallen steadily since 1980, except for an increase between early 1983 and mid-1984 (chart 5.1.4).

In the case of oil prices, the situation has been somewhat different. The fall in demand for oil in 1980-1983 led to a reduction in the average OPEC price, from $34 per barrel to $29, in March 1983. However, due to the appreciation of the dollar, many countries in western Europe did not benefit from this fall in price and their oil imports continued to decline in 1983. During 1984 the OPEC official dollar price was unchanged. But the situation of excess supply in the oil market, and a reduction in price differentials between light and heavy crudes, has led to a significant drop in spot prices since the summer of 1984. By the end of the year, spot prices were, on average, some $1.5 a barrel lower than the official OPEC prices.[276] Nevertheless, in terms of European currencies, oil prices were rising fast in 1984 (chart 5.1.5 and table 5.1.6).

TABLE 5.1.6

Changes in current crude oil import prices expressed in national currencies, 1981-1984
(Percentage change from previous year)

	1982	1983	1984[a]	1982-1984
United States	−9.0	−12.6	−2.6	−24.2
Japan	6.6	−16.1	−1.2	−11.1
Western Europe,	6.9	−3.5	9.2	12.6
of which:				
Belgium	21.2	−0.7	10.9	31.4
Denmark	8.0	−1.5	9.9	16.4
France	19.2	3.6	8.7[b]	31.5
Germany, Federal Republic of	−1.4	−6.4	7.7	−1.0
Italy	9.2	0.2	11.1	20.5
Spain	9.6	16.6	9.1	35.3
Sweden	18.0	7.2	4.7	29.9
Switzerland	−5.8	−8.5	4.7	−9.6
United Kingdom	10.4	2.9	10.9	24.2

Source: IEA, *Energy Prices and Taxes*, third quarter, 1984, Paris, 1984; for France, United Nations, *Monthly Bulletin of Statistics*, December 1984.

[a] Third quarter 1984 compared to the same quarter in 1983.

[b] Second quarter 1984 compared to the same quarter in 1983.

The impact of these price developments on world trade as a whole is not easy to determine. They acted negatively on the income and demand of those countries (other than the United States, Japan and Switzerland), that are net importers, but had a positive impact on the income and demand of the exporting countries. Despite the fact that the import propensity in the latter is probably higher than in the former, the net impact is likely to have been negative due to the large share of western Europe in world trade.

---

[275] It is worth noting that a relationship may exist between the changes in the dollar effective exchange rate and the commodity dollar prices. The IMF found that a 1 per cent appreciation of the dollar led to a decline in commodity prices of slightly more than 1 per cent (see IMF, *World Economic Outlook*, 1983, p. 158).

[276] As a consequence of this difference between the official price and the price in the spot market, the share of oil traded in the free market has steadily risen: it is now estimated to be 40 per cent of the total trade in oil, against 1 per cent ten years ago.

(c) *Outlook for 1985*

The main features of the outlook for world trade in 1985 are a slowdown in the rate of volume growth and a more balanced sharing of this growth among the major economic regions (table 5.1.7). The increase in world trade will moderate to some 5 to 6 per cent, mainly because of the weakening of the growth in the United States' economy. Import demand in the United States is anticipated to grow at a much slower pace than in the recent past, perhaps by 8 to 10 per cent. The United States' exports will continue to benefit from the dynamism of trade in the Pacific area and are expected to rise in line with world trade, despite a possible further deterioration in its competitive position.

TABLE 5.1.7

Outlook for trade volumes and balances on current account in 1985
(Percentage change and billion US dollars)

	Percentage change in trade volumes		Balance on current account (billions of dollars)
	Exports	Imports	
Developed market economies . . .	4-5	5-6	−75
of which:			
United States	4-5	8-10	−120
Western Europe	4-6	4-5	15
Japan.	7-8	6-7	40
Developing countries	4-5	4-5	−45
OPEC	2-3	5-6	−
Non-oil	5-7	4-5	−45
European centrally planned economies	5-6	5-6	10
World	4-5	5-6	−110

Source: ECE secretariat assessment, based in part on forecasts published by the OECD, IMF, NIESR and ODI.

In western Europe economic growth is foreseen to accelerate slightly, but the volume growth of the region's imports will probably be a bit lower than in 1984 as stockbuilding, which seems to have pushed imports in this year, may come to a halt. Still, the foreseen 4-5 per cent increase in the volume of west European imports will make a significant contribution to the growth in the region's exports, given the importance of intra-European trade. Morever, exports from west European countries will continue to be stimulated by the still significant growth in North American imports and by an expected acceleration in the growth of imports into the developing countries.

In the European centrally planned economies, import volume is likely to grow somewhat faster than in 1984, mainly on the strength of an expected rise in Soviet import growth; in eastern Europe, the improved current account position of most countries should allow import expansion to continue at about the 1984 pace (some 6 per cent). As the terms-of-trade movements are still running against the countries of eastern Europe, the adjustment to these changes—especially in intra-CMEA trade—is likely to result in somewhat faster growth of east European exports. Export volume growth of the Soviet Union will be largely influenced by the country's reaction to developments in world oil markets.

The recent modest revival of oil trade is projected to continue in 1985 and OPEC exports may rise in volume by 2-3 per cent. Although the OPEC official price was lowered by $1 dollar per barrel at the end of January and spot prices may continue to decline, the effect of the dollar appreciation still leaves some room for an increase in the import demand of OPEC member countries: the rise is expected to be about 5 to 6 per cent.

CHART 5.1.4

Indices of primary commodity prices
(1979–1981 = 100)

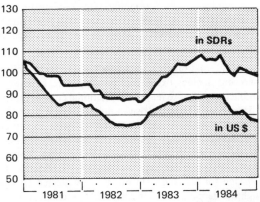

Source: UNCTAD *Monthly Commodity Price Bulletin*, vol. V, no 1, January 1985

CHART 5.1.5.

Indices of crude oil import prices
(1980 = 100)

A . Total IEA member countries [a]

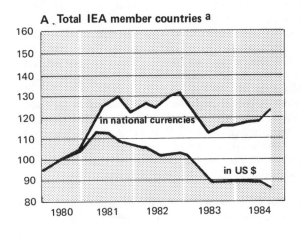

B . WESTERN EUROPE and USA
in national currencies

Source: IEA, *Energy Prices and Taxes*, third quarter 1984.

[a] OECD, excluding Iceland, Finland and France.

The import capacity of non-oil developing countries will still be limited by financial constraints in 1985. Nevertheless, as further import cuts would endanger the whole economy of these countries, some volume growth is forecast for their imports. Export prospects are not bright for a number of commodities that are important for non-oil developing countries. Furthermore, as export growth will be lowered by the slowdown in North American demand, exports of these countries are expected to increase in 1985 at a slower pace than 1984.

Prices of internationally traded goods will probably follow the path of recent changes, except for a possible increase in the prices of manufactures. These may rise, in national currency terms, by some 5 per cent;[277] but the rise in dollar terms will also reflect exchange rate movements, which are difficult to anticipate. Prices of non-oil primary commodities are expected to decline further, though less than in the second half of 1984. The combination of increased supply with a slower growth of demand is the main reason for this fall. Oil prices are expected to weaken: although the demand for oil is projected to increase, the present worldwide imbalance of oil supply over demand will continue. The difficulties of the OPEC cartel, in enforcing production quotas and official prices, are likely to continue to contribute to a weak oil market.

Against this background, the *balances on current account* are anticipated to be very much in line with the 1984 pattern. Among the developed market economies, the major changes projected for 1985 are a further widening of the deficit of the United States, by an estimated $20 billion, and a further expansion in the surplus of Japan, by some $10 billion. No significant change is expected in the combined current account of the west European countries. In the non-oil developing countries, the growth in export earnings is likely to match the rise in imports and net payments of interest and profits, leaving their current account deficit more or less unchanged. The OPEC current account deficit is expected to shrink, reflecting a higher world demand for oil and the effect of a possible further appreciation of the dollar. Efforts to imprve the current account balance of the east European countries will continue in 1985. The Soviet Union's current account is likely to remain in substantial surplus, but will probably be under downward pressure in 1985, as a result of the combined impact of oil price changes and an increased need for grain imports.

(ii) Developments in the international financial markets and the debt situation

This section comprises two parts. The first summarizes recent developments in international financing activity, which saw a substantial upswing in 1984. The second part examines the progress made towards resolution of the international debt situation. The experiences of three country groups are briefly examined and the conclusion, based on preliminary data, emerges that all have, to considerably different extents, made gains in improving their external financial positions. Nevertheless, the costs of adjustment in terms of social welfare have often been considerable and there remains a group of countries whose financial positions continue in a precarious state.

(a) *Developments in the international financial markets*

After having fallen to a low of $158 billion in 1983, international lending rebounded sharply to an all time high of nearly $230 billion in 1984 (table 5.1.8), with notable advances in the second half of the year.

---

[277] See section 2.3.

In terms of *credit instruments*, the rise in new borrowing was about equally split between bond issues and bank loans. This latter development reflects a continuation of profound structural changes in the international capital markets. In particular there has been a pronounced tendency to raise medium- and long-term funds by means of bonds, especially *floating rate notes*,[278] at the expense of bank credits. On the other hand, within the bank loan category, the use of various back-up facilities, including *syndicated note issuance facilities* (SNIFS)[279] has surged, while the volume of conventional syndicated loans has contracted considerably. Contributing to these developments has been the erosion of the traditional distinctions between various financial instruments, particularly as regards bank and bond market finance. Lower borrowing costs associated with FRN and SNIF financing have also been a factor. However, these latter options have been mainly restricted to those borrowers with the highest credit ratings (mainly developed market economies, certain corporations and some Asian developing countries), the others having been largely confined to straight syndicated loans. Overall better borrowing conditions are due to increased competition in the capital market which, in turn, stems from the decisions of banks to curtail, or cease, lending to certain countries, on the one hand, and continued liquidity in the market, on the other.

In terms of market activity by *geographical area*, countries and institutions of the *industrial market economies* were almost exclusively responsible for the $70 billion rise in global borrowing, thereby raising their share of the total market to 75 per cent (table 5.1.8). Apparently a considerable part of the new loans represent refinancing of existing debt. Lending to the *other countries*, by contrast, turned up only marginally and remained some one third below the peak in 1981. After having contracted sharply between 1981 and 1983, the volume of funds raised by *non-oil developing countries* turned up slightly in 1984 to about $28 billion. Somewhat over $15 billion of this amount was new money provided within the framework of rescheduling packages and was almost entirely accounted for by Brazil ($6.5 billion) and Mexico ($8.1 billion). Much of the balance has been "spontaneous" lending to several Asian borrowers that have maintained or even improved their creditworthiness.

The volume of funds raised by *southern Europe* has increased gradually since 1982. This appears due to the improved creditworthiness of Portugal and Turkey which has allowed them to resume or step up borrowing. By contrast, Yugoslavia has not been in a position to raise funds outside of those anticipated within the umbrella rescheduling agreements. Of the south European countries, only Spain has raised credits via syndicated loan issuance facilities while Portugal and Turkey are reported to be negotiating back-up facilities for the issuance of Euronotes and short-term bank advances respectively.

Borrowing by *eastern Europe and the Soviet Union*, largely through syndicated loans, recovered sharply in 1984 to reach the highest level ($3.3 billion) since 1979. Despite the increased activity, the east accounted for only about 1.5 per cent of total funds raised. Their presence in the syndicated loan market alone

---

[278] Among eastern borrowers, Hungary issued a $100 million floating rate note in February 1985. Also the Moscow Narodny Bank raised $50 million via the same instrument in August 1984.

[279] Syndicated note issuance facilities (SNIFS) basically represent commitments extended by banks which guarantee to the borrower the availability of medium-term credit at predetermined terms. They are to be funded through the issue on the market of short-term instruments such as promissory notes (e.g. Euronotes) or, if the borrower is a bank, certificates of deposit. For a more extensive discussion of these new facilities see OECD, *Financial Market Trends*, October 1984 pp. 47-48 and D. Shireff, "The Euronote Explosion", *Euromoney*, December 1984, pp. 31-41.

TABLE 5.1.8

Funds raised on the international markets, by instrument and borrower, 1981-1984
(In billions of US dollars)

	1981	1982	1983	1984	1984 Q3	1984 Q3
Total	200.6	179.1	157.8	227.2	49.8	63.8
By instrument:						
Issues of bonds	52.8	75.5	77.1	111.6	25.5	36.4
Bank loans	147.7	103.6	80.7	115.7	24.3	27.4
By borrower:[a]						
Industrial market economies[b]	128.3	115.6	104.4	170.7	39.1	46.8
Other countries	64.9	53.3	43.8	45.4	8.0	13.1
of which:						
Southern Europe[c]	9.1	6.8	7.8	9.3	1.9	2.6
Oil exporters	6.5	9.0	7.9	4.4	1.4	1.1
Other developing countries[d]	47.7	36.8	27.0	28.4	3.3	8.5
Eastern Europe and the Soviet Union[e]	1.6	0.7	1.1	3.3	1.4	0.9

Source: OECD, *Financial Statistics Monthly*, Part 1, Paris, February 1985.

[a] Excludes international development institutions, other countries and unattributable.

[b] OECD less Greece, Portugal, Spain and Turkey.

[c] Greece, Portugal, Spain, Turkey and Yugoslavia.

[d] Corresponds to "non-oil developing countries" used elsewhere in this section except that it excludes Bahrain, Ecuador, Gabon and Trinidad and Tobago (included in oil exporters).

[e] Includes CMEA banks.

is relatively more important with a share of almost 5 per cent. This share increased rapidly in 1984 (from less than 1 per cent in 1982) owing to the rise in eastern borrowing but also because of the shrinking of the syndicated loan market. In eastern Europe, Hungary was the first country to utilize the Euronote market (SNIF) in raising $85 million in September through a four-year facility permitting short-term maturities of three or six months. This followed a bankers's acceptance facility of $210 million obtained earlier in the year. Also it was reported that the Moscow Narodny bank has been interested in a floating rate certificates of deposit facility totalling $30 million.

(b) *Recent developments in the global debt situation*[280]

Among the more significant positive signs that the international debt situation has eased is the continued improvement in the current account deficits of debtor countries (see section 5.1(i)). In particular, the current account deficits of non-oil developing countries have contracted strongly, often at higher-than-expected rates, while the surpluses of eastern Europe and the Soviet Union have expanded. In a broad sense, these developments are due to the adjustment policies undertaken by these countries, unexpectedly buoyant import demand in the developed market economies and, to a lesser extent, to improved terms on new commercial credits.[281] Overall these factors appear to have more than offset the negative effects of higher interest rates in 1984.[282] Other indicators which have developed in a

favourable manner include a downturn in debt service burden, inflows of official credits, rising levels of international reserves and improvements in economic growth and per capita income in the non-oil developing countries. Finally, on the part of the lenders, commercial banks have managed to reduce loans-to-capital ratios from the peak levels of 1982 by slowing down lending and adding significantly to loan loss reserves.[283] On the whole, evaluations of the progress made in managing debt have tended to become more positive as 1984 advanced and the strength of economic recovery in the west became apparent. Moreover, a further easing in the international debt problem is likely as global economic recovery continues, reinforcing the contention that the current problem has basically been one of illiquidity rather than insolvency.

While considerable progress has been made, the adjustment process has often been painful. In general, imports were cut back, the growth of output slowed significantly in the non-oil developing countries (output actually declining in 1982-1983 in Latin America) and real per capita income plunged. Although growth rates accelerated in 1984, it could, nevertheless, take some countries until the end of the decade to bring real per capita income back to previous levels.[284]

Another negative aspect of the adjustment process has been net transfer of resources from debtor countries, thereby reducing the potential for economic development.[285] This situation is expected to persist in the medium-term largely because international banks are expected to limit their exposure *vis-à-vis* major debtor countries while high interest rates and growing debt will keep net interest payments rising. On the other hand, it has been pointed out that a period of net outward resource transfer is

---

[280] The section complements other parts of this *Survey* in which issues involving external payments and debt are also raised: southern Europe (chapter 3) and other sections of this chapter, especially east-west economic relationships (section 5.4).

[281] The most significant example of this has been the narrowing of the margin from 2 7/8 to 1 1/8 percentage points on new commercial bank loans to Mexico in 1984.

[282] When interest rates were rising in the first half of 1984, there was considerable concern that the gains being made in merchandise trade would be more than offset by higher interest payments. However, this did not appear to occur. For example, a recent evaluation for Latin America alone shows that exports increased by $8.4 billion in 1984 while net payments of profits and interest rose by $2.8 billion, resulting in a decline of some $5 billion in the current deficit. Economic Commission for Latin America and the Caribbean, *Preliminary Overview of the Latin American Economy during 1984*, LC/G.1336, January 17, 1985, table 1, p. 15.

[283] Morgan Guaranty Trust Co., *World Financial Markets*, October/November 1984, p. 4.

[284] Latin America's output growth recovered in 1984 at an estimated rate of 2.6 per cent. However, per capita gross national income has continued to decline, but at a much reduced rate compared to 1981-1983. ECLAC, *op. cit.*, table 1, p. 15.

[285] In this case interest outflows exceed net new borrowing. For eastern Europe and the Soviet Union combined, net new borrowing appears to have been negative in 1982, and probably very low in 1983-1984.

TABLE 5.1.9

**Gross external debt of the non-oil developing countries, southern
Europe and eastern Europe and the Soviet Union**
(*In billion of US dollars*)

	1977	1978	1979	1980	1981	1982	1983	1984
Developing countries[a]	290	349	415	492	580	668	707	749
of which:								
Non-oil developing countries . . .	250	296	349	418	502	578	611	651
Southern Europe	44	54	61	74	84	89	92	96
Eastern Europe and the Soviet Union.	60	73	86	92	97	91	89	86
Total of above	394	476	562	658	761	848	888	931

Source: Developing countries: IMF, (September), *op. cit.*, table 35; southern Europe: sme as table 3.6.1; eastern Europe and the Soviet Union: same as table 5.4.12.

[a] Developing countries and non-oil developing countries as used here differ from the IMF definition in that both exclude the group "Europe". IMF data on external debt of developing countries exclude eight oil exporting countries (Iran, Iraq, Kuwait, Libya, Oman, Quatar, Saudia Arabia and the United Arab Emirates). Data do not include debt owed to the IMF.

necessary if highly indebted countries are to bring their debt export ratios down to levels generally judged compatible with creditworthiness.[286]

Aside from these developments the global financial situation remains characterized by an uneven geographical distribution of indebtedness, significant differences in the rates of adjustment among countries, and by a group of "problem" countries which remain in a precarious financial position. Naturally, such considerable variations in country experiences tend to be obscured in any regional grouping, including those used here, and should be borne in mind whenever generalizations are made.

The indicator of trends in global debt used here is the sum of the external gross debt of the three groups of countries—non-oil developing countries,[287] southern Europe, eastern Europe and the Soviet Union. This total reached almost $890 billion at end-1983 and is estimated to have risen further to some $930 billion by end-1984 (table 5.1.9).[288] The annual increments in gross debt in 1983 and 1984 amounted to about $40 billion, significantly smaller than the annual changes of some $100 billion in the period 1979-1981.

Of the total, the developing countries account for the predominant and increasing share. Nevertheless, the contracting current account deficits of the *non-oil developing countries* have resulted in a sharp slowdown in the accumulation of their debt from an annual growth rate in the 15-20 per cent range during 1980-1982 to some 6-7 per cent in 1983-1984 (table 5.1.10). It is estimated that their debt/export ratio turned downward in 1984 after having increased considerably during the three previous years. The debt service ratio is estimated to have fallen by several

percentage points below the high level in 1982.[289] Faster-than-expected progress has also been made in rebuilding reserves because current account deficits have contracted rapidly, capital flight (a major factor contributing to debt build up in some countries in the late 1970s and early 1980s) slowed while the inflow of funds from official lending has held up better than anticipated.[290,291]

Southern Europe's current account deficit has been contracting since the peak recorded in 1980 (see chapter 3). The gross debt continued to rise, reaching some $96 billion in 1984, thereby exceeding that of eastern Europe and the Soviet Union. The debt burden, as measured by the debt-export ratio, is estimated to have turned downward in 1984 owing to a strong performance in the export of goods and services (including transfer receipts). By contrast the debt service ratio rose slightly (despite the rescheduling of some debt in this group), largely because of higher interest payments. However, the reserve position has been improving, especially in 1984 when the combined reserves of these countries covered three months' of imports again.

In contrast to the experience of the other two groups analysed here, the *European centrally planned economies'* external debt has actually been declining.[292] This is the result of the current account surpluses in convertible currencies which the group has run since 1982 and the effect of the US dollar appreciation.[293] The former have been accomplished largely through lower imports, as exports to the market economies have tended to rise sluggishly. As a result, reduction of debt has been the most important reason for the decline in the debt-export ratio. A measure of the

[286] William Cline, *International Debt: Systemic Risk and Policy Response*, Institute for International Economics, Washington, D.C., 1984, pp. 175-178.

[287] The definition of non-oil developing countries corresponds to that adopted by the IMF except that it *excludes* the group of countries which the IMF designates "Europe". See IMF, *World Economic Outlook*, Occasional Papers 27 and 32, Washington, D.C., April and September 1984. Most of the data relating to the non-oil developing countries, are based upon the *revised projections* in the September paper.

[288] It should be stressed that all figures presented here for 1984 are preliminary and based on incomplete data. This is important to bear in mind, since 1984 is likely to have been a critical year in the development of the international debt situation. More information will be required to determine the extent to which debt became more manageable and less burdensome for debtor countries.

[289] In 1983 the debt-service ratio declined because of lower interest rates and the rescheduling of maturities coming due. Relief provided by the latter amounted to some $23-24 billion (thus lowering the debt service ratio by over 5 percentage points) and a similar amount was expected to be negotiated in 1984. IMF (September), *op. cit.*, p. 16.

[290] The figures in table 5.1.10 do not include the considerable assets held by private citizens of these countries in overseas banks.

[291] IMF (September), *op. cit.*, p. 13.

[292] The external financial relations of eastern Europe and the Soviet Union are also discussed in section 5.4 in an east-west context.

[293] In comparison to the developing countries, changes in the value of the US dollar exert a considerable impact on the debt (in US dollars) of the European centrally planned economies. The reason is the significant differences in currency composition. Perhaps one half of the European centrally planned economies' debt is denominated in non-dollar currencies while a comparable figure for the total of developing country debt is only 10-15 per cent.

TABLE 5.1.10

Debt indicators, by major region

(In billions of US dollars and percentages)

	1977	1978	1979	1980	1981	1982	1983	1984
Non-oil developing countries								
Gross debt (billions)	250	296	349	418	502	578	611	651
Debt-export ratio (per cent). . . .	132	132	120	113	128	154	159	152
Debt service ratio (per cent) . . .	11.0	15.6	16.4	15.8	19.8	23.2	20.1	20.0
Interest payment ratio.	4.5	5.8	7.1	8.3	11.2	13.7	12.5	12.7
Reserves (billions)	60.0	74.1	85.1	85.8	87.4	84.8	91.6	107.2
Reserves-imports ratio.	28	28	24	19	17	18	21	22
Southern Europe								
Gross debt (billions)	44	54	61	74	84	89	92	96
Debt-export ratio (per cent). . . .	103	102	90	93	99	105	115	112
Debt service ratio (per cent) . . .	15	19	17	16	18	20	22	23
Reserves (billions)	12.1	17.6	19.6	18.7	17.1	12.4	12.6	17.3
Reserves-imports ratio.	29	41	35	26	24	18	19	25
Eastern Europe and the Soviet Union								
Gross debt[a] (billions)	60	73	86	92	97	91	89	86
Debt-export ratio[b] (per cent) . . .	151	164	149	130	135	121	115	111
Interest payment ratio (net)[b]	6	8	8	9	12	11	9	8
Reserves[c] (billions).	8.4	10.7	15.5	15.7	15.2	16.4	16.5	20.7
Reserves-imports ratio[d]	20	22	27	22	21	25	25	34

Sources: Same as table 5.1.9.

Note: Debt ratios are based upon exports of goods and services. Those of southern Europe also include transfer receipts.

[a] In convertible currencies only.

[b] Reflecting exports to the market economies only.

[c] Assets held at BIS reporting banks only.

[d] Reflecting imports from the market economies only.

debt burden, the interest payment ratios (net), has also been easing downward, owing to somewhat higher exports and lower interest payments. In 1984, the impact on interest payments of the rise in interest rates has been more than offset by the declining stock of debt on which interest is paid.

The currency composition of the European centrally planned economies external debt appears to have made the debt service burden somewhat less sensitive to recent interest rate change than, say, that of the non-oil developing countries. A considerable portion of the non-dollar debt is denominated in Deutschmarks and Swiss francs, currencies on which LIBOR rates were lower than on the dollar and considerably much more stable.

These countries have also been accumulating reserves, the build-up being notable especially in 1984. For the group as a whole they now cover about four months' imports.

The rate of improvement in the international debt situation is likely to slow somewhat given the expected slackening in the rate of growth in the developed market economies and the relative change in the geographical pattern of import demand (as already discussed in section 5.1(i)). Nevertheless, the results of several studies suggest that further easing of the debt problem would be expected at a growth rate of around the 3 per cent which is somewhat below that now projected for 1984.[294] Other factors—interest rates, domestic policies of the debtors, the value of the US dollar and changes in commercial policies—are also important to the outcome.

LIBOR rates on six-month US dollar deposits started to fall in the third quarter of 1984 and had declined to below 9 per cent in January 1985—their lowest in many years. Since movements in interest rates affect interest payments only with a lag, some relief should be felt by debtors in early 1985 and persist at least into the second half of the year.[295] On the other hand, the continuing appreciation of the US dollar, which reached record levels against several important currencies in February 1985, would tend to raise the burden of debt servicing of those countries whose debt is largely denominated in US dollars but whose exports are invoiced in other currencies.

It is generally believed that continued progress toward the resolution of the global debt will require restraint in the application of new restrictive commercial policy measures. In the past year, the resistance of governments to the pressures exerted by various sectoral interests have not always been successful as the recent spate of actions taken against particular exports of both developing and developed countries would testify. In other cases, initiatives to tighten measures controlling imports originate with governments which may place a certain priority on improving their external financial positions.

---

[294] For example see Cline, *op. cit.*, p. 46 and IMF (April) *op. cit.*, p. 68.

[295] It might be noted that a drop in interest rates does not appear to have been foreseen and consequently has not been built into any of the forecasts available for 1985. To the extent that this is correct, it would imply a greater reduction in the debt service burden of debtor countries than anticipated in the forecasts of the IMF and others.

5.2 WESTERN EUROPE AND NORTH AMERICA [296]

In 1984 there was a substantial acceleration in the growth of trade volumes in western Europe and North America. The increase in the volume of imports was, in both regions, twice as large as in 1983. This surge in import demand boosted the volume of exports from these regions, which also increased at a much faster pace than in the previous year. In particular, the rise in west European imports constituted an important stimulus to trade inside this region, owing to the large share of west European trade which is accounted for by intra-regional flows. The impact of the United States' import demand on exports from western Europe was also significant in 1984.

The weakening of trade prices on the world market, combined with the firm appreciation of the United States' dollar, entailed a decline in the unit dollar values of west European exports and imports. Still, the total value of exports tended to rise faster than that of imports, and the trade balances of most west European countries improved, resulting in a further increase in the combined current account surplus of western Europe. In North America the major change occurred in the United States, where both the trade balance and the balance on current account deteriorated substantially.

This section analyses the recent developments in west European and North American trade. Special attention is paid to trade between the two regions, in particular to the impact of the product mix of the United States' import demand on trade with western Europe.

(i) Recent developments in trade and current accounts

In the following review of recent trade developments, the focus is on regional and inter-regional trade flows, although individual countries or country-groups are referred to whenever they are relevant to the discussion. [297] In particular, reference is made to the two free trading areas in western Europe (the European Economic Community and the European Free Trade Association), as trade developments in each of them appear to have been different in the past few years.

(a) *Trade volumes and prices*

The *volume of imports* into North America, which had risen some 12 per cent in 1983, increased at an annual rate of 28 per cent in the first three quarters of 1984 (table 5.2.1 and chart 5.2.1). This import boom originated largely in the strong recovery of the United States' economy, combined with a deterioration of this country's competitiveness in the home market. It also reflected increased oil imports, partly to build up domestic stocks, as the war in the Persian Gulf raised concern that future supplies might be threatened.

In western Europe the volume of imports rose, in January-September 1984, at an annual rate more than twice as large as the 2.5 per cent increase of 1983.

The acceleration of import growth in western Europe to 6 per cent in 1984 is rather impressive when compared to a GDP growth slightly above 2 per cent. The relatively weak GDP performance, however, was partly due to the private and public service sectors, which normally have a low import content. The economies of many west European countries appear less sluggish when their performance is viewed through other cyclical indicators. In fact, output in manufacturing accelerated significantly from the end of 1983 and, in most west European countries, it rose at an annual rate of 3-4 per cent in the first three quarters of 1984. [298] The significant growth in imports into most countries of this group may thus reflect accelerating growth in west European industry. Part of this import growth is accounted for by oil—in the first half of the year, imports from OPEC member countries rose by some 3 per cent in value, suggesting a volume growth of about 8 per cent. The largest proportion of the increase in west European imports, however, corresponds to intra-European trade. This is clearly shown by the value changes for the first half of 1984 in table 5.2.2: more than 50 per cent of the rise in the value of imports into the countries of the EEC originated in western Europe, and this share was nearly 90 per cent for the EFTA member countries. Hence, west European import demand constituted a considerable stimulus for the region's exports.

The *volume of exports* from western Europe rose by 7.5 per cent in the first three quarters of 1984, an increase that also represents a noticeable acceleration from the 1983 export growth. The increase in export volumes was almost 9 per cent for EFTA, but this area had already experienced a significant export rise in the previous year, owing to the effects of currency devaluation in a number of member countries. More than half of the volume increase in west European exports may be attributed to intra-regional trade, though exports to the United States also contributed significantly. [299] The United States' import demand seems to have been particularly important for the export performance of the EEC, while for the EFTA countries shipments to western Europe appear to have accounted for most of the growth. It is worth noting that the large share of intra-regional flows in west European trade makes the region very dependent upon its own trade developments: the impact on west European exports of a 3-4 per cent rise in European imports from western Europe is equivalent to that of a 30 per cent increase in this region's exports to the United States.

In North America, export volumes increased steadily since the fourth quarter of 1983. This growth is partly accounted for by Canadian exports to the United States; but the volume of exports from the United States also rose by more than 6 per cent in the first three quarters of 1984. This is a remarkable increase given the sharp deterioration in the United States' competitive position entailed by the appreciation of the dollar (chart 5.1.3 in section 5.1.(i)). There are two reasons for this growth, however: first, most of it reflects exports to Canada and Japan (table 5.2.2), two markets where the United States' competitiveness is likely to have remained roughly unchanged, as the Canadian dollar and the Japanese yen did not depreciate significantly against the

---

[296] Western Europe includes all the European market economies, including those in southern Europe.

[297] References to trade developments of individual countries in western Europe and North America may also be found in chapters 2 and 3.

[298] See OECD, *Main Economic Indicators*, January 1985.

[299] See table 2.2.8 in section 2.2.

CHART 5.2.1.

Indices of trade volumes and unit values for western Europe and North America [a]

(1980=100)

Legend:

Import: ━━━━━   Export: ▪▪▪▪▪▪▪▪

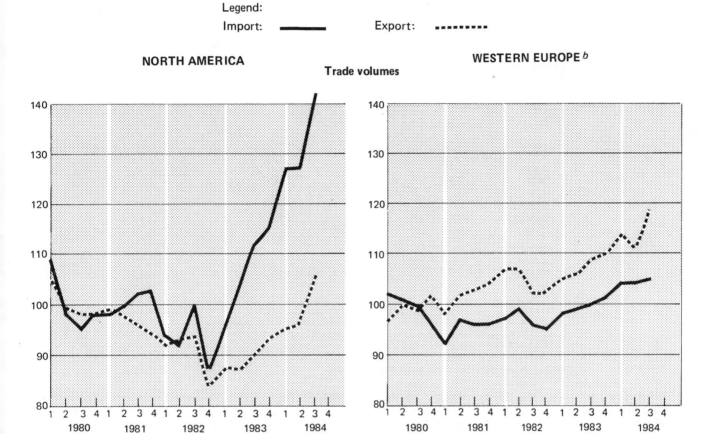

NORTH AMERICA   Trade volumes   WESTERN EUROPE [b]

Unit values

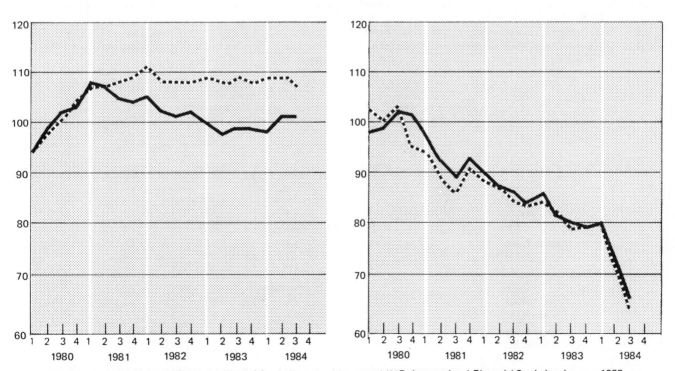

Source : United Nations, *Monthly Bulletin of Statistics,* several issues and IMF, *International Financial Statistics,* January 1985.

a Volume indices are seasonally adjusted.
b Excluding southern Europe.

TABLE 5.2.1

Trade volumes of western Europe and North America, 1982-1984
(*Percentage changes from previous year*)

	Exports			Imports		
	1982	1983	1984 (Jan.-Sept.)	1982	1983	1984 (Jan.-Sept.)
North America.	−7.7	−2.3	12.4	−7.7	12.1	28.2
of which:						
United States	−10.3	−6.9	6.2	−5.8	11.3	28.8
Western Europe	0.8	3.3	7.5	2.0	2.5	6.0
of which:						
EEC[a]	1.0	2.8	7.4	2.3	2.5	5.6
of which:						
Belgium-Luxembourg	2.0	3.9	5.8[b]	1.0	−3.1	3.3[b]
France	−2.9	3.0	5.0	3.1	−2.0	1.7
Germany, Fed. Rep. of	2.8	−	9.0	1.1	4.2	6.8
Italy	−0.9	5.7	6.9	3.4	1.1	8.1
Netherlands	−1.0	7.1	6.1	−	4.3	3.5
United Kingdom	3.0	−	7.4	4.2	8.0	8.4
EFTA	0.1	7.6	8.8	1.7	1.9	6.6
of which:						
Austria	1.0	4.7	9.0	−1.0	6.3	10.1
Finland	−2.9	4.0	11.3	1.1	3.2	2.1
Norway	−1.0	13.4	10.0	4.2	−4.0	14.4
Sweden	3.0	12.5	7.7	5.3	4.0	6.2
Switzerland	−2.9	−	7.2	−1.9	3.0	6.5

Source: United Nations, *Monthly Bulletin of Statistics*, December 1984 and January 1985; OECD, *Monthly Statistics of Foreign Trade*, Series A, January 1985 and national statistical publications.

[a] Including Greece.

[b] ECE secretariat estimate based on data for the first half of the year.

United States' dollar; secondly, an important part of United States' exports is made up of agricultural commodities and high technology manufactures—products for which demand is probably not very sensitive to price changes.

Export *prices* of western Europe continued to decline in dollar terms, due to the weakening of inflation rates in the region and to the depreciation of the European currencies *vis-à-vis* the United States' dollar (table 5.2.3 and chart 5.2.1). In the first three quarters of 1984, export prices declined more rapidly than the prices of imports—the latter reflected a small increase in primary commodity prices. Hence, the *terms of trade* of western Europe, which had improved slightly in 1982 and 1983, deteriorated in 1984. This applies to the EEC, while for the EFTA area the terms of trade deteriorated slightly in 1983 and improved in 1984.

Price developments were more favourable for the United States: a moderate rise in export prices, combined with falling import prices, entailed appreciable terms of trade gains in 1982-1983; the United States' terms of trade improved further in 1984, as a moderate rise in import prices was more than offset by the increase in the prices of exports.

TABLE 5.2.2

Changes in the value of trade of North America and western Europe:
contribution of the different areas, by origin and destination, 1984[a]
(*Percentage points*)

	Total percentage change	North America	West Europe	Japan	European CPEs	OPEC	Non-oil developing
	Exports: contribution by area of destination						
North America.	11.7	9.5	−0.1	1.3	0.2	−0.5	1.7
of which: United States.	7.8	5.1	−0.3	1.6	0.4	−0.9	1.9
Western Europe	3.4	2.8	2.1	0.1	−0.4	−1.1	−0.1
of which: EEC[b].	1.9	2.6	1.1	0.1	−0.4	−1.1	−0.4
EFTA	7.4	3.0	4.7	0.3	−0.5	−0.7	0.4
	Imports: contribution by area of origin						
North America.	31.5	8.3	6.5	7.0	0.1	2.9	6.6
of which: United States.	32.3	6.1	7.1	8.2	0.1	3.1	7.5
Western Europe	3.8	−	2.1	0.2	0.5	0.3	0.7
of which: EEC[b].	4.4	0.2	2.3	0.3	0.4	0.2	0.9
EFTA	2.7	−1.0	2.4	0.1	1.0	−0.3	0.5

Source: ECE secretariat estimates based on data published in United Nations, *Monthly Bulletin of Statistics*, December 1984.

[a] First half of the year.

[b] Including Greece.

TABLE 5.2.3

Unit trade values (in US dollars) and terms of trade of western Europe and North America, 1982-1984

(Percentage changes from the previous year)

	1982	1983	1984 (Jan.-Sept.)
Unit Export Values			
North America	0.1	—	−0.3
of which: United States	1.3	1.5	2.4
Western Europe	−4.4	−5.4	−5.8
of which: EEC[a]	−4.4	−5.2	−6.4
EFTA	−4.3	−6.9	−2.4
Unit Import Values			
North America	−1.1	−4.7	1.2
of which: United States	−1.0	−4.9	1.5
Western Europe	−6.8	−6.4	−4.6
of which: EEC[a]	−6.8	−6.4	−4.5
EFTA	−6.7	−6.3	−4.6
Terms of Trade			
North America	1.3	4.9	−1.5
of which: United States	2.3	6.7	0.8
Western Europe	2.5	1.1	−1.6
of which: EEC[a]	2.5	1.3	−2.1
EFTA	2.6	−0.7	2.2

Source: See table 5.2.1.

[a] Including Greece.

(b) *Balances on trade and current account*

As mentioned in section 5.1 above, the major change in the regional pattern of trade balances was the substantial increase in the deficit of the United States, despite the rise in its exports and favourable terms of trade developments. The United States' trade deficit is estimated to have reached $123 billion by the end of 1984, or slightly less than double the deficit in 1983 (chart 5.2.2). The increase in the trade deficit is a result of the high exchange value of the dollar, the rapid growth of the United States' economy and the weaker expansion of major trading partners, especially in Latin America. It has been estimated that each of these factors is responsible for one third of the deficit.[300] The current account balance deteriorated even more, from about $42 billion in 1983 to over $100 billion in 1984, as a result of a severe erosion in the traditional surplus on services and investment income. In 1984 net service receipts decreased, as did the receipts on direct investment income; on the other hand, interest payments on foreign investment in the United States rose strongly. In fact, the United States is experiencing a structural shift in its foreign investment position, from a large surplus to a rapidly growing burden of servicing the external debt.

No significant changes occurred in the trade and current account balances of Canada, which continued registering surpluses. The nearly $20 billion surplus on trade originates largely from the transactions with the United States.

There was a significant improvement in the trade and current account balances of many west European countries. The trade deficit of France was reduced to some $2 billion, while the deficit on the current account almost vanished. The trade and current account deficits of the south European countries were also considerably reduced (the current account of Spain moved into surplus) owing to a good export performance and, in some

---

[300] Morgan Guaranty Trust Company of New York, *World Financial Markets*, September 1984.

countries, to policies aiming to restrain imports. The trade surplus of the Federal Republic of Germany decreased by $4-5 billion in 1984, to some $18.5 billion. Almost half of this surplus originated in trade with the United States. The surplus on the current account is estimated to have been $6.5 billion, slightly larger than in 1983. In the United Kingdom there was a marked widening of the non-oil trade deficit; but an increased surplus in oil trade and in invisibles resulted in a virtually balanced current account. The smaller countries of north-west Europe registered increased trade and current account surpluses, partly owing to trade in oil and gas (Norway and the Netherlands).

(c) *Outlook for 1985*

In western Europe the growth of import volumes is expected to slow down slightly, to some 4-5 per cent (table 5.1.7 in section 5.1(i)). The rate is anticipated to be somewhat below average for France and above average for the Federal Republic of Germany. Despite the slowdown, the foreseen growth in west European imports will still constitute a significant stimulus to intra-regional trade. Exports from the west European countries will also benefit from the growth of imports into the United States. The latter is predicted to be considerably below the 1984 rate, but nevertheless somewhat above 8 per cent, reaching perhaps 10 per cent. The United States is likely to continue sharing in the trade dynamism of the Pacific area, but trade with Canada may slow down. Hence, the United States' exports will probably rise at a rate slightly slower than in 1984.

Changes in trade prices in dollar terms will very much depend on the exchange value of the United States currency. A further appreciation *vis-à-vis* the European currencies may entail another decline in the trade prices of western Europe, as the rate of inflation in the region is foreseen to decline to about 6 per cent. For both western Europe and North America export prices may rise faster than the prices of imports, as prices of manufactures are likely to increase by 5 to 6 per cent, while those of primary products and oil may stabilize or decline. Hence, there may be a terms of trade gain in both regions.

The current account deficit of the United States will probably widen: imports will grow faster than exports and the invisible balance will continue deteriorating.

The combined current account of the west European countries is expected to register a surplus of some $15 billion, or nearly as much as in 1984. France is expected to move into surplus; the current account surplus of the Federal Republic of Germany may improve slightly; the United Kingdom is forecast to remain with a balanced current account, and Italy may register a small deficit.

(ii) The structure of west European trade and the impact of United States' import demand

The impact on the European economies of the current recovery in the United States has not been as large as many expected. In fact, the "locomotive approach" of the late 1970s, and its most recent variants (e.g. the "differentiated approach")[301], assumed that growth in any of the major economic powers—the United States, Japan and the Federal Republic of Germany as the economic centre of the European Community—would induce growth in the economies of other countries. Recent trade developments suggest that it is not so simple, at least with respect to the effect of non-European "locomotives" on the European

---

[301] In the "differentiated approach", differences in the economic situation of the various countries are taken into account, with more impetus to growth being expected to come from those countries that are in a stronger economic position.

CHART 5.2.2.

Balances on trade and current account , 1981-1984
(Billions of US dollars)

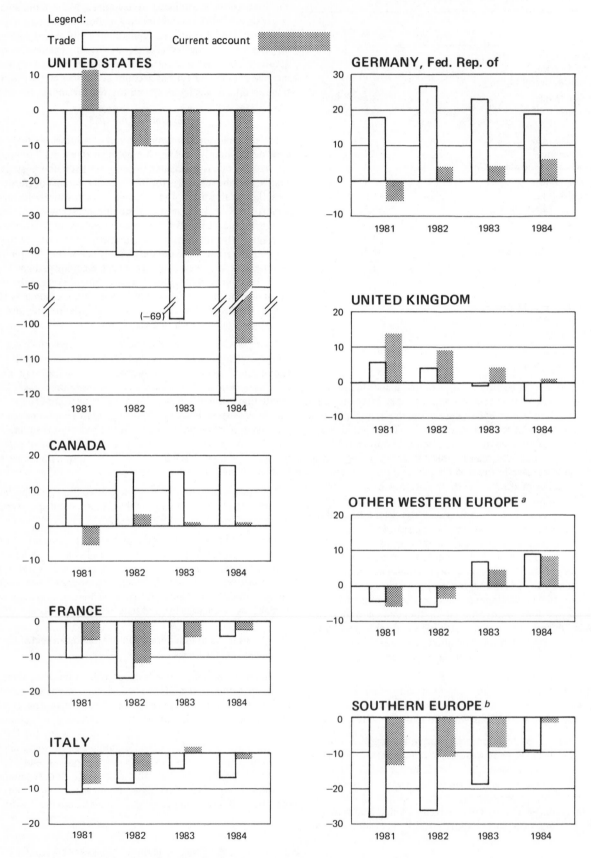

Legend:

Trade [ ]   Current account [▨]

UNITED STATES

GERMANY, Fed. Rep. of

UNITED KINGDOM

CANADA

OTHER WESTERN EUROPE [a]

FRANCE

ITALY

SOUTHERN EUROPE [b]

Source: OECD, *Economic Outlook* (36), December 1984 and national sources.

a Excluding southern Europe.
b Greece, Portugal, Spain, Turkey and Yugoslavia.

economies. The volume of United States' imports from western Europe rose by almost 40 per cent in 1984, but this increase only contributed about 2.8 percentage points to the growth in west European exports.[302] One reason for this is that Europe has become increasingly "sheltered" from external influences, as a result of a strengthening in intra-European trade, which entailed a weakening of trade relations with other regions, including North America.[303] The intensity of the trade relations between the European countries and North America declined steadily over the period 1965-1980, but there was an intensification of west European exports to the United States in 1980-1984. This recent change seems to be a reflection of the second oil shock, which apparently created increased opportunities for European shipments to that country.

This note intends to investigate these aspects of trade relations between western Europe and North America. First, these relations are viewed within the framework of the structural changes in west European trade with major economic regions. The second part focuses on the effect the product composition of the United States' imports had on trade with western Europe in 1980-1984.

(a) Structural changes in west European trade with major economic regions[304]

The structural trade links between countries and regions can be analysed by means of "trade intensity coefficients", which measure a given country or region's trade structure relative to the structure of world trade. For exporter i and market j, these coefficients may be defined as the share of market j in exports from i, normalized by the share of the same market in world exports. They can also be defined as the share of exporter i in imports into j, normalized by the share of the same exporter in world imports.[305] This ratio equals 1 whenever the share of market j in i's exports is the same as the share of that market in world exports (or the share of i in the market j equals i's share of world imports). A coefficient of less than (greater than) unity indicates a weaker (stronger) than average trade flow between i and j. Therefore, the "trade intensity coefficients" measure the relative strength of the trade links between two countries or country groups. These ratios are relatively stable: they reflect trade links deriving from geographical distances, historical ties, production patterns, and are less affected by changes in demand patterns and supply conditions than the market shares that are normally used to analyse trade relationships. Thus, changes in these structural coefficients may be expected to reflect, to a large extent, changes in the "economic distances" between trading partners, which are influenced by a number of factors, including trade policies.[306]

---

[302] See table 2.2.8 in section 2.2.

[303] The impact of the United States' recovery on the European economies was also offset by the negative effects of financial developments, which counteracted the positive effects arising from the trade revival. These aspects are discussed in chapter 2 above.

[304] For this section, the data sources and the basic approach are the same as used by the secretariat in a study on structural changes in North-South trade, published recently in *Economic Bulletin for Europe*, vol. 36, No. 4, Pergamon Press for the United Nations, December, 1984.

[305] The coefficient is calculated as:

$$d_{ij} = \frac{X_{ij}}{X_{i.}} \bigg/ \frac{X_{.j}}{X_{..}} \quad \text{or} \quad \frac{X_{ij}}{X_{.j}} \bigg/ \frac{X_{i.}}{X_{..}}$$

where, X_{ij} is exports from exporter i to market j; $X_{i.}$ is total exports from i; $X_{.j}$ is total imports into j and $X_{..}$ is total world trade value.

[306] For a more detailed discussion of the coefficients, see United Nations, Economic Commission for Europe, *Economic Bulletin for Europe*, vol. 24, No. 2, 1973, and vol. 36, No. 4, *op. cit.*, 1984.

"Trade intensity coefficients" for west European exports to and imports from major economic regions are shown in chart 5.2.3.[307] The coefficients indicate that the trade intensity is much higher for the relations between European countries than for trade between western Europe and other areas or country groups. Furthermore, intra-European trade strengthened steadily over the whole 1965-1984 period, while the intensity of trade between western Europe and other regions tended to weaken (the most significant exception to this declining trend is the rise in the intensity of west European imports from the centrally planned economies of Europe, which is likely to be due, for the most part, to trade in oil and gas).

The reinforcement of the trade relations between European countries reflects, to a certain extent, the trade creation and diversion effects of the free trade agreements established among the European countries in the 1960s and early 1970s. It may also be a consequence of the weakening of trade relations between Europe and the developing countries which followed the breaking of colonial ties. However, intra-European trade intensified significantly in 1980-1984 and this recent strengthening can hardly be explained by the above-mentioned factors, whose effects were likely dissipated by the early 1980s. It may, however, be partly the result of a shift in European oil imports from OPEC members to west European producers, although trade with other non-European partners, including exporters of manufactures, also weakened in these years.[308] This suggests that, in the early 1980s, other factors were at work, for example trade policies that discriminated against third partners.

The intensity of west European trade with North America tended to decline over the last two decades. West European imports from this region clearly weakened in 1965-1972: the intensity coefficient dropped from 0.68 to 0.55. In 1972-1982 the import intensity coefficient remained broadly unchanged (except for an increase in 1980), but in 1982-1984 it declined further. The intensity of west European exports to North America declined still more rapidly up to 1980: the coefficient fell from about 0.60 in the late 1960s to some 0.42 in the late 1970s. But in 1980-1984 there was a noticeable strengthening in exports from western Europe to North America.

This recent upturn was apparently caused by a change in the United States' sources of supply of oil and primary products in favour of west European countries. The impact of the product structure of the United States' import demand on the trade relations between that country and western Europe is analysed in the following section.

(b) The product mix of United States' imports in 1980-1984 and its impact on trade with western Europe

Since 1980, west European exports to North America, particularly to the United States, intensified noticeably. The sharp rise in the United States' imports from western Europe in 1983-1984 may explain part of this strengthening, but other factors were at work as well. In fact, the reinforcement of west European exports to the United States was already under way before the economic upturn; moreover, in those recovery years, the share of the United States in exports from western Europe rose more rapidly than that country's share in world exports (table 5.2.4).

---

[307] The coefficients refer to current trade values, because data for 1980-1984 were only available at current prices. In any case, as these coefficients stand for relative trade shares, they are not very sensitive to relative price changes.

[308] See *Economic Bulletin for Europe*, vol. 36, No. 4, *op. cit.*

CHART 5.2.3.

West European trade with major economic regions: trade intensity coefficients[a]

(1965 – 1984)

Western Europe
Less developed countries
European centrally planned economies
North America
Japan

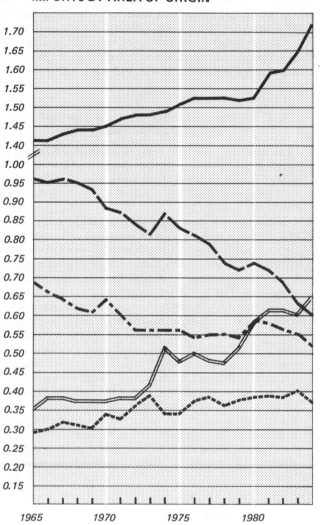

EXPORTS BY AREA OF DESTINATION

IMPORTS BY AREA OF ORIGIN

Source: ECE secretariat based on United Nations, Department of International Economic and Social Affairs, *Commodity Trade Matrix,* tape, New York, 1983 and United Nations, *Monthly Bulletin of Statistics,* December 1984.

a For exports, the coefficient is the share of a given market in exports of western Europe normalized by the share of the same market in world exports; for imports it is the share of a given exporter in west European imports, normalized by the share of that exporter in world imports.

Between 1980 and 1984, the share of the United States in west European exports rose from 5.5 per cent to nearly 9 per cent, after a steady decline in 1965-1980. This seems to have been the result of shifts in the sources of supply of the United States' imports, which apparently benefited some countries in western Europe.

Over the 1980-1984 period, the United States' imports of manufactures increased faster than total imports (table 5.2.5 and chart 5.2.4). This presumably favoured the west European coun-

tries, as manufactures account for more than 70 per cent of their exports to the United States (this proportion compares with 50 to 60 per cent in world exports to this country). Furthermore, engineering and consumer goods, which make up nearly 50 per cent of western Europe's exports to the United States, were the most rapidly growing product-groups in 1982-1984. It is noteworthy that exchange rate movements in this period clearly helped to raise the competitiveness of the west European countries *vis-à-vis* the United States and other competitors in that market (e.g.

CHART 5.2.4.

Growth in US imports by product group and area of origin, 1981 — 1984 [a]

(Percentage changes)

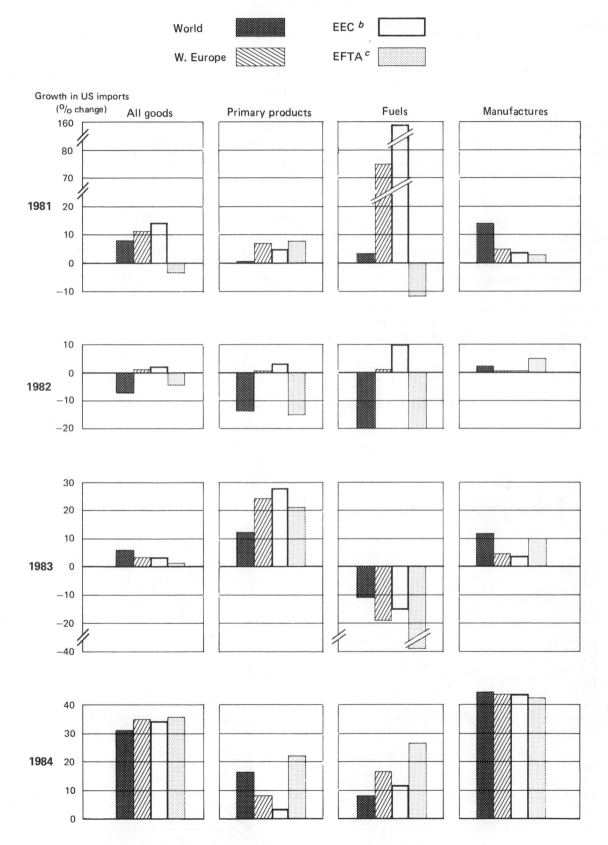

Source: United Nations, COMTRADE tape.
a 1984 January - September.
b Excluding Greece.
c Excluding Portugal.

Japan and Canada). However, it was trade in oil and primary products, not in manufactures, that strengthened west European exports to the United States.

TABLE 5.2.4

The share of the United States in world exports and in exports from western Europe, 1980-1984
(*Percentages*)

	1980	1981	1982	1983	1984[a]
World	12.2	13.1	12.5	14.0	15.8
Total western Europe . . .	5.5	6.6	6.8	7.6	8.7
of which:					
EEC	5.6	6.8	7.1	7.8	8.9
EFTA	4.9	5.5	5.6	6.6	8.1

Source: United Nations, *Monthly Bulletin of Statistics* (Special Table B), June and December 1984.

[a] January-June.

In 1981-1982 western Europe's exports of manufactured goods to the United States rose less than the United States' total imports of manufactures; but the region's exports of primary products and oil to the United States increased, while the country's total imports of these products declined. This applies only to the EEC area, as the changes in trade with the EFTA countries moved in the opposite direction: their manufactured exports to the United States rose faster than the country's total manufactured imports, while their exports of oil and primary commodi-

TABLE 5.2.5

Changes in United States' total imports by product groups, 1981-1984
(*Percentage change from previous year*)

	1981	1982	1983	1984[a]
Total	8	−7	6	31
Primary products.	−	−13	12	17
Fuels	3	−20	−11	8
Manufactures	14	2	12	44
of which:				
Semi-manufactures	20	7	1	41
Engineering goods	12	5	16	47
Consumer goods	14	5	15	42

Source: United Nations, COMTRADE tape.
[a] January-September.

ties tended to decline more rapidly than the United States' imports of these products (chart 5.2.4).

During the 1983-1984 recovery there was a change in the product mix of the United States' total import demand: in the beginning of the recovery, imports of primary products were growing faster than imports of manufactures; but in the last quarter of 1983, manufactures began to grow more rapidly (chart 5.2.5). Surprisingly, imports of primary commodities from western Europe grew even faster than the United States' total commodity imports. This higher growth originated in raw ma-

CHART 5.2.5.

Quarterly indices of US imports of primary commodities and manufactures, 1982 (IV) — 1984 (III)

1981, (I) = 100

Manufactures ――――――
Primary commodities ━ ▪ ━ ▪ ━ ▪ ▪

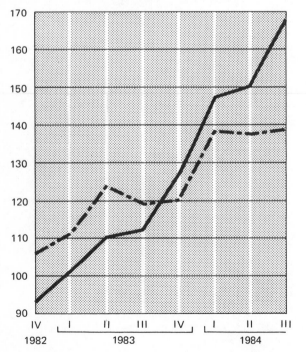

IMPORTS FROM THE WORLD

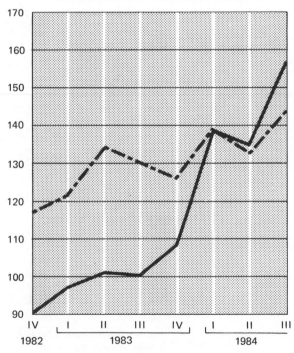

IMPORTS FROM WESTERN EUROPE

Source: United Nations, COMTRADE tape.

terials and non-ferrous metals, perhaps revealing a shift in the United States' sources of supply from the developing countries to European producers. In trade in manufactures, western Europe's exports rose at a slower pace than the United States' demand for these goods. As a whole, west European exports to the United States in 1983 rose less than this country's total imports. But in 1984 the increase in west European exports to the United States was again larger than the rise in this country's import demand, partly due to trade in oil: the United States' imports of oil from Europe increased more than its total oil imports. For the EFTA group it also reflected a faster growth in primary products (chart 5.2.4). Exports of manufactured goods from west European countries to the United States increased, in 1984, at the same high rate as the United States' total manufactured imports.

The developments described above entailed an increase in the share of western Europe in the United States' market, from 19.4 per cent in 1980 to 21.3 per cent in 1984 (table 5.2.6). This increase originated fully in a share gain of the EEC in the United States' market for primary products and oil. In the case of oil, most of the gain is accounted for by the United Kingdom and the Netherlands; in primary commodities, it was largely due to increased exports of non-ferrous metals from the United Kingdom. The share of the west European countries in the United States' market for manufactures actually declined over the 1980-1984 period, though it rose slightly in 1984 from the preceding year. This recent increase in the west European share of United States' manufactured imports stems from France's share gain in machinery and Italy's gain in chemicals and in textiles and clothing.

In short, the strengthening of west European exports to the United States in 1980-1984 seems to have been mainly the result of a shift in the United States' imports of oil, from the OPEC members to the European producers. There was also a strengthening in European exports of primary commodities. However,

TABLE 5.2.6

Share of western Europe in United States' imports, 1980-1984
(*Percentages*)

	1980	*1981*	*1982*	*1983*	*1984*[a]
All goods					
Total western Europe . . .	19.4	19.9	21.5	20.9	21.3
of which: EEC[b]	15.0	15.8	17.3	16.9	17.2
EFTA[c]	3.3	2.9	3.0	2.9	3.0
Priary commodities					
Total western Europe . . .	15.1	16.1	18.5	20.4	20.6
of which: EEC[b]	10.9	11.4	13.5	15.5	15.6
EFTA[c]	2.3	2.4	2.4	2.6	2.6
Fuels					
Total western Europe . . .	5.8	9.9	12.5	11.4	11.9
of which: EEC[b]	2.9	7.3	10.1	9.7	10.0
EFTA[c]	2.6	2.3	2.2	1.5	1.7
Manufactured goods					
Total western Europe . . .	29.0	26.6	26.1	24.3	24.8
of which: EEC[b]	24.1	22.0	21.4	19.8	20.3
EFTA[c]	3.7	3.3	3.4	3.3	3.4

Source: ECE secretariat, based on United Nations, COMTRADE tape.

[a] January-September.

[b] Excluding Greece.

[c] Excluding Portugal.

trade in manufactures, which represents nearly three quarters of western Europe's exports to the United States, did not intensify, not even in 1984 when the European countries could have benefited from the very fast growth in the United States' imports of engineering goods. Other countries exporting these goods, namely Japan and some countries in south-east Asia, seem to have profited most from that growth.

5.3 EASTERN EUROPE AND THE SOVIET UNION

Developments in the external sector of the European centrally planned economies in 1984 were broadly in continuation of those observed in the preceding year: trade volume of the region expanded at roughly the same rate in both years; export growth generally outpaced that of imports, both in volume and in value terms, and trade balances improved further.

These developments will be examined in some detail in this section. Changes in the overall volume of trade, in trade prices and the terms of trade, and in external balances in the last few years will be reviewed in succession. Thereafter, some aspects of changes in trade with the socialist countries will be examined separately.[309] A final part will be devoted to a discussion of trade policy stances and the near-term outlook. East-west trade will be dealt with in greater detail in section 5.4 below.

Throughout, the review will be conducted in terms of *volume* changes wherever feasible, even though this involves a substantial amount of estimation in the case of the data for the last year. Information on recent changes in trade *value* is shown for reference purposes in a table placed at the end of this section.[310]

(i) Growth in trade volume

The volume of imports into the European centrally planned economies grew by somewhat more than 4 per cent in 1984, only slightly faster than in 1983. Export volume growth, at over 5 per cent, was also much as in the preceding year (table 5.3.1). Import growth accelerated somewhat in eastern Europe and slowed in the Soviet Union while export expansion was approximately unchanged in both cases. This relative steadiness of pace contrasts with the world market pattern of a strong upswing in 1984 after a modest revival in the preceding year.

Underlying this steadiness of trade growth at the aggregate level were significant, partly offsetting, shifts in the regional structure of trade flows. At the same time, the focus on short-term similarities masks important differences in the macro-economic significance of these recent changes between eastern Europe and the Soviet Union, which should be noted.

An important feature among the regional shifts was a pronounced acceleration in the growth of Soviet exports to socialist countries—largely to the east European centrally planned economies, as can be seen from the fact that this was matched by a somewhat smaller rise in the volume of east European imports from socialist countries (table 5.3.2). This follows a period of several years during which the *volume* of these flows had been declining or stagnating even while their *value* was rising rapidly, in reflection of the endeavour of both the Soviet Union and its east European trade partners to adjust to the latters' deteriorating terms of trade. Since Soviet deliveries of fuels and raw materials constitute a very large part of this trade flow (some 50 per cent for fuels and energy, and another 11 per cent for minerals and metals in 1983), they are likely to have played an important role in this volume increase, and perhaps in the acceleration of output growth in eastern Europe noted elsewhere in this *Survey*. Though there was also a large rise in the volume of Soviet imports from socialist countries, this was not sufficient to prevent a deterioration in the balance of trade between the Soviet Union and eastern Europe.

The volume of Soviet exports to the market economies rose only sluggishly, reflecting an advance in exports to the developed market economies and a very sharp drop (13 per cent in value during the first three quarters) in those to the developing countries. Soviet imports from both groups of market economies stagnated. These developments, which represent a substantial break with the trends of the last few years, will be analyzed further below and in section 5.4 (east-west trade).

In the case of the east European countries jointly, the stepped up pace of imports from socialist countries was the only notable feature of change by comparison to the preceding year, but there were some significant differences in experience among the six countries. A substantial acceleration of export growth occurred in Romania, stemming entirely from a very large increase (estimated at over 20 per cent) in exports to the market economies, and imports into Romania also started to expand again after three years of contraction. Import growth accelerated also in Poland. In both countries, however, this reflects an only partial recovery from the very large import contractions they had had to undergo in the last few years to escape from severe payments crises.[311] In the remaining countries, variations in trade growth were smaller.

In Bulgaria, as in Romania, both export and import volume growth was largely carried by advances in the non-socialist markets. In Czechoslovakia, most of the strength came from trade with socialist partners. In the remaining countries, the contribution of the two markets to *export* growth was about evenly split, whereas *import* growth originated more pronouncedly from the socialist trade partners. Only in Hungary, however, was there a decline in the volume of imports from the market economies, in consequence of that country's external adjustment policy.

---

[309] For reasons of data availability for the last year in particular and for the estimation of volume and structural changes, the breakdown of *trade partners* used in the text and the tables of this section differs somewhat from that employed normally in UN statistics and especially in section 5.4 below (see table 5.3.9, note *a*). Importantly, following the practice of the national statistical sources of the European centrally planned economies, Yugoslavia is here included in the data on trade with "socialist countries". Trade with the "market economies" refers to trade with all developed and developing countries not included in the "socialist" trade aggregate.

[310] Table 5.3.9 (see also appendix tables C.4 and C.5, which provide information on trade levels, 1970-1984, in a somewhat different breakdown of trade partners). For the sake of comparability with other value data in this *Survey* and other international data sources, those shown here generally reflect values measured in US dollars even for trade flows largely conducted in other currencies (e.g., intra-CMEA trade). Consequently, value changes will differ—often substantially—from those shown in national sources. More significantly, owing to large differences between countries in exchange rate adjustments against the dollar and the rouble (and the resulting cross-rate variations), this procedure tends to reduce the cross-country comparability of value changes in rouble-area trade flows.

[311] The level of Polish import volume in 1984 was still some 18 per cent below that of 1980 (20 per cent below 1978, the prior peak). In Romania, import volume was by at least a quarter below the 1980 level.

TABLE 5.3.1

Eastern Europe and the Soviet Union: volume of foreign trade, by country, 1982-1984

(*Annual percentage change*)

	Exports			Imports		
	1982	*1983*	*1984*[a]	*1982*	*1983*	*1984*[a]
Bulgaria	11.3	4.4	7.0	3.2	5.2	3.0
Czechoslovakia	6.1	5.7	6.0	2.9	2.0	5.5
German Democratic Republic	5.4	10.6	4.0	0.4	5.3	6.0
Hungary	7.3	9.4	5.5	−0.1	3.9	1.0
Poland	8.7	10.3	9.0	−13.7	5.2	9.0
Romania	7.6	0.9	12.0	−22.8	−5.0	7.0
Eastern Europe	5.6	7.4	7.5	−4.6	3.4	5.5
Soviet Union	4.6	3.3	3.0	9.8	4.0	5.0
Eastern Europe and Soviet Union	5.1	5.7	5.2	2.2	3.7	5.2

Source: Appendix table B.15.

[a] Preliminary national data and secretariat estimates.

If apart from Romania eastern Europe did not share in the trade acceleration impulse emanating from the world market in 1984, this has to be seen against the fact that export growth—especially in trade with the market economies—had been notably strong already in 1982-1983 if compared to the prevailing current of shrinking or only weakly expanding world demand.

In fact, the determining force for the development of the east European countries' external trade in recent years had not been outside demand, but domestic policies shaped by the urgent need to effectuate an adjustment to a number of negative developments in the external sector.[312] These required a rapid turnround in the foreign balance, achieved through strong export promotion efforts as well as policies to hold down imports. The adjustment steps and their success have been analysed in earlier ECE publications.[313] What is to be retained here—to provide a perspective to this summary of short-term changes in trade volume—is the fact that whereas the real exports of the east Eu-

ropean group had in 1984 exceeded the 1980 level by some 22 per cent, real imports, in spite of the recent expansion, were still some 3 per cent below the 1980 level.

(ii) Price changes and terms of trade

Price movements in external trade continued to be detrimental for the east European countries in 1984, though to a lesser degree than in the preceding few years. The Soviet Union probably experienced another terms-of-trade gain on its overall trade, but this too is likely to have been smaller than in the past.

The trade price experience of the centrally planned economies constitutes a mixture of two price regimes frequently moving in opposite directions: the CMEA price system and current world market prices. Price determination in the intra-CMEA market, which variously affects some 45-70 per cent of the trade transactions of individual centrally planned economies (much less in the case of Romania), has been based for the last decade on a formula of gradually absorbing past changes in world market prices in the guise of five-year averages moved forward annually.[314] In 1984, energy prices under this system were still advancing at about twice the rate of the average price of most

[312] These included deteriorating terms of trade in the convertible-currency and the rouble markets, stemming to a large part from the shifts in world market prices of the 1970s, but also from unfavourable production structures and low success rates in adjusting export offer to market requirements. Sudden action was required in all countries of the group when the balance-of-payments squeeze of 1981-1982 was super-imposed on these long-term conditions.

[313] See *Economic Bulletin for Europe*, vol. 36, No. 4, *op. cit.*, chapter 1.4, and *Economic Survey of Europe in 1982*, chapter 4.3.

[314] Proposals for changes in this price formation system have been under discussion for some time. However, agreement on a new approach appears to have been difficult to reach. Early in January 1985, it was decided at the 113th meeting of the CMEA Executive Committee to maintain the system in its present form for the 1986-1990 plan period (*Pravda*, 18 January 1985).

TABLE 5.3.2

Eastern Europe and the Soviet Union: volume of foreign trade by direction, 1982-1984

(*Annual percentage change*)

	Exports			Imports		
	1982	*1983*	*1984*	*1982*	*1983*	*1984*
Eastern Europe, to or from:						
World	6	7	8	−5	3	5
Socialist economies	6	6	6	−2	3	6
Market economies	6	10	10	−13	6	6
Soviet Union, to or from:						
World	5	3	3	7	4	5
Socialist economies	−3	1	6	7	3	10
Market economies	18	7	1	6	5	1

Source and country groups: As for table 5.3.8.

TABLE 5.3.3
Eastern Europe and the Soviet Union: unit values and terms of trade
(*Annual percentage change*)

	Rouble trade[a]				Convertible currency trade[b]			
	1981	1982	1983	1984	1981	1982	1983	1984
Eastern Europe								
Export unit values	8	6	5	4	−2	−6	−7	−5
Import unit values	13	10	7	5	−3	−4	−7	−4
Terms of trade	−4	−3	−2	−1	1	−3	−	−1
Soviet Union								
Export unit values	17	12	10	7	−1	−6	−5	−4
Import unit values	8	8	6	4	1	−8	−5	−5
Terms of trade	9	5	4	2	−3	2	1	1

Source: table 5.3.8.

[a] Unit value change measured in rouble terms.

[b] Unit value change measured in US dollar terms.

other goods (over 9 per cent in rouble terms), with the result of a further shift of intra-CMEA terms of trade in favour of the Soviet Union (table 5.3.3). As this movement was somewhat smaller than expected,[315] the absorption of the 1979-1980 fuel price shock into the CMEA price system may now almost have been completed. However, residual effects remain to affect the 1985 price structure.[316]

Estimations of the centrally planned economies' price experience in trade with the market economies are rather less firm, especially as concerns the Soviet Union. East European export unit values suffered, as in 1983, from an unfavourable commodity structure of exports to the market economies—especially of the increment in exports, which for most countries indicates a strong concentration of export growth in commodity groups with a relatively weak price performance in 1984.[317] In the case of Soviet trade with the market economies, the estimate of a slight gain in the terms of trade hinges very much on the relative behaviour of the prices of fuel and energy exports and foodstuff imports.[318]

In eastern Europe, all countries but Czechoslovakia and the German Democratic Republic showed gains in the overall balance, and Bulgaria, the only country of the region still in overall deficit in 1983, attained a small surplus in its trade flows. The combined trade balance of the east European countries with the *market economies* improved by over $1 billion in 1984, following the massive gain of almost $5 billion in 1982 and a $1 billion rise in 1983. As in the preceding year, the rise in the surplus is based entirely on trade with the developed market economies, as the surplus with the developing countries declined again. As to country positions, only the substantial trade surplus of the German Democratic Republic in the convertible currency sphere appears to have eroded slightly. Hungary, which was the only country remaining in deficit with the market economies in 1983, swung into surplus for the first time.[319] The adjustments in individual country positions all were in the $100-$200 million range except for that of Romania, which accounted for two thirds of the combined $1 billion rise in the east European surplus.[320]

(iii) Trade balances

Further gains in the overall trade surplus were registered in 1984 by the east European countries in the aggregate while the Soviet Union maintained its large surplus (table 5.3.4; see also table 5.3.9 for country data).

[315] A 12-13 per cent increase had been predicted in last year's *Survey* (*op. cit.*, p. 220), based on past movements of world market oil prices.

[316] Hungarian planners reckon with a 2 per cent rise in their export prices and a 3-4 per cent rise in import prices in rouble area trade (*Tervgazdasàgi Ertesitö*, 29 December 1984), which might point to a 4-5 per cent rise in fuel prices.

[317] The dollar prices of minerals, ores and metals declined by 6 per cent and those of fuels by 5 per cent (table 5.1.2); this commodity group provided 56 per cent of the increment in Czechoslovak exports to market economies. In Poland, fuels—mainly coal—supplied 26 per cent of the increment in export value; the prices of coking and steam coal imports into the OECD area, where most of Polish coal exports go, appear to have suffered particularly steep erosion in 1984—by some 15-18 per cent in the first half of the year (IEA, *Energy Prices and Taxes*, third quarter 1984). Agricultural product prices significant in east European exports to market economies also seem to have declined at above average rates (United Nations, *Monthly Bulletin of Statistics*, December 1984, table 59). Hungary reports an 11 per cent price drop in dollar terms in its foodstuff exports to the non-rouble trading area for the first three quarters of 1984 (*Statisztikai Havi Közlemények*, 1984, No. 10, p. 95). Items in this class provided 15 per cent of the Czechoslovak, 33 per cent of the Hungarian and 18 per cent of the Polish export increment in non-socialist or non-rouble trade.

[318] The unit value of Soviet crude oil exports to the OECD area (an average of contract and spot market prices) appears to have declined rather less in 1984 than the unit value of overall OECD crude imports, mainly because Soviet price reductions in the first quarter of 1983 preceded those of other oil suppliers: for the first three quarters the price drop is just over 1 per cent, as against almost 4 per cent for total OECD crude imports (IEA, *op. cit.*, third quarter 1984). Price cuts on oil products and natural gas may have been much larger, but given the relative weights of these commodities in total Soviet energy exports, the total unit value decline is likely to have been 3 per cent or less. Since energy exports appear to provide the bulk of the Soviet export increment, this component is also decisive for the overall price change in exports to the market economies. On the import side, foodstuff imports appear to be the determining factor (26 per cent of non-socialist imports in 1983, and with a much larger share in import growth in 1984), with grains as a major component. International grain prices appear to have declined some 5 per cent in the first three quarters of 1984 (United Nations, *Monthly Bulletin of Statistics*, loc. cit.).

[319] Hungary, however, has since 1982 registered surpluses in its total convertible-currency trade, based entirely on its convertible-currency transactions with other CMEA countries (mainly the Soviet Union). As against the $160 million surplus with the market economies, this total convertible-currency surplus reached $600 million in 1984.

[320] It should be noted that the data on 1984 regional trade flows and balances for Romania (as are those for the German Democratic Republic) are ECE secretariat estimates based on a national data for the totals and rates of change in trade flows reported by CMEA and OECD partner countries. Estimates of changes in trade with developing economies and of trade balances by direction for these two countries, as residual positions, are thus less certain than those for countries where either full-year data are available or within-year reporting of trade is the practice.

TABLE 5.3.4

Eastern Europe and the Soviet Union: trade balances, 1981-1984
(Billions of US dollars)

	1981	1982	1983	Jan.-Sept. 1983	Jan.-Sept. 1984	1984[a]
Eastern Europe with:						
World	−2.7	4.4	6.0	4.3	5.0	6.8
Socialist countries	−3.1	−0.8	−0.2	−0.4	−0.4	−0.6
Developed market economies	−2.9	1.3	3.2	2.6	3.6	4.8
Developing countries	3.4	3.9	3.0	2.0	1.8	2.6
Soviet Union with:						
World	6.2	9.3	11.2	6.7	7.8	11.2
Socialist countries	6.2	4.6	5.4	3.2	3.4	4.8
Developed market economies	−1.2	−0.1	1.3	−0.4	2.2	2.1
Developing countries	1.2	4.8	4.5	2.9	2.2	4.3

Source and country groups: As for table 5.3.9.

[a] Preliminary estimates.

As already noted, the external adjustment gains of the east European countries with the market economies were partially offset by a widening of the deficit with other socialist countries, mainly in trade with the Soviet Union (table 5.3.9).

The trade surplus of the Soviet Union remained unchanged, a widening of the surplus with the developed market economies being offset by a reduction in the surplus positions with the other country groups.

(iv) Trade among socialist countries

A substantial upswing in the volume of east European and Soviet trade with other socialist economies has already been noted above. In the following section, the regional composition of the change in 1984 will be briefly reviewed. Then the question will be asked, on the basis of data for a longer term period, whether there is any sign of a turning away of the CMEA countries from the world market.

(a) *Trade rise in 1984*

The data on recent changes in trade value in dollar terms shown in table 5.3.9 suggest a severe deceleration between 1983 and 1984 in the growth of intra-socialist exchanges, especially in the case of the east European countries, but also in that of the Soviet Union. Thus, to give only two examples, value growth in east European exports to socialist countries is shown to fall from 7 per cent in 1983 to about 1 per cent in 1984 (while exports to developed market economies are shown to rise at 6 and 8 per

cent, respectively); in the case of the Soviet exports to socialist economies, value growth declines from 8 to 3 per cent over the same two years (exports to the developed market economies rising at a constant 2 per cent in both years). To illustrate the distortions—warned against in an earlier footnote—which can arise from the conversion procedure, the same data are shown as growth rates in rouble terms in table 5.3.5 below to serve at the same time—together with the further breakdown into subregions among the socialist countries—as a benchmark for the observations to follow.

Table 5.3.5 shows that *in rouble terms* the value of trade among the socialist countries, especially within the European CMEA region, expanded at a relatively constant rate. As noted earlier, price rises in rouble trade have slowed significantly between the two years, especially for those flows dominated by fuels and raw materials (Soviet exports/east European imports in the intra-area exchanges). In trade *among* the east European countries, they probably came down from some 5 per cent in 1983 to some 4 per cent in 1984; since trade value rose at an unchanged pace, volume growth will have edged up another point from some 5 to 6 per cent, thus continuing the advance in trade among the smaller centrally planned economies first observed in 1983 after some five years of stagnant or declining trade. In trade between the east European countries and the Soviet Union, the rate of advance of east European export prices probably dropped from some 5-6 to some 4 per cent and that of import prices from some 11 to some 7 per cent; on the basis of the rouble values shown this yields a rate of growth of east European export volume of some

TABLE 5.3.5

Eastern Europe and Soviet Union: value growth of trade with socialist countries, in rouble terms
(Annual percentage change)

	Eastern Europe				Soviet Union			
	Exports		Imports		Exports		Imports	
Destination or origin	1983	1984	1983	1984	1983	1984	1983	1984
Socialist countries . .	11.3	11.4	10.4	11.7	10.5	12.8	9.3	12.4
Eastern Europe. . .	10.4	10.8	10.9	10.5	10.9	12.5	13.2	10.5
Soviet Union . . .	13.3	10.1	10.3	11.8	. .	. .	. .	. .
Other	1.9	23.3	9.1	16.1	9.2	13.8	−5.1	20.1

Source: As for table 5.3.9. Growth rates for 1984 refer to January-September, relative to the same period of 1983.

CHART 5.3.1.

Eastern Europe and Soviet Union: regional structure of trade at current and 1975 prices.

(Percentage shares, five - year averages)

Legend: Market economies  Socialist economies

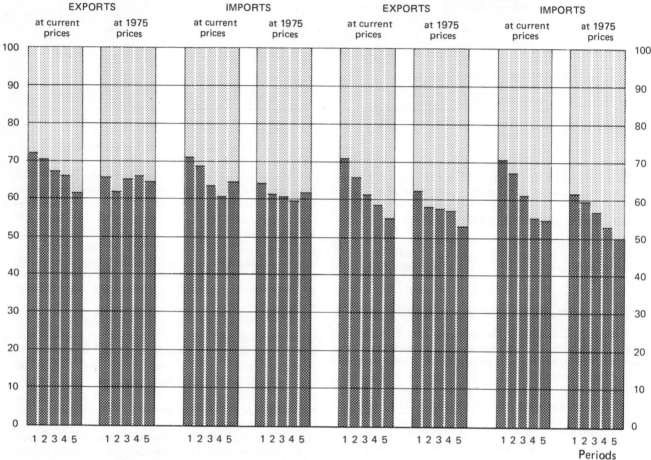

Source: National statistics (shares at current prices) and ECE secretariat estimates (shares at 1975 prices).
For definition of partner country groups, see note to chapter 5.3.
Period codes: 1:1960–1964 , 2:1965–1969, 3:1970–1974, 4:1975–1979, 5:1980–1984.

6-7 per cent for both years, while east European imports from the Soviet Union are likely to have increased by about 5 per cent in 1984, the first such rise in a number of years.

A significant advance was registered in 1984 in trade with "other" socialist countries, including the Asian CMEA countries, Cuba, Yugoslavia and China. In Soviet foreign trade, the last three account for 20 to 30 per cent of the rise in the value of socialist trade, with especially rapid growth in trade with China. Yugoslavia and China are also of growing importance in the foreign trade of a number of east European countries.[321]

(b) *Is CMEA turning inward?*

A number of developments in international economic relations have given rise to a feeling that a pronounced reversal was

under way in the trends of the past 20 years towards rising interdependence between centrally planned and market economies. The east-west political tensions and western trade sanctions of the last few years contributed to this, as did the discussions of policies for enhanced regional plan and production co-ordination at various CMEA gatherings, which at times included calls for increased regional self-reliance in certain spheres of production.[322] Indeed, on the basis of short-term movements in the trade shares of individual countries, which in some cases have been quite large,[323] some observers have concluded that a significant "inward turn" in the trade relations of the CMEA region has already taken place.

---

[321] However, as trade with these countries is usually conducted in convertible or clearing dollars, or Swiss francs, at world market prices, the derivation of volume change estimates at rouble prices would be inappropriate for this trade component.

[322] An additional element has been the tendency in several socialist countries to state annual plan targets for intra-regional trade in terms of shares in total trade which invariably appear to imply a rise in this share. However, the comparison base used is usually not well defined, and in the actual outcome trade shares at current prices are often quite stable.

[323] Especially for Poland, where the share of socialist countries in total imports rose from 56 per cent in 1980 to 65 per cent in 1981 in consequence of the sharp drop in imports from the market economies during the country's balance-of-payments crisis.

TABLE 5.3.6

Eastern Europe and the Soviet Union: share of trade with socialist countries in total trade, 1975-1984
(*Percentage*)

| | Eastern Europe | | | | Soviet Union | | | |
| | Exports | | Imports | | Exports | | Imports | |
Year	Current prices	1975 prices	Current prices	1975 prices	Current prices	1975 prices	Current prices	1975 prices
1975	67	67	60	60	61	61	52	52
1980	62	66	59	60	54	58	53	51
1981	61	65	63	62	55	58	51	48
1982	62	65	66	65	54	53	55	50
1983	63	64	68	64	56	51	57	50
1984	62	63	68	63	57	52	60	50

Source: National statistics for current price data; ECE secretariat estimates for shares at 1975 prices (see note to table 5.3.8).

A brief review of changes in the intra-group concentration of trade may therefore be useful. For the reasons noted above, data on the share of east European and Soviet trade with all socialist countries—including non-CMEA trade partners—are used as a stand-in for a more precise measure. Recent changes in this share are shown in table 5.3.6, and trends in five-year averages for the period 1960-1984 are presented in chart 5.3.1.

At this aggregate level of analysis in terms of trade shares, there does not appear any evidence for an inward re-orientation of east European and Soviet trade. In the case of eastern Europe, the share of socialist countries in total *exports* has been stable in nominal terms over the past five years and slowly declining in real terms, whereas in the case of the Soviet Union a rising share of socialist exports in nominal terms was accompanied by an even more rapid decline in the real share. These relations between nominal and real shares are consistent both with the relative movements of east European and Soviet export prices in intra-CMEA trade noted earlier, and with the above-average rate of growth of the volume of exports to the market economies.

The share of *imports* into the east European economies from socialist countries has indeed shown a pronounced rise in nominal terms over the past five years, and a more narrow one also in real terms. This rise, however, is rather the outfall—the passive reflection, as it were—of the absolute cutback in imports from the market economies required to meet the payments squeeze of 1981-1982. As noted earlier, the necessary balance-of-payments adjustment having been achieved, the volume of these imports appears to be rising again at least in pace with those from the socialist countries. In the case of the Soviet Union, the recent rise in the nominal share of socialist imports reflects entirely the lagged intra-CMEA price adjustment, the real share remaining essentially unchanged (the rise in the 1984 figure can be ignored, as it reflects very incomplete data).

(v) Outlook for 1985

Improvement of the external balance remains an important priority in the national economic plans for 1985 of most east European centrally planned economies. In their relationship with the market economies, a build-down of the external debt position continues to figure explicitly in the plan targets of several countries,[324] and is probably the intention of others. Debt

service requirements, though now somewhat eased (see section 5.4 below), still impose a substantial toll on the convertible-currency earnings even of those countries whose external debt has been rescheduled, thus necessitating continued large trade surpluses. In the relationship within the CMEA market, the reduction of the trade deficits with the Soviet Union remains on the agenda. As noted above, a further small deterioration in the east European countries' terms of trade with the Soviet Union is expected, which will add to the real cost of this adjustment.

At the same time, however, the constraints imposed by external balance considerations appear to have eased somewhat by comparison to the last few years. Thus, though the plans for 1985 continue in most countries to be fairly restrictive on domestic absorption (growth of NMP-utilized or its components), the gap between the planned growth of output and that of absorption appears to have lessened. While the national plans for 1984 in a number of cases called for or implied a substantial widening of trade surpluses, those for 1985 appear generally much less stringent.[325]

To move from these general observations to a more precise appreciation of foreign trade policy stances is difficult, however. While the annual economic plans of the centrally planned economies comprise a fully elaborated external sector, very little information is normally available on this component.[326] The published plan targets (table 5.3.7), relating to "turnover" (exports plus imports) which may be in value or in volume terms, frequently do not even permit an inference about the expected direction of change. Hence any attempt to gauge the foreign trade intentions of policy makers in the European centrally planned economies and the short-term outlook for foreign trade in this sector of the world market must rely on rather indirect evidence and remain somewhat speculative.

The bulk of the European centrally planned economies' trade is transacted in the European *intra-CMEA market* where volume growth—at some 6 per cent—has been unusually high in 1984. A somewhat lower rate of growth is likely in 1985. Annual protocols to the medium-term trade agreements between the CMEA member countries, which were negotiated in the last weeks of 1984 and determine minimum trade levels for 1985, point to an increase in trade value (in rouble terms) of some 7-8 per cent for

---

[324] Notably in Czechoslovakia, Hungary and Romania. In Czechoslovakia, continued retirement of foreign debt is to result in "full equilibrium" in the convertible currency position of the state by the end of 1985 in the sense that the country's convertible-currency liabilities will be balanced by convertible-currency claims on foreign countries (presumably including long-term claims on developing countries).

[325] See *Economic Survey of Europe in 1983*, p. 226, for 1984 targets. Though convertible-currency surplus targets of Hungary and Poland were not achieved, both countries registered increases in this surplus by $60-70 million. Targets for 1985 are at approximately the 1984 level (Poland) or a little above (Hungary).

[326] Trade targets by main direction, as well as targets for the relevant trade balances, are available only for Hungary and Poland.

TABLE 5.3.7

Eastern Europe and the Soviet Union: foreign trade, planned and actual, 1984-1985
(Annual percentage change)

| | Plan 1984 | | | Actual 1984 | | | | | | Plan 1985 | | |
| | | | | Value | | Volume | | | | | | |
	Turnover	Exports	Imports	Exports	Imports	Exports	Imports			Turnover	Exports	Imports
Bulgaria	8.1	..	..	9.0*	8.0*	6.5	3.0			4.5	..	..
Czechoslovakia	..	7.8*	9.1*	10.0	10.4	6.0	5.5			..	..	..
German Democratic Republic. . .	5.0	..	..	6.6*	9.5*	4.0	6.0			8.0	..	..
Hungary	..	5-6	—	10.7	7.0	5.5	1.0			..	5-6	2-3
Poland	..	12.3	14.8	25.8	24.8	9.0	9.0			..	7	7-8
Romania	13.8	..	..	31.6	23.3	12.0	7.0			15.0	..	..
Soviet Union	..	..	..	9.6	9.6	3.0	5.0			..	..	..

Source: Plan targets from national plan documents, explanatory speeches and other official announcements; 1984 *volumes* as for table 5.3.8, *values* as for table 5.3.9.

Note: Value changes are measured in terms of national currencies.

trade between the east European countries and the Soviet Union, and a slightly higher rise in the value of trade among the east European countries. Given an expected 3-4 per cent rise in rouble prices (somewhat higher in the case of Soviet exports), this indicates volume growth of some 4-5 per cent.[327]

---

[327] Based on data for five of the six possible bilateral agreements in the case of east European trade with the Soviet Union, and from 7 out of 15 possible bilateral agreements in intra-trade of the east European countries. Though the protocols define only minimum levels of trade, these rates of change—usually expressed relative to the previous protocol—have in the past proven fairly good predictors of the actual change in trade value.

Developments in the world market will largely determine the outlook for the trade of the European centrally planned economies with the *market economies*. Given the geographical structure of their exports, the evolution of economic activity and import demand in western Europe will be of special significance for the east European centrally planned economies. In the case of the Soviet Union, as well as Poland and Romania among the east European countries, the future course of world energy prices will also be an important determinant of export earnings. Finally, the import capacity of the developing countries is significant for some east European countries—notably Bulgaria and Romania.

TABLE 5.3.8

Eastern Europe and the Soviet Union: change in foreign trade value, volume, unit values and terms of trade, by major partner regions, 1981-1984
(Annual percentage change)

	Exports				Imports			
	1981	1982	1983	1984	1981	1982	1983	1984
	Eastern Europe							
Total trade								
Value[a]	0.5	4.0	5.0	2.8	−3.1	−4.1	3.2	1.9
Volume	1	6	7	8	−6	−5	3	5
Unit values[a]	−1	−2	−2	−4	3	—	—	−3
Terms of trade	−4	−2	−2	−1	..	..	..	..
of which:								
Trade with socialist countries								
Value[b]	8.2	12.3	11.3	9.9	11.1	7.8	10.4	10.6
Volume	—	6	6	6	−2	−2	3	6
Unit values[b]	8	6	5	4	13	10	7	5
Terms of trade	−4	−3	−2	−1	..	..	..	..
Trade with developed and developing market economies								
Value[a]	0.1	−0.5	1.9	5.1	−13.4	−16.2	−1.7	1.5
Volume	2	6	10	10	−11	−13	6	6
Unit values[a]	−2	−6	−7	−5	−3	−4	−7	−4
Terms of trade	1	−3	—	−1	..	..	..	..

TABLE 5.3.8 (*continued*)

	Exports				Imports			
	1981	1982	1983	1984	1981	1982	1983	1984
				Soviet Union				
Total trade								
Value[a]	3.8	9.6	5.1	−0.2	6.8	6.2	3.3	−0.2
Volume	−	5	3	3	8	7	4	5
Unit values[a]	3	5	3	−3	−1	−1	−1	−5
Terms of trade	5	4	2	2	..	..	..	..
of which:								
Trade with socialist countries								
Value[b]	15.9	9.4	10.5	12.6	13.1	15.2	9.3	12.3
Volume	−1	−3	1	6	5	7	3	8
Unit values[b]	17	12	10	7	8	8	6	4
Terms of trade	9	5	4	2	..	..	..	..
Trade with developed and developing market economies								
Value[a]	2.8	10.9	1.6	−3.6	12.2	−2.1	−1.1	−3.4
Volume	4	18	7	1	11	6	5	1
Unit values[a]	−1	−6	−5	−4	1	−8	−5	−5
Terms of trade	−3	2	1	1	..	..	..	..

Source: As for table 5.3.9.

Note: Value and unit value changes for total trade and for trade with the market economies are expressed in terms of US dollars, whereas value and unit value changes in trade with socialist countries reflect value measures in transferable roubles. All *unit value* and *terms-of-trade* indices were derived from the value and volume figures. Apparent inconsistencies between the four indicators for any given year reflect separate rounding after calculation from unrounded numbers. All figures for 1984 are secretariat estimates.

Eastern Europe: Volume indices for *total trade* from national statistical sources have been aggregated with weights reflecting the individual countries' shares in the total trade of the region in 1975, measured in US dollars. Volume indices for *trade with socialist countries* and *with market economies* were obtained by deflating national data (supplemented by secretariat estimates) on the value of trade in the two markets in five major commodity groups by means of Hungarian, Polish and UN price indices. This exercise was conducted in terms of transferable roubles for trade with socialist countries and in US dollars for trade with market economies; deflated commodity group data were aggregated for each country and for eastern Europe in terms of their value in 1975 transferable roubles or US dollars, respectively.

Soviet Union: Volume indices of *total trade, trade with socialist countries* and *trade with market economies* for 1981 from USSR Ministry of Foreign Trade, *Vneshniaia torgovlia SSSR 1922-1981*, Moscow, 1982. Separate indices for developed and developing market economies have been aggregated in terms of the value of these flows at 1975 US dollars in order to obtain the index for all market economies. Volume indices for 1982-1984 are secretariat estimates obtained on the procedure outlined above.

[a] In terms of US dollars.

[b] In terms of transferable roubles.

As was noted in section 5.1, current expectations are for some slowing in the import growth of developed market economies, which should nonetheless remain substantial, and some rise in the import capacity of developing countries. The outlook for fuel prices remains rather dismal from the exporters' point of view. The implications of this for east-west trade will be discussed in more detail below (section 5.4). While it is not possible to quantify the impact of these factors on the volume growth of the centrally planned economies' exports to the convertible currency markets, it seems that on balance they would tend to exert downward pressure on the high growth rates of the last two years. This clearly has planners in the east European countries worried, the more so as much of this growth reflected one-time recovery factors[328] and/or the export of raw materials and low-technology products.[329]

Unless the terms of trade in transactions with the market economies were to turn very decisively against eastern Europe, however, it would seem that even with reduced export volume growth they should be able to maintain the 1984 pace of import volume expansion without endangering their external balance targets. This also appears to be the feeling of planners, who in a number of countries have scheduled resumed growth of investment goods imports for 1985.[330]

No data at all are available on the import intentions of the Soviet Union. Given the country's large trade and current account surpluses of 1984 (section 5.4 below), balance-of-payments considerations are not likely to have much bearing on import decisions in 1985. Import volume from the market economies will be boosted by a rise in foodstuff imports following the poor grain harvest of 1984, much of which western market reports show already to be in the pipeline.

[328] E.g., Romania's resumption of large-scale petroleum products and steel exports, or Poland's regaining of its old coal markets. Polish coal production and exports, in particular, are now back at capacity level, leaving little room for further expansion.

[329] In Czechoslovakia, for instance, State Planning Committee chairman S. Potáč anticipated little growth in 1985 trade with market economies, partly for external reasons, but "to a significant degree also owing to the low adaptation of output and the organization of foreign trade to the changing requirements of demanding markets" and called for "a reduction of the reliance on fuel and raw material exports" in favour of strengthening the exports of processing branches, especially engineering (*Rudé právo*, 6 December 1984).

[330] A 14 per cent increase in machinery and equipment imports from the non-socialist countries is planned in Czechoslovakia (*Rudé právo*, 6 December 1984). For additional convertible-currency investment imports for projects with a short gestation period, the national bank makes available from a revolving-loan account convertible-currency credits which have to be repaid within three years (*Hospodárské noviny*, 1985, No. 3). With a planned increase of 5 per cent in non-rouble imports, Hungary expects machinery imports in non-rouble transactions to rise by 20-25 per cent in 1985 (*Tervgazdasàgi Ertesitö*, 29 December 1984).

TABLE 5.3.9

Eastern Europe and the Soviet Union: changes in foreign trade value and trade balances by partner region, 1982-1984

(*Growth rates in percentage; trade balances in billion US dollars*)

| | Growth rates | | | | | | Trade balance, in billion US dollars | | |
| | Exports | | | Imports | | | | | |
Country and trade partner group[a]	1982	1983	1984[b]	1982	1983	1984[b]	1982	1983	1984[b]
Bulgaria									
World	7.0	6.1	5.8	6.8	6.5	3.1	−0.1	−0.1	0.2
Socialist countries	10.6	13.5	4.6	9.4	10.0	3.3	−0.7	−0.5	−0.4
Developed market economies	−9.6	−2.5	−8.1	−11.0	−10.8	1.5	−0.6	−0.4	−0.6
Developing countries	5.3	−19.1	23.9	41.6	8.6	4.9	1.3	0.8	1.2
Czechoslovakia									
World	4.9	5.5	4.2	5.4	5.9	4.6	0.2	0.1	−
Socialist countries	8.9	6.6	6.2	10.9	9.4	6.5	−0.3	−0.6	−0.7
Developed market economies	−4.9	−2.4	2.5*	−9.8	−6.5	−6.8*	−0.1	−	0.2*
Developing countries	−4.9	12.9	−9.0*	−8.0	−1.3	14.4*	0.6	0.8	0.6*
German Democratic Republic									
World	9.5	9.4	1.3	0.1	6.6	3.4	1.5	2.3	1.8
Socialist countries	5.5	10.0	2.1*	2.2	3.4	4.4*	−	0.9	0.6*
Developed market economies	15.6	12.8	−0.9*	−7.4	12.9	1.8*	0.8	0.9	0.7*
Developing countries	24.5	−8.7	3.9*	22.1	16.5	−2.1*	0.7	0.4	0.5*
Hungary									
World	1.4	−1.0	−1.7	−3.2	−3.5	−5.0	−	0.2	0.5
Socialist countries	−0.4	−5.8	−2.6	0.1	−4.7	−4.0	0.3	0.3	0.3
Developed market economies	1.3	8.8	4.8	−12.4	−8.7	−4.1	−0.6	−0.1	0.2
Developing countries	10.5	−2.1	−14.5	19.2	20.9	−11.1	0.2	−	−
Poland									
World	6.0	3.2	1.4	−14.9	3.4	0.6	1.0	1.0	1.1
Socialist countries	17.1	5.5	−1.7	−2.1	4.8	−1.2	−0.5	−0.5	−0.5
Developed market economies	−6.6	2.5	8.1	−29.5	−3.7	3.2	0.5	0.7	0.9
Developing countries	0.2	−3.8	−2.4	−37.2	26.6	6.2	0.9	0.7	0.6
Romania									
World	−9.5	0.4	5.5	−24.2	−8.2	−1.2	1.8	2.5	3.1
Socialist countries	−2.6	1.4	−14.2*	−11.0	5.5	−13.0*	0.3	0.2	0.1
Developed market economies	−13.2	7.8	36.1*	−46.2	−30.3	6.3*	1.5	2.2	3.3*
Developing countries	−13.6	−9.3	−5.4*	−17.2	−10.9	13.1*	0.1	0.1	−0.3*
Eastern Europe									
World	4.0	5.0	2.8	−4.1	3.1	1.9	4.4	6.0	6.8
Socialist countries	7.0	6.9	1.4	3.4	5.6	2.0	−0.8	−0.2	−0.6
of this: Eastern Europe	4.1	5.7	−0.9	3.3	5.3	0.5	−	−	−
Soviet Union	8.8	9.1	2.1	4.0	6.0	2.8	−1.5	−0.7	−0.9
Developed market economies	−0.7	6.4	7.6	−19.1	−3.5	0.1	1.3	3.2	4.8
Developing countries	−	−6.7	−1.5	−6.8	3.5	5.3	3.9	3.0	2.6
Soviet Union									
World	9.6	5.1	−0.2	6.2	3.3	−0.2	9.3	11.2	11.2
Socialist countries	8.4	8.0	1.7	14.1	6.9	3.3	4.6	5.4	4.8
Developed market economies	8.2	1.9	−1.3	3.3	−3.1	−4.6	−	1.3	2.1
Developing countries	16.3	1.1	−4.8	−14.6	4.6	−4.8	4.8	4.4	4.3

Source: Secretariat of the United Nations Economic Commission for Europe, based on national foreign trade statistics. Figures for 1984 are in some cases secretariat estimates based on national trade data for the first 9-11 months, supplemented by trade partner statistics and trend analysis; these may be subject to substantial error margins and should therefore be considered first approximations only.

Note: Growth rates and trade balances are based on trade values in terms of US dollars; growth rates may therefore differ from those shown in national statistics. National trade data are converted to dollars at the conversion coefficients used for statistical purposes. In most—but not all—cases these are time-weighted averages of the official "basic" exchange rate against the dollar, as announced by national banks or other authorities.

The measurement of trade value movements over the period 1981-1982 can be distorted by the changes introduced in the foreign trade accounting regime in Poland in 1982. The conventional valuation of foreign trade flows in terms of a special accounting currency unit (*zloty dewizowy*) was abandoned in favour of expressing trade values in terms of the ordinary domestic monetary unit (*zloty*) through the use of conversion rates which, ideally, should approximate a purchasing power parity ratio. This reform also involved a substantial change in the rouble/dollar cross rate. Owing to the effect of this cross rate change, a direct comparison of trade values in the pre- and post-change year in terms of a third currency (whether this be the rouble or the dollar) will result in a biased image of value change (i.e., one that does not reflect the combined effect of price, volume and international exchange rate changes).

In order to avoid this distortion, a chain-linkage procedure has been employed here. In the case of *Poland*, the 1981 to 1982 comparison is made on the basis of the new (zloty) valuation for both years. The adjustment is also carried into the aggregation for eastern Europe.

[a] The partner country grouping follows the practice of the national statistical sources, which differs from the breakdown usually employed in United Nations publications. Thus, "socialist countries" includes Yugoslavia and Cuba, in addition to the east European countries, the Soviet Union and the Asian centrally planned economies. "Eastern Europe" refers to the six east European country members of the CMEA shown separately in the table.

[b] Preliminary.

5.4 EAST-WEST ECONOMIC RELATIONSHIPS [331]

(i) Overview of recent developments [332]

East-west trade in 1984 was characterized by a pickup in the growth of western trade with eastern Europe and—after several years as the most dynamic component of east-west trade—a slowdown in western trade with the Soviet Union. In both cases, the pace appeared to speed up somewhat as the year progressed. At the same time the western trade deficit with the east as a whole continued to widen.

The *western* trade deficit with *eastern Europe* continued to rise in 1984; it could reach some $3 billion, as compared to $1 billion in 1983. In contrast to 1981 and 1982, when a western trade surplus turned to deficit through a fall in western exports in excess of the decline in western imports, the recent pattern has been characterized by a strong recovery in *western imports* from eastern Europe: after rising by some 9 per cent in 1983 they expanded at some 19 per cent in volume terms in 1984. [333] These gains were more than sufficient to offset the cumulative 15 per cent erosion of western imports from eastern Europe during 1980-1982, bringing them above the previous peak in 1979 (see table 5.4.1 and chart 5.4.1.A). Western imports from Romania played a leading role in 1984 and, in terms of commodities, manufactured goods (particularly semi-manufactures), primary products, and possibly fuels, contributed. *Western exports* developed less favourably. An upturn of some 6 per cent in 1984 followed a cumulative decline in 1980-1982 of 22 per cent in volume terms which was arrested in 1983. The higher deliveries consisted mainly of primary products, semi-manufactures and consumer goods.

The changes in western trade balances with eastern Europe in this decade are associated with two rather different periods of east European external adjustment. While in 1981 and 1982 the east European deficit had to be turned to surplus owing to restricted access to new commercial credits and, in some cases, liquidity problems, since 1983 the trade surpluses, along with new borrowing, have been used to improve financial asset positions and/or repay some debt. [334] In 1984, this policy was most strikingly pursued by Romania.

The slackening in the expansion of *western imports* from the *Soviet Union* continued in 1984, the rate falling to some 3 per cent (table 5.4.1 and chart 5.4.1.B). Along with the continuing contribution made by higher volumes of oil and oil product imports, natural gas re-emerged as an important factor of growth in 1984.

In contrast to the strong upward trend in *western exports* to the *Soviet Union* during 1977-1982, the volume of western sales increased only slowly in 1983-1984. The 1 per cent rise in 1984 reflects a strong upturn in grain sales in the third quarter. It offset what appears to have been the tapering-off of deliveries of pipeline equipment which had caused a sharp decline in total western exports in the first half. [335] As a result of these changes in trade flows the western deficit with the Soviet Union is expected to rise by some one-half billion dollars above the $1 billion recorded in 1983.

Owing to the continuing decline in *prices* in east-west trade (as in other international markets—see section 5.1) the *value* of western exports fell again in 1984—despite the higher quantities delivered (table 5.4.1). Declining prices were also a characteristic of western imports, but quantities purchased rose strongly enough to yield the first increase in the value of this trade flow since 1980.

As regards *east-west financial activity*, the improvement which began in 1983 continued into 1984. There was a further strengthening in the eastern countries' financial position, as reflected in larger current account surpluses, a high level of assets, declining debt and increasing access to a wider variety of credit instruments. At the same time, international banks increased the availability of commercial credits and the number of banks, including United States banks, willing to participate in this lending has grown. Medium- and long-term funds raised totalled $3.3 billion—the highest level since 1979. In contrast to 1983, easier access to commercial credits appears to have lessened eastern borrowers' reliance on official and guaranteed loans.

Western imports from eastern Europe and the Soviet Union are discussed further in sub-section (ii) below. It focuses on western sub-regions of destination, eastern country of origin, and on commodity composition. A number of the factors determining these flows are also examined. Western exports are then treated in a parallel fashion. The section terminates with a discussion of the resulting changes in western trade balances. East-west financial developments are treated in sub-section (iii) in which changes in the east's current account in convertible currencies, financial assets, the upswing in borrowing from international banks and the decline in indebtedness are analysed. The section ends with a discussion of some of the factors which are likely to influence the development of east-west trade in the near future.

(ii) Trade flows by destination/origin and by commodity

Western imports

The rapid growth of the western market in 1984 contributed to the strong rise in imports from eastern Europe. However, the United States, the fastest growing western market with imports expanding by over 30 per cent, accounts for only about 5 per cent

---

[331] The term "developed market economies" (or for convenience "west" or "western") as used here refers to the countries of western Europe (including Turkey and Yugoslavia), North America and Japan. This grouping is intended only for statistical convenience. The term "eastern Europe" refers to Bulgaria, Czechoslovakia, the German Democratic Republic, Hungary, Poland and Romania taken together; the term "east" or "eastern countries" refers to eastern Europe together with the Soviet Union.

[332] An overview of developments in east-west trade and finance since the early 1980s is also given in the Introduction (chapter 1). This section serves to update the data and analysis provided earlier in the *Economic Bulletin for Europe*, vol. 36, No. 4, *op. cit.*, chapter 2, completed in October 1984.

[333] Unless otherwise stated, growth rates are for the first three quarters of 1984 relative to the same period in 1983.

[334] On these points, also see chapter 1.

[335] In the first half the volume of western exports to the Soviet Union turned down by 9 per cent (*Economic Bulletin for Europe*, vol. 36, No. 4, *op. cit.*, table 2.1).

CHART 5.4.1.

International trade of the developed market economies
with eastern Europe and the Soviet Union

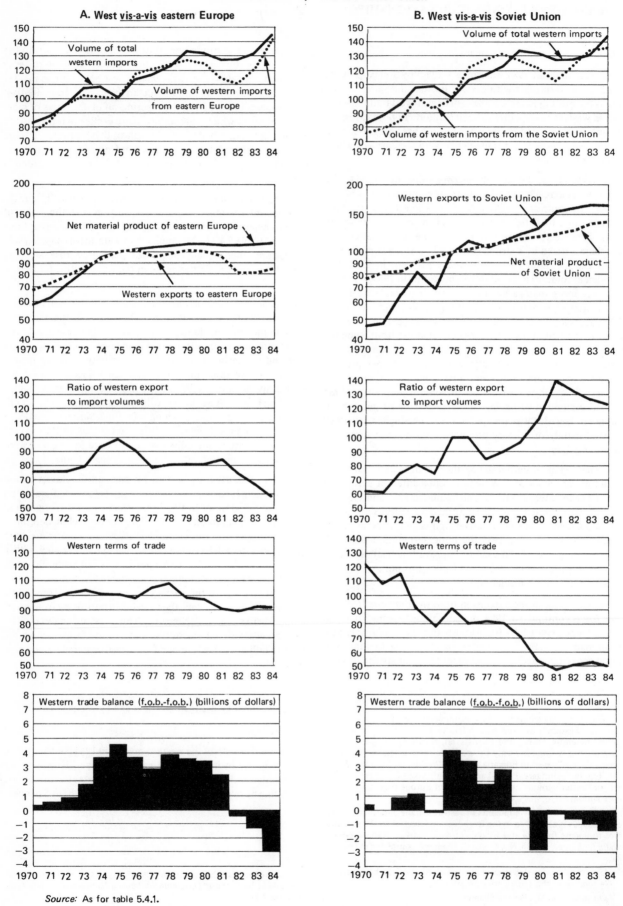

A. West vis-a-vis eastern Europe

B. West vis-a-vis Soviet Union

Source: As for table 5.4.1.

TABLE 5.4.1

East-west trade: value, volumes, prices, terms of trade

(*Percentage change over the same period of previous year*)

To/from	Western exports					Western imports				
	1980	1981	1982	1983	1984 Q1-3	1980	1981	1982	1983	1984 Q1-3
Values (in US dollars)										
Eastern Europe and the Soviet Union	11	−4	−7	−4	−3	22	−8	–	−1	4
of which:										
Eastern Europe	9	−16	−21	−5	–	12	−14	−8	1	12
Soviet Union	16	8	3	−4	−4	31	−3	5	−3	–
Volumes										
Eastern Europe and the Soviet Union	4	6	−3	2	3	−3	−8	3	8	8
of which:										
Eastern Europe	−9	−5	−16	–	6	−2	−8	−4	9	19
Soviet Union	9	15	5	2	1	−5	−8	10	7	3
Prices (in US dollars)										
Eastern Europe and the Soviet Union	7	−9	−4	−6	−5	25	1	−3	−8	−4
of which:										
Eastern Europe	11	−12	−5	−5	−6	13	−5	−4	−7	−6
Soviet Union	5	−6	−2	−6	−5	35	6	−5	−9	−3
World										
Values	18	−2	−5	−1	5	20	−5	−6	−4	8
Volumes	4	2	−1	2	8	–	−3	–	2	11

Western terms of trade (1975 = 100)					
	1980	1981	1982	1983	1984
With:					
Eastern Europe and the Soviet Union	71	64	64	65	64
of which:					
Eastern Europe	97	91	90	92	92
Soviet Union	54	49	50	52	50

Sources: United Nations commodity trade data (COMTRADE), OECD, *Statistics on Foreign Trade, Series A*, Paris; IMF, *Directions of Trade* and *International Financial Statistics*, Washington D.C.; United Nations, *Monthly Bulletin of Statistics* (volume indices of total western exports to and imports from the world); national statistics.

Price and volume indices: for the methodology and derivation, see *Economic Bulletin for Europe*, vol. 31, No. 1, United Nations, New York, 1979.

These data reflect the trade of 23 western reporting countries. Throughout, western data do not include trade between the Federal Republic of Germany and the German Democratic Republic, unless otherwise noted. The same data are used in chart 5.4.1.A and 5.4.1.B. The indices of net material product of eastern Europe and the Soviet Union used in the charts are based upon the national statistical sources of those countries.

of total western imports from eastern Europe. By contrast, western Europe, which absorbs 93 per cent of western imports from eastern Europe, expanded its total imports at a much lower rate. As a result, only about one half of western import growth from eastern Europe can be attributed to western Europe. Despite the small share of the United States, its 58 per cent growth rate of imports from eastern Europe accounted for over one quarter of total western import growth from that region.

As regards imports by *origin*, western purchases from all east European countries increased in volume terms with the possible exception of imports from Bulgaria. Data in value terms (table 5.4.2) deflated by changes in import prices (which declined by some 6 per cent) yield especially rapid rates of growth in imports from Romania (over 40 per cent), Poland (over one quarter) and from Hungary (some 16 per cent). Romania accounted for most of the growth in value terms, based largely on additional western imports of petroleum products and, to a lesser extent, of semi-manufactures.

In the first half of 1984,[336] *manufactures* accounted for a considerable portion of the increment in the value of western imports from *eastern Europe* (table 5.4.3). Within this group imports of *semi-manufactures*, including *chemicals* and particularly *iron and steel* (the latter rose by over 40 per cent in volume terms), increased rapidly. In both cases, Romania appears to have accounted for a considerable part of the incremental supplies. It is noteworthy that western imports of iron and steel from eastern Europe expanded faster than western imports of these products from the world. *Engineering* and *consumer goods* imports, although growing by some 13-15 per cent in volume terms, contributed only a small share of total incremental value.

[336] In contrast to data on total trade covering the first three quarters of 1984, commodity data (based upon COMTRADE) cover only the first half of the year. The classification used is described in table 5.4.13 which also includes a more detailed commodity breakdown of western imports by eastern country of origin.

TABLE 5.4.2

East-west trade: change in trade value, by country: 1980-1984
(*Percentage change in US dollar terms*)

	Western exports					Western imports				
	1980	1981	1982	1983	1984[a]	1980	1981	1982	1983	1984[a]
Bulgaria	31	14	−17	2	−6	12	−13	−5	−12	7
Czechoslovakia	11	−16	−3	−8	−4	18	−11	−2	1	4
German Democratic										
Republic[b]	9	−8	−11	7	−11	24	−4	4	−	−2
Hungary	11	−1	−9	−9	−3	11	−10	−7	3	10
Poland	8	−33	−24	−8	1	9	−34	−6	−	21
Romania	4	−22	−43	−23	8	6	−	−26	7	39
Eastern Europe[b] . . .	10	−16	−18	−5	−4	13	−13	−6	1	11
Soviet Union	16	8	3	−4	−4	31	−3	5	−3	−
Eastern Europe and										
Soviet Union[b] . . .	12	−4	−6	−4	−4	22	−8	−	−1	4
World	18	−2	−5	−1	5	20	−5	−6	−4	8

Source: As for table 4.5.1.

Note: Appendix tables C.6 and C.7 contain data on east-west trade for all ECE countries.

[a] January-September, over the same period in 1983.

[b] Including trade between the Federal Republic of Germany and the German Democratic Republic.

Imports of *primary products*, especially *non-ferrous metals* and *agricultural raw materials*, were important and were responsible for about 20 per cent of the incremental value of imports. As regards *fuels*, large increases were recorded in *coal*, mainly from Poland,[337] and in *petroleum and petroleum products* from Romania. As a result, fuel imports from eastern Europe as a whole appear to have risen substantially (table 5.4.3). However, this finding is tentative because of notable discrepancies in petroleum and petroleum product import data (the major component of fuels) between the two different data sources. On one hand, data as reported in COMTRADE suggest a rise in volume of some 22 per cent (19 per cent in value terms) while IEA data show

a 2 per cent decline in OECD imports.[338] Although differences between data sources are common,[339] the magnitude of the discrepancies suggests that the fuels component for imports from eastern Europe as a whole is overstated.[340]

Fuels again played the largest role in western imports from the *Soviet Union*. *Oil and oil products* and *natural gas* contributed

[337] According to the Polish Ministry of Mining and Power, Poland's exports of coal to the west rose by 47 per cent—from 15.4 million tons in 1983 to 22.6 million tons in 1984. However, coal prices fell by 10-15 per cent, rendering a smaller increase in value.

[338] International Energy Agency, *Quarterly Oil Statistics*, third quarter, Paris, 1985.

[339] For a discussion of some of the discrepancies between the United Nations trade reporting system and the IEA's oil trade reporting system, see *Economic Survey of Europe in 1983*, p. 231.

[340] The two data sources agree quite well as regards western imports of petroleum and petroleum products from Romania—COMTRADE showing an increase of about 80 per cent (in volume) and the IEA reporting 71 per cent. By contrast, COMTRADE indicates a decline in imports from other east European countries of about 13 per cent in volume terms while that reported by the IEA is significantly larger—some 24 per cent.

TABLE 5.4.3

Western imports from eastern Europe and the Soviet Union and the world, by commodity, first half 1984
(*Changes[a] and shares in per cent; increments[a] in millions of US dollars*)

	World	Eastern Europe			Soviet Union		
Origin	Change	Share	Increment	Change	Share	Increment	Change
Total	12	100	705	12	100	320	3
Primary products	9	23	139	10	12	−19	−1
Fuels[b]	4	28	257	16	78	327	4
Manufactures	17	48	304	11	8	53	7
of which:							
Semi-manufactures	14	20	188	17	6	75	13
Engineering	19	10	46	8	1	−14	−9
Consumer goods	15	19	69	6	−	−7	−16

Source and definitions: As in table 5.4.13.

Note: Shares and increments of components may not sum to the total because of incomplete reporting of commodities. Changes in total trade may not agree with the data in tables 5.4.1 and 5.4.2 because of differences in country coverage and periods.

[a] Relative to same period in 1983.

[b] See text for discussion of uncertainty regarding data on fuel imports from eastern Europe.

almost equally to the outcome. *Manufactured goods* imports rose by some 7 per cent in value terms, due exclusively to higher purchases of *chemicals* and *other machinery*. Imports of other goods declined.

In contrast with recent years, *natural gas* purchases from the *Soviet Union* were almost as important to the development of western imports in 1984 as *oil and oil products*. The latter rose by some 6 per cent in volume terms in the first half-year, down from a rate of expansion of 13-14 per cent in 1983. As 1984 progressed import growth appears to have slowed.[341] Nevertheless these commodities accounted for one half of the increment in the value of total imports from the Soviet Union. Imports of natural gas from the Soviet Union rose by 10 per cent in volume terms and accounted for about 45 per cent of the value increment in total western imports. This contrasts with 1982 and 1983, when western purchases of gas declined in volume terms (although probably only marginally in 1983) and by even more in US dollars.[342] The trend toward lower import prices appears to have been carried over into 1984, presumably because of the glut of gas supplies on the west European market and weakening reference prices. These data are largely in agreement with EEC data on imports of natural gas measured in physical units (table 5.4.4),[343] which show imports rising by over 20 per cent in the first three quarters. This owes most to a considerable rise in purchases by the Federal Republic of Germany and France.[344] These additional volumes were sufficient to reverse the decline in the Soviet Union's share of gas consumption in the EEC.

Soviet oil and oil product exports appear to play a special role as a balancing item in total Soviet hard currency exports to the west.[345] It appears, for example, that the volume of oil and oil products was increased in 1982 and 1983 not only to compensate for weakening oil prices, but also to offset falling revenues from natural gas—the result of declining west European demand for Soviet natural gas and/or lower prices in those years.

In 1984, the pressure on the Soviet Union to export additional volume of petroleum and petroleum products to gain convertible currency was probably reduced owing to higher revenues from natural gas and manufactured goods—though sagging oil prices would have tended to increase it. This might explain the lower (and falling) growth rate of Soviet oil exports in 1984, as noted. It might also be mentioned that these events took place against a background of a slight downturn in domestic oil production and a continuing rapid expansion of natural gas production (10 per cent in 1984). These supply developments suggest that the Soviet capacity to export oil to the west is increasingly a function of efforts to substitute natural gas for petroleum in domestic consumption.[346]

Unlike in 1983, Soviet imports of crude oil from OPEC countries did not appear to be a factor contributing to the additional supplies of oil and oil products available for export to the west.[347]

In addition to the role of western demand, other factors such as commercial policies and the commodity structure of eastern supplies are likely to have influenced the development of western imports from eastern Europe. Certain western commercial policies, particularly the setting of quotas on some products, may mitigate the expansionary impact of demand on eastern exports unless, of course, they are specifically adjusted in line with market developments. Mention might also be made of the initiation of anti-dumping procedures—in particular against iron and steel products, chemicals, building materials and consumer goods.[348]

On the supply side, the large contribution of primary goods and, in some cases, fuels, iron and steel to east European exports

---

[341] Data reported by the IEA suggest a sharp deceleration in the growth of oil and oil product imports throughout the year from 23 per cent in the first quarter to 8 per cent in the first half, falling to 7 per cent in the first three quarters. IEA, *op. cit.*

[342] See *Economic Bulletin for Europe*, vol. 36, No. 4, *op. cit.*, p. 440.

[343] Aside from the EEC importing countries, other major west European customers for Soviet natural gas are Austria, Finland, and Yugoslavia.

[344] The significant rise in the Federal Republic of Germany's gas imports from the Soviet Union in the first three quarters of 1984 reflects the outcome of an increase in total consumption by 6.4 per cent, lower domestic production of gas, and lower supplies from other EEC producers and Norway. EUROSTAT, *Hydrocarbons*, Brussels, 12/1984, Annex 1.

[345] See also *Economic Bulletin for Europe*, vol. 36, No. 4, *op. cit.*, pp. 440-441.

[346] It has recently been reported that the arrival of Soviet oil and oil products in western Europe had fallen to 0.5 million barrels per day early in 1985, down from normal seasonal imports of 1.9 million barrels per day. Reports attributed this decline to severe weather conditions affecting production and consequent higher demand inside the Soviet Union. *Financial Times*, 7 February 1985, p. 2.

[347] For an analysis of these flows in the first half of 1984, see *Economic Bulletin for Europe*, vol. 36, No. 4, *op. cit.*, pp. 441-443. Data on Soviet imports from OPEC in the third quarter show only a slight increase and would not change this conclusion.

[348] See also Economic Commission for Europe, *Review of Recent and Prospective Trends, Policies and Problems in Inter-regional Trade*, Trade, R.479.

TABLE 5.4.4

European Communities' imports of natural gas from the Soviet Union: 1981-1984

(*In 1,000 terajoules or percentage*)

	1981	1982	1983	1983 Q1-3	1984 Q1-3	Change[a]
European Communities	904	842	817	580	710	22.4
of which:						
Germany, Federal Republic of.	416	369	383	258	365	41.7
France	204	143	140	102	127	24.1
Italy	283	330	293	220	217	−1.1
Memoranda items:						
Apparent consumption	7714	7361	7686	5351	5848	9.3
Imports from Soviet Union as share of consumption (per cent)	11.7	11.4	10.6	10.8	12.1	..

Source: EUROSTAT, *Hydrocarbons*, Brussels, various issues.

[a] First three quarters of 1984 relative to same period in 1983.

has been noted. Officials of several eastern countries have observed that while their overall export growth targets may have been achieved, the commodity composition was less favourable than planned. In particular, the engineering goods industries are mentioned as not having achieved their planned export growth.[349] In a related development, the east European share of the western market for manufactures declined again in 1984, as it has since 1976.

Western exports

The upturn in western exports to *eastern Europe* in 1984 reflects faster rates of growth, or slower declines, in deliveries to all east European countries (except to the German Democratic Republic)[350]—and especially to Romania and Poland (table 5.4.2). With the exception of Hungary in 1981, Czechoslovakia in 1982, Bulgaria and the German Democratic Republic in 1983, export volumes to these countries had not risen since 1979.

Changes in the *commodity composition* of western exports to *eastern Europe* were characterized by higher deliveries of primary goods, semi-manufactures and consumer goods (table 5.4.5).[351] The volume of *primary product* exports to the German Democratic Republic and to Romania (mainly food) rose particularly quickly. Within this category, *raw materials* were imported in greater quantities by all eastern countries. Export volumes of *semi-manufactures*, rose by 7-8 per cent. Most of this was accounted for by exports to the German Democratic Republic, which expanded by almost one half. *Consumer goods* exports to all east European countries rose—the average being some 9-10 per cent in volume terms. Sales of *clothing* rose the fastest, followed by *textiles*, Poland being responsible for the largest share of the rise in total purchases of this item. As in every year since 1977, the overall volume of western *engineering goods* exports fell, but sales advanced to Romania (by over 20 per cent), Poland, and possibly to Czechoslovakia. Sharp reductions in exports of various types of *machinery* were mainly responsible. Contrary to this trend, the volume of *road and motor vehicles*

increased by about a quarter, with significantly higher exports to all countries except Bulgaria and Czechoslovakia.

In very general terms, the commodity pattern of western exports suggests that current production requiring imported inputs and perhaps, indirectly, consumer goods serving as incentives, had priority in eastern Europe. Improvements in domestic economic activity and in export capacity appear to have been facilitated by the more ample supply of imported inputs (see section 4.3). The continued decline of machinery imports probably reflects constraints on domestic investment activity (see section 4.4), and also on the growth of total east European imports (see below). It is often noted that imported machinery has not always been used effectively. Hence, additional large quantities of machinery imports may not be economically justifiable until absorption procedures are improved. Nevertheless it is generally recognized that imported capital goods have a role to play in the modernization of the capital stock and the improvement in industrial structure and product characteristics.

An important factor weakening the overall expansion of western exports to eastern Europe in 1984 was the priority assigned in most of these countries to a further improvement in their financial asset positions and/or the reduction of outstanding debt. Import expansion was thus held below export growth. The constraint imposed by scarce commercial import finance in 1982 and 1983 was loosened considerably in 1984.[352]

The overall decline in western exports to the *Soviet Union* was largely due to various groups of *engineering products*. The only exception in this group was *office and telecommunications equipment* (including computers), which rose by over 30 per cent in volume terms. *Semi-manufactures*, especially *iron and steel*, also fell sharply. Pipes and tubes, particularly those used for oil and gas pipelines generally account for a significant share of this category. These developments suggest that deliveries associated with pipeline projects have tapered off. Since these data are only for the first half, they do not reflect the large upswing in *food* exports in the third quarter which appears to have offset the downturn in engineering goods.

---

[349] For example in Poland engineering exports in convertible currency trade were 72 per cent of plan in 1984 (*Zycie gospodarcze*, 10 February 1985). Also see section 5.3.

[350] This downturn is due largely to lower deliveries by the Federal Republic of Germany, which declined by 23 per cent in value terms during the first three quarters of 1984.

[351] Also see table 5.4.14.

[352] However, Poland has been able to obtain only a limited amount of new commercial credits in the form of recycled interest payments. Polish authorities stress that capacity to import is seriously impeded by the unavailability of new commercial and official credits.

TABLE 5.4.5

Western exports to eastern Europe and the Soviet Union and the world, by commodity, first half 1984

(*Changes*[a] *and shares in per cent; increments*[a] *in millions of US dollars*)

Destination	World change	Eastern Europe			Soviet Union		
		Share	Increment	Change	Share	Increment	Change
Total	8	100	−96	−2	100	−1393	−13
Primary.	7	26	86	7	29	−45	−2
Fuels	1	2	−9	−8	1	14	16
Manufactures	8	70	−163	−4	66	−1423	−19
of which:							
Semi-manufactures	9	32	18	1	30	−546	−17
Engineering	8	28	−189	−12	34	−774	−20
Consumer goods	6	11	16	3	6	−49	−8

Source and definitions: As in table 5.4.13.

Note: Shares and increment may not sum to total because of incomplete reporting of commodities. Changes in total trade may not agree with the data in table 5.4.1 and 5.4.2 because of differences in country coverage and period.

[a] Relative to same period in 1983.

TABLE 5.4.6

East-west trade: trade balances, 1980-1984

(Billions of US dollars, f.o.b.-f.o.b.)

	1980	1981	1982	1983	Jan.-Sept. 1983	Jan.-Sept. 1984	1984[a]
A. Developed market economies with:[b]							
Eastern Europe and the Soviet Union	0.5	2.2	−0.9	−2.3	−1.6	−3.7	−4.7
of which:							
Eastern Europe	3.3	2.4	−0.2	−1.3	−1.2	−2.6	−3.1
Soviet Union	−2.9	−0.2	−0.7	−1.0	−0.4	−1.1	−1.6
Western Europe with:[b]							
Eastern Europe and the Soviet Union	−5.2	−4.6	−8.4	−7.4	−5.3	−7.2	−9.8
of which:							
Eastern Europe	1.2	1.1	−1.0	−1.7	−1.6	−2.1	−2.3
Soviet Union	−6.4	−5.7	−7.4	−5.7	−3.7	−5.1	−7.5
North America with:							
Eastern Europe and the Soviet Union	4.0	4.3	4.4	3.0	2.1	2.6	4.0
of which:							
Eastern Europe	1.6	0.8	0.3	−0.1	−	−0.5	−0.7
Soviet Union	2.4	3.6	4.0	3.1	2.1	3.1	4.7
Japan with:							
Eastern Europe and the Soviet Union	1.7	2.4	3.1	2.1	1.6	1.0	1.2
of which:							
Eastern Europe	0.6	0.5	0.4	0.5	0.4	0.1	−
Soviet Union	1.1	1.9	2.7	1.6	1.2	0.9	1.2
B. Developed market economies with:[c]							
Eastern Europe and the Soviet Union	0.8	3.1	−2.2	−6.3	2.3	−5.9	−7.8
of which:							
Eastern Europe	3.3	2.4	−1.7	−3.7	−2.5	−3.5	−4.8
Soviet Union	−2.4	0.7	−0.6	−2.5	0.2	−2.3	−3.0

Sources: As for table 5.4.1 (western data) and table 5.3.9 (eastern data).

Note: Section A is based on western data which have been adjusted to an *f.o.b.-f.o.b.* basis by the secretariat; section B is based on eastern national sources. A positive balance indicates a surplus for the developed market economies.

[a] Extrapolated, assuming a continuation of January-September trends of exports and imports.

[b] Excluding trade between the Federal Republic of Germany and the German Democratic Republic. For this reason the figures differ from those in table 5.4.7.

[c] Including trade between the Federal Republic of Germany and the German Democratic Republic.

Trade balances

The western trade deficit[353] recorded with the east in 1983 widened in 1984 (table 5.4.6). Extrapolations of the changes in trade flows in the first three quarters of 1984 to the year as a whole result in deficits of $3 billion with *eastern Europe*, up from over $1 billion in 1983. Both *western Europe* and *North America* recorded deficits with eastern Europe, while *Japan's* surplus disappeared.

A western surplus was again recorded with *Bulgaria*, but this was more than offset by growing deficits with the other countries. In the case of *Hungary*, the western surplus was eliminated (table 5.4.7). The largest rise in the western deficit occurred in trade with *Romania*.

In the case of the *Soviet Union*, the same procedure yields a full-year western trade deficit of under $2 billion in 1984—some $0.6 billion above the 1983 figure. The improvement in the *North American* trade surplus in the third quarter (as compared to the first half) suggests the pickup of grain exports. North America's trade surplus with the Soviet Union may approach $5 billion for the entire year, while *western Europe's* deficit probably increased. So far in this decade, the latter cumulates to over $30 billion and largely reflects rising Soviet fuel sales.

---

[353] The trade balances presented here and in panel A of table 5.4.6 are based on western data. As has generally been the case, they differ from balances calculated from eastern data sources (panel B). The reasons for these divergences, particularly the role of energy trade as an explanatory factor, have been addressed in the *Economic Survey of Europe in 1983* p. 233.

TABLE 5.4.7

East-west trade: trade balances, by eastern country, 1980-1984
(Billions of US dollars)

	1980	1981	1982	1983	Jan.-Sept. 1983	Jan.-Sept. 1984	1984[a]
A. *Developed market economies with:*							
Bulgaria	0.63	1.03	0.75	0.90	0.61	0.58	0.9
Czechoslovakia.	−0.16	−0.32	−0.33	−0.56	−0.54	−0.70	−0.7
German Democratic Republic[b] .	0.36	0.12	−0.68	−0.32	−0.16	−0.51	−0.7
Hungary	0.56	0.85	0.72	0.36	0.28	−	−
Poland	1.23	0.86	0.01	−0.27	−0.22	−0.71	−0.9
Romania	0.58	−0.36	−0.80	−1.37	−0.97	−1.64	−2.3
Eastern Europe[b]	3.19	2.18	−0.34	−1.27	−1.00	−2.94	−3.7
Soviet Union	−2.88	−0.23	−0.67	−1.02	−0.37	−1.12	−1.6
Eastern Europe and the Soviet Union[b]	0.31	1.95	−1.01	−2.28	−1.37	−4.06	−5.4

Source: As for table 4.5.1.

Notes: A negative sign indicates a western deficit. Appendix tables C.8 and C.9 contain east-west trade balances for all ECE countries.

[a] Extrapolated, assuming a continuation of January-September export and import trends.

[b] Including trade between the Federal Republic of Germany and the German Democratic Republic. For this reason the figures differ from those in table 5.4.6 section A.

(iii) Developments in east-west finance [354]

Current account

The *current account surpluses* of eastern Europe and the Soviet Union in convertible currencies [355] continued to widen in 1984 owing to larger *trade surpluses* with the market economies (table 5.4.8). *Invisibles deficits* remained largely unchanged, since the impact of higher interest rates on the investment income item was roughly offset by the effect of a falling stock of net debt. The average interest rate on the east's floating rate debt probably did not in any case rise significantly—perhaps by some one half of a percentage point for most countries in 1984. Interest rates rose only for US dollar denominated liabilities which account for about 50 per cent of total eastern debt.

[354] Also see section 5.1(ii).

[355] As an *approximation* to the trade balance component of the eastern convertible currency current account, the eastern trade balance with developed and developing market economies is used here. Beyond the west, as the term is defined in this section, this grouping also includes the developed countries of the southern hemisphere and the developing countries, most of which conduct trade on a convertible currency basis. The trade balance data shown thus include, on one hand, balances on clearing accounts (on which, in general, very little is known, especially for the current year), and on the other hand exclude balances on convertible currency transactions among the socialist countries. These are important for some east European countries.

Only Hungary, Poland, Romania publish current account data in terms of all convertible-currency transactions (in millions of US dollars):

	Hungary Current account balance	Hungary Of which: trade balance	Poland Current account balance[a]	Poland Of which: trade balance	Romania Current account balance	Romania Of which: trade balance
1982 . .	−63	766	−1016	358	655	1525
1983 . .	316	884	62	1086	922	1688
1984 . .	100[b]	868[b]	1047[b]	1047[b]	588[c]	899[c]

Source: National Bank of Hungary, *Economic Bulletin*, and Central Statistical Office, Warsaw; Romania: national sources.

[a] Excludes interest arrears on official and guaranteed debt.

[b] January-September.

[c] January-June.

Eastern Europe's current account surplus rose to about $3.7 billion in 1984, up by some $1 billion, and that of the *Soviet Union* widened by $0.6 billion to $6.7 billion. Improvements in the current account balances of Bulgaria, Czechoslovakia and Romania contributed to the east European outcome.[356]

Some noteworthy changes occurred in the regional structure of eastern trade surpluses. Whereas in 1981 the trade balance of

[356] According to Mr. Matyas Timár, President of the National Bank, Hungary ended 1984 with a $331 hard currency current account surplus—about the same as in 1983. (*Figyelö*, 14 February 1985.)

TABLE 5.4.8

Estimated current account balance of payments of eastern Europe and the Soviet Union with market economies, 1980-1984
(Billions of US dollars)

	Trade balances[a] with market economies Total	Trade balances[a] with market economies of this DME[b]	Net services plus transfers[c] Total	Net services plus transfers[c] Investment income	Current account
Bulgaria					
1980	1.0	0.1	−0.1	−0.4	1.0
1981	0.7	−0.6	−	−0.3	0.7
1982	0.7	−0.5	−0.1	−0.2	0.6
1983	0.3	−0.4	−	−0.2	0.3
1984	0.5	−0.4	−	−0.1	0.5
Czechoslovakia					
1980	0.1	−0.4	−0.4	−0.3	−0.4
1981	0.3	−0.3	−0.5	−0.5	−0.2
1982	0.4	−0.1	−0.4	−0.4	−
1983	0.8	0.1	−0.3	−0.3	0.5
1984	1.0	0.4	−0.2	−0.2	0.7
German Democratic Republic					
1980	−1.7	−1.7	−0.1	−1.2	−1.8
1981	−	−0.5	−0.4	−1.6	−0.4
1982	1.5	0.7	−	−1.3	1.5

TABLE 5.4.8 (*continued*)

	Trade balances[a] with market economies		Net services plus transfers[c]		
	Total	of this DME[b]	Total	Investment income	Current account
German Democratic Republic (continued)					
1983	1.3	0.8	0.3	−1.0	1.6
1984	1.0	0.5	0.6	−0.7	1.5
Hungary[a,d]					
1980	−0.7	−0.6	−0.6	−0.4	−1.3
1981	−0.8	−1.0	−1.2	−1.1	−1.9
1982	−0.3	−0.5	−0.8	−1.0	−1.2
1983	−0.1	−	−0.6	−0.7	−0.6
1984	0.1	0.2	−0.7	−0.7	−0.6
Poland[d]					
1980	−1.0	−0.7	−1.8	−2.3	−2.8
1981	−	−0.5	−2.1	−2.9	−2.1
1982	1.5	0.6	−2.7	−3.0	−1.2
1983	1.4	0.9	−2.3	−2.7	−0.9
1984	1.5	0.8	−2.3	−2.7	−0.9
Romania[d]					
1980	−1.9	−	−0.9	−0.8	−2.8
1981	0.2	0.5	−1.0	−1.0	−0.8
1982	1.4	1.4	−0.9	−1.0	0.5
1983	2.3	2.3	−0.8	−0.7	1.5
1984	3.0	3.3	−0.7	−0.7	2.3
Eastern Europe					
1979	−4.8	−4.6	−2.4	−3.7	−7.3
1980	−4.2	−3.2	−3.9	−5.4	−8.1
1981	0.4	−2.4	−5.3	−7.4	−4.8
1982	5.2	1.7	−4.9	−6.8	0.3
1983	6.1	3.7	−3.6	−5.5	2.5
1984	7.1	4.8	−3.4	−5.1	3.7
Soviet Union					
1979	4.2	0.6	0.1	−1.2	4.3
1980	3.4	2.4	0.2	−1.2	3.6
1981	−0.7	−0.7	−0.1	−1.4	−0.8
1982	4.3	0.6	−0.2	−1.5	4.1
1983	6.2	2.5	−0.2	−1.4	6.1
1984	6.7	3.0	−	−1.3	6.7
Eastern Europe and the Soviet Union[e]					
1979	−0.6	−4.0	−2.8	−5.3	−3.3
1980	−0.8	−0.8	−4.3	−7.1	−5.0
1981	−0.3	−3.1	−5.9	−9.4	−6.2
1982	9.5	2.2	−5.5	−8.8	4.0
1983	12.3	6.3	−4.0	−7.2	8.2
1984	13.8	7.9	−3.7	−6.7	9.6

Sources: As for table 5.3.9 (trade balances), national data and ECE secretariat estimates (net services and investment income).

Note: A positive balance indices a surplus for the eastern economies.

[a] Trade balance *f.o.b.-f.o.b.*, except for Hungarian imports which are shown *c.i.f.* in the national returns.

[b] Developed market economies (see definition in footnote at beginning of this section).

[c] Invisibles balances are ECE secretariat estimates, except in the cases of Hungary, Poland and Romania, 1979-1983. Data for these three countries reflect all interest charges incurred in convertible currencies. The invisibles data for Poland include convertible currency transfers from socialist countries of $131 million in 1980 and $328 million in 1981. Polish and Romanian official data have been adjusted to include interest arrears in the years in which they were incurred, to conform to IMF *Balance of Payments Manual* recommendations.
Investment income (inflows) for the other eastern countries reflect only interest earned on assets at BIS reporting banks.

[d] See also foot note 355 for national data covering all convertible currency transactions.

[e] Includes estimated investment income deficit of the CMEA banks.

eastern Europe with *all* market economies turned into a surplus, that with the *developed* market economies remained in deficit in that year (table 5.4.8). In subsequent years, the trade balance with the developed market economies also moved into surplus and, accounted for a growing share of the surplus with all market

economies. A similar pattern can be observed in the trade balances of the Soviet Union. Since eastern earnings on transactions with the developed market economies are more likely to result in liquid claims than those with *developing* countries, this structural shift tends to improve the eastern countries' liquidity position.

Asset positions

Eastern *assets* held at BIS reporting banks were rebuilt to relatively high levels by the end of 1983 relative to the levels recorded in the 1970s. Nevertheless they continued to accumulate in 1984, reaching a level of $22 billion (table 5.4.9). All eastern countries improved their asset positions. The advance was particularly notable in the case of the German Democratic Republic. This strong recovery follows an exceptional drawdown of assets by the east European countries in the first half of 1982 (to some $12 billion) in support of debt service obligations. This appears to have had two motives: to mitigate the unfavourable effects of any sudden changes in access to new credits, and to improve international banks' perceptions of their creditworthiness. The latter objective appears to have been met in most cases (see below).

The significantly improved asset position is also reflected in the east's liquidity ratio—measured here as assets held at BIS reporting banks as a percentage of annual imports from the market economies. For the region as a whole assets now cover over four months' imports (as opposed to only two months' in 1982). Romania's liquidity position shows a considerable improvement over the early 1980s. If all its international reserves are taken into account, Romania is approaching the three months' import coverage generally considered normal for trade-related needs. A weak liquidity position in 1981 (less than one month's import coverage) has often been cited as an important factor leading to arrears on payments at that time.

Aside from assets held at BIS reporting banks, eastern countries have other reserves. They include deposits in banks outside the BIS reporting area, short-, medium- and long-term claims on enterprises and sovereign borrowers and gold, etc., on which little information is available.[357] These assets appear to have increased recently.[358] For example in Hungary, convertible currency assets other than international reserves—probably trade-related credits—rose in 1983.[359] Also Czechoslovakia has had to lengthen maturities on export credits and increase the share of its capital goods exports financed with trade credits,

---

[357] Both Hungary and Romania regularly report their international reserve positions in convertible currencies. Hungary also reports a broader aggregate which includes other short- and long-term assets.

	Hungary		Romania,
	International reserves plus other assets[a]	Of which: international reserves[a]	international reserves[b]
1982	2.8	1.2	0.6
1983	3.7	1.9	0.7
1984	3.3[c]	1.5[c]	0.9[d]

Source: National Bank of Hungary, *Quarterly Review*; IMF, *International Financial Statistics.*

[a] Includes gold valued at $226/ounce (national valuation).

[b] Includes gold valued at SDR 35 per ounce.

[c] June.

[d] September.

[358] This would be one explanation why the eastern net debt as measured here (see below) declines less than would be expected on the basis of eastern current account surpluses. Also see *Economic Bulletin for Europe*, vol. 36, No. 4, *op. cit.*, p. 459-462.

[359] Bank of Hungary, *loc. cit.*

TABLE 5.4.9

Eastern Europe and the Soviet Union: assets held at BIS reporting banks and liquidity ratios (end of period)

	Assets (billions of US dollars)			Liquidity ratios[a] (per cent)		
	1982	1983[b]	1984[c]	1982	1983[b]	1984[c]
Bulgaria	1.0	1.2	1.3	35.2	45.0	48.1
Czechoslovakia	0.7	0.9	1.1	16.8	22.8	27.4
German Democratic Republic	1.9	3.4	4.6	27.5	44.3	58.4
Hungary	0.7	1.3	1.2	16.5	29.9	29.9
Poland	1.0	1.3	1.6	24.2	30.5	36.3
Romania	0.3	0.5	0.7	6.2	11.1	15.8
Eastern Europe	5.6	8.6	10.5	20.5	31.5	38.4
Soviet Union	10.0	11.0	11.1	25.6	29.1	31.6
Eastern Europe and the Soviet Union	16.4	19.9	21.7	24.8	31.9	34.6

Source: Secretariat estimates; BIS, *International Banking Developments (quarterly).*

[a] Assets as percentage of imports from all market economies.

[b] New series starting 1983.

[c] September.

especially in dealings with developing countries.[360] Both factors would tend to raise its stock of assets. However, some of these claims may not be as liquid as deposits held at BIS reporting banks because of their maturities or because borrowers are in financial difficulty.[361]

New lending to the east in the form of *publicized medium- and long-term funds* (bank credits and bonds) started to recover in 1983. It accelerated to $3.3 billion in 1984 (table 5.4.10). This area of east-west financial activity had fallen to particularly low levels in 1982 in the wake of the external financial difficulties experienced by a number of eastern countries and the unpropi-

tious political climate. The level recorded in 1984 was exceeded only in 1978 and 1979 when $3.8 and $4.7 billion were raised.

Borrowing has been concentrated in three eastern countries—Hungary, the German Democratic Republic, the Soviet Union—and the CMEA banks. Bulgaria and Czechoslovakia are considered highly creditworthy but have preferred, for various reasons, not to enter the market. Romania has borrowed on a bank-to-bank basis as can be seen from the rise in its liabilities *vis-à-vis* BIS reporting banks in 1984. Poland, on the other hand, has been unable to raise syndicated medium- and long-term loans, though it has obtained some funds in the form of recycled interest payments.

As 1984 progressed, terms on loan facilities negotiated by the eastern countries improved, particularly for the Soviet Union.[362]

[360] K. Hajek, "Devizové vztahy v roce 1983 a úkoly v této oblasti pro rok 1984", *Finance a Uver*, No. 6/1984, p. 367.

[361] For the Czechoslovakian experience regarding this latter point, see Hajek, *ibid.* The rescheduling by the Soviet Union of $400 million in claims on Peru may also be taken as an example—see Business International, *Business Eastern Europe*, 30 September 1983.

[362] The ECU 50 million loan (now oversubscribed) being negotiated by the Soviet Union would carry a margin of only 1/4 percentage point over LIBOR for the first three years of the loan. This compares with a spread of 5/8 percentage point at the beginning of 1984.

TABLE 5.4.10

Medium- and long-term funds raised by eastern Europe and the Soviet Union on the international financial markets

(*In millions of US dollars*)

	1980	1981	1982	1983	1984	Jan. 1985
Bulgaria	–	–	–	–	–	–
Czechoslovakia	475	30	–	50	–	–
German Democratic Republic[a]	397	516	69	386	903	–
Hungary	550	591	483	567	1 146	230
Poland	736	–	–	–	260	–
Romania	458	337	–	–	–	–
Eastern Europe	2 616	1 474	552	1 003	2 309	230
Soviet Union	50	25	153	68	867	206
CMEA banks	–	100	–	–	140	100
Eastern Europe and the Soviet Union	2 666	1 600	704	1 071	3 316	535
Memorandum item: by instrument						
Bonds	..	50	–	–	41	..
Bank loans[a]	..	1 549	563	1 000	2 980	..
Other[b]	..	–	142	72	295	..

Source: OECD, *Financial Statistics Monthly*, Paris, Part 1, Table S.2.

[a] Bank loans in eurocurrencies and in the domestic currency of lending countries, excluding officially guaranteed loans and rescheduling of debt but including loans to the German Democratic Republic guaranteed by the government of the Federal Republic of Germany.

[b] Other bank facilities, including bankers' acceptances and note issuance facilities.

Margins over LIBOR have declined and the average maturities on loans tended to lengthen. Nevertheless, for the east as a whole, terms remained less favourable than those extended to most western borrowers, but as good or better than for other groups.[363] The fact that the margins on eastern loans have been relatively high appears to have contributed to the oversubscription, sometimes by substantial margins, of several loans negotiated by the German Democratic Republic, Hungary and the Soviet Union.

The surge in funds raised by the east in 1984 appears to have been due to several factors. First, international banks have been increasingly willing to augment lending to most eastern countries. Recently this has included more United States banks which were not heavily involved in 1984. Undoubtedly this change stemmed from the recognition of the strong external adjustment measures undertaken by these countries and their improved financial positions. Second, the eastern countries appear to have benefited from the increased competition among banks for the business of creditworthy borrowers (see section 5.1(ii)). In this atmosphere, there have also been greater possibilities for them to broaden the range of borrowing instruments (floating rate notes, short-term note issuance facilities, etc.), currencies (ECU, Yen) and sources of finance (Arab and Japanese banks). Moreover it has been reported that the demonstrated capacity to diversify borrowing reinforced lenders' perceptions of the improving creditworthiness of the borrowers.[364] This is also reflected in the oversubscription of several credits. Apparently, in some cases these additional funds have been used to improve maturity structures.

The greater availability of longer-term credits has apparently also induced the eastern countries to rely less on short-term trade-related borrowing. The latter had become more important during the credit squeeze when eastern importers found it necessary to resort to supplier credits.[365]

[363] For a comparison of terms with other groups of borrowers see OECD, *Financial Market Trends*, October 1984.

[364] In the case of Hungary, IMF membership has also played a role in this regard. Moreover banks were also prepared to grant loans as a part of cofinancing schemes with the World Bank. See comment of Dr. Janos Fekete, deputy governor of the National Bank of Hungary, as reported in *Financial Times*, 6.12.1984, p. 2.

[365] On this point see L. Szamuely "The Eastern European Economic Situation and the Prospects of Foreign Trade" *The New Hungarian Quarterly*, vol. XXV, Autumn 1984, p. 71. These credits were often unguaranteed in which case they would very likely have gone unreported by the lender.

In the first half of 1984 the value of outstanding western *official and guaranteed commercial loans* to the east declined (table 5.4.11). For the region as a whole this reflects the appreciation of the US dollar as well as the reduction of debt levels. In only two eastern countries, Czechoslovakia and Romania, did new borrowing clearly exceed repayments. The situation contrasts with 1983, when eastern financing by means of these instruments was rapid enough to result in an increase in outstanding claims.[366] At the time, this type of borrowing was also relatively more important than new commercial bank credits.

While western official credit and guarantor agencies appear to have been willing to provide new credits in both 1983 and 1984 to maintain the competitiveness of domestic exporters, the greater reliance of the east on these sources of credit in 1983 is likely to have been due to the difficulties encountered in raising commercial credits. In 1984, by contrast, the increasing availability and improved terms of bank loans presumably gave eastern borrowers more options to switch away from official credit sources. In both years changes in imports of capital goods, often financed by this type of credit, appear also to have played a role (for example in the cases of Romania and the Soviet Union).

Poland and western governments have recently agreed on terms for the rescheduling of Polish official debt. The agreement provides for a rescheduling, over 11 years with a six-year grace period of principal arrears (some $9-10 billion), of debt incurred during 1982-1984. It includes provisions for the repayment of interest arrears on official debt cumulated during 1981-1984. At the end of 1983, Polish sources estimated these at $2.7 billion (including interest owed to several developing countries). Interest rates, where not previously established, and the terms of repayment of interest arrears will be subject to bilateral negotiations. After the agreement is signed, discussions are to open on the rescheduling of maturities falling due in 1985.[367]

The *gross debt* of eastern Europe and the Soviet Union in convertible currencies is estimated to have declined again in 1984 (table 5.4.12).[368] Data for mid-1984, based upon national sources and the BIS/OECD reporting system, show a $3 billion decline to $86 billion. Indebtedness fell even more in terms of a measure of

[366] See *Economic Bulletin for Europe*, vol. 36, No. 4, *op. cit.*, pp. 456-458.

[367] Based on *Financial Times*, 29 January, 1985, p. 1.

[368] These data have been discussed extensively in the *Economic Bulletin for Europe*, vol. 36, No. 4, *op. cit.*, pp. 459-462 and appendix. The BIS/OECD reported figures may be considered as *minimum* estimates since several categories of debt are excluded.

TABLE 5.4.11

Guaranteed and official debt of eastern Europe and the Soviet Union and its share in total eastern liabilities *vis-à-vis* BIS/OECD reporting countries, 1982-1984 (end of period)

(Millions of US dollars and per cent)

	Millions of US dollars			Shares		
	1982	1983	1984[a]	1982	1983	1984[a]
Bulgaria	883	808	729	31.6	34.1	33.0
Czechoslovakia	846	838	856	23.8	24.8	26.1
German Democratic Republic	2503	2930	2413	23.3	28.3	24.3
Hungary	464	536	431	6.7	7.5	6.5
Poland[b]	6067	5311	6015	34.8	34.6	45.1
Romania	1217	843	1066	24.1	19.8	25.2
Soviet Union[c]	17644	16584	14562	61.7	61.2	55.8

Source: ECE secretariat based on BIS/OECD, *Statistics on External Indebtedness, Bank and Trade-Related Non-Bank External Claims on Individual Borrowing Countries and Territories*, Basle and Paris.

[a] June.

[b] Only part of all guaranteed and official loans are reflected here.

[c] Includes CMEA banks.

TABLE 5.4.12

**Estimated convertible currency debt of eastern Europe
and the Soviet Union, 1982-1984, end of period**
(*Billions of US dollars*)

	Gross debt		
	1982	1983	1984 end-June
Bulgaria	2.8	2.4	2.2
Czechoslovakia	3.6	3.4	3.3
German Democratic Republic. .	12.7	12.3	11.5
Hungary	7.7	8.3	7.7
Poland[a]	26.2	26.4	26.6
Romania	9.8	8.9	8.4
Eastern Europe.	62.8	61.6	59.7
Soviet Union and CMEA Banks .	28.6	27.1	26.1
Eastern Europe and Soviet Union	91.4	88.7	85.8

	Net debt		
	1982	1983	1984 end-June
Bulgaria	1.8	1.3	1.0
Czechoslovakia	2.8	2.5	2.0
German Democratic Republic. .	10.7	8.8	7.3
Hungary	7.0	7.0	6.8
Poland[a]	25.2	25.2	25.3
Romania	9.4	8.4	7.8
Eastern Europe.	56.9	53.0	50.1
Soviet Union and CMEA Banks .	18.3	17.1	15.0
Eastern Europe and Soviet Union	75.1	70.2	65.1

Sources: National data for: Hungary, Poland and Romania; BIS/OECD, *loc. cit.*, for Bulgaria, Czechoslovakia, German Democratic Republic (including gross claims of the Federal Republic of Germany arising from clearing exchanges), Soviet Union, including CMEA banks.

Notes: Net debt: gross debt less eastern assets at BIS reporting banks only.

[a] Includes arrears on official debt.

net debt (defined here as gross debt less eastern assets held at BIS reporting banks) because of the continuing buildup in assets.[369] It is estimated that by the end of the year gross debt remained unchanged at $86 billion, but that the measure of net debt had declined further to some $62 billion—to almost $48 billion for eastern Europe and some $14 billion for the Soviet Union

(including CMEA banks). The further decline in the net debt reflects a seasonal buildup of assets in the final quarter of the year. The impact of the US dollar appreciation on the stock of eastern debt (in terms of US dollars) appears to have been considerable in 1984, accounting for around $6 billion of the estimated decline in net indebtedness (also see section 5.1(ii)).

(iv) Some concluding comments

Several factors which are expected to influence the near-term development of east-west trade include, among others, economic growth in the west, eastern supply capabilities and the competitiveness of exports, and the evolution of energy prices in world markets. More buoyant economic activity in western Europe, the major market for the eastern group in the ECE region, could offset to some extent the decelerating but still high rate of growth anticipated in North America. Western imports will also depend increasingly on eastern Europe's ability to imprve the competitiveness of its manufactured goods in western markets. It should be added, however, that gains in shares of western markets for certain products in which eastern Europe has developed export potential—iron and steel, textiles, clothing and some food—are in certain markets to some extent limited by commercial policy considerations or bilateral arrangements. Additional primary goods and fuels exports are apparently becoming progressively more difficult to achieve because of the exhaustion of deposits, rapidly rising costs, etc.[370] The export of petroleum products by Romania, which contributed a great deal to the dynamism of western imports in 1984, is based largely on imports of crude oil from OPEC.

Western exports to the east have been affected by eastern export revenues, funds raised from international sources and, especially in the recent past, by the fall in eastern net debt. The present eastern external financial position, characterized by a relatively high level of assets and, in most cases, a manageable debt burden, offers in some countries potential for faster import expansion. However, the latter could conflict in some countries with other objectives such as the liquidation of net debt.[371]

The delivery of grain contracted for earlier by the Soviet Union can be expected to boost western exports, but little is known about other intended purchases. Western imports (Soviet exports), consisting mainly of fuels, appear to be determined largely by the Soviet Union's own import requirements. The expansion of demand in the west is likely to further raise imports of manufactures, raw materials and natural gas from the Soviet Union. To the extent that oil and oil products exports are used as a balancing item to achieve a hard currency revenue target (as gold is also used), the volumes of these commodities exported to the west would depend on the sale of other goods and on oil prices. Since the latter have been weakening in international markets, larger quantities of oil might have to be exported.

[369] This incomplete measure of net debt is not fully satisfactory since it does not account for all eastern assets. To this extent, it tends to *overstate* true net indebtedness. Another limitation of the measure is that it does not always permit a full reconciliation with developments in the current account. On these points, see *Economic Bulletin for Europe, loc. cit.*

National data taking account of a broader range of assets are available only for Hungary and Romania (billion dollars):

	Hungary		Romania[a]
	a	b	
1982	6.5	4.9	9.2
1983	6.4	4.6	8.2
1984 (June)	6.2	4.4	7.5
1984 (December)	..	4	..

[a] Incorporating international reserves only (see footnote 357).

[b] Incorporating international reserves and other financial assets.

[370] Even in the case of Poland (with its considerable coal reserves), it has been stated by the Polish authorities that maximum feasible extraction rates are being approached.

[371] According to Mr. Jan Stejskal, President of the Czechoslovak National Bank, Czechoslovakia intends to eliminate its convertible currency debt in net terms (presumably reflecting all convertible currency claims) by the end of 1985. *Hospodářské Noviny*, No. 3, 18 January 1985, p. 4.

TABLE 5.4.13

**Western imports from the world, eastern Europe and the Soviet Union,
by commodity: growth of trade value, first half 1984[a]**

(*Percentage change*)

				Origin					
Product	*World*	*Bulgaria*	*Czecho-slovakia*	*German Democratic Republic*	*Hungary*	*Poland*	*Romania*	*Eastern Europe*	*Soviet Union*
Total	12	−13	1	−9	11	14	49	12	3
Primary products.	9	−21	7	13	10	10	42	10	−1
Food.	5	−27	11	21	5	−2	−2	−	−3
Raw materials	12	−10	1	6	−3	34	58	13	−13
Ores and minerals	15	30	13	−4	17	35	216	23	6
Non-ferrous metals	19	31	41	58	69	9	109	41	20
Fuels	4	−46	−9	−31	84	12	77	16	4
Coal.	8	..	−2	−3	186	14	..	10	15
Petroleum and products . .	5	−51	−11	−31	91	−17	77	19	3
Gas	2	−31	−26	−89	22	−82	..	−27	8
Electricity.	−5	−14	−29	..	..	244	..	56	14
Manufactures	17	20	2	2	1	20	29	11	7
Semi-manufactures . . .	14	45	−	3	7	14	84	17	13
Iron and steel	24	98	−	27	38	−	210	40	−33
Chemicals.	11	−2	−3	−4	−3	25	53	8	25
Other semi-manufactures .	15	−47	4	−3	3	18	4	4	−4
Engineering products . . .	19	−25	−2	7	−1	37	1	8	−9
Machinery.	13	−14	−2	−12	−24	3	−9	−10	−22
Office and telecommuni-cations equipment.	36	56	−11	12	11	−11	30	11	−3
Road vehicles	21	−72	−11	−11	23	−3	−2	−1	−22
Other machinery	11	−34	8	31	4	76	12	29	21
Consumer goods	15	4	8	−3	−2	13	11	6	−16
Household appliances . .	21	28	26	3	−10	−6	30	3	−16
Textiles.	11	30	10	−	2	16	10	8	−33
Clothing	18	9	12	−18	−5	18	18	9	−32
Other consumer goods . .	13	−16	3	−3	2	9	4	3	1

Source: United Nations Statistical Office, COMTRADE, Quarterly trade data, "Series D"

Note: In contrast to data used for tables 5.4.1 and 5.4.2, the coverage in tables 5.4.13 and 5.4.14 is reduced to countries for which commodity data were available for the first half of 1984 and the same period in 1983: Austria, Denmark, Finland, France, Federal Republic of Germany, Greece, Italy, Netherlands, Norway, Sweden, Switzerland, Canada, United States and Japan. These data exclude trade between the Federal Republic of Germany and the German Democratic Republic. Thus, growth rates based upon this sample of 14 countries differ from those given in table 5.4.1 and 5.4.2 because of differences in coverage but also because the data for total trade comprise the first three quarters.

Commodity groups in terms of SITC categories, based on the Standard International Trade Classification, Revised (United Nations *Statistical Papers*, Series M, No. 34):

Primary products

Food (sections 0, 1, and 4 and division 22)
Raw materials (section 2, excluding divisions 22, 27 and 28)
Ores and other minerals (divisions 27 and 28)
Non-ferrous metals (division 68).

Fuels (section 3)

Coal (division 32)
Petroleum and petroleum products (division 33)
Gas (division 34)
Electricity (division 35)

Manufactures

Semi-manufactures

Iron and steel (division 67)
Chemicals (section 5 and groups 862 and 863)
Other semi-manufactures (division 61, 62, 63, 64 and 66 excluding groups 665 and 666).

Engineering products

Machinery for specialized industries (groups 712, 715, 717, 718 and 719 excluding subgroup 719.4)
Office and telecommunications equipment and parts, including computers; (group 714 plus sub-groups 724.9 and 729.3).

Road motor vehicles (group 732)

Other machinery and transport equipment (divisions 69 excluding group 696 and 697; 73 excluding group 732, groups 711, 722, 723, 726, 729 excluding sub-groups 729.3 and 861 excluding sub-groups 861.4 and 961.4).

Consumer goods

Household appliances (groups 696, 697, 725, 864, sub-groups 719.4, 724.1, 724.2, 861.4, 861.6 and 891.1).
Textiles (division 65)
Clothing (division 84)
Other consumer goods (groups 665 and 666, section 8, less divisions 84 and 86 plus subgroup 891.1).

[a] Relative to same period in previous year.

TABLE 5.4.14

Western exports to the world, eastern Europe and the Soviet Union, by commodity: growth of trade value, first half 1984[a]

(Percentage change)

Product		Origin							
	World	Bulgaria	Czecho-slovakia	German Democratic Republic	Hungary	Poland	Romania	Eastern Europe	Soviet Union
Total	8	−9	−3	6	−5	−4	5	−2	−13
Primary products	7	−4	−3	31	−5	−5	25	7	−2
Food	3	−5	−28	34	−27	−7	51	6	−3
Raw materials	14	2	32	37	32	6	−5	19	11
Ores and minerals	13	−63	−12	74	−6	4	−9	−1	−4
Non-ferrous metals	13	19	11	−33	27	−8	−41	−	−5
Fuels	1	−35	15	15	54	16	−18	−8	16
Coal	10	−84	..	−99	−1	1 693	−25	−28	−82
Petroleum and products . .	3	−10	16	23	85	15	87	29	16
Gas	−7	−88	−35	−37	−80	..	..	−38	−59
Electricity	16	..	..	..	..	..	..	..	..
Manufactures	8	−11	−2	−6	−6	−2	2	−4	−19
Semi-manufactures	9	−	−	41	−4	−6	−4	1	−17
Iron and steel	8	−6	−6	86	−	−15	−31	3	−25
Chemical	10	8	3	16	−5	−4	9	2	−2
Other semi-manufactures .	8	−14	−8	56	−3	−7	−10	−4	−14
Engineering products . . .	8	−23	−5	−30	−11	−	16	−13	−22
Machinery	2	−28	−2	−33	−13	−9	−3	−17	−19
Office and telecommuni-cations equipment	27	31	−7	−21	12	−14	72	4	28
Road vehicles	13	−34	−20	36	16	47	98	20	−8
Other machinery	0	−16	−9	−29	−15	6	6	−12	−30
Consumer goods	6	6	2	−1	−2	11	6	3	−9
Household appliances . .	13	−13	−5	−47	−14	−2	−27	−14	−20
Textiles	5	17	−	2	3	6	8	5	−5
Clothing	4	−22	8	172	5	25	9	17	−8
Other consumer goods . .	3	16	7	−26	−14	24	1	−2	−11

Source and *Notes:* as for table 5.4.13.

[a] Relative to same period in previous year.

Statistical appendices

Introductory note

For the user's convenience, as well as to lighten the text, this year's *Economic Survey of Europe* includes a set of appendix tables showing annual changes in main economic indicators over a longer time period (1970-1984).

The data are presented in three sections, following the structure of the text: *Appendix A* provides macro-economic indicators for the ECE market economies; *Appendix B* does the same for the ECE centrally planned economies; and *Appendix C* collates time series on world trade and the development of foreign trade of the ECE countries.

Except where otherwise stated, time series reflect levels or change in *real terms*, i.e. at constant prices in case of series measured in value terms.

Data were compiled from international (United Nations, OECD, CMEA) or national statistical sources, as indicated in the notes to individual tables.

Regional aggregations are ECE secretariat calculations, based on 1975 US dollar weights in the case of the market economies and on CMEA estimates of relative per capita levels in the case of the centrally planned economies.

All figures for 1984 are preliminary estimates, based on data available in the first weeks of February 1985.

Appendix A. Western Europe and North America

APPENDIX TABLE A.1

Gross domestic product
(Annual percentage change)

	1970	1971	1972	1973	1974	1975	1976	1977	1978	1979	1980	1981	1982	1983	1984
France	5.7	5.4	5.9	5.4	3.2	0.2	5.2	3.1	3.8	3.3	1.1	0.2	2.0	1.0	1.9
Germany, Federal Republic of[a]	5.0	3.2	4.1	4.6	0.5	-1.6	5.6	2.8	3.5	4.0	1.9	-0.5	-1.1	1.3	2.6
Italy	5.3	1.6	3.2	7.0	4.1	-3.6	5.9	1.9	2.7	4.9	3.9	0.2	-0.4	-1.2	2.8
United Kingdom	2.2	2.7	2.3	7.9	-1.1	-0.7	3.9	1.0	3.6	2.1	-2.2	-1.1	1.9	3.0	2.5
Total 4 countries	4.7	3.4	4.1	5.8	1.5	-1.2	5.2	2.4	3.5	3.6	1.2	-0.2	0.5	1.1	2.4
Austria	7.1	5.1	6.2	4.9	3.9	-0.4	4.6	4.4	0.5	4.7	3.0	-0.1	1.0	2.1	2.4
Belgium	6.7	3.7	5.4	6.0	4.2	-1.4	5.3	0.5	3.1	2.1	3.3	-1.2	1.1	0.4	1.5
Denmark	2.3	2.4	5.4	3.8	-0.7	-1.0	6.5	2.3	1.8	3.7	-0.4	-0.9	3.0	2.0	4.2
Finland	7.5	2.1	7.6	6.7	3.0	1.2	0.3	0.2	2.6	7.4	5.6	1.9	2.8	2.9	3.0
Ireland	3.2	3.4	6.5	4.7	4.2	3.7	1.4	8.2	7.2	2.8	3.2	2.9	1.9	0.6	3.7
Netherlands	6.7	4.3	3.4	5.7	3.5	-1.0	5.3	2.4	2.5	2.4	0.9	-0.7	-1.7	0.6	1.5
Norway	2.0	4.6	5.2	4.1	5.2	4.2	6.8	3.6	4.5	5.1	4.2	0.9	0.9	3.2	4.3
Sweden	7.2	0.9	2.3	4.0	3.2	2.6	1.0	-1.6	1.8	3.8	1.7	-0.3	0.8	2.5	2.7
Switzerland	6.4	4.1	3.2	3.0	1.5	-7.3	-1.4	2.4	0.4	2.5	4.6	1.5	-1.1	0.7	2.4
Total 9 countries	6.0	3.3	4.4	4.8	3.0	-0.7	3.4	1.7	2.2	3.5	2.5	–	0.5	1.5	2.6
Total western Europe	5.0	3.4	4.2	5.6	1.9	-1.1	4.7	2.2	3.1	3.5	1.5	-0.1	0.5	1.2	2.5
Greece	8.0	7.1	8.9	7.3	-3.6	6.1	6.4	3.4	6.7	3.7	1.8	-0.3	-0.1	-0.3	2.3
Portugal	9.1	6.6	8.0	11.2	1.1	-4.3	6.9	5.6	3.4	6.6	4.1	0.5	3.5	0.0	-1.6
Spain	4.1	5.0	8.1	7.9	5.7	1.1	3.0	3.3	1.8	0.2	1.5	0.2	1.2	2.2	2.5
Turkey	4.9	9.1	6.6	2.0	12.5	10.1	10.8	5.1	3.2	-1.7	-0.3	4.5	5.6	3.0	5.4
Yugoslavia[b]	7.2	8.1	4.2	5.0	8.5	3.6	3.9	8.0	6.9	7.0	2.3	1.5	0.7	-1.3	1.7
Total southern Europe	6.9	8.0	6.6	5.5	5.8	5.1	7.3	5.6	5.0	3.1	1.5	2.0	2.6	0.7	2.7
Total Europe	5.1	3.6	4.3	5.6	2.1	-0.8	4.9	2.4	3.3	3.5	1.5	0.0	0.6	1.2	2.5
United States[a]	-0.2	3.4	5.7	5.8	-0.6	-1.1	5.4	5.3	5.0	2.8	-0.3	2.5	-2.1	3.7	6.8
Canada[a]	2.5	6.9	6.1	7.5	3.6	1.2	5.8	2.0	3.6	3.2	1.1	3.3	-4.4	3.3	4.2
North America[a]	–	3.7	5.7	6.0	-0.2	-0.9	5.4	5.0	4.9	2.9	-0.2	2.6	-2.3	3.7	6.6
Total above	2.5	3.7	5.0	5.8	0.9	-0.8	5.1	3.7	4.1	3.2	0.7	1.3	-0.9	2.5	4.6

Sources: National statistics; and for southern Europe, OECD *National Accounts*, vol. II. Data are calculated in 1975 prices and exchange rates.

[a] GNP.

[b] Social product.

APPENDIX TABLE A.2

Private consumption
(Annual percentage change)

	1970	1971	1972	1973	1974	1975	1976	1977	1978	1979	1980	1981	1982	1983	1984
France	4.3	6.3	6.1	5.6	3.2	3.2	5.5	3.2	4.7	3.4	1.5	2.0	3.5	1.0	0.8
Germany, Federal Republic of	7.6	5.2	4.6	2.4	0.4	3.5	3.8	3.7	3.6	3.1	1.4	-0.6	-1.4	1.1	0.8
Italy	7.3	2.9	3.4	5.8	2.6	-1.4	3.5	2.3	3.0	5.3	4.3	0.5	0.5	-0.5	2.0
United Kingdom	2.7	3.1	6.1	5.1	-1.4	-0.7	0.3	-0.5	5.5	4.5	-0.3	-0.1	1.0	4.0	1.5
Total 4 countries	5.6	4.7	5.1	4.5	1.2	1.7	3.6	2.5	4.2	3.8	1.6	0.5	0.9	1.3	1.1
Austria	4.2	6.7	6.1	5.4	3.0	3.2	4.5	5.7	-1.6	4.6	1.5	0.3	1.5	5.0	-1.0
Belgium	6.4	4.7	6.2	7.8	2.7	0.6	4.7	2.4	2.8	4.4	2.2	-1.0	0.7	-1.0	-0.8
Denmark	3.0	-0.6	1.6	5.7	-2.5	3.6	7.9	2.0	1.0	7.7	-3.7	-2.3	1.5	1.7	3.0
Finland	7.6	1.7	8.4	5.9	1.8	3.1	0.9	-1.2	2.8	5.6	1.9	1.4	4.1	2.0	3.0
Ireland	2.8	3.2	5.2	7.1	1.7	-2.7	2.8	6.8	9.0	4.3	1.5	2.1	-4.9	-3.5	1.2
Netherlands	7.7	3.0	3.2	3.9	2.7	3.4	5.7	6.4	4.3	3.0	0.0	-2.5	-1.3	-0.2	-0.5
Norway	-2.4	4.6	3.0	2.9	3.9	5.1	6.1	6.9	-1.6	3.2	2.3	1.1	1.4	1.0	1.0
Sweden	6.9	0.1	3.4	2.6	3.4	2.2	4.1	-1.0	-0.7	2.4	-0.9	-0.7	1.3	-1.7	0.8
Switzerland	5.4	4.8	5.4	2.8	-0.5	-2.9	1.1	3.0	2.2	1.3	2.6	0.4	—	1.5	1.5
Total 9 countries	5.5	3.0	4.5	4.6	1.9	1.7	4.3	3.2	1.8	3.7	0.7	-0.7	0.5	0.5	0.6
Total western Europe	5.5	4.3	5.0	4.5	1.4	1.7	3.8	2.7	3.6	3.8	1.4	0.2	0.8	1.2	1.0
Greece	8.8	5.6	7.0	7.6	0.7	5.5	5.3	4.6	5.7	2.7	-0.2	1.0	2.1	0.6	1.2
Portugal	2.6	12.7	4.0	12.0	9.7	-0.9	3.5	0.6	-1.7	0.9	2.9	2.4	2.0	-1.0	-2.0
Spain	4.2	4.9	8.3	8.0	5.2	2.4	4.7	2.5	1.3	1.2	1.3	-0.9	0.5	0.7	-0.7
Turkey	2.2	13.5	6.4	1.1	8.0	8.5	9.9	6.0	-1.1	-3.2	-5.1	0.6	4.4	4.9	4.9
Yugoslavia	14.6	8.3	4.6	2.7	7.3	3.4	4.4	7.0	7.0	5.6	0.7	-1.0	-0.1	-0.6	-1.0
Total southern Europe	6.3	10.5	5.8	4.5	6.6	5.2	6.8	5.1	1.9	0.6	-1.5	0.6	2.5	1.8	1.8
Total Europe	5.6	4.6	5.0	4.5	1.7	1.9	4.0	2.9	3.5	3.6	1.2	0.2	0.9	1.2	1.1
United States	2.2	3.7	5.8	4.3	-0.6	2.2	5.6	4.9	4.5	2.7	0.5	2.0	1.3	4.8	5.3
Canada	2.3	7.9	7.6	6.7	5.1	5.2	6.4	2.4	2.6	2.0	1.0	1.7	-2.0	3.1	3.8
North America	2.2	4.0	5.9	4.5	-0.1	2.4	5.7	4.7	4.3	2.6	0.5	2.0	1.0	4.6	5.2
Total above	3.8	4.3	5.5	4.5	0.8	2.2	4.8	3.8	3.9	3.1	0.8	1.1	1.0	3.0	3.2

Sources: National statistics; and for southern Europe, OECD *National Accounts*, vol. II. Data are calculated in 1975 prices and exchange rates.

APPENDIX TABLE A.3

Public consumption

(Annual percentage change)

	1970	1971	1972	1973	1974	1975	1976	1977	1978	1979	1980	1981	1982	1983	1984
France	4.2	3.5	2.7	3.2	1.2	4.7	6.2	1.4	4.3	1.8	1.8	2.3	2.5	1.9	1.2
Germany, Federal Republic of	4.4	5.2	4.2	5.0	4.1	3.9	1.6	0.9	3.9	3.5	2.6	1.5	-1.0	–	1.9
Italy	3.3	5.8	5.3	2.1	3.1	3.3	2.6	2.3	2.3	1.7	2.1	3.3	2.4	2.8	1.0
United Kingdom	1.6	3.0	4.2	4.9	1.5	5.5	1.3	-1.7	2.3	2.1	1.5	0.2	0.9	3.0	1.0
Total 4 countries	3.5	4.4	4.0	4.2	2.7	4.4	2.6	0.6	3.4	2.5	2.1	1.6	0.7	1.5	1.4
Austria	3.3	3.3	4.1	3.0	5.7	4.0	4.3	3.6	3.8	3.2	2.5	1.9	2.3	2.0	2.0
Belgium	10.7	5.9	5.9	5.3	3.8	4.7	4.0	2.7	5.9	2.7	1.6	1.2	-1.4	0.2	-0.3
Denmark	6.9	5.5	5.7	4.0	3.5	2.0	4.5	2.4	6.2	4.9	4.3	2.6	2.8	–	–
Finland	5.4	5.8	7.8	5.6	4.5	6.9	5.7	4.3	4.1	3.7	4.4	4.0	3.6	3.9	3.5
Ireland	7.4	8.7	7.1	6.8	7.5	6.5	2.7	2.0	8.2	6.9	6.9	2.0	4.1	–	-0.5
Netherlands	6.0	3.3	1.8	0.7	2.0	3.9	4.0	0.2	3.9	2.8	0.6	2.0	0.2	1.0	-1.0
Norway	1.0	6.0	4.5	5.5	4.0	6.4	7.4	4.9	5.3	3.5	5.4	6.1	3.7	3.7	2.6
Sweden	19.3	2.2	2.4	2.6	3.1	5.9	3.5	3.0	3.2	4.8	2.3	2.2	0.9	0.9	2.3
Switzerland	4.8	5.8	2.9	2.4	1.6	0.7	2.7	0.5	2.0	1.1	0.9	2.5	1.0	4.4	3.4
Total 9 countries	9.0	4.2	3.9	3.2	3.3	4.4	4.2	2.4	4.3	3.6	2.5	2.5	1.3	1.5	1.2
Total western Europe	5.0	4.3	4.0	3.9	2.9	4.4	3.0	1.1	3.6	2.8	2.2	1.8	0.8	1.5	1.3
Greece	5.9	4.9	5.7	6.8	12.1	11.9	5.1	6.5	3.5	5.8	0.2	6.8	1.9	2.5	3.0
Portugal	7.0	6.4	8.6	7.8	17.3	6.6	7.0	11.8	4.3	8.9	3.7	3.0	3.5	4.0	3.0
Spain	5.2	4.7	5.5	6.7	8.2	5.3	5.3	4.1	5.5	4.2	4.4	1.5	6.3	4.1	3.8
Turkey	3.6	6.1	7.3	10.3	9.9	13.5	10.8	3.2	9.9	1.6	8.8	0.8	3.2	1.8	2.9
Yugoslavia[a]	9.3	-0.1	5.1	4.1	7.3	9.3	9.5	7.4	6.5	4.5	-1.0	-4.8	-0.7	1.0	-1.6
Total southern Europe	6.2	4.2	6.5	7.4	11.1	10.8	8.3	6.6	6.4	4.7	3.3	1.5	2.1	2.2	2.0
Total Europe	5.0	4.3	4.1	4.0	3.2	4.6	3.2	1.3	3.8	2.9	2.2	1.8	0.9	1.5	1.4
United States	-2.4	-0.4	1.2	0.2	3.0	2.1	0.0	0.9	2.0	1.3	2.2	0.9	2.0	-0.3	3.5
Canada	10.4	4.1	3.1	4.6	4.0	4.0	0.9	3.2	1.7	0.3	0.4	2.5	0.7	0.3	2.3
North America	-1.6	-0.1	1.3	0.5	3.1	2.3	0.1	1.1	1.9	1.3	2.0	1.1	1.9	-0.2	3.4
Total above	1.1	1.8	2.5	2.0	3.1	3.3	1.5	1.2	2.8	2.0	2.1	1.4	1.4	0.6	2.5

Sources: National statistics; and for southern Europe, OECD *National Accounts*, vol. II. Data are calculated at 1975 prices and exchange rates.

aCollective consumption.

APPENDIX TABLE A.4

Gross domestic fixed capital formation
(Annual percentage change)

	1970	1971	1972	1973	1974	1975	1976	1977	1978	1979	1980	1981	1982	1983	1984
France	4.6	7.1	7.2	6.1	0.9	-3.2	3.7	-0.8	1.5	3.7	3.2	-1.6	-0.6	-1.4	-1.1
Germany, Federal Republic of	9.9	6.2	2.5	-0.2	-9.6	-4.9	4.6	3.8	4.9	7.3	3.2	-4.2	-4.7	3.1	1.3
Italy	3.0	-3.2	0.9	7.7	3.3	-12.7	2.3	-0.4	-0.1	5.8	9.4	0.6	-5.2	-5.3	2.2
United Kingdom	2.6	1.9	-0.3	7.2	-4.1	0.2	1.5	-2.6	3.9	2.3	-5.2	-8.5	6.7	4.0	6.5
Total 4 countries	5.9	4.2	3.1	4.1	-3.6	-4.6	3.4	0.6	2.9	5.1	2.5	-3.4	-1.7	0.6	1.9
Austria	9.8	13.8	12.1	0.3	4.0	-5.0	3.8	5.2	-3.8	3.6	3.6	-2.0	-6.8	-1.9	3.0
Belgium	9.0	-2.0	2.9	7.0	7.4	-1.8	3.8	0.1	2.6	-2.6	4.6	-16.2	-1.1	-6.4	3.3
Denmark	2.4	1.7	8.6	4.3	-9.0	-12.2	17.4	-2.3	1.4	0.5	-12.6	-19.2	5.4	3.2	11.9
Finland	12.5	3.8	6.5	8.5	3.5	5.9	-8.8	-5.1	-7.2	3.1	9.9	3.2	3.5	2.5	-1.5
Ireland	0.2	8.6	5.2	18.1	-7.5	-1.7	10.1	4.7	18.3	14.1	-6.2	6.1	-6.1	-7.7	-2.0
Netherlands	9.5	3.4	-2.8	4.5	-3.8	-4.9	-2.8	18.8	2.5	-1.7	-0.9	-10.5	-4.2	0.4	2.4
Norway	11.5	18.7	-4.1	13.6	5.1	11.9	10.1	3.6	-11.2	-5.0	-1.5	17.9	-10.2	2.8	4.4
Sweden	10.2	-0.6	4.2	2.7	-3.0	3.1	1.9	-2.9	-6.8	4.5	3.5	-5.3	-1.1	1.1	2.4
Switzerland	8.9	9.9	5.0	2.9	-4.3	-13.6	-10.5	1.6	6.1	5.1	9.9	2.4	-2.7	4.3	3.8
Total 9 countries	8.9	5.0	3.5	5.0	-0.9	-2.9	1.0	3.3	-1.0	1.1	2.0	-4.5	-2.8	0.4	3.2
Total western Europe	6.7	4.4	3.2	4.4	-2.8	-4.2	2.7	1.3	1.8	4.0	2.4	-3.7	-2.0	0.6	2.2
Greece	-1.4	14.0	15.4	7.7	-25.6	0.2	6.8	7.8	6.0	8.8	-6.5	-7.8	-1.5	-1.4	1.0
Portugal	11.5	9.8	13.5	9.5	-7.0	-11.3	0.8	12.0	7.1	-0.9	10.3	5.1	2.9	-7.5	-20.0
Spain	3.0	-2.9	15.8	14.3	6.6	-3.9	-2.0	-0.2	-2.3	-4.5	1.3	0.9	-2.0	-1.5	-1.5
Turkey	13.5	-5.0	14.8	13.0	8.1	24.2	20.2	4.6	-10.0	-3.6	-10.0	1.7	2.6	3.0	1.8
Yugoslavia	22.6	4.6	1.8	4.2	9.1	9.7	8.1	9.5	10.5	6.4	-5.9	-9.8	-5.9	-10.2	-10.0
Total southern Europe	12.7	4.8	10.1	8.2	-2.1	8.4	10.8	7.8	2.1	2.6	-4.8	-3.8	-1.1	-4.3	-6.2
Total Europe	7.1	4.4	3.6	4.6	-2.8	-3.4	3.3	1.8	1.8	3.8	1.8	-3.7	-1.9	0.2	1.6
United States	-3.5	7.1	11.5	8.4	-8.2	-12.2	9.5	13.6	9.9	3.8	-7.1	3.1	-6.8	9.7	18.2
Canada	0.3	10.0	5.6	11.1	5.4	3.8	4.0	-0.5	-0.1	6.8	3.4	6.4	-9.7	-4.9	1.0
North America	-3.0	7.5	10.7	8.7	-6.5	-10.0	8.6	11.5	8.5	4.2	-5.7	3.6	-7.2	7.7	16.1
Total above	2.9	5.6	6.4	6.3	-4.3	-6.1	5.4	5.7	4.7	4.0	-1.5	-0.6	-4.3	3.4	8.1

Sources: National statistics; and for southern Europe, OECD *National Accounts*, vol. II. Data are calculated at 1975 prices and exchange rates.

APPENDIX TABLE A.5

Volume of exports of goods and services

(Annual percentage change)

	1970	1971	1972	1973	1974	1975	1976	1977	1978	1979	1980	1981	1982	1983	1984
France	16.1	11.2	13.4	12.5	10.8	-1.5	10.7	8.5	6.1	7.3	2.4	5.3	-2.2	3.6	4.7
Germany, Federal Republic of	6.5	6.2	6.5	10.2	12.0	-6.1	10.5	3.5	4.2	4.9	5.5	8.4	4.6	-1.3	7.4
Italy	6.0	7.2	11.5	3.8	9.9	3.7	13.2	6.7	10.1	9.1	-4.3	5.2	0.8	3.9	6.0
United Kingdom	5.5	6.8	1.2	11.6	7.3	-2.7	9.0	6.5	1.9	3.8	-0.1	-1.8	0.9	1.5	6.5
Total 4 countries	8.1	7.5	7.5	10.1	10.4	-3.0	10.6	5.8	5.0	5.9	2.1	5.1	1.6	1.2	6.4
Austria	16.4	5.9	9.2	8.9	10.6	-3.0	11.6	5.1	4.4	10.9	6.6	5.1	2.1	6.2	18.3
Belgium	10.8	6.3	10.0	14.4	6.8	-8.9	12.6	12.3	3.7	8.0	4.5	3.3	3.4	0.0	4.8
Denmark	5.2	5.1	5.7	7.7	4.4	-1.7	4.2	4.8	2.0	6.2	5.2	8.2	2.6	3.4	4.8
Finland	8.7	-1.3	14.5	6.6	-14.0	12.8	16.0	8.5	0.0	9.0	8.5	6.4	-1.5	3.6	6.0
Ireland	4.4	4.1	3.6	10.9	0.7	7.2	8.1	14.0	12.3	6.7	6.5	1.8	5.5	10.6	14.2
Netherlands	12.3	11.0	10.8	12.4	2.5	-3.0	10.1	-58.3	2.5	-1.7	-0.9	-10.5	-4.2	0.4	2.4
Norway	9.5	1.1	14.1	8.3	0.7	3.1	11.3	3.6	8.4	2.6	2.1	1.4	0.2	7.0	6.1
Sweden	1.0	4.8	5.9	13.7	5.3	-9.3	4.3	1.5	7.8	6.1	-0.5	1.1	4.4	10.5	7.2
Switzerland	6.8	3.9	6.4	7.9	1.0	-6.6	9.3	9.7	3.7	2.5	5.1	4.6	-3.0	0.9	5.2
Total 9 countries	8.9	6.0	9.2	11.1	3.2	-4.0	9.8	3.3	4.4	6.6	3.5	3.3	1.2	4.3	6.7
Total western Europe . .	8.4	6.9	8.1	10.5	7.6	-3.4	10.3	4.9	4.8	6.1	2.6	4.4	1.5	2.3	6.5
Greece	12.4	11.9	22.9	23.4	0.1	10.6	16.4	1.8	16.4	6.7	6.6	-4.1	-9.0	9.8	8.0
Portugal	-1.6	9.9	18.5	4.2	-15.7	-15.6	0.0	5.9	11.1	30.2	7.6	-3.4	6.0	16.5	12.0
Spain	17.5	13.0	12.2	9.0	0.8	-1.4	10.1	8.5	10.7	6.4	0.6	6.9	7.1	7.6	18.0
Turkey	14.3	15.5	14.6	26.2	-11.0	-1.1	37.5	-21.8	12.9	-12.3	7.4	62.2	36.1	8.4	23.0
Yugoslavia	3.3	3.7	17.6	6.8	1.0	-1.8	14.9	-5.4	-0.8	5.4	11.0	12.2	-7.0	-0.6	7.7
Total southern Europe . .	4.8	8.5	18.1	12.0	-5.8	-2.5	16.5	-5.6	7.9	7.2	8.5	12.3	4.9	7.4	13.2
Total Europe	8.3	7.0	8.5	10.5	7.1	-3.4	10.5	4.5	4.9	6.2	2.8	4.7	1.6	2.5	6.8
United States	8.5	0.7	9.2	25.5	11.5	-4.5	6.3	2.5	12.2	15.4	8.8	0.7	-7.9	-5.5	4.5
Canada.	9.0	4.5	6.6	10.6	-2.0	-6.4	9.6	7.3	10.5	3.0	1.8	3.1	-1.6	6.4	18.5
North America	8.6	1.7	8.5	21.7	8.3	-4.9	7.0	3.6	11.8	12.7	7.4	1.1	-6.6	-3.1	7.7
Total above	8.4	5.6	8.5	13.3	7.5	-3.8	9.5	4.3	6.7	8.0	4.1	3.7	-0.8	4.0	7.0

Sources: National statistics; and for southern Europe, OECD *National Accounts*, Vol. II. Data are calculated at 1975 prices and exchange rates. National expenditure accounting basis is employed.

APPENDIX TABLE A.6

Volume of imports of goods and services

(Annual percentage change)

	1970	1971	1972	1973	1974	1975	1976	1977	1978	1979	1980	1981	1982	1983	1984
France	6.3	7.8	16.7	15.4	6.3	−7.5	20.7	2.2	6.2	11.4	7.2	1.6	6.3	−0.9	3.0
Germany, Federal Republic of	15.8	9.3	6.0	4.1	1.4	1.5	10.5	3.9	5.3	10.2	3.9	0.7	2.1	0.5	5.5
Italy	15.9	2.4	11.4	10.5	2.2	−9.6	15.4	−0.2	8.1	13.8	8.3	−5.3	2.0	0.8	7.2
United Kingdom	5.3	5.2	10.0	11.9	1.2	−7.1	4.2	1.2	3.9	10.4	−3.9	−3.4	3.9	5.5	8.5
Total 4 countries	11.1	7.0	9.9	9.3	2.7	−4.3	12.2	2.4	5.6	11.0	3.8	−0.7	3.6	1.1	5.6
Austria	16.9	5.8	11.1	12.9	7.5	−5.5	17.7	8.3	−2.3	11.8	6.8	−0.3	−2.6	9.9	19.1
Belgium	12.1	5.3	8.4	19.4	7.5	−9.8	12.2	14.9	3.9	9.5	1.9	−1.5	1.3	−3.0	2.3
Denmark	8.4	−0.5	0.9	15.1	−3.5	−4.3	17.0	0.2	0.6	13.4	−6.8	−1.7	2.9	0.7	6.9
Finland	20.3	−0.6	4.2	13.0	6.7	0.6	−2.0	−1.6	−3.9	18.5	8.3	−3.5	2.1	3.8	1.5
Ireland	2.4	4.7	5.1	19.0	−2.3	−10.2	14.7	13.3	15.7	14.1	−4.7	2.3	−3.1	3.9	6.8
Netherlands	14.5	6.1	5.2	10.9	−1.1	−4.1	10.3	0.3	6.3	6.0	−0.4	−5.9	0.7	4.9	3.5
Norway	18.5	6.4	−1.0	14.4	4.7	7.0	12.3	3.4	−13.5	−0.7	3.3	1.5	4.2	−1.2	1.6
Sweden	21.9	−3.3	4.0	6.9	9.9	−3.5	9.0	−3.8	−5.5	11.6	0.4	−7.1	4.3	0.0	5.7
Switzerland	13.9	6.2	7.3	6.5	−1.0	−15.4	13.1	9.3	10.9	6.9	7.2	−1.3	−2.6	4.7	6.5
Total 9 countries	14.9	3.7	5.4	12.3	3.2	−5.7	11.4	4.7	1.8	8.8	1.8	−2.8	0.9	2.2	5.4
Total western Europe	12.6	5.7	8.1	10.5	2.8	−4.8	11.9	3.3	4.1	10.2	3.0	−1.5	2.6	1.5	5.5
Greece	6.2	7.6	15.4	32.2	−16.3	6.3	6.1	8.0	7.2	7.2	−6.6	3.4	5.1	2.6	3.0
Portugal	0.9	14.5	12.0	12.7	4.8	−25.2	3.4	12.0	−0.2	11.5	11.6	0.6	5.0	−8.0	−4.4
Spain	7.0	0.6	24.7	16.4	7.7	−1.1	10.1	−4.7	−0.7	11.5	3.8	−2.8	4.5	−0.6	1.0
Turkey	22.0	9.7	19.0	10.5	1.7	11.8	21.6	−5.5	−31.2	−9.0	−2.8	11.1	7.7	12.5	15.0
Yugoslavia	27.8	9.2	−6.5	16.4	14.4	−2.8	−6.8	13.1	−1.0	20.0	−10.0	−2.3	−10.0	−5.5	4.2
Total southern Europe	15.8	10.3	8.9	16.0	2.6	−1.9	7.5	4.4	−10.9	7.4	−3.0	2.8	1.1	0.6	5.5
Total Europe	12.8	5.9	8.1	10.8	2.8	−4.7	11.6	3.3	3.2	10.0	2.7	−1.3	2.5	1.4	5.5
United States	3.9	4.1	10.7	6.5	−1.2	−11.5	18.6	7.3	13.0	6.1	−0.2	7.0	1.4	7.5	27.1
Canada	−0.7	6.9	11.2	13.6	9.8	−2.8	8.7	1.6	4.6	6.9	−2.5	4.5	−11.2	8.1	16.0
North America	2.7	4.8	10.8	8.4	1.9	−8.9	15.4	5.6	10.5	6.4	−0.8	6.3	−2.0	7.7	24.4
Total above	10.2	5.7	8.8	10.2	2.6	−5.7	12.5	3.9	5.0	9.1	1.8	0.5	1.3	3.0	10.4

Sources: National statistics; and for southern Europe, OECD *National Accounts*, vol. II. Data are calculated at 1975 prices and exchange rates. National expenditure accounting basis is employed.

APPENDIX TABLE A.7

Current account balances

(Million US dollars)

	1970	1971	1972	1973	1974	1975	1976	1977	1978	1979	1980	1981	1982	1983	1984ª
France	55	569	294	1450	-3860	2743	-3371	408	7065	5141	-4208	-4809	-12081	-4904	-66
Germany, Federal Republic of	850	770	810	4650	10360	4090	3940	4140	9270	-6190	-16000	-5720	3410	4000	6500
Italy	902	2041	1992	-2538	-8062	-580	-2901	2440	6237	5414	-9801	-8604	-5684	597	-1000
United Kingdom	1975	2742	731	-2520	-7707	-3477	-1508	147	2246	-954	8690	15068	8934	4364	-220
Total 4 countries	3782	6122	3827	1042	-9269	2776	-3840	6319	24818	3411	-21319	-4065	-5421	4057	5214
Austria	-75	-92	-157	-254	-203	-232	-1119	-2200	-706	-1141	-1725	-1526	385	-119	–
Belgium	717	647	1296	1378	774	180	435	-554	-817	-3077	-4945	-4174	-2669	-762	-500
Denmark	-544	-424	-63	-476	-980	-490	-1913	-1722	-1502	-2965	-2466	-1875	-2259	-1176	-1750
Finland	-240	-339	-118	-390	-1219	-2180	-1154	-106	671	-169	-1409	-373	-743	-945	-750
Ireland	-198	-200	-150	-253	-688	-123	-428	-522	-852	-2100	-2133	-2567	-1867	-1100	-750
Netherlands	-482	-107	1352	2419	2219	1991	2730	621	-1436	-2070	-2974	2883	3697	3681	4500
Norway	-242	-526	-58	-366	-1119	-2478	-3746	-5034	-2103	-1044	1098	2184	675	2204	3500
Sweden	-264	351	567	1429	-552	-342	-1647	-2181	-251	-2414	-4404	-2847	-3393	-938	–
Switzerland	72	82	221	279	174	2287	3134	3395	3756	1268	-1555	1498	3934	3526	3300
Total 9 countries	-1256	-608	2890	3766	-1594	-1387	-3708	-8303	-3240	-13712	-20513	-6797	-2240	4371	8300
Total western Europe	2526	5514	6717	4808	-10863	1389	-7548	-1984	21578	-10301	-41832	-10862	-7661	8428	13514
Greece	-422	-344	-400	-1188	-1143	-876	-929	-1075	-955	-1886	-2209	-2408	-1892	-1878	1900
Portugal	..	..	355	341	-829	-754	-1281	-957	-463	-54	-1064	-2605	-3250	-1620	-500
Spain	79	855	580	586	-3232	-3514	-4291	-2133	1634	1128	-5173	-4989	-4240	-2480	1945
Turkey	-44	43	211	661	-519	-1595	-1972	-3074	-1213	-1356	-3233	-1908	-790	-1747	-1000
Yugoslavia	-372	-396	431	501	-950	-626	180	-1346	-1284	-3665	-2316	-961	-475	-275	504
Total southern Europe	..	..	1177	901	-6673	-7365	-8293	-8585	-2281	-5833	-13995	-12871	-10647	-7450	-901
Total Europe	..	..	7894	5709	-17536	-5976	-15841	-10569	19297	-16134	-55827	-23733	-18308	2078	12613
United States	2320	-1450	-5780	7070	1920	18130	4170	-14490	-15490	-950	1890	6290	-9190	-41580	-105000
Canada	1078	423	-387	108	-1487	-4696	-4153	-4112	-4298	-4120	-953	-5055	2110	1365	1000
North America	3398	-1027	-6167	7178	433	13434	17	-18602	-19788	-5070	937	1235	-7080	-40215	-104000
Total above	..	..	1727	12887	-17103	7458	-15824	-29171	-491	-21204	-54890	-22488	-25388	-38137	-91387

Source: International Monetary Fund, *International Financial Statistics.*

ª 1984 provisional data from OECD, *Economic Outlook,* No. 36, December 1984. EFTA secretariat forecast, based on national sources.

APPENDIX TABLE A.8

Industrial production
(Indices, 1980 = 100)

	1970	1971	1972	1973	1974	1975	1976	1977	1978	1979	1980	1981	1982	1983	1984
France	74.0	79.0	84.0	89.0	91.0	85.0	92.0	93.0	96.0	100.0	100.0	99.0	97.0	98.0	100.0
Germany, Federal Republic of	83.2	83.9	86.9	92.3	90.8	85.2	91.1	93.4	95.1	100.0	100.0	98.5	95.6	96.3	99.6
Italy	72.2	71.8	75.3	82.6	85.9	78.3	87.4	87.4	89.1	95.1	100.0	98.4	95.4	92.3	95.4
United Kingdom	90.1	89.6	91.2	99.4	97.5	92.2	95.2	100.1	103.1	107.2	100.0	96.5	98.6	101.9	102.7
Total 4 countries	80.4	81.7	85.0	91.2	91.3	85.3	91.5	93.6	95.9	100.6	100.0	98.2	96.5	97.1	99.6
Austria	68.2	72.2	78.1	81.0	85.4	80.0	85.3	88.6	90.4	97.4	100.0	98.4	97.6	98.5	104.0
Belgium	80.2	82.3	87.3	92.8	96.2	87.0	94.6	94.5	96.8	101.2	100.0	97.2	97.0	99.0	102.0
Denmark															
Finland	64.0	67.0	73.0	78.0	82.0	79.0	80.0	80.0	84.0	93.0	100.0	102.9	103.8	106.9	112.0
Ireland[a]	64.0	67.0	70.0	77.0	78.0	75.0	82.0	88.0	95.0	102.0	100.0	102.3	102.6	109.2	123.0
Netherlands	75.0	80.0	83.0	89.0	94.0	89.0	96.0	96.0	97.0	101.0	100.0	98.0	94.0	96.0	101.0
Norway	59.0	61.0	65.0	69.0	72.0	76.0	80.0	80.0	88.0	94.0	100.0	99.0	99.0	106.0	113.0
Sweden[a]	91.0	92.0	94.0	100.0	105.0	102.0	102.0	96.0	94.0	100.0	100.0	98.0	97.0	103.0	110.0
Switzerland	90.0	92.0	94.0	99.0	100.0	87.0	88.0	93.0	93.0	95.0	100.0	99.0	96.0	95.0	99.0
Total 8 countries	77.5	80.4	84.0	89.1	92.7	86.8	90.9	91.5	93.2	98.2	100.0	98.6	97.0	99.6	104.8
Total western Europe	79.8	81.4	84.8	90.8	91.6	85.6	91.4	93.2	95.3	100.1	100.0	98.3	96.6	97.6	100.7
Greece	51.1	56.9	64.9	74.9	73.7	77.0	85.1	86.8	93.4	99.0	100.0	99.3	94.9	94.3	97.0
Portugal	53.2	57.4	64.8	72.5	74.5	70.8	73.2	82.8	88.5	94.9	100.0	100.5	105.1	106.8	104.0
Spain	63.2	65.1	75.5	86.8	94.9	86.6	91.0	95.8	98.0	98.8	100.0	99.0	97.8	100.5	102.0
Turkey															
Yugoslavia	49.0	54.0	59.0	62.0	69.0	72.0	75.0	82.0	89.0	97.0	100.0	104.0	104.0	105.0	111.0
Total southern Europe	58.0	61.1	69.8	78.8	85.2	81.0	85.2	90.7	94.7	98.1	100.0	100.3	99.6	101.5	103.8
Total Europe	77.8	79.6	83.4	89.7	91.0	85.2	90.8	92.9	95.3	99.9	100.0	98.5	96.9	98.0	101.0
United States	73.3	74.6	81.5	88.3	88.0	80.1	88.7	94.0	99.4	103.8	100.0	102.7	94.3	100.4	111.2
Canada	69.6	73.6	79.2	87.6	90.4	85.0	90.2	92.5	95.6	101.5	100.0	100.9	90.1	95.5	103.6
North America	73.0	74.5	81.3	88.2	88.2	80.5	88.8	93.9	99.1	103.6	100.0	102.5	93.9	100.0	110.5
Total above	75.7	77.4	82.5	89.1	89.8	83.2	90.0	93.3	96.9	101.5	100.0	100.2	95.6	98.8	105.1

Source: OECD, *Main Economic Indicators*, Paris (monthly).

[a] Ireland and Sweden refer to mining and manufacturing only.

APPENDIX TABLE A.9

Consumer prices
(Annual percentage change)

	1970	1971	1972	1973	1974	1975	1976	1977	1978	1979	1980	1981	1982	1983	1984
France	5.2	5.5	6.2	7.3	13.7	11.8	9.6	9.4	9.1	10.8	13.6	13.4	11.8	9.6	7.4
Germany, Federal Republic of	3.6	5.1	5.6	6.9	6.9	5.9	4.4	3.6	2.7	4.2	5.4	6.3	5.3	3.3	2.4
Italy	4.9	4.8	5.7	10.8	19.1	17.0	16.7	17.0	12.1	14.8	21.2	17.8	16.5	14.7	10.8
United Kingdom	6.4	9.4	7.1	9.1	16.0	24.2	16.5	15.8	8.3	13.4	18.0	11.9	8.6	4.6	5.0
Total 4 countries	4.8	6.0	6.1	8.2	12.9	13.2	10.5	10.1	7.3	9.8	13.0	11.5	9.8	7.4	5.8
Austria	4.4	4.7	6.3	7.6	9.5	8.4	7.3	5.5	3.6	3.7	6.4	6.8	5.4	3.3	5.6
Belgium	3.9	4.4	5.4	7.0	12.7	12.8	9.2	7.1	4.5	4.5	6.6	7.6	8.7	7.7	6.3
Denmark	6.5	5.8	6.6	9.3	15.2	9.6	9.0	11.1	10.1	9.6	12.3	11.7	10.1	6.9	6.3
Finland	2.7	6.1	7.4	10.7	16.9	17.9	14.4	12.6	7.8	7.5	11.6	12.0	9.6	8.3	7.1
Ireland	8.2	8.9	8.7	11.4	17.0	20.9	18.0	13.6	7.6	13.2	18.2	20.4	17.1	10.4	8.6
Netherlands	3.6	7.5	7.8	8.0	9.6	10.2	8.8	6.4	4.1	4.2	6.5	6.7	5.9	2.8	3.3
Norway	10.7	6.0	7.2	7.6	9.4	11.6	9.2	9.0	8.2	4.8	10.9	13.6	11.3	8.4	6.2
Sweden	7.0	7.4	6.0	6.8	9.9	9.8	10.3	11.4	10.0	7.2	13.7	12.1	8.6	9.0	8.0
Switzerland	3.6	6.6	6.7	8.7	9.8	6.7	1.8	1.2	1.1	3.6	4.0	6.5	5.6	3.0	3.0
Total 9 countries	5.0	6.3	6.7	8.0	11.3	10.7	8.6	7.7	5.7	5.5	8.7	9.2	7.9	5.9	5.5
Total western Europe	4.9	6.1	6.2	8.1	12.5	12.6	10.0	9.5	6.9	8.7	12.0	10.9	9.3	7.0	5.8
Greece	2.9	3.0	4.3	15.5	26.9	13.4	13.3	12.1	12.6	19.0	24.9	24.5	21.0	20.2	18.5
Portugal[a]	6.4	12.0	10.7	12.9	25.1	15.3	21.0[b]	27.4	22.0	24.2	16.6	20.0	22.4	25.5	29.5
Spain	5.6	8.3	8.3	11.4	15.7	16.9	14.9	24.5	19.8	15.7	15.5	14.6	14.4	12.2	11.3
Turkey[c]	8.1	16.3	12.9	16.6	18.7	20.1	15.3	28.4	49.5	56.5	116.6	35.9	27.1	31.4[b]	48.4
Yugoslavia	10.4	15.7	16.3	19.9	21.0	24.2	12.0	15.1	14.1	20.3	31.0	42.1	31.5	40.8	53.4
Total southern Europe	6.4	10.5	9.9	14.0	18.8	17.9	15.0	23.1	24.1	24.9	37.3	23.4	20.2	21.1	25.5
Total Europe	5.1	6.7	6.7	8.9	13.3	13.3	10.7	11.2	9.1	10.8	15.2	12.5	10.7	8.8	8.3
United States[d]	5.9	4.3	3.3	6.2	11.0	9.1	5.8	6.5	7.6[b]	11.3	13.5	10.4	6.1	3.2	4.3
Canada	3.3	2.9	4.7	7.7	10.9	10.8	7.5	7.9	8.8	9.2	10.2	12.5	10.8	5.8	4.4
North America	5.7	4.2	3.4	6.4	11.0	9.3	5.9	6.6	7.7	11.1	13.2	10.6	6.5	3.4	4.3
Total above	5.4	5.4	5.1	7.6	12.1	11.3	8.3	8.9	8.4	10.9	14.2	11.5	8.6	6.1	6.3

Source: National statistics with weights taken from OECD National Accounts.

a 1970-1976, Lisbon.

b Major change in coverage takes place in year noted.

c 1970-1982, Ankara; 1983-1984, total urban areas.

d 1970-1978, urban wage earners and clerical workers; 1979 and thereafter, all urban consumers.

APPENDIX TABLE A.10

Average hourly earnings in manufacturing
(Annual percentage change)

	1970	1971	1972	1973	1974	1975	1976	1977	1978	1979	1980	1981	1982	1983
France[a]	10.5	11.2	11.3	14.6	19.3	17.3	14.1	12.7	12.9	13.0	15.1	14.5	15.2	11.2
Germany, Federal Republic of	13.6	11.0	8.7	10.7	10.6	8.2	6.5	7.5	5.0	5.5	6.2	5.2	4.9	3.3
Italy[a]	21.7	13.5	10.4	24.2	22.4	26.7	20.9	27.9	16.2	19.0	22.5	23.7	17.2	15.3
United Kingdom[b]	12.8	11.3	12.8	12.7	17.2	26.1	16.9	10.3	14.3	15.7	17.8	13.3	11.2	9.0
Total 4 countries	14.4	11.6	10.7	14.8	16.5	18.5	13.7	13.5	11.3	12.5	14.4	13.0	11.2	8.9
Austria[c]	9.4	13.7	11.6	12.7	15.9	13.3	9.1	8.5	5.7	5.8	7.9	6.2	6.1	4.5
Belgium	10.5	13.6	14.9	16.2	20.7	18.6	11.7	9.8	5.8	7.5	9.3	10.9	7.4	5.9
Denmark[d]	12.0	14.5	12.6	18.8	21.5	19.1	12.7	10.3	10.4	11.3	11.2	9.5	10.0	6.6
Finland[e]	11.0	14.5	14.7	16.8	22.3	21.1	14.8	8.9	7.4	11.6	12.8	12.7	10.5	9.6
Ireland[e]	16.1	16.1	14.9	19.0	20.3	28.7	17.0	18.6	14.5	15.4	21.1	16.4	14.4	10.3
Netherlands[a]	10.8	12.0	13.3	13.0	17.7	13.5	8.6	7.3	5.7	4.3	4.6	3.0	7.2	2.2
Norway[f]	12.0	12.5	9.1	10.6	17.5	20.3	17.0	10.9	8.0	2.9	9.9	10.4	10.2	8.4
Sweden[d]	15.6	5.4	15.4	8.2	11.0	14.8	17.8	6.7	8.7	7.8	8.8	10.6	7.9	7.9
Switzerland[c]	6.2	9.7	8.8	9.2	13.9	7.4	1.6	1.7	3.4	2.1	5.2	5.1	5.9	3.7
Total 9 countries	11.0	11.7	12.8	13.0	17.1	15.6	11.2	7.9	6.8	6.7	8.6	8.3	7.9	5.8
Total western Europe	13.7	11.6	11.1	14.4	16.6	17.9	13.2	12.4	10.4	11.3	13.2	12.1	10.5	8.3
Greece	6.0	8.7	9.2	15.8	26.8	24.4	28.8	20.8	23.7	20.5	27.2	27.2	33.9	18.2
Portugal[g]					44.9	33.1	18.7	16.3	16.7	15.9	23.5	20.8	19.8	19.9
Spain[h]	14.4	14.0	15.4	19.7	25.6	28.6	30.0	30.3	26.6	23.7	18.4	19.9	15.2	16.2
Turkey														
Yugoslavia[c]	16.3	22.3	16.1	19.3	27.8	22.4	14.2	17.9	19.1	20.7	24.2	34.7	27.4	24.0
Total southern Europe	14.1	16.3	14.9	19.1	29.3	27.0	23.4	23.5	22.6	21.3	21.8	25.2	21.5	19.3
Total Europe	13.9	14.0	13.0	16.8	23.0	22.5	18.3	18.0	16.5	16.3	17.5	18.7	16.0	13.8
United States	5.2	6.2	7.2	7.0	8.3	9.0	8.1	8.8	8.7	8.5	8.7	9.8	6.3	4.0
Canada	8.0	8.9	7.8	8.9	13.5	15.7	13.7	10.9	7.2	8.8	10.1	11.8	11.8	3.5
North America	5.4	6.4	7.3	7.2	8.8	9.6	8.6	9.0	8.6	8.5	8.8	10.0	6.8	4.0
Total above	10.7	11.2	10.9	13.2	17.7	17.7	14.7	14.6	13.5	13.4	14.2	15.4	12.6	10.1

Source: National statistics, and OECD, *Economic Outlook—Historical Statistics, 1960-1982.*

[a] Wage rates.
[b] Weekly earnings of all employees—Great Britain.
[c] Monthly earnings in mining and manufacturing.
[d] Includes mining.
[e] Industry.
[f] Males only.
[g] Daily earnings. Excluded for 1970-1973.
[h] Refers to all activities.

APPENDIX TABLE A.11

Total employment

(Annual percentage change)

	1970	1971	1972	1973	1974	1975	1976	1977	1978	1979	1980	1981	1982	1983
France[a]	1.4	0.4	0.5	1.1	0.8	-1.0	0.7	0.8	0.4	-0.1	0.0	-0.8	0.2	-0.7
Germany, Federal Republic of[a]	1.2	0.6	-0.3	0.7	-1.3	-2.8	-0.8	-0.2	0.6	1.3	1.0	-0.8	-1.8	-1.7
Italy	0.4	0.0	-1.7	1.0	2.0	0.5	0.8	1.1	0.4	1.1	1.5	0.4	-0.3	0.0
United Kingdom[a]	0.5	-1.9	-0.1	2.3	0.3	-0.4	-0.8	0.1	0.6	1.3	-0.5	-3.5	-1.4	-0.8
Total 4 countries	0.6	—	-0.3	1.3	0.3	-1.0	-0.1	0.4	0.5	0.9	0.5	-1.2	-0.9	-0.8
Austria[a]	0.4	1.2	0.7	1.7	0.9	-0.5	0.6	0.9	0.2	0.2	0.2	0.1	-1.2	-1.2
Belgium[a]	1.8	1.0	-0.1	1.2	1.4	-1.5	-0.7	-0.2	0.1	1.2	-0.1	-2.1	-2.0	-1.3
Denmark	1.4	0.8	0.8	1.0	-1.4	-1.1	2.5	1.0	2.5	0.8	-1.4	-2.5	-0.4	-0.9
Finland	1.4	-0.1	-0.2	2.2	3.0	-0.4	2.6	-2.0	-1.4	2.5	3.2	1.1	1.0	0.5
Ireland	0.5	0.2	-0.5	0.7	0.9	-1.0	0.2	0.9	2.5	3.1	1.7	-1.0	-0.4	-0.8
Netherlands[b]		0.4	-0.5	0.5	0.2	-0.6	0.5	1.3	1.4	2.4	2.2	-0.1	-0.6	-1.1
Norway				0.3	0.3	2.9	4.8	2.0	1.6	1.0	2.2	1.0	0.7	0.6
Sweden	1.9	0.2	0.1	0.4	2.1	2.5	0.6	0.3	0.4	1.6	1.2	-0.2	-0.1	0.1
Switzerland	1.4	1.4	0.7	0.4	-0.5	-5.3	-3.3	0.2	0.6	0.7	1.8	1.3	-0.7	-1.3
Total 9 countries				0.9	0.8	-0.6	0.5	0.5	0.7	1.5	1.2	-0.3	-0.5	-0.7
Total western Europe				1.2	0.4	-0.9	—	0.4	0.6	0.8	0.6	-1.0	-0.8	-0.8
Greece	0.1	0.3	0.5	1.0	0.1	0.1	1.2	0.8	0.4	1.1	1.4	5.2	-1.1	0.5
Portugal	0.6	-0.3	-0.6	-0.8	14.6c	-0.9	1.5	-0.1	-0.3	2.2	1.8	1.1	-0.3	-3.8
Spain	1.0	0.6	0.1	2.5	0.5	-1.8	-0.9	-0.8	-2.5	-1.9	-3.9	-2.9	-0.5	-0.7
Turkey	1.3	1.7	2.3	1.6	1.3	0.8	2.3	1.9	1.0	0.1	0.0	0.9	0.8	0.7
Yugoslavia	1.9	-0.7	-0.4	-0.7	1.2	1.3	0.9	1.0	1.1	1.0	1.2	0.9	0.7	0.9
Total southern Europe	0.4	0.6	0.7	1.2	2.0	-0.1	0.9	0.7	-0.2	—	-0.6	0.3	0.2	-0.1
Total Europe				1.2	0.8	-0.7	0.2	0.5	0.4	0.8	0.3	-0.7	-0.6	-0.6
United States[a]	0.6	0.4	2.9	3.3	1.9	-1.1	3.3	3.6	4.3	2.8	0.5	1.1	-0.8	1.3
Canada[a]	1.1	2.3	2.9	4.9	4.1	1.7	2.1	1.8	3.3	3.9	2.7	3.2	-3.3	0.8
North America	0.6	0.6	2.9	3.4	2.1	-0.9	3.1	3.4	4.2	2.9	0.7	1.3	-1.1	1.2
Total above				2.0	1.3	-0.8	1.3	1.6	1.9	1.6	0.5	0.1	-0.8	0.2

Sources: National statistics; OECD, *Labour Force statistics*, Paris, various issues; ECE secretariat estimates.

[a] Includes the armed forces.

[b] Man-years.

[c] Break in time series.

APPENDIX TABLE A.12

Unemployment rates

(Per cent of total labour force)

	1970	1971	1972	1973	1974	1975	1976	1977	1978	1979	1980	1981	1982	1983	1984
France	2.4	2.6	2.7	2.6	2.8	4.1	4.4	4.7	5.2	5.9	6.3	7.3	8.0	8.0	9.0
Germany, Federal Republic of	0.8	0.9	0.8	0.8	1.6	3.6	3.7	3.6	3.5	3.2	3.0	4.4	6.1	8.0	8.0
Italy	5.3	5.3	6.3	6.2	5.3	5.8	6.6	7.0	7.1	7.5	7.4	8.3	9.0	9.8	10.1
United Kingdom	3.1	3.9	4.3	3.3	3.1	4.6	6.0	6.4	6.3	5.6	6.9	10.6	12.3	13.1	13.2
Total 4 countries	2.8	3.1	3.4	3.1	3.1	4.5	5.1	5.4	5.5	5.4	5.8	7.6	8.8	9.8	10.1
Austria	1.4	1.3	1.2	1.1	1.4	1.7	1.8	1.6	2.1	2.1	1.9	2.5	3.5	4.1	4.2
Belgium	2.1	2.2	2.7	2.8	3.1	5.1	6.6	7.5	8.1	8.4	9.0	11.1	13.1	14.7	15.3
Denmark	0.7	1.1	0.9	0.9	3.5	4.9	6.3	7.3	8.3	6.0	6.5	10.3	9.9	10.7	10.1
Finland	1.9	2.2	2.5	2.3	1.7	2.2	3.8[a]	5.8	7.2	5.9	4.6	5.1	5.8	6.1	6.1
Ireland	5.8	5.8	6.3	5.9	5.6	6.4	7.8	7.6	7.1	6.1	6.1	8.9	10.7	13.8	15.4
Netherlands	1.0	1.3	2.2	2.2	2.7	5.2[a]	5.5	5.3	5.3	5.4	6.0	8.6	11.4	13.7	14.0
Norway	1.6	1.5	1.7	1.5	1.5	2.3	1.8	1.5	1.8	2.0	1.7	2.0	2.6	3.3	3.0
Sweden	1.5	2.5	2.7	2.5	2.0	1.6	1.6	1.8	2.2	2.1	2.0	2.5	3.1	3.5	3.1
Switzerland	0.0	0.0	0.0	0.0	0.0	0.3	0.7	0.4	0.4	0.3	0.2	0.2	0.4	0.9	1.1
Total 9 countries	1.5	1.7	2.0	2.0	2.3	3.3	3.9	4.2	4.6	4.3	4.4	5.9	7.0	8.2	8.3
Total western Europe	2.5	2.8	3.1	2.9	3.0	4.2	4.9	5.1	5.3	5.2	5.5	7.2	8.4	9.4	9.7
Greece	4.2	3.1	2.1	2.0	2.1	2.3	1.9	1.7	1.8	1.9	2.8	4.1	5.8	7.2	7.7
Portugal	2.5	2.5	2.5	2.5	2.1	5.5	6.3	7.4	8.0	8.1	7.9	7.6	7.6	10.8	11.5
Spain	2.4	3.1	3.1	2.5	2.6	3.7[a]	4.7	5.2	6.9	8.5	11.2	14.0	15.9	17.4	20.1
Turkey	11.9	11.9	11.6	12.1	12.8	12.9	13.6	11.9	12.3	13.6	15.0	16.3	17.6	19.2	..
Yugoslavia	7.7	6.7	7.0	8.1	9.0	10.2	11.4	11.9	12.0	11.9	11.0	11.9	12.4	12.8	..
Total southern Europe	7.0	7.0	6.8	7.0	7.4	8.3	9.1	8.7	9.5	10.4	11.7	13.3	14.5	15.9	..
Total Europe	2.5	2.7	2.9	2.7	2.8	4.0	4.6	4.8	5.1	5.2	5.6	7.2	8.2	9.1	..
United States	4.8	5.8	5.5	4.8	5.5	8.3	7.6	6.9	6.0	5.8	7.0	7.5	9.5	9.5	7.4
Canada	5.6	6.1	6.2	5.5	5.3	6.9	7.1	8.0	8.3	7.4	7.4	7.5	10.9	11.8	11.2
North America	4.9	5.8	5.6	4.9	5.5	8.2	7.6	7.0	6.2	6.0	7.0	7.5	9.6	9.7	7.8
Total above	4.2	4.7	4.7	4.3	4.7	6.5	6.6	6.4	6.3	6.3	7.1	8.3	9.9	10.5	..

Source: OECD, *Quarterly Labour Force Statistics*, No. 4, 1984; *Main Economic Indicators—Historical Statistics, 1964-1983*; *Employment Outlook*, September 1984, and ILO, *Yearbook of Labour Statistics*; EUROSTAT, *Monthly Bulletin*, No. 12, January 1985.

[a] Major change in coverage takes place in year noted.

224   **Statistical appendices**

Appendix B. Eastern Europe and the Soviet Union

APPENDIX TABLE B.1

Net material product
(Annual percentage change)

	1970	1971	1972	1973	1974	1975	1976	1977	1978	1979	1980	1981	1982	1983	1984
Bulgaria	7.1	6.9	7.7	8.1	7.6	8.8	6.5	6.3	5.6	6.6	5.7	5.0	4.2	3.0	4.6
Czechoslovakia	5.7	5.5	5.7	5.2	5.9	6.2	4.2	4.2	4.1	3.1	2.9	-0.1	0.2	2.3	3.0
German Democratic Republic . . .	5.6	4.4	5.7	5.6	6.5	4.9	3.5	5.1	3.7	4.0	4.4	4.8	2.6	4.4	5.5
Hungary	4.9	5.9	6.2	7.0	5.9	6.1	3.0	7.1	4.0	1.2	-0.9	2.5	2.6	0.3	2.8-3.0
Poland	5.2	8.1	10.6	10.8	10.5	9.0	6.9	5.0	3.0	-2.3	-6.0	-12.0	-5.5	6.0	5.1
Romania	6.8	13.5	10.0	10.7	12.4	9.8	11.3	8.7	7.4	6.2	2.9	2.2	2.7	3.7	7.7
Eastern Europe	5.7	7.3	8.1	8.3	8.6	7.6	6.1	5.7	4.3	2.0	0.1	-1.9	0.1	3.9	5.1
Soviet Union	9.0	5.6	3.9	8.9	5.4	4.5	5.9	4.5	5.1	2.2	3.9	3.3	3.9	4.2	3.0*
Eastern Europe and the Soviet Union . . .	8.0	6.1	5.1	8.7	6.5	5.4	5.9	4.9	4.9	2.1	2.7	1.7	2.8	4.1	3.6

Sources: National statistics and ECE secretariat estimates.

APPENDIX TABLE B.2

Net material product used for domestic consumption and accumulation

(Annual percentage change)

	1970	1971	1972	1973	1974	1975	1976	1977	1978	1979	1980	1981	1982	1983	1984
Bulgaria															
Total	3.8	1.6	9.8	9.0	11.8	11.1	0.3	5.2	0.2	3.5	5.1	7.7	1.9	1.2	..
Consumption	5.6	7.4	6.3	6.6	7.1	7.7	6.0	4.0	3.6	3.0	3.6	5.3	3.7	2.9	..
Accumulation	-0.6	-11.5	21.0	16.0	24.2	18.7	-11.5	8.9	-9.3	5.0	9.5	14.8	-3.3	-3.6	..
Czechoslovakia															
Total	5.0	4.9	5.7	7.3	8.1	4.5	3.2	1.6	2.7	1.1	2.7	-3.4	-1.6	0.7	..
Consumption	1.9	6.6	5.2	5.8	6.2	3.0	3.4	3.7	3.8	0.9	1.0	2.6	-1.1	2.7	..
Accumulation	16.7	-0.6	7.7	12.2	14.3	9.2	2.7	-4.5	-0.5	1.8	8.2	-21.7	-3.6	-7.2	..
German Democratic Republic															
Total	7.5	3.1	5.3	6.7	6.0	2.9	5.9	4.8	1.1	1.5	5.0	1.1	-3.2	0.4	..
Consumption	4.5	4.9	6.2	5.6	6.3	4.0	4.9	4.7	3.2	3.4	3.0	2.4	1.4	0.6	..
Accumulation	17.4	-2.1	2.5	10.3	5.3	-0.8	9.5	5.2	-5.6	-5.0	12.3	-3.4	-19.9	0.2	..
Hungary															
Total	11.8	11.3	-3.7	2.0	12.7	6.4	1.3	6.0	9.2	-5.8	-1.7	0.7	-1.1	-2.7	–
Consumption	8.4	5.4	3.1	3.7	6.9	4.7	2.2	5.0	4.3	3.3	0.2	3.0	1.4	0.6	1
Accumulation	23.6	30.4	-21.4	-3.8	34.2	11.5	-1.4	9.4	24.0	-28.9	-8.7	-8.6	-12.4	-20.5	-(8-9)
Poland															
Total	5.0	9.8	12.5	14.3	12.0	9.5	6.5	2.2	0.5	-3.7	-6.0	-10.5	-10.5	5.4	5.0
Consumption	4.1	7.7	9.1	8.1	7.4	11.1	8.8	6.8	1.7	3.1	2.1	-4.6	-11.5	5.6	..
Accumulation	7.4	15.2	20.9	27.8	20.5	7.0	2.4	-6.5	-2.0	-19.2	-29.6	-27.6	-6.6	4.9	..
Romania															
Total	..	..	..	..	..	..	12.3	6.8	9.7	5.5	0.8	-6.6	1.5	0.9	..
Consumption	..	..	..	..	..	..	8.8	7.8	9.4	6.3	3.4	3.0	-1.3	0.1	..
Accumulation	..	..	..	..	..	..	18.9	5.1	10.1	3.9	-3.7	-24.7	-2.0	3.0	..
Eastern Europe															
Total	[a]6.3	[a]6.6	[a]7.2	[a]9.3	[a]9.9	[a]6.7	5.9	3.9	3.2	-0.2	-0.3	-4.2	-4.2	1.6	..
Consumption	4.3	6.5	6.7	6.5	6.7	6.8	6.4	5.7	3.9	3.3	2.2	0.5	-3.4	2.5	..
Accumulation	14.0	6.7	5.8	15.0	17.1	7.1	5.8	0.9	2.8	-7.8	-4.6	-16.0	-8.4	-2.4	..
Soviet Union															
Total	11.2	5.9	3.5	7.7	4.1	4.2	5.3	3.5	4.5	2.0	3.9	3.2	3.6	3.6	2.6
Consumption	7.5	5.8	5.8	5.2	4.8	5.5	4.3	4.0	4.6	4.5	6.0	4.0	1.2	2.9	..
Accumulation	21.3	3.4	-2.1	14.4	0.5	-1.5	6.6	3.3	5.2	-2.9	-0.6	0.9	11.0	5.8	..
Eastern Europe and the Soviet Union															
Total	[a]9.9	[a]5.5	[a]4.6	[a]8.2	[a]5.8	[a]5.0	5.3	3.6	4.1	1.3	2.5	0.8	1.2	3.1	..
Consumption	6.6	6.0	6.1	5.5	5.3	5.9	5.0	4.5	4.4	4.1	4.7	2.8	-0.3	2.8	..
Accumulation	19.6	4.2	-0.3	14.6	4.6	0.9	6.3	2.5	4.4	-4.5	-1.9	-4.4	5.7	3.9	..

Sources: National statistics and ECE secretariat estimates.

a Excluding Romania.

APPENDIX TABLE B.3

Wages
(Annual percentage change)

	1970	1971	1972	1973	1974	1975	1976	1977	1978	1979	1980	1981	1982	1983	1984
Bulgaria															
Average nominal wages	..	2.4	3.1	6.1	2.2	2.1	2.1	2.0	4.0	5.1	16.9	5.2	2.5	1.9	2.2
Real wages	6.1	1.8	3.2	5.5	1.6	2.6	0.9	0.3	0.4	1.5	-0.2	4.7	2.2	1.0	..
Czechoslovakia															
Average nominal wages	..	1.8	4.1	3.3	3.3	3.2	2.8	3.2	3.0	2.5	2.2	1.5	2.3	1.9	1.7
Real wages	1.3	4.1	4.5	3.2	2.8	2.7	1.8	1.9	1.4	-0.6	-1.0	0.8	-2.5	1.9	0.8*
German Democratic Republic															
Average nominal wages	4.6	4.0	4.0	1.8	3.7	3.4	3.5	2.9	3.2	3.0	1.5	2.4	1.9	1.3	..
Real wages[a]	4.9	3.9	4.7	2.4	4.1	3.4	3.5	3.0	3.3	2.3	1.1	2.2	1.9	1.3	..
Hungary															
Average nominal wages	..	3.5	4.5	6.8	6.8	6.3	5.5	9.8	8.2	6.3	6.1	6.4	6.7	4.9	5.8
Real wages	4.7	2.3	2.2	2.8	5.6	3.8	0.1	3.8	3.1	-1.7	-1.6	1.1	-0.7	-3.2	-2.3
Poland															
Average nominal wages	..	4.9	6.8	11.7	13.8	11.8	8.8	7.1	6.3	8.8	13.5	27.4	51.0	25.1	20.2
Real wages	1.7	5.6	6.4	8.7	6.5	8.8	4.3	2.4	-2.2	2.1	4.0	2.3	-24.9	1.1	3.6
Romania															
Average nominal wages	..	2.6	1.8	4.3	6.4	9.0	7.3	6.2	10.6	4.8	6.2	4.6	7.9	3.0	12.5
Real wages	..	1.7	1.6	3.2	4.7	7.5	6.1	5.8	8.2	2.3	3.5	1.0	-7.7	-2.1	6.0[b]
Soviet Union															
Average nominal wages	4.3	3.2	3.4	3.6	4.6	3.3	3.8	2.5	3.0	2.1	3.4	2.1	2.8	2.6	2.5
Real wages[c]	4.3	3.2	3.4	3.6	4.6	3.3	3.8	2.5	3.0	2.1	3.4	2.1	2.8	2.6	2.5

Source: Statisticheskii ezhegodnik stran-chlenov SEV (CMEA statistical yearbook), various issues.

[a] Calculated as rate of average nominal monthly wages growth / index of retail prices, service charges and fares

[b] 1984 to 1980.

[c] Average nominal wages.

APPENDIX TABLE B.4

Money incomes of population and volume of retail trade
(Annual percentage change)

	1970	1971	1972	1973	1974	1975	1976	1977	1978	1979	1980	1981	1982	1983	1984
Bulgaria															
Money incomes	..	..	..	..	..	..	..	..	..	..	..	..	..	..	..
Retail trade turnover	..	6.5	6.7	8.8	9.1	7.8	7.3	3.1	3.6	2.3	3.0	4.6	4.5	2.4	4.6
Czechoslovakia															
Money incomes	4.6	5.3	6.1	6.4	4.5	3.8	4.9	4.4	3.6	3.6	4.0	2.6	4.3	3.1	2.6
Retail trade turnover	..	5.5	6.0	5.8	7.5	2.8	2.8	2.4	3.7	-0.1	-0.3	1.5	-2.7	2.2	2.2
German Democratic Republic															
Money incomes	3.1	3.4	6.2	6.3	5.1	3.8	3.7	5.5	3.6	3.0	2.5	3.1	2.8	2.3	3.9
Retail trade turnover	..	3.9	5.9	5.8	6.2	3.4	4.6	4.4	3.3	3.5	4.5	2.5	1.0	0.7	4.1
Hungary															
Money incomes	9.6	7.9	6.8	10.0	9.7	9.7	5.6	9.2	7.6	8.4	9.1	8.1	7.4	8.7	9.0
Retail trade turnover	12.4	7.4	3.3	5.8	9.2	5.4	1.7	6.2	3.9	1.7	0.1	3.2	1.2	0.3	0.2
Poland															
Money incomes	..	10.4	13.5	14.2	14.8	14.5	12.1	12.3	8.9	9.9	12.6	31.1	64.9	23.0	19.6
Retail trade turnover	4.3	8.1	12.3	10.1	8.6	12.3	7.2	6.1	1.2	2.6	0.2	-4.6	-17.4	8.1	6
Romania															
Money incomes	..	..	..	..	..	..	10.4	8.7	13.2	7.2	9.2	6.4	9.5	5.1	..
Retail trade turnover	..	9.0	6.4	7.8	9.6	8.0	8.8	6.8	10.5	6.3	6.4	4.2	-2.5*	0.5*	4.8*
Soviet Union															
Money incomes	7.0	5.9	6.1	6.3	6.7	6.2	5.8	4.5	5.0	4.0	5.2	3.7	4.3	4.4	..
Retail trade turnover	7.4	6.8	6.8	5.3	5.9	6.9	4.6	4.5	3.9	4.1	5.2	4.3	0.3	2.7	4.2

Source: National statistics, and ECE secretariat estimates.

APPENDIX TABLE B.5

Real incomes (per head of population)
(*Annual percentage change*)

	1970	1971	1972	1973	1974	1975	1976	1977	1978	1979	1980	1981	1982	1983	1984
Bulgaria	4.9	4.3	7.0	8.6	3.3	5.3	4.6	0.6	1.3	2.9	3.4	5.8	4.1	2.8	2.7
Czechoslovakia[a]	..	5.3	6.0	5.5	3.2	2.4	3.2	2.2	1.4	-0.1	0.1	1.6	-0.7	1.7	1.3
German Democratic Republic.	..	5.4	5.7	5.7	5.8	5.8	5.0	5.9	4.2	3.4	3.1	4.0	3.3	2.3	4.0
Hungary	7.3	4.2	3.3	4.7	6.2	4.4	0.9	4.9	2.9	-0.2	0.4	2.9	0.9	1.1	1.0
Poland	..	6.1	7.8	10.3	5.0	8.9	5.7	5.3	0.4	2.4	1.0	3.3	-18.0	0.4	..
Romania	..	12.2	5.8	4.1	6.6	5.6	8.5	3.5	8.0	2.9	2.8	1.5	..	..	..
Soviet Union	5.6	4.5	4.0	5.0	4.0	4.5	3.7	3.5	3.0	3.0	3.7	3.3	0.1	2.0	3.0

Source: National statistics and ECE secretariat estimates.

[a] Real money incomes.

APPENDIX TABLE B.6

Retail prices
(Annual percentage change)

	1970	1971	1972	1973	1974	1975	1976	1977	1978	1979	1980	1981	1982	1983	1984
Bulgaria	..	–	–0.1	0.2	0.5	0.4	0.2	0.4	1.5	4.6	14.0	0.5	0.3	1.2	..
Czechoslovakia	1.2	–0.3	–0.3	0.3	0.5	0.6	0.8	1.3	1.6	3.9	2.9	0.8	5.1	0.9	0.9
German Democratic Republic .	–0.3	–	–0.8	–0.7	–0.4	–	–	–0.2	–0.1	0.4	0.4	0.3	–	–	..
Hungary	1.3	1.7	3.1	3.5	2.1	4.4	4.3	4.0	4.9	9.7	9.2	4.0	6.6	7.2	8.5
Poland	0.8	1.6	–0.4	3.3	5.2	3.5	4.0	4.5	8.4	7.3	8.5	18.4	109.4	21.9	13.0
Romania	..	..	..	..	..	..	–	1.0	1.0	0.9	1.9	2.0	16.9[a]	5.2[a]	0.2*
Soviet Union	..	–0.2	–0.2	–	–0.1	–	–	0.3	0.7	1.3	1.0	1.0	4.0	–	–3.4*

Sources: Statisticheskii ezhegodnik stran-chlenov SEV (CMEA statistical yearbook), various issues and national statistics.
[a] International Monetary Fund, *International Financial Statistics*.

APPENDIX TABLE B.7

Dwellings constructed
(Thousands)

	1970	1971	1972	1973	1974	1975	1976	1977	1978	1979	1980	1981	1982	1983	1984
Bulgaria	45.7	48.9	46.5	54.2	44.1	57.2	67.6	75.9	67.8	66.2	74.3	71.4	68.2	68.8	67.9
Czechoslovakia	112.1	107.4	115.6	118.6	129.0	144.7	132.4	134.8	129.3	122.7	128.9	95.4	101.8	95.7	91.0
German Democratic Republic	65.8	65.0	69.6	80.7	88.3	100.0	103.1	106.8	111.9	117.4	120.2	125.7	122.4	122.6	121.7
Hungary	80.3	75.3	90.2	85.2	87.8	99.6	93.9	93.4	88.2	88.2	89.1	77.0	75.6	74.2	70.4
Poland	194.0	191.0	206.0	227.0	250.0	248.0	264.0	266.0	284.0	278.0	217.0	187.0	186.0	195.5	196.0
Romania	159.0	147.0	136.0	149.0	154.0	165.0	139.0	145.0	167.0	192.0	198.0	161.0	161.0	146.7	131.9
Soviet Union	2266.0	2256.0	2233.0	2276.0	2231.0	2228.0	2113.0	2111.0	2080.0	1932.0	2004.0	1997.0	2002.0	2030.0	2081.0

Source: Statisticheskii ezhegodnik stran-chlenov SEV (CMEA statistical yearbook), various issues, plan fulfilment reports for 1984.

APPENDIX TABLE B.8

Total gross investment
(Annual percentage change)

	1970	1971	1972	1973	1974	1975	1976	1977	1978	1979	1980	1981	1982	1983	1984
Bulgaria															
Total	10.6	1.7	10.0	6.9	7.8	16.9	1.0	13.9	0.6	-2.3	7.5	10.5	3.6	0.7	-*
Material sphere	..	1.0	8.9	6.6	8.3	18.0	-1.1	16.0	0.4	1.6	5.4	12.2	2.7	-1.0	..
Non-material sphere	..	4.2	13.0	7.7	6.5	13.9	6.6	8.9	1.3	4.0	14.3	5.3	6.1	5.3	..
Czechoslovakia															
Total	5.9	4.7	8.2	10.7	9.0	7.7	4.1	5.6	4.7	1.4	1.4	-4.6	-2.3	0.6	1.5*
Material sphere	..	5.1	6.0	14.0	9.4	7.9	5.8	6.5	4.8	3.9	2.5	-2.2	-2.1	0.6	..
Non-material sphere	..	4.0	12.6	4.5	8.3	7.3	0.5	3.5	4.4	4.3	1.5	-7.3	-2.8	-1.4	..
German Democratic Republic															
Total	7.3	1.3	4.3	8.5	5.5	4.5	7.4	5.6	2.8	1.4	0.3	2.8	-5.1	-	-*
Material sphere	..	0.4	3.1	8.3	4.8	4.3	7.7	4.5	1.7	1.4	1.2	2.3	-5.1	0.5	..
Non-material sphere	..	4.9	9.3	9.1	7.8	5.3	5.9	9.8	6.8	1.2	-3.1	4.3	-5.6	-2.1	..
Hungary															
Total	16.9	10.6	-1.1	3.2	10.9	11.5	-	12.1	4.8	0.7	-5.8	-4.3	-1.6	-3.7	(-6-7)
Material sphere	17.3	8.6	-3.6	1.6	9.1	15.1	1.1	14.3	6.4	-	-7.8	-5.0	-2.6	-4.9	..
Non-material sphere	20.4	16.6	6.8	9.9	8.5	8.1	-3.1	9.1	0.9	3.9	-0.3	-5.4	-1.1	2.7	..
Poland															
Total	4.0	7.4	23.0	24.4	22.3	10.7	1.2	3.1	2.1	-7.9	-12.3	-22.4	-12.1	9.4	8
Material sphere	..	9.4	25.3	26.1	22.9	16.1	1.7	3.4	0.7	-13.6	-13.0	-23.5	-15.3	8.2	..
Non-material sphere	..	1.4	16.0	19.9	19.8	7.4	4.5	8.9	5.1	6.1	-11.0	-19.9	-5.7	11.4	..
Romania															
Total	11.6	10.5	10.4	8.2	13.4	15.1	8.5	11.7	16.0	4.1	3.0	-7.1	-3.1	2.5	6.1
Material sphere	..	12.2	10.4	8.2	12.0	13.8	9.3	13.4	17.0	3.9	3.4	-6.6	-3.2	4.9	..
Non-material sphere	..	2.1	9.3	8.1	19.3	21.2	5.2	4.4	11.0	5.2	1.1	-9.4	-2.7	-8.5	..
Eastern Europe															
Total	8.1	6.3	11.0	12.6	13.4	10.8	3.9	7.3	5.7	-1.0	-2.2	-7.2	-4.4	1.9	3.5
Material sphere	..	6.6	10.2	13.1	12.9	12.6	4.5	8.0	5.6	-2.4	-2.1	-6.6	-5.1	2.6	..
Non-material sphere	..	4.4	12.0	10.8	13.9	10.5	4.2	7.4	5.6	3.0	-3.0	-8.9	-3.0	1.7	..
Soviet Union															
Total	11.4	7.3	7.2	4.7	7.1	8.6	4.5	3.7	6.0	0.7	2.3	3.8	3.5	5.8	2.0
Material sphere	..	8.6	8.7	6.2	8.0	9.2	5.0	3.5	7.1	0.7	2.5	3.5	3.3	5.3	..
Non-material sphere	..	4.4	3.7	0.1	5.4	6.7	3.0	4.1	3.1	1.0	1.8	4.6	4.6	6.9	..
Eastern Europe and the Soviet Union															
Total	10.4	7.0	8.2	7.0	9.0	9.4	4.3	4.8	5.9	0.1	0.9	0.4	1.3	4.7	2.4
Material sphere	..	8.0	9.2	8.2	9.5	10.3	4.9	4.9	6.6	-0.3	1.0	0.4	0.9	4.6	..
Non-material sphere	..	4.4	5.8	3.1	7.9	7.9	3.4	5.2	4.0	1.7	0.2	0.1	2.3	5.4	..

Sources: National statistics and ECE secretariat estimates.

APPENDIX TABLE B.9

Gross fixed assets

(Annual percentage change)

	1970	1971	1972	1973	1974	1975	1976	1977	1978	1979	1980	1981	1982	1983
Bulgaria														
Total	8.8	7.3	7.6	7.1	8.8	8.8	7.7	8.9	7.1	6.9	7.2	7.1	7.8	7.4
Material	..	8.0	8.3	7.7	11.1	9.3	7.8	9.7	7.2	7.2	8.2	7.6	7.9	6.9
Non-material	..	5.0	6.7	7.1	4.2	6.4	8.3	7.6	6.5	6.1	5.7	7.6	7.0	8.0
Czechoslovakia														
Total	5.0	4.8	5.2	4.9	5.9	6.1	6.3	4.9	5.6	5.3	5.5	5.6	4.5	4.3
Material	..	5.0	4.8	5.4	6.0	5.7	6.9	7.9	6.0	6.3	2.4	5.7	4.9	4.7
Non-material	..	5.0	4.8	5.4	5.2	6.6	6.2	2.2	7.1	2.7	7.1	4.2	4.7	3.6
German Democratic Republic														
Total	3.6	5.6	4.0	4.5	4.3	4.7	4.5	4.3	4.1	4.5	4.3	4.2	4.5	3.8
Material	..	6.0	8.7	5.4	5.9	6.4	6.0	5.0	6.1	5.7	5.4	5.2	5.5	5.2
Non-material	..	2.0	2.0	1.9	1.9	1.9	2.7	1.8	2.6	6.0	6.0	5.2	2.3	1.5
Hungary														
Total	4.0	7.2	7.8	7.3	6.8	6.3	6.4	6.0	5.7	6.2	5.9	4.9	4.3	4.5
Material	..	7.0	7.5	7.0	8.1	6.0	8.0	6.1	5.7	7.2	6.7	5.4	4.1	4.4
Non-material	..	4.0	4.8	4.6	4.4	5.0	4.8	5.4	5.1	4.9	6.0	5.8	3.6	4.1
Poland														
Total	4.9	2.7	5.3	6.3	7.6	7.7	7.1	7.6	7.0	6.6	3.5	3.4	1.8	2.5
Material	..	5.0	6.7	8.0	10.7	9.7	8.9	9.9	8.5	7.3	1.0	3.4	1.4	2.3
Non-material	..	1.0	2.0	2.9	3.8	4.5	3.5	5.0	4.8	4.6	8.0	3.4	2.6	2.5
Romania														
Total	9.4	9.1	7.9	8.9	10.4	11.5	10.3	9.6	8.8	8.8	8.5	8.2	8.7	8.5
Material	..	12.0	9.8	10.6	12.5	14.4	12.0	10.7	10.1	9.2	9.2	8.8	9.4	9.1
Non-material	..	4.0	4.8	4.6	5.3	5.8	5.5	8.2	4.1	6.6	6.2	6.4	6.6	6.2
Soviet Union														
Total	8.0	8.8	7.7	7.9	8.1	7.8	7.0	6.8	6.9	6.5	6.6	6.4	6.3	6.3
Material	..	8.0	9.3	8.5	9.4	8.6	7.2	7.4	8.0	6.9	6.9	6.5	6.9	6.9
Non-material	..	7.0	6.5	7.0	5.7	6.2	5.8	5.5	5.9	5.6	5.8	5.0	5.3	5.0

Source: Calculated on the basis of *Statisticheskii ezhegodnik stran-chlenov SEV* (CMEA Statistical Yearbook), various issues.

APPENDIX TABLE B.10

Employment

(Annual percentage change)

	1970	1971	1972	1973	1974	1975	1976	1977	1978	1979	1980	1981	1982	1983	1984
Bulgaria															
Total	0.9	0.9	1.3	-0.1	1.0	0.4	0.2	-0.6	0.2	0.9	0.7	1.3	0.7	0.1	..
Material sphere	0.3	0.9	0.7	-0.7	0.5	-0.5	-0.5	-0.6	0.1	0.8	0.1	1.2	0.6	0.1	..
Non-material sphere	5.3	0.9	5.1	4.3	4.5	5.1	4.0	-0.6	1.5	0.7	3.7	2.1	1.3	0.1	..
Czechoslovakia															
Total	1.1	0.3	0.1	0.6	1.0	0.7	0.5	0.8	0.9	1.0	1.0	0.7	0.4	0.4	0.7
Material sphere	1.1	0.4	-0.3	0.4	0.7	0.4	–	0.3	0.5	0.6	0.4	0.3	0.1	0.5	0.5
Non-material sphere	1.1	0.1	1.9	1.0	2.2	1.8	2.1	2.3	2.1	2.4	3.0	1.9	1.3	0.3	1.1
German Democratic Republic															
Total	0.2	0.4	0.2	0.5	0.6	0.5	1.0	0.8	0.8	0.7	0.4	0.5	0.6	0.7	..
Material sphere	-0.1	-0.1	-0.1	0.1	0.3	0.3	0.8	0.6	0.6	0.4	0.2	0.2	0.2	0.4	..
Non-material sphere	1.7	2.6	1.6	2.4	1.8	1.6	1.8	1.7	1.7	2.1	1.2	1.7	2.0	1.9	..
Hungary															
Total	0.6	0.6	0.4	0.2	0.2	0.2	-0.2	-0.2	-0.2	-0.1	-1.2	-0.3	-0.6	-0.6	-0.4
Material sphere	0.3	0.2	0.1	-0.3	-0.3	-0.4	-0.9	-0.5	-0.2	-0.8	-1.7	-0.1	0.2	-1.1	-1
Non-material sphere	2.2	2.4	2.5	2.9	3.1	2.7	2.9	0.7	2.1	2.8	0.9	-0.8	0.6	-3.5	..
Poland															
Total	1.2	2.0	2.6	2.3	2.0	1.7	0.3	1.3	0.4	0.8	0.3	0.8	-2.9	0.2	..
Material sphere	2.0	1.4	2.3	1.9	1.7	1.9	–	1.2	0.1	0.5	-0.1	0.2	-3.1	-0.3	..
Non-material sphere	-3.1	5.7	4.5	4.5	3.4	4.0	1.9	2.0	2.0	2.5	2.3	4.0	-2.1	2.4	..
Romania															
Total	-0.5	0.3	–	-0.2	0.4	0.8	0.4	0.3	0.6	0.4	0.1	-0.3	0.7	0.6	..
Material sphere	-0.4	-0.1	-0.4	-0.2	0.1	0.4	-0.2	0.2	0.3	-0.2	0.3	-0.6	0.5	0.7	..
Non-material sphere	-1.0	2.9	3.0	0.1	3.1	3.6	5.0	0.7	2.5	3.8	-1.3	2.0	1.7	-0.2	..
Eastern Europe															
Total	0.6	1.0	1.0	0.9	1.1	1.0	0.4	0.6	0.5	0.6	0.2	0.5	-1.7	0.3	..
Material sphere	0.7	0.6	0.6	0.5	0.7	0.8	0.1	0.5	0.2	0.3	-0.1	0.1	-0.9	0.2	..
Non-material sphere	–	3.0	3.1	2.7	2.9	1.9	2.6	1.5	2.0	2.5	1.6	2.3	0.3	0.8	..
Soviet Union															
Total	1.2	2.2	1.7	1.3	1.6	1.2	1.3	1.5	1.6	1.3	1.2	1.0	0.9	0.7	0.6
Material sphere	0.9	1.5	1.1	0.7	1.1	1.0	1.1	1.2	1.2	0.8	0.7	0.7	0.8	0.5	0.4
Non-material sphere	2.2	4.6	3.5	3.4	3.0	2.0	2.1	2.5	2.7	2.9	2.6	1.8	1.3	1.1	1.1
Eastern Europe and the Soviet Union															
Total	1.3	1.7	1.7	1.6	1.6	1.4	1.1	1.2	1.3	1.1	0.9	0.8	0.4	0.5	..
Material sphere	1.1	1.2	1.2	1.2	1.3	1.1	1.0	1.0	0.9	0.6	0.5	0.5	0.2	0.4	..
Non-material sphere	2.5	3.4	3.4	3.3	3.0	2.7	1.5	2.2	2.5	2.2	2.3	1.9	1.0	1.0	..

Sources: National statistics and ECE secretariat estimates.

APPENDIX TABLE B.11

Gross industrial production
(Annual percentage change)

	1970	1971	1972	1973	1974	1975	1976	1977	1978	1979	1980	1981	1982	1983	1984
Bulgaria	9.6	9.2	9.1	9.0	8.2	9.6	6.8	6.8	6.9	5.4	4.2	4.9	4.6	3.9	4.6
Czechoslovakia	8.4	6.9	6.6	6.8	6.2	7.0	5.5	5.6	5.0	3.7	3.5	2.1	1.1	2.8	3.9
German Democratic Republic	6.7	5.7	6.0	6.7	7.2	6.4	5.9	4.8	4.8	4.6	4.7	4.7	3.2	4.1	4.2
Hungary	7.9	6.7	5.2	7.0	8.4	4.7	4.5	5.7	5.4	3.1	-1.7	2.4	2.5	1.4	3.0
Poland	8.1	7.9	10.7	11.3	11.4	10.9	9.3	6.9	4.9	2.7	–	-10.8	-2.1	6.4	5.3
Romania	12.1	11.6	11.8	14.7	14.6	12.0	11.4	12.6	9.0	8.1	6.5	2.6	1.1	4.7	6.7
Eastern Europe	8.4	7.6	8.3	9.2	9.4	8.8	7.6	7.1	5.8	4.5	3.0	-0.6	1.2	4.4	4.9
Soviet Union	8.5	7.7	6.5	7.5	8.0	7.6	4.8	5.7	4.8	3.4	3.6	3.4	2.9	4.2	4.2
Eastern Europe and the Soviet Union. . .	8.5	7.7	7.0	8.0	8.4	7.9	5.6	6.1	5.1	3.7	3.4	2.2	2.4	4.3	4.4

Sources: National statistics and ECE secretariat estimates.

APPENDIX TABLE B.12

Industry: gross fixed investment, gross fixed assets[a] and employment

(Annual percentage change)

	1970	1971	1972	1973	1974	1975	1976	1977	1978	1979	1980	1981	1982	1983	1984
Bulgaria															
Investment	5.4	-1.1	3.0	8.1	1.3	19.9	1.7	17.7	1.1	-0.2	9.1	10.4	10.1	-3.2	..
Fixed assets	7.3	6.8	9.3	9.2	12.9	8.9	6.7	5.8	8.6	8.2	10.2	8.1	9.8	7.5	..
Employment	1.1	3.8	2.6	1.8	2.9	2.6	1.1	0.6	1.4	1.6	1.5	2.8	2.4	1.4	0.5
Czechoslovakia															
Investment	5.5	4.6	2.9	15.6	8.1	5.0	8.4	7.3	3.2	6.6	3.6	-1.4	-4.4	-3.0	..
Fixed assets	5.7	5.3	5.0	5.7	5.7	6.3	6.9	6.2	5.6	5.9	5.9	6.7	5.2	4.9	..
Employment	1.2	0.2	0.8	0.9	0.4	0.7	0.1	0.5	0.8	0.6	0.5	0.6	0.4	0.5	0.6
German Democratic Republic															
Investment	13.3	3.5	6.7	10.2	-0.6	1.2	8.2	6.7	5.4	3.6	4.2	3.2	-1.5	4.0	..
Fixed assets	6.1	6.2	6.3	6.3	6.5	8.3	5.4	5.4	5.4	5.1	6.0	6.0	6.2	5.6	..
Employment	0.1	0.4	0.2	0.8	0.1	–	0.9	0.7	0.7	0.6	0.1	0.5	0.3	0.3	0.4*
Hungary															
Investment	9.9	11.3	0.6	-0.2	9.3	10.8	8.0	23.3	3.3	-1.8	-11.5	-8.1	0.2	-2.5	..
Fixed assets	8.0	8.4	8.1	7.4	7.2	9.9	6.7	7.3	9.1	8.1	6.4	4.3	4.9	..	..
Employment	-0.8	0.1	1.1	1.1	-0.3	-1.2	-1.4	-0.7	-1.0	-2.1	-2.6	-2.4	-2.2	-2.1	–
Poland															
Investment	0.9	10.6	34.8	27.7	22.2	11.4	2.3	-2.4	-4.7	-15.4	-13.9	-27.2	-12.9	5.4	..
Fixed assets	8.6	6.7	9.3	9.8	13.0	11.0	9.8	11.8	8.9	7.4	4.6	3.4	2.4	2.8	..
Employment	1.9	3.0	3.9	2.9	2.4	2.6	0.2	1.0	-0.2	-0.1	0.1	-0.2	-4.7	-0.1	-0.5
Romania															
Investment	3.8	12.9	15.0	19.8	3.8	10.7	4.9	16.3	20.4	7.4	2.6	-5.8	-9.6	5.5	..
Fixed assets	13.4	13.0	10.6	12.0	14.3	15.6	11.9	10.7	9.7	9.6	10.1	9.1	9.5	9.4	..
Employment	4.3	6.6	5.6	6.9	7.1	5.3	3.8	4.1	2.6	3.9	3.2	2.0	2.1	1.7	–*
Eastern Europe															
Employment	1.3	2.2	2.5	2.4	2.0	1.8	0.8	1.2	0.7	0.8	0.6	0.5	-0.9	0.4	0.1*
Soviet Union															
Investment	11.0	6.0	7.2	5.6	7.2	9.3	4.7	4.5	4.9	0.2	4.2	4.0	2.8	5.5	..
Fixed assets	9.4	9.0	8.3	8.3	7.7	9.7	8.1	7.0	7.9	7.1	7.8	7.0	6.9	6.9	..
Employment	1.4	1.4	1.3	1.3	1.7	1.9	2.2	1.7	1.7	1.3	1.1	0.9	1.0	0.6	0.4
Eastern Europe and the Soviet Union															
Employment	1.4	1.6	1.7	1.7	1.8	1.8	1.7	1.5	1.3	1.1	0.9	0.8	0.4	0.5	0.3*

Sources: National statistics and ECE secretariat estimates.

a Undepreciated.

APPENDIX TABLE B.13

Gross agricultural output
(*Annual percentage change*)

	1970	1971	1972	1973	1974	1975	1976	1977	1978	1979	1980	1981	1982	1983	1984
Bulgaria															
Total	3.9	1.9	5.6	1.3	-1.5	7.5	4.1	-4.7	4.3	6.1	-4.6	5.9	5.2	-7.2	6.8
Crop	2.3	-0.3	8.5	0.2	-7.5	7.8	5.6	-9.5	4.5	5.6	-8.8	10.2	7.9	-17.4	13.9
Animal	6.9	6.1	1.4	3.1	7.4	7.3	2.0	2.0	4.0	6.5	0.3	2.2	2.6	3.0	1.1
Czechoslovakia															
Total	1.3	2.0	4.3	3.8	2.2	1.0	3.2	9.4	2.1	-3.3	4.8	-2.5	4.4	4.2	3.6
Crop	-4.5	0.4	4.5	4.0	1.5	-2.6	-8.2	16.8	1.7	-7.2	6.2	-5.3	13.8	2.8	4.2
Animal	6.3	3.3	4.1	3.6	2.7	0.2	0.5	4.3	2.4	-0.3	3.9	-0.5	-2.0	5.4	3.2
German Democratic Republic															
Total	4.1	-0.3	10.0	-0.3	7.2	-2.5	-5.0	7.1	1.1	3.1	0.7	1.6	-4.0	4.1	8.0
Crop	10.5	-5.9	18.3	-7.8	8.8	-9.6	-12.5	20.9	—	5.3	-3.7	1.9	1.7	1.2	13.9
Animal	—	4.0	4.4	5.3	6.1	2.2	-0.7	-0.1	1.7	1.8	3.5	1.5	-7.4	6.0	5.1
Hungary															
Total	-5.7	7.6	2.6	6.3	3.2	3.7	-2.7	10.9	1.1	-1.5	4.6	2.0	7.3	-2.7	2.5-3.0
Crop	-16.4	9.5	5.8	7.8	0.5	4.8	-7.1	12.3	-1.5	-3.2	7.6	1.6	9.4	-7.5	4
Animal	10.4	5.5	-1.0	4.5	6.4	2.5	2.7	9.6	3.8	0.1	1.9	2.4	5.3	2.2	1
Poland															
Total	2.2	3.6	8.4	7.3	1.6	-2.1	-1.2	1.4	4.1	-1.5	-10.7	3.8	-2.8	3.3	5.7
Crop	4.4	1.4	7.8	6.5	-0.7	-3.0	5.0	-7.2	5.4	-3.7	-15.2	18.9	-2.5	5.9	7.6
Animal	-1.1	6.6	9.0	8.2	4.2	-1.0	-8.7	13.7	2.6	1.3	-5.6	8.9	-3.2	0.4	3.4
Romania															
Total	-4.9	18.9	9.5	0.7	1.1	3.2	17.3	-0.9	2.7	5.5	-4.4	-0.9	7.6	-1.6	13.3
Crop	-11.8	26.3	7.6	-3.2	0.7	—	22.0	-5.0	0.3	6.2	-6.1	0.6	12.8	-5.2	..
Animal	5.5	8.9	12.5	7.7	1.4	6.7	11.5	5.6	5.6	4.8	-2.3	-2.8	0.2	3.7	..
Eastern Europe															
Total	0.5	5.2	7.6	4.0	2.4	0.2	1.2	3.3	2.8	0.8	-3.7	1.8	1.6	0.8	6.9
Crop	-1.2	4.0	8.7	2.0	0.8	-1.8	1.9	1.4	2.3	-0.4	-6.0	6.7	5.0	-1.0	..
Animal	2.8	5.9	6.4	6.3	4.3	1.9	-0.8	7.4	3.2	2.1	-1.2	-2.9	-1.5	3.0	..
Soviet Union															
Total	10.3	1.1	-4.1	16.1	-2.7	-5.3	6.5	4.0	2.7	-3.1	-1.9	-1.0	5.5	6.1	..
Crop	11.9	-1.3	-7.7	27.1	-10.0	-10.5	18.4	-1.8	5.0	-5.9	-2.3	-2.4	9.2	5.9	..
Animal	8.7	3.5	-0.6	6.2	5.2	-2.5	-2.4	9.4	0.8	-0.7	-1.6	0.1	2.6	6.3	..
Eastern Europe and the Soviet Union															
Total	7.0	2.4	-0.4	11.9	-1.1	-3.5	4.6	3.8	2.7	-1.8	-2.5	-0.1	4.2	4.3	2.2
Crop	7.6	0.3	-2.5	18.3	-6.7	-7.6	12.7	-0.8	4.1	-4.2	-3.5	0.5	7.8	3.6	..
Animal	8.7	3.5	-0.6	6.2	5.2	-2.5	-2.4	9.4	0.8	-0.7	-1.2	-1.0	2.6	6.3	..

Sources: National statistical yearbooks, plan fulfilment reports for 1984. *Statisticheskii ezhegodnik stran-chlenov SEV* (CMEA statistical yearbook), various issues.

APPENDIX TABLE B.14

Agricultural gross fixed investment, gross fixed assets[a] and employment

(*Annual percentage change*)

	1970	1971	1972	1973	1974	1975	1976	1977	1978	1979	1980	1981	1982	1983	1984
Bulgaria															
Investment	6.7	3.7	11.5	3.8	17.1	5.1	1.4	10.9	−9.8	−1.7	6.9	10.7	−18.6	1.6	..
Fixed assets	6.9	6.6	6.3	6.4	−0.4	14.5	7.3	5.3	4.7	4.5	5.3	−2.3	5.3	5.2	..
Employment	−4.1	−4.2	−2.0	−4.1	−3.5	−6.4	−4.9	−4.0	−2.5	0.1	−1.8	−1.5	−2.8	−3.7	..
Czechoslovakia															
Investment	−5.0	5.3	9.7	19.3	10.2	13.3	−1.1	6.3	6.4	−6.7	−3.7	5.0	4.6	12.6	..
Fixed assets	5.7	5.5	5.5	5.5	6.3	6.8	7.2	6.4	6.8	6.3	6.0	6.1	5.3	4.9	..
Employment	−0.9	−1.4	−6.2	−3.0	−0.8	−2.3	−2.1	−2.3	−1.9	−0.7	−0.2	−	−0.8	−1.4	..
German Democratic Republic															
Investment	−0.6	2.2	−2.6	4.9	9.1	0.7	2.9	3.5	−3.3	−4.3	−0.4	2.9	−7.6	−9.3	..
Fixed assets	5.0	5.6	4.8	5.6	4.3	4.2	5.9	5.5	5.2	3.8	5.4	4.9	4.9	4.7	..
Employment	−3.3	−2.4	−3.7	−1.9	−1.4	−0.8	−1.4	−0.5	0.5	−0.2	0.3	0.4	0.6	1.5	..
Hungary															
Investment	25.0	−	−13.3	−	7.7	14.3	−5.7	8.8	9.5	−2.0	−11.2	8.0	−1.0	−15.4	..
Fixed assets	8.4	9.3	8.6	8.6	6.9	7.0	5.9	5.9	5.8	5.6	4.3	4.3	4.3	..	..
Employment	−2.2	−2.4	−2.6	−4.3	−3.1	−2.1	−1.8	−1.2	0.2	0.9	−0.6	4.4	0.4	−1.0	..
Poland															
Investment	3.1	4.4	14.3	17.6	17.6	15.7	1.3	13.5	5.1	−3.6	−17.1	−12.7	−15.6	2.6	..
Fixed assets	4.5	3.2	4.4	5.4	6.2	6.1	7.0	7.2	7.0	6.6	5.6	4.2	1.8	2.0	6.8
Employment	−0.3	−0.3	−1.4	−1.8	−1.6	1.4	−0.4	1.4	−0.2	1.7	0.2	1.1	−0.5	−0.5	0.4
Romania															
Investment	11.6	11.0	2.7	−	8.9	14.5	12.2	12.1	11.4	−1.7	4.4	10.0	−1.8	8.6	..
Fixed assets	7.3	10.0	9.1	9.2	9.2	10.5	7.6	10.6	6.9	7.0	5.6	8.8	10.1	9.9	..
Employment	−3.6	−4.4	−4.9	−4.4	−4.3	−4.5	−4.7	−4.1	−4.1	−4.7	−4.6	−2.7	−1.0	0.2	..
Eastern Europe															
Employment	−2.2	−2.4	−3.2	−3.1	−2.7	−1.9	−2.4	−1.3	−1.6	−0.7	−1.3	−	−0.7	..	..
Soviet Union															
Investment	13.5	14.8	9.5	10.3	8.7	7.2	4.2	2.6	4.6	1.6	1.6	2.6	1.6	3.5	..
Fixed assets	5.2	6.6	9.7	10.5	10.2	10.6	7.8	7.8	7.7	6.7	6.7	6.7	7.1	6.6	6.8
Employment	−1.5	−0.7	−0.6	−0.5	0.1	−1.3	0.4	−0.7	−0.2	−1.1	−0.5	−0.4	0.4	0.4	0.4
Eastern Europe and the Soviet Union															
Employment	−1.8	−1.3	−1.5	−0.8	−0.9	−1.5	−0.5	−0.9	−0.6	−1.0	−0.8	−0.4	0.1	0.2	..

Sources: National statistical yearbooks; *Statisticheskii ezhegodnik stran-chlenov SEV* (CMEA statistical yearbook), various issues.

[a] Undepreciated.

APPENDIX TABLE B.15

Export and import volumes
(*Annual percentage change*)

	1970	1971	1972	1973	1974	1975	1976	1977	1978	1979	1980	1981	1982	1983	1984*
Bulgaria															
Exports	8.7	8.0	11.6	9.6	8.3	12.4	13.4	14.3	10.7	13.7	12.2	8.4	11.3	4.4	6.5
Imports	4.7	13.3	13.3	10.7	21.9	12.6	-2.3	5.3	7.1	2.1	4.1	9.3	3.2	5.2	3.0
Czechoslovakia															
Exports	20.7	8.4	7.7	3.5	5.0	6.8	7.5	9.1	7.1	3.2	4.7	0.5	6.1	5.7	6.0
Imports	15.9	5.9	4.1	9.8	10.9	1.9	3.4	7.1	3.6	2.2	-1.6	-6.9	2.9	2.0	5.5
German Democratic Republic															
Exports	8.8	10.3	11.9	7.4	8.4	7.2	5.8	4.2	7.4	8.9	3.6	8.4	5.4	10.6	4.0
Imports	15.9	2.0	7.6	13.1	8.7	5.0	11.1	4.6	-0.2	6.5	5.1	-6.3	0.4	5.3	6.0
Hungary															
Exports	7.6	7.6	19.3	12.5	3.5	4.8	8.2	12.6	1.5	12.5	1.0	2.6	7.3	9.4	5.5
Imports	27.1	17.3	-5.1	2.9	17.5	5.7	3.9	8.5	12.5	-3.3	-1.1	0.1	-0.1	3.9	1.0
Poland															
Exports	10.1	6.5	15.2	11.0	12.8	8.3	5.3	7.0	5.7	6.8	-4.2	-19.0	8.7	10.3	9.0
Imports	10.4	13.8	22.1	22.7	14.1	5.0	10.2	0.2	1.6	-1.2	-1.9	-16.9	-13.7	5.2	9.0
Romania[a]															
Exports	5.2	10.7	8.0	18.3	6.1	3.3	9.6	9.1	4.1	2.1	4.4	13.6	-7.6	0.9	12.0
Imports	7.9	3.5	11.8	9.7	15.8	-4.2	9.7	8.6	16.1	4.0	3.7	-7.2	-22.8	-5.0	7.0
Eastern Europe															
Exports	10.8	8.6	12.2	9.6	7.7	7.1	7.6	8.6	6.1	7.6	2.9	1.2	5.6	7.4	7.0
Imports	14.3	8.6	8.6	12.5	13.6	4.2	6.9	4.9	5.2	1.7	1.2	-6.4	-4.6	3.4	5.5
Soviet Union															
Exports	6.1	3.2	2.7	14.4	2.6	2.5	8.6	10.6	3.4	0.6	1.6	1.9	4.6	3.3	3.0
Imports	7.8	5.9	17.2	14.6	1.0	14.8	7.0	0.9	13.3	1.1	7.5	6.4	9.8	4.0	5.0
Eastern Europe and the Soviet Union															
Exports	8.5	6.0	7.8	11.7	5.4	5.1	8.0	9.5	4.9	4.6	2.4	1.5	5.1	5.7	5.0
Imports	11.6	7.5	12.1	13.4	8.3	8.4	6.9	3.2	8.6	1.5	3.9	-0.7	2.2	3.7	5.2

Sources: National statistics and ECE secretariat estimates for Romania.

a ECE secretariat estimates.

APPENDIX TABLE B.16

Energy production: electricity, coal and crude oil
(Billion kWh, million tons)

	1970	1971	1972	1973	1974	1975	1976	1977	1978	1979	1980	1981	1982	1983	1984
Bulgaria															
Electricity	19.5	21.0	22.3	21.9	22.8	25.2	27.7	29.7	31.5	32.5	34.8	37.0	40.5	42.6	44.6
Coal	29.2	27.0	27.3	26.8	24.3	27.8	25.5	25.2	25.8	28.2	30.2	29.2	32.2	32.4	33.6*
Oil	0.3	0.3	0.2	0.2	0.1	0.1	0.1	..	..	..	..	..	..	..	..
Czechoslovakia															
Electricity	45.2	47.2	51.4	53.5	56.0	59.3	62.7	66.5	69.1	68.1	72.7	73.5	74.7	76.3	78.3
Coal	109.5	113.0	112.9	109.0	110.1	114.4	117.7	121.2	123.2	124.7	123.1	122.8	124.6	127.4	129.3
Oil	0.2	0.2	0.2	0.2	0.1	0.1	0.1	0.1	0.1	0.1	0.1	0.1	0.1	0.1	0.1*
German Democratic Republic															
Electricity	67.7	69.4	72.8	76.9	80.3	84.5	89.1	92.0	96.0	96.8	98.8	100.7	102.9	104.9	110.1
Coal	262.5	263.7	249.2	247.0	244.1	247.2	247.3	254.0	253.3	256.1	258.1	266.7	276.0	278.0	296.3
Oil	..	..	..	..	..	..	..	..	..	..	..	..	..	..	..
Hungary															
Electricity	14.5	15.0	16.3	17.6	19.0	20.5	22.0	23.4	25.6	24.5	23.9	24.3	24.7	25.7	26.2
Coal	27.8	27.4	25.8	26.8	25.8	24.9	25.3	25.5	25.7	25.7	25.7	25.9	26.1	25.2	25.0
Oil[a]	1.9	2.0	2.0	2.0	2.0	2.0	2.1	2.2	2.2	2.0	2.0	2.5	2.5	2.5	2.5*
Poland															
Electricity	64.5	69.9	76.5	84.3	91.6	97.2	104.1	109.4	115.6	117.5	121.9	115.0	117.6	125.8	134.8
Coal	172.9	180.0	188.9	195.8	201.8	211.5	218.6	226.9	233.6	239.1	230.0	198.6	227.0	233.6	242.0
Oil	0.4	0.4	0.3	0.4	0.5	0.5	0.5	0.4	0.4	0.3	0.3	0.3	0.2	0.2	0.2*
Romania															
Electricity	35.1	39.4	43.3	46.8	49.1	53.7	58.3	59.9	64.3	64.9	67.5	70.1	68.9	70.3	71.6
Coal	20.5	20.6	23.2	24.8	26.9	27.1	25.8	26.8	29.3	32.8	35.2	36.9	37.9	44.5	44.3
Oil	13.4	13.8	14.1	14.3	14.5	14.6	14.7	14.6	13.7	12.3	11.5	11.6	11.7	11.6	11.4
Eastern Europe															
Electricity	246.5	261.9	282.6	301.0	318.8	340.4	363.9	380.9	402.1	404.3	419.6	420.6	429.3	445.6	465.5
Coal	622.4	631.7	627.3	630.2	633.0	652.9	660.2	679.5	690.9	706.6	702.3	680.1	723.8	741.1	770.5
Oil	16.3	16.6	16.9	17.0	17.3	17.5	17.5	17.3	16.4	14.8	14.4	14.5	14.6	14.4	14.2
Soviet Union															
Electricity	740.9	800.4	857.4	914.6	975.7	1038.6	1111.4	1150.1	1201.9	1238.2	1294.0	1326.0	1367.0	1418.0	1493.0
Coal	577.5	591.5	603.6	614.7	630.5	644.9	654.4	663.3	664.4	657.6	652.9	637.8	647.3	641.6	638.4
Oil	353.0	377.1	400.4	429.0	458.9	490.8	519.7	545.8	571.5	585.6	603.2	608.8	612.6	616.3	613.0
Eastern Europe and the Soviet Union															
Electricity	987.4	1062.3	1140.0	1215.6	1294.5	1379.0	1475.3	1531.0	1604.0	1642.5	1713.6	1746.6	1796.3	1863.6	1958.5
Coal	1199.9	1223.2	1230.9	1244.9	1263.5	1297.8	1314.6	1342.8	1355.3	1364.2	1355.2	1317.9	1371.1	1382.7	1408.9
Oil	369.3	393.7	417.3	446.0	476.2	508.3	537.2	563.1	587.9	600.4	617.6	623.4	627.2	630.7	627.2

Sources: Staticheskii ezhegodnik stran-chlenov SEV, (CMEA Statistical Yearbook), various issues, plan fulfilment report for 1984 and ECE secretariat estimates.

a Since 1981, including gas condensate.

APPENDIX TABLE B.17

Steel production
(*Million tons*)

	1970	1971	1972	1973	1974	1975	1976	1977	1978	1979	1980	1981	1982	1983	1984
Bulgaria	1.8	1.9	2.1	2.2	2.2	2.3	2.5	2.6	2.5	2.5	2.6	2.5	2.6	2.8	2.9*
Czechoslovakia	11.5	12.1	12.7	13.2	13.6	14.3	14.7	15.1	15.3	14.8	15.2	15.3	15.0	15.0	14.8
German Democratic Republic	5.0	5.3	5.7	5.9	6.2	6.5	6.7	6.8	7.0	7.0	7.3	7.5	7.2	7.2	7.7
Hungary	3.1	3.1	3.3	3.3	3.5	3.7	3.7	3.7	3.9	3.9	3.8	3.6	3.7	3.6	3.8
Poland	11.8	12.7	13.5	14.1	14.6	15.0	15.6	17.8	19.2	19.2	19.5	15.7	14.8	16.2	16.5
Romania	6.5	6.8	7.4	8.2	8.8	9.5	10.7	11.5	11.8	12.9	13.2	13.0	13.0	12.6	14.4
Eastern Europe	39.7	41.9	44.7	46.9	48.9	51.3	53.8	57.5	59.7	60.3	61.6	57.6	56.3	57.4	59.8
Soviet Union	115.9	120.7	125.6	131.5	136.2	141.3	144.8	146.7	151.4	149.1	147.9	148.4	147.2	152.5	154.0
Eastern Europe and the Soviet Union	155.6	162.6	170.3	178.4	185.1	192.6	198.6	204.2	211.1	209.4	209.5	206.0	203.5	209.9	213.8

Sources: As for Appendix table B.16.

APPENDIX TABLE B.18

Grain production
(Million tons)

	1970	1971	1972	1973	1974	1975	1976	1977	1978	1979	1980	1981	1982	1983	1984
Bulgaria															
Total	6.9	7.2	8.2	7.4	6.7	7.8	8.6	7.7	7.6	8.4	7.7	8.5	10.1	8.0	9.3
Wheat	3.0	3.1	3.6	3.3	2.9	2.8	3.5	3.4	3.5	3.4	3.8	4.4	4.9	3.6	..
Maize	2.4	2.5	3.0	2.6	1.6	2.8	3.0	2.5	2.2	3.2	2.3	2.4	3.4	3.1	..
Czechoslovakia															
Total	7.3	8.9	8.7	9.7	10.5	9.4	9.2	10.5	11.1	9.3	10.9	9.5	10.4	11.2	12.0
Wheat	3.2	3.9	4.0	4.6	5.1	4.2	4.8	5.2	5.6	3.7	5.4	4.3	4.6	5.8	..
Maize	0.5	0.5	0.6	0.6	0.6	0.8	0.5	0.8	0.6	0.9	0.7	0.7	0.9	0.7	..
German Democratic Republic															
Total	6.5	7.8	8.6	8.6	9.8	9.0	8.2	8.8	9.9	9.0	9.7	8.9	10.1	10.2	11.5
Wheat	2.1	2.5	2.7	2.9	3.2	2.7	2.7	2.9	3.1	3.1	3.1	2.9	2.7	3.6	3.9
Maize	–	–	–	–	–	–	–	–	–	–	–	–	–	–	–
Hungary															
Total	7.8	10.0	10.9	11.8	12.6	12.4	11.5	12.4	13.5	12.2	14.2	13.0	15.1	13.9	15.7
Wheat	2.7	3.9	4.1	4.5	5.0	4.0	5.1	5.3	5.7	3.7	6.1	4.6	5.8	6.0	7.3
Maize	4.1	4.7	5.6	6.0	6.2	7.2	5.1	6.0	6.7	7.4	6.7	7.0	8.0	6.4	6.7
Poland															
Total	16.6	20.2	20.7	22.2	23.3	19.8	21.1	19.6	21.8	17.6	18.5	19.9	21.4	22.4	24.4
Wheat	4.6	5.5	5.1	5.8	6.4	5.2	5.7	5.3	6.0	4.2	4.2	4.2	4.5	5.2	..
Maize	–	–	–	–	–	–	–	–	–	–	–	–	–	–	–
Romania															
Total	10.9	14.8	17.1	14.0	13.7	15.4	19.9	18.7	19.1	19.4	20.3	20.1	22.5	19.6	23.6
Wheat	3.4	5.6	6.0	5.5	5.0	4.9	6.8	6.5	6.3	4.7	6.5	5.3	6.5	5.1	..
Maize	6.5	7.9	9.8	7.4	7.4	9.2	11.6	10.1	10.2	12.4	11.2	11.9	12.6	11.5*	..
Eastern Europe															
Total	56.0	68.9	74.2	73.7	76.6	73.8	78.5	77.7	83.0	75.9	81.3	79.9	89.6	85.3	99.5
Wheat	19.0	24.5	25.5	26.6	27.6	23.8	28.6	28.6	30.2	22.8	29.1	25.7	29.0	29.3	..
Maize	13.5	15.6	19.0	16.6	15.8	20.0	20.2	19.4	19.7	23.9	20.9	22.0	24.9	21.7*	..
Soviet Union															
Total	186.8	181.2	168.2	222.5	195.7	140.1	223.8	195.7	237.4	179.3	189.1	160.0[a]	179.0[a]	200.0[a]	170.0[a]
Wheat	99.7	98.8	86.0	109.8	83.9	66.2	96.9	92.2	120.9	90.3	98.2	80.0	84.0[a]	87.0[a]	..
Maize	9.4	8.6	9.8	13.2	12.1	7.3	10.1	11.0	8.9	8.4	9.5	8.0[a]	11.0[a]	14.0[a]	..
Eastern Europe and the Soviet Union															
Total	242.8	250.1	242.4	296.2	272.3	213.9	302.3	273.4	320.4	255.2	270.4	239.9	268.6	285.3	269.5
Wheat	118.7	123.3	111.5	136.4	111.5	90.0	125.5	120.8	151.1	113.1	127.3	105.7	113.0	116.3*	..
Maize	22.9	24.2	28.8	29.8	27.9	27.3	30.3	30.4	28.6	32.3	30.4	30.0	35.9	35.7	..

Sources: Statisticheskii ezhegodnik stran-chlenov SEV (CMEA statistical yearbook), 1976, 1981, 1984; plan fulfilment reports.

[a] FAO estimate.

APPENDIX TABLE B.19

Meat production[a]
(*Million tons*)

	1970	1971	1972	1973	1974	1975	1976	1977	1978	1979	1980	1981	1982	1983	1984
Bulgaria	0.48	0.52	0.57	0.57	0.56	0.66	0.73	0.70	0.73	0.78	0.78	0.79	0.81	0.84	..
Czechoslovakia	1.10	1.16	1.23	1.24	1.31	1.35	1.32	1.38	1.45	1.47	1.50	1.53	1.41	1.49	..
German Democratic Republic	1.35	1.41	1.52	1.59	1.71	1.84	1.81	1.77	1.81	1.82	1.90	2.00	1.84	1.87	..
Hungary	1.04	1.22	1.29	1.22	1.34	1.42	1.32	1.47	1.48	1.52	1.57	1.58	1.69	1.79	..
Poland	2.18	2.21	2.48	2.73	3.06	3.06	2.90	2.88	3.14	3.26	3.14	2.53	2.58	2.50	..
Romania	0.88	0.90	1.06	1.20	1.31	1.37	1.45	1.55	1.58	1.76	1.77	1.79	..	..	..
Eastern Europe	7.03	7.42	8.15	8.55	9.29	9.70	9.53	9.75	10.19	10.61	10.66	10.22	..	..	..
Soviet Union	12.28	13.27	13.63	13.53	14.62	14.97	13.58	14.72	15.50	15.34	15.07	15.20	15.37	16.45	16.7
Eastern Europe and the Soviet Union .	19.31	20.69	21.78	22.08	23.91	24.67	23.11	24.47	25.69	25.95	25.73	25.42	..	..	..

Sources: Statisticheskii ezhegodnik stran-chlenov SEV, (CMEA statistical yearbook) 1976, 1981, 1983.

[a] Slaughter weight.

Appendix C. International trade and payments

APPENDIX TABLE C.1

World trade: value, by region
(Billion US dollars)

	1970	1971	1972	1973	1974	1975	1976	1977	1978	1979	1980	1981	1982	1983	1984ᵃ
Exports															
Developed market economies	225.4	252.7	298.5	407.9	544.0	580.3	644.9	730.2	874.6	1074.4	1265.2	1243.2	1179.3	1163.6	909.3
North America	59.1	62.0	69.8	96.4	131.2	140.0	153.2	162.0	189.1	236.3	283.3	300.1	276.6	270.7	223.3
Western Europe	138.4	157.8	188.8	258.6	338.9	365.3	402.9	463.6	559.4	698.6	809.8	750.1	724.7	708.3	530.5
Asia	20.1	24.7	29.4	37.9	56.5	56.9	68.8	82.8	100.5	106.5	133.8	156.1	142.6	150.4	127.9
Developing market economies	54.9	61.2	73.1	108.9	223.8	208.1	251.3	287.0	300.3	415.6	553.4	544.9	480.2	444.9	334.8
OPEC	17.5	23.1	27.3	41.9	126.0	113.4	137.5	151.4	145.8	218.3	307.0	281.2	225.8	183.1	138.1
Non-oil developing countries	37.4	38.2	45.8	67.0	97.8	94.7	113.9	135.6	154.5	197.3	246.3	263.7	254.4	261.8	196.7
European centrally planned economies	30.9	33.7	40.0	52.4	65.3	78.1	85.0	98.9	113.0	135.7	156.2	158.0	166.0	174.3	128.7
Eastern Europe	18.1	19.9	24.6	31.1	37.9	44.8	47.9	53.8	60.6	71.0	79.7	78.7	79.0	82.9	61.0
Soviet Union	12.8	13.8	15.5	21.3	27.4	33.3	37.2	45.2	52.4	64.7	76.5	79.4	87.0	91.4	67.7
Total above	311.2	347.7	411.7	569.2	833.1	866.5	981.3	1116.1	1287.9	1625.7	1974.8	1946.2	1825.5	1782.8	1372.8
Memorandum item															
ECE region	228.4	253.4	298.6	407.3	535.4	583.4	641.1	724.6	861.6	1070.7	1249.2	1208.3	1167.3	1153.4	882.5
Imports															
Developed market economies	241.5	265.7	317.0	436.3	619.2	618.5	708.5	801.2	926.0	1192.9	1432.5	1362.4	1277.1	1252.3	1009.6
North America	58.8	65.1	83.2	102.5	144.0	138.7	170.1	197.8	230.4	276.3	315.8	338.6	307.4	329.6	310.8
Western Europe	152.2	168.7	199.3	278.0	385.7	396.7	447.9	506.1	585.6	765.1	924.0	821.1	782.5	748.3	557.0
Asia	20.3	21.3	25.2	40.9	65.5	61.3	68.2	74.9	84.2	117.2	147.1	149.9	138.6	133.6	107.6
Developing market economies	55.0	62.1	70.0	97.1	158.5	183.3	202.0	245.4	286.1	338.5	437.2	491.1	463.4	437.4	306.6
OPEC	9.9	11.5	14.1	20.7	33.4	52.0	63.9	85.8	96.0	98.3	128.4	152.9	156.4	143.1	100.7
Non-oil developing countries	45.1	50.6	55.9	76.4	125.1	131.3	138.1	159.6	190.1	240.2	308.8	338.2	307.0	294.2	205.8
European centrally planned economies	30.2	32.7	40.4	53.1	67.5	87.8	92.1	100.9	118.0	133.9	154.0	154.5	152.3	157.2	116.0
Eastern Europe	18.4	20.2	24.2	32.2	42.7	50.8	54.0	60.0	67.3	76.1	85.4	81.3	74.6	77.0	56.0
Soviet Union	11.7	12.5	16.2	20.9	24.8	36.9	38.1	40.9	50.7	57.8	68.5	73.2	77.7	80.2	60.0
Total above	326.7	360.5	427.5	586.6	845.3	889.5	1002.6	1147.6	1330.2	1665.2	2023.7	2007.9	1892.8	1846.8	1432.2
Memorandum item															
ECE region	241.2	266.5	322.0	433.6	597.2	623.1	710.2	804.8	934.0	1175.3	1393.8	1314.2	1242.2	1235.2	983.7

Source: United Nations, *Monthly Bulletin of Statistics*, New York, January 1985; for centrally planned economies, ECE secretariat calculations based on national statistical publications.

ᵃ January-September.

APPENDIX TABLE C.2

World trade: volume change, by region
(*Annual percentage change*)

	1970	1971	1972	1973	1974	1975	1976	1977	1978	1979	1980	1981	1982	1983	1984
Exports															
Developed market economies	8.8	6.8	10.1	12.6	7.1	-4.8	11.0	4.5	6.0	7.3	3.8	1.5	-1.0	2.0	8.0
North America	7.1	1.3	9.2	19.3	6.1	-4.8	6.0	2.8	11.0	8.3	5.3	-2.2	-7.7	-2.3	12.4[a]
Western Europe	10.1	6.6	9.9	12.4	6.0	-5.7	11.0	4.5	6.0	7.3	2.3	1.5	0.8	3.3	7.5[a]
Asia	14.8	21.0	6.7	6.3	17.6		22.0	9.0	0.8	-1.5	16.7	10.4	-3.5	9.1	14.7
Developing market economies	12.6	0.6	11.7	12.0	-0.9	-6.5	12.9	2.1	2.7	4.6	-2.6	-4.8	-9.3	-1.4	7.4
OPEC	16.5	–	11.3	14.2	-1.6	-11.7	14.3	0.4	-3.2	1.6	-12.2	-15.2	-18.5	-7.5	6.0
Non-oil developing countries	8.0	1.2	12.2	9.3	-0.1	-0.3	11.3	4.2	9.7	8.1	9.0	7.7	1.7	5.8	9.1
European centrally planned economies	8.5	6.0	7.8	11.7	5.4	5.1	8.0	9.5	4.9	4.6	2.4	1.5	5.1	5.7	5.0
Eastern Europe	10.8	8.6	12.2	9.6	7.7	7.1	7.6	8.6	6.1	7.6	2.9	1.2	5.6	7.4	7.5
Soviet Union	6.1	3.2	2.7	14.4	2.6	2.5	8.6	10.6	3.4	0.6	1.6	1.9	4.5	3.3	3.0
Total above	9.7	5.2	10.3	12.4	5.1	-4.3	11.2	4.4	5.1	6.4	2.1	–	-2.4	1.5	7.6
Memorandum item															
ECE region	9.2	5.2	9.4	13.9	5.9	-4.0	9.4	4.8	7.1	7.2	3.0	0.6	-0.7	2.3	8.4
Imports															
Developed market economies	9.3	6.1	9.2	12.6	0.9	-7.4	13.0	3.5	5.1	8.1	-0.8	-3.0	–	2.1	10.5
North America	1.2	11.1	13.3	6.9	1.8	-9.9	18.0	9.3	7.0	2.9	-7.0	1.5	-7.7	12.1	28.2[a]
Western Europe	12.2	3.6	9.3	11.7	–	-4.8	13.0	2.7	3.4	10.8	0.8	-4.5	2.0	2.5	6.0[a]
Asia	17.6	1.2	12.3	29.7	-5.1	-10.7	8.0	2.8	5.4	12.8	-7.6	-1.6	–	–	13.3
Developing market economies	10.0	5.7	3.0	14.1	16.4	8.8	9.1	10.0	7.1	5.2	8.7	8.3	-4.2	-4.4	3.8
OPEC	10.0	6.8	10.6	20.6	38.5	41.4	20.6	16.7	3.4	-8.5	12.4	21.3	5.9	-10.9	-2.7
Non-oil developing countries	10.0	5.2	–	11.5	7.6	-4.1	4.5	7.4	8.6	10.6	7.3	3.1	-8.2	-1.8	6.4
European centrally planned economies	11.6	7.5	12.1	13.4	8.3	8.4	6.9	3.2	8.6	1.5	3.9	-0.7	2.2	3.7	5.2
Eastern Europe	14.3	8.6	8.6	12.5	13.6	4.2	6.9	4.9	5.2	1.7	1.2	-6.4	-4.6	3.4	5.5
Soviet Union	7.8	5.9	17.2	14.6	1.0	14.8	7.0	0.9	13.3	1.1	7.5	6.4	9.7	4.0	5.0
Total above	9.7	6.1	8.2	13.0	4.8	-2.5	11.6	4.8	5.9	6.9	1.7	-0.5	-0.6	0.9	8.5
Memorandum item															
ECE region	9.6	5.8	10.6	10.9	1.6	-4.1	13.3	4.2	5.0	7.7	-0.5	-2.6	-0.1	4.8	10.7

Sources: For developed market economies, United Nations, *Monthly Bulletin of Statistics*, New York, various issues; for oil exporting and non-oil exporting developing market economies, UNCTAD, *Handbook of International Trade and Development Statistics*, Geneva 1984 for 1970-1972 and IMF, *World Economic Outlook*, Washington D.C., various issues for 1973-1984 (total developing market economies is obtained as a weighted average of the two country groups); for centrally planned economies, ECE secretariat calculations based on national statistical publications.

[a] January-September.

APPENDIX TABLE C.3

Western Europe and North America: trade volume change

(Annual percentage change)

	1970	1971	1972	1973	1974	1975	1976	1977	1978	1979	1980	1981	1982	1983	1984[a]
Exports															
France	16.1	8.1	14.3	10.3	9.6	-4.1	9.0	6.6	6.1	10.0	2.1	2.9	-3.0	3.7	5.0
Germany, Federal Republic of	7.6	4.8	6.3	14.0	11.0	-11.2	18.6	4.0	3.2	4.5	2.0	6.6	3.3	-0.3	9.0
Italy	7.2	7.8	12.4	1.2	7.7	3.7	11.8	7.6	10.8	7.7	7.8	5.5	-0.5	5.2	6.9
United Kingdom	1.8	8.6	1.8	14.0	4.8	-2.6	8.8	9.3	2.8	3.8	0.8	-1.1	2.7	0.6	7.4
Total 4 countries	8.1	6.8	8.2	11.2	8.9	-5.4	13.2	6.3	5.0	6.2	0.2	3.9	1.1	1.7	7.4
Austria	7.9	3.2	11.8	7.9	12.5	-7.1	15.7	3.0	10.3	13.0	4.7	5.2	1.1	4.5	9.0
Belgium	9.6	10.5	14.3	13.9	–	-8.5	14.7	4.7	3.3	4.3	3.1	–	2.0	3.9	...
Denmark	7.3	5.1	8.1	6.0	7.0	-3.9	4.1	3.9	6.3	10.7	7.5	3.0	1.9	7.6	5.1
Finland	8.8	-4.8	15.3	7.4	–	-17.8	18.3	9.9	7.7	9.5	8.7	3.0	-1.9	3.0	11.3
Ireland	8.2	7.2	6.3	9.4	5.6	7.7	3.9	18.2	10.3	8.4	7.5	0.8	7.2	12.0	18.7
Netherlands	14.3	8.9	9.8	13.4	9.2	-4.8	13.9	-2.2	3.4	8.8	1.0	–	-1.0	7.1	5.8
Norway	4.2	2.0	11.8	10.5	–	3.2	15.4	-2.7	23.3	5.6	5.3	-2.0	-1.0	12.4	10.0
Sweden	10.2	6.2	7.2	17.6	5.7	-9.8	4.8	1.1	8.0	7.4	-2.0	1.0	3.0	12.5	7.7
Switzerland	6.8	3.2	6.2	11.6	3.9	-8.8	12.3	12.2	4.3	2.1	2.0	4.0	-2.9	–	7.2
Total 9 countries	9.9	6.4	10.5	12.3	5.0	-6.5	12.4	3.2	6.5	7.1	2.8	1.1	0.4	6.4	7.3
Total 13 countries	8.8	6.7	9.0	11.6	7.5	-5.8	12.9	5.2	5.5	6.5	1.2	2.9	0.9	3.4	7.4
United States	8.3	-1.0	8.9	23.9	8.7	-2.2	3.6	0.4	12.0	11.3	6.7	-3.1	-10.6	-6.4	6.2
Canada	9.9	5.2	9.5	10.7	-3.7	-7.3	11.9	9.0	9.9	1.8	-1.3	2.7	0.2	9.6	26.7
Total	8.7	5.0	9.0	14.1	7.0	-5.0	10.9	4.5	7.3	7.3	2.2	1.5	-1.8	1.6	8.3
Imports															
France	6.6	7.6	13.9	13.7	4.3	-7.1	20.8	0.8	5.2	11.6	6.3	-3.4	3.6	-1.9	1.7
Germany, Federal Republic of	12.9	7.9	6.4	5.6	-4.0	-0.3	17.7	2.4	6.8	7.5	–	-5.0	1.4	3.9	6.8
Italy	14.5	0.5	10.9	11.2	-5.6	-10.7	15.7	-0.4	7.5	13.1	2.8	-11.3	3.3	1.4	8.1
United Kingdom	10.4	5.2	9.8	13.9	0.3	-8.6	6.4	0.3	6.7	8.4	-3.8	-3.9	4.2	7.7	8.4
Total 4 countries	11.1	5.8	9.9	10.4	-1.3	-5.7	15.7	1.0	6.5	9.8	1.3	-5.6	2.9	2.8	6.1
Austria	18.2	8.6	14.4	10.6	2.7	-6.7	23.0	9.8	-1.6	10.7	6.3	-4.1	-1.3	6.3	10.1
Belgium	9.6	8.8	9.7	14.7	2.6	-3.8	11.7	4.7	3.3	5.4	2.0	-4.0	1.0	-3.1	...
Denmark	11.0	-3.7	3.8	19.8	-6.2	-6.6	20.0	-2.9	4.0	5.8	-8.3	-5.0	3.2	5.1	7.0
Finland	22.0	-1.4	4.2	12.2	8.4	–	-4.4	-8.1	-5.1	18.7	12.4	-6.0	1.1	3.2	2.1
Ireland	3.1	5.4	6.2	20.1	-1.9	-13.4	15.1	12.9	14.5	14.4	-4.5	2.1	-3.4	3.1	7.6
Netherlands	11.9	3.0	4.4	12.7	3.7	-4.8	11.4	2.3	6.7	6.3	-2.0	-7.0	–	4.3	8.5
Norway	12.1	1.5	–	12.1	9.5	–	11.1	7.8	-11.3	4.7	11.1	-4.0	4.2	-5.0	14.4
Sweden	11.5	-4.4	6.2	8.7	14.7	2.3	5.7	-3.2	-5.6	15.3	2.0	-6.0	5.3	4.0	6.2
Switzerland	13.8	6.1	5.7	6.8	-1.3	-17.9	15.6	9.5	9.9	9.0	3.1	3.0	-1.9	3.0	6.5
Total 9 countries	12.2	3.7	6.5	12.6	3.7	-5.4	12.1	3.5	2.7	8.5	1.6	-4.1	0.9	2.0	6.7
Total 13 countries	11.4	5.1	8.7	11.2	0.5	-5.6	14.4	1.9	5.2	9.4	1.4	-5.0	2.2	2.5	6.3
United States	3.2	8.7	13.4	4.8	-1.4	11.9	21.7	10.8	10.2	0.2	-7.1	2.5	-5.0	10.4	28.8
Canada	-3.2	10.0	16.7	16.2	10.1	-5.4	7.9	0.5	3.1	11.1	-5.7	2.8	-16.0	15.5	25.3
Total	8.9	6.1	10.1	10.0	0.6	-7.0	15.7	3.8	6.3	7.4	-0.8	-2.9	-0.4	4.9	12.3

Sources: United Nations, *Monthly Bulletin of Statistics*, New York, January 1985; IMF, *International Financial Statistics*, Washington D.C., January 1985, and *International Financial Statistics Yearbook 1983*; national statistical publications.

[a] January-September.

APPENDIX TABLE C.4

Eastern Europe and USSR: export value, by main destinations

(Billion US dollars)

Exports from/to:	1970	1971	1972	1973	1974	1975	1976	1977	1978	1979	1980	1981	1982	1983	1984a
Bulgaria															
World	2.00	2.18	2.63	3.24	3.84	4.69	5.38	6.35	7.45	8.86	10.39	10.70	11.44	12.14	12.90
ECE-East	1.51	1.64	2.01	2.46	2.73	3.50	4.10	4.81	5.51	6.18	6.90	6.95	7.75	8.87	9.30
ECE-West	0.32	0.34	0.39	0.48	0.55	0.55	0.69	0.75	0.87	1.54	1.92	1.70	1.53	1.48	1.50
Other	0.17	0.20	0.22	0.30	0.55	0.64	0.59	0.79	1.07	1.14	1.57	2.05	2.16	1.78	2.10
Czechoslovakia															
World	3.79	4.18	4.92	5.99	7.03	8.36	9.03	10.27	11.75	13.19	14.93	14.91	15.64	16.50	17.20
ECE-East	2.43	2.66	3.26	3.89	4.27	5.47	6.18	6.95	7.95	8.69	9.46	9.60	10.42	11.19	11.90
ECE-West	0.92	1.00	1.12	1.51	1.98	1.97	1.98	2.30	2.57	3.15	3.82	3.53	3.51	3.53	3.50
Other	0.43	0.52	0.54	0.60	0.78	0.92	0.87	1.02	1.23	1.35	1.64	1.77	1.70	1.78	1.80
German Democratic Republic															
World	4.58	5.08	6.18	7.52	8.75	10.09	11.36	12.02	13.27	15.06	17.31	19.86	21.74	23.79	24.10
ECE-East	3.13	3.50	4.39	5.20	5.60	6.84	7.46	8.29	9.21	10.30	11.05	12.20	12.90	14.27	14.60
ECE-West	1.10	1.20	1.43	1.87	2.60	2.51	3.04	2.81	2.96	3.48	4.60	5.89	6.72	7.54	7.40
Other	0.36	0.37	0.37	0.45	0.56	0.73	0.87	0.92	1.10	1.28	1.67	1.77	2.13	1.98	2.10
Hungary															
World	2.32	2.50	3.29	4.37	5.13	6.06	4.93	5.82	6.35	7.93	8.61	8.73	8.86	8.77	8.60
ECE-East	1.44	1.62	2.15	2.80	3.22	4.10	2.73	3.25	3.45	4.14	4.33	4.65	4.62	4.32	4.20
ECE-West	0.69	0.68	0.89	1.26	1.49	1.45	1.68	1.97	2.22	2.91	3.27	2.90	2.93	3.19	3.30
Other	0.33	0.34	0.35	0.40	0.77	0.98	1.01	1.15	0.68	0.88	1.01	1.18	1.31	1.25	1.20
Poland															
World	3.55	3.87	4.93	6.35	8.32	10.29	11.02	12.27	13.77	16.22	17.02	13.29	11.22	11.58	11.80
ECE-East	2.13	2.29	2.97	3.67	4.38	5.82	6.25	6.99	7.90	9.25	8.90	7.41	5.51	5.84	5.70
ECE-West	1.09	1.24	1.60	2.28	3.17	3.49	3.76	4.13	4.66	5.42	6.21	4.22	3.99	4.17	4.40
Other	0.33	0.34	0.35	0.40	0.77	0.98	1.01	1.15	1.21	1.54	1.91	1.66	1.71	1.57	1.70
Romania															
World	1.85	2.10	2.60	3.67	4.87	5.34	6.14	7.02	8.05	9.72	11.40	11.18	10.12	10.16	10.70
ECE-East	0.92	1.00	1.23	1.65	1.75	2.04	2.33	2.92	3.29	3.48	4.24	3.35	3.24	3.42	2.70
ECE-West	0.66	0.80	0.97	1.42	2.22	2.03	2.40	2.37	2.95	3.93	4.39	4.16	3.48	3.77	4.90
Other	0.27	0.30	0.40	0.60	0.90	1.27	1.40	1.73	1.81	2.31	2.77	3.67	3.40	2.98	3.10
Eastern Europe															
World	18.09	19.91	24.56	31.14	37.94	44.83	47.86	53.76	60.64	70.99	79.66	78.66	79.02	82.94	85.20
ECE-East	11.56	12.71	16.02	19.66	21.96	27.77	29.05	33.21	37.31	42.05	44.89	44.16	44.43	47.92	48.40
ECE-West	4.78	5.25	6.41	8.83	12.01	12.00	13.55	14.34	16.22	20.44	24.21	22.40	22.16	23.67	24.90
Other	1.75	1.95	2.13	2.64	3.98	5.06	5.26	6.21	7.11	8.50	10.56	12.10	12.43	11.35	11.90
USSR															
World	12.80	13.81	15.47	21.26	27.36	33.29	37.16	45.18	52.38	64.71	76.50	79.39	86.97	91.38	91.20
ECE-East	6.76	7.24	8.17	9.93	11.48	16.44	17.38	20.74	24.88	28.29	32.24	33.78	36.21	39.24	39.80
ECE-West	2.78	3.16	3.44	5.62	9.24	9.63	11.68	13.55	14.52	21.78	28.13	27.49	29.55	30.20	29.90
Other	3.26	3.41	3.86	5.71	6.64	7.22	8.11	10.89	12.97	14.64	16.13	18.12	21.21	21.94	21.50
Eastern Europe and USSR															
World	30.89	33.72	40.02	52.40	65.30	78.12	85.03	98.94	113.02	135.71	156.16	158.05	165.99	174.32	176.40
ECE-East	18.32	19.95	24.19	29.59	33.44	44.21	46.43	53.96	62.19	70.34	77.13	77.94	80.64	87.16	88.20
ECE-West	7.56	8.41	9.85	14.45	21.25	21.63	25.23	27.89	30.75	42.22	52.34	49.89	51.71	53.87	54.90
Other	5.01	5.35	5.99	8.36	10.62	12.27	13.36	17.10	20.08	23.15	26.69	30.22	33.64	33.29	33.40

Source: Secretariat of the United Nations Economic Commission for Europe, based on national foreign trade statistics. Partner country grouping: ECE-East—east European member countries of CMEA and the Soviet Union; ECE-West—ECE market economies and Japan; Other—all remaining countries.

[a] Preliminary data or secretariat estimates.

APPENDIX TABLE C.5

Eastern Europe and USSR: import value by main origins

(Billion US dollars)

Imports to/from:	1970	1971	1972	1973	1974	1975	1976	1977	1978	1979	1980	1981	1982	1983	1984a
Bulgaria															
World	1.83	2.12	2.57	3.21	4.33	5.40	5.63	6.39	7.62	8.51	9.67	10.80	11.54	12.29	12.70
ECE-East	1.33	1.57	1.97	2.40	2.83	3.71	4.13	4.91	5.96	6.59	7.29	7.76	8.56	9.41	9.70
ECE-West	0.38	0.39	0.43	0.56	1.07	1.35	1.12	1.08	1.20	1.42	1.79	2.29	2.04	1.86	1.90
Other	0.13	0.16	0.17	0.24	0.43	0.34	0.37	0.41	0.47	0.50	0.59	0.75	0.95	1.02	1.10
Czechoslovakia															
World	3.70	4.01	4.67	6.07	7.51	9.09	9.70	11.15	12.57	14.25	15.18	14.67	15.45	16.37	17.10
ECE-East	2.33	2.54	3.04	3.81	4.41	5.85	6.30	7.31	8.43	9.39	9.83	9.79	10.82	11.92	12.90
ECE-West	1.01	1.12	1.22	1.69	2.34	2.52	2.68	2.87	3.23	3.84	4.21	3.80	3.59	3.39	3.10
Other	0.35	0.34	0.41	0.57	0.76	0.71	0.72	0.97	0.91	1.02	1.14	1.08	1.04	1.06	1.10
German Democratic Republic															
World	4.85	4.96	5.90	7.85	9.65	11.29	13.20	14.33	14.57	16.21	19.08	20.18	20.20	21.52	22.20
ECE-East	3.19	3.23	3.71	4.81	5.40	7.09	9.97	9.28	9.52	9.82	11.27	12.60	12.97	13.38	13.90
ECE-West	1.35	1.44	1.93	2.67	3.45	3.50	4.44	4.07	4.02	5.35	6.30	6.41	5.99	6.70	6.90
Other	0.30	0.29	0.27	0.38	0.79	0.69	0.78	0.99	1.03	1.04	1.52	1.17	1.24	1.45	1.40
Hungary															
World	2.51	2.99	3.15	3.88	5.58	7.15	5.53	6.52	7.94	8.68	9.19	9.16	8.87	8.55	8.10
ECE-East	1.56	1.88	1.98	2.33	3.00	4.48	2.81	3.23	3.86	4.33	4.31	4.30	4.33	4.12	3.90
ECE-West	0.72	0.89	0.93	1.21	2.05	2.03	2.09	2.52	3.20	3.46	3.88	3.93	3.48	3.23	3.10
Other	0.22	0.22	0.25	0.34	0.53	0.64	0.64	0.77	0.88	0.89	1.01	0.93	1.06	1.21	1.10
Poland															
World	3.61	4.04	5.33	7.76	10.49	12.55	13.88	14.63	15.70	17.55	19.12	15.53	10.25	10.60	10.60
ECE-East	2.36	2.58	3.08	3.81	4.40	5.45	6.20	7.25	8.06	8.99	10.09	9.59	5.98	6.25	6.10
ECE-West	0.98	1.18	1.89	3.49	5.41	6.31	6.92	6.44	6.52	6.87	6.92	4.72	3.35	3.29	3.50
Other	0.27	0.28	0.35	0.46	0.68	0.78	0.75	0.94	1.12	1.68	2.11	1.22	0.92	1.06	1.00
Romania															
World	1.96	2.10	2.62	3.44	5.14	5.34	6.10	7.02	8.88	10.92	13.20	10.98	8.32	7.64	7.60
ECE-East	0.94	0.97	1.17	1.37	1.64	1.97	2.42	2.92	3.27	3.69	4.05	3.44	3.08	3.28	2.80
ECE-West	0.81	0.89	1.14	1.58	2.64	2.39	2.32	2.65	3.56	4.07	4.35	3.63	2.05	1.48	1.60
Other	0.21	0.25	0.31	0.49	0.86	0.99	1.36	1.45	2.06	3.15	4.79	3.91	3.20	2.88	3.20
Eastern Europe															
World	18.45	20.22	24.25	32.21	42.69	50.82	54.03	60.04	67.29	76.12	85.44	81.32	74.63	76.98	78.40
ECE-East	11.71	12.77	14.95	18.53	21.67	28.56	29.82	34.88	39.10	42.82	46.83	47.48	45.73	48.35	49.30
ECE-West	5.25	5.91	7.53	11.20	16.97	18.10	19.58	19.63	21.73	25.01	27.45	24.78	20.49	19.95	20.10
Other	1.48	1.54	1.76	2.49	4.05	4.16	4.62	5.52	6.46	8.29	11.16	9.06	8.40	8.67	9.00
USSR															
World	11.73	12.48	16.16	20.91	24.85	36.94	38.11	40.89	50.74	57.78	68.53	73.16	77.67	80.20	80.10
ECE-East	6.63	7.26	9.34	10.89	11.35	15.67	16.22	18.82	24.63	26.68	29.43	29.40	33.49	37.05	37.60
ECE-West	3.02	3.11	4.46	6.37	8.61	14.10	14.98	14.26	17.33	21.21	25.70	28.24	28.98	27.65	26.90
Other	2.08	2.12	2.36	3.66	4.89	7.17	6.91	7.80	8.78	9.89	13.40	15.52	15.21	15.50	15.50
Eastern Europe and USSR															
World	30.18	32.70	40.40	53.13	67.53	87.76	92.13	100.92	118.03	133.90	153.97	154.48	152.30	157.18	158.50
ECE-East	18.35	20.03	24.29	29.42	33.02	44.23	46.04	53.70	63.74	69.50	76.26	76.88	79.22	85.40	86.90
ECE-West	8.27	9.02	11.99	17.56	25.58	32.20	34.57	33.90	39.06	46.23	53.15	53.02	49.47	47.60	47.00
Other	3.56	3.65	4.13	6.15	8.94	11.33	11.53	13.33	15.24	18.17	24.56	24.59	23.61	24.17	24.50

Source: Secretariat of the United Nations Economic Commission for Europe, based on national foreign trade statistics. Partner country grouping: ECE-East—east European member countries of CMEA and the Soviet Union; ECE-West—ECE market economies and Japan; Other—all remaining countries.

a Preliminary data or secretariat estimates.

APPENDIX TABLE C.6

East-west trade: value of western exports, by country of origin

(Million US dollars)

	1970	1971	1972	1973	1974	1975	1976	1977	1978	1979	1980	1981	1982	1983	1984[a]
Austria	368	387	457	627	1 078	1 279	1 286	1 418	1 671	1 998	2 108	1 808	1 742	1 867	2 009
Belgium-Luxembourg	170	183	268	498	821	846	791	760	851	1 058	1 307	1 106	907	1 090	926
Denmark	113	141	140	188	265	293	268	270	318	354	370	269	213	213	278
Finland	361	329	448	530	898	1 312	1 504	1 707	1 754	1 810	2 814	3 707	3 755	3 460	2 866
France	647	730	950	1 306	1 604	2 601	2 732	2 782	2 919	4 031	4 643	3 905	2 810	3 331	2 867
Germany Federal Republic of[b]	1 296	1 527	2 199	3 753	5 562	6 458	6 247	6 647	7 714	8 692	9 443	7 587	7 525	7 719	7 175
Greece	106	85	117	166	239	261	288	337	388	359	520	342	332	317	344
Iceland	14	16	22	24	41	41	41	62	49	64	82	70	57	59	70
Ireland	7	6	7	12	30	33	20	29	38	71	110	75	62	81	38
Italy	701	740	780	983	1 647	2 167	1 960	2 271	2 413	2 637	2 728	2 468	2 445	2 709	2 421
Netherlands	210	251	354	495	754	792	762	816	942	1 145	1 420	1 385	993	1 077	816
Norway	60	62	94	139	198	254	274	275	319	246	265	262	210	218	161
Portugal	7	6	7	10	19	42	82	80	74	95	91	83	85	78	62
Spain	67	64	121	115	201	255	302	284	354	547	545	787	428	515	583
Sweden	337	310	327	524	786	1 094	1 033	943	984	1 176	1 195	1 035	813	698	766
Switzerland	209	213	285	427	598	744	794	885	1 069	1 069	1 063	852	810	773	758
Turkey	83	81	87	101	145	122	166	174	323	301	480	320	311	228	288
United Kingdom	595	591	654	762	992	1 292	1 178	1 456	1 872	2 049	2 627	2 028	1 505	1 430	1 700
Yugoslavia	538	669	785	968	1 451	1 871	2 028	1 904	2 327	2 663	3 975	5 347	5 354	4 550	4 550
Western Europe[c]	6 560	7 116	9 027	12 758	18 755	23 359	23 469	24 990	28 647	32 993	38 706	35 912	32 999	33 145	30 785
Canada	132	165	350	371	162	599	786	545	743	991	1 773	1 893	2 035	1 679	1 845
United States	352	382	817	1 797	1 428	2 778	3 497	2 531	3 664	5 660	3 842	4 255	3 585	2 878	4 508
North America	485	548	1 167	2 168	1 590	3 377	4 283	3 076	4 408	6 652	5 615	6 148	5 620	4 558	6 353
Japan	446	536	735	810	1 674	2 198	2 798	2 669	3 197	3 264	3 583	4 011	4 472	3 563	2 921
Developed market economies[c]	7 492	8 200	10 930	15 736	22 020	28 935	30 552	30 736	36 252	42 910	47 906	46 072	43 092	41 266	40 061

Source: United Nations commodity trade data (COMTRADE). Data cover reported exports to six east European countries (Bulgaria, Czechoslovakia, German Democratic Republic, Hungary, Poland, Romania) and the Soviet Union.

[a] Extrapolations, based on January-September growth rates.

[b] Excluding trade between the Federal Republic of Germany and the German Democratic Republic.

[c] Including trade between the Federal Republic of Germany and the German Democratic Republic.

APPENDIX TABLE C.7

East-west trade: value of western imports, by country of destination

(Million US dollars)

	1970	1971	1972	1973	1974	1975	1976	1977	1978	1979	1980	1981	1982	1983	1984a
Austria	322	369	427	578	843	919	1 053	1 208	1 345	1 706	2 287	2 414	2 092	1 954	2 241
Belgium-Luxembourg	170	208	255	375	538	580	558	683	785	1 009	1 540	1 389	1 765	1 461	1 557
Denmark	138	130	149	258	397	494	541	457	528	712	784	561	625	571	673
Finland	397	468	465	615	1 414	1 470	1 504	1 674	1 676	2 463	3 564	3 521	3 475	3 425	3 367
France	424	535	667	940	1 253	1 615	1 901	2 118	2 448	3 141	5 075	4 770	4 116	3 893	3 554
Germany Federal Republic ofb	1 032	1 188	1 441	2 180	2 862	3 083	3 880	4 331	5 434	7 722	8 258	7 312	7 484	7 347	7 947
Greece	91	92	111	161	174	242	359	344	584	522	535	517	469	422	393
Iceland	14	18	21	26	65	55	59	67	62	94	101	86	88	84	76
Ireland	28	33	38	50	90	87	87	113	126	183	137	107	123	128	132
Italy	733	799	1 005	1 354	1 766	1 780	2 298	2 424	2 606	3 450	4 873	4 369	4 790	4 849	5 481
Netherlands	200	239	294	416	610	749	888	986	1 148	1 711	2 163	2 507	3 090	3 138	2 870
Norway	79	159	132	173	220	242	334	385	311	386	359	387	558	472	551
Portugal	8	20	18	25	31	76	149	150	121	188	203	249	115	113	110
Spain	59	57	121	176	306	425	396	321	352	519	712	793	798	807	859
Sweden	307	312	333	473	779	1 017	1 055	1 062	1 008	1 645	1 506	1 187	1 441	1 601	1 433
Switzerland	130	137	154	239	353	334	484	582	818	1 098	1 372	1 189	1 096	953	864
Turkey	102	100	146	156	229	217	282	297	335	536	656	691	351	644	666
United Kingdom	550	562	620	812	1 048	1 394	1 758	2 060	2 140	2 777	2 754	1 555	1 835	1 808	2 034
Yugoslavia	539	716	726	1 059	1 553	1 691	1 971	2 319	2 577	3 169	4 047	4 436	4 388	4 049	3 703
Western Europec	5 876	6 815	7 878	11 069	15 796	17 838	21 107	23 300	26 361	35 551	44 004	40 727	41 441	40 422	41 298
Canada	64	79	101	131	182	153	182	176	188	251	224	226	155	161	196
United States	225	222	320	525	890	728	864	915	1 254	1 354	1 413	1 596	1 105	1 404	2 180
North America	290	302	421	656	1 073	882	1 047	1 091	1 443	1 606	1 638	1 822	1 260	1 565	2 376
Japan	493	487	589	1 061	1 493	1 213	1 216	1 466	1 479	1 983	1 895	1 570	1 385	1 502	1 757
Developed market economiesc	6 660	7 605	8 889	12 787	18 362	19 933	23 371	25 857	29 284	39 141	47 538	44 120	44 087	43 490	45 432

Source: United Nations commodity trade data (COMTRADE). Data cover reported imports from six east European countries (Bulgaria, Czechoslovakia, German Democratic Republic, Hungary, Poland, Romania) and the Soviet Union. Imports are converted to f.o.b. terms wherever appropriate.

a Extrapolations, based on January-September growth rates.

b Excluding trade between the Federal Republic of Germany and the German Democratic Republic.

c Including trade between the Federal Republic of Germany and the German Democratic Republic.

APPENDIX TABLE C.8

East-west trade: western trade balances by western country
(Million US dollars)

	1970	1971	1972	1973	1974	1975	1976	1977	1978	1979	1980	1981	1982	1983	1984[a]
Austria	46	17	29	49	234	359	233	209	325	291	-179	-606	-349	-87	-231
Belgium-Luxembourg	-	-24	12	123	283	265	232	76	65	48	-232	-283	-858	-370	-631
Denmark	-24	10	-9	-69	-132	-200	-273	-186	-209	-358	-414	-292	-411	-358	-395
Finland	-36	-139	-16	-85	-515	-157	-	32	77	-652	-750	185	280	34	-500
France	222	195	282	365	350	986	831	663	470	890	-431	-864	-1 305	-562	-686
Germany Federal Republic of[b]	263	339	757	1 572	2 700	3 374	2 366	2 316	2 280	970	1 184	274	41	371	-772
Greece	15	-6	5	4	64	18	-71	-6	-195	-163	-15	-175	-136	-104	-48
Iceland	-	-2	1	-1	-23	-13	-17	-5	-13	-30	-18	-15	-30	-24	-5
Ireland	-21	-26	-30	-37	-59	-53	-67	-84	-88	-112	-26	-32	-60	-47	-93
Italy	-31	-58	-224	-370	-119	386	-338	-153	-193	-813	-2 145	-1 900	-2 344	-2 139	-3 059
Netherlands	9	11	59	79	144	43	-125	-169	-205	-566	-742	-1 121	-2 096	-2 060	-2 053
Norway	-19	-97	-37	-34	-22	11	-59	-109	7	-140	-93	-125	-347	-253	-389
Portugal	7	-13	-10	-14	-11	-33	-67	-69	-46	-92	-112	-165	-30	-34	-47
Spain	7	7	-	-61	-104	-170	-93	-36	2	28	-167	-6	-369	-291	-276
Sweden	30	-2	-5	50	6	76	-22	-118	-24	-469	-311	-152	-627	-902	-667
Switzerland	79	76	130	187	245	410	310	302	250	-29	-309	-337	-285	-179	-106
Turkey	-18	-19	-58	-55	-84	-95	-115	-123	-11	-235	-175	-371	-39	-416	-377
United Kingdom	45	28	33	-49	-56	-101	-580	-603	-268	-727	-127	472	-330	-377	-334
Yugoslavia	-1	-46	59	-91	-101	180	57	-415	-249	-505	-72	910	966	501	846
Western Europe[c]	684	300	1 149	1 688	2 959	5 520	2 362	1 690	2 286	-2 558	-5 297	-4 814	-8 442	-7 277	-10 512
Canada	67	86	248	240	-20	446	603	369	554	739	1 548	1 666	1 879	1 517	1 648
United States	126	159	497	1 271	538	2 049	2 633	1 616	2 410	4 306	2 429	2 658	2 480	1 474	2 328
North America	194	246	745	1 511	517	2 495	3 236	1 985	2 964	5 046	3 977	4 325	4 359	2 992	3 976
Japan	-46	48	146	-250	181	984	1 582	1 202	1 717	1 280	1 688	2 440	3 086	2 061	1 164
Developed market economies[c]	832	595	2 041	299	3 657	9 001	7 181	4 879	6 968	3 768	367	1 951	-995	-2 223	-5 371

Source: United Nations commodity trade data (COMTRADE). Data cover balances (*f.o.b.-f.o.b.*) with six east European countries (Bulgaria, Czechoslovakia, German Democratic Republic, Hungary, Poland, Romania) and the Soviet Union. Imports are converted to *f.o.b.* terms wherever appropriate.

[a] Extrapolations, based on January-September growth rates.

[b] Excluding trade between the Federal Republic of Germany and the German Democratic Republic.

[c] Including trade between the Federal Republic of Germany and the German Democratic Republic.

APPENDIX TABLE C.9

East-west trade: western exports, imports and balances by eastern trade partner
(Millions US dollars)

	1970	1971	1972	1973	1974	1975	1976	1977	1978	1979	1980	1981	1982	1983	1984ᵃ
Western exports to:															
Bulgaria	349	352	383	537	913	1 154	1 002	942	1 147	1 307	1 709	1 966	1 641	1 679	1 603
Czechoslovakia	865	1 026	1 118	1 461	1 914	2 101	2 295	2 250	2 565	3 066	3 375	2 850	2 773	2 559	2 449
German Democratic Republicᵇ	1 143	1 274	1 626	1 955	2 541	2 909	3 190	3 264	3 986	5 270	5 717	5 272	4 692	5 040	4 589
Hungary	671	799	884	1 163	1 878	1 912	1 903	2 405	3 104	3 133	3 468	3 461	3 139	2 856	2 774
Poland	922	1 113	1 746	3 232	4 668	5 593	5 633	5 144	5 725	6 210	6 670	4 469	3 385	3 114	3 204
Romania	727	786	1 038	1 431	2 157	2 091	2 103	2 394	3 081	3 881	4 015	3 108	1 770	1 366	1 499
Eastern Europeᵇ	4 680	5 353	6 797	9 782	14 074	15 762	16 129	16 403	19 610	22 870	24 957	21 128	17 402	16 617	16 121
Soviet Union	2 812	2 847	4 133	5 954	7 946	13 173	14 422	14 333	16 642	20 039	22 948	24 943	25 689	24 649	23 939
Totalᵇ	7 492	8 200	10 930	15 736	22 020	28 935	30 552	30 736	36 252	42 910	47 906	46 072	43 092	41 266	40 061
Western imports (f.o.b.) from:															
Bulgaria	246	267	289	387	462	428	522	556	634	972	1 071	939	889	774	731
Czechoslovakia	807	909	1 024	1 373	1 703	1 825	1 899	2 078	2 390	3 041	3 528	3 169	3 100	3 096	3 196
German Democratic Republicᵇ	988	1 142	1 312	1 749	2 302	2 533	2 753	3 045	3 509	4 351	5 356	5 154	5 377	5 360	5 259
Hungary	540	603	812	1 119	1 376	1 287	1 483	1 792	2 068	2 635	2 904	2 612	2 423	2 499	2 751
Poland	1 032	1 197	1 490	2 116	2 819	3 182	3 611	3 851	4 329	5 035	5 438	3 604	3 382	3 377	4 088
Romania	543	624	795	1 136	1 619	1 676	2 059	1 978	2 401	3 258	3 439	3 469	2 571	2 731	3 838
Eastern Europeᵇ	4 159	4 745	5 725	7 883	10 284	10 934	12 330	13 303	15 334	19 295	21 739	18 949	17 745	17 838	19 865
Soviet Union	2 501	2 860	3 163	4 904	8 078	8 999	11 040	12 553	13 949	19 846	25 798	25 171	26 342	25 651	25 567
Totalᵇ	6 660	7 605	8 889	12 787	18 362	19 933	23 371	25 857	29 284	39 141	47 538	44 120	44 087	43 490	45 432
Western trade balances with:															
Bulgaria	102	84	93	149	450	725	480	386	512	334	637	1 027	751	905	872
Czechoslovakia	57	116	94	87	210	275	395	172	174	25	–153	–318	–327	–536	–746
German Democratic Republicᵇ	155	132	314	205	239	375	437	218	477	918	361	118	–685	–319	–669
Hungary	130	196	71	44	502	625	419	613	1 035	498	563	848	715	356	22
Poland	–110	–83	255	1 116	1 848	2 410	2 021	1 292	1 395	1 174	1 231	864	3	–262	–883
Romania	184	162	242	295	537	414	44	416	680	622	576	–360	–800	–1 365	–2 338
Eastern Europeᵇ	520	608	1 071	1 899	3 789	4 828	3 799	3 099	4 275	3 575	3 217	2 179	–343	–1 221	–3 743
Soviet Union	311	–12	969	1 050	–131	4 173	3 381	1 779	2 693	193	–2 849	–227	–652	–1 002	–1 627
Totalᵇ	832	595	2 041	2 949	3 657	9 001	7 181	4 879	6 968	3 768	367	1 951	–995	–2 223	–5 371

ᵃ Extrapolations, based on January-September growth rates.
ᵇ Including trade between the Federal Republic of Germany and the German Democratic Republic.